Acclaim for *Joe Papp*

"A terrific book. To those of us attempting to build theater companies that will endure, this biography is almost a handbook of what it is possible to achieve and of what should be avoided at all costs. In fact, for anyone starting out in theater, I should say 'Read this book!'"
—**Tina Packer,** Artistic Director, Shakespeare & Company

"The book reflects Mr. Papp's sensibility in a significant way. . . . [The author] shines a light into previously hidden corners of his life . . . Epstein has assembled a wealth of observations, anecdotes, and institutional detail that are invaluable for anyone interested in the producer. And in the book's final chapters she achieves the fluid, richly shaded narrative momentum found in the best biographies." —*New York Times*

"A riveting story . . . [Told] with exemplary honesty, verve and intelligence." —**Meryle Secrest,** author of *Salvador Dali*

"Epstein adds a wealth of new detail about Papp's early struggles and later achievements, and, more disturbingly, about his personal relationships. . . . [She] tells it with utter frankness."
—**Robert Brustein,** *New Republic*

"Some may consider this marvelous biography as a New York book, with little relevance for the rest of America. . . . But this is more than a biography. It is a story of passion, of a lifelong love affair with the stage, of ego, pride and power. In short, this is a book with universal themes featuring a larger-than-life, extremely complicated protagonist. Epstein fully explores Papp's dark side. . . . [A] brilliant biography."
—*Kansas City Star*

"Epstein has done an excellent job of providing a journalistic account of Papp's career, interviewing hundreds of actors, directors, writers, critics, colleagues, and rivals, many of whom were on bitter terms with the producer; the multiplicity of perspectives gives the book depth. . . . Her account of his lengthy struggle with cancer is exhaustive and ultimately quite sensitive." —*Christian Science Monitor*

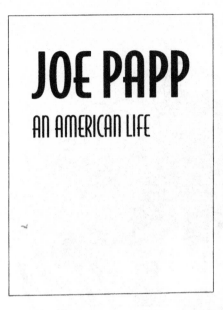

JOE PAPP

AN AMERICAN LIFE

JOE PAPP

AN AMERICAN LIFE

by Helen Epstein

DA CAPO PRESS

For Patrick, Daniel, and Sam

Also by Helen Epstein
CHILDREN OF THE HOLOCAUST
THE COMPANIES SHE KEEPS
MUSIC TALKS

Library of Congress Cataloging in Publication Data

Epstein, Helen, 1947–
    Joe Papp: an American life / by Helen Epstein.—1st Da Capo
Press ed.
        p.   cm.
    Originally published: Boston: Little, Brown, c1994.
    Includes bibliographical references and index.
    ISBN 0-306-80676-2 (alk. paper)
    1. Papp, Joseph. 2. Theatrical producers and directors—
United States—Biography. Title.
PN2287.P23E67 1996
792'.0232'092—dc20   95-43018
[B]   CIP

First Da Capo Press edition 1996

This Da Capo Press paperback edition of *Joe Papp* is an
unabridged republication of the edition originally published
in Boston in 1994. It is reprinted by arrangement with
Little, Brown and Company.

Published by Da Capo Press
A Member of the Perseus Books Group
http://www.dacapopress.com

Manufactured in the United States of America

10 9 8 7

Contents

CONTENTS

Introduction

AT MIDDAY November 1, 1991, Lafayette Street in downtown Manhattan was closed to traffic. People who could not get inside the Public Theater spilled over the steps and onto the sidewalk, standing beneath the large purple-and-black banners, listening to the loudspeakers that broadcast the funeral service. Throughout New York City, radio and television stations had been repeating the same bulletin since early morning:

"Broadway theaters will dim their lights tonight for Joseph Papp. . . . The legendary producer and creator of the New York Shakespeare Festival died of cancer yesterday at the age of seventy . . ." and "Not only are the lights dimmed on Broadway but they dimmed from Avon to Central Park. . . . The giant of the theater, creator of Shakespeare in the Park and so much more, was seventy and had cancer."

The *New York Times* ran Joseph Papp's photograph and obituary on its front page. Across the country, newspapers cited his thirty-five years of producing Shakespeare free of charge as well as the contemporary plays that had originated at his theater: *A Chorus Line, Hair, Sticks and Bones, for colored girls who have considered suicide/when the rainbow is enuf, The Mystery of Edwin Drood* and *The Normal Heart,* one of the first dramas to deal with AIDS.

Inside the Public Theater, standing beside the plain pine coffin that dominated the stage, Papp's longtime friend Bernard Gersten told the mourners, "Joe was not a long-term planner. Joe didn't really know that he was setting out to build a theater when he created the Shakespearean Theater Workshop in 1954. *We* know it *now.* He couldn't have conceived or imagined the course that the next thirty-five years would take or how brilliantly he would stay that course. . . .

"Joe was not a theoretician or a philosopher. Joe leapt into action driven by passion and rage and adrenaline and explained himself — if he felt like it — after the fact. . . . Great numbers of us here spring from him, have learned from him, have loved and hated him, each in turn, have fought and argued with him, have wept because of him and have triumphed with him. And we are his legacy. . . ."

Actress Meryl Streep, looking tired and pale, had flown in from Los Angeles to speak at the funeral. She had first auditioned for Papp while still a drama student in the mid 1970s, worked at the Festival for several years and regarded her time there as the wellspring of her professional life. Like many of the people who had converged on Lafayette Street, Streep viewed Joseph Papp as far more than her first boss or mentor. "What Joe became to me goes way beyond our professional relationship," she said. "After I began working at the theater, my boyfriend John Cazale had developed some disturbing symptoms and I called Joe to get the name of a good doctor. Joe scooped us up, took us to his own doctor and got that doctor to drive us around town in his Rolls-Royce to all the cancer specialists you could possibly see in one day. He checked us in at the hospital, sat in the chair for hours and waited for the results of the tests. He asked the questions we were too freaked out or too ignorant to ask. He stayed with me through the course of John's illness and helped me when I couldn't even negotiate the stairs to organize the memorial after John's death. After the memorial I went to Canada to an old friend's house in the country and over and over I sketched two faces, John's and Joe's. My feelings for him have always been stoked by memories of that time. These feelings are unconditional."

There were others at the funeral who were feeling emotions far too complex to articulate. One was Merle Debuskey, Papp's former press agent. Another was Ming Cho Lee, a former principal designer at the Festival. Another was Gerald Freedman, a former artistic director, who had left at about the same time as Lee. Another was David Rabe, once

Papp's premier playwright, who had not worked at the Festival for many years.

"I've never known anyone as contradictory," Rabe later said. "He had a powerful artistic, human side that was in unresolved conflict with a tremendous ambition and desire for power and control. I've met people who were as generous and helpful and creative as Joe, and I've met people who were as dangerous as Joe, but I've never encountered these things in any other single person. He gave me an opportunity that I would probably never have had if he weren't there, but it wasn't free."

Director Stuart Vaughan, the Festival's artistic director during the 1950s, when it first burst into the city's consciousness, sat at home reading the obituaries and fulminating. "Left a cultural void! *What void?* Most of the 'exciting' new plays he developed at the Public never had and never would find a real public! Who would cite the empty houses, the lack of a sustaining membership? Who would say, today or tomorrow, that the emperor had no clothes — that Joe Papp was just one more fast-talking con man who latched onto the nonprofit structure? That after a great artistic start, he offered up a series of badly spoken, incompetently acted, ill-conceived productions! Charm boy, huckster, liar, bandwagon climber, shameless exploiter of the talents and affections of others, driven by your bottomless need for love and recompense for all the injustices suffered by poor little Joseph Papirofsky. Arrogant and anti-intellectual autodidact, have done with you!"

The seven pallbearers moved the coffin off the stage, out onto the sidewalk, into the waiting hearse. The doors were shut and the motorcade made a slow turn toward downtown. Led by a New York City Police Department squad car with its sirens blaring, flanked on both sides by police riding motorcycles, the long line of cars turned east not far from the church on East 6th Street where, in 1954, the producer had established his original Shakespearean Theater Workshop, then sped down the Bowery, toward the Brooklyn-Battery tunnel.

In Washington that morning, Representative Ted Weiss had read into the *Congressional Record:* "As Chairman of the Congressional Arts Caucus, I cannot overstate the important role Joseph Papp has played as a champion of the arts — not only in New York City but in the United States. Joe Papp stood up to those who would try to censor artistic expression; he stood up for the principle of free speech and the integrity of the written word.

"Joe Papp struggled to make our city and country a more liveable place; to uplift our spirits, to challenge our minds, and to see us through to another day."

In Colorado, composer David Amram was just hearing the news. "I couldn't believe he was dead," he later said. "I had just written to him to say we were starting rehearsals for the opera version of *Twelfth Night* that we had written together in 1958. For thirty-five years, I was always talking about Joe Papp. He was someone I carried around inside me — like Charlie Parker, Jackson Pollack and Jack Kerouac. It doesn't feel like they're dead. It just feels like I haven't seen them in a while."

Playwright and president of Czechoslovakia Václav Havel, who had spoken with Papp three days before he died, felt much the same way. Papp had produced one of Havel's first plays and brought him to the United States in 1968, when the Communist regime was making it difficult for him to leave his country. Later he would write:

> I was eternally grateful to Joe Papp, because it was my first and for a long time last visit to America, which I fell in love with. It was the time of the hippies, the student strikes and a thoroughly interesting election campaign. Thanks to him I saw *Hair.* . . . Thanks to him I caught a glimpse of the atmosphere of those days. After that, I didn't see him for many years until he appeared in Czechoslovakia sometime in 1984 just in order to visit me.
>
> Despite the fact that we hadn't seen one another for so long, it seemed like we just started up where we had left off in our last conversation. We talked about many things — politics, spiritual things, cultural matters, theater. Then we met again when I was in America as a president on a state visit. He was a man who belonged to the same blood group as my own.

John Simon, the New York theater critic who had been reviewing Papp's productions for nearly thirty years, had no such feelings of affinity. "There were times when Papp and I were friendly — whenever I gave him a good review," Simon would later say. "But I'm a snob and an elitist. I believe culture is like ballet-dancing — you do not start at the age of twenty. You have to start as a small child, get it in the family, at the right schools, live with it, grow up with it, feel at ease with it, and then you *may* be the kind of person who can run a great theater.

"Joe came out of the gutter and he had a gutter mentality. He came to culture too late and had vulgar, nouveau riche, insecure notions of what culture is. His genius was for organization, publicity, raising money. He was an impresario of considerable accomplishment. But I think his taste was deplorable from beginning to end. Papp had all the problems one has when one hasn't been educated: you can easily be manipulated by people who sell you snake oil. You can never entirely trust your instincts. Or you become defiant in order to compensate for the insecurity you always feel."

The funeral cortege sped through the Brooklyn-Battery tunnel, coming up in Brooklyn, the borough where Joseph Papp had been born and where all of his siblings continued to live. Then it turned south on the Brooklyn Queens Expressway, away from Williamsburg, Brownsville, Crown Heights and Bedford-Stuyvesant, neighborhoods once inhabited by poor Jews, Italians, Irish and Poles — now by poor African Americans and Latinos — neighborhoods whose streets and rooftops Joseph Papp knew in his bones and where, during the 1960s, he had taken Free Shakespeare to patches of park and asphalt playgrounds.

"I understood that Joseph was mortal but I just could not imagine anyone or anything striking him a lethal blow," said Roscoe Lee Browne, whose life Papp had changed by hiring him as an actor in 1956. "He was always so vital and forward looking, always trying to make the best of the human condition available to everyone. He stood for a sense of freedom and understood that we are not free yet — none of us."

"Joseph Papp was ahead of the pack," wrote novelist Thulani Davis, who worked for Papp one generation later. "He was one of the few people who understood that Martin Luther King Jr. was talking about multiculturalism. Joe insisted that Shakespeare could be played by the gorgeous mosaic of this city and do just fine, thank-you. It may seem silly now, but as I recall, it shook the ground for a minute. In the mid-seventies, one could find at the Public Theater what we now call multiculturalism being practiced in a way that still has not been tried by most American theaters."

For years, Joseph Papp had been a de facto citizens' representative of many New Yorkers in despair over problems ranging from ever-larger potholes to interracial violence. Where other people talked, Papp acted. Where other people were silent, the producer spoke out. He and the New York Shakespeare Festival had been a symbol of everything that was right with the city and it seemed only fitting that New York was now clearing an unobstructed path for him. "A lot of people believe that one person can't make a difference," said Emmett Foster, a performance artist and Papp's personal assistant for seventeen years. "But Joe took huge chances for what he believed in and he proved that one human being can change the world, because he *did* change it."

The motorcade sped past the police barriers across the top level of the Verazzano Narrows Bridge, over the great expanse of New York Harbor, toward the outlying sleepy borough of Staten Island. Although Papp's Mobile Theater had trucked Free Shakespeare to Staten Island as well as to the other four boroughs, few of the Manhattan drivers had ever been in this part of New York City before.

The funeral cortege pulled into the Baron Hirsch cemetery, where Shmuel and Yetta Papirofsky, Papp's parents, were buried in the family plot. It was a working-class cemetery, largely untended, overgrown, suggesting the abandoned Jewish cemeteries of Central and Eastern Europe. Many of the children of those buried here, like Joseph Papp himself, had moved up and far away, to the city, to the suburbs, to other parts of America.

In addition to his theater family, there were members of Joseph Papp's large and complicated personal family gathered in the cemetery — who had never before been assembled in one place. There were Papp's three siblings: elder sister, Rhoda, younger brother, Phillip, and younger sister, Anna; his wife and long-time colleague Gail Merrifield Papp; his non-marital daughter, Barbara Mosser, and her children; his first ex-wife, Betty Ball, their daughter, Susan Papp Lippman, and her son; Papp's son Michael Faulkner, whose mother, Papp's second ex-wife, Sylvia Faulkner, had not spoken to the producer for several decades; his third ex-wife, Peggy Papp, and Papp's third daughter, Miranda Papp Adani. Everyone gathered around the grave was conscious of the absence of Tony, Papp's fifth child and second son, who had died of AIDS five months earlier at the age of twenty-eight.

The coffin was lowered into the ground. A shovel was passed from hand to hand. The rabbi led the group in reciting the Kaddish. The grandchildren placed pots of ivy around the covered grave and the mourners returned to Manhattan.

I had been out early that morning, buying those pots of ivy. Fifteen years earlier, I had been assigned by the Sunday *New York Times* to write about the New York Shakespeare Festival. After several weeks of research, I had spent twelve hours accompanying Joe Papp on a "typical" day. At 9:00 P.M., on the spur of the moment, he had invited me home for dinner and I had accepted.

Papp's wife, Gail Merrifield, took my coat at the apartment door. She was the head of the Play Development Department and we had already met during an interview in which I had noted that she possessed a quirky and intriguing intelligence. Now she ushered me into the living room. The table in the dining alcove was set with candelabra and flowers. They told me it was their first wedding anniversary.

Neither of the Papps would listen to my embarrassed proposals to come back another time. They were, I was to learn, unconventional in the celebration of anniversaries, birthdays and holidays. They often invited people they liked home on impulse — and their living room offered up as assorted a group as ever appeared on the old television show *What's My Line?* When I rang their doorbell — as I was to do for the next fifteen years — the door might be opened by one of the squad of nutritionally correct Papp trainers, who watched over the Papps' physiques and eventually persuaded them to convert their living room into a gym. Or the fascinating Jesuit college president who was Gail Merrifield's cousin. Or a distraught actor, playwright, director or playreader — clad in a towel — who had been recovering in the closet sauna from some personal catastrophe. Or the Papps' horse-trainer neighbor from Westchester County — in town to see a Broadway musical. Or a maintenance man taking a break from fixing the elaborate telephone system or one of the many new high-tech gadgets — audio equipment, automatic bread-machine or sorbet-maker — that both Papps favored. Or the children — Tony and Miranda Papp — and their friends, sprawled out on the two brightly patterned couches.

The cluttered living room, with its hodgepodge of people, mirrors, pictures, bookshelves, exercise equipment, lamps, weird *objets*, and the small dining alcove bore no resemblance to the grand, expensive rooms in which I had conducted other interviews and which belonged to other men whose names had become household words. For by the late seventies, news about the producer and his Festival was a regular item not only in the American media but in newspapers and magazines around the world. Oral history libraries were trying to get him on tape. University students were writing dissertations about him. Publishers were asking him to write books.

The producer had no time or patience to write a book and he did not make an easy subject. He refused to be interviewed for an oral history and, although he tried to accommodate journalists, would often get antsy and find it difficult to keep his mind set on answering questions. On those occasions when he agreed to cooperate on a long project, as he did for a *New Yorker* profile in 1973, he overwhelmed the writer with so much — and so much *contradictory* — material that the writer gave up, complaining, "This fellow is in motion all the time and I can't keep up with him."

By the time he had become a famous producer, keeping up with him, even when he sat for an interview, was difficult. Papp talked in a rapid-fire, digressive and volatile way, punning, quoting from Shakespeare, sometimes jumping up to illustrate a point. Unlike many celebrities who dined out on their famous exploits, the producer got bored recounting the highlights of his career again and again. He took to embroidering on the narrative with such urgency, charm and conviction that, year after year, journalists as well as academics wrote his life story as if it were being told for the first time.

Like many New York City children, I had grown up hearing that story and seeing Papp's photograph in the newspapers, alongside such other handsome young public figures as musician Leonard Bernstein and President John F. Kennedy. In the early 1960s, Papp often visited city high schools to speak about Shakespeare and impressed a generation of teenagers with his intensity and idealism. Many of us, including a young African-American girl who would become the actress Whoopi Goldberg, first saw Shakespeare because of him, stood on line for free tickets in Central Park, cheered when he fought the political establishment and perceived him as a kind of contemporary Robin Hood who stole art from the rich and gave it to the poor.

Then the 1960s ended. By the time I was assigned to write about Papp, in 1976, he was no longer anti-Establishment but part of it, producing on Broadway as well as in Central Park. He had become a powerful man — now photographed in tuxedos as well as in shirtsleeves, behind an enormous desk, smoking a cigar. I had interviewed several such men in the course of my work and did not look forward to it. Such interviewees often had enormous egos, a slick presentation and a slimy way of interacting with female reporters. Imagining that a theater producer, in particular, would be cavalier with women, I was prepared for sleaze and a hard time.

Papp surprised me. His ego was huge, but instead of slickness, he exuded reserve and a sobriety that made me think of Old Testament patriarchs. Some people he worked with found his seriousness almost unrelieved. His colleague Bernard Gersten said Papp suffered from anhedonia — an inability to take pleasure. Papp did take pleasure in life but his approach to it was serious and somewhat wary. He was not a smiler and I always felt a sense of accomplishment after eliciting his laughter. I also felt free. He gave me a lot of room and, when I later mentioned that to women who had worked for him, they understood what I meant.

"Joe Papp had perfect pitch when it came to dealing with women," said actress Ellen Holly. "He made you feel that you were a gorgeous woman and a magnificent talent. But he was only interested in those assets as they enhanced the business at hand. There was never any kind of sexual innuendo, no double entendre, none of the varieties of sexual abuse that are so frequent in show business among both men and women in power. It was business all the way. Even back in the fifties. I knew that I was safe and that was very important to me."

Papp was, all his life, inordinately curious about people. He could read a face, tone of voice or body posture as if it were text — and had no compunction about cutting through convention and asking an intimate, direct question, not only of friends but of actors, journalists, elevator men, taxi drivers and anyone else who caught his interest. Strangers talked to him with the freedom one feels on a long train ride with a person one will never see again. He would offer comments that addressed the most vulnerable places of the speaker's psyche and, I thought, he had to be extremely vulnerable himself.

That habit of going to the heart of the emotional matter co-existed with a playfulness of mind that was fast, urban and American — and a product of the 1930s. Papp was unable to let five minutes go by without constructing some pun or play on words whose meaning eluded me and made me feel like a fool. In that, I was to discover, I was not alone. "I'd say I just got back from Washington and he'd say, 'How's George?'" a playwright would later tell me. "And I'd think: *That's stupid*. But then he'd make thirteen more puns in two and a half minutes. I was in his office once when they were rehearsing *Hamlet*. Someone came in to say an actor had been injured and he said, as though automatically, 'Well you can't make a *Hamlet* without breaking legs.'" Didn't I know that punning was a poor man's way of showing off his intellect, Papp asked me. He had grown up extremely poor.

Papp fell into no standard category. He was neither performer nor politician, not an impresario nor an arts bureaucrat, but a prodigiously creative cultural entrepreneur, who had built up an institution from scratch. Like the great American inventors, he had started with nothing but a notion; like the great American tycoons, he had devoted his life to giving it form. The odds for his success were not good. Joseph Papp had no family money, no higher education (he had never attended college), no network of social or political contacts. The financial underpinning of government endowments and private foundations for the arts that came into existence during the 1960s was unavailable to him when he began. Nonetheless, Joseph Papp had influenced a huge number of his contemporaries and younger people in the arts. Hundreds of writers, actors, directors, composers, designers, producers, arts administrators, stage managers, journalists and critics traced the beginnings of their careers to the Festival. Thousands more dated their first exposure to Shakespeare to a production in Central Park. Millions of others had seen his productions on television and on Broadway. The name Joseph Papp embodied the history and the very best possibilities of New York. When he died, in the fall of 1991, he had survived several newspapers, *four* mayors, *six* city parks commissioners and at least a dozen New York theater critics.

Because of the revenues from such commercial hits as *Hair, Two Gentlemen of Verona* and *A Chorus Line,* the New York Shakespeare Festival had become one of the largest arts institutions in the United States. At Lincoln Center, it became a constituent alongside the venerable New York Philharmonic and the Metropolitan Opera. The view of these old and long-exclusive institutions of what constituted art and its inter-preters was, with few exceptions, taken from the European model, as were their conventions, their programming, the expectations of their audience. Those audiences included New York City's wealthiest inhabi-tants, as well as a large dollop of tourists, expense-account business visitors and suburbanites who patronized them provided that they could park their cars in a protected lot.

The New York Shakespeare Festival and its audience was, by contrast, composed of men and women whose diversity was uncommon not only in New York City, but anywhere else on the American cultural scene. The audience for Free Shakespeare was the only one in the world in which it was not inconceivable that a welfare recipient might be seated beside an investment banker, a Brooklyn native beside a Parisian tourist. Papp had anticipated multiculturalism by a few decades and the evolution of this alternative to the dominant American cultural institutions interested me. In 1977, I told Joseph Papp that I envisaged a biography that would explain it.

I had, at the time, never written a book — a fact that would have ended discussions with almost anyone else but that, typically, intrigued the producer. I was twenty-nine years old and an untenured journalism professor, but inexperience, I discovered, could be an asset in Papp's eyes. What was important, it seemed, was that he could see himself in me: a first-generation American Jew, the child of Holocaust survivors — some members of his family had been murdered by the Nazis during World War II — a product of New York City public schools. My first love, like his, had been music. I had studied at the Columbia Graduate School of Journalism, which he had wished to attend, and was pursuing the career that he, as a young man, had wished to pursue. Like Papp, I was intense, impatient and focused on my work. We discussed the book I envisaged, chapter by chapter. Then he asked me where I'd like to see it published, picked up the telephone and dialed the editor-in-chief of that publishing house. As it happened, the editor's wife was an actress who had started out as an usher in his Central Park theater.

"Hello. This is Joseph Papp," I watched him say. "I've got a girl here with whom I'm going to write a book. I'd like you to see her."

The editor saw me within the week. Like many others, he was eager to publish a book about Joseph Papp but wise enough to ask for a written statement of his cooperation. It was then that Joe changed his mind.

"I'm not ready to write a book," he said. "I'm still writing my life. That man from *The New Yorker* followed me for months and months and then told me he couldn't write my story because it seemed to have no ending. That surprised me. I thought certainly he could write something. But he didn't. He didn't have an ending. The ending will be when I die."

"You can't be my friend and my biographer," he said, when I expressed disappointment. Or, "I don't have to address my life now. I'm not a raconteur. Under the best of circumstances I don't like recollecting." Or, "A book is a lie. Nobody remains the same. You're at a different stage of life with every day that passes. Things are always changing around you and in you. For me, to find those moments and remember how I felt then, what can I say? I'm sorry. Write another book."

I wrote another book. Instead of becoming Papp's biographer, I became a family friend. After writing my profile of the New York Shakespeare Festival, I continued working as a cultural reporter but had no further involvement in the New York theater world. I saw the plays Joe produced, heard about new projects he was considering and sometimes listened to him give interviews. He gave hundreds of them — to the local, national and international press, to graduate students writing dissertations on the history of American theater, to teenagers doing reports for school, to brash television talk show hosts fresh from the provinces. *What first drew you to Shakespeare, Mr. Papp? How did you come up with the idea of presenting performances for free?*

Joseph Papp typically took charge — sometimes without the interviewer's grasping that he was doing so. He focused in on his questioner, probing, assessing motive, sizing up, making a casual, transitory exchange a vivid encounter, like the quick, intense connection between players of opposing teams during a basketball game. He lived as though he was playing basketball, I thought, reversing directions abruptly, turning on a dime. I understood why writers sometimes gave up trying to capture him on paper.

Although he did not remain in one place for very long, it was long enough to affect the course of other people's lives. There were artists who felt that their work had been transformed by one word he had uttered at a key moment or by a moment during which, instead of speaking, he had said nothing at all. There were others who were bitter, who felt that

Joseph Papp had let them down. Some saw him, as per Lord Acton's dictum, as a man corrupted by absolute power in the theater. Others saw him as incorruptible. Some found him intensely vulnerable; others, seemingly walled off from feeling. Some saw his consistency; others his self-contradiction. Some saw his nurturing side; others a savage, unpredictable anger. Joseph Papp had a terrible temper and a sharp tongue; he often spoke carelessly or with great cruelty. But the producer was also a man of tremendous compassion. He offered help and solace more consistently than anyone else I knew.

Occasionally, I heard that yet another writer or editor had approached Papp about a biography, but he had turned the project down. Then, in 1985, he told me with great excitement that he had conceived of producing an oral history of the New York Shakespeare Festival, a book of interviews with some one hundred people — actors, directors, technicians, administrators, critics, politicians — who had been involved with it over the years. An interviewer was hired. He traveled the country, recorded hundreds of hours of oral history and produced a first draft.

Within a few days of reading it, Papp decided to cancel the project.

The themes he felt were crucial to the development of the Festival were not apparent to him and subjects that he did not consider important — such as who did what to whom backstage in such and such a production — were all too evident. The publisher wanted a gossipy bestseller, he said, not the historical theater document he had in mind. In July of 1989, he terminated the project over which, typically, he had retained editorial control. Then he revived the decade-old idea of my writing his biography.

In 1989, that plan felt very different to me than it had in 1977. Joseph Papp was now sixty-eight and, for two years, had been living with an advanced state of prostate cancer. Although it had already metastasized into his spine and rib cage, very few people knew he was ill. He was traveling abroad. He was leading a vigorous battle against congressional restrictions on the National Endowment for the Arts. He had announced a Shakespeare Marathon during which he would produce all of Shakespeare's plays. And he was commuting to Boston, where my husband had found him an oncologist at the Dana-Farber Institute.

I did not take up his suggestion with alacrity. Instead, I suggested he follow the model of many other celebrities and tell me his story. I would then organize it and write it. He thought that was a good idea. It gave him an alibi for his repeated trips to Boston. On those occasions when a reporter spotted him and asked what he was doing here, Joe replied that he was working with me on his autobiography.

Once again, we put together a book proposal.

"When I read about the Joe Papp the press portrays, I find, as the song from *A Chorus Line* goes, 'A person I don't know,'" it read.

Again and again I find a misrepresentation of who I am and what I do. I've been portrayed as a man with low-brow taste and no aesthetic vision who destroys playwrights and is nothing but an artistic midwife. I've been attacked for being too anti-Establishment as well as for being the Establishment, for giving too much or not enough support to minorities, for showing too much or not enough loyalty to the people with whom I work.

But as we enter the 1990s, I'm engaged in combat on several fronts. I'm struggling with the bureaucracy that is New York City government and the monopoly that is the *New York Times*. I'm fighting a state of mind that has struck a blow at the very source of the creative enterprise. Writers are abandoning the theater for venues which will allow them to earn a living. The plague of AIDS has hit hard at the arts community; at the New York Shakespeare Festival, several of our most experienced, key people have died of the disease. At the same time that we are feeling the loss of people and financial support, we are under attack by critics for principles we have held since our beginnings such as multiracial casting, free or low-cost tickets, a quest for ever-broader audiences.

Together, we produced two sample chapters. Then, Joe hesitated.

"I cannot be an active participant in the writing of this book," he told me. "I'm not a writer. I don't have a compelling need to do it. If I needed the money, if I were broke, I'd do it. If I had something I needed to say, if I wanted to put my life's effort into perspective, I'd do it. But, do I want to do that? Why? For me — the past is dead. The present interests me far more than the past. I want to start from scratch every day. Why tell the same stories over and over again? Robert Moses and the grass. How I found *Hair* and *A Chorus Line*. That was years ago! I'm trying to get away from old structures."

"The worst thing about it," he said one day, "is that I'm in the center of the book. I have to go back into old areas and find out that the things that I decided to accept about myself — especially the positive things — might prove to me not so positive at all or else outweighed by negative things. There are things in everyone's life they don't talk about. My life includes four marriages and five children. Now everything seems to be okay but there's no question that those children were influenced and perhaps scarred by those broken marriages."

Or, on another occasion: "I don't want to hold myself up as a kind of ideal. My life has been made up of many things. It may have had more bad than good in it. I've not been at all praiseworthy in my private life. My brother, my sisters — they have what I'd call *good character*. I used to think that the worst thing you could do would be to be disloyal to your mate, play around with women. And yet I had a period in my life when I did exactly that. I cannot take seriously what some public figure says if I know he has a terrible private life. I have a very high regard for people that are true. I can't believe someone who is an extraordinary fighter for civil rights if I know he beats his wife; I cannot take what they say with a total amount of seriousness. I had trouble with the Kennedys for that reason and even with Martin Luther King. I expect people who speak out publicly on issues to be pure. I apply that same high standard to myself and for much of my life I don't meet it. I was perceived as doing something heroic in my public life at the same time that I was being very unheroic in private. I'm not like that now. I'm the best I've been. But the book will take me into the past, where I've been the worst. Why should I do it? I don't have a need to tell that truth. I have the energy to talk to you about it but I'd probably drop dead when I read it."

Death was, in fact, the subtext. Although he had had advanced cancer for two years by then, Joseph Papp refused to contemplate the possibility of his death. He had, after much procrastination, made out a will. He had begun to confer with possible successors to him at the Festival, but writing a memoir? That would be too continual a reminder of his mortality.

So our second collaboration fell into a kind of limbo. We continued to talk but I began work on another book. By this time I had a clearer picture of what he termed his "unheroic" private life. There were his complicated personal relationships with his five children — one of whom was dying of AIDS, one of whom had been conceived out of wedlock when Joe was in the navy and had first established a relationship with her birth father at the age of thirty-five. Then there were Papp's three ex-wives, from whom he had separated with great bitterness, and several ex-colleagues who had left him or whom he had fired. And there was the question of discussing his politics, especially since the mood of the country had, Papp felt, drifted sharply to the right.

From the age of fifteen till he was in his early thirties, Joe had been a Communist. He rarely spoke publicly about the subject, believing that doing so would endanger his theater. His theater was the house he had built, his alter ego. One of the sample chapters we had worked on together focused on his communism, his encounters with the FBI and his testimony before the House Committee on Un-American Activities.

It was hard for me to understand this part of Papp. I was born in Prague. My parents had survived the Nazis but, in 1948, left the country that had been their families' home for centuries because of the Communists. Joe had been a Communist in 1948. He had supported the Communist takeover of Czechoslovakia that had forced my parents to leave it. In fact, he had not formally broken with the Communist party until the mid-1950s.

Although he spoke at length to me about what communism had meant to him as an adolescent and adult, Papp was ambivalent about publishing what he said — even in 1989. The NEA controversy, the politics of the Reagan and Bush administrations and the ascent of such conservative figures as Senator Jesse Helms had raised his guard. He was not sure whether publishing this chapter of his life was worth the risk to the Festival he might incur.

Then there was a personal insecurity that I had begun to sense only after years of observing him at close hand. He could not tolerate being alone. He needed to command an audience and to be reminded of his accomplishments, his stature, his power. He was, I realized with surprise, what psychologists term "counterphobic," often frightened but striding purposefully into fear. Although Joseph Papp often seemed a pillar of certainty, he was often not sure that he had earned his position. He took many risks, but he was also a man who defended his flanks. And although he had come to trust me somewhat, I knew that he did not trust anyone enough to undertake an examination of his life.

By 1991, his cancer — which had been under control for four years — resurged with great force. He was in constant pain. He required heavy medication. At times, he could not walk. At others, he could not eat or think or speak clearly. His physician thought that keeping a journal might help. So, Joe began to write. Although he sometimes asked me technical questions about writing — what did I do if I felt I had nothing to say? how did I make my writing sound like speech? — we never again spoke about writing a book together. To do so would have been to confront the reality that he was dying, and that, until the very last few weeks, was something Joe was unwilling to do.

It was a few months after his death that Gail Merrifield Papp asked me to finish what Joe and I had begun. This is an "authorized" biography, which means that I was given full access to both the vast New York Shakespeare Festival archive and to boxloads of private papers. However, it is atypical in that I was also given full editorial control of the content. It is a "friendly" biography in the sense that I admired Joseph Papp, enjoyed many productions in his theater and shared many of his ideas — most importantly a belief in art *not* for "art's sake" but for "life's sake," art that was inclusive rather than exclusive, art that was urgent, that made you feel as though the artist needed to convey it now or else blow his or her brains out. When colleagues pointedly asked whether it would be a "whitewash," I replied that I hoped not. On the other hand, I did not set out to demolish my subject.

We all see the people and events that pass before our eyes through the prism of our personalities, our histories, our genders, our prejudices. Joseph Papp understood and honored that. Even if he had not brought me home to his first wedding anniversary dinner nearly two decades ago, even if I had not known him personally, I would have wanted to write a book about him because of who I am. I wanted to discover what kind of conditions created Joe. Where did he get his ideas? How was he able to turn them into a reality? Who influenced him and how? Why were there so few people like him?

"Critics often claim I'm inconsistent, that I have no central aesthetic," Joe had written in a note that I had kept apart from the others. "What is consistent in my work is that I have always wanted to provide access to the best human endeavor to the greatest number of people. This has always been my central idea, my aesthetic. I am not an academic, not an intellectual, not some kind of cultural missionary bringing Shakespeare to the natives. I believe that great art is for everyone — not just the rich or the middle class. When I go into East Harlem or Bedford-Stuyvesant and see the kids who come to our shows, I see nothing so clearly as myself."

I began writing this book for a third time, fifteen years after I had started, looking for the child who grew up to become Joseph Papp.

ONE

A Jewish Boyhood in Brooklyn

WHEN in later years Joe Papp would talk about his childhood, he did so in grim, Dickensian terms that some of his Jewish contemporaries found self-dramatizing and extreme. Papp's memories of childhood did not correspond to their own. They seemed too raw. They seemed to belong to the world of their fathers — powerless, penniless, sometimes illiterate immigrant Jews, who had exchanged the miseries of European towns and villages for the urban ghettos of the New World.

By the late twentieth century, most American Jews of Joe Papp's generation — the men and women who had grown up during the Great Depression and the Second World War — were comfortably middle class. They viewed themselves as part of the American majority, well established and secure. Many did not remember or wish to remember that it had ever been any other way.

For Joe Papp, however, Jewishness, poverty, marginality and danger were inextricably entwined. His early experience as a Jew would remain vivid and available to him, coloring his responses and decisions. A few years before he died, Papp interviewed a new accountant, who had come highly recommended. At the door, without so much as a "hello," Papp demanded, "Why do you want to represent me? I don't have any money and I'm difficult."

Aaron Shapiro, who would become co-executor of Papp's estate, replied frankly, "I was just wondering the same thing."

Papp let him into his living room. "You represent a lot of people — you probably don't return phone calls."

Shapiro assured him he returned calls within twenty-four hours.

"Why so long?" Papp demanded. "Where'd you go to school?"

"City College," said Shapiro.

"Oh, one of those *smart* Jewish kids. Where'd you grow up?"

"Brooklyn," said Shapiro.

"Where?" demanded Papp.

"Williamsburg."

Papp's face relaxed, Shapiro recalled. "None of my other credentials or references made any difference," he said. "Now he knew who I was."

Joseph Papp was born Joseph, or, as his parents called him, "Yussel," Papirofsky — after his maternal grandfather — on June 22, 1921, at home in Williamsburg. "I thought it was a Jewish name," he would later quip, "My father always pronounced it *Viliamsburg*. It was much later that I would learn it was Jeffersonian."

The Williamsburg into which Joseph Papirofsky was born in 1921 was not yet the cohesive Chassidic enclave it would become after the Second World War. There was no organized Jewish community there. There were not even enough Jews on every block to give the neighborhood the kind of security in numbers that emanated from the streets of the Lower East Side — the most densely populated neighborhood in the United States — or from the streets of Brownsville, called the "Jerusalem of America" because of its large number of synagogues.

In the socioeconomic hierarchy of American Jewish neighborhoods, Williamsburg ranked near the bottom. Its rows of multifamily houses and tenements were home to a mix of poor ethnic groups — Jewish, Italian, Ukrainian, Polish, Irish, Negro and some Arab families whom the children called "Mohammedans." They observed one another's religious ceremonies, wedding celebrations and funeral processions with suspicion. By the time boys were six or seven, they had already been beaten up a few times and had mastered the fight-or-flight response. Every block "belonged" to one immigrant group or another. Schoolchildren were acutely aware of their turf and their names, and Papirofsky was clearly not Irish or Italian.

By 1921, more than two million Jews like the Papirofskys had left

Eastern Europe for the United States. Those with family connections or money or extraordinary energy ventured beyond New York City. The majority settled in the crowded Lower East Side of Manhattan. Then they spilled over to Brooklyn, crossing the East River in such numbers that the Williamsburg Bridge was dubbed "Jews' Bridge" by the yellow press. These new immigrants were regarded with contempt not only by the older German and Irish communities. They were despised by the "uptown" Jewish community, established Jews of Portuguese and German descent, whose newspaper, the *Hebrew Standard,* described the immigrants as "miserably darkened Hebrews," with whom "the thoroughly acclimatized American Jew . . . has no religious, social or intellectual ties."

As a small boy, Yussel Papirofsky saw daily evidence of their marginality. Sam and Yetta Papirofsky had brought with them from Poland and Lithuania the centuries-old culture of the traditional Jewish community. But, in Brooklyn, that culture's values and assumptions were as irrelevant as its calendar of holidays and rituals. The Papirofskys' finances were shaky, their frames of reference all but useless, their names unstable and subject to the whim of immigration officials. The family papers would, for years, offer up several variants of their name: Papirofsky, Papierowski, Papirovski, Paprovsky, Papiroski.

Migration had severed the Papirofskys from family history, place in community and most other springs of security and self-worth. Most radically, it had turned upside down the traditional roles of parent and child. The Papirofsky children, particularly the elder son and daughter, took on the roles of interpreters, guides, arbitrators and protectors. "There were never any instructions, never anybody yelling 'It's getting dark, come upstairs!'" Papp's younger brother Phillip would recall. "There was no supervision. We were out in the street until all hours and Joe could stay out all night. We raised ourselves."

When he was much older, the producer would sometimes marvel at playwright Neil Simon's or filmmaker Woody Allen's paradigms of Jewish family relations, the abundance of good food, the music lessons, the involvement of parents in children's lives. His contemporary, Irving Howe, might write, "The Jews formed a genuine community, reaching half-unseen into a dozen neighborhoods and a multitude of institutions within the shadows of which we have found protection of a kind," but Papp drew a sharp distinction between that world and his own.

"I come from a sector of Judaism that was poor in every sense," he would say. "I always wondered how we got to Williamsburg, we were so isolated. There was no network of connections among the Jews, no sense of being protected. My father was a member of the Workmen's Circle but he didn't go to meetings.

"My parents had no friends that I knew of and not many relations. The phone was in the corner candy store so you always knew who got a call and they never got a phone call. There was very little conversation at home and almost nothing was said about the past." It would be five decades later, when Papp was sixty and the *Jewish Forward* ran an article comparing him to his paternal grandfather, that the producer first began to examine his family history.

The Papirofskys came from Kielce, Poland. Notorious as one of the Eastern European cities to have had a pogrom *after* the Holocaust, it had belonged for centuries to the estates of the bishops of Kraków, who had prevented Jews from living there since the 1500s. In the mid-nineteenth century, Kielce had one hundred legally resident Jews. By the turn of the century, migration from the countryside had swelled that number to a thousand. All Jewish children passed through the *cheder* of Papp's paternal grandfather, Moshe Papirofsky, where, under a portrait of the Tsar, they learned religion and Hebrew as well as some Russian. Both Moshe the *Melamed,* or Moses the Teacher, and his students were desperately poor. At least half of his charges did not pay tuition. Eventually the school was closed and Moshe Papirofsky and his family were evicted from their home.

One of his sons went to Austria to work as a baker. Another moved to Kraków, where he worked as a photographer. At twenty, short and spunky, with the erect, compact frame that was a family characteristic, Shmuel Papirofsky escaped conscription into the army by making his way through the forests to Austria, then to the port of Hamburg, then to America. When he arrived in New York City in 1913, he found work as a trunkmaker. Four years later, he married Yetta Miritch, whom he had met at Goldberg's Farm, a restaurant and dance hall in Brooklyn.

Yetta Miritch — or Mirisch or Morris — had been a fifteen-year-old orphan when she left Kovno, Lithuania, for America, sponsored by one of her aunts. She communicated little about her family and nothing about Joseph Miritch, the father for whom she had named her eldest son. She had arrived in New York in 1909 and, unable to read or write, was put to work in a Brooklyn shirtwaist factory.

Papp told interviewers that his mother was a beautiful, gracious woman, with a style of her own. "She was raised very poor," he said, "but she always had a certain kind of aristocracy about her. She spoke very little and her energy was amazing. Her rhythm was rapid — like mine. She used to go up and down those five flights of stairs like a whiz — carrying coal or chunks of ice for the icebox or groceries — keeping the house immaculate. She did everything herself, would never let anybody touch anything. She was not a stereotypical Jewish mother. She was a Jewish wife. What I remember most about her was a certain aloofness, an elegance and pride. She was always impeccably clean, everything starched and ironed because when you're poor, you try to dress well."

He also said that his interaction with her was mostly nonverbal and characterized by desires left unexpressed. "She seemed to want so much from me — I saw it in her eyes. And I'd do anything for her — I once climbed to the fifth floor, up this pole I had to shimmy up, just to put up this laundry line for her. If she'd asked me to jump off, I would have jumped. The thing is, you give a lot and sometimes you get nothing back in return. There's this fear where you're called upon to give and give and there's no payment at all."

The familial pattern offered up in Jewish immigrant literature — the remote, passive father; the intrusive, overcompensating mother — did not pertain to the Papirofskys. Shmuel Papirofsky was a warm, demonstrative man, an extrovert who loved to sing and share jokes with his children. Yetta Papirofsky, as described by her children, was loving but reserved and chronically ill. "She kept mainly to herself, relative to the flock of *yentas* who tried to become her friends," her younger son would recall. Her orphanhood, the long journey in steerage alone, lifelong circulatory problems and the bearing and care of four children — Rhoda in 1918; Joseph in 1921; Phillip in 1924; Anna in 1930 — had contributed to what Papp would later come to understand not only as his mother's aloof nature but possibly her depression. As a very small child, Joe Papirofsky adapted to his mother's emotional distance. "He tended to somatize, even as a small child," recalled a close friend. "Rather than call his mother, he developed physical symptoms of distress — like not being able to breathe. One of his few early memories was of being a toddler on the kitchen floor. He remembered the sight of his mother's legs as she went about her housework and his longing for his father to come home."

"Sometimes, when I watch my face on television, I see my father's face on one side and my mother's on the other," Papp said. "My father's is the extremely human side of me, the side where I identify with people's feelings and can express my own. I see the unfulfilled side of me as coming from my mother. I hooked into her sense of isolation and feeling disconnected from the world. Also into the way she kept striving because she never really felt she had accomplished anything. That has its advantages: it creates a drive. But its disadvantage is that you're never satisfied.

She was always setting goals for me. And I would do anything for her. I wanted her to pay some attention to me."

Yetta Papirofsky reserved what emotional resources she had for Sam, as he was called in Brooklyn, and it was he who spent time with the children. "My father was solidly of the earth," Papp would later say, "Warm. Open. Very loving. Generous in spirit and religious in the best sense of the word. His relation to God was as natural to him as eating or drinking, and he never tried to push it onto anyone else, not even onto me, his eldest son." Sam Papirofsky would rise early in order to lay *tefillin*, the ancient Jewish prayer custom that religiously observant Jewish males practice from the age of thirteen on. Yussel Papirofsky liked to watch his father take out two small black leather boxes containing bits of parchment inscribed with biblical text, attach one to his forehead and the second to the inside of his left arm. "He told me that even in the forest, he never forgot to pray," Papp later said. "He went to a very poor *shul* on our block and I would go with him. I used to feel good there, being with my father as he was communicating with God. I was the only little boy there in that crowd of men and I used to sit and listen."

Years later, when asked by a child about his belief in God, the producer made no mention of the nearly twenty years he chose to pass as a Christian. He wrote: "When I was your age, God was to be found in the synagogue, a small storefront *shul* in Brooklyn. He was everywhere . . . in the cracked voice of the neighborhood cantor who was a glazier by trade, in the chanting of the small, poor, devoted congregation. But, most of all, I saw God in the ark which housed the precious Torahs, the scrolls covered with soft velvet material and decorated in gold thread with the great lion of Judah. When these huge scrolls were lifted high into the air, I held my breath. 'If a Torah is dropped,' my father would say, 'it would be a tragedy of immense proportions. We would have to fast for forty days and nights to compensate. . . .' Today I still find God in *shul* and in the memory of my parents, plain and simple Jewish folk who gave me an everlasting gift of cultural continuity."

His father's *shul*, Joseph Papp would often point out, was nothing like the "uptown" Manhattan synagogues, which required tickets of admission on High Holidays, and where people spoke what he perceived as a fancy, postwar Hebrew, pronounced in the Israeli manner, sanitized of the Yiddish intonation redolent of European ghetto life. Until his death Papp would point out the difference between his own poor, marginal, Williamsburg kind of Jew and the "uptown," middle-class, mainstream, educated "doctors and lawyers" who lived in Manhattan or in the suburbs. "There are no doctors or lawyers in my family," he would often say.

"My brother and sisters all live in Brooklyn. Their kids live in Brooklyn. We're all working-class people."

Six mornings a week in the 1920s, Sam Papirofsky would travel two hours to the shop where he sat on a bench, cutting pieces of metal and hammering nails into trunks. The workshop was, in his son's recollection, no bigger than four telephone booths, filled with sheets of tin and kegs of copper nails. The work was steady and suited Sam's temperament but it barely supported a family that comprised, by 1930, four children.

"The twenties, you remember, was a period of parties," Papp later read with bemusement in a memoir by theater director Harold Clurman. For Clurman, the twenties were the Jazz Age, embodied by F. Scott Fitzgerald, Ernest Hemingway and Noël Coward and a golden age for the American theater. "It was a prosperous time, and it seemed that all distinction between people, all struggle, and all natural unpleasantness were to be liquidated in the polite booze of the party ritual. . . . It was the time for fun. It was the time of the good time."

For people like the Papirofskys, of course, the twenties were not a good time. The family lived in a series of tenements, moving four times before Joe turned twelve. Their flats were the cheapest: located on the top floor, with two tiny bedrooms, and a toilet in the hall. Yetta and her daughters slept in one bedroom; Sam and his sons in the other; the kitchen served as bathroom, dining room and living room. During the winters, when the only source of heat was a coal stove, the flat was cold; during the summers, so hot that Joe and his younger brother would drench themselves with citronella and brave the mosquitoes out on the fire escape.

Like so many Orthodox Jewish women of the time, Yetta Papirofsky's life revolved around keeping her family and its living quarters clean. "My mother was as clean as any German housewife," wrote Michael Gold, whose autobiographical novel *Jews Without Money* was, during his adolescence, one of Joe Papirofksy's favorites:

> She slaved, she worked herself to the bone keeping us fresh and neat. The bedbugs were a torment to her. She doused the beds with kerosene, changed the sheets, sprayed the mattresses in an endless frantic war with the bedbugs. What was the use? Nothing could help; it was Poverty; it was the Tenement. . . . The bedbugs lived and bred in the rotten walls of the tenement, with the rats, fleas, roaches; the whole rotten structure needed to be torn down; a kerosene bottle would not help.

Neither poverty nor the break from her community deflected Yetta Papirofsky from keeping house according to strict Jewish ritual law, with two sets of dishes and eating utensils — one for meals made with dairy food, one for meals that contained meat. She taught her children to put pennies in the family's traditional *zedakah* (charity) box, to give money to beggars and to treat all people with respect — particularly people less fortunate than themselves. With four children and no parents or siblings of her own to help her, there was always work for Yetta Papirofsky: cooking, cleaning, mending clothes. Not until the mid-1950s did she learn to read and write English and painstakingly to sign her name. By then, she was over sixty years old.

Except for Friday nights, when Yetta Papirofsky lit Sabbath candles, put a white cloth on the kitchen table and cooked a chicken, the family rarely ate a full meal. Snacks were pieces of *matzoh* dipped in chicken fat. Children's birthdays came and went without cakes, presents, photographs or parties. Joseph Papp would recall a time when his family had no knives and forks, but ate with *leffels* or spoons and sat down to meals on fruit boxes, under the light of one bleak ceiling bulb.

Years later, visitors to his home would admire the many beautiful lamps in his apartment and be startled by the sight of kitchen shelves crammed with food. While he did not lecture his children about his own hungry childhood or allude to it in ordinary conversation, Joseph Papp did not wish to be caught short on offering hospitality to his guests or ever to find his larder bare. When he took over the Public Theater, one of the first things he installed was a refrigerator. During a press conference announcing his move to Lincoln Center, he baffled reporters by breaking off in midsentence to comment on the wonderful softness of the recessed lighting in the lobby.

Warm lighting would retain a special meaning for him all his life. Although he was not particular about furniture, his home environment always contained comfortable couches and beautiful lamps. As a small child, he had read Hans Christian Andersen's "The Little Match Girl," which had become his favorite fairy tale and which he remembered in the following way:

"It's about a little girl, very poor, evidently parentless, and she's very cold. It's Christmas Eve or maybe Christmas Day and she's blue with cold. She looks into a window and she sees a Christmas tree inside, and little kids dressed up and having a good time, playing with toys, and there's something steaming on the table — a Christmas goose — and the place is full of food and light and there's a smiling father and mother — all the things that mean family and warmth and wealth. And outside, a few snowflakes start to fall and all she has left is three matches and her hands are freezing. So she lights one of her matches and some fantasy takes place where she sees herself as part of this thing. Then she dies of cold.

"I was so moved by that. I can always see that little girl looking into a restaurant. I used to do that myself, when people were eating on Christmas and you could see people having a good time, well-dressed, and you're looking in from the outside. I wasn't freezing to death exactly but it was cold."

Although he never sold matches, Joseph Papp all but lived his childhood in the streets. He rarely brought friends home and long remembered being invited to the apartment of his Irish schoolfriend, Jerry Winthrop, which always had the sweet smell of butter in the air, where there were chairs instead of fruit boxes and lamps instead of bare light bulbs. He remembered mothers who spoke what seemed to be flawless English and phrases like "Please come in" and "How are you." He remembered that there had been no English at home until his elder sister Rhoda had brought it home from school. "That embarrassed me," the producer would confess. "I always wanted to be out of the house, on my own, free of any kind of connection."

Rhoda Papirofsky, two years older than Joe, took on the responsibility of supervising her brother. "I always had a lot of responsibility," she recalled. "When I was five years old, I came home from kindergarten into a hallway full of blood. The neighbors told me a vein in my mother's leg had burst and that she had to be taken to the emergency room. My father was in bed recovering from appendicitis. Joe must have been around two years old then. I had to take care of him. But, later on, he was never around. He was always involved with a wild gang of kids. I remember him falling off a roof once and scarring his head. Nobody really kept track of him."

Joe Papp would later speak with a mixture of affection and wariness of his "bossy older sister," who irritated him by searching him out and trying to get him to come home. He would be in the Lindsay Park playground, or hanging out on some rooftop where a friend kept pigeons, stealing coal from the coalyards, or in the street — playing skelly, a game based on bottle caps, or marbles, boxball, punchball — or in a fight. Although his block of Williamsburg was only a few minutes' trolley ride from the East River, he was unaware of the river, unaware of the Manhattan skyline. "I didn't get across the Williamsburg Bridge into Manhattan until I was at least ten," he told an interviewer, "and I still have a nightmare about the Canarsie BMT. I'm inside the train, my father is still on the platform and the door has closed between us." His landscape was made of asphalt, concrete, chicken wire and the dirt in his yard and the cellar, where he organized clubs such as the I-Findem Detective Agency. "Our most auspicious case," his younger brother recalled, "was a prospect we followed through the streets, a park, a schoolyard . . . until we finally lost him when he entered a synagogue." Every January, he collected the Christmas trees that neighbors threw away and used them to build his own clubhouse. "That's very much connected with the theater for me," the producer would later say. "My own roof over my head. From the time I was a very small child, I always wanted to have my own place."

The only regular community event in Joseph Papp's childhood was going to the movies. Every Saturday after *shul,* he took the money he had won playing marbles and — in disregard of the prohibitions of Orthodox Judaism — spent six hours at the Progress or Alba, watching one or two feature films, a couple of serials, the newsreel and everyone else in the neighborhood. Papp would later recall the manager's call: *"Baby crying outside!"* which would prompt three or four mothers to run out into the lobby to check their prams. At the Folly, one of the one hundred or so vaudeville houses still left in the United States, the movie was supplemented with a stage show, one of them featuring the Silver Lady, a dancer entirely painted in silver, and four or five singers, magicians, jugglers and comedians. "I was reared chiefly on vaudeville," he later told an interviewer. "The great Houdini was my idol and I wanted to be a magician. In those vaudeville houses, there was an exhilarating rapport between the headliners and the spectators that makes theater what it should be, with the audience participating with what is set before them."

Along with the rest of the neighborhood kids, Joe watched the Marx Brothers, Charlie Chaplin and Buster Keaton, Tom Mix, Bob Steele, Ken Maynard, Hoot Gibson and a whole series of Tarzans. As a teenager, he would admire a series of tough-talking leading men: James Cagney, Clark Gable, Spencer Tracy. But the first with whom he identified was Al Jolson in *The Jazz Singer,* which he saw with his father.

The Jazz Singer was the first talkie as well as a film with special meaning for the Jewish community. It had begun as a short story in *Everybody's Magazine* about a seventh-generation Orthodox Jewish cantor on the Lower East Side and his musical son, Jakie Rabinowitz, who loves the jazzy, secular music of the neighborhood saloon. The cantor forbids his son to sing in the saloon. Jakie runs away and becomes the nightclub singer Jack Robin. Jack Robin finds that his lucky break — the opening of his first Broadway show — conflicts with the holiest day of the Jewish calendar, Yom Kippur, the Day of Atonement. That afternoon, he returns home to find his father on his deathbed, imploring him to take his place as cantor for the evening service. Jack Robin chooses to miss his opening night and takes his father's place in the synagogue, becoming the eighth generation of Rabinowitzes to serve as cantor.

At least, that was how the story and the play read. In the Warner Brothers film, which became a milestone of movie history, Jack Robin remains Jack Robin. The son returns home to find his father on his deathbed and winds up chanting most of the *Kol Nidrei* prayer onscreen with his (Gentile) girlfriend Mary listening in the wings. But the next day (the opening having been postponed for his convenience), Jack Robin goes on to become a smash success on the Broadway stage. What writer Neal Gabler rightly calls "an assimilationist fable" was, in fact, close to the true story of Al Jolson as well as a paradigm for a generation of sons of all kinds of immigrants.

For American Jews like the Papirofskys, *The Jazz Singer* was a big deal, much discussed at home, with the neighbors and in the Jewish press. There on the big screen, for the first time, was an Orthodox Jewish family and a cantor draped in a prayer shawl, chanting the holiest and most intimate of Jewish prayers! And, because Jack Robin was a star of vaudeville, the scene of his final triumph showed him in blackface, a Jew taking on the convention of a Negro minstrel singer to succeed as an American.

What did eight-year-old Joe Papirofsky make of this bizarre configuration of identities? There is no record of it. But the *Jazz Singer*'s message, many of the producer's Jewish contemporaries would later recall, was that success in America entailed the jettisoning of Jewish law, Jewish women and a Jewish way of life. It was a message that was reinforced daily over the radio, by such comedians as Eddie Cantor and Jack Benny.

The Papirofskys did not own a radio until Joe was a teenager, but in the evenings Joe and his siblings would go to the homes of their neighbors, who charged them a penny for the privilege of listening. Every Jewish kid knew that Eddie Cantor, born Edward Israel Iskowitz, and Jack Benny, born Benjamin Kubelsky, were the sons of immigrant Jews. In a neighborhood like Williamsburg, the two comedians were regarded not only with the respect accorded self-made millionaires but with a deference toward the very few Jews of the time who had America listening to them. Their routines, their gags, their timing and plays on words were to influence Joe Papirofsky's as well as a generation of Americans' speech patterns as well as their notion of what was funny. They would also implicitly reinforce the message of *The Jazz Singer*: If they wished to make it in America, they needed to take the Jewishness out of their intonations, their names and their pasts — all of which the producer would later do.

At the time, though, Joe Papirofsky was immersed in Jewish culture. One spring before his voice changed, a dapper, Yiddish-speaking man arrived in Williamsburg looking for a boy soloist for High Holiday services at his synagogue. He said that he would provide training in liturgical chant, pay subway fare to rehearsals and pay for the final performance on Yom Kippur. One of Joe Papirofsky's friends recommended Joe. Sam Papirofsky was pleased, Joe was excited by the prospect of earning money by singing and a deal was struck.

Weeks of practice followed until the day father and son took the long ride across Brooklyn to the prosperous neighborhood of Ocean Parkway where he was to perform in an imposing stone synagogue. They were stopped at the door by a man who asked to see their tickets. At first, Sam Papirofsky did not understand what he was talking about; in his storefront *shul*, there were no reserved seats, let alone an admission fee. Joe angrily identified himself as the boy soloist and insisted that his father be allowed to hear him free of charge.

In the end, Sam Papirofsky was admitted to the splendid synagogue, and sat alone in a sea of well-dressed strangers. The producer Joseph Papp would retain a vivid memory of his own feelings of sadness, indignation and embarrassment, the injustice of his father's predicament and the contrast of entitlement and poverty that existed within the Jewish community just as it did outside.

In the 1920s and early 1930s, Joe Papirofsky's ideas about that outside world came to him via movies, vaudeville and the radio. Once they had acquired their own Philco, the Papirofskys would often listen to the news as well as to musical programs together. "Music — to me — is the source of all art," Papp would later say. "If you ask me what I missed most in my childhood, it was that I didn't learn an instrument. I wanted to play the violin." But Joe Papirofsky knew there was no money for either a violin or violin lessons. Instead, Sam Papirofsky taught his son how to play the harmonica — an instrument Joe Papp enjoyed playing all his life. He also led the Papirofskys in whole evenings of singing, harmonizing Stephen Foster songs and songs from the movies like "Keep Your Sunny Side Up" or "I'm in the Market for You." One of his earliest major purchases for the family had been an RCA Victor console record player, which Joe remembered as costing $150 and taking forever to pay off on the installment plan. They had found the bulk of their record collection one day in the street. It included 78 rpm disks by opera singers Fyodor Chaliapin, Enrico Caruso and John McCormick, the Beethoven symphonies, and the Mendelssohn violin concerto. The radio offered Benny Goodman, Ted Lewis, Bing Crosby, Rudy Vallee, Duke Ellington.

Sam Papirofsky, who had performed with a *klezmer* band in his youth, loved it all as did his children. During the summers, he would take them to Prospect Park to hear the Goldman Band. Goldman was a horn player with the Metropolitan Opera orchestra who presented an all-wind ensemble playing a mixed repertoire of symphonic music, military marches, popular songs and operatic overtures — free of charge. Joe Papirofsky came to love Russian symphonies, Italian opera, Negro gospel and Jewish liturgical music equally. With no teacher to draw distinctions between high and low culture, European and American, no one who said, with authority, "This is good; this is bad," he discovered his own taste.

His reading proceeded in the same way. There were no books at home but Sam Papirofsky's prayer book and a few other religious volumes. But by the time the Papirofsky children were six years old, following the example of their eldest sister Rhoda, each had obtained his or her own library card at the Bushwick Public Library. There, each of them alone, they showed the palms and the backs of their hands to the librarian, who often sent them home to wash, then made their way through the shelves unaided, picking up and borrowing whatever struck their fancy. Joe read through everything: mysteries, westerns, Charles Dickens, Tom Swift, and later, the turn-of-the-century muckrakers, Thomas Wolfe, Machiavelli and Shakespeare, on whose work he would later base his career.

But it was probably by listening to radio comedians that Joe Papirofsky began to connect his father's offbeat habit of playing with words to a widely appreciated form of entertainment. He began to create his own plays on words and to pun, a form of amusement that he held all his life. Like children of London's working class, Williamsburg kids loved to talk in the equivalent of rhyming slang: "Hey's your father a glazier?" they would ask when they meant "Get out of my way. I can't see through you." Joe Papirofsky quickly understood that he had a gift for language and that language, quite apart from being fun to play with, could confer power on the person who used it.

That power was apparent in the context of school as well as in the streets. In Williamsburg in 1928, school was a world that children did not share with their parents. There was no PTA, few parent-teacher conferences or other bridges between the institution and the home. At school, Williamsburg's first-generation immigrant children were socialized, taught to become Americans. They were checked for lice, drilled in penmanship, taught in ways that had been popular throughout the nineteenth century. However, by the late 1920s, the mainly Irish Catholic teachers were also influenced by new educational theory that stressed "learning by *doing*" rather than passively taking in. They encouraged pupils to express themselves, gave them plays and poetry to recite and lavished praise on those children of immigrants who learned to speak well and publicly.

Some of their pupils, like the future literary critic Alfred Kazin, were miserable in this environment. "Our families and teachers seemed tacitly agreed that we were somehow to be a little ashamed of what we were," he wrote later. "Yet it was always hard to say why this should be so. It was certainly not because we were Jews, or simply because we spoke another language at home, or were absent on our holy days. It was rather that a 'refined,' 'correct,' 'nice,' English was required of us at school that we did not naturally speak, and that our teachers could never be quite sure we would keep. This English was peculiarly the ladder of advancement. . . . It was bright and clean and polished. We were expected to show it off like a pair of new shoes. When the teacher sharply called a question out, then your name, you were expected to leap up, face the class, and eject those new words fluently off the tongue."

Joe Papirofsky was one of those who leaped up with confidence. He soaked up verse like a sponge, loved to memorize things, and became an exemplar of the civilizing power of public schooling. He preferred the classroom to his home and became the pet of a series of teachers who found in him a responsive student. Most smart kids in Brooklyn knew they needed to acquire "nice" speech. But there were probably few children who found as much joy in the acquisition as Joe.

"There were little poems that I learned by heart when I was very young, maybe five or six years old," he would recall sixty years later, "poems that dealt with nature which I loved":

> *Hurry, Scurry*
> *Helter, skelter,*
> *the storm has come,*
> *Let us take shelter*

or

> *Who has seen the wind?*
> *Neither you nor I*
> *But when the trees bow down their heads,*
> *the wind is passing by*

When Joe was eight, his class put on a production of *A Christmas Carol*, adding the pleasures of drama to the sounds and rhythms of words. He was cast as Scrooge and required to memorize his part. Sixty years later, Joseph Papp was able to perform his own and everybody else's lines:

"Merry Christmas, Uncle," he would begin, playing the nephew.

"Bah, humbug!" he would reply as Scrooge.

"Christmas a humbug, Uncle? You don't mean that I'm sure."

"I do. Merry Christmas indeed. What right have you to be merry. You're poor enough."

"Come then, what right have you to be cross? You're rich enough."

"Bah, humbug. You're just like my clerk, Bob Cratchit. He wished me a Merry Christmas today. Merry Christmas indeed. Why, he hasn't one sixpence to rub against another."

"Bob Cratchit has something better than sixpence. He has a heart full of kindness and love. Come, don't be cross, Uncle."

"What else can I be when I live in such a foolish world? Merry Christmas!"

"Oh no, Uncle, come have dinner with us."

"I never give dinners for anyone. I never take them from anyone. A foolish custom! If you have nothing better to say, good night!"

But his most significant encounter with language came in Isaac Remson Junior High School when Joe Papirofsky was twelve years old and his English teacher gave her class of boys some Shakespeare to memorize. Remson was known as a tough school. Instead of a class president, kids there elected a class sheriff. Papp would later recall one of his classmates "pissing in the back of the classroom." Miss McKay shrewdly chose *Julius Caesar* and, rather than having them read the whole play, assigned the class one speech to memorize. Years later, Joseph Papp could still recite it at will, introducing it by explaining that the city official Marullus is castigating the Romans for so quickly shifting their love of the general Pompey to the new conquering hero, Caesar.

> *Wherefore rejoice? What conquest brings he home?*
> *What tributaries follow him to Rome,*
> *To grace in captive bonds his chariot-wheels?*
> *You blocks, you stones, you worse than senseless things!*
> *O you hard hearts, you cruel men of Rome,*
> *Knew you not Pompey? . . .*

Shakespeare was, Joseph Papp later wrote, "a stranger to me. I had no particular interest in him, for I was from a different cultural tradition," but he knew a good speech when he heard one. Julius was such a common name in Williamsburg, Papp later said, that he had been sure Caesar was Jewish. And memorizing Shakespeare's words was so pleasurable for him — "It all sounded like music" — that he continued to read the play aloud. He fastened on the figure of Marc Antony, who by the power of his language made the Romans understand what they had lost. In one of the speeches he memorized, Marc Antony held up the murdered Julius Caesar's bloody coat, and told the Romans:

> *If you have tears, prepare to shed them now.*
> *You all do know this mantle: I remember*
> *The first time Caesar ever put it on;*
> *'Twas on a summer's evening, in his tent,*
> *That day he overcame the Nervii:*
> *Look, in this place ran Cassius' dagger through:*
> *See what a rent the envious Casca made:*
> *Through this the well-beloved Brutus stabb'd,*
> *And as he pluck'd his cursed steel away,*
> *Mark how the blood of Caesar followed it,*
> *As rushing out of doors, to be resolved*
> *If Brutus so unkindly knock'd, or no;*
> *For Brutus, as you know, was Caesar's angel:*
> *Judge, O you gods, how dearly Caesar loved him!*
> *This was the most unkindest cut of all. . . .*

There was enough violent, graphic detail here to bridge the gap between Elizabethan English and Brooklynese, school and street, and to excite a young teenager who carried a knife and ran with a gang. In fact, Joe Papirofsky was a textbook case of the slum kid whom educational reformers such as John Dewey and Jane Addams had written about one generation earlier.

While many reformers focused on the need to monitor health problems and provide children with after-school activities to keep them off the streets, Addams wished to provide artistic outlets for their energies. From the slums of Chicago, she wrote:

"Going to the show" for thousands of young people in every industrialized city is the only possible road to the realms of mystery and romance; the theater is the only place where they can satisfy that craving for a conception of life higher than that which the actual world offers them. . . . The theater becomes to them a "veritable house of dreams" infinitely more real than the noisy streets and the crowded factories.

The contemporary American city, Jane Addams argued, had abdicated its responsibility to provide its citizens with recreation:

> The classical city promoted play with careful solicitude, building the theater and stadium as it built the market place and the temple. . . . In the medieval city, the knights held their tourneys, the guilds their pageants, the people their dances, and the church . . . presented a drama in which no less a theme than the history of creation became a matter of thrilling interest. Only in the modern city have men concluded that it is no longer necessary for the municipality to provide for the insatiable desire for play. . . . We forget how new the modern city is and how short the span of time in which we have assumed that we can eliminate public provision for recreation.

Although Joe Papirofsky never read Jane Addams, it is likely that Miss McKay, Miss O'Brian and others of his teachers had. Throughout his time in New York City public schools, they would provide him with theatrical outlets in English classes, after-school drama clubs and all-school musicals designed to, as Addams put it, satisfy "that craving for a conception of life higher than that which the actual world offers them."

The actual world offered Joe Papirofsky a bleak and simple view of life in which strong and violent people won and weaker people fell by the wayside. When he was in his sixties and asked to recall the one most powerful lesson from his childhood, Joseph Papp did not hesitate to recount the story of Whitey.

"By the time I was in junior high school," he said, "I'd beaten up and gotten beaten up by all kinds of people. There was an Arab called The Crutch — if you went anywhere near him, he'd knock you down with that thing. There was Jetta, an Italian girl who beat me up, and Eustace Baily, a big fat black guy who beat the hell out of me. But with all of them, no matter how hard you were hit, you never had a sense that it was meant personally. Whitey was different.

"He was a wiry Irish kid with dirty blond hair, about seventeen when I was fourteen, who was always after me, trying to shake me down because I was Jewish. It was impossible to avoid him because we lived in the same building. Whitey was such a gangster that even the adults were afraid of him and, in fact, he later wound up in prison. His father was a drunk: all the neighbors could hear it when he beat him. Well, one day Whitey punched me in the face, so hard he made my whole mouth bleed. I've always remembered the shock of it, what it did to me psychologically. But that was only the first part: the second was that my father was standing there and could not help me. I felt so sad. I was so sorry for him.

"Whitey showed total brutality, with no hesitation, no remorse. He provided my first encounter with quintessential violence, what I would later connect to nazism and fascism. I felt crushed by Whitey and I saw my father was crushed too. He acted like a European Jew after a pogrom: he packed his bags."

The incident with Whitey, Papp said fifty years later, was the formative experience of his childhood. At fourteen, Joe Papirofsky had learned two lessons that he would remember all his life: First, "If you want to make an impact, you hit first, hard, and without any kind of feeling. *Hit hard.* That gives you a immense psychological advantage." And second, "I couldn't depend on anyone else to defend me: I had to learn to do it on my own, and that realization separated me from my family." The Papirofskys viewed the incident as a New World version of a pogrom. Joe's elder sister Rhoda immediately looked for a flat in a new neighborhood for the family. In 1936, in an act that spoke far more than words, the Papirofskys moved out of Williamsburg to another neighborhood.

TWO

From Moses to Marx

WHEN the Papirofsky family moved from Williamsburg to Browns-ville in the wake of Whitey's attack on Joe, the family was moving a step up. In 1936, Brownsville was a bustling, largely Jewish section of Brook-lyn that included a large working-class population, a prosperous middle class, and everyone on the political spectrum from the antireligious, radical left to the antiradical, religious right. Margaret Sanger had chosen the neighborhood for the first public birth control clinic in America because, she said, "Here there would be at least no breaking of windows, no hurling of insults." Its main thoroughfare, Pitkin Avenue, was a virtual midway of soapbox orators representing every shade of progressive poli-tics. It was a neighborhood where the police had been called in to shut down a provocative Yom Kippur ball organized by the New York Anar-chists Club, and where the Socialist candidate for the presidency, Norman Thomas, taught classes in adult education. It was home to a boy who would become the preeminent art historian Meyer Shapiro as well as to a generation of Jewish gangsters.

In Brownsville, Sam Papirofsky immediately found another storefront *shul* in which to pray and his son Joe found communism. "They were putting people out on the street in the dead of winter," he later recalled. "The sheriff would go in with a few men and they'd take the stuff out — pillows, mattresses, all the household goods, sometimes three or four or five children — and you could see them standing there, right in front of your house, helpless, as though there had been a fire. One of the guys in my building came to me and said, 'Listen, we want to get a group of guys together to put this stuff back in the building. You want to do something about that?' And I said, 'Okay, sure.'

"As soon as the sheriff and his deputies would leave, we'd take the stuff back into the house. And if they came back again, we'd do exactly the same thing. They were anywhere from fifteen to eighteen years old. They belonged to the Young Communist League, which had a storefront on my block, and they asked me to come to a meeting."

In 1934, when Papirofsky turned thirteen, he had had a bar mitzvah, the Jewish coming of age ceremony. He shared the honor with a friend from a family as poor as his own and — in place of the elaborate reception favored by uptown Jews — had been showered with peanuts and raisins by his friends. For two years after that, he continued to observe Jewish ritual with his father. But, by the time he was seventeen, he appeared in *shul* only on the High Holidays. Sam Papirofsky did not ask for explanations. Father and son had none of the protracted battles that were waged in other Jewish households over religion and politics. Marxism replaced Judaism as a guide to Joe Papirofsky's conduct and became his ideology of social justice.

His sense of vulnerability as a Jew remained. He tracked each step of Adolf Hitler's rise to power. He was aware of the strong movement for American neutrality in European affairs, and of a pervasive, national anti-Semitism, exemplified by the regular, vituperative radio broadcasts of Father Coughlin. Communists stood in opposition to all that.

"The word *Communist* — which sounds so reprehensible to many people today because it's been used as a maligning word, even a death word — was a beautiful word to me," he said. "To me, in the 1930s, it represented fearlessness, a stand against appalling social conditions, a way of creating a world that was free of injustice. I joined the Young Communist League when I was about sixteen. It wasn't illegal. But it was clearly tied into illegal action like moving those people back into their homes. I began to speak on street corners and at rallies about conditions on the block and to learn about the theory of communism.

"Soviet Russia was, at the time, the prime example of a country that had undergone a remarkable change. My ideology came out of my personal feelings. It was clear to me that there were two classes: the haves and the have-nots, the rich and the poor. For me it was not an intellectual matter. I was one of the poorest kids in my high school class."

Joe Papirofsky took what interested him from communism and ig-nored the rest. Unlike the intellectuals drawn to Communist theory in the thirties, his interest was pragmatic. His own family's experience un-derscored the need for social security, unemployment and health insur-ance. He was intrigued by stories of the Soviet Union, where these needs were reportedly being addressed. He was impatient with meetings — he later claimed to have attended no more than four — and interested in action, not theory. The American Communist party was then only two years older than Joe. Its members, he was told, had been harassed by the government since its inception just like the fur workers who had taken on the Mafia and had successfully unionized the fur industry, or the Brownsville boys who joined the Abraham Lincoln Brigade and went off to fight against Franco in the Spanish Civil War. The rough YCL manner that so many other leftists found repugnant did not bother him. He was used to it. As for the tedium of meetings, Papp said, he always stood a chance of meeting a pretty girl.

His father had lost his trunk-maker's job shortly after the stock market crash of 1929 and would remain unemployed for most of the 1930s. Joe Papirofsky used to pray for snow so that his father might have a chance at some shoveling jobs. He wore a used winter coat donated by a more fortunate family at his Hebrew School and had what he later called "perennial poor people's problems" with his teeth. "There was no such thing as a filling when I was a kid. You waited until the tooth was gone and then you went to a roughneck dentist who pulled it out."

In later life, Joe Papp would remember his family's helplessness during the depression. Until 1933, when the Federal Emergency Relief Admini-stration began to disburse home relief, the Papirofskys had no steady source of income. Sam Papirofsky found odd jobs as a porter or florist's assistant but, with his gentle nature and few contacts, he was unsuited to hustling work. Mornings and evenings found him at prayer. He was compliant when the home relief investigator asked him questions his son found intrusive and improper, or asked to examine Yetta Papirofsky's wedding ring. He followed instructions when told he had to cash in the $1,000 life insurance policy he had been paying installments on for fifteen years in order to qualify for government subsidy.

"As a child, Joe felt unprotected," a close friend later emphasized. "His mother was, emotionally, not around. His father — who feared authority and had no sense of entitlement — could not protect him. Two things can happen to children of such parents. They either look for a parent in their partner and/or they assume the role of parenting themselves."

Long before he turned thirteen, Joe Papirofsky began to support his family. First he was a chicken-flicker. Working Sundays and after school, he went to the poultry market where Jewish housewives had the live chickens they bought slaughtered according to ritual law. After each chicken was bled dry, his job was to pluck off its feathers, then haggle with the customer about whether it was clean enough. His fingers grew raw from the work, his shoes were caked with chicken shit and the stench was impossible to wash out of his clothes, but it was work that brought money in to his family and, to its eldest son, a feeling of pride.

Joseph Papp would later recall trying to hawk tomatoes from a push-cart, lollypops, pretzels and peanuts from a basket, selling newspapers, delivering groceries and telegrams, working as a short-order cook, as a janitor for his apartment house and even as a barker at Coney Island. In the entrepreneurial venture he recounted most often, he built himself a shoebox and walked the avenues of his neighborhood calling out, "*Shine! Nickel a shine.*" His first customer, as he told the story, had been a woman wearing shoes so dainty and small that he missed them entirely and, instead, smeared his first wad of polish onto her silk stocking. She stalked off before he could do any more damage and he wandered around Grand Avenue sobbing "*Shine! Nickel a shine!*" until a nattily dressed Negro replied, "Yeah."

The man was what Joe Papirofsky would later recall as a "sport," with black and white shoes — "black tip, white in the center," the producer would remember — and he polished them very carefully, tears rolling down his cheeks. The man asked why he was crying and Papirofsky gave him a detailed account of the mess he had made of his first job. The man then smiled and, instead of a nickel, gave him a quarter for his work.

Encounters with sympathetic African Americans were, in Joseph Papp's memory, a recurring event in his childhood. In his account, whenever he went to the A&P for the Negro woman who lived behind his own house or delivered telegrams to Negro families, they — like so many of the poor people to whom he brought bad news — responded with generous tips. Although Sam Papirofsky had brought with him from Eastern Europe tales of pogroms and the assumption of a chasm dividing Jews from Gentiles, and a sense of them as "others," he did not instill fear of them in his children. And in his adolescence, like his childhood, he took in more from school than from family.

Although he was short, looked young and was actually two years younger than some of the other boys in his class, Joe thrived at Eastern District High School. He worked on the student newspaper and senior yearbook, led the debating team, served as president of the Dramatics Society and was voted "Most Talented" by his 370 classmates. He also sang in the tenor section of the glee club, performed the male leads in many school plays, and toyed with the notion of adopting the stage name Joel Parker. One of his senior yearbook photographs shows a somber, slim boy in the robes of a Student Court judge. Under his formal class picture is the epigraph: *On the stage, he's won renown and fame; all of Eastern knows his name.* Although he failed math and did poorly in science, Joe excelled in almost every other area, seemingly without effort. Until his height precluded playing for the school team, he was also an excellent basketball player, "*fast,* aggressive and cool under pressure," recalled his brother. "I can see him racing downcourt, handling the ball and yelling out directions to his teammates, more than making up for his lack of size and height with his smarts."

His slim good looks and passionate way of speaking made him an object of interest to several dozen girls. But his reserve — a characteristic he had inherited from his mother — made conversation he did not want difficult and they pestered his older sister, Rhoda, for information. One classmate who rode the trolley to school with him every morning for four years remembers Joe Papirofsky as a purposeful, preoccupied boy whose head was always buried in a book. Another took his aloofness for vanity and once wrote a friend: "My dear. I nearly died when it happened. The honorable Joe Papirofsky actually spoke to me. Can you imagine my surprise?"

Bina Rothfeld, who alternated with Joe as president of the Dramatics Society, thought him "adorable, very cute, with these dark eyes and long lashes, but totally self-involved — a real smart aleck. He was different from all the other boys. He knew it and he didn't hide in the woodwork. He needed to be heard. He always had something to say, often something ironic or sarcastic, and he was not careful about whom he hurt."

The one person Joe Papirofsky looked up to was Philip Lerner, re-garded then and in retrospect by his classmates as a "genius." Voted "Brightest Boy" and "Best Writer" at Eastern, Lerner was a stocky, introspective boy of average height with the broad forehead and combed-back hair of a Central European middle-aged intellectual. "Phil Lerner lived to write poetry," Joseph Papp would remember, "but he was also a brilliant student and a scientist. There'd always be smoke coming out of his window and fire engines around his house." The Lerners were better off than the Papirofskys during the depression, thanks to the regular government payments that continued to come to Phil's father, a wounded veteran of the Great War. "He'd be sitting there in his wheelchair, always muttering, always angry. The implication, that was never talked about, was that he had had his genitalia shot off. I used to hear him talk to himself about Phil's mother screwing around, he was so jealous. And he had no cause. She was a wonderful woman."

Philip Lerner and Joe Papirofsky became inseparable. Lerner was clumsy at sports; Papirofsky taught him how to ride a bike and to smack a punchball past two sewers. Papirofsky was, as the producer later put it, "uneducated." Lerner opened up the world of academic knowledge to him: introducing him to free verse, taking him to a music library in Manhattan where they put on earphones and listened to Tchaikovsky, Stravinsky, Ravel and Bach. Lerner was senior yearbook editor; Papirofsky was his right hand. Of course, they featured their own poetry, including a poem by Joe Papirofsky called "The Museum":

> *Curious pretenders*
> *Gaze with wonder*
> *Affected nonchalance*
> *superficial ponder*
> *Nodding assent*
> *to false comprehension*
> *of works of art*
> *and queer invention*
> *medieval pageantry*
> *in conspicuous display*
> *Asia's ancient lore*
> *the polished walls array*
> *They look with awe*
> *At color, beauty blending —*
> *ignorant individuals*
> *still pretending*

"He and Joe made a perfect team," Papp's younger brother, Phillip, recalled. "Lerner was all acerbic wit and brain, an unimpressive physique but so ironic and sarcastic. Joe was smart too, but he was more physical and popular with girls."

Joe Papirofsky was, early on, involved in a wide variety of ways with a wide variety of girls but, even as a teenager, kept his private life private. He spent a great deal of time at the home of Beatrice "Red" Reed, a "plain, bright, musical girl with bright red hair" with whom he enjoyed talking, singing and jitterbugging. Like many of the women with whom Papp would later become involved, Red Reed had a large family that welcomed Joe and a mother who was warm and hospitable. "But at that stage of my life, I didn't fall in love with girls like that," Joe Papp later said with a smile. "I fell in love with a beautiful, black-haired girl who sat on the handlebars of my bicycle." His friend Phil Lerner was in love with Bina Rothfeld, the girl who alternated with Papp as president of the Dramatics Society, and, at seventeen, both wrote her letters.

"and then came the dawn," wrote Lerner. "you speak as though hope for humanity were a universal belief . . . and my idea of hope is yes different different different . . . wherein lies the salvation . . . not in religion . . . not in the fulfillment of a code of puritanism . . . not in strict moral rigidity. . . ."

"Hello Beets," wrote Papirofsky. "Just to let you know I have that old feeling for Rita but I believe mutuality is lacking. Ho hum, cruel fate. Don't think for a minute that I'll be as damned persistent as that goofy friend of mine. I know when I'm not wanted. . . . A hint: he misinterprets your deep friendship and interest as affection. Don't lead him on unless you are serious, you amazon."

Bina Rothfeld rehearsed several days a week with Joe Papirofsky, preparing a potpourri of "semi-annuals": plays by contemporary American women poets Edna St. Vincent Millay and Mary Carolyn Davie; Gilbert and Sullivan musicals such as *Yeoman of the Guard, The Mikado* and *The Gondoliers;* and Molière's *The Doctor in Spite of Himself.* Later she would invite him to direct her community theater group in the church that would become the New York Shakespeare Festival's first home. But in high school, Bina Rothfeld was just another girl from an immigrant Jewish family, who spoke Yiddish with her parents and was a Zionist — all good reasons, in Joe Papirofsky's view, for ridicule. "Joe liked to tease people," she later recalled. "He was a terrible show-off and many kids did not like him."

His teachers, however, were drawn to Joe Papirofsky. Several of them saw in him that one rewarding student in one thousand, who loved to learn and would soak up and use any information or guidance they gave him. They invited Joe into their homes, helped him find work, tutored him outside class. "I remember that, even at 17, you were impatient with the trite and the obvious, and your tastes ran way above those of the ordinary ghetto kid," wrote Esther Hersh in 1972, noting that although her letter was ostensibly intended for *him,* she thought this would be a "nice quote" for his biographer. Papp received no letters from the only

African-American teacher at Eastern, the one who was his mentor and adviser to the Dramatics Society. But Eulalie Spence was one of the few people in Joe Papp's early life whom he continued to talk about at length and admiringly throughout his career.

It was this high school English teacher who, in a variation on *Pygmalion,* put an end to what one classmate called "Joe's gutter speech." Unmarried and extremely serious about her teaching duties, Miss Spence *worked* on her pupils. Even fifty years later, Joseph Papp's voice would drop in deference to the woman he regarded as the most influential force in his life.

"Miss Spence was a tall, dignified, coffee-colored woman who spoke so well, I used to love to just listen and hear her speak," he said. "Many years later, at a museum exhibit in Harlem, I discovered she had been a rising young poet and a published playwright. She wore her hair in a beautiful way, very close to her head. She dressed very tastefully — she'd wear brown snakeskin shoes and silk stockings at a time when I was going around the neighborhood telling people to boycott silk and stop supporting Japan. But I loved the fact she wore silk stockings. She wasn't pretty, like the girls I used to fall in love with at that time, but everything about her was just right. She had natural wonderful enunciation, impeccable speech and wonderful posture. She spoke and moved with real authority. When she smiled, her whole face would illuminate.

"Miss Spence called me Joseph — unlike all the other teachers who called me Joe — and boy did you hear the 'ph' at the end of my name. She was interested in me. She made me feel real good about myself. She took me under her wing. And she was interested in an area that I seemed to find interesting: language. Although she never said it in words, she had that look in her eye, a little bit like my mother did, which meant: There are goals for you."

At the time, Papp's speech was full of Brooklyn "deses" and "deres." Miss Spence taught him grammar as well as correct enunciation, brought actors to the school to visit and gave her students plays and poetry to read. It was probably thanks to Miss Spence that Joe Papirofsky saw his first two performances of Shakespeare when he was fifteen. Two productions of *Hamlet* were playing on Broadway during the winter of 1936, and, thanks to philanthropist Mrs. August Belmont, Eastern District High School students were taken to both of them.

The British stage actor John Gielgud, then thirty-two and trained in classical theater, was one Hamlet; film star Leslie Howard, then forty-three and with no classical training, was the second. "He speaks the King's English as well as Shakespeare's, with exactitude of phrasing and pronunciation," Brooks Atkinson wrote about Gielgud. "But the main point is that Shakespearean verse is not only lyric but bold and stormy, coined from the common speech and flung off with fury." As for Leslie Howard: "He is frank and unstudied. . . . In gesture he is sparing, after the fashion of the modern stage. . . . [T]here is in his acting none of the bite, savage irony, mental turmoil, raging despair the part calls for."

Neither actor impressed Joe Papirofsky. "I remember listening to Gielgud and thinking why can't he talk English?" he said. "He looked terrific but he'd talk in this high-flown way. I compared him to the actors I was used to seeing in the movies and he was too elaborate. I liked Leslie Howard better, because even though he was very British, he was much more naturalistic. There was something phony about the stage and the way people in the theater spoke that I didn't like. But I went home and put up a picture of Gielgud on my wall. Theater became Shakespeare to me."

He had no idea what an anomaly Shakespeare on Broadway was. Broadway, in 1936, was enjoying an excellent season, but its more typical menu was Rodgers and Hart's musical *On Your Toes*, Kaufman and Hart's *You Can't Take It with You*, and the latest installments of the musical extravaganzas, *New Faces* and *The Ziegfield Follies*. Joe Papirofsky knew nothing about these productions. Later on, he would surprise associates by his ignorance of songs from the musical theater of the twenties and thirties. The songs he knew came from the radio, from the movies or from the political arena.

At sixteen, Joe Papirofsky's cultural view was conditioned by what he read in the *Daily Worker*. With his friend Phil Lerner, he debated every speech given by President Franklin Delano Roosevelt but he was even more involved in following international affairs: the rise of totalitarian dictators Adolf Hitler and Benito Mussolini, Japan's incursions into China and Manchuria, Italy's invasion of Ethiopia and — most important to him then — the Spanish Civil War.

Too young to join the Abraham Lincoln Brigade and go off, like some of his neighbors, to fight against fascism in Spain, he became one of the soapbox orators on Pitkin Avenue, warning that the Germans were arming Franco and using Spain as a testing ground for a wider war. He also spent hours wending his way through subway cars beneath the streets of New York City, shaking a can of coins. His slogans were "Stop Franco!" "Do not sell scrap iron to Japan!" and, increasingly, "Stop Hitler!"

Often, his presence would provoke a fistfight or taunts of "Why don't you go back to Russia?" or "Why don't you sing the national anthem?" which gave Joe an opportunity to display his extraordinary memory for words.

"I'll sing the first verse if you sing the third," he'd say, and when his heckler fell silent, sang out:

Oh thus be it ever when free man shall stand
Between their loved homes and the war's desolation!
Blessed with vict'ry and peace may the Heav'n-rescued land
Praise the pow'r that hath made and preserved us a Nation.
Then conquer we must, for our cause it is just
And this be our motto: "In God is our Trust."
And the Star-Spangled Banner in triumph shall wave
O'er the land of the free and the home of the brave.

He sang the words without irony. As a first-generation American growing up in the 1930s, Joe Papirofsky viewed himself as a patriot. The late thirties were the years of the Popular Front, when the Communist party supported President Franklin Delano Roosevelt. They were also years when the interests of the nation and the interests of American Jews were, for Joe Papirofsky, clearly aligned.

"The years of the depression were a dramatic time for any child," he later said, "but they were particularly so if you were a Jewish child. Jews were being murdered abroad and seeking refuge in the United States. My father's family was stuck in Poland. The world seemed polarized between the Fascist states of Germany, Italy and Japan on the one hand, and the wishy-washy western democracies on the other — those democracies that, in 1938, sold out Czechoslovakia to Hitler in the Munich Pact. I remember being devastated by that. People tend to forget that it was the Allies who made a deal with Germany first."

The Communists, he felt, had been on to Hitler from the very beginning. Unlike droves of other Americans — young and old — who had already embraced and abandoned communism, Papirofsky continued to be a believer. The Moscow Show Trials of 1936 disaffected many American Communists; then, in 1939, news of Russia's mutual nonaggression pact with Germany led many more to repudiate communism, but Joe Papirofsky, who had just turned eighteen, was not one of them.

"I never believed it," he said. "I believed Russia was buying time, moving to protect itself against the Germans. When Germany attacked Russia on the morning of my birthday in 1940, that only corroborated my view. I could then and I can now only think of the Russians as heroes. Nobody stopped Franco in Spain. Nobody stopped Mussolini in Abyssinia. Nobody stopped the Japanese from going into Manchuria in 1931 or into China in 1937. Nobody stopped Hitler from marching into Austria, then Czechoslovakia, then Poland. The Communists were the first to oppose the Nazis, and the reason Russia continued to be a symbol for me was not only because it represented a vision of social justice but because it bore the brunt of the German attack. During those first five months, the German army went forward like a hot knife through butter. They claimed to have wounded or captured three million Russians. Until 1943, well after the United States entered the war I thought: We don't stand a chance. Germany will take over this country. They were winning. The Luftwaffe and the Wehrmacht seemed unstoppable."

Another reason Joe Papirofsky remained a Communist at a time when so many American intellectuals left the fold was that he was interested in its culture. He skimmed the many pamphlets and political books he was assigned at YCL meetings, and found *The History of the Communist Party of the Soviet Union* "one of the longest, most difficult, most boring books on record." He carried Karl Marx's *Das Kapital* under his arm for a few years but never got through it. He did, however, begin to devour, pell-mell, the literature he was fed: the great Russian novelists Gorky and Gogol, the American muckrakers, books by James Farrell, Howard Fast, Jack London and Michael Gold.

At the same time, his party friends introduced him to the films of Sergei Eisenstein — *Strike, Potemkin, Ten Days That Shook the World* — and the new, politically correct music of Shostakovitch and Moussorgsky. But, oddly, he did not attend any theater — none of the "workers' theaters" being established in New York, not the Federal Theater, which had begun to bring mobile theater into neighborhoods in the way Joseph Papp himself would twenty years later, or even the Group Theater's productions of plays by Clifford Odets. When Joe Papirofsky went to Broadway in the 1930s, it was to attend a left-wing demonstration in Times Square. Until he graduated high school, his world was confined to Eastern District, Pitkin Avenue and the subways. Theater was something for rich people that happened across the river, in New York, and somewhere "uptown."

Joe Papirofsky graduated high school in June of 1938, just as he turned seventeen, and for the next few years — until America entered the Second World War and he joined the navy — he did little that would indicate his ultimate career. His academic record was unacceptable to Brooklyn College, the only institution of higher learning to which he applied, for he had failed his last math course and also lacked the required science credits. He took a night course in playwriting. And he worked at a lackluster job in a Manhattan laundry service owned by a relative of one of his Eastern District teachers.

"A lot of people have said to me that I was lucky not to go to college," he later said, "that I had the opportunity of finding myself on my own. I don't think that's true. I wanted to be well educated. I felt I could have learned more in that situation, learned to structure things better." Instead, Joe Papirofsky began his first full-time job handling and delivering bags of laundry and keeping an eye out for other opportunities.

Nothing developed.

"Greetings Beets," Joe wrote eight months after graduation.

It's so gloomy and dismal outdoors, that I can barely discern what I am typing. My kid brother is trying to memorize some speech for school. I'll tell him to shut up. . . . The Philharmonic is playing Schumann's Piano Concerto; in this din it sounds more like a garbage truck on a cobble-stoned street. My soeur is discussing some teacher she had gone out with. Boy is she bragging. . . . I can hear my mother mashing potatoes and I can smell it too. My room, a hovel, one by nothing, is in a frowzy state. On the floor are my sneakers and basketball. The ceiling is peeling. On the wall I've pasted a few items. For instance, I see a faded banner "1st. Most Talented Senior." On my right is a picture of Leslie Howard and Norma Shearer in a scene from *Romeo and Juliet*. Close by is the photograph of some vivacious model. Right next to her is my graduation photo. Underneath that is a small black painting called "Trees against Miami Sky." Near that is the Bill of Rights. There are a few more pictures of Robert Frost, Confucious [*sic*], John Gielgud in a scene from *Hamlet* and a few others. On my dresser is a pair of drumsticks, a ruler, a broken harmonica, a dictionary, a copy of Wells' Outline of History, also another by Hazlitt called Characters of Shakespeare's Plays which I'm now reading. . . . I am extremely active in dramatics and have become an ardent idoloter [*sic*] of Shakespeare. I even memorized an eighty-five line selection from one of his plays. I intend knowing an excerpt from every one of his works. I am consuming all his masterpieces rapidly. I wrote a play. Despite its having a good plot, fast-moving dialogue and a good structure, my teacher gave me a technical explanation of its fault. "It steenks," she said impassively. After much cogitation, I am inclined to agree with her. Well, the World's Fair wasn't built in a day. See, I've been reading my newspapers. Do me a little favor won't you? During the next war, when you glance at the casualty list and see Joseph Papirofsky Killed in Action, say, You know, I once knew that guy. He was going to do big things. Too bad he had to die.

Papirofsky's daily life was a far cry from his readings in Shakespeare. Every Monday morning, he would pick up towels and jockstraps from the Delahanty Institute for Fitness, where policemen and firemen worked out at the gym, as well as laundry from a variety of other customers. On the way, he bantered with policemen, elevator operators, delivery men and dozens of other people — some well educated or highly trained — who were still out of work. "I picked up a hell of a lot," he later said. "It was a time when everything you did had a certain importance. There was a lot of waiting and hanging around but I felt I was alive and witness to something vital. I went to rallies and concerts. I heard Earl Browder speak. I heard Paul Robeson and Pete Seeger sing. It didn't matter so much that I was delivering laundry." He delivered it until, one Saturday night, he refused to work an extra two hours and was fired on the spot.

His next job was as shipping clerk with Dinhofer Brothers, Manufacturing Jewelers. A few doors down Lafayette Street from what would, thirty years later, become the Public Theater, Dinhofer's sold and repaired watches and jewelry, and also operated a small diamond-cutting annex on Prince Street. Typically, Joe Papirofsky became friendly with the Swiss watchmaker and tried working with the diamonds, platinum and gold in the same way that, as a child, he had learned to cut tin for trunks. By February of 1941, he had been promoted to work in the office.

"Dear Doc," he wrote that month to the pharmacist who owned the corner drugstore in his old neighborhood, in a letter that shows Joe Papirofsky's approach to learning new skills. "As I've been very busy during the past few months, I have been unable to make my usual visits to Williamsburg. I'm progressing slowly and surely. A few years ago, I borrowed from you a book on shorthand. My job now requires that I take dictation. However, as the time is short and the need immediate, I find it impossible to take a lengthy course in stenography. Consequently, I thought it would be a good idea to learn the short course offered in that book. I'd appreciate it very much if you could let me have the book for a few weeks. . . ." He taught himself shorthand and used it for the rest of his life.

His new position at Dinhofer's left him time to attend political meetings and to moonlight. Often, in the company of Phil Lerner and his own younger brother, Joe Papirofsky attended Communist rallies and meetings. Lerner now worked for a man who organized a lecture series at the Ansonia Hotel on the Upper West Side, where well-known personalities talked about psychiatry or political subjects before a group of single people looking for dates. Papirofsky would help Lerner hand out leaflets advertising the series at Carnegie Hall and Town Hall, then help him run the cloakroom at the hotel. Following the lecture, Joe Papirofsky would serve as disk jockey for the dancing. "The saddest thing was when you'd come down to the end of the evening and watched the people hoping to make some kind of contact," he recalled. "They were not teenagers. They were in their thirties and forties. I was about to get married and could hardly wait to get home. There were always women trying to end up with us, they were so desperate, and there were these guys on the prowl, you'd see them there every week."

Seeing a business opportunity, the two friends rented a room of their own, hired a lecturer, had leaflets printed. But the Lerner-Papirofsky joint venture flopped. The evening they had chosen to open was Sunday, December 7, 1941. The Japanese bombed Pearl Harbor and nobody showed up.

By then, Joe Papirofsky was Dinhofer's office manager, supervising — among others — his younger brother, for whom he secured a job there directly after his graduation from high school. He was also a husband. In June, he had married Betty Ball, the Orthodox Jewish girl-next-door in Brownsville, one week after his twentieth birthday. Their elder son's marriage had startled the Papirofskys. He had never brought any of his girlfriends home or even mentioned the possibility of getting married. His brother later remembered Betty Ball as one of the "rare blondes" in the neighborhood who, like "Red" Reed, had a hospitable mother and a large, welcoming family. The young couple moved into their own flat and Joe Papirofsky seemed to be headed for a career at Dinhofer Brothers, Manufacturing Jewelers.

"When I was young," he later said, "all I wanted was a good job and a good job meant what every working person thinks of as a good job: a salary that could support a family. I never thought of anything past that. I never thought of getting rich. Or of winning the lottery. I was satisfied with not much, actually."

Papp was alluding to material satisfaction. Politically, his satisfaction with his job ended when he discovered what Dinhofer's workers, some of whom had been there for decades, were getting paid. In February of 1942, just after the United States entered the Second World War, he paid a visit to the United Office and Professional Workers of America to inquire as to how he might organize his office.

"I still can't see how Joe got eight other office workers to give up several hours of Friday night to speak to the United Office Workers and Professional Workers Union Organizer," his eighteen-year-old brother Phillip wrote in his diary. "But, after all, that's how the union movement moves! An appointed committee: Joe, Chairman, Ann treasurer and Sally, will meet Monday to figure out our next step. It's hard to wait until we all walk in one morning with union buttons on our coat lapels! Damn the b———. $11.09 a week!"

The union organizers had instructed Papirofsky to hold a number of secret meetings and to persuade his coworkers that joining the union would result in a wage hike. Although they were frightened of losing their jobs, they liked and trusted their twenty-one-year-old office manager and agreed on March 3 as the day they would strike.

"March 3, 1942: The explosion came off today as expected," Phillip recorded in his diary. "10:30. An important rrring was heard 'round the office. I was out at the time so I didn't know how he reacted but from what I gathered, he immediately hung up after he had been told where his office help stood and stormed wildly into the preoccupied atmosphere screaming something about anything missing from the safe."

One week later, following his union organizer's instructions, Joe Papi-rofsky — office manager and therefore management — went in to Jules Dinhofer and told him he was going to join the union.

"He was astonished," Papp later said. "He was sure my brother had influenced me.

"'No,' I said, 'I've been in on this for a long time.'

"He said, 'You should be ashamed of yourself. I had great plans for you.'

"I said, 'You're fulla shit. The way you treat people here is ridiculous. You pay people shit.' Jules Dinhofer was a tough boss, terrible with his workers. You'd drop a tiny diamond chip and you'd have your nose to the floor for ten hours until you found that thing. 'I'm ashamed of you,' I said to him. 'You're a Jew and you should represent something much higher. Our country is fighting against Hitler and we have our own Hitler right here.' And I walked out.

"In the end, what happens? I'm fired. The union leader calls me over and says, 'Joe, I'm very sorry, but we have no jurisdiction over you. You're management.'" A few hours later, his brother was fired as well.

"Now I know how it feels to be unemployed!" he wrote in his diary.

This morning the bitch called me into the office and snapped he had no use for me. . . . Joe and I walked down Sixth Avenue as the sun shone down on a Friday shopping crowd near Macy's. We bought a hot dog in a kosher restaurant.

For myself, things were ok. I could easily get a 16-dollar job but Joe needs a $22 job.

March 24, 1942: Depressing what? From 9 to 3 o'clock, Joe and I literally saw New York . . . we walked all over town, covering probably

more than 5 or 6 miles, without success. . . . #16 had nothing. . . . #65
had some beautiful jobs but we simply could not get into the union
so we trudged up Fourth Avenue to 40th Street where we found the
U.S. Employment service useless, next stop the Channin Building on
Lexington and 42nd . . . to State Building 80 Center St. . . . to Pitkin
Ave Unemployment Insurance . . . to Joe's draft board . . . to no avail.

For me, it's not important . . . but I'm worried for Joe. He has a
wife . . . a home . . . rent . . . and each day goes by without a cent into
the family coffer. . . .

March 25, 1942: Hey Georgie this is no laughing matter . . . spent
almost entire day at Hamilton Agency . . . Registered with Joe . . . all
of a sudden I'm a Christian, looka me!

After no luck with a string of employment agencies, the two brothers
had discovered, as Phillip later put it, "that if you weren't blond, they
didn't want to talk to you." Finally, they came up with a strategy. In the
designated space on the employment form, both put down their religion
as Protestant and finally landed a day's work.

In high school, Joe Papirofsky had toyed with the stage name Joel
Parker but it was not until March 25, 1942, that he first lied about his
background and "passed." Like other Jewish men of his time, he began
"passing" regularly as a strategy to get a job. Later, it became a precau-
tion against personal rejection, or a joke, or a game just to see how much
he could get away with. Although his bond with Judaism would eventually prove stronger than his wish to jettison his background of Jewishness,
poverty and vulnerability, from the late 1930s into the early 1950s, Joe
Papirofsky chose to escape from it.

"I don't believe that poverty, when it comes together with good family
support, has to destroy you — in fact it can make you stronger," he later
said. "What I experienced more intensely was anti-Semitism. I always feel
it's just below the surface, skin-deep, and if you scratch it a lot of it will
come out. A lot of it. I was more affected by the Holocaust than I was
by poverty. I feel that I can't get comfortable, that I'm a Jew and my
fortunes can change tomorrow. To me, intolerance is a greater threat
than poverty."

By 1942, that intolerance had become more than a social issue for
many American Jewish men in the military. They were thinking twice
before having H for Hebrew printed on their dog tags, for fear of being
captured by the Nazis. There is no record of what kind of tag Joe
Papirofsky wore or whether he told the military that he was Jewish. But
he would soon become so successful at passing that two of his subsequent

wives and several close associates would believe that he had been born a Polish Catholic.

After a few weeks of looking for work in Manhattan, he finally found a job at Samson Naval Base in upstate New York, where he had come to the attention of an officer who recommended that he enlist. "He thought, based on even my limited education," Joseph Papp later said, "that because I was articulate and could type, I could come in as a third-class petty officer, the equivalent of an army sergeant."

Although Papp was initially ambivalent about joining the navy and the navy would not accept him until he had six months of work done on his teeth, he did not want to be drafted. He also wanted to escape from a marriage that — in less than a year — he already knew had been a mistake. On November 27, 1942, Joe Papirofsky began service in the United States Navy.

THREE

The War and After

IF THERE HADN'T been a war, Joseph Papp would later say, he never would have wound up in the theater. Within a month of his arrival at Bainbridge Naval Base, in Maryland — while he was still in boot camp — Joe Papirofsky was organizing the men in his barracks and putting on skits to amuse himself. There was a theater on base and a group of officers who had been trying to start an entertainment unit. At their request, he put together a series of variety shows, drawing on the vaudeville he had seen as a child. He continued producing shows for the duration of the war, in airplane hangars, aboard aircraft carriers, on open stages, inside officers' clubs, in the North Atlantic and South Pacific and, finally, at the Brooklyn Navy Yard in New York City, across the river from the church where he would later establish his Shakespearean Theater Workshop.

"Perhaps you do not remember me, but I remember you well," a former navy buddy wrote to Papp years later. "You would strut around the barracks clad in skivvies, brushing your crew cut, trying to flatten it down after it was mutilated by the Navy barber. I remember your singing voice. . . . I remember, too, the song for which you composed both the words and the music. . . . You were interested in music and the theater while I was a frustrated writer. In Boot Camp, I began to write a book but never did get beyond the third chapter. You were the only one who ever read it."

It was in Bainbridge, during auditions, that the twenty-one-year-old met Irene Ball, a WAVE from New Jersey, who — improbably — shared his wife's maiden name. Irene Ball was nineteen years old, a daughter of English immigrants, who worked as a hospital attendant on the base. Like Joe Papirofsky, she had married early; like him, she was already regretting the marriage. They had a navy romance that lasted for two years.

"He looked," Irene Ball later said, "like that singer Paul Simon. He'd always push his hair back off his forehead and he had such beautiful hands. He used to recite poetry and talk about Shakespeare — until I'd say I couldn't handle it." Irene Ball and Joe Papirofsky lived in an apartment off-base together while both were at Bainbridge and talked about having a child. Joe Papirofsky was shipped out overseas. She discovered she was pregnant in the spring of 1945, after one of his home leaves, and gave birth to a daughter, Barbara, that December. The letter she wrote Joe Papirofsky went astray, she later said, and Joe Papp would not meet their daughter until she was thirty-five years old.

Joe Papirofsky's first assignment was the aircraft carrier U.S.S. *Solomons*, a slow-moving converted tanker, hastily assembled for duty in the North Atlantic and dubbed a "Kaiser coffin" by its crew. He spent much of his time on ship wearing a "Mae West" life-preserver, and later he would recall hours of staring at the water, wondering what had possessed him to join the navy when he did not know how to swim. It is unclear whether the navy knew it. He had, in his official papers, written that he had completed two years of college, majoring in journalism, and had worked from March until November 1942 as a radio writer for NBC in New York. Years later, when traveling with a group of Vietnam war veterans in Hanoi and consoling a veteran who had fabricated a story about his military service and had been found out, Joseph Papp told him that he, too, had sometimes lied but that the only lies worth worrying about were those that hurt someone else or cost them money.

Joseph Papp later told playwrights who had come of age in the sixties that they were "victims" of rock 'n' roll, just as he, Joseph Papp, was a "victim" of World War Two. By this he meant that his war experience was seminal. It opened up the world to him, introduced him to men he would never have met in Brooklyn or Manhattan, and gave him tools for what would become his career. For weeks at a time, bombers would take

off from the U.S.S. *Solomons* with the mission of depth-bombing German
submarines. When they landed, they might hit the deck hard or miss it
altogether, occasioning searches or fires. In between missions, there was
little of interest for the men to do, and the ship's chaplain, who had read
in Papirofsky's record that he had put on variety shows in Bainbridge,
asked him to provide some entertainment aboard ship.

His stage was the elevator on which planes were raised to the flight
deck. His theater, the huge hangar deck, was outfitted with five or six
hundred folding chairs. He chose his performers — a machinist's mate,
a third-class boatswain — put mops on their heads and taught them how
to lip-synch to records by the Andrews Sisters. He made up jokes, did
imitations of such movie stars as Edward G. Robinson, James Cagney
and James Stewart, wrote skits and served as master of ceremonies. He
was soon promoted to chief petty officer.

In many ways, Joe Papirofsky loved life on the U.S.S. *Solomons* because, for the first time in his life, he felt secure and well cared for. His
bunk was near a porthole. He valued the free medical services, the fresh
uniforms, the pride of belonging to his unit, and the three square meals
a day. The precariousness of every aircraft's takeoff and landing provided
daily excitement. Although he would later say that in the military there
had been little room for individuality and individual assertion, "As far as
I personally was concerned, I had everything I needed. There was not
much more."

In the spring of 1945, Joe Papirofsky was sent to California. The navy
had decided to establish an entertainment unit like those of the army's
Special Services, which would fly from island to island in the Pacific
performing for the troops. The chief petty officer was posted to Treasure
Island. There he put together a more elaborate group of musicians,
singers and dancers, including a young sailor named Bob Fosse, who
worshipped the dancer Gene Kelly. Once again, he wrote skits, rehearsed
his performers, taught them how to lip-synch to recorded music. Then
they set out on a long tour of islands, beginning in Honolulu and taking
in Guam, Truk, Japan, the Aleutian Islands and Alaska.

It was in the military that Joe Papirofsky began to take on a mentor's
role to other men. He read aloud to Bob Fosse, loaned him books,
advised him on his career, treated him to lectures on politics and provided
him with the encouragement that he would subsequently provide for
hundreds of other aspiring performers. Although Joe Papirofsky revealed
as little of his personal life to his shipmates as he had to his Brooklyn
classmates, men liked his ready sense of humor and sense of justice. They
also noted that he was easily bored, and had a penchant for stirring things

up, acting as an instigator or provocateur. Although his navy record makes no mention of the incident, the Chief, as Irene Ball called him, spoke up loudly in debates over international politics as well as the situation of Negroes in the military. "A black guy had been put in the brig for reasons that were unfair," he recalled. "There were no black officers to stand up for him, and no black petty officers. All the blacks were cooks and bakers. I raised a fuss about it and I was told to shut the hell up if I didn't want to end up in the brig." The military record notes only that Papirofsky left the navy with five medals, none of which he ever displayed or discussed.

His last show, starring Bob Fosse, played the Brooklyn Navy Yard in 1946. On August 8, he was discharged in New York City with no job and no skills but, as he later recalled, in "a kind of marvelous euphoria. The war was over and I was out of the navy. Fascism had been defeated. It was a tremendous victory for democracy. The world was moving in the right direction now."

At the time of his release, Joe Papirofsky was twenty-five years old. His wife had, that April, initiated divorce proceedings, which would be finalized in September. He was responsible for alimony and child support payments and unemployed. It was then, remembering a shipmate who had invited him to California, that he bluffed his way onto a military plane and flew west. On arrival in Bakersfield, he changed clothes, left his uniform in a men's room and took a bus to Hollywood.

His former shipmate put him up for a few days and advised him to check out the Actors' Lab, a new theater school in Los Angeles that was accepting veterans tuition-free as per the G.I. Bill. If he was lucky, he'd even get a small stipend for attending the school. "This is where my journey really begins," Joe Papp would later say. "This was the beginning of my life in the theater."

The Actors' Laboratory Workshop in Los Angeles had been founded shortly before the Actors Studio in New York by some of the most respected actors in the United States, including several members of the Group Theater. Founded in 1931 by Harold Clurman, Lee Strasberg and Cheryl Crawford, the Group was, for its time, a radical phenomenon. Departing from both the Broadway and British theater traditions and deeply aware of the unemployment and social devastation caused by the depression, its members were committed to a theater that brought onto the stage current political, economic and social realities. In order to do so, its leaders drew on acting techniques developed at the Moscow Art Theater by Constantin Stanislavsky and a repertoire of politically engaged plays. Members of the Group lived communally on next to nothing, with the aim of developing a permanent acting ensemble, an indigenous American acting technique and their own playwrights. They were committed to "art for the people" rather than "art for art's sake" and strongly averse to the money-making ethos of Broadway. Most were "left wing"; several were members of the Communist party.

Their experiment lasted ten years. The first defectors from the Group went out to Los Angeles in the late 1930s, part of a great exodus of actors, musicians, stagehands and technicians from Broadway to Hollywood looking for work as movies began to edge out theater as the predominant form of drama. Having shunned the glitz of Broadway, many were uneasy with what they found on the West Coast and sent back portions of their paychecks along with such impressions as "It's truly capitalism gone mad out here. Everybody talks salary, pictures, graft, drag, the whole spirit of the place is fake, the acting is fake, the art is synthetic." They found local artistic life barren and, wanting "to reform Hollywood's working environment," began to meet informally in 1940 to work on their craft. By 1941, when Harold Clurman published an obituary for the Group Theater in the *New York Times*, its L.A. offshoot included more than seventy people.

"The Actors' Lab is an organization with the primary purpose of developing for actors a real understanding of and participation in the life of our times — based on an intelligent appraisal of the social forces at work in this particular period," read the Actors' Laboratory Statement of Policy that spring. "This understanding of and participation in today's world is inextricably tied up with the development of our craft as actors."

A few years later, this policy would be augmented by a ten-point program that included giving war veterans theater training, building their own theater, pushing for the creation of a "Minister of Fine Arts" in the federal government and supporting "those forces in America who are vigilant against the emergence of native forms of Fascism." On December 8, the day after Pearl Harbor was bombed, the Lab gave its first performance to an invited audience of eighteen. During the next four years, Lab members offered their services to the USO and the Hollywood Victory Committee, producing hospital and overseas shows that played to thousands of servicemen and women. They were the only theater group in Hollywood who consistently presented the classics.

"Some of the most skillful acting in the United States today is being done in Hollywood by some part-time refugees from the movies," reported *Life* magazine. In June of 1946, they received rave reviews for their production of Clifford Odets' *Awake and Sing*. When Joe Papirofsky arrived, they were doing an early play by Arthur Laurents, who would later become known as one of the authors of the musicals *West Side Story* and *Gypsy*. By then, the Lab had evolved into a unique institution that was at once a not-for-profit theater, a workshop where screen actors could work informally on their craft and a theater school, where former soldiers as well as Hollywood starlets could study.

It had also become a target of Hollywood's Red-baiters. A year earlier, the *Hollywood Reporter*, the principal journal of the film industry, reported that the Lab was "the object of some pretty serious accusations being made quite openly, by people of repute, contending that the group is dominated by people who are as red as a burlesque queen's garters." The rumors were of public concern because "the major studios are paying weekly fees to the Lab to train young players and the school is accredited to teach veterans under the G.I. Bill. A denial of communistic affiliations of members of the faculty is due, and vital to the Lab itself."

Joe Papirofsky knew almost nothing about Lab history when he walked into the collection of small wooden buildings behind Schwab's Drugstore at the intersection of North Laurel Avenue and Sunset Boulevard. "Here I was in Hollywood on a beautiful sunny southern California day," he later recalled. "The air smelled good and it felt great to be free. I was just out of the navy. I felt I could do anything or nothing and be just as happy. I had no great goals. I was trying to unwind. Before the war, it had never occurred to me to join a theater. But suddenly, after the war, there was this tremendous optimism in the air: anything seemed possible."

When he inquired about how to be admitted to the G.I. course in acting, Joe Papirofsky was told that he had arrived too late: over five hundred people had auditioned and twenty-five had already been chosen as students. There were two or three more auditions previously scheduled for that day but no more applicants would be considered.

Joe Papirofsky sat down on a bench in the alleyway furnished with bits of scenery from old shows, where actors sat for hours nursing lukewarm cups of coffee, and had struck up a conversation when the receptionist called him back. One of the scheduled applicants had arrived without her audition partner. Could Joe read in his place? The play was Eugene O'Neill's *Desire under the Elms*. Joe Papirofsky had never heard of it.

He read the scene cold in a small auditorium where actors Phoebe Brand and Anthony Quinn were sitting in the dark. When he and his partner finished, a voice said "Thank you." As he began to walk offstage, Phoebe Brand said "Miss, you can go on. Mr. Papirofsky . . . why do you want to be in the theater?"

Joe began improvising. He knew nothing about Phoebe Brand or her husband, Morris Carnovsky, who had been key members of the Group Theater, or about the Mexican film star Anthony Quinn. He talked about his time in the navy, his feelings about nazism, his first exposure to Shakespeare as a high school student.

Brand and Quinn, both a generation his senior, liked what he had to say. Most of the men auditioning wanted to become successful screen actors. Papirofsky had no clear idea of what he wanted to do professionally but his background and his politics were tailor-made for the Lab. "I think I was a kind of symbol for them," he said, "of what the Lab believed in."

Joe Papirofsky quickly became one of the Lab's most popular students. His blend of intensity and reserve attracted his women teachers, who treated him like a favorite nephew, as well as many women his own age. He dated several and, years later, when seated at a Manhattan dinner party beside a former "fiancée" whom he had promised to meet in front of Schwab's Drugstore on the way to a justice of the peace, he did not, at first, recognize her.

He continued to see other women even after he married Sylvia Ostroff, a former WAC, who had come to L.A. after demobilization from the army. "He wasn't particularly aggressive but he was a very magnetic guy," she said. "He was nice-looking, eloquent, persuasive, talented — he had an energy that captivated people and I fell madly in love with him."

A small, dark-haired, attractive woman, Sylvia Ostroff was — like Joe Papirofsky — the child of Jewish immigrants from Russia and Poland. She had studied piano since the age of six and, after her father lost his job during the depression, had supported her family on a WPA job playing piano in settlement houses and children's recreation facilities. She, too, had been married before the war and had sought a divorce while in the service. When the war was over, she had started a new life as the Lab's receptionist.

"You have to understand it was an unusual place for its time: a nonprofit organization," she later recalled. "No one was there for the money. It was a magnet where people worked long hours and felt it was their home. Lots of people — some of them movie stars — congregated there. Sam Levene, the comedian, paid for a tonsillectomy I needed! He heard me talking on the phone to my doctor and when I said I didn't have a hundred dollars and hung up, Sam Levene said 'Call him back!' and pulled a hundred dollars out of his pocket. I also saw some of the best theater I ever saw in my life at the Lab — both the workshops that the students did and the professional productions."

Joe and Sylvia Papirofsky first lived in a rented garden room, then in a sparsely furnished shack in Laurel Canyon. Like most returning veterans, they had few possessions. They ate at the soda counter of Schwab's Drugstore and spent most of their time at the Lab. Their first acquisition was a blue convertible, which he raced up and down the California hills with the abandon of a city boy who had just learned to drive. Their second was a record player for which they bought dozens of records. Although it was Sylvia who had been a conservatory student, she would later say that it was Joe who taught her how to listen to music and introduced her to jazz as well as to some of the modern classical repertory.

Her new husband, she recalled, behaved like many young men just out of the military. He ran wild. After drinking all night, he and Jimmy Anderson, "a good ol' boy from Alabama," would often strip to the waist and at five or six in the morning go into the deserted Lab classrooms to fence for an hour or two, then have a cup of coffee and start their morning classes. Four years older than her husband, Sylvia Papirofsky would look back on her role as a kind of "mother figure" rather than wife.

"I was madly in love. I didn't ask him any questions and I believed everything he told me: that he came from Brooklyn, that his father was Russian and his mother was British and had tea every afternoon at four with a silver service. I never met anyone in his family and I did not know then that he was Jewish — *he used to ask me what Yiddish words meant!* I did not know he was a Communist. I did not know he had ever been married until we started sending eight dollars a week to his first wife for child support."

Sylvia Papirofsky did know that her husband was seeing other women: "Always. And the women he went for were not the Marilyn Monroes and not the women who were focused on their careers. They were the kind of women he could shape and mold and make his own. He was happiest with me when he had something else good going on outside. Those were the times he'd come home and hug me."

The Actors' Lab was Joe Papirofsky's university and he focused on acquiring an education in the theater with a singlemindedness absent from his private life. The twenty-five-year-old from Brooklyn understood that he had stumbled upon an extraordinary community of people, less formal than the military organization he had just left, but with its own code of behavior that was in some ways more demanding. The Lab had a constitution specifying that every member perform duties for the good of the organization. Members who performed there typically turned back their paychecks. Its school, theater and workshop operated at a deliberate deficit of about $200,000 per year. Until the United States established a cabinet minister of fine arts to foot such bills, one of its leaders told a reporter, Lab members would be obliged to make motion pictures in order to subsidize the operation.

Joe Papirofsky soaked up this socialist theater ideology along with acting technique. He spent all his time at the Lab, rehearsing and taking classes with about one hundred other students including Audie Murphy, a veteran who talked incessantly about the men he had killed, and Marilyn Monroe, who, Papp said, came to class with a small dog and was so shy that she barely talked at all. He took Body Training with Lotte Goslar and Jacobina Caro, Acting with Phoebe Brand, Anthony Quinn and Mary Tarcai, and Literature of Theater. His favorite subject, as in high school, was Speech. His teacher was Margaret Prendergast McLean, a frail, silver-haired woman born in Colorado. She had written two classic texts on "good American dramatic speech" which could stand on its own alongside British diction. Mrs. McLean teamed Joe Papirofsky up with Audie Murphy. The first worked on ridding himself of the vestiges of Brooklyn; the second, of a southern drawl.

Some of his teachers taught the acting technique known as the Method, new to Hollywood at the time. This method of work devised by the Russian director Constantin Stanislavsky had been brought to the Lab by members of the Group Theater, who had learned it a decade earlier from Lee Strasberg in New York, who had, in turn, learned it in the twenties from members of the Moscow Art Theater. Using the Method, Lab G.I.s and starlets were taught to perform exercises in sense memory — trying to remember and reconstruct how a cup of coffee tasted or the way a cold doorknob or hard pencil felt in their hand — to do animal improvisations and to make use of memories of deep emotions. "The Method was all trying to work from the inside out — shoveling around in your own innards — and I didn't know how to really do that," Papp said. "I don't think anybody really knew. They tried. We would cheer and shout, 'He's breaking through! She's breaking through!' That meant you had touched an emotional area that you hadn't touched before. They certainly *talked* about the Method all the time. You hardly could get them to talk about anything else. But I don't think you learn to act by being trained to act. People are good actors because they were born with the talent. It's true in all creative fields. But I had to experience that to learn it."

Not all the Lab's acting teachers were wedded to the Method. Phoebe Brand felt it was destructive and developed her own milder version. Roman Bohnen preferred to work on monologues. Anthony Quinn had never learned it. All were wary of fooling with their veterans' "emotional memory." But as in acting classes elsewhere, even the non-Method preparatory exercises caused much upheaval; some of the students confused them with therapy. Joe Papirofsky felt that his emotions were too volatile for them. When Phoebe Brand cast him as Romeo with a Juliet he felt attracted to, "I couldn't play the scene too well. See, you have to be careful to not really feel those things, particularly if you're a new actor, you get confused when your emotions get in the way. We'd be backstage together — you know, sort of hugging behind the scenes. And then I went on and suddenly I didn't know what was life. Was it backstage? Or when I went onstage? Reality struck me because you are onstage and the lights are on you. I felt awful." When the scene was presented at the Lab's theater, Joe Papirofsky ran out of the Lab complex instead of taking his bow, and did not come back that night. Whenever he was asked why he did not become an actor, Papp recalled that experience and said that he could not tolerate making himself so vulnerable.

Apart from his aversion to personal vulnerability, the student grasped that developing an obsession with the nonverbal Method relegated language to second place. "You can't do Shakespeare with the Method," he would say for the rest of his life. "Learning Shakespeare is like learning to play an instrument." He grew bored with his classmates' search for emotional truth, and impatient with their cinematic ambitions. They, in turn, were impatient with his focus on language and bored by the phonetics taught by Mrs. McLean. Most of them wanted to be movie stars; why did they need to learn how to enunciate?

Joe Papirofsky soon became identified with his teachers rather than with his peers and, in the egalitarian spirit of the Lab, they accepted him. He became a close friend to actors Phoebe Brand and Morris Carnovsky, and on walks and over dinner, spent hours discussing politics, Shakespeare and how to run a theater. He watched actors Lee J. Cobb — "I used to admire him tremendously," Papp would recall; "he was so moving, so powerful" — Lloyd Bridges, Franchot Tone, John Garfield and Roman Bohnen. He observed Bertolt Brecht when the playwright directed his *Galileo* at the Lab. He became particularly friendly with Lloyd Gough, the first in a long line of hard-drinking Irish friends, who played the concertina and sang Irish folksongs far into the night. Through that older generation of actors, he was introduced to Sean O'Casey's plays and autobiography, and to the importance of supporting new work for the theater. After two years as a student, he also began to direct and to take on some of the work of management.

"We would all turn to him for help, even though he was fifteen or twenty years younger than we were," recalled Phoebe Brand. "We felt right away: Here's somebody who knows what to do. There's no doubt in my mind that if the Lab had gone on, Joe would have run it. He was a very intelligent man, a morale-builder. He did his best to keep things steady, organized and happy. He was passionate but calm."

The G.I. stipend did not suffice to cover his expenses so, early on, Joe Papirofsky volunteered to work in whatever capacity was needed. When the Lab's old janitor had too much work, Joe filled in as a janitor's assistant; when actors Brand or Carnovsky were directing and needed help, he became a production assistant; when Lab director Mary Tarcai needed him, he was a ticket-taker. He turned out an in-house newspaper called *Curtain Call,* which featured interviews with students and faculty members. He organized fundraisers, wrote letters, distributed flyers. Soon, he was the Lab's de facto managing director.

The people who organized and participated in the Lab were regarded by many as free spirits with a predilection for anarchy rather than organization, discussion rather than action. "They were like the 'wise men' from Chelm," recalled Bernard Gersten, who worked almost a year as their tech director before returning back East. "It was the Group Theater with its leadership removed. They were reflecters, talmudists — not doers. They needed someone to take charge."

They found that person in Joe Papirofsky who, unlike Gersten, was caught up in their idealism. "I was among people who had made theater their *life,*" he said. "They all had a commitment to theater that articulated a serious point of view and it allowed me to think about making it my life and my profession even at a time when it looked like there was no support for it. Theater seems to me the most basic, true representation of life. In contrast, working on a movie is for me like working on a corpse. You capture something and you move the parts around. Theater is a little bit like baseball: It's a dangerous field. There's no security. You can't be an actor or start a theater if you're thinking about security. I like that."

In addition to attending classes, taking on management responsibilities at the Lab, drinking and conducting multiple love affairs, Joe Papirofsky continued to do the "political work" he had begun as a teenager, attending meetings and rallies, delivering leaflets and *The People's World* — the West Coast Communist newspaper — door to door. "For me, in the years after the war, Russia remained our heroic partner," he later said. "Russia had been our ally. They helped us win the war and they died by the millions. They represented something good and I wanted the alliance to continue. I thought Churchill's speech in 1946 about an iron curtain coming down over Europe was a *bad* speech. I felt that Russia was trying to prevent the countries from going back to the prewar fascist regimes. I *wanted* a wall dividing Germany."

His views, in the late 1940s, put Joe Papirofsky in a dwindling group of die-hard Communists in the United States. American perceptions of Soviet sacrifices during World War II had been superseded by revelations of Soviet show trials and concentration camps and fears that the Russians had developed their own atomic bomb. The American Left distanced itself from the Communists; the Right attacked them. In 1947, President Truman signed Executive Order 9835 that revived the attorney general's old list of subversive organizations and required two million federal workers to sign a loyalty oath. The theater and movie industries came under the scrutiny of several state and federal committees bent on ferreting out Communists. It had been the House Committee on Un-American Activities hearings of 1938 that had destroyed the Federal Theater. Conceived by President Roosevelt's aide Harry Hopkins and directed by Vassar College professor Hallie Flanagan, the Federal Theater was part of the Works Progress Administration. It had presented more than a thousand productions in twenty-two states, most of them free, and mostly to people who had never seen live theater before. But "the notion of singling out for subsidy several thousand writers and actors strained the generous impulses of many Congressmen," as an historian of the committee later wrote. Although it enjoyed grassroots support throughout the United States, from actors, unions, newspapers, local colleges, community theaters and artists in every field, it was not "a program that the Democrats could count on the nation to support with passion." Six months after the Dies Committee concluded that the Federal Theater was "infested with radicals from top to bottom," and constituted "one more link in the vast and unparalleled New Deal propaganda machine," Congress voted to terminate its funding.

By 1944, the committee had published a six-volume report containing the names of 22,000 alleged Communists, including a broad spectrum of New Dealers, liberals and radicals. By January of 1945, Congress voted to make HUAC its first permanent standing committee to investigate alleged Communists in the civil service, the labor unions, the schools and universities, the scientific community and the entertainment industry. The publicity it received encouraged several state imitations, the most prominent of which was the California Committee, chaired by Jack Tenney, a former pianist and president of Local 47 of the Musicians' Union, who had become a politician.

In its first report, Tenney's committee investigated the German-American Bund, the America First Committee and the Ku Klux Klan. Then it began to assist the House committee in its investigation of Hollywood.

In March of 1947, Jack Tenney accused actors Charles Chaplin, Fredric

March, John Garfield, Edward G. Robinson and singer Frank Sinatra of aiding communism. It was then that Joseph R. McCarthy, a freshman senator, first took part in the witch-hunt that would bear his name. That May, HUAC came to Los Angeles to hold hearings and interview heads of major studios. In the fall, forty-one Hollywood people were subpoenaed to appear in Washington. Nineteen said they would not cooperate and were dubbed the "unfriendly nineteen." Ten men — almost all associated with the Actors' Laboratory — went to Washington to testify.

Despite protests on their behalf, the "Hollywood Ten" were cited for contempt of Congress on November 24, 1947. The Motion Picture Producers Association, which had previously been critical of HUAC, bowed to its pressure and announced: "We will forthwith discharge or suspend without compensation those in our employ, and we will not re-employ any of the ten until such time as he is acquitted, or has purged himself of contempt, and declares under oath that he is not a Communist." For Hollywood, it was the beginning of the blacklist; for the Actors' Laboratory Theater, it was the beginning of the end.

"Unless you were part of it, it's impossible to understand just how grim those times were," Joseph Papp would later recall. "The attack by HUAC froze Hollywood into one great Frigidaire. It was the coldest place in the world. Everyone was terrified. I would read the papers and I would see people I had respected naming names.

"The committee was interested in people with a recognizable reputation like Lloyd Bridges, Edward Bromberg, Morris Carnovsky, Hume Cronyn, Anthony Quinn, Waldo Salt — all of whom were on the Executive Board of the Lab — or Alvah Bessie, Dalton Trumbo, Ring Lardner, Jr., who were listed as Lab sponsors and directors. I remember feeling how ironic it was that there they were, subpoenaed, and I wasn't.

"On Sundays, when they would be sleeping late, I'd be out selling *The People's World,* a thankless newspaper route where after you'd ring the doorbell, someone might come out and punch you in the face. After class, I'd sweep the Lab, then go downtown and make speeches or pass on whatever I'd learned to students at the California Labor School. I had felt I was the one who was an activist and that their greatest danger as Communists was falling into a swimming pool. I made speeches and I signed petitions, but I didn't have many venues. Reporters did not call me up the way they do today and ask, 'Tell me, Mr. Papp, what do you think?'"

It was only a matter of time before the Actors' Laboratory was formally named as a Communist Front organization. In February of 1948, four Lab elders — Joe Bromberg, Rose Hobart, Roman Bohnen and Will Lee — were called to testify before the California Committee. They refused to say whether they had ever been members of the Communist party and found themselves unemployable. That month, the *American Mercury* reported:

In the past ten years, the Hollywood–Los Angeles area has become the mouthpiece, heart and pocketbook of the American Communist Party. In terms of Party membership, Los Angeles now ranks second only to New York City. . . .

In pumping its propaganda into Hollywood, the Party has been aided considerably by two "fronts," known respectively, as the Peoples Educational Center and the Actors' Laboratory, Inc. . . . Its primary function apparently is to draw ambitious young actors and actresses into the orbit of Communist front organizations. Ostensibly the Actors' Laboratory is a combination training school and experimental theater, but in fact it has always been more political than artistic.

Communist Party literature is always available at the Actors' Lab and the organization has frequently donated funds and talent to help put across pro-Communist demonstrations. Its activities are well-publicized in the *People's World*.

The list of sponsors and directors of the Actors' Laboratory comprises a representative cross section of Hollywood Stalinism. The "audience sponsors" include Alvah Bessie, Ring Lardner Jr., Albert Maltz, Dalton Trumbo, Donald Ogden Stewart, Mr. and Mrs. Sam Ornitz, Gale Sondergaard and Sidney Buchman.

The members of the Actors' Lab executive board and faculty include: J. Edward Bromberg, who came to Hollywood from the Group Theater in New York, where, according to testimony received by the house committee, he was a member of the local party faction; actor Morris Carnovsky . . . Rose Hobart . . . Larry Parks, the actor who has become notorious for his ardent defense of Soviet and Communist policies in the past two years . . . Hy Kraft, who was a sponsor of the Hollywood Anti-Nazi League, who signed a petition in 1938 justifying Stalin's purges in Russia, and who has been a frequent speaker at front meetings; Abraham L. Polonsky, a screen and radio writer who was (according to the *People's World* of September 24, 1946) Secretary of the Hollywood Writers Mobilization, and who was also active in the Hollywood Community Radio Group, another Communist front; Anthony Quinn, a popular Mexican-born screen star who is a favorite of the *People's World;* and Jacobina Caro, whose husband is Sidney Davison of the PEC, and who was registered as a Communist in Los Angeles in 1940, under the name of Mrs. Jacobina Davison.

The Tenney Report of 1948 reprinted all these names, exacerbating existing tensions within the Lab. For years, Lab members had been wrestling with problems typical of theater groups: egos, rank, varying teaching methods, the tensions between teaching and performing. Both the students and the professionals wanted to be *seen.* The students wanted to be cast alongside the professionals. The professionals wanted to do their own productions. Some Lab members had no interest in politics but now mere attendance at the Lab took on political connotations. The local columnists flocked to it like vultures to a dying animal.

In September, the Lab held a carnival, which aimed both to raise money and to give thousands of Angelenos the opportunity to meet Lab actors and staff. Held in its parking lot, the carnival featured a bazaar, food stalls, performances and outdoor dancing. But the *Hollywood Reporter* as well as the *Los Angeles Times* attacked even this innocuous event. "The Actors' Lab made no friends when they gave an open-air barbecue, which included dancing between whites and Negroes . . . where one and all could see," wrote columnist Hedda Hopper:

> This group's corny idea of being liberal will eventually lead them into trouble. The situation has nothing whatever to do with racial prejudice or discrimination; everyone in the world is as good as he is in his heart regardless of his race, creed or color. But that doesn't mean they have to intermix. Right or wrong the great balance of the community has this deep-rooted conviction, and they were shocked at this public display on the part of the Actors' Lab. That's the sort of thing that leads to race riots.

It was in response that Joe Papirofsky made his first foray into the adult press. Following the lesson in power that he had learned as an adolescent from Whitey, he hit fast and hard, writing to the *Hollywood Reporter,* the *L.A. Times,* the *Los Angeles Daily News,* the *California Eagle,* the local Negro newspaper, the *Los Angeles Daily People's World,* the local branch of the NAACP and the Urban League.

In September, the *L.A. Daily News* published part of his letter:

> Mothers, fathers, kids and old folks, Catholics, Protestants, Jews joined together this day and had a good time. Certainly there were Negro people present. The Negro veterans who attend classes here under the G.I. Bill "mix" everyday. The Negro actors from the cast of *Freight*

were present. Negro artists from the community were present. Joel Fluellen, Negro actor, who prepared a delicious Creole dinner, was present. Negroes who are part of our audience were present. . . . There were no back doors or separate entrances for Negroes. In the best tradition of theater and democracy, there was no discrimination against fellow human beings.

We, as a theater, are part of the tremendous struggles being waged by Equity and the Dramatists' Guild against segregation in theaters. . . .

In fact, Joe Papirofsky had long been impatient with what he saw as the Lab's negligence regarding racial integration in the theater. With the exception of Jimmie Davis, his friend who wrote the song "Lover Man" for Billie Holiday, another actor and the actress Dorothy Dandridge, there were no Negro students at the Lab and proposals for color-blind casting in Lab productions were routinely rejected as "historically inappropriate." In 1945, Lab elders had met with Paul Robeson to discuss "the problems of the Negro actor" and, during the summer of 1947, had given a special night class for eighteen Negro actors. "They talked about a problem with minorities, a lot of these people," Papp later said. "But they *did* nothing."

At the time, he himself was still "passing," and channeling his outrage at discrimination — like many Jews of his generation — into the service of the Negro cause. Although some of the most successful men in Hollywood were Jews, he did not identify with them. The Jewish actors, directors and studio heads who held power in the film industry were, for him, another incarnation of the Eastern Parkway Jews who had stopped his father at the synagogue entrance on Yom Kippur because he did not have a ticket. When Bernard Gersten met him at the Lab in the spring of 1948, "Joe never used a Yiddish expression and never responded to one. He never talked about his parents — I thought maybe they were dead. It was obvious that he was Polish, a hard-drinking, brash, fiery Gentile, married to a Jewish wife."

Joe Papirofsky's efforts to marshal the press in support of the Lab were unsuccessful. The major studios pulled their starlets out of the Lab's school in 1947, following the testimony of the Hollywood Ten. In October 1948, the Internal Revenue Service revoked the Lab's tax-exempt status. The Lab appealed for a hearing, to no avail. Private students, who had formerly put their names on long waiting lists in order to be accepted at the Lab, disappeared. The Lab's theater, which had formerly played to standing room only, was suddenly unable to find an audience. People were afraid to appear on Lab premises lest their names or faces be reported to a government committee or, worse, to columnist Hedda Hopper.

The Lab community broke apart under the unremitting pressure. Almost all of its members were unable to find work. In 1949, the year he turned twenty-eight, Joe Papirofsky watched his adopted home crumbling despite his best efforts to keep it together.

In February, Roman Bohnen, the Lab's guiding spirit, died of a heart attack during a performance. Lab members blamed the death on mounting financial and political pressures. Then the Veterans Administration announced that enrolling at the Lab was no longer acceptable to the administrators of the G.I. Bill. In June, what remained of the student body organized a strike to protest faculty disorganization as well as some of the techniques being taught. "I didn't come to the Actors' Lab to learn to do Rin Tin Tin," read one of the pickets, in a reference to Phoebe Brand's use of animal improvisations. When a gossip columnist asked Brand to comment and the actress refused, she was promptly dubbed "Clam Brand" in a column citing G.I. bitterness with the curriculum as well as a report that the Lab's facilities had failed city inspection. The Lab school's director, Mary Tarcai, became embroiled in a bitter dispute with several of the other Lab elders that paralyzed the administration.

"You have to understand our state of mind then," recalled Phoebe Brand forty years later. "The Lab was a wonderful, successful place that we had created. It and we were wiped out. I felt then that Hitler had done a job on America as well as Europe. He killed all the people who opposed him and people here believed that it could happen to them too. It was a reign of terror. The fear was incredible. I believe Bud Bohnen died because of it. And other people."

Without its veterans, starlets and private students, the Lab was forced to close its school. It regrouped as a producing organization and, led by actor Lloyd Gough, bought an old nightclub at Beverly and La Brea boulevards. There was no money with which to hire professional builders, so Gough's brother, who was in the construction business, instructed a group of Lab volunteers working with jackhammers and shovels, to break up the floor, regrade it and to install seats. Joe Papirofsky was a regular member of the crew who "hauled dirt, drove to the other side of town to dump it into a canyon, returned and started all over again" — a process of creating a theater by hand that he would later repeat several times in New York. The Lab's new theater was named the New Globe. The organization could no longer use the name Actors' Lab Inc. since it had filed for bankruptcy a few months earlier. When they opened their first play, a musical adaptation of Dion Boucicault's *Streets of New York,* in February of 1950, reviews were tepid and attendance was low. Those Lab stalwarts who remained — Morris Carnovsky, Phoebe Brand, Howard Da Silva, Will Lee — finally gave up trying to make it work and returned to New York. In May of 1950, three and a half years after he had first auditioned before Quinn and Brand, Lab manager/janitor Joe Papirofsky locked its door for the last time.

The destruction of the first professional home he had ever known was a key experience for the man who would become Joe Papp. At the Lab, he had found a community of like-minded people, a philosophy he could live by, work he could do. At the Lab, he had learned the politics of nonprofit theater: how to enlist the support of government agencies such as the State Board of Regents; how to fundraise; how to transfer the profits of successful productions toward the support of noncommercial work; how to attract an audience. It was at the Lab that he developed professional relationships and friendships that would last all his life.

"Living among these people," Joseph Papp would later say, "I learned about the very best and the worst of human beings and a lot about what sustains a theater. The Lab never had a clear identity, except as a place of quality. A theater needs that. It also needs a board of directors who are not performers or directors, who don't have a particular artistic ax to grind. A board's fundamental function is to raise money."

And, "There are so many needs that actors and directors and people in the theater have so they go at each other. It's clear that a theater needs strong leadership. People can leave but one person has to be the mainstay and stay on. Shakespeare understood it: If you have a strong monarch, you don't have revolutions. I never stand in the way of talent. But after a while, people naturally feel that they want more of a say in the organization. And I always feel that they cannot. The running of the organization clearly has to be mine. I am the producer. I cannot permit the institution to fall apart."

FOUR

The Floor Manager Who Loved Shakespeare

ON OCTOBER 8, 1948, Joe Papirofsky had become a father for the third time. Now, with the Lab closed, he needed a job and found work in a sheet-metal factory to support himself, his wife Sylvia, and their one-year-old son, Michael. Three months later, a Lab friend called: The national company of Arthur Miller's *Death of a Salesman* had a job for someone doubling as assistant stage manager and understudy for the roles of the salesman's two sons. In September of 1950, the twenty-nine-year-old Joe Papirofsky embarked on a national tour that would take *Salesman* from Pasadena to Salt Lake City to Peoria to Boston and New York City. During that time he would gain his first professional credits as stage manager and actor and fall in love with his third wife, Peggy Bennion.

Peggy Bennion was a dark-haired, dark-eyed aspiring actress from Manila, Utah, playing one of the call girls in *Salesman*. Her father was a Mormon bishop who would later run for governor; her mother, a rancher's wife who would herself become a political activist. Peggy had grown up on her parents' ranch, graduated from the University of Utah and then made her way to Hollywood, where she worked for a fan magazine.

In part because he was married, in part because he looked so young, in part because, in high school, Peggy Bennion had always ignored boys under six feet tall, the two struck up a friendship rather than a romance. They went bicycle riding in the cities where they performed. They spent hours talking on the train. "He had the answers to everything in the world," she said. "He was brilliant, perceptive, shrewd about people, imaginative, energetic. He was also very, very funny."

Joe Papirofsky was capable of listening for hours to stories of the Bennion homestead in Utah, so intently that she gained a new appreciation of her family. But when Peggy Bennion asked about his family, Joe Papirofsky had little to say. He described his mother as English, his father as Polish and himself as the youngest graduate ever of Columbia University. He said he had married at nineteen, and that he had a daughter named Susan in addition to his son Michael.

As the tour made its way through the Midwest, Papirofsky became a determined suitor. He told Peggy Bennion that he and Sylvia had not lived together as man and wife for some time, that he was married in name only. "And when Joe wanted something," she recalled, "there was no obstacle. I had never lived with anybody and, in those days, for me, that was stepping over the line." But Peggy Bennion fell in love for the first time in her life and agreed to marry him.

The trouble was, he was still married. In October 1950, Sylvia Papirofsky packed up her belongings and her son and drove to Peoria to join her husband. For the next few months, as the tour moved from city to city, Joe Papirofsky tried to make up his mind whether to live with his wife and son, or with his lover. By the time they arrived in New York in February 1951, he had chosen to live with Peggy Bennion. Sylvia and Michael Papirofsky moved in temporarily with Lab friend Bernard Gersten. He and Peggy moved in with another Lab alumnus. Both looked for work in the theater, he as an assistant director, she as an actress. Neither found employment until Joe took a part-time job as a floor manager for CBS.

In between those day jobs, Joe Papirofsky looked for opportunities to direct. Through his Irish friends, he had met members of the James Connolly Association, for whom he directed a play about the execution of four I.R.A. leaders. He taught classes for his former Lab teacher Morris Carnovsky at the Neighborhood Playhouse. During the summer, he served as social director at Camp Arrowhead, a left-wing camp for adults in the Catskills, where, in addition to scheduling tennis games and dances, he persuaded an elderly, leftist Daughter of the American Revolution to give him money to start a theater. With $1,000, Joe turned a barn into a playhouse, paid three friends to come up to the Catskills and produced a series of plays.

Then, during the winter of 1951, he ran into his former high school classmate and Dramatics Club copresident, "Beets" Rothfeld. She lived in a then-new Manhattan housing project called Stuyvesant Town, where she belonged to an amateur theatrical group called the Oval Players. They were looking for a director; she urged him to meet them. Joe Papirofsky contracted for $25 to direct John Patrick's *The Curious Savage* and, in December 1951, read, in the *Villager*, his first review: "Under the able direction of Joe Papirofsky, the eleven characters are brought to life with what at times might be called powerful performances."

By then, Joe and Peggy Bennion were married and living in a tiny Greenwich Village flat. They had had a small wedding, with none of the Bennion family and only Papp's brother in attendance. Peggy Bennion met the elder Papirofskys only later, and then because of a family emergency. Joe Papirofsky had gone alone to his parents' home in Brooklyn and when his new wife telephoned him there, she had difficulty understanding Yetta Papirofsky's English. "It was then Joe told me his parents were immigrants and that he was Jewish," Peggy Papp recalled. "He told me he had started lying about his background during the depression, when many firms would not hire Jews and he needed to get a job. But I also understood that Joe was ashamed of his family history."

Joe Papirofsky's first meeting with the Bennions was the result of another telephone call, one that Peggy made to inform her parents that she was getting married. For months, she had been sending them clippings from the *Daily Worker*. "They seemed to be about the same things my father believed in," she said. "He was very idealistic, like Joe. Against powerful monopolies and on the side of the disadvantaged. I was terribly naive. I thought he'd be interested. My father was secretary of the state of Utah then — he later ran for governor — and he got very nervous. He called the FBI in Washington and asked for a dossier on Joe. When the message came from Washington that Joe was an active Communist, he called me and told me that the family wanted to meet Joe before I married him. I said, 'Daddy that's impossible. We're busy. We can't get away. . . .' And he said, 'Then I'm taking the next plane to New York.' So I said, 'I'll come home.'"

Before she left for Utah, Joe Papirofsky promised, at her insistence, to resign from the party if she married him. "I was terrified," she recalled. "The Rosenbergs had been sentenced to death that spring for espionage. McCarthy hysteria was at its height. People were being put in jail. My

father was liberal, and liberal was liberal, you know, but Communist was
Communist.

"When I got to Utah, my father took me for a ride in the car and said
it was wonderful I had fallen in love and that they were very happy for
me. He then asked whether I knew everything there was to know about
Joe. When I said I did, he was very calm and he asked me whether I knew
that both of us could go to jail if things got bad. I said yes. And then he
said, 'There's nothing wrong with going to jail for your beliefs.' He said
that the Mormons had done that, as well as many other wonderful
people. But he wanted to make sure that I believed what Joe believed.

"There followed ten days with my family during which we discussed
the situation. My mother just cried. At one point, she said: *'Oh Peggy was
always so pretty and now she's going to marry a Communist!'* My mother
wanted me to marry a doctor, a pillar of the community. And who did I
want to marry? A Jew, who was a Communist, who had been married
twice before, who had two children, who had no steady job, and who
was living on unemployment insurance. What mother would be happy
about that? For ten days, I barely ate. I went to bed every night saying:
'My family will not accept Joe because he's a Communist and I may end
up in jail through guilt by association and I have to break it off.' And
then another part of me would say: 'I love him; I will share his fate.'"

Joe Papirofsky flew to Utah to meet the Bennions and proved so
likable that the family retained affectionate relations with him even after
the couple divorced over twenty years later. "All their stereotypes about
Communists vanished," Peggy Papp later said. "They saw Joe as a young,
dedicated idealist." Her father and her thirty-year-old prospective husband rode horseback together, camped, fished, sang folk songs and found
they agreed on almost everything except communism. They hit it off so
well that Heber Bennion gave the marriage his blessing. For Joe Papirofsky, the Bennions came to represent America at its best. Joe Papp would
later say that his Mormon father-in-law was one of the few men he had
ever trusted.

On October 27, 1951, Peggy Bennion became Peggy Papirofsky. A
few months later, her husband was hired full-time at CBS. "Television
was the last place I wanted to go," he later said. "It was amateur night
in Dixie as far as we were concerned. No self-respecting person would be
caught dead in a television show. But CBS employed a lot of theater
people and I needed the money."

Joe Papirofsky began work for CBS just as television was entering what
would later be called its "Golden Age of Drama." Up to a dozen original

plays were telecast live every week, with writers, directors and actors all in attendance. Stage managers worked for whichever show needed them and Papirofsky bounced from such television classics as *Studio One* to *Omnibus* to *The Jackie Gleason Show* to *Person to Person*, running into veterans of the Actors' Lab as well as meeting people he would later employ. He watched Sidney Lumet and Yul Brynner direct episodes of *Danger*. He watched Peter Brook direct *King Lear* starring Orson Welles. He met the cohost of *Mike and Buff*, Mike Wallace, who would become America's preeminent television reporter, and the chatty celebrity panelists of Garry Moore's *I've Got a Secret*, whose Kitty Carlisle would later chair the New York State Council on the Arts.

The work required of a stage manager varied greatly from show to show. If he was assigned to a news broadcast, the stage manager was expected half an hour before air time, merely to cue the anchorman. For a variety show or "special," he was required to confer with the director and serve as his stage voice, working with earphones, coordinating people and sets.

Joseph Papp would later remember being exhilarated by the pace of the work, by helping directors with casting, and getting to know actors and stagehands. He smoked cigars with Ernie Kovacs, Burl Ives and Orson Welles. He met the musical comedy creators Richard Rodgers and Oscar Hammerstein and actress Julie Andrews — people who would later help him raise money for the New York Shakespeare Festival. "I even liked the shows that made demands on me," he later said. "But I did not want to be in television."

Joe Papirofsky did not then talk much about his disdain for the medium. He did his work and was known as a very good stage manager: steady, calm, cool under pressure, unlikely to waste his own or anybody else's time. He became an active union man, member of the Radio and Television Directors Guild, and an employee who got along well with everyone on the set. Men who worked with him then would later remark on his warmth, his wit and an idealism that bordered on naiveté.

They were all aware of his passionate interest in Shakespeare. He seemed to know all the plays by heart — he was always declaiming speeches — and, unlike other television people who talked about doing theater, Joe Papirofsky seemed to be training himself to do it. TV crews would typically see three or four run-throughs of a show before a telecast. Whenever the fledgling stage manager found someone with something to teach him, he would pick his brain, spending hours analyzing the casting, the acting, the production values of a show. After hours, he continued to look for directing jobs, and in May of 1952, he worked with the Irish-American James Connolly Association once again, producing three one-act plays — *Hall of Healing, Bedtime Story* and *Time to Go* — by Sean O'Casey.

He had first seen O'Casey performed at the Actors' Lab, when Sara Allgood of Dublin's Abbey Theater had played in *Juno and the Paycock,* and he had been impressed by the power of O'Casey's language and politics. "O'Casey seemed to be in the same place I was," he later said. "He was considered a Communist playwright but he was hardly dogmatic or doctrinaire. I always had a strong connection with the Irish. Jerry Winthrop, my friend when I was six years old, was Irish. His father had a brogue and I loved the sound of his voice. Later I loved Yeats, John Synge, Lady Gregory. The Irish people I knew were lively and spent all their nights reading poetry. I wrote to O'Casey, explaining that I wanted to produce some of his one-act plays, but I had no money to pay him. I received a nice letter back which read, 'I make my living by writing. I can't give you anything for nothing.' So I raised some money."

He persuaded three friends he had met through the Lab — stage manager Bernard Gersten, actor Charles Cooper and producer Peter Lawrence — to put in a couple of hundred dollars each and the four of them produced the plays with Papirofsky directing. They rented space in Yugoslav-American Hall at 405 West 41st Street, near the Hudson River wharves, where the James Connolly Association sometimes held meetings. "That hall was not the most attractive place," he recalled. "Those Yugoslavs were drinking and rousing it up and arguing in Serbo-Croatian. But we got it cheap. We agreed to pay O'Casey a royalty for three one-act plays; and I began casting." The actors he chose included Irish actors Liam Lenihan, Padear Noonan, Benedict MacQuarrie, and African-American actors William Marshall and Osceola Archer.

Interracial casting in 1952 was rare. Interracial casting for a Sean O'Casey play, unheard of. But, at the Lab, Joe Papirofsky had listened to Lab elders talk about expanding the range of roles for Negroes and do nothing about it. "I did not cast blacks with deep Southern accents," Joseph Papp later said. "All the actors — Irish, black and Jewish — spoke with a very slight brogue. Still, Sean O'Casey would have dropped dead if he had known."

Although his characters were ordinary people struggling with poverty and Catholicism, their joy, suffering and the cadence of their speech was so intrinsically Irish that they seemed to defy translation to an American stage. Few Americans had attempted O'Casey plays. Joe Papirofsky, however, plowed ahead, rehearsing in the hours that he was not working at CBS.

It was on the O'Casey project that the young producer met Merle Debuskey, soon to become one of his staunchest supporters. Debuskey was a tall, dignified press agent from a Baltimore Jewish family who, like Joe Papirofsky, had once had ambitions to become a reporter. An outstanding college athlete, then a navy gunner, he had come to New York after his military discharge, drifted into theater circles and wound up as a press agent. Although he earned his living representing Broadway producers, Debuskey had worked off-Broadway and was interested in socially meaningful theater. He loved O'Casey and volunteered his services to do publicity.

When the two men first met, Debuskey was impressed by Joe Papirofsky's sense of purpose as well as fun. Although they were about the same age, Papirofsky viewed the calm, measured press agent as far older than he actually was. Debuskey, on his side, was taken with the engaging and energetic stage manager who spouted speeches from O'Casey and Shakespeare. "It was *life* to him," Debuskey later said. "He was enormously exciting to talk with and masterful at bad puns. They came out in an endless stream. His ideas were spontaneous, impromptu, not carefully considered. He would jump up on a chair and say, 'Let's go to Washington!' and forget he had said it five minutes later. He never censored himself and had so many ideas that even if most never went anywhere, at least one of them did."

Debuskey, who would oversee Joseph Papp's publicity for the next twenty-five years, obtained a few paragraphs in the press announcing the O'Casey plays and the promise of several critics to attend.

On the evening of the dress rehearsal, Joe was astonished to see Brooks Atkinson walk in. *New York Times* chief drama critic since 1926, he had won a Pulitzer Prize as war correspondent in the Soviet Union. He was the most respected critic of his time, and he was to figure prominently in Joseph Papp's fortunes. His appearance, now, at the O'Casey dress rehearsal was a mixed blessing. To have a major critic present was a big deal for an unknown theater group. On the other hand, Joe Papirofsky had a feeling O'Casey had written and asked Atkinson to check up on him. "I was worried but I couldn't very well ask him to leave," he later said. "Everything was riding on that play for me. It was my first real professional undertaking."

"Eighteen years having elapsed since a new O'Casey play was done in this town, a patron of the arts instinctively rises to attention when a new bill is announced," Atkinson wrote. "Although the actors and impresarios of the current bill have Mr. O'Casey's best interests at heart . . . the acting is frantically inadequate. Neither the director of the first two plays nor the actors who are in them have any sense of genre style for Irish drama. If there were no Equity actors among them, you would assume that they were amateurs, taking a fling at something for which they have little talent."

The following morning, Joe Papirofsky walked into Central Park with the newspaper and sat down on a bench. Although another critic later put the evening of one-acts on his list of Ten Best Plays of 1952, Joseph Papp remembered that morning as one of the worst moments in his life. "I thought maybe I should do something else. Then I tried to think of what else, but there was nothing else I knew. Doing these plays had been a tremendous investment for me: of all the money I had, of my hopes for the future. I had put such effort into it. What was I supposed to do now? I was nearly thirty-one years old and not qualified for anything except giving cues on television. I had very little training. I'd been on the road with one show. I wasn't even a highly trained stage manager. I had made such a strong effort — everything was riding on that play."

At the same time, he was struggling with another blow. His second wife, Sylvia, had married the lawyer who had handled their divorce, a widower with two young children. The divorce had been exceptionally bitter, with his ex-wife destroying every vestige of Joe Papirofsky in her possession. In an effort to consolidate their new family, she and her husband planned to legally adopt one another's children and change Michael's family name. They also discouraged Joe Papirofsky's visits to his son, arguing that they were disruptive and confusing to Michael. Now, they asked him to stop seeing Michael entirely and, when Joe refused, proposed that they consult what they considered an impartial authority: a child psychologist. The psychologist recommended that the father give up all rights to his son and, for reasons he never fully made clear, Joe Papirofsky accepted his decision. In May 1953, the adoption papers were finalized and his visits to his son were terminated. Although he would later recall his profound grief at the separation and the days he spent drunk at home, few of the people he worked with knew anything about it.

"It's characteristic of Joe that when anything was painful he closed the door on it," said Peggy Papp. "That's what he did with Michael. That's what he did with his first wife and child. He wiped the memory out. Joe had always had terrible depressions where he had the feeling he was dying, sinking into a black hole. The way he overcame depression was to go fast and hard, to produce, to put his mark on the world, to make a difference and to create himself. His psychic life depended on him being somebody. It was a desperate thing. It was a matter of life and death. Personal ambition is too narrow a word to describe it because his need to succeed was tied to a deep commitment to society. In order for him to find meaning in his life, Joe had to effect a change in the society in which he lived. The more appropriate words are *fanatical, driven.*"

In the aftermath of the Brooks Atkinson review and the separation from his first son, Joe Papirofsky began to think about leaving New York and finding a job teaching theater at a college. At the age of thirty-two, he felt his life was still ungrounded. He worked at CBS, looked for freelance directing jobs and tried to figure out how he could create his own theater. And despite the promise he had made Peggy and the Bennions to leave the Communist party, he was still attending meetings and demonstrations, aware that, like other left-wing people, he was being tailed by the FBI.

The Los Angeles Bureau of the Federal Bureau of Investigation had been tracking Joe Papirofsky since 1948. By 1953, it had amassed a dossier that recorded the minutiae of his life.

June 24, 1953: Due to the irregular working hours and the varied schedule of subject, efforts to interview him directly have thus far been unsuccessful. Surveillances have been conducted to ascertain his travel routes and his daily working habits.

June 25, 1953: Subject was observed leaving the CBS Television Studio, 15 Vanderbilt Ave at 1:30 P.M. and was thereafter surveilled for approximately five minutes. He was approached for interview by SAS on East 43rd Street at approximately 1:35 P.M.

The agents identified themselves and it was noted that subject appeared to be cooperative in the initial overtures and stated although he was in somewhat of a hurry for an appointment, he had several minutes to speak to the agents. When asked if he would have more time at a later contact, he stated he wanted to know what the interview was about before he made any commitments. The subject was asked whether he would be willing to furnish any information concerning his activities and associates in California. It is to be noted that up to this point the word "Communist" had not been mentioned. The subject stated he had a lot of associates in California and he wanted to know what the agents wanted to know about them. He was then told the agents were interested in Communist activities in California. At this point the subject paled somewhat and seemed to become nervous.

The subject stated that "in these times" he would not make any statements without consulting his lawyer for fear of "incriminating himself." . . . It was noted that the subject was casually friendly and appeared to be sincere in his answers.

August 6, 1953: Subject was recontacted on Seventh Avenue between 49th and 50th Streets. After the agents identified themselves the subject stated that he did not wish to discuss his own activities or those of his associates with the FBI under any circumstances. The interview was immediately terminated.

The FBI file notes that in April of 1953, Joe Papirofsky had directed an Actors Equity showcase production of *Deep Are the Roots,* in which a Negro G.I. returning home after the war is framed for a crime he did not commit. The file also contains clippings of an advertisement Papirofsky placed for an actor to work intensively with him on Sean O'Casey's work; missing is his continuing relationship with Bina Rothfeld's group, the Oval Players, written up in the *Villager* a few months earlier. The *Villager* described Papirofsky as "ambitious for the Oval Players to establish a permanent playhouse" in the neighborhood, and planning a production of Federico García Lorca's *The House of Bernarda Alba.* But the plans never reached fruition. The Oval Players disbanded and Joe Papirofsky decided he would establish his own theater in the place where the group had met: the Sunday School room of Emmanuel Church.

Seymour Hall was a large, shabby room, which had been used as a Sunday School since 1873. It had a shallow stage, no wings, no curtains over the windows or altar and no division between the audience and actor. There was a gymnasium on the other side of one wall and a nursery school above it. Two nights a week the church Missionary Society and the Women's Sewing Group used the space; Saturdays and in August, it was used by the Bible School.

The neighborhood of Emmanuel Church was even farther off the beaten track than Yugoslav-American Hall. It was situated at 729 East 6th Street near Avenue D, in the place where Manhattan island bulges out so far that the avenues have been alphabetized. Composer David Amram, who lived between avenues B and C, would later recall the chant of elderly Polish Jews in synagogue mixing with the guitars and accordions of the Ukrainians in Tomkins Square Park. They, the growing population of African Americans and Puerto Ricans, and the small community of musicians and artists who had started to settle there "cooked along amazingly well," Amram said. "Most of us were in the same boat. We

lived there because that was the rent we could afford. Although there
were a few bad gangs, they would leave you alone if they knew you
weren't going to bother them. There was a certain kind of honor present
in the neighborhood."

Joe Papirofsky, who was still living on West 8th Street, about a fifteen
minutes' walk away, liked Emmanuel Church. It was small, with a peaked
roof, and a style reminiscent of New England. The space he wanted had
already met the extensive regulations of the New York City Fire Department. He talked with other alternative theater people such as Stella Holt,
who had been producing plays in a church-based theater beneath the
sanctuary of the Village Presbyterian Church and Brotherhood Synagogue for many years. Early in 1954, he went to see the Presbyterian
minister, Reverend Clarence F. Boyer, to talk about the venture which
he was calling "Wooden O Productions" — the "wooden O" being a
reference to Shakespeare's Globe Theater and to the prologue of *Henry V*:

> *Can this cockpit hold*
> *the vasty fields of France? Or may we cram*
> *Within this wooden O the very casques*
> *That did affright the air at Agincourt?*

Joseph Papp later recapitulated their meeting in this way: He had rung
the church doorbell and Reverend Boyer, "a cheerful, big-bellied man
with red cheeks," who looked "right out of the pages of Dickens," came
to the door.

"Reverend Boyer?" Papirofsky said. "Do you have a moment?"

"Sure," said Reverend Boyer, and waved him into a cluttered office
with a roll-top desk and almost no room to sit.

"I want to start a Shakespeare workshop in your theater," said Papirofsky. "I want to put on plays of Shakespeare and other Elizabethans
and perform without charge."

"Aha!" said Reverend Boyer. "You realize you'll have to pay for the
heat?"

The fledgling producer tried to look distressed. "Really?"

"That'll be around ten dollars a week," said the pastor.

"That's not too bad," he said casually, trying to digest the fact that
he apparently was not going to pay any rent.

"Do you think anyone will come to hear Shakespeare?" Reverend
Boyer asked.

"I really don't know."

"Wooden O Productions wants to do plays of the Elizabethan period. Why in God's name?" Joe Papirofsky wrote in an early prospectus.

Well, let me tell you why. Most of us speak English — maybe not so good — but we can pass. A few hundred years ago a little country — that blessed plot, that earth, that realm, that England — underwent a transformation. Amongst better people it was called a "cultural renaissance." This period in the reign of Elizabeth produced with miraculous abundance great tomes of works which were performed before the multitudes and the leisure classes. Characteristic of these plays was the breaking away from earlier and cruder forms of writing as well as from a content that dwelt on morality themes. This age was swept by energetic interests in the world around men — and in the men themselves. The writing it produced reflected this energy and interest and gave rise to a score of playwrights who discovered in effect the English language and its possibilities.

Their plays were rich in ideas, language, movement, pageantry — all those facets which skilfully blended produce entertainment. There were no prosceniums separating audience from actor. The entire wooden o was the theater and scenes moved fluidly from one playing area to another (somewhat like our TV sets) without long delays for changes. . . . I think you will agree with me that there is an audience for Shakespeare — maybe not as many as for Marilyn Monroe — but not everybody likes Beethoven. The point is that there is at present a sizable audience existing that would support an Elizabethan theater . . . [and] in addition to this ready-made audience there exists a vast potential for increasing it.

Shakespeare was part of the American cultural canon. There were even a few institutions exclusively devoted to Shakespeare's plays, such as the Oregon Shakespeare Festival in Ashland and the San Diego Shakespeare Festival in California. But most Americans read rather than saw Shakespeare. Joseph Papirofsky, like millions of other boys in the countries that had once belonged to the British Empire, memorized speeches from *Julius Caesar* in school. But, unlike every other one of them, he would transform a homework assignment into a life's work. His brother and sisters, wives, navy buddies, friends and professional colleagues all recalled that Papp had always slipped into Shakespeare the way other people slipped into Yiddish, Spanish or French.

From the time he had memorized the rabble-rousing speeches of Marullus and Marc Antony in junior high school, Joe Papirofsky had been reading and rereading his Shakespeare. Coworkers at CBS in the early 1950s were accustomed to the stage manager comparing colleagues to Shakespearean characters and salting his speech with Shakespearean lines the way observant Jews quoted the Bible. "If you have loved wisely but not too well, if you have felt the unkindest cut of all, if you have held the mirror up to nature and asked what's in a name," he would declaim, "you are thinking Shakespeare. If you have considered yourself of this happy breed of men, or of this sceptered isle — when you have demanded your pound of flesh or called down a plague on both your houses, you are thinking Shakespeare. If you suspect we are pigeon-livered or believe the play's the thing, you are thinking Shakespeare. If you believe music is the food of love and that you should first kill all the lawyers, you are thinking Shakespeare."

Shakespeare's characters seemed more convincing to Joe Papirofsky than those written by any other writer. Their ambiguities of character and the way those ambiguities played out in their relationships fascinated him in the way the behavior of close friends fascinated other people. "He identified all the stories in the plays with stories in his life," said Peggy Papp. "When he read *Romeo and Juliet,* he was Romeo. When he did *Hamlet,* he believed that Hamlet had grown up in Brooklyn! When he did *Henry V,* he became Henry. Every director uses the material of his or her own life in their work — look at Ingmar Bergman — but most of them develop some distance from it. Joe's involvement was very personal. He had no distance." He would talk about Romeo and Rosalind and Petruchio as if gossiping about friends. "Why did Iago do what he did to Othello?" he would ask. "The answer to me is very, very simple — because that's the way he is. That's his nature. Shakespeare never dealt with psychological reasons for things. He was interested in ambiguous people, like people in real life, people with imperfections. You take Shakespeare at his word. What you see is what you get."

Joe Papirofsky's enthusiasm captivated Reverend Boyer. But who would pay for the Shakespeare?

His financial plan for running the theater, the aspiring young director told Reverend Boyer, was standard for off-Broadway. His Shakespeare Workshop would pay no one for services and charge no admission. Restricting his theater to the Elizabethan had several advantages: There would be no need to pay author's royalties; actors were more likely to work without pay to gain experience in rarely performed classical plays; and the theater might attract press, funds and audiences by organizing around sixteenth-century work. Joseph Papirofsky himself would, of course, bear the expense of renovating Seymour Hall.

Reverend Boyer said yes.

Once he had Reverend Boyer's backing, Papirofsky set about applying for a charter from the New York State Department of Education. He remembered how the California Board of Regents imprimatur had lent a certain distinction to the Actors' Laboratory stationery. In New York State, in 1953, educational charters were rarely granted to theaters, which were regarded as places of entertainment rather than education. He drafted a statement of goals for the Workshop, which read:

1. To encourage and cultivate interest in poetic drama, with emphasis on the work of Shakespeare and his Elizabethan contemporaries, through the presentation of plays, the conduct of classes in the technique of Shakespearean acting and stagecraft, reading of plays at high schools, colleges, community centers and similar institutions
2. To establish an annual Shakespeare Festival
3. To construct a replica of the Elizabethan playhouse

By law, a nonprofit institution chartered by the Board of Regents needed a board of no less than five trustees. The first included two men with whom he worked at CBS; Leo Brody, who had grown up in the neighborhood, and now ran an Army-Navy store; himself and Reverend Boyer. The venue also needed to pass inspection. At the Lab, he had helped transform a nightclub into a theater; in the Catskills, he had started with a barn. Now, he addressed himself to the former Sunday School room of the church.

Working evenings and on weekends, drawing on the skills of his colleagues at CBS, Joe Papirofsky cleaned up Seymour Hall, covered the windows, radiators, exits, altar and religious decorations with black velour curtains and hired an electrician to hook up a rudimentary lighting system. The Sunday School children had been crammed onto long benches that could not serve a theater audience. Leo Brody, however, knew of a wrecking company that was then taking apart the Windsor Theater in the Bronx and, together with Papirofsky, bargained for the seats. The wrecker offered to sell at $25 per seat; they counteroffered 25 cents, finally buying 200 seats at $1 each, with Brody supplying the cash. A crew of CBS stagehand volunteers drove to the Bronx to move them.

The Windsor was unlit, its cement floor was wet and the nuts that fastened the seats to the floor were rusted. None of the men had tools suitable for the task at hand and it took two and half days working with hammers, chisels and screwdrivers by the light of flashlights to get the chairs out. After they had installed the seats in Emmanuel Church, about fourteen fell over backwards because the floorboards were rotten, and several subsequent weekends were spent replacing the boards and then bolting them in, one by one. A CBS lighting man put together a sound and lighting system from parts scavenged from the studios. By the time the Workshop's provisional charter was granted in November 1954 for five years, many actors had made the long, inconvenient trek to East 6th Street at least once.

Joe Papirofsky's plan had been to perform *Romeo and Juliet* during the second weekend in November, and then present, in quick succession, Thomas Middleton's *The Changeling*, Shakespeare's *Much Ado About Nothing*, Christopher Marlowe's *Edward II* and Shakespeare's *Troilus and Cressida*. He soon discovered that was impossible. He worked full-time. So did his volunteers and many of his potential actors. His inability to pay people, the inconvenience of his location and the unlikelihood of any visibility for his project created a high actor turnover. Papirofsky could find no director willing to work at Emmanuel Church, and although a steady stream of actors kept coming down to see what was going on, most left. "The thing would get competitive and people would leave," he later said. "Or they would leave because they didn't find the rest of us congenial. You have to work with people who are compatible if you're really going to create something. So anyone who joined us for a couple of evenings and found he wasn't happy there, just naturally didn't come back."

Joe sat down at his Remington Standard typewriter and wrote letters to several famous actors such as Alfred Drake who, he thought, might wish to direct:

Dear ——— ,
    In the past few years, there have been a number of attempts to corral actors to work on the problems of playing Shakespeare. Most of these dwindled away for the reasons most groups dwindle away, but I think there were additional factors. The theoretical problems of poetic theater can hold an actor's interest for a little while — but not for long. The actor finds it necessary to test himself and the new problems in front of an audience. . . .
    In examining the problem last year, I decided that a place to work was of great importance, not any place but a stage conducive to the Shakespearean staging. I found such quarters — an archaic church with an ideal 250-seat intimate auditorium. It is laid out in amphitheater style with a raked floor down to the main playing area. There are three side balconies — all within perfect sight lines. There are complete

cross-over passages circling the entire theater making entrances and exits possible from all parts of the house. We are in the midst of making the theater habitable by installing a dimmer board, hanging curtains, improving the seating, building step and platform units to increase the flexibility of the playing area. . . .

Our initial project will be *Romeo and Juliet*. . . . I would like very much to discuss with you the possibility of your directing the first project. I can assure you of an excellent cast and an exciting experience. I trust you feel that the objectives as outlined have validity. There are other objectives a little more far reaching such as a Shakespeare Festival under a tent next summer in one of the city's parks. Investigations are already underway. Please let me hear from you. . . .

P.S. I think I mentioned that for the past three years, I've been a stage manager at CBS TV. I need fresh air badly. . . .

Joe Papirofsky

When this letter yielded no directors, Joe began to direct *Romeo and Juliet* himself. He took out advertisements in the trade papers to announce auditions, and Peggy Papp brought over friends from the acting class she was taking with Harold Clurman. But actors kept dropping out after they had been cast. The Romeos, in particular, kept leaving. Actress Bryarly Lee rehearsed with eight of them, as well as three Fathers, four Nurses, and an assortment of Benvolios, Mercutios and Tybalts, and later told an interviewer she could remember only one rehearsal with the full cast and rarely two with the same principals.

Papirofsky, who was working full-time at CBS while he put together his production, adapted. He began scheduling *Romeo and Juliet* rehearsals in his own apartment because it seemed foolish to trek all the way down to the Lower East Side just for Juliet and the Nurse. "If I dwelled on setbacks, I'd be paralyzed," he later said. "You always have to take the next step. You have to come up with a solution and most of the time you come up with a better solution. Romeo's gone? Well, he wasn't that great. I replaced that Romeo. I replaced him with a *fat* Romeo. But he spoke so gorgeously and I thought: Why does Romeo have to be handsome? Why shouldn't he be fat? Why? There's nothing in the play that says that he has to be handsome."

As September became October, the heating system began to add to the actors' discomfort. "As soon as Juliet would say, 'Romeo wherefore art thou Romeo, deny thy father and refuse thy name,' *clang-clang-clang* — the steam heat would begin to clang," Joseph Papp recalled. "It would happen every night around the same time and the actors would take it personally and blame it on me!" After the eighth Romeo defected, the exasperated director/producer decided to postpone his production of *Romeo and Juliet*. He had been talking to noted Shakespearean actor Whitford Kane, whom he had met at the Lab, and decided that the most practical course of action would be to inaugurate the Workshop with an evening of "scenes" from Shakespeare.

On November 4, 1954, Joe Papirofsky's first Shakespeare production opened at Seymour Hall. The only review was written by Eugene Burr, CBS technician, board member and sometime *Playbill* columnist, who wrote: "On a Friday night several weeks ago, in a church near the East River, Mr. Whitford Kane buried his 36th Ophelia. . . . It is one of the most heartening and exciting experiences to hit the professional stage in years. No conclave of impassioned amateurs, no off-Broadway promotion for the benefit of submerged semi-pros, it is a strictly professional project, of, by, and for professional players and audiences who are interested in the American acting tradition. . . ."

There were, however, few neighborhood people in the audience. The thirty-three-year-old director sat down at his Remington and typed invitations to a second evening to neighborhood merchants, hospitals and schools, and to the drama critics of the *New York Times,* the *New York Herald Tribune*, the *New York Post* and *Time* magazine. He signed them Joseph Papp, Managing Director. CBS, he would later say, had shortened Papirofsky to Papp, because the name did not fit on the credit line and communications between control room and the stage were difficult enough without having to pronounce a four-syllable name. He had been called "Pappy" at school, liked the sound of Joseph Papp, and had his name legally changed five years later.

In February 1955, Joseph Papp presented a second evening of scenes titled "An Evening with Shakespeare's Women" with an accompanying lecture by a Rutgers University professor. Once again, Whitford Kane performed a monologue. After months of rehearsals, Bryarly Lee and Sylvia Gassell were finally able to perform a scene from *Romeo and Juliet,* and Gassell and Colleen Dewhurst performed a scene from *Henry V.* There were 185 people in Seymour Hall, a capacity house. Contributions totaled $55 but there was not a single review.

The following week, Joseph Papp held the first meeting of the Shakespeare Workshop's board of trustees. As chairman, he introduced new members, reported on the successful acquisition of a charter from the New York State Board of Regents, the opening of the Workshop's first bank account and its current financial situation. He told the other men that he had paid the church $100 each month for heat and $20 for electricity. He noted that trustee Leo Brody had, to date, invested over $700 into the project and that he, Joseph Papp, had put in $941.

It was agreed, the minutes of that first meeting record, that if in the future the Workshop achieved some financial stability, the two outlays would be refunded.

FIVE

Becoming Joseph Papp

THE THEATER landscape during 1955, the first full year of the Shakespeare Workshop, was crowded. The musicals *The Boy Friend, Damn Yankees, Fanny, Silk Stockings* and *The Pajama Game,* the one-man shows of Maurice Chevalier and Danish comic Victor Borge and serious dramas such as an adaptation of *The Diary of Anne Frank,* Arthur Miller's *A View from the Bridge* and Tennessee Williams's *Cat on a Hot Tin Roof* were offered on the Broadway stage. Off-Broadway was also thriving, its growth fueled largely by veterans who had worked on the stage during their military service and established dozens of new theaters when they came home. In 1950, Actors Equity formally recognized off-Broadway by setting union regulations for theaters containing under 300 seats and located outside the official theater district.

People who worked off-Broadway in the postwar period were interested in an alternative kind of theater. They aimed to take more risks than mainstream theater, to produce new work and give established playwrights and actors a second stage. They were interested in reviving the plays of Sean O'Casey, George Bernard Shaw, August Strindberg, Gertrude Stein, Henrik Ibsen, Anton Chekhov and the Elizabethans. Actors received the off-Broadway standard payment of $5 per week when they rehearsed and $25 a week when they performed — a salary scale that reinforced the prejudice that they were amateurs rather than theater professionals — but they viewed the opportunity to do serious theater as more important than money.

There were also theater groups organized exclusively around the plays of William Shakespeare, whose work was then enjoying a small vogue in North America. New Shakespeare festivals had been established in Stratford, Ontario, as well as at Antioch College in Ohio. A small Manhattan group called the Shakespearewrights had opened on the Upper East Side. And a mammoth, well-publicized effort was under way to establish an American Shakespeare Festival at Stratford, Connecticut.

The ASF was the project of several prominent New Yorkers, supported by $600,000 in start-up funds, half of which came from the Rockefeller Foundation. It had been chartered as a nonprofit, educational institution by a special bill passed in the Connecticut State Legislature. Its master plan called for a three-part institution: a theater, an acting company and an academy. Its staff included two prestigious British directors who would be charged with performance and training.

Whenever theater people like press agent Merle Debuskey or stage manager Bernard Gersten — who would work in Stratford — ran into Joseph Papp in those early years, they were struck by the personable CBS employee's ambition despite his lack of money and connections. Ever a man who chose action over reflection, he relied on gut instinct and only later filled in the blanks. "Usually, when someone seeks a job in the theater," Gersten would later reflect, "he or she thinks: Where will I work? As a set designer? An actor? A director? I don't believe Joe had one career line in mind. He was not, at first, a director. He was certainly not a conventional producer — he had no money. He created his own job by, in effect, opening his own business."

Even more striking to his contemporaries was Papp's energy. Despite the fact that he had no actors and no audience, Papp was brimming over with ideas, which he set down in writing. "The theater in New York is a business," he wrote in one of his many papers of the early 1950s.

On Broadway it's a big business — off-Broadway it's a smaller business. Regardless of scope both have a product to sell to customers. If it's a good product (and the critics think it is) then people come to it; but if it's a poor product (and the critics think it is) nobody buys. Unlike other products, theater productions are highly perishable. They can't keep on the shelves or in refrigerators. Once they hit the lights they have to be consumed nightly and with great relish — so enough with this analogy.

Theater must also be an art and there's the rub. With art there are a great number of intangibles that have little relation to budgets and bucks and therefore those misty-eyed people who invest in a Broadway show are prepared to take a calculated risk. That's the way it works on Broadway and some people make a million dollars. . . .

Now off-Broadway, though dwarfed by the aforementioned scale of activity, operates with similar laws in a smaller framework. . . . I think it is safe to say that any off-Broadway theater that can manage its operating expenses week after week can be considered a howling success yet at its very best, the off-Broadway theater can never make a great deal of money. . . .

His theater, Papp told Debuskey, would be different from Broadway, off-Broadway and the American Shakespeare Festival. It took as its model such institutions as the New York Public Library and New York City's Goldman Band. At the band concerts he had attended as a child in Prospect Park, there were no assigned seats, no ticket-takers, no admission fee — just green lawns and music. At the Actors' Lab, Roman Bohnen had talked about that kind of theater, a theater to which money was irrelevant.

Presenting theater for free was no interim measure, Papp told Debuskey, but a cornerstone of his project. Both Broadway and off-Broadway, he wrote later, lived in the realm of "the quick buck, the overnight success, here today, gone tomorrow. There's a reason it's called show *business*. A business must stay out of the red to exist. I had a different idea. I wanted to reach audiences who might never have seen a play before and who were unable or unwilling to pay. I wanted my theater to be free. . . ."

Another of Papp's ideas that appealed to Merle Debuskey was multiracial casting and the development of multiracial audiences. In 1955, African-Americans were not a conspicuous presence on Broadway. There had been some "all-Negro" musicals; the thirties had witnessed Federal Theater and Mercury Theater productions with integrated casts. But in 1955, mainstream theater meant "white" theater played by white actors before white audiences. Such theaters as the Negro Ensemble Company were yet to be formed and many actors — some whites included — viewed New York theater as a closed club. "There were very few producing organizations and a place like the Theatre Guild had its own coterie of performers," Merle Debuskey recalled. "If you came from Iowa with no connections, your chances were very slim indeed. If you were black or Latino you had a very difficult time. But, from the start, anybody could walk into Joe's workshop and feel welcome. There were enough black people walking around there for a black to say, 'Well, it's *not hopeless'* — and *not hopeless* is a great step up in the world of theater."

Gloria Foster, the African-American actress who first worked for Papp in February of 1955 and continued to do so through the 1980s, recalled that when she first came to New York from Chicago and auditioned at Emmanuel Church, she thought *"This is the way theater is supposed to function,* not knowing that Joe was unique. He gained the loyalty of actors all around the world. They wouldn't want to work for numerous other people because they knew they weren't welcome — that they were filling up a quota, that they were doing something odd and that after the production was over, they would no longer be welcome in that theater. Joe always made you feel that you had an open invitation to return many times."

All sorts of actors were intrigued by Papp's vision of an American kind of Shakespeare. "At the time I was starting out, the Anglophilic myth was that only the British could properly do Shakespeare," Papp recalled, "but there was no reliable evidence that the present mode of English speech was the speech of Shakespeare's time. When I first heard Laurence Olivier doing Shakespeare, I found it pompous and horribly artificial. Much of the British tradition was a kind of singing tradition, declamatory, oratorical.

"I wanted the verse to be American, the language handled without too much singing. I remember calling up Stratford, Connecticut, one time and having a terribly clipped voice answer, 'American Shakespeare Festival.' I told her, *'You don't sound American at all!'* If you present Shakespeare to American high school kids in British English, you convey the message that the Bard is something strange, for the elite and out of their ken. You do Shakespeare a disservice if you worship him. You have to see him as you would see a contemporary writer: someone who's speaking to you. But the real point is that nobody has a corner on Shakespeare. The artistic impulse, not the accent, is what matters."

The American Shakespeare Festival in Stratford, Connecticut, had a strong, "external" British orientation, which relied on a rigorous training program. The most important American training ground for actors in New York, the Actors Studio, stressed the "internal" and discouraged their members from attempting Shakespeare, just as the Group Theater had. "Lee Strasberg didn't believe we were good enough to do it," recalled actress Phoebe Brand. "Well, the only way you can *get* good is to do it, and Joe just went and did."

Papp's way of doing was impetuous, make-do — critics would say makeshift — and philosophically inconsistent. Although he often reiterated his stated position on developing an American Shakespeare style, from the very inception of his Workshop, he engaged the services of well-known British actors such as Whitford Kane and, later, actors who had undergone classical British training. Papp's inconsistency was integral to his personality, infuriating many, a source of delight to others. Rather than having one idea at a time, he tended to have several. Rather than developing and adhering to a master plan, he relished his ability to turn on a dime. He was criticized as a man who found easy solutions, whose work was "un-thought-through." But during the thirty-five years that he directed a theater, many of the best thought-through theaters died. Neither the tiny Shakespearewrights nor the massive American Shakespeare Festival was able to survive, while the Shakespeare Workshop grew and thrived.

"The reason was, simply, Joe," recalled Merle Debuskey. "Joe was a bottomless well of fierce conviction and evangelical righteousness. Not only was his theater free, but he was supporting it with his salary. Skeptics would have a hard time finding the Achilles' heel in this activity. It was a beautiful, altruistic venture, with no profit in it for anyone. It offered things that had never been offered before on this scale. It was marvelously imaginative, brave, human and civilizing."

In February of 1955, however, the venture was still more a vision than a reality. The Shakespeare Workshop had staged two evenings of "scenes" and had had one board meeting, but it had no artistic director and no stable of actors. "Joe certainly wished to direct," actress Sylvia Gassell, who for months rehearsed the role of the Nurse in Papp's revolving-door *Romeo and Juliet,* later said. "It was his foremost desire. Nor did he relinquish that desire for many years to come. In my opinion, it was his Achilles' heel." But even Joe Papp could not work a full-time job, put together a theater, and direct at the same time. Professional actors such as Alfred Ryder, Olive Deering, Leo Penn and Anthony Franciosa appeared at the church, read and then disappeared. Directors came to investigate the premises, then drifted away. Finally, Gassell asked Papp to let her husband, Joel Friedman, direct the Workshop.

Friedman was a Bronx-born actor and freelance director who had been well schooled in theater. After returning from the war, he had used the G.I. Bill to study with former Federal Theater director Hallie Flanagan at Smith College. He had directed there, in summer stock and off-Broadway, and was then making his living as lighting director for a nightclub in the St. Regis Hotel.

If there was any divergence in theatrical outlook between Gassell, Friedman and Papp, it was, as the actress later put it, "very small." Friedman believed that Method acting was ruining American theater. It was of no use, he told Papp, in performing Shakespeare, where every nuance of the drama is expressed in the words. The problem with American actors was getting them to pay as much attention to the text as they did to their feelings about it. Papp, whose own devotion to text had been reinforced by a line of teachers that included Miss McKay, Eulalie Spence and Margaret Prendergast McLean, liked what he heard. All three were interested in developing an American way of performing Shakespeare. Moreover, Gassell, who had worked with Harold Clurman and Sanford Meisner, had already organized a small troupe of actors who had performed Shakespeare.

That troupe constituted the core of the company at Seymour Hall. Colleen Dewhurst did not join, because she had a job working as a telephone operator, but she sent her husband, James Vickery, and her friend Jack Cannon, who read with Papp's wife, Peggy Bennion. The only misfit was a young man who both the Friedmans and Papp assumed had been invited by the other party. It turned out that Joseph Spagnuolo was a neighborhood regular who played basketball at the church and had wandered into Seymour Hall to see what was going on. But Friedman had asked him to read from a script, so he had. Spagnuolo was the first of a series of walk-ins who worked at the Festival. He later parlayed that experience into a career as film actor Joe Spinell.

For his first production, Friedman selected *Much Ado About Nothing*. In April of 1955, the *New York Times* carried a small notice of the production, which was scheduled to run Friday and Saturday nights for three weeks. The men in the cast all wore black trousers and white shirts; the women wore damaged wedding gowns from Bonwit Teller, where Papp's sister-in-law, Marsha Martel, worked as a bridal consultant and obtained them for a few dollars apiece. The fights were performed without foils and there were almost no props.

There were also no reviews. The neighborhood newspaper, *Town and Village*, and the *New York Post* merely noted the final performances, and on April 30, the cast disbanded. If the producer could not come up with money for carfare at the very least, some said, they could make no promise to come back.

Left only with the services of Peggy Bennion and actor William Major, Papp decided that he himself would direct one of Shakespeare's least popular plays, *Cymbeline*. It opened in July in very hot weather. The fans donated by a neighborhood butcher were unequal to the heat. The producer climbed up on the roof and ran a water hose over the tiles to cool them off. But people stayed away. Peggy Bennion would later remember playing to an audience of eight — and there was no press notice at all.

Nevertheless, in the fall, Joel Friedman, Sylvia Gassell and company returned to Emmanuel Church. Although the Friedmans would later say they knew next to nothing about Joe Papp, they were taken by his idealism, his energy and his evident love of Shakespeare. Papp supplied everything Friedman asked for, and kept the organization running smoothly, despite his full-time job at CBS. Papp attended the Shakespeare classes that Friedman instituted at Emmanuel Church and would later credit the director with teaching him directing techniques that made the plays accessible, easily understood and swiftly performed.

But, Gassell noted, once the company got going, Joe Papp found himself in a peculiar position. "Here he was in his own theater with an acting company formed by another director and his wife, and no role for himself. 'What am *I* supposed to do?' Joe asked us. *'Produce,'* we answered. The right thing to suggest, as it turned out, though he knew next to nothing about it at the time."

One of the areas of which Papp knew nothing was publicity. Friedman and Gassell demanded that he get critics to review productions, and the fledgling producer called on his friend Merle Debuskey to help. Debuskey, a professional Broadway press agent, knew his way around the cultural departments of the major city newspapers. He introduced him to reporters and critics and coached him on how to interest them. "Actors and directors come and go," he told Papp. "And institutions can't speak for themselves. *You* have to speak for the Workshop. *You* have to be its voice." In junior high school, Papp had dreamed of becoming a journalist. Now, following Debuskey's pointers, he began to write, telephone and visit the offices of New York City critics and reporters, embarking on what would become a long and mostly successful love affair with the press.

Workshop actors were both thrilled and frightened by their producer's forays into the pressroom. They knew he had a hot temper and, while they wanted publicity, they didn't want to offend anyone. But Joseph Papp liked reporters and understood the interplay between a major city newspaper, its subjects and its readers. That understanding and knack for providing good copy would help the Shakespeare Workshop become a city institution.

When *As You Like It* opened in October of 1955, after being heralded about town by both Papp and Debuskey, it received four press notices, including one by Louis Calta of the *New York Times*. But Joseph Papp was not one to rest on any laurels.

"Dear Mr. Atkinson," he wrote to the *Times* chief critic:

I must confess that when I approached you at your office two weeks ago, I expected to be brushed off. Your kindness and attention were very warming and I want you to know that I deeply appreciate it. The "infectious exuberance" attributed to our work by Mr. Calta and such words as "boldness" and "enthusiasm" however . . . are not the result of youthful vitality but a calculated point of view. . . . Attuning the ear to Shakespearean language takes practice for actor and audience. It is one of the problems Joel Friedman who directed the play, and myself are strongly interested in. If you could take some time in your busy schedule, we would love to have you come down. You'll see what I'm talking about and I think you'll enjoy yourself. I shall take the liberty of keeping you informed of our subsequent productions.

> Sincerely,
> Joseph Papp

In his Sunday *Times* column the first week of December, Brooks Atkinson noted: "Louis Calta likes *As You Like It* at the Shakespearean Workshop Theatre as well as an 'ebullient' *Macbeth,* presented by the Shakespearewrights at Hus Auditorium." By that time, Papp had two other productions in the works: *Two Gentlemen of Verona* and, at long last, *Romeo and Juliet*. Neither one was reviewed, Gassell and Friedman were furious and Papp redoubled his press efforts.

"Dear Sir," he wrote to the drama editor of the *Times:*

Since I must explain to the fifteen Equity actors who have devoted more than a year of their time and talent to build a Shakespeare Repertory Company why the *New York Times* will not review our new production, I have to understand the basis for your decision. . . . Do you require that the group be a paid Equity company? Evidently not, as an amateur presentation of three Saroyan plays was reviewed some weeks ago and others have been systematically covered. . . . Is it that you require a more commercial operation? . . . Must the event be newsworthy? . . . Perhaps a paid press agent is necessary or a higher advertising budget is a consideration? . . . Maybe you now insist that the last play of a bona fide off-Broadway producing group receive favorable press notices? . . . Why are we being singled out? . . .

We feel that the *New York Times* Drama section has a stake in our proceedings; that our activity is vital to the theater — its very life blood; that if we are successful in developing one good Shakespearean actor or influencing one high school student to appreciate Shakespeare, we have done our job. And even if this is not accomplished, our struggle to achieve it must be recognized and supported.

Mr. Atkinson has imbued the drama section of the *New York Times* with a quality that transcends the commercialism of the legitimate theater. He speaks of horizons and perspectives. Your arbitrary refusal to review our play is hardly consistent with this enlightened approach to the problems of the theater and we regret it sincerely.

> Very truly yours,
> Joseph Papp

By then, the Shakespeare Workshop had given almost one hundred performances of six plays, charging no admission, with a total cash expenditure of less than three thousand dollars. His actors were happy to be doing Shakespeare. And audiences, which veered between full houses during favorable weather and a handful of stalwarts when it was bad, had been broadened by an amalgam of mailing lists including that of the Police Athletic League and the local hospitals. In June, the *Village Voice,* then in its first summer of publication, would award the Workshop a special Obie citation for "the passion, the good humor, the clarity" with which it produced Shakespeare. But Joseph Papp was dissatisfied. For the past half year, he had been thinking of a new venue.

As the FBI had discovered, the producer liked to walk. He walked all over Manhattan, but especially in and around Greenwich Village and the Lower East Side. He remembered trips to the area with his father when he was small, the Workmen's Circle building, the stalls where his father had bargained for suits, the synagogues, the barrels of pickles. He was walking along Grand Street one winter day and, at its end, crossed a footbridge over the East River Drive. There, between the highway and the river, he discovered a 2,000-seat amphitheater directly facing the Brooklyn Navy Yard where he had put on his last navy show. He could hear the loudspeakers: *"Now hear this . . . Now hear this . . . Report on the quarterdeck immediately, Seaman First Class Perkins. . . ."* The site was noisy. There was traffic on the East River Drive, boats on the river, airplanes on their way to and from New York's two busiest airports. But there were also poplar trees on both sides of the amphitheater, which rustled in the breeze.

"I wasn't thinking of leaving the church — pardon the expression," he would later quip. But the heat made summer productions impossible and Papp had been disturbed by the fact that the neighborhood people on East Sixth Street did not come into Emmanuel Church. They had not, he thought, been taught the ritual of dressing up and going into an auditorium to sit among strangers. They might prefer to watch a play outside. He remembered the breeze and trees and lake of Prospect Park on those evenings that he went with his father to hear the Goldman Band. The amphitheater and river with its cacophony of sounds seemed to him like "a very soothing place."

The park attendant with whom he struck up a conversation told him that the amphitheater had been built under the La Guardia administration by the WPA and was now administered by the New York City Department of Parks. It was sometimes used for dances or concerts sponsored by the Lower East Side Neighborhood Association. He told Papp to go up to the Arsenal Building in Central Park for more information. There, the producer filed an application to present three plays with a sympathetic Parks Department clerk whose son wished to become an actor.

In March of 1956, the *Times* reported that the Shakespeare Workshop, operating under a charter from the State Education Department, would present *As You Like It, Much Ado About Nothing, The Taming of the Shrew* and *Twelfth Night* in the East River Amphitheater during the summer. Should the experiment prove successful, it added, the Parks Department intended to bring Shakespeare to parks in other boroughs. Joseph Papp, originator of the plan and managing director of the Workshop, was trying to raise $15,000 for actors' salaries.

Shortly after that report appeared, director Joel Friedman decided to leave the enterprise. Later, Sylvia Gassell would explain that they had been broke and discouraged, that they had neither Papp's optimism nor his talent for ignoring a "no." They wanted year-round employment. They wanted to be treated like theater professionals earning a professional wage and receiving regular reviews. The Workshop's State Board of Regents charter bothered them — the word "educational" made it seem as though they were amateur actors, and it seemed to be emphasized in each of the rare reviews. Papp seemed not to care. In Gassell's view, the fledgling producer "seemed to have an aura of another era about him — the time when great causes were rallied for with exhortation and collection baskets. Joel and I and some of the actors were all in favor of theater for the masses but we also felt we were entitled to the dignity of performers and the importance of our art. We were also a little snobby. Taking up a collection made us look like we were street actors. If you were a professional actor, you didn't pass the hat."

Gassell and Friedman left the Workshop amicably — both would later return to the Festival — but Papp, who was still working full-time at CBS, needed a director fast. Gassell recommended Stuart Vaughan.

Stuart Vaughan had actually been down to Emmanuel Church twice before. In 1954, he was one of the dozens of men who had auditioned for the role of Romeo. Vaughan was from a working-class background in Indiana and had recently studied repertory companies in England on a Fulbright Fellowship. Papp regarded him with some suspicion as "a quintessential WASP" and an "intellectual" and insisted on calling Vaughan by his rarely used given name, John.

"I remember a short, slender, fast-talking New Yorker," Vaughan recalled — much later, after the two men had parted, reconciled and parted angrily again. "I felt I was in the presence of a huckster. It was hard for me to understand why he wanted to do Shakespeare at all." The second time Vaughan had gone to Emmanuel Church, it had been to investigate the Workshop group being organized by Joel Friedman and Sylvia Gassell. He had decided against joining.

Now, just at the time Friedman had given Papp notice, Vaughan had directed an adaptation of Sean O'Casey's *I Knock at the Door* at the 92nd Street YMHA and received a warm review from Brooks Atkinson. The two men met, Papp showed Vaughan the amphitheater and they discussed collaborating. "What I thought we were doing then," Vaughan recalled, "was a fusion of the best American and British traditions. We were hitching external control to the splendid inner training of American actors. We wanted them to sound like real people — not Brooklynites or Californians or other regional Americans — but human beings, not merely the mouthers of verse. Playing in the amphitheater rather than indoors made sense to me. I was a sort of New Deal Democrat and I was in total sympathy with what I could sense of Joe's political and philosophical goals."

Papp had already chosen *Julius Caesar* as his first play in the amphitheater. Vaughan had directed it in Indiana, and felt it was a good choice. But he said Papp would have to forget Joel Friedman's black-and-white costumed, chamber Shakespeare and mount a spectacle that would fill the space. Papp replied he had no budget with which to raise production values, but Vaughan countered that he had no choice. "In the amphitheater unlike the church, you start in daylight," Vaughan argued. "There's no lighting to concentrate the audience's attention. We need costumes and enough extras to fill the stage."

Papp agreed, and he and Vaughan sealed their agreement with a handshake. Vaughan had just finished a Broadway show and was receiving unemployment insurance: he could afford to serve as artistic director without pay. Papp persuaded Henry May, a CBS colleague, to design the show, and assembled a company of actors that included some eighty people.

One was Roscoe Lee Browne, a tall, handsome former athlete and college instructor then working in public relations for a liquor concern. Browne had, at the age of thirty-five, decided to embark on a career in the theater. He had announced his decision at a dinner with three theatrical friends, actresses Josephine Premice and Susan Fonda and soprano Leontyne Price, and they had been appalled. How could a Negro in a secure, cushy job even contemplate becoming an actor? Was he so naive and self-absorbed as to think he would be welcomed into the theater? Josephine Premice brought out trade papers to demonstrate the idiocy of his plan. Meanwhile, Leontyne Price warned him that, at best, he would be cast as a torchbearer.

Perusing *Variety* and *Show Business,* Browne picked out a casting notice for Shakespeare and decided that he would audition the next day. After reading for Vaughan and Papp, he was asked how long he had been working as an actor. Browne replied, "Twelve hours, but I have no intention of bearing torches." Papp laughed and assured him that he would have words to speak. He subsequently cast Browne not only in *Julius Caesar* but in *The Taming of the Shrew, Titus Andronicus, The Winter's Tale, Romeo and Juliet, Othello, King Lear* and *Troilus and Cressida* — providing him with a full apprenticeship in theater. "It would not have taken much to discourage me," Browne would later say. "For Joseph Papp to say yes instantly, knowing that I was without craft and an ancient thirty-five years old — he changed my life."

Stuart Vaughan wanted a fully costumed cast. Papp had hired a young actor named Chester Dougherty, whose parents owned a costume company that rented such items as armor. They donated it to the enterprise, and Vaughan's wife, Gladys, supplied the rest. Rummaging through the stalls on nearby Orchard Street, Gladys Vaughan found a white, lightweight curtain backing for 25 cents a yard from which to make togas. She bought up several dozen yards, then sewed togas on her mother's sewing machine. Between these two sources, the company was fully costumed.

Julius Caesar also required far more staff than anything Papp had done in Emmanuel Church. But the theater grapevine was loaded with bulletins about the upcoming production and volunteers were pouring in. Elsa Raven, a young woman who was running an organization to encourage new playwrights, initially called to ask about an acting job and was enlisted as a one-woman production department, using her office at the City Center in the service of what was now being called the New York Summer Shakespeare Festival.

Raven recruited others, including an executive from Blue Cross to run the sound equipment. She herself typed up the program and then farmed it out among friends who worked at advertising agencies, billing the 2,000 pieces required per night to various accounts. She worked as carpenter, grip, house manager and usher, visited public libraries to talk up the Festival to librarians, put up posters all over the city and ran errands, picking up the props and equipment that Papp managed to coax various people and agencies into donating.

"If you want to build a theater and you start from scratch," Papp would later say, "you need a lot of things and a lot of people. It's not like being a writer, where it's you and a sheet of paper; or a painter, where it's you and the canvas. You need an instinct for finding the right people. And not only the right people — but the right people at the right *time*. I would not call it luck, because it happened consistently. There were many people who laid the groundwork of this theater. I had relationships with many of them for a very long period of time. But it's hard to sustain relationships in the theater because people have so many needs and they are so tied into their own egos. My role was to try to keep those people and to build an institution."

The Workshop's board of trustees was a motley group that included press agent Merle Debuskey, lawyer Alexander Racolin, playwright Joseph Carroll and Gregory Majzlin, a gynecologist who had recently invented an intrauterine device. Leo Brody, who had helped Papp refurbish Seymour Hall, was unhappy about the move to the amphitheater and demanded a greater role in making decisions. Papp refused, and Brody quit. His role had to be filled by other members of the board, none of whom had much money.

Again, Papp scrounged up much of the technical equipment and talent from CBS. In addition to set designer Henry May, his CBS colleague Ralph Holmes once again supplied network lighting equipment that was no longer state-of-the-art and supervised lighting. Tape, studio space and sound engineers were donated by a recording company to record music mostly taken from the soundtrack of the movie *Quo Vadis?*, and Tele-funken was persuaded to loan a thousand-dollar speaker.

There was no budget for advertising and publicity. The $15,000 fundraiser that Papp had announced in the *New York Times* in March had failed to raise even $1,000. The head of the Lower East Side Neighbor-hood Association proved uncooperative. Most of the neighborhood people, she said, didn't even speak English. Mayor Robert Wagner had launched a 1956 advertising campaign called "New York Is a Summer Festival," but the producer was unable to obtain any money from the New York City Convention and Visitors Bureau, nor from the celebrities and many foundations he tried. He had even approached policeman Redmond O'Hanlon, who had won $16,000 on the CBS television show *$64,000 Question* answering questions about Shakespeare. He suggested that O'Hanlon give fencing demonstrations in the amphitheater before performances, and join the Workshop's Sponsoring Committee. He even succeeded in getting the *Times* to run a story about O'Hanlon, but the policeman, like so many others, did not come up with any cash.

"Until then, when people asked me what I was, I never knew what to say," Papp later recalled. "By that time I *felt* I was a producer. A producer without any money maybe, but a real producer." He and Vaughan to-gether contributed $800 for *Julius Caesar*.

In June, Stuart Vaughan began rehearsals in the amphitheater. The cast assembled wearing straw hats and sunglasses, carrying bottles of suntan lotion and water. Rehearsals were scheduled to run all day long, there was no telephone within two blocks and the actors were nervous. Then, they noticed, up above them, a gang of teenagers, aiming stones.

"Hey Caesar, hey Caesar!" And the stones came down.

"If the teenagers had expected a group of cowering artists, they were mistaken," Vaughan later wrote. "And with no more nonsense, they fled. Attendance by neighborhood children at rehearsals did not stop, but as they watched us go about our work the jeers turned to friendly greetings. They stopped calling down interruptions, and as we rehearsed they hung about the gates and watched with interest. Soon they began to run errands and to help with some of the heavy work."

Morale in the amphitheater was extraordinarily high. Free Shakespeare seemed to be a rare theater phenomenon, free of ego or malice. Actors and volunteers alike performed work they had never done before. Joseph Papp, still working at CBS, was seldom there but when he was and the cast or production crew was feeling defeated, Joseph Papp would appear and spin out a series of puns and jokes, forcing them to laugh instead of complain. People who worked there that summer would later remember the improbable emergencies and their even more improbable solutions. Anything that was not nailed down would be stolen during the night, including heavy concrete blocks. Dr. Majzlin's medical skills were called upon more than once as electrical equipment meant for indoor use backfired outside and caused injuries. Their most vivid memories were of the audience, the unusual mix of Puerto Ricans, Italians, African Americans, Chinese and Jews who came to see the finished production.

They included, Stuart Vaughan would write, "grade school kids, couples, oldsters, whole families, people carrying portable radios so they could turn on the ball game if the performance flagged. Most of them had never seen a live performance. Few of them knew who Shakespeare was. Someone heard a wife ask her husband 'Who was this Julius Caesar?' He answered, 'Oh, some guy who lived at the time they built the Second Temple.'"

The Festival was scheduled to open on June 20. On June 13, the press reported a delay in the opening of *Julius Caesar* for lack of funds. That week, Joseph Papp telephoned everyone he knew, begging for money so that he could rent those costumes and props he had been unable to get for free. He collected money in dribs and drabs, quitting only when he had gathered enough to pay his bills for at least one week.

At 7:30 on June 29, an hour before curtain time, the trickle of pedestrians across the footbridge toward the amphitheater became a flood.

"Every seat in the place was taken," the *Village Voice* reported. "Over 2000 people had turned out from the new projects and the old tenements . . . and the concrete semi-circle was seething and crackling with expectancy. Then the lights went up, though it was not fully dark, and tearing down the aisles from the rim of the bowl came a gleefully howling score of wreath-toting Roman citizens into the playing area where they capered and yowled some more. . . ."

Then, as Marullus the Tribune began to berate the mob — with the speech Joe Papirofsky had memorized in junior high school — the audience became absolutely still:

> *Wherefore rejoice? What conquest brings he home?*
> *What tributaries follow him to Rome*
> *To grace in captive bonds his chariot wheels?*
> *You blocks, you stones, you worse than senseless things!*

"Frankly, I was scared to death," Joe told the *New Yorker*. "I didn't have the faintest notion what to expect. Obviously most of the people out there had never seen live actors before." When the speech was met by a great cheer, Papp understood that "Here was an audience that really identified. I've never felt so relieved in my life."

"The venture is loaded with lure qualities in a social, cultural, economic and offbeat vein," reported *Variety*.

> The no-charge aspect is a natural come-on while the unusual locale is also a draw. . . . Most important, though, is the caliber of the performance. It's strictly professional. The "Caesar" acting contingent does a fine job. . . . Although the cast is primarily comprised of Equity members, the union does not require salaries since the show is a cuffo deal. It's assumed the actors are participating for a variety of reasons that take in the showcasing aspect, a desire to remain in the city, and possibly the hope that the project may catch on and be repeated in future seasons. . . .
>
> In general, it stacks up as not only a novelty, but as a commendable project, and it should be maintained, either by the city or by the support of private groups.

Theater people were moved to compare the shoestring production with productions at the Stratford, Connecticut, festival, then presenting *King John* and *Measure for Measure*. The *Voice*, mocking Stratford's country club atmosphere, came out strongly for the local festival. "In many ways, it has all the excitement of youth, of high purpose, of fidelity to the original," wrote Jerry Tallmer. "And for communication with its audience, I challenge anyone to suggest its rival. Roughhewn as things may be at the foot of Grand Street, there is something in the wind there that smells and tastes of human excitement."

By the time those two notices appeared, rehearsals for *The Taming of the Shrew* had begun.

Papp had originally selected the play so that his wife could play the starring role. But he ran into unexpected opposition from Stuart Vaughan. "Peggy Bennion was playing Portia in *Caesar*," Vaughan recalled, "but she seemed to lack the fire, earthiness and energy Katherine requires." Actor Jack Cannon suggested he cast actress Colleen Dewhurst instead.

"It was a hard thing to bring up but we did," Vaughan recalled.

Papp, ever one to improvise an argument on the spot, said, "Do you realize that the reason I started this theater was to give my wife a place to act?"

Vaughan said, "'No, but we have a chance at something important here, and this is the moment when you have to decide whether this is going to be a professional theater with a mission, or your own branch of vanity productions.' It was as if I'd slapped him. He said he needed to sleep on it. The next day, he told me to go ahead. It was a strong and right decision and a turning point of some kind, I believe."

The decision to cast Colleen Dewhurst instead of Peggy Bennion had several important consequences. It marked the beginning of Dewhurst's career. It put the New York Shakespeare Festival in the spotlight. And it changed the Papp marriage. Peggy Bennion, who had been promised the role of Kate, left the city to vacation in Utah, leaving Joe Papp alone in New York to deal with the problems occasioned by his first real success.

The Festival now had a large audience. Parks Department and other city officials who had not bothered to show up for *Caesar* were asking for reserved seating for *Shrew*. Papp's financial problems were worse than before, due to the costs of renting costumes, props, and equipment, and taking out advertisements for his second production. Suppliers began to withhold needed goods — such as posters — until debts were paid. On July 11, a news brief in the *Times* reported that unless $850 were found, Mr. Papp would be forced to delay *Shrew*. ANTA — the Greater New York Chapter of the American National Theatre and Academy — came up with a $500 grant, the Workshop's first.

The producer's anxieties were compounded by his sense that he was being followed. He did not know if the FBI had reported the fact that he was under surveillance to his employers, but Papp knew that CBS, like the other two television networks, would not hesitate to fire an employee if he proved to be an embarrassment.

In public, Papp kept up his persona of a wisecracking, irrepressible Robin Hood, who punned away problems and kept people so busy that they had no time to worry about the larger picture. But, in private, Joseph Papp suffered increasingly serious anxiety attacks, whose symptoms resembled those of a heart attack. "He lived on the edge of crisis," Peggy Papp would recall. "He would take an enormous chance that was far beyond his capacity and somehow or other he'd gear himself up to that leap. The energy required to do that came of a profound feeling of worthlessness and depression. He could have moods in which he would almost pass out from depression and lose all sense of himself. His nightmares were horrible and grotesque. I think success was a life-or-death issue for him. He literally would have died had he not succeeded."

The Taming of the Shrew opened August 3, 1956. By seven that evening, a line had formed at the gates although the amphitheater did not even begin seating people until an hour later. Those waiting included a large contingent of "uptown" people, who had arrived at the foot of Grand Street in taxicabs and chauffeured limousines. Colleen Dewhurst, Roscoe

Lee Browne and Jack Cannon gave performances that were to mark the beginning of their careers, but that first weekend there were no critics in attendance.

On Monday morning, Papp strode into the Drama Department of the *New York Times,* demanding to see Brooks Atkinson. The men in the "culture gulch" as well as Atkinson's secretary, Clara Rotter, told him that Mr. Atkinson was in London, but Papp did not believe them. He said he would wait until the critic returned, and sat down.

Papp knew that Atkinson was the dean of theater critics, all the more for announcing, during World War II, that theater reviewing was "kid stuff" and going on to win a Pulitzer for reporting from the Soviet Union. Atkinson was regarded by some as "the conscience of the *Times,*" a man whom even the publisher consulted on ethical matters. Papp remembered, word for word, the devastating review Atkinson had written of the O'Casey plays he had directed four years earlier. He wanted Atkinson to endorse *Shrew.*

By that time, everyone in the Drama Department knew Joseph Papp as one of the more persistent pests who came up to the third floor. They were used to press agents, aspiring actors, worried producers, even celebrities like actress Helen Hayes or director Moss Hart who dropped in to see Atkinson. But this guy was something else. Now, seeing that Papp had settled comfortably into a seat, second-string critic Arthur Gelb struck up a conversation with him, repeating that Atkinson was on vacation and would not be back for another few days.

"Joe said he had run out of money and that if someone didn't review the production, he'd have to pack up at the end of the week," Gelb recalled. "'If Mr. Atkinson isn't here, why don't you come down?' he said to me." Gelb agreed to go to the amphitheater that night.

The Taming of the Shrew was interrupted at intermission by a sudden thunderstorm. As the audience scrambled for shelter, Gelb went up onto the stage and, in the pouring rain, listened to Papp argue that the critic should write a review of the first act. Or didn't Gelb think this was a project worth saving?

"It started to rain at 9:45 o'clock last night," Gelb began what he figured was his newspaper's first review of half a show.

For most heat-weary New Yorkers, it was a blessing. But for the 1,800 spectators and 45 actors at the East River Amphitheatre on the Lower East Side the downpour had the effect of a slap in the face.

The Taming of the Shrew was being lustily performed there against a background of tooting tugboats and flashes of heat lightning. Petruchio had just finished giving Kate a sound trouncing. The audience was leaning raptly forward on tiers of long wooden benches. If ever an audience was with a play, this one was.

When Joseph Papp . . . announced over a loudspeaker that the show could not continue because of the rain, exclamations of dismay resounded in a blending of dialects that could be heard only on the Lower East Side. Many of the disappointed shouts came from young children.

This was an audience that had paid no admission. They knew the chance of getting a raincheck was slim since there is a danger that this Summer Shakespeare Festival may soon be forced to shut down because of a scarcity of operating funds. The merits of the performance must be judged on one act alone. But even from this abortive look, the production could be rated as a resourceful one. . . . It seems a shame that a project evidently bringing so much joy to so many people should be permitted to die a-borning.

Herman Levin, producer of *My Fair Lady,* then Broadway's biggest hit, came forward with a check for $750. Thousands of *Times* readers flocked to the amphitheater. But the most important consequence involved the newspaper's chief critic. When Brooks Atkinson returned from his vacation, Gelb suggested that he visit the amphitheater.

On August 23, Joseph Papp, driving the clunky old Festival truck, fetched Brooks Atkinson from the Harvard Club and drove him downtown. The amphitheater was located between the uptown side of the East River Drive and the East River, and Papp was accustomed to saving time by jumping the divider when there was a break in the traffic. "*Hold on,* Mr. Atkinson," he said. He jumped the divider, negotiated the truck to the amphitheater parking area and escorted the critic to his seat.

The following Sunday, Atkinson devoted his first column of the new season to praising *Shrew* and enlisting support for the New York Shakespeare Festival. Nearly everything that was picturesque about outdoor Shakespeare, Atkinson wrote, weighed against Papp's theater. He cited the rumble of traffic, the drone of planes, the cough of diesel engines on the river, the problems of voice amplification. But the audience of which he was a part sat, for two and a half hours, fully absorbed by the performance. "The company that has been recruited under the management of Joseph Papp is as sound as the audience," he wrote. Stuart Vaughan had directed "with taste and exuberance." Colleen Dewhurst was "excellent"; Jack Cannon "plays with a sardonic swagger."

Atkinson concluded his column with an appeal for funds.

Two months of Shakespeare in a park have cost $2,000, chiefly for costumes, scenery and amplifying equipment. Nobody has contributed so much as the actors, the dancers, the backstage crew and the staff. They have given skill, time and energy. But other people have given enough money to make this quixotic enterprise possible. It began with contributions of $100 each from two well-wishers, $500 from the local chapter of ANTA and some other friendly donations. About three weeks ago, the company found itself hopelessly in debt for $750 for expenses. . . . It looked as if the bailiffs would make off with everything and put a dismal end to a unique midsummer night's entertainment.

When Arthur Gelb included that bit of gloomy news in his comments on the production in these columns, the catastrophe was miraculously avoided. Herman Levin, producer of *My Fair Lady*, sent his check for the full amount the next day. He made it possible for some actors to continue working free. Next year, Mr. Papp would like to raise $25,000 to put on his productions in several of the city parks and pay the actors $40 a week, which is Actors Equity's minimum rate for off-Broadway actors. That seems like the least New York could do for a good deed in a heedless city.

By the end of the summer, the two plays had been performed before more than 25,000 people. On closing night, Joseph Papp made a short speech, explaining that the large company of actors that the audience had been watching represented only the "tip of the iceberg," that behind them stood a virtual army of technicians and administrative staff. Then, he introduced the tiny crew that had provided the support.

After the audience had dispersed and the cast party was over, Joseph Papp and those few people were at the amphitheater, cleaning up. It was early morning by the time he and Elsa Raven — his young Jill-of-all-trades — finished loading up props and equipment that Raven had borrowed from the New Dramatists Guild into his station wagon and, for the first time, Joseph Papp told her that for the past three years, the FBI had been trailing him and that he might soon be subpoenaed to appear before the House Un-American Activities Committee. If he was asked to name names, Papp told her, he would refuse and he was not sure what effect that might have on the Festival. Would she consider taking over from him as producer?

Elsa Raven was taken aback. She had a full-time job and was commuting to Baltimore on alternate weekends to see her boyfriend. She could not imagine taking on the Festival and said so. Joseph Papp did not mention it again.

In September, Stuart Vaughan and the company of actors dispersed in search of paying jobs and Papp settled in for another season as stage manager at CBS. He sent a new round of letters to foundations on New York Shakespeare Festival letterhead, enclosing the effusive Brooks Atkinson column. He began rehearsing *Titus Andronicus* at Emmanuel Church, with his wife *and* Colleen Dewhurst. But Seymour Hall already felt like history to him. "There will always be a need for a place like East 6th Street in New York," he would say later, "because there's a constant need for young people who need to act, need to direct, need to write music. That's why they come to New York. But those people all leave unless you provide a place for them to grow artistically. The question I had to think about was: How do you build an institution?"

SIX

Taking the Fifth

EVEN BEFORE Joseph Papp had completed his first summer season of Free Shakespeare, he told Stuart Vaughan that he wished to move the enterprise out of the East River Amphitheater. "He had two impulses," Vaughan later said. "One was that he wanted to be mobile and bring Shakespeare into all five boroughs instead of forcing the audience to come to him. Two, he wanted an uptown Manhattan audience and a site in Central Park that would be easily accessible and afford high visibility. Both ideas made sense to me. I began to design a truck stage."

The 35-foot trailer truck had sides that folded out and, Vaughan wrote, was "reminiscent of some of the Renaissance theatres, particularly the 1539 Theatre at Ghent and the 1561 Theatre at Antwerp." Joseph Papp remembered contacting an old classmate who ran a body shop. "This guy said, 'I have some old bodies back there. I'll do it for three or four thousand.' So I went to Brooklyn a couple of times. I began to look at trucks. I went crazy about trucks for a while. Mine looked like it came out of Eastern Europe, with all the plywood and rubber and hinges that couldn't really support the weight of the sides. We'd look awfully strange going through the city streets and when we got to the parks, the whole thing would start to sink, but for the money, you couldn't go wrong."

He arranged his CBS schedule so as to benefit Free Shakespeare, spending hours typing up on his Remington a barrage of letters to individuals, foundations and various municipal agencies, trying to find help from within the city bureaucracy. That fall of 1956, Papp managed to get through to the man who became his first political ally, Deputy Mayor Stanley Lowell.

Stanley Lowell was in his mid-thirties — about the same age as Papp and Vaughan — a liberal who had gravitated to Manhattan's Young Democratic Club in the postwar period and a graduate of Harvard Law School. Lowell had worked for Robert Wagner, Jr., when he ran for borough president in 1949; he had worked for his mayoral campaign in 1953 and was now Wagner's sole deputy mayor.

As the mayor's deputy, it was Lowell's job to field complaints to City Hall and to address problems that ranged from civil rights conflicts to the problems of film crews making movies in the city. In the course of working with community groups, Lowell had become accustomed to a wide range of demanding people. But none, he later said, had conveyed the intensity and urgency of Joseph Papp.

"He called me up and said he had an idea he wanted to talk to me about," Lowell recalled. "When I asked him what it was, he said, 'I don't want to tell you on the phone. I need to see you face to face.' That's typical Joe Papp. But the mayor had an open door policy. I said, 'Okay, When do you want to come?' And we made a time."

Lowell was not particularly interested in the theater. He had not been to the East River Amphitheater. He did not remember reading about it. When Papp said he wanted to do free Shakespeare in the city's parks, Lowell's first question was: "What d'ya mean *free?*

"He said, 'I don't want any money from the city. I just want some help in kind.' And he pulled out a list. There were about seven departments he wanted to borrow stuff from. He said he had called up all of them and had been turned down.

"I said, 'How many people do you expect to come to this?'

"He said, 'Several hundred a night.'

"'For a week? Ten days?'

"'No, *all summer.*'

"I told him I thought it was a great idea, that he should give me two or three days and call me back. He thought I was sloughing him off. His face got flushed. I could see the ire. And I said, 'You know, I'm only the *executive assistant* to the mayor. The mayor can lend the city's property like this — not I.' So he calmed down and he said he'd call. And the next time the mayor was rushing out someplace, I stuck my foot in front of him and said, 'Bob, what would you think if somebody wanted to put on free Shakespeare plays all summer?'

"He looked at me and said, 'What d'ya mean, *free?*'

"I told him there'd be no charge to the people and that the city wouldn't have to put up any money and the mayor said, 'Sounds good to me.'

"When Joe called back, I said, 'Give me that laundry list of yours — you're in business. But don't call the commissioners for at least three days because it's going to take me a while to get hold of them all.' "

Stanley Lowell called up the commissioners of the Department of Gas and Electricity, the Department of Parks, the Department of Sanitation, the Department of Public Events, the Department of Welfare, the Office of Civil Defense and the head of the municipal radio station, WNYC. He told them, "You're going to get a call from a man named Joseph Papp. The mayor knows all about it and would like you to help him out." Within a few weeks, Joe had a promise of electric current, chairs and permits, a generator from the Office of Civil Defense, a sound system from WNYC, and a truck from Sanitation that would pull his new Mobile Theater from site to site during the summer. Papp would later estimate that the city contributed the equivalent of $15,000 to $20,000 in man-power and equipment toward his Mobile Theater.

With municipal cooperation secured, Papp determined that his crea-tive people would no longer work without pay. He managed to raise $30,000 for the 1957 summer season to pay his actors the off-Broadway minimum wage. Although he himself continued working for free, he paid his artistic director, Stuart Vaughan, as well. "About money, he was always fair to a fault — it was one of his most admirable qualities," Vaughan later said. "In fact, people had to gang up on him to get him to start taking a salary."

Papp and Vaughan had managed to hold together a loose-knit group of about forty actors. Like Joel Friedman before him, Vaughan directed a biweekly Shakespeare workshop for his company of actors. Meanwhile, Papp mapped out a 1957 summer schedule in which *Romeo and Juliet, Two Gentlemen of Verona* and *Macbeth* would tour the five boroughs, going from Central Park in Manhattan to the Brooklyn War Memorial Park to the Williamsbridge Oval Park in the Bronx, to the Clove Lakes Park on Staten Island and to the King Park in Queens.

Some actors were immediately taken with the public spirit of the project; others were dubious. When Vaughan asked Jerry Stiller, who had been working at the American Shakespeare Company at Stratford, Connecticut, to join the cast, Stiller recalled, "I didn't know what to say. One season I'm up in Connecticut and now I'm getting hired to go on a truck throughout the city and play the parks? And against my own conceit, my own sense of ego, I said, *'Well, why not?'* They gave me things to do that I never dreamed I could do and that I could never have done up in Stratford. In my head, I kept saying: *'What am I doing in Staten Island? What am I doing under the Brooklyn Bridge? This is where I used to live!'* I used to fall asleep when I saw Shakespeare because of the way they used to read the lines. But these people were so unjaded about what they were seeing. In the love scenes, the Hispanic kids would holler: *'Give it to her, Romeo! Give it to her, man!'* We had to connect to those audiences and it forced us to understand what we were saying."

Papp's small staff was zealous about the Mobile Theater. Most ardent was press agent and board member Merle Debuskey, considered the "purist" of the group. "Leaf by leaf," he wrote, the Festival was "peeling away" those impediments that had, in the past, "deterred many people from going to the theater: cost, unfamiliarity, indifference, distrust and even antagonism. The presentations are free of any admission charge, the physical environment is convenient, convivial and conducive. It is there for anyone, merely for the asking."

By the time summer arrived, the Festival's Mobile Theater — New York City's first since the Federal Theater's tours in the 1930s — had become major local news. In addition to the newspaper and magazine reporters, CBS and NBC radio and television followed it through the boroughs. *New Yorker* writer J. M. Flagler telephoned Joseph Papp — whose home telephone was then published in advertisements and served as the source of ticket information — asking to accompany him by subway to Queens, which he had formerly associated more with used-car lots than with theater.

"Any attempt to reclaim even a few corners of our parks from the muggers and the teen-age wolf packs is all right with me," he wrote in the *New Yorker,* "and to enlist the drama in aiding our more peaceful citizens to enjoy evenings in their rightful greenery struck me as highly felicitous, for the attractions that still keep me a fascinated, hidebound resident of New York, at a time when everyone else seems to be moving to Westport, settling in Mallorca, or taking up sports cars, are its theatres, its parks, and its people in their infinite variety. The prospect of finding all these combined in one package was pleasing indeed."

Like all the writers who covered the Festival that summer, Flagler was as fascinated by the audience as the actors.

In front of me sat three spectators whose conversation left no doubt
that each of them represented a generation of an Italian family —
grandfather, daughter, and small grandson. In back of me were two
high-spirited old ladies chattering half in Yiddish, half in English. . . .
On my right, a slim colored boy wearing a flashy sports coat and a
narrow tie was displaying a keen interest in a teen-age girl with skin
the color of brown sugar who, sitting directly in front of him, beside
a girl friend, was trying to ignore a sporadic line of sweet talk that he
was softly directing toward her. Beyond the preoccupied youth, an old
Chinese fastidiously spread a newspaper over a seat and lowered himself
into it. . . .

When *Romeo and Juliet* opened in Central Park, even the *Herald
Tribune*'s crotchety Walter Kerr wrote that although few of the best
things in life were, in fact, free, the Festival's *Romeo and Juliet* was the
best he had ever seen.

While the popular and critical response to the Mobile Theater encouraged Papp, the problems — up to eighteen hours of set-up time, the
actors' reluctance to travel to remote parts of the city, bad weather,
unpredictable attendance — proved burdensome. On July 5, Papp wrote
the Department of Parks:

> As per our telephone conversation of Wednesday, I have notified our
> cast and technical crew that we will conclude the touring phase of our
> program on July 15, the final performance of *Romeo and Juliet* at the
> East River Park Amphitheater. I have further informed them that we
> plan to present the balance of our performances at the Belvedere site
> in Central Park. . . . To win audiences for two night stands requires a
> bang up publicity campaign. This requires funds and a staff of which
> we have neither. . . . Remaining in Central Park will add some fifteen
> performance nights to our schedule or some 30,000 more patrons. . . .
> All in all, our settling down at the Belvedere will benefit our audiences,
> the Park Department and ourselves.

That letter was all the notice Joseph Papp gave the municipality of his
plan to establish a base in Central Park. "One night, at about two in the
morning," Papp would recall, "I drove the mobile theater, hooked up to
a truck we had borrowed from the Sanitation Department, into the park.
There was a cop on horseback who looked at me kind of strangely but
he must have assumed nobody would come in with a huge thirty-five-foot
platform trailer hitched to a garbage truck without a permit. I waved to
him and we went on."

On July 18, the Department of Parks announced a revised schedule for the Mobile. "Beginning July 22 and through September 4," it read, "all performances will be held at the Belvedere Tower area." There, with no permit to remain on the site that would five years later accommodate the Delacorte Theater, the young company presented two more plays — *Two Gentlemen of Verona* and *Macbeth* — to excellent reviews.

Papp and Vaughan both wished to extend the run of *Macbeth*, with Colleen Dewhurst, into the fall season, and the producer had found an unused theater that the Department of Welfare had agreed to lend him, rent-free. It was the Heckscher Children's Center, located at Fifth Avenue and 104th Street, part of a complex of classrooms and dormitories used to house wards of the court. The 650-seat Heckscher Theater had a proscenium arch, orchestra pit and large, bright murals of Jack and the Beanstalk, Little Red Riding Hood and Cinderella by the artist Willy Pogany. It had been used for children's performances by the Federal Theater in the 1930s and seemed, Vaughan recalled, "like a gift from heaven."

In November, Stuart Vaughan directed an actor named George C. Scott in *Richard III* before audiences of restless high school students bused in by the Board of Education in the afternoons and audiences of adults in the evenings. The actor who would later become famous for his portrayal of General Patton routinely mesmerized his rowdy teenage audiences and garnered enthusiastic reviews. And Papp, who continued to put aside his own directorial ambitions, established a small office in the theater where he continued to type out hundreds of letters, asking foundations and potential donors for money, and lobbying the mayor, several municipal departments and the powerful parks commissioner, Robert Moses, for various kinds of support.

It was the Parks Department that had approved Papp's use of the East River Amphitheater and issued him permits to perform in the various city parks. Moses had written admiringly about the Festival in an article for the *Herald Tribune* and had even asked his personal friend Howard Cullman to raise money for the Festival. But Cullman's efforts to raise private money were a failure and the producer determined to obtain more funding from the city.

In January of 1958, he lobbied the New York City Board of Estimate to appropriate $40,000 for the Festival — which it refused to do. "It's a worthy cause," Mayor Wagner told the *New York Post*, "but we have to recognize that it is simply not an operation of government. We've been telling all departments they are not to fill vacancies. We are faced with finding $6,000,000."

Later that month, when Papp and Vaughan previewed *As You Like It,* $1,400 arrived in the mail, mostly in small amounts, including a check from one municipal employee who wrote that he sent it because he knew how hard it was to get any money out of the city. During February, the production was sustained by proceeds from a collection basket through the audience. But when it closed at the end of the month, Papp canceled plans to produce *Antony and Cleopatra.*

The demands on his time were becoming overwhelming. On March 2, Peggy Bennion gave birth to a daughter — Miranda — and Joseph Papp became a father for the fourth time. He continued working at CBS, continued fundraising and, with Stuart Vaughan, planning for the 1958 summer Shakespeare productions, *Othello* and *Twelfth Night.* "I couldn't do that again," Joseph Papp said later. "But then, I had the energy and the commitment. I enjoyed doing those big shows at CBS. I met a lot of actors on the shows to feed into the theater and I had no other income — CBS gave me money: $150 per week."

Merle Debuskey kept the press supplied with continual reminders of the Festival's precarious financial situation. A one-million-dollar fund drive was announced and sank into oblivion. "Mr. Papp stands at the point of no return," Henry Hewes, one of the Festival's first supporters, wrote the *Saturday Review.*

> It is obvious that he cannot go on indefinitely scrounging funds, producing, and putting in a full week's work at CBS. . . . That the New York Shakespeare Festival will continue this summer seems most likely. But the raising of $1,000,000 to insure a year-round operation and a permanent park theatre will be tougher. It can be done only if the foundations contribute a fair share of the load (as they have for the Shakespeare Festivals in Canada and Connecticut) and if the New York businessmen fully comprehend the importance of having such a Public Theatre in their city.

The Festival's financial problems were so pressing that, that spring, Papp accepted an invitation from the city of Philadelphia to present *Othello* there before opening in Central Park on July 5, garnering the headline "EVICTED BARD FINDS HOME." Parks commissioner Robert Moses as well as drama critic Walter Kerr pressed Papp to charge admission, with Kerr offering the producer his Sunday column in the *New York Herald Tribune* to defend his philosophy of Free Shakespeare.

On March 16, in what was the most comprehensive public formulation of his thinking so far, Joseph Papp wrote: "Thank you very much [Mr. Kerr] for your very thoughtful article in which you offer some

formidable arguments for a change in our policy of free admissions. . . .
If, by charging admission, I was convinced we would have a 'minimum
stability' I would do it. I would have done it long ago. It would certainly
be a less painful method of operation for me, personally. . . ."

If the festival were to charge admission, Papp explained, the entertainment unions would revise their concessions and he would be forced to
charge between $3.60 and $5.50 for tickets, thus defeating the primary
purpose of the Festival's existence: creating large, new audiences for the
classics. He continued:

Up to this point we have been very lucky. We have had a string of
consecutive critical successes. On a paying basis it would take just one
or two "failures" to wipe us out — one or two rainy nights in the park
to wash us out. Off-Broadway and Broadway economics do not give
us the right to fail from time to time and still stay alive. If we are to
strive for stability we must develop a structure that gives us this right.
It would be an act of irresponsibility on my part to subject the organization to the chaotic gambling of show business.

What may seem an idealistic approach to the theater is in reality the
most practical for what we are trying to build. Broadway and off-
Broadway live in a world of romance; the quick buck, the overnight
success, the one big break, here today and gone tomorrow — hardly a
solid base for operations.

I am trying to build our theater on the bedrock of municipal and
civic responsibility — not on the quicksands of show business economics. I am interested in a popular theater — not a theater for the few. I
am interested in establishing a classical repertory company with a
guaranteed annual wage for performers. This is impossible under the
present conditions on or off Broadway. . . .

The only practical means of insuring the permanence of our theater
is to tie it in with civic responsibility. The public library, an institution
for enlightenment and entertainment, is a case in point. No charge is
made for books. If people had to pay, most of the books would gather
dust on the shelves. I know that if I had had to pay for books at the
Williamsburg (Brooklyn) Public Library, it is doubtful that I would
have read the plays of Shakespeare.

The important thing about the library is that it is free and available
to people if they want to use it. I do not know how much they
appreciate it, but nobody suggests charging for books as a method of
obtaining appreciation nor as a way of getting stability. The library is
an institution for the people and it stands. This is how I want our

theater to stand, supported by two pillars — the city and private donors. This is the only economic base that can insure permanence for
our kind of theater. . . .

We are now engaged in a campaign to raise one million dollars. . . .
Though we do not have enough funds to keep our curtain up right
now, we have enough potential to keep it up for ten years. I am far
from ready to throw in my towel over the city's reluctance to come to
our aid. Conditions change and so do attitudes. I have every reason to
believe that support from the city will come, and if I were a gambling
man I would lay odds that it will. . . .

Papp would have been able to capitalize on his much-talked-about
exchange with Kerr had his politics not, one month later, become the
focus of his energy. "They've landed," Papp told Merle Debuskey, after
he was finally served with a subpoena to appear before the House Committee on Un-American Activities. The press agent noted a certain jaunti-
ness in Papp's tone. "He was not defeated or deflated. If you worked in
film or broadcasting, the day you got subpoenaed you were dead."

In fact, he was terrified. His life was very different from what it had
been ten years earlier, when the Tenney Committee had investigated the
Actors' Lab. "I was a student then," Joseph Papp would recall. "My
picture could appear on the front page of the *Los Angeles Examiner* and
nobody knew or cared. I was twenty-seven years old, tough, just out of
the military. Also, I had the kind of resilience you have when you're in
your twenties, no money, no investment in my job. I didn't mind going
to jail. Now I was thirty-seven. I had a wife and an infant daughter and
this young theater. I thought no large organization would ever give us
money again and I would probably lose the job that was supporting the
Festival."

Joseph Papp did not inform CBS that he had been subpoenaed. He
told his wife, Peggy Bennion, who was at home with their six-week-old
daughter, and scared. "I wondered what we would live on and I wondered at Joe's courage. He said he wasn't scared for himself but for the
whole country. I know it sounds corny now but that's what he said."

Next, Papp informed his artistic director, Stuart Vaughan, who was far
less admiring. During the two years of their association, Papp and Vaughan
had made their differences work for them, but their relationship was not
easy. "I'm a college-educated person, a WASP and, as Joe was fond of
jibing, a quintessential WASP," Vaughan later said. "I'm a classicist in my
art and Joe was always wanting to reinvent the wheel. And, right away,
Joseph Papp Presents was up there. I thought it was an unseemly, commer-

cial tag for a not-for-profit operation, indicating Napoleonic tendencies and a wish for personal aggrandizement. He was *not* the Shakespeare Festival. There were many people who were responsible for its early success."

Also, Vaughan was not a political activist but an artist who viewed the committee's subpoena of his producer as an unwelcome distraction from the project at hand. Later, he would recall Papp telling him, "'I was a member of the party until Peggy and I got married and she convinced me it was stupid to be any longer.' And I said, 'Well I'm glad to hear the truth from you and it certainly doesn't affect our relationship, and thank you for telling me.' What I didn't say was 'Anybody who still held a Communist party card after the Hitler-Stalin pact seems to me to have been either a fool or something much worse.'"

Papp later said that he had asked Stuart Vaughan to take over the Festival if it became necessary but Vaughan had no recollection of the conversation. He had joined the Festival on the understanding that he and Papp would form a permanent company. That did not seem to be forthcoming. He needed Papp to solve and finance production problems; instead, Papp was preoccupied with legal and political matters. When, that spring, Vaughan received a call from the managers of the Phoenix Theater, he was quick to respond. He told Papp that he planned to take the job at the Phoenix and that he would not be able to direct that summer's second production, *Twelfth Night,* as planned.

At the time, Joseph Papp said that he understood. Only years later did he accuse Vaughan of defection, saying, "*You* left us, we didn't leave *you.*" Vaughan responded that he had never thought that working at the Phoenix and at the Festival would be mutually exclusive. "He expects a loyalty that no thinking person can give easily," the director later said. "It's a Mafia loyalty, a loyalty of the street. Well, an artist can't do that. An artist is loyal to the art. He'll work together with the most arrogant bastard so long as he's working with the art. That separated me from Joe."

In the spring of 1958, Joseph Papp was too busy dealing with HUAC to give much thought to Vaughan. Merle Debuskey knew others who had been subpoenaed — including Papp's old Lab friend Bernard Gersten — and got him a good lawyer, who explained to him the intricacies of testifying before the committee, particularly the consequences of acknowledging Communist party membership and naming other party members.

In 1990, the producer would say that, while some people found the committee's demand that they name names a complicated problem, he himself did not. "I knew I would not cooperate," he recalled. "For better or worse, I tend to see most things in black and white; only occasionally are there areas of gray. I did not believe that the Communists I knew posed a threat to the security of the United States. They were people interested in social justice. As far as my own activities were concerned, I had no secrets to give to the enemy. I'd never burned an American flag. The most radical thing I'd ever done was Free Shakespeare.

"The word 'Communist,' which sounds so reprehensible to so many people today — because it's been used so often as the death word, the maligning word — was, to me, a beautiful word. It represented fearlessness, changing abysmal living conditions, creating a world which was free of social injustice. I don't wish in any way to soften the feelings I had during the depression, during the war, and even later. I'll always feel indebted to Russia for what they did during the Second World War. For a year and a half they were fighting alone. The Germans came within ten miles of Moscow. Even in 1956, when Khrushchev denounced Stalinism and during the Hungarian Revolution, I understood rationally what they were saying but emotionally I was skeptical. What was Hungary before the war? What was Romania before the war? I saw Cuba under Battista and I saw Cuba under Castro. There was a reason for *all* those revolutions.

"I'm terribly critical of things that have happened in the Communist countries but I never had the kind of bitter disappointment with the Communist party that some people — perhaps those better educated than myself — had. When people quit something that has been a major sustaining belief, often they turn against it. I couldn't turn against it. I still have a fundamental belief in a world that has no violence in it, a world which gives everyone an equal chance. That belief — maybe it's a variation of the belief in the Messiah — is still with me. And also a desire to be part of something larger than the block. And so I've never been sure who the heroes were in the wars between the American Stalinists and anti-Stalinists."

Papp had thought a great deal about informers. He had been impressed by Roberto Rossellini's film *Open City*, in which a Communist is captured in Italy and tortured by the Nazis, and had wondered what he himself would do. "How would I respond under torture? Would I name people? I liked to think not. It was a matter of pride with me not to be a stool pigeon. That was the lowest form of life. I had read about informers throughout history. I had *seen* informers trying to break up unions. Then I had watched good people, people I had known and admired at the Lab, inform."

Of the people he had known there, director Elia Kazan, actors Lloyd Bridges, Lee J. Cobb and Larry Parks, chose to name names. Howard Da Silva — with whom Joe Papirofsky had performed an evening of limericks at the California Labor School — Joe Bromberg and Abe Polansky had refused. The emnity between who had informed and those who had not was strong even in the 1990s.

"Parks at first said, *'Don't present me with the choice of either being in contempt of this committee and going to jail, or forcing me to really crawl through the mud to be an informer. . . .'* Then he named names. But Parks was not a political person. I was and that background certainly helped me. Some people feel it was heroic to take the Fifth; others think it was the act of a traitor. At the time, I can tell you, it was simply grim.

"The fifties — like the period preceding our entry into the war — looked like the end of the world, with no light at the end of the tunnel. People forced to choose between informing on other people or saving themselves, people scared into silence. People stopped writing. Some of those who were blacklisted tried to clear their names, some committed suicide, some were unemployed for years. On the other hand, you had people who had escaped the blacklist, who were still working and enjoying success, terrified that any day they would be exposed."

What was hard for Papp was his uncertainty about whether the FBI had informed CBS of his subpoena. He did not allow himself to ask. He gritted his teeth and waited. Later, he would say that he was tougher in his thirties than he would be later on.

Ephraim London, his tall, distinguished-looking lawyer, made Papp feel at ease, in part because of his familiarity with constitutional law, in part because of his direct, plain-spoken manner. He never billed Papp for his services and advised the producer that "taking the Fifth Amendment" — saying he could not answer a question because the answer might incriminate him — was his constitutional prerogative. London told Papp that once a witness began to answer *any* question about communism in the affirmative, he would be placed in a position where he could not refuse to name names. "It was a ticklish situation for me and one which did not appeal to my temperament. But we mapped out a strategy: By answering some questions that I viewed as legitimate but refusing to answer others on the grounds of constitutional privilege, I hoped to avoid being cited for contempt of Congress and receiving a jail sentence."

Meanwhile, Papp appeared at CBS every day, continued raising money for the Festival and, with Stuart Vaughan, continued work on the summer productions. In May, Vaughan began rehearsals for *Othello*, which was scheduled to open July 2. Hollywood, which paid far more than the

$55 a week that was the current Equity minimum, had already begun to draw away Festival actors. George C. Scott and Frank Silvera had been slated to play Othello and Iago but pulled out and had to be replaced at the last minute. Composer David Amram was working on the music. Designer Eldon Elder was providing the costumes and scenery. Papp gave his usual pre-season interviews as though Shakespeare was the only thing on his mind. On May 25, Judith Crist published a long article in the *Herald Tribune* that detailed the Festival's financial problems, noting that the $15,500 Papp had in hand was one-third of what he needed for the summer.

Finally, on June 19, Papp took the subway to the U.S. courthouse in Foley Square, in downtown Manhattan. "When I took the stand to testify, strange to say, I felt very high," he recalled. "It was a totally unrealistic, romantic notion but somehow I thought that these people questioning me would understand my patriotism — I was a *veteran*, after all — and that they would look for some way to comprehend my point of view. They did not do that, of course. They insisted on getting what they wanted for their own purposes. But I felt very emotional and I tried to be very straight, not aggressive, to try to make them understand me."

By 1958, HUAC had finished with Hollywood and turned its attention to the powerful new medium of television. A host of publications — notably *Red Channels* — had sprung up to help, listing confirmed and suspected members of the Communist party. Eight years earlier, CBS had instituted a mandatory loyalty oath for its employees, requiring them to swear that they had not belonged to any organization listed as subversive by the attorney general and, if they had, to explain why their membership should not be construed as meaningful. The network had subsequently canceled its popular situation comedy *The Goldbergs* because its sponsor, General Foods, was alarmed that one of its stars, Philip Loeb, had been listed in *Red Channels*. Television personalities whose names were listed in such publications had to be cleared. Loeb — an older actor whom Joe Papirofsky had known and admired — had testified under oath that he had not been a Communist and appealed to his union and to the Television Authority. But he was unable to continue working in television and in 1955, he committed suicide.

Loeb's death brought to three the number of men Papp knew personally who had died as a result of political harassment. The first had been Roman Bohnen, guiding spirit of the Actors' Lab. The second was Joe Bromberg, who had also died of a heart attack — in London where, because of the American blacklist, he was appearing in a play by Dalton Trumbo. "*Red Channels* lists more than 15 CP Front connections of the late Mr. Bromberg," a self-styled watchdog had written in the *New York World Telegram and Sun* after his death. "With American soldiers dying in the Far East and the nation's economy and welfare threatened by worldwide Soviet aggression, the Communist in America, surrounded by his chosen enemies, is subjected to a certain stress and strain nowadays. To the end, the ailing Mr. Bromberg chose not to take sides against the Communist enemy."

When Joseph Papp arrived at the federal courthouse along with eight other witnesses, there were virulent articles in the right-wing press. Charles Dubin, director of the NBC quiz show *Twenty-One,* had appeared before the committee the day before and had repeatedly taken the Fifth. Within a few hours of his testimony, NBC had fired him.

The subcommittee of the Committee on Un-American Activities was chaired by Congressman Morgan M. Moulder of Missouri and conducted largely by his staff director, Richard Arens, who began by asking the producer to identify himself.

"My name is Joseph Papirofsky," said Joe Papp, who had not yet gotten around to changing his name legally.

"Would you be good enough to spell that for us please?"

"P-a-p-i-r-o-f-s-k-y. I reside at 410 Central Park West, in Manhattan, and I am a producer of Shakespearean plays for Central Park. . . .

"My present work is primarily centered around the New York Shakespeare Festival, which is an educational nonprofit organization chartered by the State education department, established for the purpose of producing plays for the general public without admission charge. The programs also include free performances of Shakespeare for high school students. . . ."

"Does it enjoy tax-free status?"

"Yes, it does."

"Do you receive a salary?"

"I began to receive a salary five months ago. For the first three years, I received no salary. . . . I am still employed by CBS as a stage manager. . . . The last show I did last night was *I've Got a Secret.* . . . Prior to that I was in California and I worked for the Actors' Laboratory, Inc. . . ."

"Were there any other schools with which you were connected in California?"

"Yes, I also taught acting to working people at the California Labor School."

The course, as the committe knew, was titled "Preparation for and

Participation in a People's Theater" and was listed among such offerings as "The Fight for Negro Freedom," "The Jewish People in the Struggle for Democracy," "Mimeographing, Leaflet and Poster Design," "Building Trade Union Leadership," "Writing People's Songs" and "What to Do Until the Lawyer Comes."

"Mr. Papirofsky, are you now, or have you ever been, a member of the Communist party?" continued Mr. Arens.

"I am not now a member of the Communist party. . . ."

"Have you been a member of the Communist party in the course of the last year?"

"No, sir. Would you specify the years — 1957 and 1958 — no sir; I have not."

"Have you been a member of the Communist party any time since January 1955?"

"I must decline to answer that question on the grounds of self-incrimination."

"Have you been a member of the Communist party since June 1955?"

"No, sir."

"Have you been a member of the Communist party any time since February 1955?"

"I must decline to answer that question on the same grounds."

"Are there persons presently in the entertainment industry who, to your certain knowledge, are or in the recent past have been members of the Communist party?"

Papp conferred with London.

"I am afraid I do not know the answer to that question."

"Have you resigned from the Communist party?"

"The assumption is that I was a member of the Communist party; and, therefore, I must respectfully decline to answer that on the basis of the Fifth Amendment."

"Are you a Communist, though not a member of the Communist party?"

"The answer to that is 'No.'"

"Although the question distinguished a card-carrying member of the party from a person committed to the ideals of communism," Joseph Papp recalled, "it was clear to me that the committee would make no such distinction and there followed a series of questions to get me to admit that I was a Communist: Did I know that the California Labor School was controlled by the Communist conspiracy? Had I signed a telegram of support along with the rest of the Executive Committee of

Actors' Laboratory Theater which was reported in the newspaper *The Daily Worker?*"

The questioning continued.

"Is your opinion — and I'm not trying to probe your opinion — still in condemnation of Larry Parks, who broke from the Communist party and came before the committee and identified a number of Communists? Are you still hostile to that man?"

"The feeling I have about Mr. Parks would be the same feeling I would have about anybody who would gratuitously injure the people who work with him in the way he did."

"What if Mr. Parks, instead of having been in the Communist conspiracy, had been in a narcotics ring and came before the appropriate investigating committee and identified persons active in the narcotics ring? Would you be in opposition to him then?"

"I am afraid I cannot go into that question because the one case you mentioned with Mr. Parks has to do with a man [who] because of the way he functioned, hurt the employment of people, innocent people, by mentioning names and so forth. Whereas the narcotic situation is hurting men's bodies and not their thinking."

"You acclaimed Mr. Parks publicly at one time and used your prestige and used the glamour of your position to acclaim Mr. Parks when he at first refused to cooperate with the Committee on Un-American Activities."

"I have no glamour and prestige. I think it is a misnomer to use that."

"You let your name be used, in acclaim of Larry Parks when he refused to cooperate with the Committee on Un-American Activities, is that correct?"

"Yes, if you have a record of it there, I would have to say I did."

"They then presented me with a reproduction of a petition," Papp later recalled, "which I had signed and long forgotten titled 'THE THOMAS RANKIN COMMITTEE MUST GO!' which read 'We, the undersigned members of the acting profession, acclaim Larry Parks, one of the "unfriendly nineteen." We acclaim those actors who appeared in Washington to protest the star chamber proceedings . . . those others who broadcast their indignation on the air in the press. . . . We are proud that they are upholding the finest traditions of our profession and our country.' Then they asked whether I had been a Communist when I signed that petition."

Papp said, "I must refuse to answer on the same grounds as I mentioned before."

"I respectfully suggest that would conclude the staff interrogation of this witness."

Congressman Moulder asked, "Did counsel ask you your age?"

"I gave my date of birth, Representative Moulder. I would like to submit this, if you do not mind, sir. This is a magazine published by the State Department and sent to Russia — an example of American democracy at work. The work of this cover is the work of the New York Shakespeare Festival. Inside there is a series of pictures describing our work as descriptive of the free democratic culture. I see no mention of the Un-American Activities Committee, so I must assume what we are doing, the department feels, is a much more important function. I also submit the Voice of America tapes that I have made to various countries as an example of free democracy in this country. I feel that what I believe can be best stated this way."

"When you were making those Voice of America tapes, were you a member of the Communist party?"

"No, sir, I was not a member of the Communist party when I was making the Voice of America tapes. . . ."

"I had forgotten what you said your age to be."

"I will be thirty-seven this coming Sunday."

"Are you married?"

"Yes, sir, and I have a three and a half month daughter."

"Were you in the armed forces?"

"Yes sir, I was in the navy. I was in the service for three years."

"At any time during your professional career or in connection with the work that you are doing at the present time, do you have the opportunity to inject into your plays or into the acting or the entertainment supervision which you have, any propaganda in any way which would influence others to be sympathetic with the Communist philosophy or the beliefs of communism?"

"Sir, the plays we do are Shakespeare's plays. Shakespeare said, 'To thine own self be true,' and various other lines from Shakespeare can hardly be said to be 'subversive' of 'influencing minds.' I cannot control the writings of Shakespeare. He wrote plays five hundred years ago. I am in no position in any plays where I work to influence what the final product will be, except artistically and except in terms of my job as a producer."

"My point is, do you intentionally control the operation of the entertainment which you produce or supervise for the purpose of influencing sympathy toward communism? That is my point."

"The answer to that is obviously no. The plays speak for themselves. I began to mention the plays that we did. Maybe some of these plays might be considered propagandistic."

"We are not concerned with the plays," interjected Mr. Arens, "and you know we are not, and there is no suggestion here by this chairman or anyone else that Shakespeare was a Communist. That is ludicrous and absurd. That is the Commie lie . . . and for you to twist this testimony in the presence of the public press here is to give an implication that the chairman is trying to elicit information from you that Shakespeare was subversive or this committee is investigating Shakespeare, investigating that type of thing, is not only ludicrous, but it is highly unfair."

"I am sorry. I think you misunderstand me."

"I did not misunderstand you. . . ."

"I was very much impressed by your straightforward and honest replies to counsel regarding your background and your work," noted Congressman Moulder. "When it comes to the question of whether you have been actively connected with the Communist party, that is a different matter. . . . Have you undergone any change in your beliefs and the form of government we should have, during the past two or three years? Have you changed your opinion in that connection?"

"Changed my opinion from what?"

"In your philosophy of government or form of government we should have."

"My opinions change constantly, and they have changed from time to time on many subjects."

"You understand, of course, the Communist philosophy is antispiritual, antireligious, and is very much in conflict with our system . . . do you agree with that?"

"I am not antispiritual or antireligious in any way."

"You mentioned a while ago that to give names of other people, such as Larry Parks, you considered wrong, when it does injury to other people. . . . If communism is not subversive or a danger to our American form of government and our way of life, then what harm is done by revealing the names of people who are active in the Communist party and the Communist movement?"

"I understand the question, Representative Moulder. You know there is a blacklisting device that lists [suspected Communists] in the industry and the naming of people this way does deny these people the right to work, which I think is terribly unfair and un-American."

"Who denies them the right to work? . . . Do you think it is wrong to disassociate from public media of expression, in this country, people who are secret members of a conspiracy which has as its vowed objective the overthrow of this government by force and violence?"

Papp conferred again with London.

"I just think it is wrong to deny anybody employment because of their political beliefs," he said.

After one more question, the witness was excused. He took the subway back to CBS, planning how he would greet his coworkers. "The worst thing about it was the fear," he would later recall. "Once you were linked with HUAC, people were afraid to talk to you. It was as though you had a contagious disease. So as soon as I got back to the studio, the first thing I did was call together the stagehands and cameramen. They were a group of mostly Irish and Italian men, with whom I had been working six years. I was pretty well liked there because I worked hard and, a few years before, I had succeeded in getting our job designation renamed from 'floor manager,' which made us sound as though we worked in a department store, to 'stage manager.' I told them that the committee had wanted me to name names. I said I had answered questions about myself but refused to answer any question that would lead to anybody else. Most people have an aversion to informing that goes back to Jesus Christ. I said that was the reason I took the Fifth Amendment twelve times.

"Most of them understood. One old, hard-drinking Irish electrician said to me, shaking his head: 'You know, Joe, you shouldn't have gotten mixed up with those guys in Yugoslav Hall.' Another man called me a Communist and walked away. A third — someone I had helped with a play he was writing — was, above all, worried that I had mentioned *his* name. The others were uncomfortable but supportive.

"I had started to prepare for the evening news show that I was scheduled to do when the phone rang. The head stage manager wanted to see me right away. I said no, I'd talk to him later. I finished the show and then I went up to his office."

The head stage manager told him, "We're going to have to let you go."

"'Why?' I say. He's squirming.

"'We're cutting back,' he said. 'You know we're overstaffed.'

"'What has that got to do with me? I have seniority here.'

"'Well you're fired, Joe,' he says.

"I said, 'I don't accept this.'

"He said, 'What do you mean?'

"'I'm going to fight this,' I said, and I left the studio."

That same afternoon, the Associated Press sent out a story titled "Broadway Red Probe Gets More 5th Pleas" featuring "TV figure" Joseph Papirovsky [*sic*]. The following day, UPI led its story, "The stage manager of the Columbia Broadcasting System's *I've Got a Secret* television show kept his own secret today when Congressional investigators asked about his alleged Communist affiliation. CBS promptly fired him." Other stories on the two-day HUAC subcommittee hearings, listing the names, addresses and telephone numbers of the witnesses, appeared in all the major New York City newspapers. The *New York Post* described the producer sitting with his wife in his "tiny" apartment, holding his infant daughter and saying — between telephone calls from concerned friends — "It didn't come as a surprise. It's like waiting for someone to die — you get a twinge. My worst sorrow is that I feel the Festival may be lost because contributors will be afraid of the adverse publicity I've gotten. All my energies for the past four years have gone into the Festival. It is the most satisfactory part of my life."

"Papp says he needs $35,000 more to complete the festival's season. . . . *Othello* was reduced from a four-week engagement to one. 'The project itself will come to an end unless we are able to raise more money,' Papp said."

There had, in 1958, been no case in which a blacklisted employee had ever succeeded in challenging the network's right to dismiss him or her. Charles S. Dubin, the director who had been fired by NBC the previous day, was not an NBC employee and could not appeal. At the American Shakespeare Festival, where Papp's Lab friend Bernard Gersten worked, plans to dismiss Gersten for his failure to cooperate with the committee were quashed when actress Katharine Hepburn and director John Houseman threatened to leave with him. Joseph Papp decided to appeal to his union, the Radio and Television Directors Guild.

"Some of those union officials had a reputation as Red-baiters," recalled Debuskey. "It was alleged that they cooperated with the blacklisting organizations." Nonetheless, Papp called Lamar Caselli, an RTDG board member and the man who had helped Papp create the theater on East 6th Street. Caselli advised Papp that if the union supported him, CBS would cave in. Because the reason given for Papp's termination had been "overstaffing," the two men decided to find a stage manager who had never worked for CBS before and have him apply for Papp's job. CBS hired him.

Meanwhile, on the nights before and after Papp's HUAC appearance, *Othello* had played to audiences at Philadelphia's Playhouse-in-the-Park and, on July 2, was scheduled to open in Central Park. The Festival's finances that summer were actually in worse shape than they had been the summer before. *Othello* was the Festival's most expensive production to date, not only because of its large cast but because, for the first time, Papp was required to employ union stagehands. He did not have enough money on hand to pay for the four weeks in Central Park. And, because Stuart Vaughan had left, he had no director for his second summer play, *Twelfth Night*, in which Peggy Bennion was to star.

So it was with "a somewhat cluttered mind," as Papp later recalled, that he went to see the executive director of his union. The director was reluctant to help but, finally, Papp persuaded him to hold a board meeting. It voted to hold a referendum of the membership to determine "whether it constitutes 'good and sufficient cause' to terminate a contract when a person avails himself of his constitutional privileges."

On July 2, the day *Othello* opened, the *New York Post* reported that the New York chapter of the Radio and Television Directors Guild would hold a national referendum on whether to contest the dismissals of both Joseph Papp and Charles Dubin, and interviewed both men. Dubin said he hoped to direct an off-Broadway show. Papp used the opportunity to fundraise. "We have $24,000 now," he told the reporter. "We need $50,000 to run through the entire season. I think our chances of getting it are good, from the contributions we've received in the last ten days." Jobless, he rehearsed *Twelfth Night* and tried to find work.

The officials in charge of the union vote had phrased the question in so confusing a way that Papp was not sure how it would go. "I didn't know any of the West Coast people," Papp recalled, "and I thought that, given how scared everyone was, how beaten down by McCarthyism, they'd never vote to challenge CBS, to hire a lawyer and essentially fight the blacklist. Even if they voted to take on my case, I doubted whether we could win."

When the results were tallied, the vote was more than 2 to 1 in favor of challenging CBS. On July 29, the RTDG announced that, under the terms of its contract, the union was submitting the case of Joseph Papirofsky to binding arbitration. In its brief, CBS held that like all its employees, Joe Papirofsky had filled out and signed a mandatory employment questionnaire. His testimony before HUAC indicated that he had misrepresented his background and deliberately concealed his connection with the Actors' Lab, and the California Labor School, constituting "just and sufficient cause for discharge."

While the lawyers prepared their briefs, Joseph Papp directed *Twelfth Night*, which opened on August 6 to mixed reviews. The ever-impartial Brooks Atkinson found Papp's work as a director "below the able standard . . . the organization, the brisk dry pace and the authority of Mr. Vaughan's work." But this time, Papp had no time to sit on a park bench and brood.

"I had thought that contributions to the Festival would fall off completely because of my testimony," he said later, "but I was wrong. Money did not exactly rain down on us but it did not stop coming." Rachel Armour Klein — later to become a Festival board member — sent one major contribution: "My husband and I felt rather strongly about your being victimized recently. We did some thinking about what we might do about it and decided that the best thing we could do was to express our admiration of your work by making the enclosed contribution. We hope that the Festival won't fold and that things will be ok for you personally."

Papp wrote back: "Your $1000 contribution is certainly the best expression of your concern for what happened to me recently, because as you probably know, my whole life is tied up with this work . . . we are determined to continue the Festival and survive the obstacles confronting us. In fact, our plans include a much more expanded program. With deepest gratitude, Joseph Papp."

His public posture, in contrast, was calculatedly pessimistic. In a newsbrief that appeared in the Sunday *New York Times* in August, the newspaper reported that "After three years of crying 'wolf' Joseph Papp is ready to say 'Uncle.' In other words, having begged, pleaded and borrowed funds for his ideal of a free Shakespeare festival in this city, Mr. Papp has reached the end of the line. He was saying with characteristic determination last week that unless there are sufficient funds available in advance next season, he will not reopen the New York Shakespeare Festival."

In November, CBS was ordered to reinstate Joseph Papp by arbitrator Emanuel Stein, chairman of the Economics Department at New York University. He ruled that Papp's dismissal did not constitute a Fifth Amendment case at all. CBS contended that it had discharged Papp because he had concealed information in his employment application. "We have no way of knowing whether CBS would have hired Papp in March, 1952, if he included these institutions in his employment application. But even if we assume that it would not have hired him, then it does not follow that six and a half years later, it might rely on these omissions to justify a dismissal," Stein told the *Herald Tribune*, "thus upholding the union's contention that the dismissal had not been for good and sufficient cause."

There was no winter season at the Heckscher that winter. Papp's only production was a staged reading of *Antony and Cleopatra,* with Colleen Dewhurst and George C. Scott. Papp, who told the *New York Times* he regarded his CBS reinstatement as "common sense," went back to work as a stage manager. In December, his request for a $50,000 appropriation from the New York City Board of Estimate was denied. Exactly one year earlier, he had asked for $40,000 and had been refused.

In January of 1959, with Festival finances dismal, a wife who had decided to give up acting and go to graduate school, and a new baby, Papp might have determined to hold on to the job he had fought to get back. But, instead, a few months after his reinstatement at CBS, Joseph Papp quit.

"I realized very soon," he later said, "that they were not only watching me very carefully but assigning me to minimal tasks. When I complained, the head stage manager said directors had stopped asking for me. I went to a few directors and asked them outright. They said they had been asking for me all the time.

"It was then I decided to devote all my time to Shakespeare. It was a jump off the high board. But from that moment on, the Festival became my life."

SEVEN

Winning the Park

NO SOONER had Joseph Papp given up his CBS job and linked his livelihood to Shakespeare than the roof caved in. In March, as he had done for the past three years, the producer formally requested his summer performance permit.

"Dear Sir," Commissioner Robert Moses replied:

I have your letter of March 11, in which you ask that we permit you this summer to operate your New York Shakespeare Festival in Central Park, as you have in the past, on a free admission basis.

I regret that we cannot do this. First, there is no control in the area you have been using and a considerable park acreage is being damaged by your operation. We must have fencing for control if your operation is to continue.

Second, there are no sanitary or dressing facilities for your actors and others employed in your productions and no electric current is available for lighting. We were forced to run a portable generator at the site during your operating season. Adequate sanitary and dressing facilities must be supplied if you are to continue in Central Park.

Third, the area used by your audience needs seats and paving. We cannot permit your audience to continue to use lawn areas in Central Park as theater seating areas . . . serious erosion problems will soon face us unless the area is paved.

The cost of the work the City must do if your Shakespeare in Central Park is to continue is between $100,000 and $150,000. If your performances are worthwhile, people will pay a reasonable charge to see them.

The concession agreement we have offered you will, if you have even moderate success, return about $10,000 annually to the City which will help to amortize the cost of necessary improvements and pay in part at least the cost of City help assigned to control and service your operation.

Unless, therefore, you are prepared to agree to charge admission and to enter into a regular concession agreement with the Department of Parks (10% of the gross receipts to go to the Dept. of Parks) we cannot give you a permit to operate in the City Park system in 1959.

Very truly yours,

And over the single word *Commissioner* was a scrawl that might be construed to read *R. Moses*.

In later years, when repetition of the saga had polished its contours to anecdote, Joseph Papp would say that Commissioner Moses's letter came "out of the blue," surprising him like "a hit in the *kishkes*." But, in fact, the commissioner and the producer had been on a potential collision course over the issue of public subsidy for Papp's theater for three years. Moses refused to meet with Papp, view his productions or even speak to him over the telephone. The two men communicated by letter, and the story of their conflict reads like an epistolary novel.

In March of 1959, Joseph Papp was thirty-seven years old and Robert Moses was seventy. Although Moses had never been elected to public office, he was one of the most powerful nonelected public officials in the United States. Ruling from a nondescript building below the toll plaza of the Triborough Bridge — which he had built and whose enormous revenues he controlled — Moses was not only New York City parks commissioner but chairman of the New York State Council of Parks, New York City construction coordinator, chairman of the New York State Power Authority, and director of the mayor's Slum Clearance Committee. He had started out in 1919 as the protégé of Governor Al Smith, for whom he had reorganized state government. Then he had begun remaking Long Island, transforming the estates of some of America's wealthiest families into public parks and parkways. Like Papp, he had at first been perceived as an idealist and a dreamer. Like Papp, he had been indefatigable and persistent. He had harnessed the power of the press and the courts to his cause, taking one opponent to court twenty-five times until he got what he wanted.

Robert Moses had built miles of public state parks, miles of public beaches, miles of parkways — on an unprecedented scale and at unprecedented cost. Around New York City alone, he had built sixteen of the seventeen highways and seven bridges. It was the commissioner who had reconstructed Central Park after sixty years of neglect, created Riverside Park, built six hundred city playgrounds, dozens of public swimming pools, ice-skating rinks, baseball diamonds, zoos, soccer fields and golf courses. He was lionized by the two newspapers of the elite, the *New York Times* and the *Herald Tribune,* enjoyed a job security unknown to politicians and had an unsullied reputation as a public servant.

Joe Papirofsky had been thirteen years old when Mayor Fiorello La Guardia created the office of Parks Department commissioner in 1934 and appointed Moses to it. The commissioner had improved much of the landscape Joe Papirofsky knew. He had rehabilitated Prospect Park, where Papp first heard the Goldman Band. He had built Stuyvesant Town, home to the Oval Players. He had built the East River Amphitheater where Joe Papp had produced his first outdoor Shakespeare.

Papp admired the commissioner but sensed that Moses had passed the peak of his power. The press had recently featured photos of a group of clever West Side mothers who had prevented Moses from building a parking lot near their children's playground on 67th Street and Central Park West. Nonetheless, Moses was very powerful, not the kind of man that Joseph Papp, with his gift for sizing up whoever stood before him, would choose for an enemy.

Moses's letter threw the producer into an unaccustomed state of confusion. "I didn't know how to deal with it," Papp later recalled. "I had thought that I had the support of this man and I couldn't understand what had changed his mind. I wanted to avoid a fight. Who would want to fight Robert Moses? He ran his department like a military organization. Here I was enmeshed in this thing and I never understood why."

Although both Moses and Papp were New York Jews, they came from opposite ends of the community. For all his life, Papp would loudly identify himself as working class and, later, as the son of poor, Eastern European Jewish immigrants. For all his life, Moses would more subtly define himself as an aristocrat, the son of a wealthy German Jewish family. His grandparents had immigrated sixty years before the Papirofskys and had quickly assimilated to their new surroundings. His mother had lost no time in replacing Judaism with Ethical Culture, sending Moses not to a New York City public school but to an out-of-town prep school, then to Yale and Oxford. Robert Moses, unlike Joseph Papp, had never heard a word of Yiddish at home.

But both were uncommonly ambitious, driven and audacious men. Both were pragmatists, so wedded to creating that neither, at first, cared about being paid for his work. Both inspired unusual devotion, long working hours and loyalty from their staffs. Both were impatient and sometimes abrasive men who made irreconcilable enemies. But perhaps most important, both were uncommonly shrewd in exploiting existing governmental structures to achieve their goals and, by March 1959, Moses was feeling that the Parks Department — the municipal body he viewed as his own — had been so exploited.

Moses felt, rightly, that Papp had shrewdly used *his* Parks Department to advance his cause. In January of 1956, he had applied for a permit to use an underutilized amphitheater in a slum on the Lower East Side. Papp had agreed to abide by Parks Department policy that no tickets be issued and no charges made. But even before his first production had opened, he had asked Mayor Wagner for financial support, the mayor had referred the letter to Moses, and Moses's deputy commissioner, Stuart Constable, had written, "I regret that I must tell you we have no funds available which could be used for the production of any sort of theatrical performance by your group."

In December of that year, Papp had for the first time contacted the commissioner directly. The New York Foundation and the Doris Duke Foundation were considering support of the Festival. "It would be helpful to have from you an expression of interest in the project," Papp wrote. "The trustees of the foundations mentioned above will be greatly influenced by your opinion of this civic-cultural venture." Moses had replied the next day: "We are much interested in your proposal to provide a five-borough program of Shakespeare in the parks next summer. If you are successful in efforts to obtain the needed financial support, we can work out a mutually satisfying program."

In the spring of 1957, Papp asked the Parks Department for a permit to put on three productions — *Romeo and Juliet, Two Gentlemen of Verona* and *Macbeth* — each of which would open in Central Park and then tour parks in the four outlying boroughs. That April, Stuart Constable had granted him the permit, warning that "it is prohibited to solicit funds or collect contributions within or adjacent to any park area."

At the very outset of the tour, Papp had written the department that he was encountering difficulties. "Our technical staff as it stands is woefully inadequate. . . . Unless we can get five men from the city assigned to the project for a ten week period, I say right now that we will not be able to move out of Central Park. Our physical set-up is gigantic. While it was possible to envisage the scope of a touring company, we did not anticipate the enormity of the moves. Financially, we are in no position to hire anybody."

On July 5, the producer again wrote a department official:

As per our telephone conversation . . . we will conclude the touring phase of our program on July 15. . . . The choice of continuing a back-breaking tour to reach a few hundred people a night as against remaining in an area already established by extraordinary publicity and playing for thousands is quite obvious.

By eliminating the physical drain of the elaborate and highly complex moves, we will be able to channel the energies presently diverted into the productions themselves. . . . As for the savings to the Department of Parks, well, it is incalculable as you well know. . . . All in all, our settling down at the Belvedere will benefit our audiences, the Park Department and ourselves.

The Festival, in Moses's view, had taken over the site like a squatter. Papp's Mobile Theater had "collapsed" at Belvedere Lake and become firmly established in the public mind as "Free Shakespeare in the Park." Moses might have noted that Papp had acquired his site in much the way he himself had acquired his first plots of land on Long Island, by moving in first and worrying about legal and financial details later. But Papp had gone farther: after what amounted to squatting on city property, he had tried to solicit money from his audiences by passing a basket. When Moses's people informed him that he was violating department regulations, Papp found out that the department controlled only three corners of 81st Street and Central Park West. The northwest corner was regulated by the Department of Welfare. He obtained the necessary permit, then had his staff dress in Elizabethan costume and solicit money there. And he continued to badger the Parks Department for outright financial support — in addition to aid-in-kind such as use of city space, electricity, water and personnel.

Repeated refusals from Moses and Deputy Commissioner Stuart Constable had no effect on the producer. On the contrary. During that same summer of 1957, Papp had the nerve to propose that the commissioner build him a permanent theater in the park:

Dear Commissioner Moses,

I was interested to learn of certain efforts made by your department to win support from foundations for the construction of a children's Marionette theater in Central Park. By coincidence, we have also embarked on a program for a permanent structure for our free presentations.

What is your reaction to a combined fund raising campaign for a single building project with facilities for the Marionette Theater and a Shakespeare Theater on an all year round basis? . . . We are ready to sit down with you at your convenience to go into some of the details of starting the campaign.

Papp did not understand that in the parks as in other parts of his empire, Moses delegated authority to his "executive officers" — in this case, to Stuart Constable, the fifty-nine-year-old, Ohio-born-and-bred, Harvard-educated landscape architect who had been chief designer of the Parks Department since 1936. It was Constable who conducted the correspondence with Papp, even when Moses signed it. It was Constable who had written: "We cannot agree to provide a site in the park system for a theater suitable for year-round use. If what you are after is a subsidized or partly subsidized Shakespeare playhouse . . . such a venture should not be maintained by or operated as part of the City park system."

Joseph Papp ignored the letter. He sent preliminary designs for the construction of a theater to another officer of the department, who announced to the press that plans to build such a theater were under consideration. Papp referred to those plans in letter after letter to Robert Moses. And he repeatedly tried to enlist the commissioner's support in everything from obtaining foundation grants to helping him "getting in on the ground floor" at the huge new cultural complex that would become Lincoln Center, which Moses was then building.

Dear Commissioner Moses:

For the past several weeks I have been trying, without success, to reach Mr. John D. Rockefeller III, regarding a proposal for the Lincoln Square project. . . . If it is no imposition I would be grateful if you could help to arrange for me to speak to Mr. Rockefeller. Our classical

repertory plans would undoubtedly be of great interest to him. . . .
Many, many thanks for all your kindness and assistance.

Robert Moses — via Constable — responded to those of Papp's overtures that did not require an outlay of cash. Although the commissioner
rarely attended the theater, he knew some Shakespeare, and was not
averse to theater in "his" parks. Moreover, he was sympathetic to the
wishes of two women of his social set — actress Cornelia Otis Skinner
and UNICEF activist Helenka Panteleone — who supported the Festival
and interceded when they could on Papp's behalf. In one of Moses's
frequent newspaper articles, he wrote:

> When it comes to Shakespeare, we've been tremendously interested in
> the company which performed this year. They have youth and enthu-
> siasm. They are uninhibited and free from ham traditions. They have
> been a conspicuous and widely heralded success, but they haven't got
> enough money to reopen next year, so we are setting about to raise
> funds to support them. Certainly a great deal of it, most of it, should
> come from private sources. . . . Perhaps, eventually, the city should
> contribute something. . . .

However, the commissioner himself had no interest in subsidizing any
non-revenue-producing venture on park property. Repeatedly, Moses
insisted on seeing a written guarantee that Papp could finance his proposed productions. Papp could not provide it, and Moses concluded he
was unreliable. That did not stop Papp from writing:

> We are now in rehearsal for our second play of the season without
> sufficient capital to open. I have proceeded with commitments to
> actors, high schools, organizations, and the general public, on the basis
> of general assurances from City Hall that operating funds for our
> winter season would be forthcoming. At this moment, our request for
> funds had been received favorably by the Mayor and had been chan-
> neled to the budget commissioner Mr. Beame. . . .
>   Our operating costs are minimal because the salaries we pay cannot
> be considered anything near a living wage. If we were to proceed on
> a fully unionized basis, our costs would be comparable to that of the
> Metropolitan Opera Company. . . .
>   Therefore, while private donations and grants from foundations are
> essential, I am of the belief that at least half of the basic support must
> emanate from either the city or the state; the other half to be matched
> by the aforementioned foundations and patrons of the arts.

Moses replied that his department could not raise money for Papp. And, more than one year before what was to be known as the Moses affair began, suggested, "If you cannot raise the funds required to produce the summer program free to the public, we suggest that the program be moved to the Corlears Hook [East River] amphitheatre and that a charge be made — say 50 to 75 cents per seat. There are about 2000 seats in this amphitheatre and you should be able to operate there successfully."

Ignoring the suggestion to return downtown, Papp replied, "I am prepared to take immediate steps to raise the necessary operating costs. However, in order to do this with any degree of effectiveness, it will be necessary for me to assure the interested parties that the newly-designated Central Park amphitheater is going ahead as scheduled."

In January of 1958, Moses wrote, "The estimated cost of the work in Central Park necessary to provide a permanent outdoor theatre suitable for your productions is about $200,000. I regret that we cannot ask the City to spend such a sum at this time." And he added, "Meanwhile our offer to allow you to charge for admission at Corlears Hook is still open."

Joseph Papp sent back a reply, which Moses himself annotated. Where the producer wrote, "I am starting a campaign to raise funds for next summer's productions in the parks . . . ," Moses scrawled, "Won't work. RM." And where he wrote, "I am also seeking long range support to justify an outlay of city funds for a permanent outdoor amphitheater in Central Park as we originally planned," Moses scrawled, "We are not leaving this to him."

Throughout 1958, in letters to the producer as well as to various friends, Moses expressed his opposition to public subsidy for Joe Papp's theater. "I think the City should not do this," Moses wrote to Stanley Lowell in February. "We suggested that Mr. Papp make a charge for his performances if he was unable to raise funds from foundations or individuals to carry on what is certainly very popular free entertainment in our parks. He says this is impossible. . . . I think this sort of thing should be either privately supported or supported by a charge for admission . . . the City shouldn't subsidize free theatre in the parks or elsewhere." When, in April, Papp pointed out that the Festival would be presenting *Othello* in Philadelphia to a paying audience in June and asked whether he might solicit contributions from his park audiences during the coming summer, Moses replied, "If we granted your request, we would have to do the same for representatives of every worthy cause in the city."

In June, Papp had testified before HUAC. A few days earlier, actress Helen Hayes had invited the commissioner to cochair a telecast tribute to the Festival. One day after the hearings, Moses replied, "Frankly I don't care to take a leading part in further celebrating and advertising Mr. Papp."

That was the commissioner's only negative allusion to Papp's testimony at the time. When a theatergoer concerned about the impact of the hearings on the Festival wrote to Moses, "How far we have come from the thinking of Jefferson and the other founding fathers whose love of freedom is so nobly embodied in our Constitution and especially in the Bill of Rights," Moses replied cooly, "Our understanding with Mr. Joseph Papp is that he may produce Shakespeare in Central Park this summer if he is able to raise funds from private sources to defray his costs. At this time we propose no change." Stuart Constable also told the press that the department would not be affected by the hearings in regard to its policy toward the Festival.

Throughout the rest of 1958, while battling CBS, producing *Othello* and directing *Twelfth Night,* Papp kept up his end of what he persisted in believing was a cordial relationship with Moses and Constable. In August, Constable wrote Papp, "We are glad to hear that our cooperation has been satisfactory and that you believe you are going to be able to put the financing of your summer Shakespeare Festival on a sound basis. We, of course, shall continue to cooperate as we have in the past."

But, in fact, Constable was scheming like a Shakespearean villain to outwit Papp. "Commissioner Moses is still trying to move Papp to some other place and to make him charge for Shakespeare," he wrote to one of his assistant executive officers in October.

> One of the reasons Papp always gives for doing no such thing is that the Unions would make demands which would necessitate his charging prices he could not collect for the show. What Unions are involved and can you get representatives to attend a meeting here to discuss Shakespeare? I don't want Papp present at the discussion and I'd rather the Unions do not know we're going to discuss Papp's Shakespeare before they get here.

After Constable held his meeting with the theatrical unions, he reported to Moses that the unions didn't "like Papp," wanted the producer to charge admission and thought he would accept an admission of $1 or $1.50 if the department made that a condition for obtaining a permit. "We made a study of fencing, paving and seats for the area he now uses which would make possible a charge," he added. Then he noted, for the first time, "The estimated cost of this work is about $250,000 [*sic*]. Will you consider doing this work if Papp will agree to the charge?" When

Moses read this, he had drawn an arrow pointing to the last sentences and scrawled: "Where in hell would it come from? I still believe in Corlears Hook."

In December, Constable informed Moses that Papp refused to charge at Corlears Hook and that the East River Amphitheater was already booked. "Papp is now willing to discuss a $1.00 charge at his present location," Constable reported. "His change in attitude is not due to anything we have said or done but to some pressure put on him by Newbold Morris and your good friend Eleanor Roosevelt. . . . It seems to me we have to go along with Papp in Central Park."

In January 1959, there was a routine letter from the commissioner to Papp; in February, more correspondence regarding the producer's meetings with the Fact-Finding Committee of Entertainment Unions. Using as a model the agreement between the Musicians Union and the city, which subsidized free live concerts in New York parks and schools, Papp had proposed a plan whereby a $50,000 city contribution would be matched by the theatrical unions to subsidize the Festival.

Then, on March 9, Constable informed his boss:

Joe Papp is, I think, trying to figure a way to embarrass us and go on with his free show business. He called today and wanted to know why we had changed our position in regard to his free plays. I told him we thought any theatrical performance in the parks should be at least self-supporting and that we objected to his solicitation of funds at every performance in spite of our protests and in defiance of park regulations. He then asked what right we had to take an area in Central Park which had been free and turn it into an area which would provide revenue for the City. I referred him to the Charter and he then said they might have to give up the whole thing. I'm for this and for getting rid of Papp any way we can but you can see what he's up to. We will be the dogs who drove art and culture for the masses out of Central Park.

On this last letter, Moses scrawled, "To hell with him. Get up memo explaining matter to the public. Our power under the Charter is unquestionable. We don't have to stand being blackmailed by that bastard. RM."

The following day, Constable told Papp that he would have to charge admission or get out of Central Park, and the fight began.

On March 11, Papp wrote a carefully worded letter "on behalf of the Board of Directors and on advice of *pro bono* counsel John Wharton" asking permission to operate in Central Park "on the basis of free admissions." On March 18, he received the reply: "Unless, therefore, you are prepared to agree to charge admission and to enter into a regular concession agreement with the Department of Parks (10% of the gross receipts to go to the Dept. of Parks) we cannot give you a permit to operate in the City Park system in 1959."

That first week, Papp, his counsel and press agent Merle Debuskey tried to clarify what was going on. "Joe knew few important people then," recalled Debuskey. "We could not believe that the mayor would let Moses have his way but we weren't sure who had what authority and we knew no one important who could tell us. We didn't want to attack Moses in public because we thought it would get his back up. There was also no point embarrassing the mayor. And we also had to be discreet because we had three shows scheduled for that summer and if we announced that we were having problems, we would scare off the creative people working on the shows.

"The mayor asked the city corporation counsel to research his options, and the counsel told him he had no jurisdiction over the parks. Joe did not panic. He never beat his breast — that was just not part of his character. He took his lumps, didn't cry about them. He'd undercut the gloom with another bad pun. He was optimistic."

"I know that a man who can write with such depth of feeling about O'Casey will certainly understand the dilemma of our organization," Papp wrote the commissioner.

"This matter is entirely in the hands of Stuart Constable who has been in close touch with me and speaks for the Department in this matter," Moses replied.

Papp proposed that half the house be charged and the other half be admitted free.

Moses replied, "We cannot agree to any such arrangement. There must be a charge for all seats and the charge must be approved by the Department of Parks."

Papp struggled with the idea of making free Shakespeare into paying Shakespeare. Charging admission was not only contrary to his purpose but impractical. Off-Broadway institutions such as the Phoenix Theater, the City Center and the Stratford Shakespeare Festival were "always tottering on the brink" despite stars and magnificent seasons. If he began to charge, he would have to incur the enormous ancillary expenses. But on March 31, Papp capitulated. He submitted a scale of admissions to the deputy commissioner: "1000 Bleacher Seats at 50 cents each; 1000 Chair Seats at $1.00 each."

Then, Moses upped the ante. He would grant the permit, provided Papp charged $1.00 and $2.00.

By this time, Robert Montgomery had joined John Wharton as legal counsel and Merle Debuskey had been organizing a press campaign. Debuskey represented the purist wing of the Festival board. "*Free* is the Festival's spine," he argued. "If you fracture it, you're inviting other kinds of death. The difference between free and charging is not 25 cents. It's miles apart. Legions apart. A universe apart."

Papp vacillated. "Why don't we give them a fucking 50 cents a ticket?"

Debuskey would run through the reasons once again. On April 7, Papp rejected the commissioner's proposal to charge admission.

Once decided, the producer put to use the lesson in strategy he had learned from Whitey: *If you want to make an impact, hit first, hit hard, and without any kind of feeling.* On April 15, he sent the commissioner the press kit that Debuskey had sent to the four major morning newspapers in the city — the *New York Times,* the *Herald Tribune,* the *Daily Mirror,* the *Daily News* — and the three major afternoon papers — the *World Telegram and Sun,* the *Journal-American* and the *New York Post.* The producer had also sent out a "Dear Friend" letter to his supporters, urging them to send telegrams to Mayor Wagner, Moses and newspaper editors and to call ten friends and ask them to do the same. For the next two months, all New York would follow the evolving drama that attracted radio and television coverage and, eventually, the national press. "MOSES STIRS TEMPEST OVER SHAKESPEARE FEE" ran one headline. "ALL THE WORLD'S A STAGE — BUT HOW ABOUT THE PARK?" ran another. "Nothing like it had ever been seen before," Debuskey recalled. "For the media to engage in covering a hassle over producing Shakespeare? A battle over culture on the front pages day after day after day for two months? It turned the town upside down. That battle was the most significant media event that had ever involved the American theater."

The Parks Department issued a statement immediately. "Mr. Papp is an enthusiastic, I might almost say fanatical, very temperamental Shakespeare producer with real talent but no conception of Park administration," the commissioner wrote. "In Mr. Papp's philosophy the sole and overriding duty of the Park Commissioner is to brush up his Shakespeare, and all other responsibilities and considerations must yield to this categorical imperative. I have considerable respect for Mr. Papp's singleness of purpose but can't adopt it as a principle and shall certainly not direct Mr. Constable to do so. . . . I believe I have the Mayor's confidence. Mr. Constable has mine."

Brooks Atkinson, the Festival's staunch supporter, wrote with customary elegance, "Say this for Parks Commissioner Robert Moses. He is never boring. He does not let his admirers get in a rut."

The city's editorial pages were less subtle. "Fiorello La Guardia once said: 'When I make a mistake, it's a beaut.' The same goes, we think, for Bob Moses," wrote the *Tribune*.

"We assume," wrote the *New York Post*, "that as in other great decisions, Mr. Moses reached this one after an extended consultation with himself."

"Mr. Moses is being not merely inconsistent," wrote the *World Telegram and Sun*, "but capriciously unreasonable, even for him."

In ecologically ignorant 1959, Moses's concern for grass erosion made him an object of ridicule. Pranksters sent him packets of grass seed and Papp was quick to present erosion rather than money as the key issue. "Do people sitting and watching a play create more of an erosion problem than football, softball, soccer and similar sports encouraged by the parks at no cost to the players?" he asked in the *Times*. In a letter to Moses representing some 300,000 New York City parents, and published in the *Herald Tribune*, the president of the United Parents Association wrote, "As parents and citizens we have been heartened to see our city expand its all too meager public cultural programs. We are much more concerned with the erosion of men's souls than the park's soil."

The theater community was unanimous in its support for the Festival. Statements and letters from Actors Equity, the League of New York Theaters and even the American Shakespeare Festival in Stratford poured into editorial offices. Schoolchildren and their teachers who had been bused to the Heckscher Theater collected nickels and dimes and organized petitions. City politicians leaped into the fray, with Manhattan Borough President Hulan Jack and City Council President Abe Stark supporting Joseph Papp and City Councilman Louis Okin announcing his proposal for a law that would prevent Moses from "demanding or requiring that admission fees be charged by groups licensed to use park facilities for theatrical presentations." Papp received ten offers of alternate venues, including a tent at Palisades Amusement Park, a deck on the Hudson River Day line and a Long Island restaurant owned by Nathan's Famous, a New York hot-dog chain. "I have nothing to say at this time," Papp was quoted as saying, "except that I enjoy Nathan's hot dogs very much."

Joseph Papp became a household name. Moses disappeared from public view. His unavailability for comment or consultation inspired another set of headlines: "WHEREFORE ART THOU? MAYOR'S CALL TO MOSES" and "MAYOR CAN'T FIND MOSES IN SHAKESPEARE TEMPEST" and an editorial titled "AMONG THE MISSING": "When we checked late last night, Mayor Wagner was still trying to locate Parks

Commissioner Moses to talk to him about his sudden decision to bar the free Shakespeare productions from Central Park. We certainly hope the Parks Commissioner will find time to grant his boss an audience." On April 21, according to the *Herald Tribune:* "MAYOR SAYS HE'S UN-ABLE TO FIND MOSES FOR 5TH DAY" and Eleanor Roosevelt wrote in her weekly column: "It seems strange to me that Robert Moses, who once was enthusiastic about such things, should now want to ban the Shakespeare Festival from Central Park." Even Red-baiting Hollywood columnist Hedda Hopper, who had helped kill off the Actors' Lab a decade earlier, wrote in support of the Festival.

By April 29, there were reports that the commissioner tried a bit of Red-baiting himself. During the 1930s, Moses had been proficient at using anti-Red hysteria to get rid of men he disliked or who were in his way. He had publicly called New Dealer Rexford Tugwell a "Planning Red," claimed that architect Frank Lloyd Wright was "regarded in Russia as our greatest builder," and labeled his greatest critic, urban planner Lewis Mumford, "an outspoken revolutionary." Now, Moses said, "some-one who worked with the New York Shakespeare Festival and saw its operations first-hand" had written a two-page, single-spaced letter to the commissioner, complaining that Papp paid his actors only $10 per week. "It is indeed strange that he expects even more cooperation with govern-ment," the letter continued, "when it is a matter of record that he was unwilling to cooperate with government when it attempted to investigate Communist subversion and penetration into the theater."

The commissioner had this letter mimeographed and enclosed it with the following letter of his own: "Just for your further information, this fellow Papp became more and more rambunctious, unwilling to conform to rules, uncertain of support and threatening in the usual left-wing technique. As a result of recent experiences we have looked him up more carefully. He turns out to be typical of the breed. He took the Fifth Amendment twelve times in June, 1958 before the House Un-American Activities Committee. At the time of the hearing he was a Stage Manager for C.B.S., was fired, ordered reinstated."

Moses mailed the two letters to F. M. Flynn, president-publisher of the *Daily News,* Charles B. McCabe of the *Daily Mirror,* Mayor Robert Wagner, Deputy Mayor Paul O'Keefe and corporation counsel Charles Tenney, one of whom leaked it to the press.

The circulation of the unsigned letter kindled a second month of front-page controversy, with the *Journal-American,* the *Mirror* and the *News* supporting Moses. Just after the HUAC hearings, Stuart Constable had told the press that Papp's testimony would have no impact on the

Parks Department's sponsorship of Festival productions. Now, when asked by a reporter whether his boss's tactics smacked of McCarthyism, Constable replied, "What's wrong with McCarthy?"

Forty-five actors who had worked at the Festival sent a petition to the mayor protesting the circulation of the letter. The American Civil Liberties Union demanded that Mayor Wagner extract an apology from Moses. "We think that if Mr. Moses disapproved of Mr. Papp he ought to come right out and say so instead of passing around letters from persons unnamed," wrote the *Herald Tribune*. The New York assistant superintendent of schools, Clare Baldwin, announced that his department planned to go ahead with the Festival's tour through the schools in the fall and told the press, "As far as I know, Shakespeare was never a Communist but I suppose if he were alive today someone might call him that."

After two and a half weeks of raucous press coverage, the press reported that Moses had been hospitalized with a bad cold and was resting at home in Babylon, Long Island. But he had been dictating letters from his hospital bed. On April 28, he had written to the city corporation counsel, Charles Tenney:

> This man came to us originally with a committee of reputable citizens who said they would fully support his ambitious, amateur Shakespeare enterprise. I was foolish enough to say they could make a start if they had enough money. . . . They never had enough to operate a season. . . . The situation got worse with the starvation pay of the kids employed. The place is dark and impossible to police adequately. How many couples on the grass came for Shakespeare and how many for other reasons I don't know. Papp even passed the hat in the audience, something we don't permit and we never knew what became of his receipts. There were increasing evidences of small, jeering groups — the kind who wander in and start trouble. . . .
>
> Papp in recent months had become more and more truculent, and unreasonable. He first agrees to follow rules and then refuses. He adopts the old left-wing techniques of the agitator among artistic and so-called liberal groups, the big lie, etc. He was a communist of long standing, affiliated with all the radicals, took the Fifth Amendment again and again, etc. I hardly need to tell you that I don't propose to be intimidated by him, that he will have to charge admission in a fenced area with seats, etc, as long as I am Commissioner. . . .

Then, the commissioner made a surprising statement. "It's too late to do a proper job this summer which would cost about $125,000 in capital funds. Twenty thousand dollars in expense budget funds would do a makeshift job."

On that same day Moses wrote to New York senator Jacob K. Javits, urging him to stay away from Papp supporters, but again mentioning that he could make do with $20,000 instead of $125,000. And on May 1, he wrote to Papp saying a makeshift arrangement for the summer would be possible if the mayor provided $20,000 and Papp agreed to a two-scale admission charge of 50 cents and $1.

On May 4, it was reported that Mayor Wagner had finally been able to reach the commissioner by telephone, and, on May 5, Moses made public a letter to Papp in which he asked the producer to meet two conditions: persuade the city to provide $20,000 for fencing, ticket booths, seats and sanitary facilities and charge admission fees of 50 cents and $1.

Sensing victory, Papp refused. "Paying for the use of Central Park is like paying tax on a tax," he told the *New York Times,* and made public a letter he had written to the commissioner which began:

> That you still hold to the proposition that the Shakespeare audience must be singled out to pay for the privilege of using public facilities which are free to baseball players, zoo goers and concert audiences is regrettable and we have no other course than to reject this discriminatory and anti-popular concept. . . .
>
> While we acknowledge your authority to regulate our operation in the park, we feel it does not extend to the workings of the Festival. Since we are dedicated to a principle of free admissions, it is hardly within your purview to insist that we alter the basic purpose of our organization. . . .
>
> I think everyone is growing tired of the distortions, outright fabrications and anonymous allegations put out by your office. No new excuse you can conjure up will stop us from pressing for the right to continue to have free presentations of Shakespeare in Central Park.

Papp's summer productions of *Julius Caesar, Henry IV, Part I* and *The Merchant of Venice* went on indefinite hold. He wrote to the mayor, "I know that you did not create the controversy . . . [but] while Moses is stalling and changing his reasons every other day (he has changed them four times already) we are going into the summer without preparations for our program. . . . It's now up to you, Mr. Mayor, to call an end to this political game of musical chairs and insist that the Festival be permitted to operate free in Central Park."

On May 11, the mayor and the commissioner finally met face to face at the Player's Club and held a meeting whose content remained private. It was reported that Moses — who had a history of offering to resign if he did not get his way — used this threat once again. "While I can't approve of all the ways this has been handled," the mayor told the press after lunch, "the only alternative is to get another Parks Commissioner. I certainly won't do that." But an assistant to the mayor called Debuskey to suggest that Papp meet once again with officials of the Parks Department.

On May 14, Papp, Debuskey and one of the Festival's *pro bono* lawyers, Robert Montgomery, went up to the Arsenal at the entrance to the Central Park Zoo to meet with Stuart Constable.

Even in less strained circumstances, Constable was considered to be one of the most insufferable bureaucrats in New York City. "Constable was sitting behind his desk with a 'colonial officer in India' look," Debuskey recalled. "He had a Band-Aid on his finger which he kept picking at. During the whole time we were there he never once looked us directly in the eye." Neither Papp nor Debuskey nor Montgomery could engage him in dialogue or figure out what, exactly, his demands were.

"I didn't like Constable at all," Papp would recall. "I could see he was an anti-Semite and an anti-Communist, one of those red-faced people. He had a big walrus mustache and was unbelievably pompous — I would have cast him as the Constable in *Pirates of Penzance*. I was sitting there and he made some kind of accusation. I got up and said, 'Now, *listen*.' He got scared I was going to hit him. Now, I'm not a large man. But he called in four police guards who were standing watch outside and had us thrown out."

Debuskey, Papp and Montgomery were escorted out of the building, where the press agent had arranged for reporters to be waiting. They went back to their papers with yet another story.

Papp and Debuskey walked down Fifth Avenue together, Papp telling Debuskey that the only answer was to charge admission. "He was desperate. He thought it was all over," Debuskey recalled. But in a long conversation that night, the press agent once again pointed out the ramifications. "I told him the power had always been in the *free*. I reminded him that if we charged admission we would see an extraordinary rise in costs. If he started charging admission, my union would step in and demand that I be paid. The stagehands would have to be paid. A box office would have to be established. And what would we do when we toured the boroughs? Charge in Central Park and do it for free elsewhere? If the public is deprived of this, who is the villain? How long will Moses be parks commissioner? How long will Mayor Wagner take this nonsense?"

It was better to take Moses to court and lose, Debuskey argued, than to accept a compromise. Papp agreed with him but did not believe he could win. Moses had told the press he regarded the Shakespeare issue as closed and had left for Bermuda. But the Festival's lawyers at Paul, Weiss, Rifkind & Garrison had consulted their colleagues in the litigation department and advised Papp to sue.

Samuel Silverman had been a partner in the firm for thirteen years. Born in Odessa, he had come to the United States in 1913 — the same year as Yetta Papirofsky — and was the product of New York City public schools. Although he admired Robert Moses, he thought the commissioner's attitude arrogant. And although he had previously not heard of Free Shakespeare, he thought it a wonderful idea. And he was astounded that Stuart Constable had ejected his colleague Bob Montgomery from the Arsenal — a public building! Silverman had, many years before, been an assistant corporation counsel to the city, *defending* officials like Robert Moses. There was, he knew, an "Article 78 proceeding" available that could be brought against an administrative officer who had exceeded or was abusing his powers. Preparing the case would require minimal time and work.

On May 18, the Festival brought suit against Robert Moses.

Once again, the media circus resumed. People and groups with long-standing grudges against the commissioner spontaneously made calls and wrote letters on behalf of the Festival. Raymond S. Rubinow, a real estate broker who had led a citizens' committee to prevent Moses from opening Washington Square to traffic, now organized a *We Want Will* committee and opened an office on Fifth Avenue. Former Manhattan borough president Stanley Isaacs, one of the many public officials who, years before, Moses had "smeared," now spoke out against the commissioner.

"It seemed to me that the commissioner had no business insisting that Joe charge admission, that he was proceeding beyond his job and his function," Silverman later recalled. "He was there to protect the people of the city and to protect the parks. He was not there to protect or produce theater. There's a doctrine of law that an administrative officer must not be — in the legal phrase — *arbitrary and capricious*. I felt I had a respectable case and a fair chance of winning. And when everybody tells you you're a great guy for the litigation you're involved in — I must say it was nice to feel I was on the right side."

By May 29, Robert Moses was complaining in the press that Papp had "miscast" him and that, because of his history of helping the Festival, he did not deserve the role of villain.

On June 2 *Shakespeare Workshop* vs. *Moses* was heard in court and, just as Papp had feared, Moses won the case. His counsel had argued "hard and well," according to Silverman, and Justice Samuel Gold — "a good judge and a nice man" — ruled that Moses had not acted improperly. The parks commissioner had "full discretion" to make decisions regarding the municipal parks.

Papp was stunned by the court decision. "When you're jumping off a mountain, you don't stop to think what it'll do to you," he said later. "Whatever happened, happened, and then I would react to it. The only real initiative I took was to go to court and then I lost. It looked like I had lost everything. I just felt helpless. It was dismal."

Montgomery believed that the decision was correct, that they had done all they could. But Samuel Silverman insisted on appeal.

"We were now in the middle of June," he would later recall with relish, "when the courts customarily go into recess. If we didn't get to the appellate division right away, there would be no Shakespeare. The court calendars were all filled up. All the briefs had been in thirty to forty-five days before. But courts are a good deal more flexible than the public thinks — we said that if the case was put off till the fall, the project was dead. Corporate counsel objected but was overruled."

During the first court procedure, Moses was represented by first assistant corporation counsel Larkin. But on appeal, the corporation counsel himself, Charles Tenney, spoke for the city. Silverman knew that Tenney was a close friend to Mayor Wagner. "I had the feeling that he was not so bitterly opposed to us. He represented the city — not Moses himself. I suspected that Mayor Wagner felt that enough was enough. It's sheer speculation on my part, but Tenney may have sympathized with our legal position that it was none of the commissioner's business to insist on an admission fee. And also, it was a rather unpopular position to insist on charging fees if the people who were running it were willing to foot the bill. If the public could have free Shakespeare, why not?"

The fact that the Festival was "a nonprofit, educational corporation" — the very quality that drove some actors and directors away from it — proved to be a major asset in the suit. The commissioner had, in print, acknowledged the Festival's artistic and popular success. The deputy commissioner had estimated that 110,000 people had seen the performances in 1958 alone and had never contended that the productions of Shakespeare plays was not within the scope of park uses and purposes.

On June 17, the appellate division voted 5–0 in favor of the Festival.

"In no aspect of the case do we perceive a rational basis for the respondent's insistence upon an admission charge contrary to the wishes, policy and purposes of the petitioner," wrote Judge J. McNally.

> No useful park purpose is served by the requirement that petitioner make an admission charge and retain 90% thereof when petitioner desires no part of it. Such a requirement incident to the issuance of a park permit is clearly arbitrary, capricious and unreasonable.
>
> Petitioner concedes respondent may impose reasonable conditions toward proper and reasonable reimbursement. Under the circumstances, respondent is entitled to the opportunity to act thereon and we may not at this time mandate the issuance of the permit . . . the matter [is] remanded to the respondent for further proceedings consistent with the opinion filed herein.

The decision did not order the commissioner to issue a permit; it merely found his requirements "arbitrary, capricious and unreasonable" and ordered him to reconsider. Had Commissioner Moses wished to do so, he could have stuck to his demand of charging admission — thus provoking the wrath of public opinion. He could have taken the case to the court of appeals. Or he could have used the delaying tactics he had used so often before, forcing Papp to lose the summer season.

But instead, the day after the decision was rendered, Robert Moses said he would abide by it. "Dear Sir," he wrote in a letter delivered to Papp by hand:

> We are prepared to issue a permit for the presentation of Shakespeare in Central Park upon the basis of the Appellate Division decision.
>
> This means that funds in the minimum amount of $20,000 must be provided by you to put the area in condition for safe, controllable and reasonably satisfactory temporary use. . . . We must have these funds or a performance bond, or as an alternative in accordance with the Appellate Division decision, if you prefer, an entrance charge which will produce at least $20,000.
>
> In any event if you do not have $20,000 in cash available for construction, a request for this sum will have to be made to, and a sum advanced by, the Board of Estimate at its next meeting. As soon as construction funds are available, from whatever source, work will proceed as rapidly as possible.

"It was then that Joe had an absolute stroke of genius," Debuskey recalled. "By that time Moses had taken an awful beating. Joe knew it, and his instinct was to offer Moses an opportunity to appear generous, to join with the Festival in making the production possible." Papp replied by telegram:

> I would like to advise you that we have all the necessary funds to produce and operate one production, *Julius Caesar,* in the time that remains this summer. You must realize, of course, that lacking sufficient time, it is virtually impossible for us to raise the $20,000 you request in your letter.
>
> In any event, whether the necessary sum is 20,000 dollars, 10,000 dollars, or 5,000, it is apparent that every ounce of our energy and every moment of our time must immediately be directed toward the complex task of producing the play and cannot be diverted into an additional fund-raising campaign to meet your proviso.
>
> Therefore, in view of your reasonable alternative to request the appropriate sum and to have it advanced by the Board of Estimate at its next meeting, the Festival would be pleased to join with the Park Department to make this request as you think this is advisable. Since we are understandably anxious to obtain a permit without further delay we would sincerely appreciate to hear from you how best to proceed to achieve this end.

Moses had made no offer to request the sum from the Board of Estimate himself. But Papp's carefully worded telegram gave him an opportunity to end the controversy graciously. The following day, Moses formally asked the Board of Estimate to give the Department of Parks $20,000 to prepare Central Park for Shakespeare, and on June 25, the board approved a special resolution to approve the money.

Some people would later conclude that the commissioner had capitulated, embarrassed both by public opinion and the disapproval of many of the members of his social set. Others, who found capitulation inconsistent with over fifty years of Moses's behavior, thought the commissioner believed that neither Papp nor the Board of Estimate would come up with the $20,000.

Variants of "MOSES SURRENDERS!" were the headlines in all seven newspapers that day and, from Papp's point of view, the Festival was indeed the winner. Free Shakespeare was now a New York slogan, and Joseph Papp, a municipal hero. He was seen as a modern David who had vanquished the giant Goliath. His victory not only garnered thousands of contributions but the admiration of many of his contemporaries who would recall the battle for the rest of his life.

Two wealthy New Yorkers — neither of whom had ever attended a Festival production — offered Mayor Wagner $10,000 each to support the Festival. The first was Edward Bernays, a man who had started out as a theatrical press agent and was widely regarded as "the father of public relations." A nephew of Sigmund Freud and adviser to international leaders, Bernays was outraged by the commissioner's arrogance. "I had never heard of Papp before this controversy," he later said. "I didn't know if he was doing this because he loved Shakespeare, for the fame, or to satisfy his ego or because he was an idealist. I gave him the money because I felt he was setting a sound precedent that might be followed by others in New York as well as in other cities throughout the United States."

The second donor to step forward was Florence Sutro Anspacher, widow of poet and dramatist Louis K. Anspacher. She would become one of the Festival's principal donors. Mayor Robert Wagner emerged from the fray as Joseph Papp's most powerful ally, hosting Festival fundraisers, chairing a Mayor's Committee for Free Shakespeare, facilitating the construction of a permanent theater and persuading the municipality to vote it appropriations. In 1965, when he completed his last term of office, the municipality was allocating $420,000 to the Festival.

The first week in July, actors, stagehands, staff and director Stuart Vaughan — all of whom had been awaiting the outcome of the Papp-Moses controversy in various parts of the country — converged on the city to begin rehearsals of *Julius Caesar*. Vaughan, who had directed *Caesar* at the East River Amphitheater in 1956, pulled it together in no time and on opening night, August 3, the folding chairs and bleachers were packed. The producer walked out onto the stage and was greeted with a roar of a kind he had never before heard.

"I just stood there, let it wash over me," Papp remembered. "It was the most amazing experience to hear a couple of thousand people just yell at you. I felt they felt it was their triumph. Everything that subsequently happened in the play brought responses that you would never get otherwise, had there not been the background of the fight with Moses."

The reviewers did not miss the opportunity to poke fun at the commissioner. "Holy Moses, what a civilized institution the Central Park free Shakespeare is!" one wrote, and "This judge scores a solid victory for Joseph Papp in his tussle with Robert Moses," and "Worth the fight and worth a visit. But get there early to beat the crowds."

Six weeks past Papp's thirty-eighth birthday, the themes of *Julius Caesar* were as pertinent as they had been when he was twelve.

He wrote Moses a letter, thanking him for his request to the Board of Estimate. Then — almost as an afterthought — he added, "Having read in the newspapers that city departments are now preparing to submit requests for the 1960 capital budget, may I respectfully ask that the Department of Parks project the plan for a permanent amphitheatre at the Belvedere site, designs of which were drawn up by the Parks Department architects two years ago, at an estimated cost of $150,000."

On August 19, 1959, Robert Moses asked the New York City Planning Commission to allocate not $150,000 but one quarter of a million dollars for a Central Park amphitheater. The $250,000 project was approved by the Board of Estimate. And although the commissioner continued to put obstacles in Papp's way, Moses set in motion the process of building the Central Park amphitheater that would establish the New York Shakespeare Festival as a New York City institution.

EIGHT

The Making of the Delacorte

DURING THE FIRST MONTHS of 1960, Joseph Papp would hurry down Fifth Avenue from the Heckscher Theater to meet his designer, Eldon Elder, near the Metropolitan Museum of Art. Then, the producer would lead the way into Central Park, walking so fast that Elder had to strain to keep up with him. The two men would stride along the frozen playing fields of the Great Lawn to Belvedere Lake, then climb up the cliff beside it to the Tower, a castle-like structure that had been built in 1869 and now housed the equipment of the United States Weather Service.

The Tower, the lake and the dramatic cityscape behind them would later be reproduced in hundreds of posters, advertisements, photographs and cartoons. But in 1960 the site was just another place in a park that many New Yorkers viewed as too dangerous to enter, an empty plot of land on which Papp and Elder hoped an amphitheater would be built.

Although Robert Moses had personally requested that it be funded, the commissioner still refused to meet with the producer or to speak with him over the telephone. He continued to regard Papp, he wrote to a friend, as "an irresponsible Commie who doesn't keep his word or obey the rules." Stuart Constable continued to be antagonistic. The Parks Department would control the design and the construction and hold the authority to determine who used the structure. Papp would have no official claim on the theater. He would need to apply for a permit every year and, in order to receive it, provide the city with written proof of his solvency.

When, anxious to secure his position, the producer applied for his 1960 summer season in August of 1959 — nearly an entire year before he would use it — Moses replied coolly:

> Whether or not a permit will be issued at all depends upon the action of the Board of Estimate in connection with our request for permanent facilities. So far as your group is concerned, if the City does decide to provide permanent facilities, we would require definite, reliable, written assurance that you have the financial underwriting necessary to produce the theatre program you propose, whether on a free or low-charge basis.

Papp kept Moses regularly apprised of his fundraising efforts, sending him, among other things, a press release announcing the formation of "a permanent Mayor's Committee of distinguished citizens to assist the Festival in its annual campaign for funds." Moses had read it, then scrawled over the top: "Mr. Constable: What does this add up to?" Constable replied: "This adds up to City Hall support for a fellow who took the 5th Amendment 12 times in one day's testimony concerning whether or not he was or ever had been a Communist Party member or had recruited members for the Party. I'm afraid I no longer understand the meaning of the word 'distinguished' as applied to citizens of this town."

In February of 1960, Papp once again requested a permit for the summer. Like the biblical Jacob who had labored long to earn Rachel as his wife, he enumerated the conditions he had met:

> To date, the sum of $40,000 has been raised to finance the 1960 summer program (A corroborating bank statement is available upon request). The balance of the money required to complete the summer's underwriting is assured by the newly-formed Mayor's Committee . . . a fundraising dinner at the Commodore Hotel under the chairmanship of Joan Crawford, Sir Laurence Olivier and Howard Lindsay and the Festival's own Audience Sponsor Plan. We trust this meets with your approval and look forward to receiving the necessary permit.

Moses finally ordered a permit issued but shifted his opposition to new ground. Whenever Papp tried to meet with department engineers to discuss the amphitheater, Moses found an excuse for postponement. "We shall be happy to have your suggestions," Moses wrote on one occasion, "after a design contract has been awarded."

The commissioner's continuing obstructionism enraged Papp. The boyish producer was so sensitive to being patronized that he bristled whenever the Festival's lawyer affectionately called him "kiddo." Moses was such a frustration to him that Papp announced to his trustees, "We do not need the amphitheater in order to operate. If the building interferes, we'll do without it." So long as he trucked his theater around New York City, Papp reasoned, he was able to move quickly in or out. In the amphitheater, he would be a "tenant" and tenancy was an unacceptably vulnerable condition. "I never wanted a lease with the Parks Department and I never signed one," Papp noted later. "Technically, the Parks Department could throw me out at any time."

But Papp spared Eldon Elder a discussion of his problems with Moses. Since childhood, he had compartmentalized his life, keeping his own problems from his family as he now took pains to keep them from his artists. When he visited the Belvedere site with Elder, he discussed only the possibilities of the new amphitheater.

A tall, blond Kansan, Elder was three months older than Papp and the most accomplished theater professional then with the Festival. He had attended Emporia State College in the early 1940s with director Gladys Vaughan, studied theater design at Yale and had been hired by the Theatre Guild directly out of school. In 1958, when Vaughan brought him to see Papp, Elder had been designing Broadway shows for five years.

"When I met him," Joseph Papp would later write, "I was somewhat in awe. Here was a seasoned and successful Broadway designer with his own sparkling studio, showing a real interest in a poor and ragged outfit, with little credit to its name. . . ."

Elder later recalled that he was eager to work for the only man in New York regularly producing Shakespeare. He was inspired by Papp's dual vision of bringing theater to "dispossessed audiences" and developing an "American" approach to Shakespeare, as well as eager to be part of an artistic community. "I had the unusual experience of beginning my career on Broadway," he said, "and in some ways that was not a good thing. Working with Joe then, you had a sense that you were making a contribution to society."

The site, Elder thought, was ideal: picturesque, located in the very center of Central Park, easily accessible by bus and subway from any part of the city. Theatergoers wary of entering the Park at night were reassured by well-lit entrances and walkways and the familiarity of the Museum of Natural History on the West Side and the Metropolitan Museum on the East Side. Once at the Lake, there was plenty of level ground on which to picnic.

Access and safety were of primary importance to Papp. He talked to Elder about his childhood summers in Williamsburg and Brownsville, when air conditioning was unknown and anyone who could afford to get out of the city packed up and left. Those families like the Papirofskys who had no money for vacations and no car took the trolley to Prospect Park for relief from the heat and the oppressive absence of nature. He told Elder that city parks were probably New York's most democratic institution and that he wanted his theater to have a democratic design.

Two years earlier, Elder had designed the plain 40 foot by 40 foot platform on the grass that had replaced Papp's original tractor-trailer truck. The sun made rehearsals on it grueling. The wind and traffic wreaked havoc with the acoustics. The rain often interrupted performances and rehearsals and made the stage as slippery as a skating rink. Each production played about two and a half weeks, giving the crews a scant week to strike, set up and rehearse. The carpenters brought their own tools and built the sets on the lawn. The costume shop was a tent. "We couldn't have tech rehearsals during the day because of the light," Elder remembered, "so we'd come staggering out of the park at dawn."

When Papp and Elder talked in the frozen park, they discussed ways to minimize the problems. Papp had visited the theater Tyrone Guthrie had built at Stratford, Ontario. He was familiar with the acoustics and seating at the Hollywood Bowl in Los Angeles. Elder had worked at the open-air Municipal Opera Theater in St. Louis. Ambient noise, they agreed, had been part of the Festival since its debut at the East River Amphitheater. They could do nothing about the elements or the traffic or the din of yells and cheers coming from the neighboring ballfields. But since his theater lay directly beneath the helicopter route between La Guardia and Newark airports, Papp negotiated to have it rerouted for the summer. And he persuaded the owners of the Carlyle Hotel on 77th Street and Madison Avenue to turn off the floodlight that lit up their towers while his plays were running.

The notion of a "democratic theater," moreover, was something Elder could implement. There would be more than two thousand seats but Papp wanted no one to feel he or she had to use opera glasses to understand what was happening onstage. He wanted each seat to be as good as the next, comfortable to sit in for three hours, offering an unobstructed view. He wanted the amphitheater to be comfortable for the actors as well, with ample dressing rooms and easy access to and from the stage. Theatergoers would wait for their tickets on one of the curving walkways and, if they got tired, could sit down on a bench or on the grass to ease the wait.

Elder got so fired up by these discussions with Papp that he would hurry back to his studio to translate them into design. Papp would hurry back to the Heckscher, which he had been given rent-free by the New York City Department of Welfare. Some days he found the lobby filled with cots accommodating an overflow of children who were wards of the department. Always, he found waiting for him the endless tasks of building up his organization.

As 1960 began, there was a marked discrepancy between Papp's situation and his public image. Despite his great victory over Moses, the producer was relatively powerless. He worked at a desk crammed under a staircase in the windowless box office of the Heckscher Theater. He made less of a salary than he had made as a stage manager at CBS — in 1961, his annual income was $8,807. He had one female assistant to do secretarial work and a male staff of three, all devoted to him and to the theater and able to make do on subsistence salaries.

The first was Hilmar Sallee, later described by a colleague as the kind of eccentric southerner Truman Capote might have invented. A temperamental perfectionist, Sallee came from Arkansas, favored straw hats and seersucker suits and had an impressive knowledge of both politics and theater. He had come to Emmanuel Church in 1955 as an actor, then worked as stage manager. By 1960, he was general manager. For ten years, Sallee was Papp's righthand man, negotiating contracts and maintaining relations with the various city agencies, startling bureaucrats with his sudden cackle. He managed the office, and kept Papp's schedule as well as a vase on his desk filled with gladioli.

Sallee was assisted by David Black, an affable young midwesterner whose graduate studies in drama were forever interrupted when a friend told him about an odd theater job in Central Park. Papp hired Black to manage the Park crowds, and to restrain, as Black would later say, "the little old ladies who claimed they had seats in the front row." In the eighteen years that followed, he became bookkeeper, budget-maker, audience development director and official chronicler of the Festival in addition to house manager, learning on the job as the Festival grew into a million-dollar enterprise.

"I basically did not like Joe Papp," Black recalled. "As a gay man, I did not find him sexually attractive. I learned early on that he could be very cold and cruel. People who were close to him could be cut off at a moment's notice with no regret. I saw him hurt people's feelings.

"But while I didn't *like* him, I did admire him. My time in the military had conditioned me to the importance of culture to the general public. I was stationed in Germany when Stuttgart, Mannheim and Frankfurt were in ruins. The first things they rebuilt were the train stations, the opera houses and the theaters. Joe believed that government has an obligation to support theater and I found him to be a man of his convictions. I shared some of his anger toward the establishment and I worked hard not so much for him but for the dream. It was Joe's belief — often expressed — that any theater company that settled for the status quo and stopped growing was already in the process of dying. That meant for us on the staff there was no such thing as rest. It was not like any other theater job. I remember Joe saying that our responsibility was to encourage the health and growth of the art of theater and I found myself performing work I never dreamed I could do."

The third man was Bernard Gersten, who joined the Festival in 1960, becoming Papp's associate producer four years later and, as many theater people thought, his alter ego. The ebullient, articulate and somewhat maternal Gersten was Papp's perfect complement: playful where Papp was serious, gregarious where Papp was reserved, conciliatory where Papp was brusque. "Bernie was a diplomat of great proportion," recalled a colleague. "That was very important: it made him able over a period of many years to adapt to Joe's ego and sudden changes of strategy."

As associate producer, Gersten had most of the responsibilities that, in other theaters, come with the title managing director, but because of his long, close friendship with Papp and the mutual dependency that evolved between them, he had more. He supervised the elements of theater production, orchestrating people, schedules, resources, the availability and flow of capital. He oversaw the administration of the Festival and was principally responsible for its finances and budget, its contracts, its marketing, its advertising, its graphics, its fundraising and — importantly — its relations with the city, the New York State Council for the Arts and the National Endowment for the Arts. He became Papp's right hand.

Gersten shared many things with Papp. He was about the same age, came from a Jewish immigrant — albeit more prosperous — family, had served in the special services during the war. He had been a Communist, worked at the Actors' Lab and had even testified before HUAC on the same day as Papp. In Los Angeles, where the two had first met, Gersten had lived briefly with the Papirofskys and driven them to the hospital the night their son, Michael, was born. When Joe and Sylvia Papirofsky separated, she and the baby had moved into Gersten's bachelor apartment.

Professionally, Gersten had worked on Broadway and at the American Shakespeare Festival in Stratford, as stage manager, lighting director, technical director, production and general manager. Where Papp had always been on the fringe of the theater community, Gersten was in its mainstream. Where Papp was to some extent a loner, with few ties to either the academic or the commercial spheres, Gersten was well connected. Rather than taking on a separate department of his own, Gersten became what he called "the board against which Joe bounced his ideas" and "his handler in the sense boxers have handlers — to encourage or restrain them as they did it, to whisper in their ear, not to let them get into trouble or to show them an opening."

What Papp required more than anything else, Gersten later recalled, "was someone to be a buddy, to pick up the slack, play good cop when he was a bad cop." Much later, when the two had parted ways Gersten would describe himself as Kent to Papp's King Lear. "What would you with me, sir?" Lear asks Kent. "I would serve you, sir," Kent replies. Some Festival members viewed their relation as an unconsummated love affair; others as the happiest of partnerships, the best in the business.

During 1960 and 1961, however, even the "good cop–bad cop" team was unable to prod the City of New York into addressing the amphitheater with anything other than glacial slowness. Apart from the design, every step in the planning process had to be discussed by committee, contracts had to be announced and awarded, the site had to be prepared. The landfill on which the amphitheater was to be built was wet, due to seepage from Belvedere Lake. Before engineers could put in the concrete foundation for the stage and piers for the amphitheater, they had to construct a riprap wall consisting of stones to dam up the water. For that wall, they planned to use boulders that were dug up at other city construction sites. Each one of *those* sites had its own planning, contractual and scheduling problems.

Meanwhile, artistic director Stuart Vaughan had left the Festival to take a full-time job and Papp had to plan the 1960 summer season alone. Having established the precedent of mounting three plays per summer and unwilling to break it, he had to find three directors. He decided to direct *Henry V* himself, engaged Alan Schneider to direct *Measure for Measure* and Gerald Freedman to direct *The Taming of the Shrew*.

Schneider remained a busy freelancer. Gerald Freedman, however, would spend the next decade working closely with Papp. A versatile artist who had a cantorial tenor voice and had originally wished to become a painter, Freedman was from Lorain, Ohio. He had entered theater by painting sets for student productions at Northwestern University, arrived in New York in 1950 and had been director Jerome Robbins's assistant on the musicals *Bells Are Ringing* and *West Side Story*. He had also already directed two productions of Shakespeare, and after seeing the Festival's production of *As You Like It* wrote Papp a letter saying that he could have directed it better. Papp invited Freedman to stop by.

"Joe's office was tiny and you had to stoop when you went in because the ceiling sloped at the angle of the stairs," Freedman later recalled. "I wasn't accustomed to luxury but I was used to producers having an *office*. This was not a big operation, I thought. But I was very excited by Joe. There was no formality about him, no barriers at all. The most compelling thing was his directness. He was unequivocal. *Immediate.* There was no 'I'll get back to you.' He took me into the theater that very first time and said, 'You're going to direct here.'"

Freedman then heard nothing from Papp for two full years until, in February of 1960, Papp called. "He said 'Hello.' Then, 'How would you like to direct *Taming of the Shrew* in Central Park?'" Freedman directed regularly at the Festival for over a decade, eventually becoming artistic director, working for next to nothing, as did Gladys Vaughan.

Vaughan had first arrived at the Festival as "Stuart's wife," taking notes for his productions, doing his errands and serving as a sounding board for his ideas. The daughter of a well-known midwestern Mennonite minister, she had memorized stories from the King James version of the Bible as a child, and dated her ease with Shakespearean language to that time. Gladys Vaughan had a graduate degree in theater from Stanford and had studied theater companies in England on a Fulbright Scholarship. But, in the manner of the time, she supported her husband's ambitions rather than her own. She took jobs as a television women's news editor and talk-show host to support them but quit when asked.

Now divorced, and with her husband working elsewhere, Gladys Vaughan worked as Papp's and Gerald Freedman's assistant, taking *their* notes, giving them feedback on their ideas. But Papp came to rely on her eye and to value both her casting ability and her nurturing of actors. Many Festival actors found her more interesting, patient and wiser than her male counterparts. It was Vaughan who cast James Earl Jones as Othello and worked with him for months. Papp codirected with Vaughan. Then, he gave her separate billing, making her the first female director at the Festival and one of the few women directors then working in America.

Although the producer could not offer them year-round employment or even pay them more than a token fee, both Vaughan and Freedman were thrilled to work regularly on Shakespeare, personally drawn to Papp and excited by his vision of an alternative theater.

In 1960, American voters replaced Dwight D. Eisenhower with Papp's contemporary John F. Kennedy. During his campaign, Kennedy reiterated a message of service, self-sacrifice and generational change. In his inaugural address, Kennedy urged Americans to "ask not what your country can do for you; ask what you can do for your country." To theater people, twelve-hour days in Central Park working on Free Shakespeare was a version of Kennedy's New Frontier.

In January 1961, as the new president took office, the Parks Department announced that the lowest construction bid for the Central Park amphitheater had come in at $370,000 — $120,000 over the budget appropriation that the city had made. The project looked dead. But the new parks commissioner, Newbold Morris, the old-line civic leader who had replaced Robert Moses, invited publisher and philanthropist George Delacorte to lunch and persuaded him to supply the needed funds.

People would later describe the Festival of that time as a place of many such small miracles, an oasis, an artistic Camelot. "I count it as a blessing in my life to have been there," David Amram, who composed music for twenty-nine Shakespeare productions, recalled. "Those years in the park taught me to say a prayer of thanks that I could make my living in the arts, feed my children, do something that I loved and something that would make other people happy." Amram reworked his Festival music into concert pieces and borrowed Papp's idea of Free Shakespeare, organizing free young people's concerts across the country.

Papp exerted an even greater influence on actors. He employed large numbers of them and tried hard to make auditions a less painful process. Between his summer and winter seasons, he might cast up to five large productions every year. It was regular, satisfying employment and could keep actors performing until they were "discovered." If Papp found an actor interesting but not right for a role, he communicated to that actor the real possibility that he or she would be called back for another. Actors also noted that, even at the very beginning of his career, Papp was willing to advocate publicly for their concerns.

"The nomadic existence of the player in the United States remains pretty much as it was before the establishment of permanent acting companies during the reign of Queen Elizabeth," he testified before a congressional committee in 1961. "Today he isn't being thrown into jail with thieves and vagabonds for touring without a crest of patronage, but he still has great difficulty in taking out a loan or signing a lease. Banks and landlords consider him a credit risk without visible means of support. . . .

"To belabor the economic conditions of the performer without examining its devastating effect on his skills is to treat only a small part of the problem. Imagine, if you will, what would happen to the techniques of a surgeon who was able to practice only thirty days out of the year. Julie Harris — one of our most talented actresses — gave a total of 152 perfomances on Broadway in the last five years! How many others, like Uta Hagen, have given fewer?

"A hit show has as many pitfalls for the creative performer as unemployment. The necessity for Broadway producers to run a play as long as it is profitable subjects the actor to repeated performances without relief. A large, rich role can sustain an actor over longer periods of time; however, parts in the classics, where most of these roles exist, are few and far between. Broadway as a rule shies away from the noncommercial plays of Shakespeare, Ibsen, Chekhov, Molière and Aeschylus, just to name a few.

"But how many actors obtain large roles of any kind? Pity the poor Equity member who has been seeking employment for eight months and then lands a five-line part in a Broadway hit play. Sure, it's nice to have the take-home pay, but without the means of keeping his techniques sharp, his chances of growing as an actor are considerably diminished. . . .

"'Off-season' is the norm for actors; 'full-time employment,' an alien-sounding phrase in the theater. As for other desirable employment to take the place of working in a play, there is no such thing. Actors must act. Their art, like any other, is a lifetime affair. There are no off-seasons in the creative development of a serious performer. The only way the actor can be assured of continuity and development is within the structure of a permanent repertory theater. Society must be prepared to offer him this security. Lawyers have courts; doctors, hospitals. The actor's institution is the theater."

In private, Papp emphasized that actors were forced to sell themselves over and over again in "barbaric, undignified and intolerable" conditions. "The kind of nature you need is something that's very difficult," he said. "You yourself are the instrument and aside from all the sociological problems that an actor has — the unemployment and financial problems — the concentration on self is something which I feel is not conducive to a happy life. A good actor is going to feel things very, very hard. A lot of the very sensitive ones cannot bear the indignities of the profession and disappear. A lot of those who remain because of their thick skins are not very good.

"I didn't want to lead that kind of life so I felt I would take the lesser role in the theater of administrator and director. It is a lesser role because the main figure in the theater is the actor."

When he said that, Papp had a very specific kind of actor in mind. He and his codirectors thought that actors should look more like Festival audiences, that they should have the same physical imperfections and that they should reflect the same ethnic diversity. "Our audience is made up largely of people who have never seen professional theater," he wrote for a symposium featuring directors of Shakespeare in which he emphasized the centrality of casting to his aesthetic. "But they have been to the movies and they watch television . . . [and] insist that we serve them a style of Shakespeare they can relate to, a Shakespeare that is believable.

"We look for the answer in our casting. In the choice of the actor, we determine the style of our productions. To imbue our plays with the kind of reality understood by our modern audiences, we select the actor who best communicates it. We seek blood-and-guts actors . . . actors who have the stamp of truth on everything they say or do. This humanizes the language and replaces verse-reading and singsong recitation — the mark of old-fashioned classical acting — with an understandable, living speech. The English tradition will not satisfy an American audience. What we have developed in this country through the influence of the Russian Stanislavsky is a more human form of acting. . . ."

Colleen Dewhurst was the first of Papp's blood-and-guts actors to become a star. In 1954, the Canadian-born, husky-voiced actress was living in a cold-water flat on West 50th Street between Ninth and Tenth avenues with "a bathtub in the kitchen, a john in the hallway, and no heat" during what she would look back on as the "most excruciating" period of her life. She had no agent and no résumé to speak of when she received what she later called the most important telephone call of her life. On the line was Joseph Papp, who said he was the husband of Peggy Bennion, an actress in Harold Clurman's late-night acting class, and the director of a fledgling Shakespeare workshop in a Lower East Side church. The producer, who was then desperately trying to stem the turnover of actors in his first, ultimately no-show *Romeo and Juliet,* offered her the role of Juliet.

Dewhurst was stunned. For years, she had been told that she was too strong, too large-boned and too tall to be a leading lady. "I couldn't have done Juliet when I was twelve," Dewhurst told Papp and hung up. But the producer called back. He asked her to come down to Emmanuel Church anyway and cast her in an evening of scenes he called "Shakespeare's Women." One year later, while Dewhurst was on summer tour in Pennsylvania, Papp tracked her down and offered her the role of Kate in *The Taming of the Shrew* at the East River Amphitheater.

The producer was candid about the rudimentary rehearsal conditions, the lack of even token pay and the likely absence in the audience of other producers, agents or theater critics. Against all advice, because she felt what Papp was doing to be "real theater," Dewhurst left her paying job and took the role that she considered the start of her theater career.

George C. Scott arrived at the Festival a few months later. For seven years he had been trying to make a living as an actor, and when he walked into the Heckscher Theater to audition for the title role in *Richard III*, he was unemployed and desperate. At twenty-nine, Scott had worked as a waiter, a construction worker and an IBM proof machine operator. He had spent four years in the marines, earned a journalism degree and played in more than 130 stock and repertory companies. After reading for Richard, he was called back for a second audition, which he later remembered as dismal. He was so upset, he recalled, that he asked Papp for a third audition. He won the role, and one of the actresses who came to see his performance was Colleen Dewhurst.

Dewhurst and Scott later married. Both maintained a strong connection to the Festival and felt indebted to Papp. Although both became icons of the American theater, they remembered years of exclusion from it and the fight to maintain their self-esteem in the face of repeated rejection. That rejection, they felt, was not only for their failure to correspond to the features of a given role that every actor faces but in the knowledge that their very essence as actors was unacceptable.

There was, of course, an entire group of actors whose essence was unacceptable. It included Gloria Foster, Ellen Holly, James Earl Jones and Roscoe Lee Browne — all African-American actors — as well as actors who were Latino or Asian. Minority actors were generally deemed inappropriate for Shakespearean roles. When James Earl Jones approached the Festival in 1961, he thought it prudent to request the role of Abhorson in *Measure for Measure*, because his face was covered with an executioner's mask.

Ellen Holly had been twenty-six and, like Colleen Dewhurst, out of work when Papp telephoned in 1957. "I had made a splashy, critically acclaimed Broadway debut in a play based on Alan Paton's book *Too Late the Phalarope*," she said, "in which a South African native girl mesmerizes a pillar of the Afrikaaner community, enmeshes him in an affair and brings him to wrack and ruin. But I was commercially unmarketable, caught in a Catch-22, considered inappropriate for white roles because I was black and inappropriate for black roles because I looked too much like white. When I played black, I would always be required to wear dark face and body makeup.

"Given this mind-bending scenario in which your own personhood has to be constantly obliterated for you to be deemed acceptable, the Festival fell into my lap as something of a miracle — not only the sole venue where I could work with some kind of consistency, but the sole venue in which it was okay to work with my own face. The most remarkable thing about Joe was the color-blind casting he practiced as naturally as breathing, decades before it became the chic thing to do. Talent was the sole casting criterion and skin color was, for him, a completely irrelevant issue. For anyone to cast this way, not just once or twice as a matter of political posturing but as a matter of routine over the course of a career, was unprecedented."

Most Festival actors — black and white — loved Papp for creating a place where they could work. They forgave him his abruptness, his bad temper, his acerbic remarks. Ed Sherin, then an actor in *Twelfth Night,* would later recall an incident not atypical of Papp as a director. Puzzled over why his character came onstage when he did, Sherin decided to ask Papp. "Because I'm paying you, that's why," Papp snapped angrily.

Later a director himself, Sherin would say, "A director works better with tunnel vision and Joe could never involve himself totally in anything he directed. He was often impatient and he could be peremptory and unsubtle. He was the kind of man who could say to an actor: *'Do it because I'm telling you to do it. I don't have the time to screw around with you right now!'* But that doesn't change the fact that I, too, felt it was a Camelot."

People who worked at the Festival in the early 1960s found Papp's ideology reflected by a community that was, even by theater standards, extraordinarily mixed. Festival members came from a wide variety of racial, social and ethnic groups; both their general education and specific training in theater skills ranged from the minimal to the most accomplished; and no one school of thought or wellspring of talent seemed to prevail. Papp seemed determinedly egalitarian and inclusive, discouraging hierarchy, encouraging raw talent in everything from carpentry to singing and urging his impatient professionals to be generous and to teach their skills to novitiates.

"I found Joe one of the few people I could talk to in New York," recalled an actress then apprenticing at the Festival. "I was studying with Lee Strasberg and trying very hard to hide a background of Kentucky poverty. With Strasberg, I felt like I had to remake myself every day. I remember Joe, on the other hand, talked like a woman, about feelings as well as ideas. He would read me Shakespeare's sonnets. He also seemed to stand behind his opinions. I didn't know anyone else like that. And next to Strasberg, he seemed so sane."

But while many early Festival members would remember those years with nostalgia, Papp would remember them also as years when he was desperate for money and raising it alone. After performances, the producer always came out on the stage to make an appeal for contributions. Sometimes, there would be calls of "Author!" from the audience and Papp would get into his pitch by announcing that although he had not written the play, he needed the money to produce it.

But the joke wore thin. "He used to come home and say: 'I can't face another year of it,'" Peggy Papp recalled. "He had felt humiliated in his childhood by the lack of money. And, unlike other producers who raised what they needed on the gamble that they'd get a lot back, Joe raised money just to see it disappear."

In a paradox that was to become more acute over the decades, the more successful the New York Shakespeare Festival became, the more money Papp needed. In 1955, he had been able to establish the Shakespeare Workshop with a few hundred dollars and contributions in kind. In 1961, when he produced Shakespeare at The Heckscher and at The Wollman Memorial Skating Rink, the producer spent $160,000. He told everyone he knew about his dilemma, and that fall, a friend sent him a professional fundraiser.

Herta Danis was the first nontheater person to join the Festival. A short, impeccably coiffed woman who had raised hundreds of thousands of dollars for Jewish charities, she was ten years older than Papp and appalled by what she called "that hole in the wall at the Heckscher." But Papp cleared a place for her to sit under the sloping ceiling and she soon forgot her surroundings. "He was just an enchanting young man," Danis recalled. "I saw he had a tremendous ego and would be difficult to work for. But he charmed me and when you're fundraising, charm is important."

In January 1962, Danis joined the staff as the Festival's first fundraiser. Until that time, raising money had been a prolonged act of legerdemain by a producer who believed "Money will follow art." As Robert Moses had noted, Papp never had the cash in hand to pay for his projects and most of his attempts at fundraising had failed. Papp knew no rich people. He had no contacts in the foundation world and, because he knew no one, sent in his hundreds of grant applications cold.

Many of those letters elicited no response at all; others, curt rejections.

(*From L to R*) Vetta, Joseph, Sam and Rhoda Papirofsky, 1925 *(Rhoda Lifschutz)*

Joe Papirofsky and his speech teacher, Eulalie Spence, 1938 *(Lee Cahn)*

Joe Papirofsky's playground: Lindsey Park in 1929 *(Brooklyn Historical Society)*

Newlyweds Joe Papirofsky
and Betty Ball in 1941
(Nadine Weiss Bianco)

Joe Papirofsky and
daughter Susan, 1945
(Phillip Martel)

Papirofsky daughter
Barbara and her mother,
Irene Ball *(Barbara Mosser)*

The Papirofsky brothers
on leave from World War
II *(Phillip Martel)*

(*From L to R*) Joe Papirofsky, Roman "Bud" Bohnen, Robert Karnes and Bernard Gersten at the Actors' Laboratory, 1948 *(Papp Estate)*

Joe Papirofsky teaching at the California Labor School, 1948 *(Papp Estate)*

CBS stage manager Joe
Papirofsky at work *(Papp
Estate)*

Emmanuel Presbyterian
Church: Joe Papirofsky's
first theater *(George E.
Joseph)*

Hauling equipment into the East River Amphitheater, 1956 *(Mort Schreiber)*

Stuart Vaughan directing *Romeo and Juliet*, 1957 *(George E. Joseph)*

With Colleen Dewhurst reading *Taming of the Shrew* review, 1956 *(Papp Estate)*

Tony, Peggy, Joseph and Miranda Papp, 1962 *(George E. Joseph)*

George C. Scott in *The Merchant of Venice*, 1962 *(George E. Joseph)*

Free Shakespeare at the Delacorte *(George E. Joseph)*

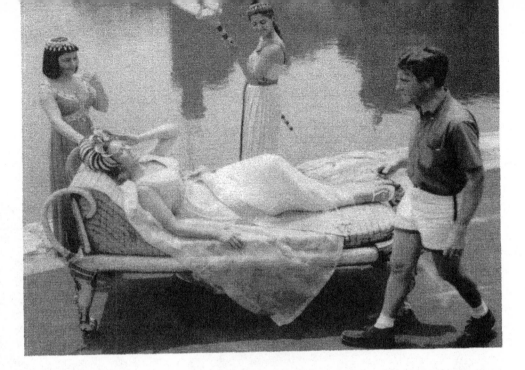

Papp directing Colleen
Dewhurst (reclining) as
Cleopatra, 1963 (*Papp
Estate*)

James Earl Jones and
Julienne Marie in *Othello*,
1964 (*Bert Andrews*)

The Mobile rolls into a neighborhood, 1964 *(George E. Joseph)*

Early architectural drawing adapting former reading room of Astor Library for use as the Anspacher Theater *(Giorgio Cavaglieri)*

The Public Theater *(New York Shakespeare Festival)*

Theatrial poster for *Hair,*
1967 *(New York Shakespeare
Festival)*

Nathan George and Ron
O'Neal in Charles
Gordone's *No Place to Be
Somebody,* 1969 *(George E.
Joseph)*

Asa Gim and David Selby
in David Rabe's *Sticks and
Bones*, 1971
(Friedman-Abeles)

(*From L to R*) Michael
McGuire, Paul Sorvino,
Richard A. Dysart, Charles
Durning and Walter
McGinn in Jason Miller's
That Championship Season,
1972 *(Friedman-Abeles)*

Papp and playwrights *(L to R)* Jason Miller,
John Guare and David Rabe
(Friedman-Abeles)

Papp, Gersten and company of *Two Gents*,
1972 *(New York Shakespeare Festival)*

But by refusing to take no for an answer, Papp had managed to get two $10,000 grants in 1957 and a $25,000 grant in 1959. The influential Ford Foundation, under the leadership of W. McNeil Lowry, steadily refused to give Papp a grant of any kind. Lowry believed institutional theaters should support themselves through their box-office receipts — a condition that made the Festival, with its credo of "Free Shakespeare," ineligible. In 1962, the Ford Foundation would grant $6.1 million to nine American repertory theater companies — including $250,000 to the Shakespeare Festival at Stratford, Connecticut — but not a dime to Papp. The producer was so enraged that he took his case to the press, thereby antagonizing Ford Foundation executives, who refused him funds for nearly a decade more.

When Lowry himself was asked to describe Joseph Papp for a foundation memoir, he first replied, "On this tape, I can't," then called him, "one of the greatest politicians I know. His first ambition was to be parks commissioner, then mayor. . . . He's not afflicted with modesty but he has always been a tremendous wheeler and dealer and promoter and innovator and a horrible force to contend with because — well, for example, the description of his reception by Mr. Pusey at the Mellon Foundation was that he ended up practically throwing the furniture at Pusey. . . . Pusey is not the type of person who is used to that kind of applicant and he thought he was dealing with a madman. . . . [Papp's] relations with the Ford Foundation have been those of complete antagonism on his part and coolness on my part."

Danis long recalled the expletives Papp would emit when asked about the Ford Foundation, the letters he wrote that she persuaded him to put in a drawer, the rages and moods she could not always predict and took pains to avoid. "He was very vulnerable, not sure of himself most of the time and he covered up with this shield of tremendous arrogance," she said. "I remember, early on, I asked him whether he knew anyone British whom he could get to come to a function. He said, quite seriously, *You want the queen? I'll write her.*' And he would have done it. He could be smooth as silk.

"But then he could get rubbed the wrong way, feel criticized or challenged in a way he didn't like and then he'd cut you dead. One of my friends whom I'd solicited as a donor came out of meeting with him furious. She said: 'Why do I bother with such a *schmuck?*'"

Papp said he always tried to avoid feeling like a beggar when talking to potential donors: "Whether I was talking to an individual or to a foundation executive, my attitude was: nobody's doing me a favor by giving my theater money. 'You're *set up* to give money!' I would say to foundation executives: 'You don't *have* to give your money to me, but let's understand each other. You can't exist without people like me. You are mandated by law to spend your money, and I'm giving you an opportunity to put it into something very important.'"

In 1960, the producer determined to raise money through an Audience Sponsor Program, a subscription plan which guaranteed a limited number of theatergoers seats to three shows for $7.50. This innocuous proposal provoked an impassioned ideological debate among the trustees. Merle Debuskey, citing the Moses affair and the entire history of the Festival to date, argued that the Festival's policy of free unreserved seats had kept it pure and pristine. "All the way down the line, from the reviews and the public's being aroused, we were very specific that we are in no way commercial," he said. "In effect, we're advertising reserved seats. We're departing from our little ivory tower."

"Let's dirty the tower a little bit," countered another trustee. And Joseph Papp concluded, "We need the money to sustain us." In 1960, proceeds from the Audience Sponsor Program accounted for about one-third of the Festival's income.

One of the reasons for that was that the Festival's board of trustees did not give the Festival much money. It had evolved from the small group of men who had met in Reverend Boyer's church to a larger group but still contained no major donor. The Festival's most public benefactors to date — Edward Bernays and Florence Anspacher — had supported the Festival because they disliked Robert Moses, *not* because they loved Free Shakespeare. George Delacorte had given his money to the Parks Department, not to the Festival. Board chairman Burt Martinson, heir to Martinson's Coffee, was primarily a patron of the dance. Stanley Lowell, who did *pro bono* political work, Debuskey, who did *pro bono* publicity, Robert Montgomery, who did *pro bono* legal work, and Robert Whitehead, a prestigious figure in the theater community, were all assets, but none gave money.

The absence of box-office receipts, major donors and foundations left government funding as Papp's main hope of support. The producer had, from the start, envisaged building his theater "on the bedrock of civic responsibility," approaching New York City's Board of Estimate as early as 1958. He had been rejected. But in 1959, he asked the Board of Education for $50,000 for a schools tour and got it. His success prompted him to repeat the Board of Education request the following year, together with a request for $60,000 from the mayor — making a total of $110,000 in municipal funds to meet his operating expenses for the summer of 1961.

"The fact that the city is investing a quarter of a million dollars to construct permanent facilities in Central Park makes it all the more important that it help to guarantee part of the operating costs," Papp explained to his board members. "In addition it has become absolutely neccessary to raise actors' salaries from the ridiculous $45 a week to the little less ridiculous $75 a week."

Papp's request of $110,000 in direct municipal subsidy caused a stir. When the Board of Estimate held its hearing on the school tour funds, Bronx borough president James Lyons and Queens borough president John Clancy once again cited Papp's HUAC testimony and refused their support. When the Board of Education held its public hearing, nine of the fifteen people who spoke raised the issue, and Charles Silver, the board president, asked Papp to issue a public statement denouncing communism. By that time, Papp had had fifteen years of Red-baiting and he was fed up.

In a draft of a press statement, Papp wrote:

In all good conscience I cannot submit to the tyranny of those office-holders seeking political advancement, holier-than-thou-veterans organizations and self-appointed super-patriots who have taken upon themselves the role of establishing criteria for my opinions, politics and associations. . . . I exercised a constitutional privilege when questioned by the House Un-American Activities Committee on my past associations. I invoked the Fifth Amendment to protect myself and others from unjust abuse and persecution. The public record will show my statement under oath that I am not a Communist. It will further show that one congressman congratulated me for being so open and free. But those whose hatred cannot abide unorthodoxy turn their venom on me — howl that I "hid behind the Fifth." Not having the thumb-screw and the rack they resort to the modern devices of vilification, character assassination and mud-slinging to extract the confession. And nothing less will satisfy them but crawling and penance. As an American, this I cannot and will not do.

Finally, both appropriations were approved by the Board of Estimate, *over and above* the $250,000 pledged for construction of the amphitheater. But it was clear to both Papp and fundraiser Danis that the Festival needed to develop a base of private donors. They planned a reception at the mayor's residence: Gracie Mansion.

The guest list included people who would otherwise never have been in the same room: foundation directors; mainstream Jewish philanthropists; the (at that time) tiny contingent of Wall Street CEOs who gave money to the arts; "Left-Wingers with Money"; a sprinkling of Republicans and Democrats active in city politics.

The major glitch in the effort, however, was the producer himself. Although Papp would earn a reputation for extraordinary fundraising, he disliked it as much as other financial matters. When he left his CBS job, Papp had been earning $16,000 a year. At the Festival, he paid himself only $10,000. When the board, concerned about his family, voted Papp a salary of $300 per week, Papp first refused it, then agreed to accept $250.

Peggy Papp disliked fundraising and finances as much as her husband. As a girl, she had preferred herding cattle or even milking cows to cooking for the hired hands the way *her* mother did. Mrs. Papp had, in 1958, left the theater to study social work, and was now embarked on a career as a psychotherapist. Although she was willing to attend openings with her husband, pose for family photographs and even chat with women's page reporters about chicken recipes, she was unavailable as hostess.

Mrs. Danis arranged for the producer to meet with potential donors in the clubs and restaurants of midtown Manhattan and made sure to be there herself to keep an eye on him. When a prominent New Yorker arranged a luncheon with a few of his associates at the Yale Club and Papp arrived in muddy boots — straight from Central Park — she sent him into the men's room to clean up. "He met with the group and he was fine," she recalled. "No one ever knew he was quaking inside. But I knew it. I knew he was thinking: *Why am I here begging for money? They should be throwing it at me! Who are all these people? They're not my kind.* But *his* kind of people couldn't help him and he knew it. So he had to learn to deal with rich people. And he became more tolerant of the rich as the years went by."

After a few months of such luncheons, a photograph of Papp wedged between two young society women appeared in the *New York Times*. "Springtime Cocktail Dance on May 6 is planned by Miss Catherine O'Brien, left, and Miss Edwardina O'Brien, with Joseph Papp, president of the New York Shakespeare Festival," read the caption. "The event is scheduled to take place at the Harwyn Club."

Mrs. Danis was also responsible for moving the Festival to midtown Manhattan. By late spring of 1962, Papp was renting an eighth-floor suite in the Great Northern, a raggedy hotel on West 57th Street just south of Central Park. The Russian Tea Room was a few doors to the west; Henri Bendel, Bonwit Teller and Bergdorf Goodman two blocks to the east. Soon there was a group of well-dressed volunteers working on the files.

The move coincided with the long-awaited completion of the Central Park amphitheater, for which Eldon Elder did not design the sets. That winter, Elder had received an emergency call, asking him to fix the new stage at the Stratford Festival. "It was February or March," Elder said. "All the work would have been done before Joe's season in the park, and I said yes. I should have gone to Joe and told him I was doing it. But I didn't. Maybe I knew it would be a problem and wanted to avoid a confrontation. Instead, he heard about it from other people. We finally had a meeting and Joe told me I had to choose between him and Langner. I chose Langner, who had given me my first job."

Elder never understood how Papp could view his helping out his first employer as disloyalty. But Papp was resolute. He hired designer Ming Cho Lee, who had initially inquired about working for the Festival a few years earlier, to design the sets for the inaugural production, and Elder never worked at the Festival again.

Press coverage of the new, as yet unnamed, 2,300-seat amphitheater began with Brooks Atkinson reporting that it looked "like the most useful Shakespeare stage in the country." But, almost immediately, attention shifted to Papp's choice of production: *The Merchant of Venice*, starring George C. Scott as Shylock.

Merchant was a provocative choice. Many Jews found it offensive, and its presentation had often been accompanied by protest. His choice of George C. Scott to play Shylock was also unorthodox. The producer thought Shylock should be consumed with a "magisterial, biblical rage" at centuries of mistreatment by Christians. "Never turn the other cheek," Papp directed the actor who would soon portray General Patton. "You want to hurt these people that have hurt you. Don't softsell it. People will understand your anger."

He may have been describing his own anger, for *The Merchant of Venice* was Papp's official coming out as a Jew. Since the late 1930s, he had not corrected people who assumed that he was of Polish or Russian or Greek extraction. Although the producer rarely missed a Passover *seder* with his brother Phillip and his parents in Brooklyn, he rarely saw his parents during the rest of the year. He never proffered the information that he was Jewish. Reporter Arthur Gelb and Deputy Mayor Stanley Lowell — himself a Jew who had changed his name from Lowenbraun a few years before — would both recall asking but obtaining no reply.

In 1962, when WCBS-TV announced that it would televise *The Merchant of Venice* live, the New York Board of Rabbis demanded cancellation of the program, calling the play "a distortion and defamity of our people and our faith." The president of the board published an angry letter in the *Times*, describing Shylock as "an amalgam of vindictiveness, cruelty and avarice" and expressed his concern that an impressionable television audience might assume he was prototypical. Members of the Jewish War Veterans picketed CBS executive offices, and the story was picked up by the national press.

Papp had no sympathy for the rabbis. He viewed them as establishment Jews of the type that had, when he was a boy, refused to allow outsiders like his father into synagogue without a $35 ticket. The rabbis took their case to the mayor and, once again, Papp was the center of a controversy.

"As a Jew," Papp told the press, "I have always considered Shylock representative of the thesis that all people are alike and suffer in the same way. . . . Our production is not going to create any new anti-Semites or increase the virulence of those who already exist." And, "I'm glad we've got a non-Jewish Shylock. Jewish actors tend to play Shylock as if he were terribly misunderstood. In fact, when I started rehearsing the play, I found *myself* trying to justify his behavior probably because I was self-conscious about criticism. . . . But I decided we'd reached a stage of maturity in race relations where there was no reason to ignore one of Shakespeare's best plays."

On June 18, *The Merchant of Venice* opened the new theater. Joseph Papp read a congratulatory telegram from Jacqueline Kennedy, the president's wife. Mayor Wagner announced that it would be named the Delacorte, in honor of the philanthropist who had donated $150,000 toward its completion.

When *Merchant* was reviewed a few days later, the production was praised for the clarity of speech and movement that, some critics said, had become the hallmark of the Festival's style. "This is how the Athenians and the Elizabethans must have felt," exulted one writer. "It is not the least of Mr. Papp's accomplishments that he has given back to his fellow New Yorkers at least a trace of the civic dignity that one feared was drowned forever in the humiliations of megalopolitan life."

According to Arbitron, in addition to the thousands of theatergoers who saw *Merchant* in Central Park, the televised broadcast was seen in 800,000 homes, by an estimated audience of two million viewers. It was probably the largest American audience to have ever seen a production of Shakespeare at one time.

November 1962 marked eight years since the Shakespeare Workshop had received its charter from the New York State Board of Regents and three years since the amphitheater project had been approved. During that time, Papp had been working without a break building up the Festival. Now that all its components were in place, he might have slowed down or taken a vacation. He had turned forty-one that summer and, apart from his stint in the military, had never traveled abroad. But instead of consolidating his gains — or savoring them — Papp was already planning for a year-round, permanent place of his own.

NINE

The Astor Library

THE DELACORTE could be used only during the summers, and Papp wanted a theater where he could, as he later put it, "live — a place to go to every day." Less than a year after the Delacorte had opened, he became aware of plans to build a large civic center in downtown Manhattan and immediately wrote Mayor Wagner that he would like to run a 1,000-seat theater in it. "The necessity for a roof at this juncture is not merely the question of a building. (Stone and mortar do not a theater make)," he wrote. "It is essentially an artistic development, nurtured in the sun of public approval and now ready for picking."

In 1963, New York governor Nelson Rockefeller signed a bill that provided a way of linking nonprofit civic and cultural projects to urban renewal programs. The producer collected news clippings on this development, and continued to lobby the mayor and city planning officials for a municipal theater. That August, he sent a letter to two hundred actors, inviting them to join a Classical Reading Workshop: "If all goes according to plan, we will have a new, year-round playhouse within the next four years. The open stage will be built within the Civic Center Complex in the City Hall area. Before an ounce of cement is poured, we must begin to lay the groundwork for a 'permanent' acting company." A group of actors began to read at the home of fundraiser Herta Danis, hoping to be cast in Festival productions.

After opening the Delacorte with *Merchant of Venice,* over three seasons Papp produced *The Tempest, King Lear, Antony and Cleopatra, As You Like It, The Winter's Tale, Hamlet, Othello* and Sophocles' *Electra* to summer audiences that averaged two thousand per night. In the winters, he toured *Macbeth, Twelfth Night* and *A Midsummer Night's Dream,* bringing Shakespeare to thousands of city high school pupils. And, beginning in 1964, Papp resuscitated the project closest to his heart: trucking Shakespeare into the poorer city neighborhoods.

Although Papp liked the look and feel of the Delacorte, he found its audience too conventional. Although younger, more racially integrated, more urban than the typical audience on Broadway, theatergoers at the Delacorte were still predominantly white, educated and middle class — unrepresentative of the city's demographics. Papp wanted working-class, uneducated people as well — people like his parents, who never attended the theater and almost never left their neighborhood to "go into the city." Extrapolating from what he knew of his family, Papp assumed that many of New York's African-American and Spanish-speaking residents were also reluctant to leave their neighborhoods for an unknown destination and that going to the theater would never become a part of their lives unless he brought theater to them.

"Much of my time with Joe was spent in this discussion of audience," Bernard Gersten recalled. "He romanticized the Mobile audience, which I felt was one of the great headaches of the Western World. He didn't see what was there. It's hard enough to get *any* people into the theater, *any* time. Joe wanted to persuade people who did not want to go to the theater to see plays he felt they should see."

Papp persuaded publisher George Delacorte to fund a Mobile Theater, and Ming Cho Lee designed a sleek caravan of vehicles, including one — forty feet long — that contained a fold-out thrust stage, two others fitted with dressing tables, mirrors, washbowls and toilets, another carrying folding chairs and tiers of bleachers to accommodate 1,600 viewers; another that served as lighting and sound control center. A sixth vehicle contained a city-supplied generator. The seventh was a bus carrying the cast; the eighth carried extra equipment. "That theater was genius," said Lee. Festival outreach staff notified schools, community centers, churches, political clubs, recreation centers and neighborhood publications of the coming event. Then the caravan would roll into obscure parts of the city, preceded by Papp's station wagon, announcing by loudspeaker the time and place of that evening's play. In 1964, *A Midsummer Night's Dream* played 54 performances to an estimated seventy thousand people, including many teenagers and children.

In some neighborhoods, such as the Brooklyn slum Bedford-Stuyvesant, the audience was mostly African-American. In others, such as Manhattan's Chelsea section, it was fully integrated. Some audiences were indistinguishable in their behavior from Delacorte audiences, but in some locations performances were interrupted by the hurling of bottles or bricks onto the stage. Special Actors Equity meetings were held to discuss the safety of the performers. Gersten coined the term "rock-out" to mean cancellation of a performance due to rock-throwing, and four performances were "rocked-out." Papp himself kept a small bowl on his desk that contained a collection of the rocks thrown at the Mobile stage. Some actors never worked on the Mobile twice, while others found it the most meaningful theater they had ever performed.

"The Mobile was a high risk/high reward venture," actress Ellen Holly would recall, "and when you were in direct sync with that audience, you experienced the voltage of the second half of that equation in a way that the managerial types on the periphery could never hope to. For all Joe's efforts to freshen Shakespeare, a faint odor of the museum still clung to the Delacorte as audiences worried about laughing 'in the right place.' Playing the Mobile was like being in a time capsule as the raucous spontaneity of the audiences was closer to what it was probably like back in the days of the Globe Theatre.

"There is a special hunger in all true people of the theater, not just to play for the dressed-up society audience but to engage in a form of theater that is much more basic and immediate — the itinerant circus, the *barracas* of García Lorca's day. The Mobile satisfied that hunger. And that was only one of its rewards. I chose to perform on the Mobile because of the largely black and Hispanic audiences and because my deepest satisfactions come from playing for my own people."

There were some 750,000 Spanish-speaking New York residents that Papp was also interested in reaching. In 1964, he engaged Osvaldo Riofrancos, an Argentine actor and director, to direct the first of several Spanish-language tours. That summer, Riofrancos directed performances of Federico García Lorca's *The Puppet Theatre of Don Cristobal* and *The Shoemaker's Prodigious Wife,* plays that García Lorca himself had once taken on tour through the Spanish countryside.

All the Mobile activity, however, was no substitute for a permanent home. Papp continued to push his plan for a municipal theater with the

mayor, the architect of the proposed civic center, and the City Planning
Board, with an optimism that was totally misplaced. In October 1964,
he took four Festival trustees to Gracie Mansion to discuss the municipal
theater. By December, he had worked out a revised plan, with one
1,200-seat theater, a second 200-seat theater, and a thirty- to thirty-five-
week program of drama in repertory, ten weeks of dance and five weeks
of "new scripts." Board member Florence Anspacher agreed to donate
$200,000 toward the project.

The civic center was never built, and other Papp projects never got off
the ground, including two unusual ways of celebrating Shakespeare's four
hundredth birthday. The first was with an opera of *Twelfth Night*. David
Amram had first written incidental music for the play in 1958, completing
an opera to Papp's libretto in 1962. The producer then set about raising
money to finance it, inviting a large group of theater, music and opera
people to a reading at the home of Herta Danis. "No one showed up,"
Amram later recalled, "but two secretaries from an opera festival in Ohio
and the head of a cultural center not yet built." Six months later, Papp
tried again, organizing a fundraiser at the elegant Fifth Avenue apartment
of a supporter. "Engraved invitations were sent out," Amram recalled.
"White satin chairs were put in the music room; a fantastic feast was
prepared with champagne by candlelight." Years later, Amram would
remember the mix of expensive perfume and cigar smoke in the air and,
after everyone had left without offering the Festival a dime, Papp saying,
"Looks like we'll have to wait a little longer to put this opera on."

A second plan that had not materialized was "The Southern Tour."
In the spring of 1963, when much of the American South was still posted
with "Whites Only" signs, Joseph Papp had come up with the idea of
celebrating Shakespeare's quadricentennial with an integrated company
of *Antony and Cleopatra*. He had long regarded segregation as a personal
affront. In the navy, he had contested the racial status quo; at the Lab he
had argued for recruiting African-American students; in 1963, he would
bring suit against a New Jersey motel for refusing to provide accommodations to his black housekeeper and win. His Southern Tour would
travel to twenty American cities. It would, he told the *Times*, feature
"Michael Higgins, a white actor, and Diana Sands, a Negro actress," as
Romeo and Juliet, in "a graphic illustration of interracial harmony. . . ."

"Wherever we play, Negro and white audiences will be encouraged to
buy tickets on an integrated seating basis. If a civic auditorium is denied
to us, we will give the play in the nearest Negro college and invite white
audiences to buy tickets."

Papp contacted officials in the Kennedy administration and 285 southern educational institutions and sent 423 appeals for funds to southern foundations. But he could not raise the funds and the Southern Tour fell by the wayside along with dozens of other ideas. But the project of a year-round theater remained.

Papp's desire for a theater of his own was whetted by his first trip to Europe in the fall of 1964. With Festival board chairman Burt Martinson paying, Papp, his wife, Peggy, his associate producer, Bernard Gersten, and Martinson flew from New York to London to Paris, then on to East Berlin, Prague and Warsaw for a one-month tour. "Martinson felt it was important that I go to Europe," Papp recalled. "He'd been raised wealthy so he had this marvelous kind of foreign education and he tried to educate me. I had never been to London or Paris and I was kind of awed by it."

The four Americans viewed thirty productions. In London, Papp met with Sean O'Casey's widow, Eileen, and then visited the Royal Shakespeare Company. He saw the Roundhouse Theater, where the playwright Arnold Wesker had, in an early example of what would later be called "adaptive reuse," converted a locomotive roundhouse into a theater. In Paris, he saw the Comédie Française; in East Berlin, he met with Bertolt Brecht's widow, Helene Weigel, and members of the Berliner Ensemble. It was, Papp noted, a showpiece of the Communist regime, lavishly subsidized by the state, with enough stagehands, as a visiting American later wrote, "to people a banana republic." Like the Royal Shakespeare Company, the Berliner Ensemble performed a mix of classical and contemporary plays and were housed in their own large building.

Flying on to Warsaw, the four Americans saw Jerzy Grotowski's avant-garde Polish Theater Laboratory, then continued to Prague for what Papp called "a poor, tired, heavy-handed *Death of a Salesman*" and an "imitation West Side Story *Romeo and Juliet*." Although Papp had for much of his life considered himself a Communist, he had never been in a Communist country before and what he saw surprised him. "Having gone through the McCarthy period in the United States," he later said, "I began to see, in the sixties, that there was a connection between that and Stalinism. In the United States, I was always fighting for all the liberal progressive things. And I saw a contradiction: Why wasn't I doing that for the people in the Communist countries? I knew I was changing because when I met someone who was not, the contrast was so amazing. I'd think: *Nothing happened to his brain.*"

Another consequence of Martinson's Grand Tour was providing Papp with a personal connection to British and European theater, a connection that would soften his anti-British bias and pique his interest in the plays of Czech dissident Václav Havel. A third consequence of the trip was its exacerbation of strains in the Papp marriage.

In New York, Peggy Papp led her own professional life. On the month-long tour, she would later complain, she felt like an unseen satellite of her husband. Martinson and Gersten attended to Papp's every whim, vying to carry his luggage at airports, ensuring that he had the best seat at restaurants, the best cigars, the best brandy. She left the tour and went to Paris alone, in one of the first open indications that the marriage was falling apart.

When Joseph Papp returned from Europe, his office suite in the Great Northern Hotel suddenly seemed small and shabby. He began to tell his board that the Festival was at a turning point. Every theater he had admired in Europe produced a mix of classics and contemporary plays. Every theater he admired had a year-round physical plant. He could no longer wait for the civic center to be built. Papp determined he would find a year-round theater right away.

By the mid-1960s, Joseph Papp had moved from the margins of the theater world to its center. Instead of grabbing a sandwich at his desk, he now often lunched at the Russian Tea Room, a restaurant frequented by many of New York's musicians, dancers and theater people. Lit by red-shaded sconces festooned with tinsel, crammed with paintings by Russian émigrés, it was the kind of warm, nineteenth-century room at whose door the Little Match Girl might have stationed herself. But instead of peering in the window, Papp was now a regular.

Papp would be seated at a front table where actors could see him and stop by to chat. Some were looking for work but many were happy just to say hello. Joseph Papp had become a local hero, a man who had created one of the most appealing landmarks of city life. His theater employed about six hundred actors on a budget that had grown to nearly one million dollars. And although he clearly had the skills to become a successful Broadway producer, he refused that route as well as the money, glamour and lifestyle that went with it.

To Mrs. Danis's chagrin, Papp continued living "like a gypsy." Apart from smoking cigars — an expensive habit he had picked up from Ernie Kovacs and Orson Welles while at CBS — the producer still walked and talked like a wisecracking Brooklyn teenager who loved racing down a basketball court. The New York Shakespeare Festival had ratty office furniture and kept its money in a savings account. At forty-three, Papp still earned the equivalent of an entry-level lawyer's salary and accepted raises only after the board proposed them.

"I was charmed by him," recalled Robert Brustein, then a theater critic

and professor of drama who was one of the Festival's staunchest supporters. "He could have been a thirties' leading man. Very masculine, direct,
handsome. He had an energy that seemed to pour out of that compact
frame."

Much of that energy and charm was focused on fundraising. Judy
Peabody, then a young blonde socialite, remembered "swooning with
delight" when the producer walked up to her table in the Russian Tea
Room and asked if they might lunch. "In my eyes, he was already the big
time," she said. "He was so attractive and had such a magnetic personality
that when he asked me to be on his board, I had to say yes. I told him
I was a terrible fundraiser. But Joe was so persuasive and charismatic and
warm, it would have been impossible to say no. He saw in me something
that I myself did not see. He made me feel that he really wanted me and
that one way or another, I was going to wind up on his board. I felt it
was a great honor and I became concerned about how I would measure
up."

Papp was just as persistent in searching for a year-round home. He
told his staff he was looking for a not-yet-fashionable section of Manhattan where the Festival could serve as a fulcrum for neighborhood rede-
velopment. Ideally, it would be close to a university, both for the advantages of institutional affiliation as well as for the potential of young
audiences. One day, Hilmar Sallee came into the office with a copy of the
Times real estate section. On the front page was the headline *"Landmarks
for Sale — or the Wrecker's Ball"* and photographs of two old buildings:
one was the Friends Meeting House off Gramercy Park; the other, the
old Astor Library on Lafayette Street.

Gramercy Park was a quiet, residential neighborhood centered around
the city's only private garden — accessible only to residents who were
given keys. Lafayette Street was a kind of no-man's-land of industrial
buildings that ran between Greenwich Village and the East Village. There
was no question as to which location Papp preferred. In the 1930s, Papp
had walked Lafayette Street between Dinhofer's and Union Square. He
remembered the proximity of the Bowery as well as the secondhand
bookshops on Fourth Avenue, a vestige of the book trade that had grown
up around the Astor Library. The building was not far from East 6th
Street, where Ukrainian immigrants were being displaced by hippies. It
was located between Cooper Union College and New York University,
the largest private university in the country.

Papp and Gersten took the subway downtown to have a look at it.
The dark red Italianate structure looked just as dirty and dreary as the
rest of Lafayette Street. The two men rang the doorbell and, after what

seemed a long time, a slight but feisty old man with a strong Yiddish accent opened the door.

He was Arthur Abraham, caretaker for the Hebrew Immigrant Aid Society. The HIAS had purchased the building in 1921, a few weeks before Joe Papirofsky's birth. During the depression, it had served as a soup kitchen, then as a processing center for Jews escaping Nazi-occupied Europe. In the late 1940s and early 1950s, it had housed Holocaust survivors, then the Jews fleeing Hungary and Egypt in 1956. Abraham made it clear that he thought neither Papp nor Gersten had the cash to buy the building, but grudgingly let them in.

The interior was not well lighted. The fine moldings were barely visible through the rows of low-hanging fluorescent lights. The walls were covered in pink and green paint. The glass ceiling of the main reading room was boarded over and the room's structure obscured by a warren of cubicles. Some had served as offices for HIAS administrators. File drawers stood open, as if abandoned in a hurry, and 3 × 5-inch index cards were scattered across the floor. "The place was littered with those cards," Papp later remembered. "Some said 'Germany.' Some said 'Austria.' Some said 'Poland,' and there were lists of people who had apparently never made it out of Nazi-occupied Europe."

Arthur Abraham led them through the tiny rooms that had housed or processed 250,000 immigrants, rooms containing a bare cot, a chair, a portrait of an American president — Theodore Roosevelt, Abraham Lincoln or George Washington — with an instructive quotation ascribed to him. There were two kitchens — one for meat and one for dairy — a synagogue with prayer books scattered across the floor, and more tiny rooms with bassinets in them. "It was such a mess," Papp remembered. "There were children's things, baby rattles. It reminded me so much of the Holocaust. It couldn't help but do that. It looked like there had been a pogrom in that place. But you could also see the glory of the building."

As the three men walked through the cold, dark structure, Gersten could tell that the building spoke to Papp. Although the producer would not, until later, uncover all the threads that bound him and it together, it already seemed auspicious to him that Arthur Abraham had seen the original production of Brecht and Weill's *Threepenny Opera* in Berlin.

Quite apart from the fact that it had sheltered thousands of immigrants, the massive brown structure had been built as New York City's first free public library. John Jacob Astor, an eighteenth-century German immigrant, had, in the 1820s, developed Lafayette Place as an enclave of palatial homes, with a garden, a theater and an opera house. But opera proved unsuccessful there and the house was soon presenting Shakespeare. In 1849, riots were triggered by the appearance of a leading British actor in *Macbeth*. Rioters shouting "America for the Americans" and "Workingmen! Shall Americans or English rule in this city?" entered the theater, broke its windows and brought down its great crystal chandelier. Police, vastly outnumbered, fired on the crowd, wounding 150 people and killing twenty-two. The actor escaped.

A few years later, John Jacob Astor had bequeathed $400,000 to establish the public library. When it opened its doors in 1854, the number of people who rushed to read its 100,000 books was so great that second and third buildings had to be added and, in 1895, the collection moved uptown to Fifth Avenue and 42nd Street. Astor Place and Lafayette Street began to deteriorate, and the Italianate building had stood vacant for twenty-five years before HIAS bought it. Now it was vacant again.

When Papp and Gersten emerged from the Astor Library, Gersten noted that the place was beautiful but far too big. Papp said that in three years it would prove too small. Gersten argued that, besides the high cost of acquisition, there would be a staggering conversion cost. Papp said that money was never a problem. Gersten pointed out that every few minutes the subway roared and shook the building. Papp brushed it off. This was the right building. He called HIAS. He met with an architect. He took his set designer, Ming Cho Lee, to the library to make drawings.

Viewing the building as one of Papp's transient enthusiasms, Gersten drafted a memo describing what the Festival needed: a property suitable for conversion to a 300-seat theater, which the Festival might lease for five to ten years until the municipal theater was finally built.

During 1965, while producing *Love's Labor's Lost, Coriolanus* and *Troilus and Cressida* at the Delacorte, and *Henry V* and *The Taming of the Shrew* on the Mobile, Gersten and Papp looked at the Friends Meeting House on Gramercy Park, at the Presbyterian Church at Spring and Varick streets in SoHo, at a warehouse on 13th Street in Greenwich Village, and at the old RKO movie theater at 81st and Broadway on the Upper West Side — and Papp pursued his correspondence with Mayor Wagner.

In July, faced with a set of disappointing reviews and frustrated by his inability to get the municipal theater project moving, the producer wrote: "While we are no longer a young, struggling theater, we have great problems for the future. If we do not grow artistically, we will soon disappear. . . . We need the assurance of year-round operation and we can turn only to the source with whom we have the most in common — the City of New York. A major grant of four million dollars to cover the construction and operation of a 1,200 seat Public Theater for a period of five years is needed."

Mayor Wagner passed the letter on to his coordinator of policy planning, who asked, "How did you arrive at your $4 [million] figure? What is the rough outline of the budget? Could you supply me with this information without delay?"

On August 10, Papp sent him a detailed plan and budget. "A Public Theater in New York City," Papp wrote, "must accommodate 1,600 to 1,800 people; It must be priced at levels which allow the non-theater-going public to attend. . . . It must be readily accessible to public transportation; It must be organically linked to the educational apparatus of the City. . . . It must be a pacesetter; and . . . it must reflect in every area of its operation the multi-racial composition of the City." Papp suggested that, for the short term, the Festival take over the ANTA Washington Square Theater, which the Repertory Company of Lincoln Center had occupied while awaiting completion of their theater uptown.

Although New York City would never build a civic center, government was, in 1965, moving closer to Papp's conviction that theater should be built "on the bedrock of civic responsibility." That year, two new pieces of legislation were signed into law — both crucial to the future of the Festival. The first was the bill creating what would become the National Endowment for the Arts. The second was a New York City law creating the Landmarks Preservation Commission, which enjoyed widespread support among New Yorkers dismayed over the demolition of Pennsylvania Station and the proposed demolition of the old Metropolitan Opera House.

Papp had been following the preservation debate since the rescue of Carnegie Hall in 1960. As Lincoln Center neared completion, Carnegie Hall had been slated for demolition, and had been saved from the wrecker's ball by a coalition of artists and civic leaders led by violinist Isaac Stern. A committee of prominent citizens had then persuaded New York City to buy it for $5 million. The city leased it back to a nonprofit corporation under the terms of a special bill signed into law by Governor Nelson Rockefeller. That September, it occurred to Papp that he could use the new law to save the Astor Library and build his theater.

He called the head of the commission and followed up by letter: "The NYSF is most interested in obtaining a structure to house its winter theater operation. The idea of collaborating with the Landmarks Commission of the City stems from our devout concern for the preservation of significant historical buildings as well as our present need for a theater. . . ."

The producer noted that he had looked at the Presbyterian church and the Friends Meeting House, either of which could house a 300-seat theater.

> There may be other buildings about which you have some knowledge that may suit our purpose and, if there are any, I would appreciate knowing about them. Since the Festival enjoys a quasi-official relationship with the City of New York (almost half our financing is obtained from the City), we would propose a similar arrangement should we find a suitable site. This means that we would ask that the City purchase the property at its present value, while the Festival would undertake the expense of reconstruction and refurbishing of the interior.

On October 5, the head of the Landmarks Commission advised Papp to look into the Astor Library. In July, HIAS had contracted to sell it to a developer, who planned to tear it down. The commission, at its first hearing, had accorded twenty other city buildings landmark status but the final decision on the Astor Library had been tabled until the next meeting. The Washington Square Association had testified that the building was "one of the most important Victorian public buildings remaining today in New York City," and could serve as an anchor to "the anticipated renewal of an otherwise rundown section at the edge of our neighborhood." The developer planned to build a high-rise on the site. Five potential buyers, including millionaire art collector Joseph Hirshhorn, had already considered and rejected the building. If no one showed up to rescue the library, it would be destroyed.

This prospect, Papp later said, was what galvanized him. In the three weeks between that telephone call and the second meeting of the Landmarks Commission, Papp met with his lawyers, with HIAS leaders and with his trustees.

"We are proceeding with steps to acquire the Astor Library (HIAS) on Lafayette Street," he wrote on October 15.

> The technicalities, though troublesome, are not formidable. . . . It is more than likely that it will be designated as a landmark within the next two weeks. In the meantime, our attorneys will examine the status of the contract between HIAS and the purchaser. . . . If the people who bought it are still the legal owners, we are convinced that they will be anxious to call it quits, since their sole interest in buying it was to tear it down for high rise apartments. . . . In a week or so we should be

able to provide you with an estimate of the cost of conversion and restoration. . . . The figure of two million dollars, I think, is not far-fetched. But we will get a clearer picture after our architect and designer draw up preliminary plans.

Festival trustees received letters explaining the urgent need for money. "It has been no secret that for the past four years I have been seeking to link the Central Park, Mobile Unit and public school program with a permanent home for the New York Shakespeare Festival," Papp wrote October 18 to George Delacorte.

As you know the City has designated a site for our year-round theater in the West Side urban renewal project. There is no doubt that the location is highly desirable as it becomes an adjunct of other cultural structures — the Museum of Natural History, the Hayden Planetarium and, of course, the Delacorte Theater. If such a theater were to be built for the Festival within a year, it would be hard to resist accepting it. The drawback, however, is the schedule of demolition and construction. Predictable estimates run from five to seven years.

There are other stumbling blocks — the fact that several million dollars would have to be appropriated by the City and/or Federal government to make the building possible. And then the occupying organization, us, would be responsible for operating a theater on the scale of the Vivian Beaumont — a fantastically expensive undertaking. With such huge financing, the theater becomes tied to a high-pressure concept of total success — the "hit" philosophy. . . . This is hardly a climate for creative work, which must have the luxury of occasional "failure."

Another important consideration is my feeling that there are enough cultural centers being built today — too many, in fact. Most of them will end up as cultural supermarkets, catering to popular taste. . . . The threat of censorship in too dependent a relationship with the municipality or with the new government agencies being formed to support the arts is apparent. The Festival's ability to keep the balance is made possible by a delicately evolved relationship with the City and private supporters like yourself. . . .

With the national tendency in culture moving toward "bigness" and "togetherness" my instincts begin to act up the other way. I feel the need for a moderate-sized theater, producing plays that do not necessarily have great popular appeal but are significant in their reflection of the present. New York City has a large, intelligent core of playgoers who would support a theater of this kind. . . . We will gear this theater to realizable deficit, which means we can raise the subsidy within our present and extended fund-raising efforts. . . .

The structure we have in mind is the former Astor Free Library on Lafayette Street, which we learn will soon be declared a landmark. It is certainly appropriate for the Festival, the first free professional theater in the United States, to acquire the property which housed the first free public library. . . . The cost of the structure is $550,000, a preposterously low price.

Papp wrote George Delacorte that he already had a foundation lined up willing to purchase the library for the Festival — although no such foundation appears in the Festival archives — but that he wished to give the publisher the opportunity to buy it first.

Our theater in Central park and our Mobile Unit carry the name: Delacorte. We would be proud to preserve the name and the association in our move toward "permanency." I hope that you will be interested in acquiring the property for the Festival. . . .

We have less than two weeks to make the decision.

Delacorte did not rise to the occasion, but trustee Florence Anspacher did by pledging the money she had promised for the municipal theater toward the acquisition of the Library.

On October 26, during its second hearing, the Landmarks Commission designated the former Astor Library as a historical landmark. The developer had six months in which to appeal. Papp had been badgering the offices of Lithos Properties for two weeks. He had researched the company's principals and discovered that the daughter of one had been a Festival contributor. After a few more days of calls, Papp obtained an appointment. "He had a small office, nothing extravagant, and he smoked a cigar," Papp later told the story about that meeting. "I told him I wanted his building.

"'What do you mean, you want the building?' he said, and began explaining that he had already put some $50,000 into the deal.

"I said he had to realize that the building had already been landmarked, that it was there to stay, that he had made a great living as a real estate developer in New York City and it was time for him to give the city something back.

"'You must be crazy, Mr. Papp!' he said. 'I'm a businessman.' And so forth. I kept arguing with him. I was passionate and very angry. I talked about his daughter and how she supported the Festival. I talked about the history of HIAS. I talked about his being Jewish. I talked about the obligations of good citizenship. I was not going to leave his office without that building."

The speed at which events were moving alarmed the Festival staff. Everyone — Gersten, Lee, Debuskey, Danis — that the producer dragged down to tour the red, Italianate building agreed that it was beautiful. Everyone was moved by the vestiges of the HIAS refugees. Everyone agreed that the rough, quasi-industrial neighborhood might turn out to be a new artistic community. But what was Papp's hurry? The Delacorte Theater had only been open for four seasons. The Mobile Theater had been up for only two. And $575,000! Where would it come from?

Hilmar Sallee was particularly incensed. The Festival had no resources with which to acquire, let alone convert, the Astor Library! And *two* subway lines! No matter where you stood in the immense building, you could not only hear but *feel* the rattle of the RR and IRT. If Papp bought the building, Sallee would quit.

Bernard Gersten agreed with Sallee. The building was far too large — at 54,000 square feet, it was the size of a small shopping mall! Papp planned a major theater on the second floor. The only access was a long and narrow staircase and one elevator that carried six. The most basic renovation would cost hundreds of thousands of dollars. "At the time," Gersten recalled, "we were living like a poor family with an aggressive breadwinner. We never had to postpone a payroll but with a permanent staff of only five or six people and a monthly rent of $800, we were very lightweight."

Designer Ming Cho Lee, who had become devoted to designing Shakespeare for the Delacorte and Mobile, was puzzled. The Festival just needed space to tide it over from summer to summer. "I was still thinking that the Delacorte was the main event and the winter home would be the workshop that fed the summer theater," he said. "What did we need the Astor Library for?"

Merle Debuskey, somewhat jaded from feeding plans for overly ambitious projects to the press, thought this one was unlikely. The excitement and repeated trips down to Astor Place would soon be a memory, like the opera of *Twelfth Night* and the Southern Tour and the hundreds of other brilliant Papp ideas that had fizzled by the wayside. After all, the building was still under contract to a developer who had gotten the bargain of the century. Why would he give it up?

Just after Thanksgiving, he did. "Our clients took the position that the Contract of Sale has a value well in excess of $45,000," wrote their attorney. "You asked our clients to make a contribution to the Festival by agreeing to accept a price for the assignment of the Contract of Sale which is lower than its true value. After further discussion, our clients suggested that they would be willing to assign the contract to the Festival for $30,000 thereby making a contribution of at least $15,000 to the Festival."

Meanwhile there had been a municipal election in which John Lindsay had replaced Robert Wagner as mayor. The producer moved quickly to establish a relationship. "Dear Congressman Lindsay," he wrote before Lindsay's inauguration. "The New York Shakespeare Festival is about to acquire an historic landmark which it has saved from demolition in cooperation with the City Landmarks Preservation Commission." Although the project would cost about three million dollars, Papp noted that he did not contemplate asking the city for any funds over and above those the Festival had received in the past, adding, "It would be a great privilege and of incalculable assistance to our efforts to have you make the announcement of our new theater at the very beginning of your Mayoralty reign. . . . Enclosed is a suggested approach to the announcement."

The day before, Papp had announced to his board that he planned to acquire the Library. Papp told the trustees that the price of the building was $575,000 and the cost of reconstruction an estimated $1.8 million. He said he had submitted a request to the city for $100,000 toward the conversion costs and asked for $750,000 in federal funds from the new National Foundation for the Arts and Humanities. Half of Florence Anspacher's contribution of $250,000 would be used as the down payment and the balance held for operating funds. He distributed floor plans showing how the building could be reconstructed to house one 800-seat theater, an experimental 200-seat theater, offices, rehearsal halls, costume and prop shops. He talked about an acting company, audience subsidy, performing both contemporary plays and classics.

General manager Hilmar Sallee would indeed quit the Festival when it moved downtown, but everyone else adjusted. "Other people would have said: 'Where do we get the money?'" Bernard Gersten recalled. "Joe said: 'Let's get the building, then we'll try to get the money.' His attitude sprang from a childhood as a poor person. His family owned nothing, not their own house, not much property. No one worried about the long-term. And Joe never asked himself: *'What if we fail?'* When Macbeth asks that question, his wife replies: *'We fail? But screw your courage to the sticking point and we'll not fail.'* Well, Joe always screwed his courage to the sticking point."

To skeptics, Papp repeated his conviction: Money follows art. Since

1954, he had been starting projects without the money in hand to pay for them. That's what all investors did. "If I had to wait for guarantees of funding," he said, "I'd never get anything done."

A second conviction was that his theater would be built on "the bedrock of civic responsibility." For years in Europe, Papp argued, cultural costs had been assumed by the state or municipality. Government, Papp argued, must be "prepared to accept the concept practiced by most of the civilized countries of the world — support for the arts." And it had to be permanent. "Unlike developing a rocket to get a man to the moon, we cannot organize a crash program for the theater. It is a living, growing thing and, like a garden, requires cultivation and tender care."

Papp's third conviction was that he would succeed only if he proceeded slowly, one step at a time. He would not try to renovate the entire building immediately but reconstruct the interior bit by bit, paying as he went.

On January 5, 1966, Papp announced the acquisition to the press, describing the Astor Library as the first building saved from demolition under the New York City Landmarks Preservation Law. Reporters viewed the announcement as a victory for all New Yorkers. Ada Louise Huxtable wrote:

> The Astor Library was New York's most celebrated cultural and architectural monument when it was constructed in the 1850s. A century of urban change turned it into one of the city's more notable white elephants, fated to go the way of Penn Station. . . .
>
> All of the conventional strikes were against it — age, awkwardness, unfashionable Victorian style, expense and technical problems of remodeling and a neighborhood teetering between improvement and further deterioration. It was a familiar episode to New Yorkers grown accustomed to seeing the city's history systematically reduced to rubble. Only the ending of the story was different.

On January 28, 1966, Papp and his associates met Lithos lawyers for the closing. The producer signed checks for $30,000 to the developer and $85,000 to HIAS as well as documents that spelled out the terms of a $460,000 mortgage.

"It seemed like an impossible thing," Papp would recall. "But I think almost everything you do in life — if you want to make any changes — is an enormous thing. It becomes manageable once you start to deal with it on a step-by-step basis. You have to have a sense of the end but you don't operate from that point of view: you deal with the moments just as though you were cutting a hole into the side of a mountain. You have to start with a few strokes and take satisfaction in the fact that you've loosened a few shards. It's always hard to start something, but once I get into it, I know I'm going to see it through. I know I sound like Teddy Roosevelt, but this is true of all hard-thinking people who get things done."

With his mortgage secured, Papp hired an architect. Giorgio Cavaglieri was a Venetian born into a privileged family before the First World War. The slim, elegant specialist in Italian Renaissance style had practiced architecture in Italy until March 1939, when he left his country one week before he would have had to register as a Jew. He fled to the United States, fought in Normandy with the American forces and, when he was demobilized, chose to live in New York.

"Joseph Papp appeared in my office one day," he recalled, "and said I was one of three architects whose names he had from Ada Louise Huxtable. He was a very quick, abrupt, frank person and I knew right away that of the three, he would have only related to me — who had a tiny, bare office with no staff, no plush chairs, no conference room and no pomp of any kind. We went down to the Astor Library to visit, we shook hands and that was it. No documents to sign, no lawyers. Nothing. Also not too much money but the job seemed to me exceptionally attractive."

Although he had never before designed a theater, Cavaglieri had been attending Festival productions since 1956, was an early advocate of "adaptive reuse" and had worked on historic buildings long before the Landmarks Commission was established. At the time, he was converting the Jefferson Market Courthouse in Greenwich Village into a working library. "The concept of preservation existed then," Cavaglieri recalled, "but largely in terms of freezing the form or preserving it in its traditional function, like a museum. I said: Why freeze a form if it is obsolete? I believed in the transformation of function for buildings and the Festival provided me with a teaching model — an example through which to demonstrate my philosophy."

Cavaglieri drew up office plans first. Then, working with designer Ming Cho Lee, plans for the theaters. Papp had scaled down his plans from the 1,800-seat municipal theater he had proposed to Mayor Wagner to a 1,200-seat, then an 800-seat theater — about the size of the smallest Broadway house — that had the possibility of making some productions self-supporting. Cavaglieri told him it would cost $2 million and require complete fireproofing. The interior of the building would have to be fully gutted. Although, curiously, that was permissible under the terms of the Landmark Commission's rules, Papp felt it sacrilegious as well as too expensive. "I have $300,000," Cavaglieri recalled Papp saying and the architect — who later characterized his client as a man "with exceptional imagination but no overall budget" — went back to the drawing board.

After much discussion, two 300-seat theaters were planned. Under municipal regulations, they required only a sprinkler system. The first, containing a thrust stage, would be called the Anspacher in honor of the donor.

Papp left the reconstruction to Lee and Cavaglieri, whose collaboration was marked by what the designer would later call "drag-out" fights. Lee despised architectural renderings and thought Cavaglieri knew little about theater design. Cavaglieri thought Lee knew nothing about architecture. One of their many battles concerned the two rows of Corinthian columns that traversed the space and included two columns in the middle of the stage area. Cavaglieri was committed to preserving them. Lee wanted them gone. "We're not doing Neoclassical opera here!" the Chinese designer later remembered shouting at the equally voluble Italian architect. In the end, the two columns in the performing area were stripped down to bare iron and Lee was impressed by the care of Cavaglieri's work.

Papp was unskilled at mediation and did not try to referee between Lee and Cavaglieri. But every day, he would hurry into the former reading room to see how the new theater was emerging from the ruins. He had always loved construction; now he watched as workers excavated original walls and ceilings of the building, some going back over one hundred years.

In addition to immersing himself in the physical process, Cavaglieri recalled, Papp was one of his few clients who consistently knew what he wanted and was surprisingly easy to work for. "He was unlike so many people who want things they cannot afford and refuse to take no for an answer," Cavaglieri said. "He trusted me."

The architect, like most people who had professional dealings with the producer, saw very little of his private side. Papp maintained a strict separation between his personal and professional lives and Cavaglieri had no idea that his brilliant, energetic client was becoming increasingly troubled by nightmares, depressions and a variety of unexplained physical symptoms.

As a child, Papp had had what he later called "seizures," episodes of fright that would leave him gasping for breath and his heart pounding. Those seizures had disappeared during the war and while he was on the West Coast but had come back when he returned to New York. In January 1964 he had been hospitalized after experiencing chest pains but tests found nothing physically wrong. Papp concluded that his problems were psychological.

He had first sought out psychotherapy in 1955, when he was thirty-four years old, troubled by a pattern of marital infidelity that had begun when he was in the navy and that continued through three marriages. He found a therapist at Bellevue Hospital who advised him that there was nothing to be done about his womanizing and counseled discretion. But discretion, Papp knew, was not the issue. Even as a boisterous teenager, Joe Papirofsky had cultivated no reputation as a Don Juan. He had kept his romances private. In Hollywood, he had conducted his love affairs so discreetly that even his drinking buddies were unaware of them. Although he thought his therapist wrong, and "a cold fish" to boot, he continued therapy with him for ten years.

By June 1965, Papp's personal problems had come to a head. He had just turned forty-four. Both his parents had died — his son Tony was three years old — the age his son Michael had been when Papp was separated from him. He and his wife led separate lives — "He was not at all interested in my work," Peggy later recalled, "and I was unwilling to devote my life and attention to his" — and his lover was in the process of leaving him. It was Peggy Papp, herself a family therapist, who insisted that they seek marital counseling. "I was always hoping to recreate what we had had in the beginning," she recalled. "People in my line of work always hope to keep a marriage together, and what kept me there was the hope that I would find again the person I had married, where we had these feelings together."

The Papps went to a few sessions of therapy together. Then he refused to go back. A few months later, he collapsed with what once again appeared to be the symptoms of a heart attack, and was, once again, hospitalized for tests. The marital therapist, whom Peggy Papp had continued to see, took the unusual step of calling Papp at the hospital and asking whether he would like her to visit.

She was a warm, attractive Jewish woman in her mid-fifties, whose poise and understated style gave no indication of her background. In fact, she, too, had been the child of poor immigrants, raised in a tough city neighborhood. She loved theater, felt a kinship with the producer and told him that during her meetings with him, she had felt he had been hiding something. Papp burst into tears. After leaving the hospital, the producer finally left his therapist of ten years and began a new course of treatment with her.

Until he began this second course of psychotherapy, Joseph Papp had managed to avoid examining his past. As a child, he had adapted to his parents' needs, protecting them, not demanding what he knew they were unable to provide. Toward the world, he cultivated a bravado that compensated for his small size and slight frame. Instead of confronting painful situations, he left them, disconnecting from people who hurt him or whom he felt guilty about hurting. He also kept himself so busy that there was never time to look back. Although he had paid out years of child support, Papp had put in a minimal amount of time as a father. His first daughter, Susan, and his first son, Michael, had grown up without him. Anthony and Miranda had been born just as he was getting the Shakespeare Festival off the ground. And he had yet to meet Barbara, the daughter conceived at Bainbridge Naval Base in 1945. His behavior as a husband and a father ran counter to the model of Sam Papirofsky as well as to Jewish family tradition. Although he had continued to see his parents and family in Brooklyn as he became more and more prominent in the world of the theater, he visited rarely and viewed them as living in a world he had left.

"He was totally cut off from his feelings before he started therapy," Peggy Papp recalled. "And then, when he began to get in touch, the effect was catastrophic."

The public never saw this vulnerable Joseph Papp, embarked on the long process of sifting through his life and remaking his self. For the press, as for Giorgio Cavaglieri, he remained the feisty, irrepressible, indefatigable man who had brought Free Shakespeare to Central Park and was now engaged in a second, seemingly impossible adventure.

On August 15, 1966, though sheets of tin still covered the first-floor windows of the Astor Library, Joseph Papp and his staff of eight moved into the Public Theater. They did not have much to unpack: a few desks and chairs, a mimeograph and stamp machine, the uncomfortable sofa on which Papp seated his guests, a few typewriters and file cabinets. Large steel girders had been rammed through the exterior wall and across the office, leaving large, drafty holes. Mice came in at night, got trapped in desk drawers, and chewed up the corners of papers left on desks. For the next year, a fine white plaster would dust Papp's hair and hands and clothing as he paced his new office and the dark corridors of his new theater and turned his attention to a baffling question: What kind of new plays and new playwrights would he introduce?

TEN

from
Hamlet to *Hair*

IN THE FALL of 1966, although he had just embarked on building the Public Theater, Papp began teaching at Yale. Earlier that year, a theater professor and critic, Robert Brustein, had been appointed dean of its School of Drama with a mandate to overhaul its curriculum. Passionate, enterprising and as dismissive of Broadway as Papp, Brustein came to Yale with the goal of preparing students for the regional theater, which, he argued, would be based on art rather than profit. For years, he had admired and supported Free Shakespeare in the Park even though, in 1957, he had been one of the auditioning actors who lost out to George C. Scott for the role of Richard III.

"I had heard Joe was down on his luck," Brustein recalled. "The Festival was receiving poor reviews, his financial situation was impossible and I thought I saw a chance to have him in New Haven full-time as a teacher and director." At forty-five, with no college education himself, Papp became a faculty member at the Yale Graduate School of Drama.

Alonso Alegria, the Peruvian writer who became Papp's teaching assistant, noticed at once that Papp did not fit in. "He had no interest in socializing with any of the faculty and he didn't have the time," he said. "I believe he was mostly amused by Yale, its traditions and its mores. He came in on the train from New York every Thursday morning, neatly dressed in a suit and tie, with his cigar in hand. He went over the text of the play we were doing, in the train on the way to New Haven, talked to a few students before class and then responded to the work.

"I had taken Drama 130 the year before with Frank MacMullen, who had a syllabus, a textbook he had written, a set of conventional, old-fashioned lectures and exams. Joe was not into any of that. He watched student scenes chewing on the cigar or nervously rolling up a piece of paper between his fingers, then stood up and critiqued them. He was funny and witty sometimes, but in a subdued kind of way. He was more often earnest, emphatic. I think he was trying things out for himself at Yale. He even changed projects midstream. We started working on the First Quarto *Hamlet*, then he lost interest in that and changed to the standard version — this, after starting out the year with *Troilus and Cressida*. When it came to grades, Joe pulled them out of his head — he didn't grade scenes like other instructors, kept no notes. But he wasn't frivolous about grades. He thought them over carefully, and it was a grade given as much to the student as a person as to his or her work on the stage."

Papp's Drama 130 students that first semester were a talented group, mostly young men, including Jeff Bleckner, Dick Place, Tom Moore and Ted Cornell — who was struck by what he perceived as Papp's Jewish, urban energy and the fact that he was a theater activist rather than an academic. "He didn't sit around discussing Brecht and Artaud — he was *building* a theater," recalled Cornell. "At Yale everybody was always talking about the need to find an American counterpart to the British angry young men, but we directors weren't getting to work on original plays. For Joe, theater was about the word. Playwrights were the name of the game and we directors were their servitors.

"There was also a class thing. To me, the ticket Joe had was that he was *not* middle class. At Yale, he flaunted it. He was the person without degrees, small, feisty, not tweedy at all. In 1966, I didn't want to be an upper-class person from Wellesley, Massachusetts. I was in the process of trying to de-class myself. I was attracted to him because — like Stella Adler, who taught acting — he was the real thing."

Jeff Bleckner would later remember Papp's confrontational style and his feeling that the producer enjoyed being a provocateur. "I had done a piece of work that made me the class genius," he recalled. "A month later, Joe was sitting next to me watching another student's work that was brilliant. He turned to me and said, 'How does it feel to be a has-been?' He was letting me know what life was going to be like in this business. He would do that kind of stuff all the time."

Papp became a seminal figure to his students. Ted Cornell, Alonso Alegria and Jeff Bleckner competed with one another for his attention as well as for jobs at the Public, and formed deep attachments to him. "I loved the man," Alegria said. "He was the center of my life. Every Thursday morning, I met Joe at the station and told him what had gone on during the week. I took notes in his classes and, in the evening, he treated me to dinner. What I learned from him was not so much a way to make theater but a way to be. A way to think — which was more personal, much deeper and more meaningful. To be totally frank, I even became a little worried if this attachment, this devotion, might not be a latent homosexual thing I was developing at age twenty-six. If it was, it stayed latent. Joe once said to me: 'It's called looking for your father.'"

It was at Yale that Papp established the first of a series of involved father-son relationships with directors, as well as a pipeline to young talented actors who would later work at the New York Shakespeare Festival. Also, thanks to Brustein, he met leading members of the theater's avant-garde. Brustein was a champion of the experimental theater, advocating for off off-Broadway where Caffe Cino, La Mama Experimental Theater Club, and the Judson Poets' Theatre were spawning young, unknown playwrights John Guare, Sam Shepard, Megan Terry, Rochelle Owens and Lanford Wilson. Like Papp, he wanted theater to connect to American social and political reality. Reviewing an Arthur Miller play, he wrote:

> The nation's cities are in total disarray, drowning in swill, torn by riots, seething with violence; our disgraceful involvement in the Vietnam conflict is making large numbers ashamed of being American. Our sense of reality is disintegrating, our illusion of freedom faltering, our expectation of disaster increasing — yet Arthur Miller, the most public-spirited of dramatists, continues to write social-psychological melodramas about Family Responsibility. . . .
>
> How can a new play fail to be affected, if only indirectly, by the events of its time? Even the atmosphere of a middle-class living room is charged with special tensions these days. Even conflicts within the family are inevitably informed by the frustrations that are driving the country mad.

Brustein found the plays he was seeking off off-Broadway. Where Broadway exuded a slick professionalism, OOB flaunted the antithesis of polish. Where Broadway played it safe and apolitical, OOB was politically engaged. Where the Broadway economy operated under tight union regulations and a system designed to turn a profit for investors, OOB was anti-organizational and proud of being a theater of poverty.

Brustein and Papp were both admirers of the Living Theater, established by Judith Malina and Julian Beck in the late 1940s, which had, from its inception, focused on some of the ugliest social issues of the day. In 1959, it opened with *The Connection,* a straightforward depiction of junkies waiting for their fixes to a monotonous jazz accompaniment. In 1963, their production of *The Brig* was described by a critic as "a-fact-for-fact duplication of life in a Marine Corps prison." It was the rare uptown theatergoer who was comfortable watching the theater's bleak productions, who endorsed their acts of civil disobedience or supported their ongoing conflict with the New York City police. But Papp felt, "It was truly the most living of all theaters that existed in New York. It had a point of view. It was alive. It had an attitude toward society and life, and to me a theater means nothing without that." The kind of theater Papp admired, as he later put it, was a "form of education, where you should be engaged spiritually and emotionally, and feel you know more when you leave than you did when you came in. You get your money's worth not by looking at the scenery but inside your soul." He wanted to establish a theater that was the opposite of complacent, that was "doubting, questioning, gray not pink."

Robert Brustein was looking for that kind of theater too. He invited both Joseph Chaikin and André Gregory to bring their companies to New Haven for residencies at Yale and it was there that Papp first met both directors, saw the Open Theater's production of Megan Terry's *Viet Rock* and met Gerome Ragni, an Open Theater actor, who handed him the script of what would become the musical *Hair.*

The contrast between the state of American society and mainstream American theater seemed, to both Papp and Brustein, obscene. By 1966, President Kennedy and Black Muslim leader Malcolm X had been murdered, and the nation had watched on television more than a decade of violence attending desegregation. Now, they were watching Vietnam. There were 285,000 Americans in Vietnam by 1966, over five thousand casualties and a growing student movement challenging U.S. involvement in Southeast Asia. Walking on the Yale campus or Lafayette Street, Joseph Papp took note of the white kids sporting improbably long hair, the black kids equally improbable Afros, the hippies dressed in the most fantastic of clothing, and the marijuana everywhere. He listened to the music of Bob Dylan as well as the Beatles and grasped that traditional attitudes toward authority, sex, race and gender were changing fast. The neighborhood in which his theater was located — now called the East Village — would become a hub of this change as the Fillmore East music hall and the Odyssey House rehabilitation center consolidated its reputation as a center for sex, drugs and rock-and-roll.

Unlike many middle-aged liberals, Papp did not embrace the youth culture. He did not smoke marijuana or experiment with psychedelic drugs, although he did, for a time, grow his hair fashionably long. His political engagement had long predated the sixties. "In a general sense, I suppose I belong to the New Left," he said. "I march in peace parades. I help out the hippies when they're arrested. I do whatever I can, but no matter how you look at it, political action comes from the young and I'm not twenty-one anymore."

But if he did not see himself as part of the counterculture, Papp became its theater facilitator. On his birthday in 1966 he told an interviewer: "We are concerned with the young people today who are active in the civil rights movements, who are very conscious of these times whether they are active or not," he said. "We'll probably have two new young directors in their twenties and playwrights in their twenties too — a whole revitalization — young people. I'm getting a little old, you see, I'm forty-five today. . . ."

"I am looking for plays that have some passionate statement to make that is commensurate with the times we are living in," he would later say. "I don't like plays that give me pat answers — there aren't any. I don't like story plays. I don't like sentimental plays. But I like plays that are hard to explain, that leave you with more questions than answers, plays that have abstractions that I don't totally understand."

Papp and Brustein competed for new plays. But the way they proceeded reflected their very different positions, personalities, education and connections. Brustein, like Papp, was a New York Jew, a product of its public schools. But, unlike Papp, he had grown up in the middle class, graduated college, taken a doctoral degree, and chosen a career in the academy. As director of the Yale Repertory Theater, he was interested in reviving the classics of the Western dramatic tradition he had studied. He planned productions of Jonson's *Volpone* and John Ford's *'Tis Pity She's a Whore* and commissioned distinguished poet Robert Lowell to write an adaptation of Aeschylus's *Prometheus Bound*. In contrast, when an agent sent him Lowell's translation of the *Oresteia*, Papp wrote brashly: "The only reason we would have for producing a Greek classic would be to illuminate values which are in some way connected to our present dilemma. I don't feel Mr. Lowell's script does this."

There were also tremendous differences in each man's social circle. Brustein's included colleagues and summer neighbors on Martha's Vineyard, among them libretto-composer team Arnold Weinstein and William Bolcom, successful mainstream novelists Philip Roth, William Styron and Joseph Heller, humorists Jules Feiffer and Art Buchwald, poet Robert Lowell, journalist John Hersey and long-established playwright Lillian Hellman.

Joseph Papp had no celebrated neighbors and no acquaintance with playwrights. He rented a series of summer cottages on the unfashionable Jersey shore where one of his old Irish friends had a beach house. But perhaps the most important difference between Papp and Brustein was Papp's mode of operating on sheer instinct. "If Joe had relied on his brain, he would have done everything wrong," said Bernard Gersten. Papp had no preconceptions about what kind of person could be a playwright. He, Joseph Papp, had learned about theater on the job; why shouldn't a playwright learn the same way?

"A playwright does not have to be steeped in theater. In fact, it's better that you not be," Papp said. "It can seduce you and give you the wrong idea. You should do just the opposite. Hold on to your own intellectual integrity and your own ideas. People can have a sense of the theater without ever having been in the theater. You don't have to be in the theater for your ideas to be theatrical. You think Brecht watched an actor before he wrote a play? He had an idea — and it changed theater. Forms change because the content changes. Actors and directors don't change theater. They may tamper with it, fool around with it, make experiments with it. But unless the playwrights change, the theater does not change. The intellectual base of the theater is the playwright. The playwright is the one who has the ideas."

Commuting between New York and Yale every Thursday, Papp read scripts, some of which had been passed on to him by artistic director Gerald Freedman. Agents — taking their cue from twelve years of Shakespeare in the Park — sent him thoughtful, respectable plays by Italian writer Mario Fratti, German novelist Günter Grass, and by playwrights of the British avant-garde — "Angry Young Men" such as John Osborne, Harold Pinter, Arnold Wesker and John Arden. He liked Pinter's work, just as he liked Genet and Samuel Beckett. But he felt all three were too academic for his theater. John Arden's plays, in Papp's mind, were right. It would be best, Papp initially thought, to start off with a "literary" British playwright to ease the transition from Shakespeare to contemporary work. Arden was both provocative and safe. His *Serjeant Musgrave's Dance* had been produced that March at New York's Theater de Lys and

Washington's Arena Stage. Sean O'Casey had called it "far and away the finest play of the present day, full of power, protest and frantic compassion." Arden's new pacifist play, *Armstrong's Last Goodnight,* could be construed as making a statement about the American engagement in Vietnam. Papp optioned it.

Among American playwrights, Papp did not, at first, find any who spoke to his political or social interests. Like Brustein, he thought Arthur Miller and Tennessee Williams belonged to a generation whose time had passed. He liked some of what he saw off-Broadway but, for the most part, he found it too stodgy and safe. He offered space and financial support to off off-Broadway figures such as George Bartenieff and Crystal Field, Joseph Chaikin and André Gregory. But he was both too eclectic and too interested in reaching large audiences to restrict himself to it. His taste in theater was like his taste in music: wide-ranging, ungoverned by schooling, extremely personal. It was hard, in 1966, for Papp's associates to predict exactly what kind of new plays the Public Theater would produce. He had never produced a play that had not been produced before. In fact, the total number of modern plays that he had ever produced *or* directed could be counted on one hand.

One Thursday on the train between New York and New Haven, Papp chose for his first production the work of a Bowery bum named Frank Zajac.

"Frank Zajac was a beer alcoholic in his mid-thirties," said actor Tom Aldredge, who would win an Obie portraying a character based on him. "An anarchic, self-educated paranoid, who was convinced that the entire world was out to get him, including Joe Papp. He lived 'on the Sally' — at Salvation Army flophouses — and would work as a dishwasher in some greasy spoon until he got drunk and into a fight with the cook. When he was sober, he wrote — on anything: toilet paper, napkins. He'd carry his plays around in a paper bag."

Zajac gave Papp a script titled *Stock Up on Pepper Cause Turkey's Going to War.* "It was the craziest, funniest, saddest thing I ever read," Aldredge recalled. "There were two bums, McKoater and McKeating, who were two halves of the playwright. The play was his way of arguing with himself: an outrageous, totally contemporary dialogue between the practical man who just wants to survive another day and the man of the arts, the dreamer. I thought it was brilliant but obviously unproduceable."

Papp decided to direct *Stock Up on Pepper* himself, and spent hours rehearsing his actors in the unheated space of what would one day become the Martinson Theater, cutting away huge portions of the text, thinking he was working on the Public's inaugural play. But construction of the first theater was taking much longer than expected and Papp asked Ellen Stewart of La Mama if he could direct the play there.

With his very first contemporary production, Papp provoked the kind of artistic controversy that characterized the Public Theater for the following two and a half decades. "He had an intensely passionate response to certain work and to certain people," said Papp's artistic director Gerald Freedman. "If he loved you, he loved you and let you do your thing. He wanted to affirm what the playwright had to say and to enable him to say it. He was so loyal. It didn't make aesthetic sense to me, but it did make emotional sense. Frank Zajac did not impress me as the future of American theater. His play had rich language and good acting roles, but it was not a play. And although I was not enthusiastic about Zajac, as long as I could do what I wanted to do, I thought there was room in our theater for him."

For the first season, Gerald Freedman planned to direct Franco Brusati's *La Pietà di Novembre,* based on the diary of Lee Harvey Oswald, which had won the Italian National award for best play of 1966. Papp planned to direct *The Line of Least Existence* by Rosalyn Drexler because, said Freedman, "she was the kind of character Joe liked — an independent, individualistic, pugilistic lady wrestler."

From the start, Papp looked for "blood and guts" in his playwrights, just as he had in his actors. He reacted as much if not more to the playwright than to the play, and his taste in people was extremely eclectic. He disliked receiving finished plays from agents and preferred an interactive relationship with the playwright in which he could help shape a play. For his inaugural season, Papp would ultimately reject agent-sent work in favor of plays he had come upon through personal encounters, such as one with novelist Jakov Lind, whom he met at the home of a mutual friend.

Lind was a Viennese Jew who had been evacuated to Holland on a children's transport after Hitler annexed Austria. He had survived the war by passing as a Dutch sailor in Nazi Germany, emigrated to what was then Palestine, and finally settled in London. A member of the prestigious German writers' workshop, Group 47, and an anti-Marxist socialist, he had written a collection of stories called *Soul of Wood.* "Jakov was an absolutely fascinating, ruggedly handsome, funny man," according to Peggy Papp, "and Joe just fell in love with him."

"I am still reading your collection of stories which are devastating, fascinating and skillfully written," Papp wrote Lind in July of 1966. "Do you remember our conversation at Bill Birnbaum's? I expressed an interest in your plays then and I do so again . . . I am deeply interested and concerned with the things you are saying and the way you are saying them and I want our theater to say them also."

The two men spent hours together when Lind was in New York, and Papp commissioned him to turn his new novel, *Ergo,* into a play. A year later, Papp was writing: "How are you, you forty-year-old son of a bitch? . . . I wish you were here but I will wait until after the new year when we can have a bottle and talk about the play. Jerry Freedman, who is directing *Ergo,* had a magnificent season. His technique and craftsmanship have grown to an all-time high and I think he will serve your play very well. We have done no casting as yet but we are feeling around. . . ."

Gerald Freedman would later recall the difficult, poetic language of the play, its surreal situations and political focus. Harold Clurman would later write that *Ergo* was a "savagely anti-German comedy in a typically German vein. . . . What gives such satire relevance beyond the immediate accusations of neo-Nazism and not dissimilar strains of thought, feeling and behavior (police brutality and punitive bigotry in education) is our suspicion that the Germans may not be the only ones so infected."

At the time he was corresponding with Lind, Papp was introduced to Adrienne Kennedy by actress Ellen Holly. Kennedy was thirty-five years old, African-American, a divorced mother of two small children with a degree in elementary education from Ohio State University. She had been writing for fifteen years when, in 1962, playwright Edward Albee had accepted her to his small playwriting workshop on the strength of a script titled *Funnyhouse of a Negro.* When it came time to do a workshop production of the play, she had tried to drop out of class. "I got scared," she said. "My play seemed so violent, and far too revealing. I had used the word 'nigger' throughout and I went through the pages, crossing the word out every time it appeared." Albee produced *Funnyhouse of a Negro.* Then Kennedy's one-act called *The Owl Answers,* a one-woman show starring Holly, had been produced at the Theater de Lys. It had been a critical success but a commercial flop and, apart from receiving a foundation grant, Kennedy had few prospects.

Her elliptical style and preoccupation with issues of identity had more in common with Central European than African-American playwrights. Nonrealistic and nonideological, they were more like re-enactments of a trauma. "Always the same one — the mongrel schizoid about its identity — the same one bred into my own bones over my lifetime," wrote Ellen Holly.

To be neither black nor white is to live one's life in double focus. One is neither fish nor fowl, belongs in both worlds and in neither. To relieve the stress of being split in two, one is forced to choose one heritage, one identity and let the other go in the desperate hope of becoming whole. . . . The truth, of course, is that one belongs nowhere and lives in limbo like those curious people who have to constantly move from one place to another by boat but can never land because as stateless persons they have no passports.

As "SHE who is CLARA PASSMORE who is the VIRGIN MARY who is the BASTARD who is the OWL," Holly spoke the lines:

> *I who am the ancestor of Shakespeare,*
> *Chaucer and William the Conqueror, I went to London —*
> *the Queen Elizabeth. London. They all said who ever heard*
> *of anybody going to London but I went. I stayed in my*
> *cabin the whole crossing, solitary. I was the only Negro*
> *there. . . . I was married*
> *once briefly. On my wedding day the Reverend's Wife*
> *came to me and said when I see Marys I cry for their deaths*
> *when I see brides, Clara, I cry for their deaths. But the past*
> *years I've spent teaching alone in Savannah. And alone I'm*
> *almost thirty-four, I who am the ancestor of somebody that*
> *cooked for somebody and Wiliam the Conqueror.*

Over lunch with the playwright, Papp commissioned Kennedy to write him a play.

At about the same time, Papp was investigating Václav Havel, who had been recommended to him by the London *Times* critic Henry Popkin. At the time Papp requested to see his plays, Václav Havel was the thirty-year-old literary manager of the avant-garde Balustrade Theater in Prague. Born into a wealthy family in Czechoslovakia, Havel had been a child during the Second World War and an adolescent during the Communist takeover of the country. He had been barred from attending an academic high school and university because of this "bourgeois" background and, like Papp, had been employed in a series of menial jobs as a young man.

Like Papp, too, he had become a theater person by doing theater, creating for himself a position at the Balustrade Theater. His first play, *The Garden Party,* was produced in 1963 and described by critic Kenneth Tynan in this way:

The hero, Hugo Pludek, is a student whose consuming interest is playing chess against himself. "Such a player," his mother says sagely, "will always stay in the game." His parents, a solid bourgeois couple, base their values on a storehouse of demented proverbs that they never tire of repeating. . . . They worry about Hugo, since he shows no inclination to apply for work in the ruling bureaucracy. Under their pressure, he attends a garden party thrown by the Liquidation Office, where he poses as a bureaucrat so successfully that before long he is put in charge of liquidating the Liquidation Office.

Many Czechs viewed the play as a realistic depiction of their daily lives. It became a hit in Prague and was produced in several European countries. Two years later, the Balustrade Theater produced *The Memorandum*, in which Havel examined the workings of bureaucracy and created a cast of characters that might have been lifted from New York City's Parks Department as easily as from a state-run Czech enterprise. It introduces a new, bureaucratic language called Ptydepe, which allegedly contains no emotional, national or religious resonances. The only catch is: one has to already speak or understand the language in order to apply to learn it. By 1966, the American periodical *Drama Review*, as well as Grove Press, was planning to publish *The Memorandum* and it was scheduled to be produced at the State University of New York at Albany and by the BBC as a radio play. In *The Memorandum*, the teacher tells an audience of clerks:

Ptydepe, as you know, is a synthetic language, built on a strictly scientific basis. Its grammar is constructed with maximum rationality, its vocabulary is unusually broad. It is a thoroughly exact language, capable of expressing with far greater precision than any current natural tongue all the minutest nuances in the formulation of important office documents. . . .

Papp optioned it that December and was drawn into what would become two decades of involvement with Václav Havel.

All the plays Papp chose reflected his fascination with poetic language, his attraction to plays with political themes that sidestepped accepted doctrines and his indifference to traditional form. None of the playwrights he initially chose told their story in a conventional way. Lind, Havel and Kennedy were all strong, individualistic voices, not easily pigeonholed, grounded in political material but not ideological. They featured one isolated protagonist standing against the Establishment, whether it was an African-American woman standing against the field of European history or a Central European Everyman caught in the bureaucracy of a totalitarian state. "Joe was not given to frivolity or fun in his work," said Bernard Gersten. "To be frivolous was to be irresponsible or bad. To learn something was good. That *shtetl* strain was translated into Marxist terms. Art had to serve a useful social or political purpose, to have a cutting edge. Pleasure, the purity of aesthetic experience, was not good enough, did not justify the effort."

To some of his colleagues, the most consistent feature of Papp's taste was his unpredictability. But even Freedman and Gersten, accustomed to Papp's eclectic tastes, were astounded by the play with which he ultimately decided to inaugurate his new theater. Gerome Ragni, the Open Theater actor who had handed Papp a script of *Hair* in October 1966, kept pestering the producer to read it. Papp seemed to have consigned it to the bottom of his pile. But, during one of his trips from Yale back to Manhattan, Ragni spotted him on the train and asked whether he might sit down.

Ragni was then a young man with a Medusa-like head of curls, whom Papp identified as "a genuine — not bourgeois — hippie." He had spent years auditioning for the Delacorte before being hired as a spear-carrier in *Julius Caesar*, had a rudimentary acquaintance with the producer and now pressed his cause, handing the producer a few pages of lyrics to read.

"They were handwritten pages on yellow paper," Papp recalled. "One of the songs was called 'Hair.' There was another song about basketball. I wasn't quite sure whether I liked it or not. Some of the lyrics sounded smart and some absolutely silly. But there was also a sad little scene about a guy talking about going off to war. The thing that struck me was that it had to do with the loneliness of young people. I thought: 'I want to do something that comes out of the times we are living in.' And then: 'I've never done a musical before.' And then: 'A musical is going to cost a lot of money.' But I told Ragni to come in and show me more."

Ragni and his collaborator, James Rado, came in to the Public Theater. They had been working on *Hair* for over two years by then. After they had picked out a few of their songs on the piano for Papp and Freedman, Freedman told them to find a composer. "The tunes were terrible," he said "You can't do a musical without good music."

They came back with composer Galt MacDermot, who looked, Papp later put it, as straight as a bank clerk. "I was thirty-nine years old and living in Staten Island," MacDermot recalled. "I was an ex-organist and choir director from Montreal who had received my music degree in Capetown, South Africa, and had spent most of my life playing jazz and rock-and-roll on the piano. I was into Motown and rhythm and blues. Having grown up in Canada, I wasn't familiar with many Rodgers and Hammerstein musicals. I had had one hit song called 'African Waltz' in England and here. To be honest, there was a lot of African and West

Indian influence in what I was writing, but people didn't know too much about that kind of music then. It was all rock-and-roll to them."

MacDermot sang his songs alone, accompanying himself on the piano. He had not yet written "Aquarius," but played the tunes to about two dozen other songs, including one that began: "Welcome, sulfur dioxide; hello, carbon monoxide," another that began: "Good morning starshine," and another that began: "How can people be so heartless? How can people be so cruel?"

Papp made out that some songs were sung by a character named Berger, who had been thrown out of high school, and others by Claude, who had been drafted. "I loved the music," Papp said. "And I liked them, especially Galt. He looked so square, so proper and correct. The whole thing seemed extremely provocative and I said to myself: *'Why the hell am I doing an English play?'*" The construction of the Public was still going much slower than expected and it began to look as though only one theater would be operative in the 1967–68 season, halving the number of plays Papp would need.

In March of 1967, Papp was planning to have two theaters operating at the Public. He wished to open with Arden's *Armstrong's Last Goodnight*, followed by Brusati's *La Pietà di Novembre*, Václav Havel's *The Memorandum* and Drexler's *The Line of Least Existence*, *Hair*, Adrienne Kennedy's *The Owl Answers*, the new script from Jakov Lind and another play. But in July, Papp informed his associates that he was ditching Arden, as well as Brusati and Drexler, and would open his new theater with a rock musical — then a newly coined term.

Gerald Freedman, an accomplished musician, was delighted, but almost everyone else was appalled. A musical was far more expensive to produce than a drama and, given the state of Festival finances, an unwarranted outlay of money. Chairman of the board Burt Martinson argued that by the time of production, nobody would be interested in hippies and long hair. Bernard Gersten argued that the core of subscribers to the new theater were Shakespeare aficionados, who were not likely to enjoy rock-and-roll. Merle Debuskey, who had already sent out press releases about the first tier of contemporary playwrights, thought that Rado and Ragni were "really crazy. They may not have been druggies but they looked and acted like they were. They were East Village characters. La Mama types. And it wasn't an accident that their play was called *Hair*."

The process of getting *Hair* produced was chaotic, even by theatrical norms. Ragni and Rado not only fought for every word they had written but wanted to choose the director and star in the production as well. Papp, who was busy preparing his stripped-down version of *Hamlet* to follow *Hair*, assigned it to his associate artistic director, Gerald Freedman.

"To me, it was a terrific artistic challenge," Freedman recalled. "There was the music and there were characters but I was taken aback by the lack of form and lack of credible writing ability. It had practically no scenes or anything you could call an event. It had so many musical numbers that you couldn't separate out what you wanted the audience to remember. And they kept bringing in rewrites everyday — on the backs of envelopes."

Hair casting notices were put in trade papers in May 1967. During the next three months, group after group of actors and hippies — some stoned — meandered through the empty building to audition. Freedman asked choreographer Anna Sokolow to help choreograph the production. She agreed but almost immediately was hospitalized with appendicitis, leaving Freedman to stage most of the show himself. She would reappear at the end of the process to contest what he had done.

Meanwhile, Freedman tried to keep the script to himself. When general manager David Black had read it, he had concluded that Papp had lost his mind and that the Public Theater would be the laughingstock of the business. Designer Ming Cho Lee, then working on the summer productions, kept asking Freedman for a script and Freedman refused to give him one. "Finally I told Jerry that if he didn't get me the script, I couldn't design the show," Lee recalled. "My approach, after reading the script, is to question the director about an overall production scheme, discussing choices: Should it be realistic or abstract? Should it be period or not? Should the material be metal, wood, granite? Then I do a rough sketch for the director to find out if I'm going in the right direction. Then I make a one-half-inch-scale model and paint it up. All this takes time. So I need to see the script.

"But Jerry kept saying that it didn't matter, that I wouldn't understand it anyhow, and he was right. When I finally got the script, I opened it up and there — for two pages — was one word: *Hair.* Hair. Hair. Hair. Hair. Hair. Right down the page. And the next page also. I thought Joe had gone crazy. If there is a plot, it is so deconstructed that you cannot see it. I said — 'This is beyond me. How do I design this show?'"

Freedman had worked on several Broadway musicals. He was a meticulous craftsman, careful, well prepared. Within the first few hours of rehearsals Freedman collided head-on with writer-actors Ragni and Rado, who often came to rehearsals stoned and kept changing their minds about issues Freedman thought he had settled the day before. The resident team — Freedman, Ming Cho Lee, costume designer Theoni Aldredge and lighting designer Martin Aronstein — came to view Ragni and Rado as hippies who lacked the professional skills to write anything resembling a play. Both wished to play the leading roles. Freedman thought they were too old to pass as high school kids but finally compromised by casting Ragni. The authors kept revising their material; choreographer Anna Sokolow, recovered, began her dance work and soon was not speaking to Freedman. Freedman would stage a scene one way; Sokolow would stage the same scene differently. The authors spun intrigues between the two, presenting the producer with so many conflicts and memos (such as one on "the spirit and the nature of *Hair*") that Papp began to rip them up unread. Ragni and Rado had written a nude scene; Papp cut it out. And the hippie ethos began to take over everyone connected with the project.

"I had an assistant from Tulane University," recalled Ming Cho Lee. "He was very neat and clean. We used to work on a table in my bedroom and it did not bother me to have him in there. Well, first it was a poncho. Then he let his hair grow. Then he stopped bathing. Then it was reflector glasses. Then he started burning incense in the room. Eventually I couldn't stand it anymore."

The conflict between Sokolow and Freedman became so heated that, during the final week of rehearsal, Gerald Freedman withdrew from the show. "I told Joe that I felt we had invested so much in the opening of the theater that it was better for me to resign," Freedman recalled. "But, of course, I expected Joe to say: *'No Way!'* To fight for me unto the death. I was, after all, his artistic director. But he didn't do that. Something about the enormity of opening the theater seemed to make him lose his nerve and he didn't come through. So I left. I went to Washington."

Papp appointed Anna Sokolow as director. She promptly installed co-author Jim Rado in the role he desired and he began giving interviews, telling reporters such things as "Joe Papp is a love person. You know the Diggers just opened a new free store in the East Village? Well Joe Papp has been doing it for years."

The staff at the Public was dismayed. "My own feeling at the time of the dress rehearsal was that we should not open the play, let alone open the theater with this play," said associate producer Bernard Gersten. But Papp remained optimistic. "You wanna talk disaster?" he asked a reporter. Then, with uncanny prescience, "Actually success will be our greatest problem. Each of our plays is scheduled to run for eight weeks. What if we have a hit? Where do we put it?"

The first performance of *Hair* was set for October 17. A few days before the first preview, Local 829 of the Scenic Artists and Brotherhood of Painters and Allied Workers voted to go on strike. A strike would trap the half-painted *Hair* sets in a warehouse behind a picket line. Ming Cho Lee and technical director Andy Mihok rented a truck and just before midnight dragged the sets out of the shop. They lugged them up to the third floor of the library and finished the painting themselves.

"The final dress rehearsal was hopeless," said Ming Cho Lee. "Nineteen thirties modern dance with half-finished scenery set to rock-and-roll." After seeing it, Papp fired Anna Sokolow and sent a telegram to Freedman that read: "PLEASE COME BACK." Anna Sokolow in turn sent Papp a telegram that read: "DEMAND PUBLIC ANNOUNCEMENT OF REMOVAL OF MY NAME FROM HAIR." Two days before the opening, Freedman fired Rado and changed the entire show back to the way he had staged it. The first preview featured staging of the first half by Freedman and of the second by Sokolow. By the second, the staging was entirely his.

Papp, who had shrewdly staggered press previews from October 26 through October 29 so as to keep the percentage of critics at each show as low as possible, sent a memo to *Hair*'s cast and crew: "Clive Barnes of the *Times* will be reviewing the 3 PM Sunday matinee performance on October 29th. We have deliberately kept out subscribers so that we can get a choice and vigorous audience. We ask that you invite your friends to buy tickets for this performance. Please be aware that everyone over thirty will be suspect."

The reviews of Papp's first production at the Public Theater and what many called "the first hippie musical" were mixed. "If only good intentions were golden," wrote Clive Barnes (who, to Papp's chagrin, attended the evening show, not the matinee, and whose review was representative), "*Hair* would be great . . . but [it] is still very much worth seeing."

If it had a story, most reviewers suggested, *Hair* might be very good. It had life, charm, innocence, energy, likable actors, good direction and design and music that was new to musicals. They had no idea just how popular that music would become. Songs such as "Aquarius," "Good Morning Starshine" and "Frank Mills" would be recorded by dozens of singers and groups all over the world, and the musical itself would become a pacifist symbol, particularly in Eastern Europe, where it was produced in such places as the former Yugoslavia during its civil war.

Its music and cheerful lack of structure were, in fact, the innovations *Hair* brought to the American musical theater. Although jazz and music hall music played their part, the Broadway musical had since the First

World War been dominated by a Central European tradition that was rooted in the operettas of Johann Strauss and Franz Lehár. "It has been increasingly evident that the musical theater, sooner or later, was going to have to face up to the fact that fashions in popular music have changed," wrote John Wilson, reviewing the album. "As the 1967–68 season started, nothing that has happened in popular music since World War II — the folk fad, the rise of rock (much less the numerous developments in jazz) — had effectively reached the musical theater. But now *Hair* . . . has plunged into this vacuum."

The mainstream theater critics did not grasp this radical shift nor did they appreciate the amplified beat of the six-piece rock band situated ten feet above the stage. Clive Barnes, Papp recalled, fell asleep during the show. Walter Kerr, at the Sunday *Times* since the *Herald Tribune* had folded, resented being solicited by actors wandering through the audience offering him marijuana. But the only expression of real outrage came from the *Village Voice*. "Hair is bald opportunism," their critic wrote. "It exploits every obvious up-to-date issue — the draft, the war, even negritude — in a crass effort to be both timely and tidy. . . . Let it be forgotten. Let the Public Theater begin again."

Hair did not please audiences accustomed to Shakespeare either. "This particular play was so disgusting in every way we were astonished that Mr. Papp would have produced it. All of the standard common vulgar words are openly used on the stage and all of the common sexual actions are carried out," wrote one businessman/subscriber. "In addition to this, ridicule is brought upon Jesus Christ, the Catholic Religion and the American Flag. . . ." A questionnaire distributed by the Festival elicited mostly favorable responses but also such comments as "WHY? Why did you go to all this trouble and expense to produce such an inane show? Two thousand years of dramatic literature and you choose this one! It's not art. It's not even entertaining."

Joseph Papp responded:

I can understand how some people are shocked to hear a four-letter word uttered from a public platform. I can also understand how a manifestation of disrespect for religion or for the flag will cause many people to react negatively. But the fact is that the young people of the play in real life have grown to distrust institutions and patriotism, sexual standards, standards of dress and deportment. This is the truthful manifestation of their rejection of old values, which have produced four wars in the past fifty years, killing thousands of young Americans like themselves — and now subjecting them to the draft and the possibility of annihilation before having the chance to grow up and live their lives.

As the producer, I need not subscribe to every statement uttered from our stage. I am concerned with veracity and theatricality — and *Hair* possesses both of these attributes.

Despite the critics and subscribers, *Hair* became a downtown hit. Its run in the new Anspacher Theater was immediately sold out and the writers begged Papp to extend it. Papp, however, was deep into rehearsals for his deconstructed *Hamlet*. He had only one theater, he had scheduled only eight weeks of running time for each show and extending the run of *Hair* meant reorganizing the timetable of his inaugural season. "I decided to close it," he recalled. "It was a bad decision, which I would never make again. We had a major success on our hands. We could have made millions and millions of dollars. Instead, we let it go. But I didn't know what a hit was then. I didn't realize that something we produced could be a hit."

At the time, the anti-Broadway ethos of the New York Shakespeare Festival was such that when someone proposed that *Hair* be moved to the small Henry Miller Theater on West 43rd Street, the suggestion was quickly shot down. Gerald Freedman believed that *Hair* would not work on a proscenium stage. Trustee Burt Martinson offered Papp $50,000 to move the show, but the producer replied that he could not take money that Martinson might otherwise donate to nonprofit work and waste it on a speculative Broadway venture.

It was while *Hair* was still running that Papp received a telephone call from a stranger named Michael Butler. Butler wanted a copy of the *Hair* poster. A few days later, Papp received in the mail a thick, cream-colored envelope bearing the letterhead *International Sports Core, Oak Brook, IL.* Butler, president of the ISC, enclosed two copies of the Oak Brook Annuals and the brochure of his polo club. In the accompanying letter, Butler lamented the fact that *Hair* could not travel to Oak Brook and, in a postscript that could have been written by a stagestruck child, asked again for the poster.

Papp answered the letter, and always alert to a fundraising opportunity, gave Butler a crash correspondence course in producing:

There is the fact that the production has been mounted in a special kind of space and staged accordingly. The scenic elements which alone cost $14,000 do not take into account the existing architectural elements to which they have been attached. To create a new scenic space would be very expensive. Road salaries are high for actors, musicians, stagehands, designers, etc. Percentages to the authors and designers add substantially to the cost. Then there is transportation and whatnot. It is mainly money and secondarily schedule and lastly the doubt I have at present to put our energies into moving about when we are just settling down in a new theater.

Even if all the money were available to pay for the cost of moving the show, I would wish to tie it in with our campaign to raise funds for our activities. As you may know, our annual budget is $1,700,000 which is painfully raised from a great variety of sources. . . .

If you could conceive an occasion which includes *Hair* (all paid for) and a major social event which could produce $50,000 in tax-exempt gifts toward the work we are performing I would be very interested. In any event, I would enjoy talking to you when you are in New York — lunch perhaps.

Michael Butler lunched with Papp. He offered to coproduce *Hair* with the Festival and, after investigating the probable costs of moving it to the Village Gate, Papp agreed to move it to a Broadway discothèque called the Cheetah. Butler put up $50,000 that Papp would not accept from Martinson and the venture was billed as a coproduction. Prices at the Cheetah were reasonable, "young people" gathered there nightly to dance and the producer liked the idea of, once again, attracting a new kind of audience. *Hair* opened at the Cheetah a few days before Christmas and almost no one came to see it. "What I failed to understand," Papp later said, "was that *Hair* was a white man's show and that the blacks and Hispanics who came to the Cheetah wanted to dance, not see a show. It was a total failure." At that point, the show closed and the Festival's rights to produce the play reverted to the authors. "Everyone thought the show was deader than a doornail — except Michael," recalled Bernard Gersten. With no competition from any experienced theater professional, Butler acquired the Broadway rights and went ahead with a third production.

In May 1968, *Hair* became a Broadway hit. Under the terms of the original contract, the Festival received 1.5 percent of the gross and 10 percent of subsidiary rights. Six months later, with two companies grossing $200,000 per week, the Festival was earning an income of $1,500 to $1,800. In the two years that followed, the musical opened in England, France, West Germany, Finland, Spain, Yugoslavia, Czechoslovakia, Israel, Italy, Japan, Canada and Australia, its various companies grossing more than $350,000 per week. Dozens of recordings of *Hair* songs were made. Eventually there was a movie. Over the years, the New York

Shakespeare Festival alone would receive more than one and a half million dollars in revenues from *Hair*.

Papp's critics would later pinpoint the *Hair* episode as the producer's awakening to the possibilities of Broadway. But at the time, Papp's mind was on other things. He was directing Václav Havel's *The Memorandum* and still engaged by the consequences of his stripped-down *Hamlet* that had followed *Hair* at the Public.

Hamlet was also a by-product of his teaching at Yale. When he first met with his group of student directors, they complained that their usual assignments — a series of short scenes from different plays — gave them little sense of how to approach a play as a whole. Papp summarily changed the curriculum. He decided to spend most of the semester examining one play and chose *Hamlet,* with the object of identifying episodes of conflict in the text and cutting it so that it could be done with six actors in forty-five minutes. The result that had most interested Papp was the work turned in by Ted Cornell, who had smashed the play to pieces and reconstituted its shards. He had offered Cornell a job at the Delacorte during the summer of 1967 and now employed him as his directing assistant.

Papp would produce *Hamlet* eight times in his career, but in 1967, his view of the play was strongly influenced by the death of his father. He created a *Hamlet* who was not a prince of Denmark but a Puerto Rican street prince. He turned his back on Shakespearean convention and unabashedly drew on the traditions of basic American popular culture that he had experienced as a child.

"Is the death of a father one of the most shattering experiences a son could have?" Papp wrote.

> Is the loss of the key male link with the past an irreparable one? Is there fear in the hidden realization that the boy has become the father? . . . Hamlet chooses to remain the eternal son, to hold back the process of nature and live outside the pale of humankind. He will not be reconciled, and chooses his own death rather than fall in line with the common theme — the death of fathers. He dies a son. . . . This production aims radioactive ididium 192 at the nineteenth century HAMLET statue and by gamma ray shadowgraphing seeks to discover the veins of the living original, buried under accumulated layers of reverential varnish.

The production that emerged was a free variation on Shakespeare that many remember as *Hellzapoppin* set to the kind of music Galt MacDermot had composed for *Hair*. It ran an uninterrupted ninety minutes, using a set of sequences rather than Shakespeare's scenes, and incorporating vaudeville and burlesque routines and lots of modern gadgets. As Hamlet, Martin Sheen walked through the audience shaking hands, eating peanuts, discarding peanut shells and giving away balloons. He began the famous "To be or not to be" soliloquy in a thick Puerto Rican accent (Sheen, half Puerto Rican, was born Ramon Estevez), which shocked some members of the audience and made others laugh but resulted in a soliloquy that was, for many, both moving and brand new. Ophelia, clad in cutaway and tights, sang her mad songs into a hand-held microphone; Hamlet filmed the play-within-a-play with a home movie camera. As in *Hair*, the actors moved through the audience and solicited their participation, culminating in the last scene when a spectator was invited to help Hamlet in the game of Russian roulette with which Papp had replaced the play's ultimate swordplay.

The major reviewers as well as many Delacorte supporters hated it. Papp later wrote:

> Most of our 10,000 subscribers committed themselves to our first four plays with expectations that the work would in some way reflect the "high moral tone" and visual splendor of the Bard's plays. *Hair* was the opening gun. Cries of outrage and indignation resounded from amidst the ranks of the 10,000. The rock *Hamlet* disaffected even more of the faithful. *Ergo* dwindled the ranks still further. *Memorandum* recouped a few because it was a more conventional play with lighter demands on an audience's commitment. There was never a performance during the run of our first three plays at which anywhere from five to fifty people didn't storm out of their seats in protest. We even developed a spot in *Hamlet* to accommodate these angry departures.

Schools superintendent Bernard E. Donovan, charged with administering a three-year touring contract with the Festival, refused to allow *Hamlet* to tour the schools, claiming it was unsuitable. Papp charged Donovan with "artistic censorship," staged a special matinee for teachers and members of the Board of Education followed by a discussion of his production and, of course, invited the press.

Superintendent Donovan, who doubtless remembered the Moses affair, changed his position. Rather than impose *Hamlet* on the schools, he would leave it up to the individual school to decide whether or not to see the play at the Public Theater. Papp was delighted. The cancellation of the tour saved him money and left him with surplus cash in hand. He asked Ted Cornell to hang a rudimentary light grid and put up a set of bleachers downstairs in the room that had served as the HIAS *shul*. After the schools' production, it would serve as an experimental, 100-seat theater.

Shortly after the Donovan decision, the Rockefeller Foundation offered Papp a one-year $25,000 grant to do six new plays in his experimental theater. Under the Equity agreement that provided for workshops, each playwright would receive $100 for the play; each director and actor would receive a total of $100. The run would be three weekends or nine performances. In the fall of 1968, the producer turned his attention to a second season of contemporary plays upstairs and downstairs. It was during that year that he began to work closely with playwrights and began to develop the emotional, complicated set of personal relationships with them that would characterize his theater.

ELEVEN

The
Private Man

IN APRIL 1968, civil rights leader Martin Luther King was murdered in Memphis, Tennessee. In June, New York senator Robert F. Kennedy was assassinated in Los Angeles, California. Summer violence in the urban ghettos had been commonplace across the nation for four years when, during the summer of 1968, the entire city of Chicago became an armed camp. A seven-foot barbed-wire fence was erected around the hall where the Democratic National Convention took place, a mandatory curfew was set for the thousands of demonstrators who had come to the city protesting the Vietnam War and eleven thousand Chicago policemen were put on alert. As Hubert Humphrey was nominated for president, Americans watched police battle demonstrators on television screens and argued the issues in their kitchens and living rooms. The antiwar movement, the student movement, the feminist movement and the black militant movement divided families all over the country. Papp wanted to address those divisions and conflicts inside his theater.

In 1968, Papp's own family was less divided than frozen into a set of unchanging and unsatisfactory relationships. The producer had no contact with his first two wives, infrequent meetings with two of his grown children and none with the third. Photographs taken of his third family in the 1960s show a boyish, handsome father, a pretty, smiling, wife and two lively, dark-eyed children. But by 1968, husband and wife were contemplating divorce. Their good times together had become a memory, set at the ranch in Manila, Utah, surrounded by the Bennions.

Utah vacations were, Peggy Papp later said, "truly golden days which brought out the best in Joe, his sweetest, most caring side." The Papps and the Bennions went horseback riding and hiking, built campfires, sang and danced. Papp played with Miranda and Tony and particularly enjoyed the time he spent with his father-in-law, Heber Bennion, whom he viewed as an archetype of the American hero. The two men would ride horseback or work together in the sheepfold and the producer would feel as though he were living a life out of a movie.

In New York, however, Papp saw little of his family. His daughter Miranda routinely stayed up late waiting for her father to come home from the theater. His son Tony viewed it as a rival for his father's attention. His wife withdrew. The couple had initially sought marital therapy in 1965, but when Papp began intensive individual therapy with the marital therapist, Peggy — who had brought her husband to the process — felt left out and betrayed.

Down on Lafayette Street, at what Papp had named the Public Theater, staffers became more aware of Papp's therapist than of Papp's wife. Peggy Papp came to opening-night parties and enjoyed talking with actors and playwrights but she rarely visited or called the office. In contrast, the producer took the subway to see his therapist up to four times per week and staffers remember seeing her at the theater. "I had been through Freudian analysis and the idea of a therapist having that much time available to a patient and so personal an involvement with him seemed suspect to me," recalled Gerald Freedman. "But she was like a life jacket for Joe. I thought he was dependent upon her in a lot of ways."

When Joseph Papp awoke in the middle of the night suffering from one of his anxiety attacks he called his therapist. He invited her to theater openings, family *seders*, even to the Bennions' home in Utah. "I remember her saying that if she did not accompany us, Joe might go into a profound depression," Peggy Papp would later recall. "She also went with us on other vacations. I experienced this as an intrusion into our personal life but I was in a bind. If I protested, I would be held responsible for Joe's depression. She encouraged Joe's dependency on her to such a degree it had a destructive effect on our marriage and family life. She became his mother rather than his therapist."

Papp himself would later describe his therapist as the person who saved his life. He had no intimates. Although he enjoyed warm relationships with Gerald Freedman and Bernard Gersten, he rarely discussed personal matters with them. At work, his energies were focused on work. "When I got to know Joe," playwright David Rabe later said, "I thought it might be nice to go hang out with him sometime. But Joe did not hang out. When we had a drink, it was always in his office. I knew he was in therapy but it came up in the course of talking about a play, not in any kind of personal confidence."

In fact, his therapist had become Papp's closest friend, and the pyscho-analytically oriented therapeutic process, a model for the way he worked as a producer. "I am using my body as a laboratory," he told an inter-viewer during the course of his treatment. "The play is the nub of my inquiry. I am looking for self-knowledge. . . . It doesn't matter whether the play fails or not. . . . The truth is internal and turns out to be one's personal truth. I am the one seeking the truth and doing the investiga-tion. . . ."

As his directing students at Yale noted, Joseph Papp honored play-wrights in a way he did not honor directors or even actors. He saw writers as people of special insight, bearers of the word, whose talent had to be nurtured and protected. It was with playwrights that the producer was at his most passionate, loving and possessive. Shakespeare had not needed him as a father: There was no call for Papp to explain him, ensure his plays got written, find him a way to earn a living or worry about his physical and psychological well-being. He did all these things for his new playwrights. "The older one learns, not from being on the same wave-length as the young, but through his mature understanding" was the way he formulated the relationship. "That's the way I learn. Then his job, the older one, is to lend his material resources, if he has them, his expertise, if he has it, so that he can put the young person in the foreground, downstage center."

Papp depended on playwrights. He needed them not only to supply product for his theater but to articulate for him his deepest feelings and voice his concerns. He knew that every institutional theater in history had been defined by its playwright. Shakespeare had been the voice of the Globe; Molière, the voice of the Comédie Française; Chekhov, the voice of the Moscow Art Theater; Odets, the voice of the Group Theater. In order for the New York Shakespeare Festival to join their ranks, Papp needed such a voice.

Toward those candidates Papp discovered and took in, he assumed a generous, paternalistic role. At the Shakespeare Workshop downstown,

Papp had provided subway fare for his technicians, lunch money for his actors, new-sweater money for composer David Amram. By the late sixties, Papp was a benefactor on a larger scale, giving some people jobs to keep them going, lending them money, allowing them to live temporarily at the Public Theater, listing them on the Festival's group health insurance when they had no other medical coverage. When he had taken possession of the Public Theater, the seventy-year-old HIAS caretaker handed him his keys, saying, "I guess I'm out now." Papp had replied, "No, you're not. I bought the building and you come with it." Arthur Abraham continued to live in his small basement apartment with his dog. Papp would, over the next two decades, offer shelter to many individual artists and theater companies including Peter Schumann's Bread and Puppet Theater, Joseph Chaikin's Open Theater, André Gregory's Manhattan Project, Mabou Mines, Doug Dyer's Commune, and Felix Camillo's The Family.

Playwrights, however, were given even more than shelter. They were given opportunities, productions, various forms of stipends and — most important — large doses of Papp's attention. Some of his associates came to feel that the producer's relationship with his playwrights resembled the relationship of an indulgent father to a brood of children. He gave them the equivalent of a blank check, provided they met his requirements of the relationship.

That relationship was complicated. Although the producer was himself a prolific and often captivating writer, he never saw himself as an author but as a kind of muse-editor-facilitator who exercised his creativity by transforming a script into a theatrical event.

"There was no other person then in the theater world who would involve himself with a playwright in this way," recalled Gail Merrifield, who often witnessed that interaction. "He adapted himself to each play and playwright. He read personalities in an uncanny way, and every time, he was all there with the aim of finding the heart of the play. He came up with hundreds of ideas but did not insist on any of them. He liked for the playwright to discover his or her own solutions.

"Joe did speak very rapidly and with great intensity and some playwrights simply took his critique for gospel. Others, who managed to get it all down, sifted through the ideas and chose those they found useful."

Most of Papp's playwrights basked in Papp's attention, even if they were not always comfortable with the degree of emotional engagement the process required. In their twenties and thirties, suffering from the insecurity that comes with marginality and lack of recognition, they competed for his time and support. Each writer would bring out a different facet of Papp's patriarchal style, trigger his soft and hot spots, cause him elation and disappointment. And, of course, every playwright Papp mentored would bring his or her own temperament, ambition and history of being parented to the process. The result was a set of relationships loaded with complex interpersonal issues, risk, problems of ownership — issues that would occupy and sometimes plague Papp for the rest of his life.

Almost without exception, Papp was introduced to a playwright by virtue of a strong personal recommendation, such as the one that actress Ellen Holly had made in regard to the work of Adrienne Kennedy. He then met or corresponded with the playwright and commissioned a play. Then began the process of coaxing the writer to deliver the work. "Please consider this a gentle nudge," Papp wrote to Kennedy more than a year after commissioning a new play. "We are making plans for our next season and have the need to know. . . . Is there a completed portion of it that I could have? If not, when do you think I could have something?" When Kennedy wrote back asking for more time, Papp replied indulgently, "It is important to me that you be satisfied with what you are doing and the fact that you won't settle for less is positive."

When *Cities in Bezique* finally arrived, it looked like nothing Papp had ever seen. It was handwritten on a variety of paper, some of it tissue paper, with cutouts from newspapers and Bezique playing cards pasted onto its pages. Although it looked more like an art object than a script, Papp regarded it as a serious submission. Rather than asking the playwright what she was doing and requesting that she try to submit something more intelligible, he tried to grasp it on her terms and discussed what to do with it with Gerald Freedman. "Adrienne isn't writing plays; she's writing poems and I admire them," said Freedman, who was to direct the play. "Do you force her to try to write like somebody else? Or do you try to deal with it?" They dealt with it by using only the name *Cities in Bezique* and producing Kennedy's earlier two one-acts, *The Owl Answers* and *The Beast's Story,* under that title.

"I don't know if I'd ever told you that Havel was in trouble with the regime," Václav Havel's translator wrote the producer at the same time Papp was corresponding with Kennedy.

It started the time he was supposed to come to New York with me last June — when his passport was taken away from him — and it's been getting worse ever since. The Balustrade Theatre is cagey about renewing his contract. All his applications to go abroad (on business) are being turned down. He was investigated by the police for 48 hours nonstop — rather vigorously, I hear. So — in other words — all one can do for him in the way of publicity abroad may be more than just a natural reaction to the discovery of a young writer of considerable talent. It may prove to be — literally — a life-saving endeavor. . . .

Papp promptly invited Havel to come to New York. "There are two problems," Havel replied.

The formalities connected with the obtaining of travelling permission, as well as of the visa, take some time. The second problem is a financial one: I cannot pay for my airplane tickets with the royalties, of which I dispose abroad, and in our currency their price surpasses my possibilities. It is rather embarrassing for me to talk about this but I am obliged to, as I do not know whether your invitation includes the covering of expenses. . . . I could accept your invitation only provided that some American institution paid my expenses.

The situation is even such, that I can obtain my travelling permission only if the respective invitation expressly includes this point. Please, do not take this as a request to pay for my visit, but merely as information about the situation over here and about my possibilities. . . .

Papp, ever sensitive to the humiliation associated with having to ask anyone for money, wrote back that the Festival would assume the cost of Havel's living expenses and "Naturally, we will also assume the cost of your plane fare. Perhaps also during the time you spend here I will arrange one or two speaking engagements for you at nearby universities."

Papp contacted people he knew at New York University, Columbia and Yale, arranging for the lectures as well as for an interpreter. Playwright and producer hit it off and Havel later viewed his stay in the United States as the opportunity of a lifetime. "Dear Joe," reads Havel's letter on his return to Prague:

I was extremely sorry not to be able to say goodbye to you in New York. . . . I should like to thank you again very, very much for all you have done for me. . . . I think New York is amazing and am quite smitten with this city and never cease to thank you in my heart; without you, I would hardly ever have had the chance to see it. It has been all so awfully interesting for me and I often think of those wonderful days. . . . In the hope to be given the opportunity to welcome you in Prague some day, or to meet you in New York again in the future, I remain. . . .

On August 12, Papp wrote back that *The Memorandum* had been named Best Foreign Play of the Year. Nine days later, the Soviet Union invaded Czechoslovakia. Havel's plays were officially banned within the country and foreign productions blocked by the Czechoslovak State Literary Agency. In what was perhaps his most consistent demonstration of loyalty to a playwright, Joseph Papp kept in touch with Havel for twenty years, during which time Havel worked as a manual laborer, became a leading Czech dissident, was jailed and later elected president of his country.

"When I was in custody facing trial," Havel would write when he was a famous Czech dissident, "it was at Joe Papp's initiative that I received an offer to go to the United States to study. That offer — although I did not take advantage of it and chose trial and prison instead — was of immense political significance: our state was thus compelled to offer me the trip to the United States in exchange for not disgracing itself by bringing me to trial. That, in turn, gave me the opportunity to humiliate the totalitarian power by declining the offer."

From the time he began producing plays at the Public Theater, Papp's taste straddled a range that reached from Havel's absurdist Czechoslovak *Memorandum* to what staffers called " angry street stuff" written by American blacks and whites. "The better plays we received at that time were written by blacks," Papp's assistant Ted Cornell later recalled. "It was likely that a good black play would get overlooked elsewhere and because it did not get overlooked at the Festival, we began to get a reputation for being a theater in which black playwrights could feel comfortable." Among the early playwrights Papp produced were Edgar White and Charles Gordone — both African-Americans.

Gordone's *No Place to Be Somebody* — Papp's first major success after *Hair* — was brought to the Festival by Walter Jones, an actor and director who had worked at the Public for several years. Papp looked at the script and said he couldn't read it. It was typed on standard paper but written in "black dialect" with every letter capitalized to emphasize its confrontational quality:

YES! THEY'S MO' TO BEIN' BLACK THAN MEETS THE EYE!
    BEIN' BLACK HAS A WAY'A MAKIN' YA MAD MOS' OF THE TIME, HURT ALL THE TIME AN' HAVIN' SO MANY HANGUPS, THE PROBLEM' A SOO-SIDE DON'T EVEN ENTER YO' MIN'!

Gordone had spent seven years writing *No Place,* revising it, taking it around to directors and producers and actors, assembling casts, trying to get it on. Born in Cleveland to a family of devout Seventh-Day Adventists, he had been to college and had served in the air force. In 1969, however, Gordone walked around barefoot, with most of his head shaved, wearing beads and a vest over his bare chest. "Why am I dressed this way?" he told a reporter. "Why the hell not? Since I'm part Indian, part French, part Irish and part nigger, I take a little here and little there and it should come out American."

Papp was intrigued by Gordone. "A very strange, interesting guy," he said. "He had a nice warmth about him and he was very, very offbeat. Even for *that* time, he was outrageous. And it was such a relief to find a play that said black is not necessarily beautiful and white is not just terrible. Attacking white people was the fashion at that time for black writers. I agreed with some of that point of view but I wasn't going to stand there being attacked because I'm white. There were too many liberals that just loved being in that position."

Papp saw himself as clearly in *No Place,* as he had seen himself one year earlier in his production of *Hamlet,* and decided on the spot to produce it. Then, he assigned it to his former student Ted Cornell. It was the first of Papp's many problematic match-ups of playwright and director, which critics would call hasty and unthought-through and supporters would view as an example of his penchant for mixing people of wildly contrasting backgrounds and styles and hoping for the best.

"It was with some trepidation that black playwright Charles Gordone handed the manuscript of his play *No Place to Be Somebody* over to Ted Cornell, the very WASP director of the Public Experimental Theater of the New York Shakespeare Festival," Papp later wrote.

> A more unlikely combination would be hard to find: Gordone, barefoot, bare-chested and pigtailed, looking more Iroquois-Chinese than African; Cornell, a blue-eyed, 24-year-old shaggy-haired Yale Drama student. Gordone must have thought, what could Cornell know about the black man's anger and what makes him laugh? And what about this Public Theater? True, it did produce *Hair* and several other contemporary plays, but its main reputation was grounded in Shakespeare. All this seemed far from Gordone's idea of the right place for *No Place.* But, Mr. Gordone was hungry and desperate, and after three [*sic*] years of trying to place his play, felt he could no longer afford too many quibbles.

The marriage of Gordone and Cornell seemed a surefire recipe for disaster and, according to those who were there, it was. Gordone felt he had nothing to learn from Cornell, behaved like a desperado, drank, prowled the theater during rehearsals, stalked out during arguments, came in one day with a revolver and so frightened the racially mixed company that they began to rally around their novice director.

"I had going for me that I was as angry and alienated as he was, as highly energized and maybe even as verbally articulate," Cornell would later recall. "I was incredibly green, however. I didn't know that a marijuana cigarette was called a roach. I suppose if I had been a lieutenant in Vietnam, I might have been shot. In the theater I was given enough rope to survive."

"They began to carry on a dialogue — direct, intense, often angry, never casual," Papp wrote. "Nobody was polite. The stage erupted with bursts of verbal violence, ghetto style, reflecting the strong feelings and emotions the play engendered among the black and white members of the cast. The transition from the text to rehearsal to performance was almost indiscernible. . . . What it did achieve was a rich confrontation of the black man and himself, the white man and himself, and then placed those selves face to face with each other."

No Place to Be Somebody opened on May 4, 1969, at the Other Stage to rave reviews and then ran for several months at the Anspacher. It was, *Newsweek*'s Jack Kroll wrote, "the first new black play I have seen that comes close to putting everything together. It is ambitious, written with a mixture of white heat and intellectual clarity . . . it is funny and sad, angry and stoical, revolutionary and conciliatory. And perhaps most important, it unmistakably sounds, feels, smells and tastes like a play." Papp took *No Place* to Broadway for a limited, two-week engagement at the ANTA Theater as part of a festival of performances from America's resident professional theaters. Then, in the spring of 1970, the playwright won the Pulitzer Prize for drama.

It was the first time either an African-American dramatist or an off-Broadway production had won the Pulitzer Prize, and Papp later described himself, as a father would, as "stunned" and "very proud." He saw the award as validation of his new play policy at the New York Shakespeare Festival, validation of his taste in new work, validation of his effort to bring work by African-Americans to the stage.

The success of *No Place* was to illustrate the complications of Papp's dependence on playwrights. Gordone succumbed to the "Pulitzer Curse," and never again enjoyed a success of that kind. Ted Cornell, who had helped Gordone shape the script and bring it to fruition, was eclipsed by the media's attention to playwright and producer. *No Place*, like *Hair* and subsequent Festival productions, became "a Joseph Papp production." The director's credit would enhance his résumé but at the time,

Cornell felt cheated, locked out of a success that he had helped create and aware that in Papp's Festival family, the siblings — actors, technicians, designers, administrative staff — were far from equal. Playwrights were the favored elder sons, and directors, the second sons, were taken for granted and, sometimes, sacrificed.

Some Festival veterans believed that because Papp viewed himself as a competent director but never a writer, he was not as impressed by directors, did not honor them or find their work mysterious enough to qualify for his awe. "I don't know any really fine American stage directors," he had told an interviewer. "The stage director I most admire is Michael Langham. I think he has the most delicate hand for Shakespeare that I've seen around, better than Peter Brook whom I also consider an excellent director. As far as American directors are concerned, I hate to say it but it's pretty sad. You see, we have no theater — we aren't going to have good directors."

Papp often credited Joel Friedman, Stuart Vaughan, Gerald Freedman and Gladys Vaughan as the people who had taught him to direct. He never fired any of them from a production. But he had jettisoned Gladys Vaughan in 1967 by not assigning her a summer production and would jettison her husband three years later, after Stuart Vaughan had organized and directed a mammoth three-play project. "We got great reviews," Vaughan recalled, "but Joe called me in afterwards and said, 'I'm not going to ask you to do any more work for the Festival.' I was surprised. Despite our many differences, I thought he was a good producer, maybe the best around. He didn't interfere in my work. I didn't take any crap from him. But he said, 'It's just like at the Actors' Lab when I was working with Howard Da Silva and Morris Carnovsky. They hated each other so that nothing could get done. You couldn't have them standing in the same room. Well, that's the way I feel about you.'"

Gerald Freedman would observe, "It was hard for Joe to give directors credit. He enjoyed directing and, although he never said as much, was competitive with other directors and did not go out of his way to credit the directors who worked at his theater." The reviews Papp himself received as a director were mixed. Some actors praised him for his endlessly innovative ideas. Many saw him as competent but impatient, a text-based director with little interest in visual "concepts." Others found his constant stream of new ideas chaotic and difficult to follow and complained that he lacked the patience and the time needed to be a good director.

As a patron, Papp could do comparatively little for his directors. Off-Broadway, they earned minuscule fees that looked ludicrous compared to those offered by Broadway, film and television. "You have to be a young and idealistic person with no family to support in order to work regularly as a director of serious drama," said Jeff Bleckner, Papp's student at Yale and later director of three Festival plays. "Except for the guys who direct big-budget musicals or the exception that proves the rule, like Mike Nichols, it's a young person's game. Very few can afford to stay in it."

For his playwrights, Papp could do a lot. His attention was then focused on three: Myrna Lamb, through whom Papp began to tap into the women's movement; and Dennis Reardon and David Rabe, through whom Papp began to explore the military experience of a generation younger than his own.

Myrna Lamb fit the feminist profile of 1970: she was thirty-nine years old, Jewish, married with two children and living in a New Jersey suburb when her play, *What Have You Done for Me Lately?* was performed at the New Feminist Theater. She brought Papp *Mod Donna,* a musical whose subject was the obsession with sexual desirability that American society exacted from its heterosexual women.

"The heart of *Mod Donna* is the heart of the male-female relationship in our society," wrote Papp in his director's notes.

> The use of sex as the ultimate weapon, the final solution in the bedroom and on the launching pad. Sex and murder are partners in crime. Whores and Wars are head and tail of the same coin. Orgasm is substituted for fulfillment and Penis Power corrupts both men and women, turning them both into objects. Having more options, the man finds alternatives outside the boudoir, while the wife, who has been turned into a witch, wields the knife of castration.

As he did with all his playwrights, Papp fell in love with Myrna Lamb's work and thought her a genius. Gerald Freedman liked the playwright but hated her play. "Let her work on it a couple more years," he told Papp. "There were ideas there that could create a play, but they weren't developed. Once again, I was concerned with craft. Joe was more concerned with content."

Papp worked day and night with the playwright. "Unlike most producers, Joe would live the process of script development," Gail Merrifield recalled. "The play he was involved with was the most important thing in the world for him at that moment. It was urgent. It involved 150 percent of himself. He developed a somatic connection to the playwright. He astonished and sometimes overwhelmed him or her with his total response."

"You come into the male camp/theatre establishment with your

women's liberation musical. Only it's different because it's Joe Papp and
he is rumored to react less defensively than other producers to such items
as hippies, militant blacks and even female playwrights," wrote Myrna
Lamb, just before her play opened.

Okay, you find the director very attractive; not because, as he assumes
and you presume, he represents power and opportunity, but because
he's recognizing and sentient and intelligent and enthusiastic and daring and entertaining and committed and vital. And because he's very
Renaissance and digs and knows it all, and has a really nice speaking
voice and a surprisingly good singing voice and is hellishly intense and
appealing and troubled and sleepless and cigarsmoking so that you
want to mother him and rock him to sleep in your arms and soothe
away the tired places beneath his eyes. And is, all in all, quite a yummy
guy. And there are so few guys who qualify in your psyche for that
appellation. (Are there any?)

As for the play, Lamb wrote,

It's obvious to you that the thing has to be a collaboration. Your play.
His editing, his concepts . . . you look for undermining, even sabotage.
You're very sensitive to every cut. What's this? You mutter to yourself.
A very important line. A very important line. The crux of the whole
thing, in fact. . . . But then you find that Joe Papp is husbanding every
word and ideological line and that whether it's feminist cant or cho-
rus-woman chant, he regards it as infinitely precious. . . . Then, crisis
happens. B-movie showbiz drama. The play isn't working. Not only
must material be reinstated, but clarification and amplification must
occur where they have not yet existed. It was reduced to one act
originally because he felt there wasn't enough of a second act. Now
there must be a second act. . . . Further, there must be more scenes
for the first act. The first day is a shock. You don't want to look at the
wound, and you know you must work and survive. . . . He says, not
in so many words, be a person. Don't fail me when I need you. Do
what I know you can do. . . . So you do it. You feel that now you want
to take more risks, like he does, like they do.

By the spring of 1970, when Lamb's musical was produced, the
Festival was working like a well-oiled machine. Papp, Freedman and
Gersten headed a skilled administrative and technical team, there was a
costume and prop shop on the premises and Merle Debuskey had long
perfected the art of attracting media attention. *Mod Donna* received
excellent coverage. Consciousness-raising sessions followed performances

on special "Men's Nights," and assorted feminists as well as the publisher of *Screw* swelled the ranks of regular reviewers. Their reviews were mixed — *Cue*'s Marilyn Stasio described it as "a conventional ménage à trois in which two archetypical modern females, Super-Castrator and Super-Whore, lock claws over a booby prize Male," which seemed "unlikely to advance the cause of either feminism or the theater." But even before the reviews came in, Papp assured Lamb — as he would assure every one of his playwrights — that no matter what the critical reception would be, he was committed to doing her next play.

If Myrna Lamb fit the profile of the sixties feminist, Dennis Reardon was the disaffected student. Blond, blue-eyed and barely out of college, Reardon was a soldier and the young author of *The Happiness Cage*. His play was set in a VA hospital and examined the ethics of military medical experiments on unsuspecting soldiers, which dated back to 1955.

Papp thought Reardon a major find. "He was so authentic," he said. "It was all truth, dug out of his bowels. The characters were so real. The topic was of great interest and I was fascinated by the power of his language." By the time Papp scheduled a date for *The Happiness Cage*, Reardon had been posted to Okinawa. When he received the news in December 1969, he was more excited about using the production as a way of getting out of the army early than about any career breakthrough. "The Army offers something known as an early separation for seasonal employment," Reardon wrote his agent. "The farm boys use it to get back in time to plant the winter wheat or whatever they feel inclined to plant. But my inquiries reveal that a playwright may also qualify under conditions such as Mr. Papp presents."

Three days later Papp wrote a letter to PFC Reardon calculated to obtain his early release:

> I was dismayed to learn that your date of discharge is sometime in March. Our schedule calls for rehearsals to begin January 15th. With some inconvenience we could stretch it a week, but anything later would make the production of your play just impossible. I say this with regret since we want to do the work very much. But without you here for planning and rewriting, I cannot see how we could undertake it.

Reardon was discharged seventy-seven days early and arrived in Papp's office ten days later, hair short, back straight, clearly disoriented.

"Joe looked like my idea of a mogul," he recalled. "He had a desk the size of the state of Montana. He offered me a gigantic cigar. I didn't know what to do with a cigar and that cigar became the focal point of that first meeting. I thought you were supposed to bite one end off and the tobacco got between my teeth and I thought I wouldn't be able to focus on anything else until I got rid of it. So I excused myself, wandered around looking for a place to spit it out and finally found a restroom with an open window."

When he returned, Reardon found himself liking Joseph Papp. The producer was usually courteous to playwrights but, in addition, he must have felt a special bond with this young man who had never set foot in New York City before. Papp himself had been twenty-five years old and just out of the navy when he had arrived, similarly disoriented, at the Actors' Lab in Los Angeles. Reardon — college educated, a lapsed Catholic of Irish descent, faintly midwestern — became the first of what would become a coterie of young male playwrights that would come to include David Rabe, Tom Babe, John Guare, John Ford Noonan, Anthony Scully and Jason Miller.

"I was immensely relieved by our first encounter," Reardon remembered. "He said nice things about my writing, told me we had a wonderful cast, including Martin Sheen. At the time, I had never even had a reading of one of my plays and I wouldn't have known a wonderful cast if it bit me in the ass. But I was grateful that Joe was not a precious, posturing homosexual dilettante of the type I had run into in academic theater. I was dealing with life-and-death issues in my plays. I had a sense of high purpose. I was not frivolous and neither was Joe. There was a pugnaciousness about him that appealed to me and that I could identify with. He was my father's age, and he gave me a sense of security. I'd go out to dinner with Joe and it was very soothing."

Reardon worked on rewrites for about a month. The process was punctuated by Papp's brief visits to rehearsals followed by intense discussions in his office. "He had a quicksilver mind," Reardon recalled. "He was also a good play doctor. He was *real specific* where another producer would just lean back in his chair, stare at the ceiling and say, 'I dunno . . . somethin' about the second act bothers me.' He recognized stage poetry. He was also smart about casting. We had an actor that Joe wanted to fire. The director and I overruled him and later we saw that Joe was right. Joe was frequently right. My problem was filtering out his brilliant insights from the bad ones."

During rehearsals, Papp decided to move *The Happiness Cage* from the 100-seat Other Stage to the 300-seat Anspacher. To help fill the theater, he sent out a personalized letter to friends and trustees:

A theatrical agent sent me a new script a few months ago, a first play by a young soldier stationed in Okinawa. I by-passed the growing pile

of unread manuscripts on my desk. . . . Ninety minutes later I phoned
the agent and said we would like to produce the play. . . . It poses one
of the great moral issues of our day. For anyone interested in fine
writing, a major contemporary theme and first-rate acting, it must be
seen.

Then, just before opening the play, Papp decided that he would,
instead, have Reardon work on yet another rewrite and then inaugurate
his new, third theater with it in the fall. In September, *The Happiness
Cage* opened the Newman, Papp's third theater at the Public. Both the
theater and the play got generally good reviews and *New York*'s John
Simon wrote a rave. Audiences were small; the play was thought to be
depressing. Nevertheless, Papp assured Reardon, as he had Myrna Lamb,
that his next play would be welcome at Papp's theater.

At the time, Papp had in hand another military play, one he had read
once and then set aside on his desk. It was called *The Basic Training of
Pavlo Hummel* and Papp thought it brilliant but problematic. It was only
when Mel Shapiro, a director Papp admired, indicated interest in it that
the producer looked at *Pavlo* again. "I didn't know what to do with it,"
Papp later said. "Complex, enigmatic and I didn't understand parts of it
at all. I was an antiwar activist. Almost everyone I knew was against the
war and here was this playwright who was not for the war but had written
a play about a guy who *liked* fighting in Vietnam. I tend to see things in
black and white. David brought shadows into my thinking. It was through
him that I began to look at both the veterans and those who refused to
fight in different ways."

Papp telephoned David Rabe, who was then living outside Philadelphia. The playwright was feeling hopeless about his career: the script of
Pavlo had been turned down by several theaters.

"David Rabe?" the producer's voice came over the line. "This is Joe
Papp. I'm interested in doing your play."

Rabe was then thirty-one years old and teaching at Villanova University. A thickset, thoughtful and wary man from Dubuque, Iowa, Rabe
began writing plays as an undergraduate. In 1965, he was drafted into
the army and later served in a hospital unit outside Saigon during 1966.
"There was something about him that was very pure," Papp said later.
"He was this all-American ex–football player with this bright, modern
mind that seemed to be dipped into some primordial past. He was both
extremely articulate and difficult to follow. That quality imbued his plays
and had a profound effect on me. He was the only white writer who
wrote a black character that I believed and one of the few male writers

who could really write women. He could articulate for the inarticulate, the people who are the most hurt by things. He taught me that an enigma is closer to life than any kind of explained thing and I became so connected with his plays that I felt I would protect them from anything. Producing his work was the most important thing I did at the Public Theater."

At first, Rabe viewed Papp in unsentimental, purely pragmatic terms, as his best hope for getting his work produced. He had seen Gordone's *No Place* and Reardon's *Happiness Cage*. "The kinds of plays Joe chose reflected a combination of intellect, heterosexual male energy, and political concern," he said; later he wrote:

> My particular brand of playwriting suited Joe. The trouble was that we were people and as people we were very different. There was a purity of anger and rebellion in Joe the producer, the director, the lover of Shakespeare, the artist, and there certainly was a matching aggression and dissension in my work. . . . But Joe was also compelled to possess, to assimilate, to put his stamp on things, and this was a tendency frequently capable of generating negative consequences that counterbalanced his virtues. . . .
>
> I was not looking for a benefactor in the beginning, at least not in any conscious way. I was looking for a producer, I thought, and Joe had a theater dedicated to the production of new work. But he liked to function in a patriarchal way, and the possibilities available in the bounty of theatrical resources to which he was proposing to give me access aroused in me a lurking filial response. So we would be father and son in some artistic way. But this is a relationship that is never simple, whatever its realm.

The pacing and energy level of the two men were also vastly different. Rabe spoke extremely slowly, with pauses that Papp joked "you could turn a battleship around in." The image of Papp that remained with Rabe was an early glimpse of the producer storming through the lobby of the Public Theater, followed by three people who couldn't quite keep stride. Those two initial images would characterize their interactions.

Papp teamed Rabe up with his former Yale student, director Jeff Bleckner, and at the beginning of 1971 they began rehearsing the play as a workshop production. Five weeks into the process, both men recognized that something was wrong and asked Papp to see a run-through.

"At the end of the first act, he was pleased though clearly not thrilled," Rabe wrote. "An hour and a half later, when the actors had been dismissed, Jeff and I headed, in a state of some apprehension, up the stairs to Joe's office for a sip of scotch and the labor of analysis and judgment. . . . He amazed me with the ability to go to the heart of my play. At this point in our relations, I half expected him to be unable to keep my own play separate from all the others he was reading and working on. . . ."

Rabe had seen Papp's production of Robert Montgomery's *Subject to Fits,* and knew that, during its development process, Papp had suggested scrambling its structure. When the producer now suggested that Rabe break down *Pavlo*'s narrative line, the playwright suspected him of applying a formula fix, ignoring his play's different style and subject. "Joe called us to a second conference. His question was simple: What scenes in the second act could be moved into the first? I felt a real anger beginning. I accused Joe of wanting to risk harm to the play in order to avoid appearing in some way outside the current theatrical fashion. Did a realistic play seem to him like an old narrow tie? Did he think form was something you started from or could change on whim like a shirt or tie?"

Papp replied mildly that he was uninterested in theatrical fashions but wanted Bleckner and Rabe to do something more than talk. If they moved a scene and they didn't like the way it played, they could always move it back to its original place. But if they regarded the play as cast in stone, he told them, they were closing their minds at a time they could least afford to do so.

"It was important for me to hear that we could change things back if we didn't like them," Rabe recalled. "It did unfreeze us and it was key to the play's success. In fact it was the ideal situation: the director and playwright working together and Joe coming in at the end as an objective third eye with on-the-fly, accurate, startling insights. I knew he was right and the fact that he was right helped break down my suspicion of him. I felt that production of *Pavlo* was about as good as it could get. As a playwright, you have a great longing for someone in whose hands you can place your work. When he helped us then, that's when I started thinking of him in that way."

About ten days later, just before the opening, Papp took Rabe into his office and told him, as he had told Gordone, Lamb and Reardon, that whatever the critical response to *Pavlo*, he wanted to do the playwright's next project. Rabe already had a script written called *Sticks and Bones,* and shortly after *Pavlo* opened to excellent reviews, Papp decided to produce it the following fall.

During the summer of 1971, while *Timon of Athens* and *Cymbeline* played at the Delacorte, followed by a musical version of *Two Gentlemen of Verona,* with music by Galt MacDermot, which began attracting major attention, *The Basic Training of Pavlo Hummel* continued playing at the Public and Rabe readied *Sticks and Bones* to open the Festival's fall season at the Anspacher. It opened to even better notices than *Pavlo* and, for a time, Rabe had two of his plays running at the Public. He had become the paradigm of Papp's New American Playwright, and the producer held his work up as a model to the ever-larger group of new playwrights. "When I fall in love with a play, I do a lot for it," Papp would later say. "It becomes like my own life, I identify so deeply with it. And certainly David's plays were among those plays."

In 1969, the producer had also fallen in love with The Combine, a Texas-based commune of college dropouts, who had created a rock musical called *Stomp,* and invited them to live at the Public Theater. The twenty-three-member Combine performed, ate, used a variety of drugs and slept in various combinations in Martinson Hall, on the third floor, where they kept their sleeping bags under the bleachers on which the audience sat. "I cannot tell from their stomping whether they are actually talented," Harold Clurman wrote kindly in the *Nation.* "They are still only raw material but as such they are by no means ungracious."

Gerald Freedman, who had helped Doug Dyer shape *Stomp* at the Public, found himself using the words "raw material" in a pejorative way in discussions with Papp. When they were selecting their first group of new plays, Freedman thought, Papp had been guided by his choices. "I may have smarted a little bit when shows I had done became known as 'Joseph Papp productions,'" he recalled. "But that went with the territory. I never felt I had to be a yes-man and I was never scared of Joe.

"It was in the second tier of material that we began to have our differences. I wanted plays that were really plays, that reflected the playwright's work and craft. Joe was more concerned with the ideas in a play or the language of a play or its politics. I always felt equal with Joe but deferred to him in the final decisions because he was out there raising the money and because, psychologically, it suited me to have him fight the battles while I could be the artist. The first season, there had been plenty for me to do without getting involved in some of the half-baked plays that needed more work. The second season, I did. They all had some originality and flair, but that, in itself, doesn't make a theater piece."

As the sixties became the seventies, Papp's choices became increasingly distant from Freedman's. One of the last productions Freedman directed at the Public, in January 1970, was a jazz opera called *Sambo.* John Lahr, reviewing it in the *Village Voice,* wrote enthusiastically that the piece might be "one of the crucial first steps in revolutionizing our musical stage. There is no book, no plot line, none of the linear accoutrements

which simplify the stage experience and make it safe. .... *Sambo*'s structure is as abstract yet emotionally specific as its jazz idiom." But Freedman wanted to keep it in workshop longer. "*Sambo* wasn't yet a show
when it opened," he recalled. "I thought there was more there and
wanted to develop it, but Joe was impatient to get it on. The last straw
was another rock musical which had originated at Amherst College called
The Dream Engine, written by another young, talented kid. I loved the
project but it wasn't ready to be done. I didn't want to put on stuff that
needed work."

Much later, Freedman would remember there had been another issue
as well, one to which he had not given a second thought at the time.
Papp had decided to do both parts of *Henry VI* and *Richard III* as one
project called *The Wars of the Roses*. He had asked Freedman to codirect
them all for the summer of 1970, and Freedman had declined. "He
didn't take that very well," Freedman recalled. "I think he was surprised.
I told him I wouldn't be comfortable codirecting and I didn't know how
it could work. Our tastes were very similar but our methods were different. But I had forgotten all about that when one day, when we were
discussing the new project over lunch, and I said I thought it was too
raw, Joe said, 'Maybe we should separate for a while.'"

Freedman was stunned. "I had been working at the Festival for over
ten years by then. I had never had a written contract but I helped build
this thing. I expected Joe to say: 'We're not going to fight over a play,
are we? Stay!' But he didn't ask me to stay and, oddly enough, I didn't
resent it at the time. I got work immediately on a Broadway show and I
retained my relationship with Joe. A few years later, I directed for him
again. But I realized that our being a family was predicated on Joe's
wishes. And I began to wonder: How could I be kicked out?"

Like Stuart Vaughan, Gerald Freedman developed a directorial career
independent of the Festival. After he left, the Festival's expansion, the
move from Shakespeare to contemporary playwrights and a generational
change began to displace other family members. "We started to feel we
needed a schedule," general manager David Black recalled. "Joe would
talk to a playwright and say, 'I love that. We're going to do it,' and
schedule a work that hadn't been scheduled before. Those of us who
were charged with the operation of these things, of seeing that the details
got done, asked him for a meeting and at that meeting asked him to
organize himself better, to set a schedule and stick to it. He agreed but
then things went on the same way and that made it very difficult.

"It also became harder to get to Joe, not only to physically get to see him in his office but to get his attention. Everyone wanted it. It was then that he began both to protect himself and to sift out what he would and would not deal with."

Set designer Ming Cho Lee was concerned about the effect of the increased activity on artistic quality. "From the very beginning, I understood that Joe liked to do theater on the run," he said. "He believed in it as a style of operation, and he did it consistently — at the beginning when he had no other option but to get a show on and later, when he did. He liked the fact that everything was temporary. He was not interested in continuity. But I felt differently. At some point, just to get a show on is an accomplishment. But later you start to want the quality to improve. I began to think: Joe's investment in each show needs to be greater. But he did not wish to 'overthink' a production. No play became super-important to him. It was always just a play.

"And then, with the new playwrights, the whole direction of the theater changed. Joe changed direction and none of us realized for a while that he had changed direction. The Public Theater became more important than the Delacorte. The new playwrights became more interesting to Joe than Shakespeare. Although the Festival had become a year-round theater, to me it created a fragmentation rather than a continuity."

Papp's interest in new talent also displaced many actors in the family. "In the beginning," actress Ellen Holly recalled, "I never auditioned. I felt cosseted and remarkably valued — one of the golden children of Joe's first ten years. The high point for me was the year I went out as leading lady on the Mobile playing Catherine of Aragon in *Henry V* and Kate in *Shrew*. Joe directed me in both plays and was absolutely marvelous to work with. But my relationship with him would change from one that was idealistic, even idyllic, to one that was disillusioned, prickly and cautious. I was required to audition for Adrienne Kennedy's *The Owl Answers* after bringing her to Joe's attention myself, and the circumstances that surrounded the audition were so grotesque that I fled the Festival as a matter of principle. Some years later I came back, but my feelings about Joe had permanently altered. I still admired him greatly and thought him an extraordinary man but had opened my eyes to the fact that he was somewhat more complex than the creature I thought I knew, and was almost frivolously capable of betrayal."

Part of the transient nature of the Festival family was the nature of theater itself. But Bernard Gersten would later ascribe changes at the Festival to what he called "Joe's Periodic Table of Restlessness and Impatience." Every few years, Gersten thought, Papp outgrew the phase he had been in before, became impatient with old projects and started new ones, often reversing principles that he had loudly proclaimed earlier.

The new phase that the Festival was moving into would be a crucial one. The mortgage on the Public and the costs of its renovation had saddled the Festival with a debt of nearly one million dollars. For more than a decade, New Yorkers had been reading that Papp's enterprise was on the brink of collapse. This time, however, it actually *was,* and Papp turned to the mayor of New York City for help.

TWELVE

A Theater
for a Dollar

JOSEPH PAPP kept his playwrights insulated from the details of his fiscal worries. None of them understood that even as Papp seemed totally absorbed by their plays, discussing characters and rewrites as though his life depended on it, planning productions without scrimping on costs, he was engaged in an endless and debilitating battle for funds to keep his enterprise afloat.

Most New Yorkers and even most theater people assumed Papp was thriving because the Festival generated so many shows. But the number of productions masked the fact that Papp's shows generated no significant revenue. The two thousand seats at the Delacorte were free of charge. The small theaters at the Public — 100 to 299 seats — and their ticket price of $2.50 made box-office earnings a joke. Moreover, Papp had taken out a $475,000 mortgage and faced huge construction costs. In 1967–68, the Festival budget was more than two million dollars.

Papp's key people knew that he had only half of those two million dollars within reach. Shortly after signing the papers for the acquisition of the Astor Library in January 1966, he had announced a major fund-

raising effort headed by August Heckscher. But Heckscher had raised as
little money as Howard Cullman had nearly a decade earlier. Unable to
attract major foundation support, Papp had personally courted private
donors and relied on Bernard Gersten and Herta Danis to come up with
a series of fundraising events. They had organized the "Saved From the
Wrecker's Ball," with tickets at $1,000 per couple; benefit dinners at the
Plaza Hotel with prominent theater stars such as Paul Scofield, Richard
Burton and Elizabeth Taylor and one featuring prominent New York
women dressed as Shakespeare's characters. "Luis Estevez already has a
dress in the works that Gloria Steinem will wear as Lady Macbeth,"
reported the *Herald Tribune*. "Bill Blass will turn Chessie Raynor into
Titania . . . Simonetta has gone back to Paris to make an Ariel costume
for Baby Jane Holzer. . . ." But the size of the current debt made such
strategies obsolete. Once again, the producer turned to the City of New
York.

"I think Joe just viewed it as the natural thing to do," recalled general
manager David Black. "We had started off with Parks Department support. At the Heckscher, we were guests of the Department of Welfare.
Then the city built us the Delacorte. Joe never wavered in his belief that
government should support the arts. He was confident that he would get
the support. And if he wasn't confident, he acted as though he were. The
numbers had gotten much bigger but it was essentially the same situation
we had been in ten years earlier."

By the late sixties, Papp had learned much about the city's budgetary
processes. He also had a powerful ally in August Heckscher, the patrician
grandson of the philanthropist who had endowed the Heckscher Children's Center, whom Mayor Lindsay had appointed administrator of the
Parks, Recreation and Cultural Affairs Administration. August Heckscher's mandate was to help make New York a more livable city, and he
viewed the producer as an asset to his work.

In January 1967, Heckscher told a Festival gathering that men like
Papp should be cherished as "God-given." As director of the well-
endowed Twentieth Century Fund, Heckscher had often reflected on what
he called the "humiliating impotence" of money. "It couldn't buy the
kind of truth that would make a better social order, or the kind of beauty
that would make the city habitable," he wrote. "These things had to exist
in the will and imagination of individual men and women. Only . . .
where men of genius were prepared to act did money become helpful."

Papp did not share Heckscher's views. For him, money was anything
but humiliatingly impotent. He needed it to survive. When he told this
to Heckscher, the commissioner replied that the Festival required far

more money than the Parks, Recreation and Cultural Affairs Administration could provide. The PRCA was responsible for funding not only parks, but art museums, libraries, historical and scientific societies *and* performing arts groups. Its combined capital and expense budget in the late 1960s was $75 million — seemingly a large amount but actually, as Heckscher wrote, "torturously small given the cultural expectations of the city and the condition of most of the institutions."

The commissioner explained to the producer that they were in the same predicament — always in the position of having to raise funds. Although the city's expense budget ranged from $5.2 billion in 1967 to $6.6 billion in 1969 and was second only to the federal budget in size, its revenues rarely kept up with the city's expenditures. Well over half the budget went to human resources, elementary and secondary education and health services, while just over one percent went to the PRCA. When it came to competing with police protection, garbage collection, hospital crises or the chronic funding problems of the city's schools, funding for cultural institutions inevitably came in close to last.

Heckscher advised Papp that the city's capital budget was more easily accessible and that he should try to do what Isaac Stern had done for Carnegie Hall: persuade the city to buy the Public Theater. Some degree of municipal funding would be assured for what would then be a city-owned building. Because the capital budget was funded by bonds, and because the city had ample bond-issuing authority under the state constitution, capital money was not as tight. If a capital appropriation were proposed by the mayor and duly approved by the City Council and Board of Estimate, the city could fund it when money became necessary, irrespective of what was happening in the local economy or in the operating budget. Although Papp was reluctant to become a tenant, he decided that selling the Public Theater to the city was his only way out of debt.

In March, he wrote to the mayor, asking whether "we might conceive of an arrangement with the City of New York whereby the developed property, which when completed will have a book value of over $3,000,000, will after a specified number of years be deeded to the city. . . ."

The following month, a mayoral assistant wrote back, "I spoke to the Mayor about the City's purchase of your property and leasing it back to you for ninety-nine years. The Mayor is very enthused about this idea. . . . I have discussed it with the Commissioner of Real Estate who advised me that we can very easily put this proposition together. . . ."

"The mayor's commitment to buy the Public Theater was relatively unusual," recalled David Grossman, then deputy budget director. "The mayor tended to be cautious about such commitments. He was fairly conservative about money — not a spendthrift, despite his reputation. But Papp was an effective spellbinder — as effective in his way as Tom Hoving at the Metropolitan Museum, who would invite us to lavish lunches to look at a new Greek vase. They both wanted everything they could get their hands on and we had to balance what they wanted with such things as a new hall at the Museum of Natural History or money for the Schomberg Collection at the Public Library in Harlem. But we had a relative surplus of capital funds then and what we liked was that Papp provided real return."

In May 1967, Papp formally applied to the Department of Real Estate to sell the Public Theater to the City of New York, thinking that the sale — and the prospect of paying off Festival debts — would be finalized within a few months. But, with his customary impatience and refusal to acknowledge obstacles to his plans, Papp did not grasp the Kafkaesque politics of the system. "The rules of the game," Heckscher later wrote, "required everyone to call for the [capital budget] money to be spent — for the mayor to boast that it was being spent rapidly and for the opposition always to complain that it wasn't being spent rapidly enough — and yet, at the same time, to make sure that enormous obstacles were placed in the way of its disbursement. . . . My own department would begin the process by putting in a range of projects that, in sober fact, it did not expect to see approved by the Planning Department or Budget. . . . Planning and Budget would then begin cutting away. . . . The fundamental point is that we [were] all performing as part of a system that puts a high premium on delay — a system designed from many points of view to curtail, rather than expedite, the achievement of public works. It seemed odd, but how else could expenditures be kept in line while the eager public was kept hopeful?" Papp's effort to have the city purchase the Public would extend over four years, from March 1967 to April 1971, "rather long for a city project," Grossman noted, "but not unheard of."

During those long and nerve-racking four years, Papp behaved like two different people. With his creative staff, he gave himself fully to the work on new plays and productions, rarely exuding any hint that he was in trouble. But his administrative staff, particularly David Black who kept the books, knew that Papp was operating on sheer nerve. "Between the mortgage and the construction costs, we were soon carrying $800,000 in debt," Black later recalled, "and we were lucky in that our contractor, Victor Goldberg, had become a friend and a devotee of the Festival. He never pressed us for money and Joe kept assuring him that the city would come through. The rest of our debts were financed the way other non-profits do it — I learned how to hold off creditors by paying them small increments on what we owed them and holding off those I could.

"What made the situation at the Festival different from other non-profits was that Joe went on expanding the artistic side and that the board did not restrict him. The Festival board was not a governing body in the sense that it is at other nonprofit organizations. Most boards say no when the deficit looms large. Joe always said, *'I must do this! Now!'* and the board never overruled him. As far as I was personally concerned, even though I knew how desperate the situation really was, I was confident so long as Joe was confident. I must say he never showed any sign of giving up. It may have been mere bravado, but it worked."

Papp's response to dire straits was to press forward with his artistic plans, borrowing the money if necessary, and to barrage city officials and reporters like a madman, with threats, entreaties, and passionate manifestos. "UNABLE TO COPE WITH PROCRASTINATION OF YOUR DEPARTMENT," he wired to the real estate commissioner, who would take two years to *engage* an architect to appraise the Public Theater. "UNLESS SPECIFIC ACTION MATERIALIZES IMMEDIATELY WE WILL HAVE TO RE-CONSIDER THE ARRANGEMENTS." Such headlines as "Summer Dramas Curtailed by City" and "Papp Eliminates a Volpone and Cuts Schools Hamlet" became a staple of the city's newspapers and, no matter how many times he was told "No" or "There is no money," Papp went back to the city again, demanding it. When one government agency turned him down, he appealed to another. When that one did too, he turned to a small coterie of patrons and foundations to bail him out. In public, he raged; in private, he beseeched, bargained and begged with a tenacity and energy that was as strong as it had been a decade before.

At the same time, as the sounds of *Hair* auditions filled the building, Papp was writing passionate letters. "Dear John," he wrote to Mayor Lindsay, who was walking through city neighborhoods in an effort to keep New York riot-free:

> Although I know that the Festival is the last thing in the world you want to think about at this moment, I hope you will hear me out the length of this letter. We are in a sad way financially and unless something happens quickly, we will have to consider drastic alternatives to our programs in New York. The one obvious alternative offered us is dissolution and it is one I am prepared to take. Others include moving the operation elsewhere — another city or a university, or just dropping the whole thing and taking a personal interest in my own and my

family's future by accepting one of many opportunities from college president to a cushy job as dean of drama with a prominent mid-western university. . . .

A tear or two might be shed at our departure; a few voices raised — but in a very short time the overwhelming problems of living in this city will bury all sorrow under an avalanche of polluted air, traffic jams, income tax, race riots and rotten buildings. Who can consider Hamlet's puny problems under these horrendous conditions? Who can worry about King Lear and ingratitude when ingratitude abounds in calamitous proportions? Who can concern himself with the frustrations of the artist striving to find some light in this dark chaos, when his own frustrations are greater and his darkness blacker?

And you, who have the responsibility of holding this edifice together; who must make decisions which affect not only the environment and the purse of every citizen here, but the very lives of children and the aged, what Herculean labors must you bring forth merely to sustain what already exists, let alone to pursue and implement necessary changes. No doubt you felt totally justified in cutting our budget request — why not? Yes — the arts are important, you believe; but what about the cuts that had to be made in education, hospitals, welfare, poverty programs, police, garbage disposal, and the thousands of services that affect our lives from the cradle to the grave. . . .

While we are waiting for the City to work out the arrangements for the purchase of our building, the completion of which I have been told by Dick Rosen is some six months away, we need $250,000 to ward off our demise. I hope that in this interim period you will be able to find a way of providing us with half of this amount — $125,000, so that we can complete our first season at the Public Theater and pave the way for matching financial support.

You have been kind. You have been generous. You have shown concern and understanding. In the name of these wonderful attributes, I appeal to you for succor. Figures are available at your request and so am I. Looking forward to your encouraging reply.

Yours truly,
Joseph Papp

It is unlikely that Lindsay ever read his letter. "I have to tell you that I received requests demanding financial aid every day," Lindsay later said. "Most were not as well written." Budget director David Grossman noted that Papp was just like every other petitioner "in that what he wanted

came first. Where he was unlike them was in his *persistence*, his access to
the media to get his story across and his ability to sell the idea that he
was not out for any personal gain." The mayor did not come to his aid,
and a few months later, Papp told reporters that Robert Wagner, who
preferred baseball to Shakespeare and Verdi, was instrumental in having
the city increase its allocation to the Festival while John Lindsay seemed
bent on cutting the city's appropriation to the Festival.

Such pronouncements angered city administrators. "Papp was consti-
tutionally unable to exist anywhere except at the outer limit of a tenuous
financial branch," Heckscher later wrote, "and some thought he made it
a practice to saw away at that branch assiduously. The mayor's aides were
almost uniformly hostile to him. I did all I could to support him, though
the annual city appropriation to the summer festival was stabilized at a
point lower than it had been under the Wagner administration. . . . He
angered me by saying several times in public that we had cut his appropriation. Actually he had the same amount as the previous year. 'Well,'
he said, 'I asked for a fifty per cent increase, didn't I? And I didn't get
it.' He promised not to use that particular argument again."

Mayor John Lindsay raised Papp's hackles. The producer saw the tall,
glamorous, WASP mayor as the maverick liberal he was, but also as the
product of St. Paul's School and Yale, a man born into privilege, part of
that circle into whose clubs Herta Danis had introduced him a few years
earlier. Papp would often remark that he distrusted liberals, that he'd
rather deal with a conservative than a liberal anytime, that both his
organization and the arts in general ultimately fared better under leaders
who did *not* profess to love the arts than under those who did. Besides,
he would later say, "The Lindsay administration people were like the
yuppies of their time. They wanted to show they were the leading cultural
figures in the city and I was already established. We were in competition.
So though the emotional support from John seemed to be positive, the
actual support was not so great."

Heckscher and Lindsay, for their part, resented the fact that Papp was
fixated on his Festival to the exclusion of all other projects and that he
was not, as Lindsay later put it, "a team player." Both the mayor and the
commissioner were idealistic men who loved the city, were committed to
its people and were beset by financial problems far greater and more
varied than those the producer was facing. The Lindsay administration
seemed, at times, to be working in a permanent crisis mode, moving from
summer racial problems to fall teachers' and sanitation workers' strikes
to winter snow emergencies without a break. They knew that Papp always
had his own agenda and that he was as insistent, indefatigable and

practiced as any Washington lobbyist. By the mid-1960s, a mayor and three parks commissioners had come and gone. Papp was still there, a veteran who knew the ropes, while Heckscher and many Lindsay staffers were new to the game.

"I thought it was clearly understood that the City would not be able to make any contributions to the Public Theater," one of the new mayor's assistants, Richard Rosen, wrote to Papp. "Again, we must repeat that the financial burdens of the City have reached enormous proportions and you must look for your help to private financing as well as the State and Federal governments. . . ."

"You must realize . . . that it is impossible for me to rule the City of New York out as a major source of support," Papp wrote back.

> Your advice to look for help to private financing as well as the state and federal government is all very good, but you must know as well as I do that's all I've been doing for the last ten years. . . . I have badgered the state and federal governments to such a point that whenever John Hightower or Roger Stevens sees me coming, they run away as fast as they can. . . .

When Rosen suggested that Papp advertise in the *New York Times* for funds and charge admission to Shakespeare in the Park — an issue the producer had thought settled almost a decade earlier — Papp replied, "Richard, I do not think these suggestions are well advised but I do appreciate the fact that you are giving the matter deep and serious thought. . . . P.S. Since you live across the street, drop in one morning and catch one of our rehearsals of *Hair.* It's wild, authentic and it will make you glad to be alive."

But if Papp was forgiving of Lindsay's young assistants, he was ever more critical of the mayor himself. "Dear John," he wrote in a sharp letter that he never mailed:

> There was little comfort in the hour-long talk we had at the Public Theater. . . . You cited with great admiration that your close friend Tom Hoving was instituting an admission charge at the Metropolitan Museum for special exhibitions. My reaction to this is that it's deplorable. Conservatism has been moving very swiftly over the past few years (taking advantage of the fiscal crisis existing in education) and posing tuition as the solution in the city and state colleges. The glorious concept of free and universal education is a cornerstone of our democracy. What you and they propose is to chip away at this basic freedom in the name of economic policy.

In the vanguard of your budget, and rightly so, stands education. The fact is that this huge slice of the fiscal pie is greater than funds for hospitals . . . [and] you certainly would not consider asking Ballantine Beer or Clairol or Con Edison to foot the bill. Yet when one of the most effective forms of education, the theater & Shakespeare, appeals for meaningful support . . . it makes you angry and your only answer is charge admission.

Permit me to say that I differ. . . . A city like New York, which lives and thrives in an environment served in the main by cultural resources — a 2 1/2 BILLION dollar operation if it is necessary to put it into money terms — must be served and supported. It must be regarded in the same way you look at a particular industry threatening to leave the city for other pastures. . . . To make an important social and educational force dependent upon the whim of philanthropy is poor leadership indeed. The pittance of City money allocated annually for the performing arts reveals how far removed the thinking is from the reality. A realistic appraisal of what the performing arts means to the city's cultural and economic life would prompt a creative leader in city politics to propose an annual budget of 15 million dollars to aid and abet the creative movements in New York. To the practical minded man, this appropriation would represent sound business policy. To the man who cares about education and enrichment of our people, this appropriation would signify a meaningful effort to break out of static and unimaginative educational forms.

When Papp looked at the agency-by-agency allocation in the city's expense budget, what he saw drove him crazy. The line item budget for 1968–69 included appropriations he supported, such as $10 million for the New York Public Library. But it also contained clearly pork barrel items such as $89,000 for the obscure Staten Island Institute of Arts and Science or $120,000 for the little-used Perkins Gardens in the Bronx — without which the mayor could not get his budget passed. He realized that the Public Theater needed to be made a "line item" and pressed Lindsay hard. In January, the mayor formally proposed that the city buy the Public for $3.5 million and lease it back to the Festival.

Meanwhile, Papp pressed ahead with his own plans. In 1968, he added to the schedule of Anspacher productions the program of experimental theater at The Other Stage. In 1969, he reduced the usual three productions in Central Park to two but borrowed money to finance the $1.1 million construction of a second 300-seat theater. Even though Papp owed creditors $1 million, he told a reporter in October that "the problem of money has always been too enormous to worry about continually."

But Papp did worry continually. The acquisition process dragged on. The Festival had, during the summer of 1969, received the largest grant in its fifteen-year history — $400,000 from the prestigious Rockefeller Foundation. The grant validated Papp's dictum that money followed art, but had little effect on the basic economics of the Festival. Yet Papp proceeded with *The Happiness Cage* and *Mod Donna*, bought the rights to tour *Stomp* in Europe, proceeded with his $500,000 summer project of mounting the *Wars of the Roses* plays at the Delacorte and, in April, received a special Antoinette Perry Award for his contribution to American theater.

Within moments of accepting it, he was told that the City Council had voted down Mayor Lindsay's request to acquire the Public. Papp vented his frustration on the closest target — the man who presented him the award. It was *Times* chief drama critic Clive Barnes and Papp, who usually made no apologies, made one then. "It was so insensitive of me to make you the target of all the pent-up feelings I have about the injustices of the system," he wrote Barnes.

> All of our plans over the past two years have hinged on this taking place. We borrowed hundreds of thousands of dollars and incurred enormous construction cost debts, all with the certain knowledge and assurances by the Mayor that the transaction would materialize. . . . In your country the government bestows high honors on its artists; here we get kicked in the ass. . . .
>
> All of this, I brought into your dressing room the other night. It had been stirring in me and rose to the surface in that tinsel fakey atmosphere of the Tonys. The contradiction, somehow, of worth, merit and value in this silvered Coney Island milieu, struck me with great force. And there you were, innocent and really very kind, but having the power of a mammoth newspaper on which a great deal of our life depends — well, I just couldn't take it out on Cary Grant or his faithful valet. It had to be you, dear friend and colleague. . . .

At the time he wrote Barnes that letter, Papp had no funds to mount his summer season and his closest staff — assistant Gail Merrifield, associate producer Bernard Gersten and associate artistic director Gerald Freedman — took to joking that they would sublet most of the building and take up residence in the basement with Arthur Abraham and his dog.

Papp placed the blame for his situation squarely on the city. In an article headlined "CUTBACK IMPERILS PARK SHAKESPEARE," the

New York Times reported that because of New York's financial crisis and because of the City Council's action, the Festival would be unable to meet its payroll and might have to cancel its summer season in Central Park. In fact, the New York Shakespeare Festival never failed to meet its payroll but, as a subsequent Festival press release put it, "this defeat, after two years of expectation, created a crisis in the Festival's ability to operate."

To dramatize the seriousness of *this* crisis — as opposed to the long string of crises that had characterized the Festival since its inception — Papp, in conjunction with Bernard Gersten and press agent Merle Debuskey, came up with the idea of gaining public attention with a twelve-hour marathon of Shakespeare in Central Park — the *Wars of the Roses* plays playing back to back, beginning at dusk and ending at dawn.

On Saturday night, June 27, 1970, two thousand people, outfitted with blankets and thermos bottles, converged on the Delacorte. The following Monday, newstands around the city featured front-page photographs and articles about the marathon, provoking an immediate grant of $100,000 from the State Council on the Arts to underwrite four more weeks of *The Wars of the Roses* and thousands of small donations.

One of the few reporters who evinced skepticism amid the hoopla was John J. O'Conner, theater critic for the *Wall Street Journal,* who grasped, as Robert Moses had, Papp's modus operandi as one of moving ahead with his theater and betting on New York City to pick up his costs. To his glowing review of Stuart Vaughan's *Wars of the Roses,* O'Conner added:

> It will no doubt seem a touch churlish to add some reservations on the performance of producer Joseph Papp. . . . Mr. Papp is obviously on the side of purity and virtue, winning in the process the unquestioning support of certain publications and critics. Over the years, however, Mr. Papp's financial crises, with their last-minute resolutions, have become more than a little tedious. Following a couple of pre-play speeches last week, the producer just might get to be known as Calamity Joe.
>
> Mr. Papp's achievements have been impressive, both with the park productions and his Public Theater efforts, which have included the original *Hair* and the Pulitzer-prize-winning *No Place to Be Somebody* (although few of his coterie mention the much longer list of pretentious flops). His methods have nonetheless been at least questionable, seemingly based on a plan of spending now and getting someone else to pay later. . . . Perhaps the park audience, which this observer has

always found to be largely white and middle class, should pay a token price of $1 or $2 per ticket. It would still represent one of the best bargains in town. If Mr. Papp is worried about attracting young people, he might consider that they are rushing to pay $5 a ticket to see the "Woodstock" film. As with free lunch — as perhaps with free theater — it just doesn't exist. Someone has to pay. . . .

Papp's response was swift and angry. "Dear Sir," he wrote O'Connor:

It behooves you as a newspaperman to acquaint yourself with the facts before using theater review space for an unwarranted attack on my "questionable methods." Aside from this being an absolutely false accusation, it is indeed surprising that a critic for the big business Bible has the temerity to question a holy and familiar Wall Street technique — "investment" I think it is called. The stock market as you know, sir, is a gambling casino. High stakes are played on the basis of "optimism." A cheerful outlook about the financial conditions in this country can turn a small investment into a huge sum of money. This year as in previous years I proceeded to mount our plays, true, without cash in hand, but with more than Wall Street optimism. If you would check with Dun and Bradstreet you would find that we have an excellent credit rating. Our guarantor is no fly by night corporation, but the City government.

The involvement of the City in supporting the Festival came about only because I made it happen, because I yelled and carried on and turned out some very good work on the stage at the same time. If I had not done so, you would not have been sitting in an unpaid seat in Central Park last week writing that laudatory review; you would not have sat in that unpaid seat at the Public Theater watching *Hair, No Place to Be Somebody* and those other plays you label "pretentious flops": *Hamlet,* which is being performed all over Europe; *The Memorandum,* which won the Obie for the best foreign play; *Stomp,* which is gathering accolades throughout Europe and has been invited by Olivier to open his new Young Vic in the fall; *Ergo,* an extraordinary work by a brilliant writer who has achieved international recognition. Occasional failures, which are certainly the lot of any theater that moves outward, do not deserve your label. The stock market hasn't been much of a hit either these days, and I haven't seen any derogatory reference in your reviews on the subject. . . .

You have the notion, and it is only a notion springing from a prejudice that people should pay for everything, that if we did charge a dollar or two, there would be no financial crisis. Do you realize that the Met charges $15 in a 3,000-seat house and plays to virtual capacity, but must raise several millions of dollars above the box office take every year? You have no awareness, it is evident, that an institution of our size requires a guaranteed subsidy of two million dollars a year! You are also unaware that my lamentations for support are not limited to the summer months but go on all year round. You are apparently insensitive to the fact that as an artistic person I abhor the role of beggar and resent the fact that after fifteen years of arduous labor I must continue to suffer the indignities of begging for money.

You find it tedious! What in hell do you think I find it? If you had any good sense, you would not be attacking me; you would be venting your churlishness on those huge corporations that subscribe to the paper that pays your salary to give some money to the arts. Big business in New York gets all the benefits of the cultural atmosphere we create, without taking any of the responsibility for our continuance.

As for charging admission to our performances, I guess you have been on freebees so long, you have no idea what it is to shell out money for theater tickets. . . . What you also fail to realize is that the creation of a paid ticket for Shakespeare in the Park would double our budget. The craft unions have over the years grudgingly permitted us to operate with minimum union people because we are free. Once we start charging, the game changes. That's first. Second, most of the money I have raised over the years (millions of private dollars) has come to us only because we do not charge admission. Once we do, most of these funds will dry up. Next, we are an outdoor theater subject to weather. Rain or threat of rain cuts down on attendance. A few consistent rainy nights can wipe us out. And this is something you might grasp: Once we depend on box office, we needs must have one objective — to sell out. If this is the reality, our tendency would be to select the most popular of Shakespeare's plays — *A Midsummer Night's Dream, Romeo and Juliet* etc. We certainly would not risk a *Wars of the Roses,* or a *Troilus and Cressida* or a *Titus Andronicus.* We certainly would think twice about doing *Timon of Athens* or *Cymbeline* or *Pericles.* Well, sir, we cherish the right to present plays on the basis of their merit, not on their popularity alone. Finally, the principle of charging for free Shakespeare is abhorrent to me and to many others. I would rather subject myself to your unkind and thoughtless criticism, than submit to your pay-as-you-go philosophy. If someone in the library and museum systems had raised a big fuss there might have been no reduction in library and museum hours.

It is clear that such carryings on would be tedious to you. But you should be grateful, not churlish, that there are people who subject themselves to indignities for you . . . so that you can have something to write about in your newspaper. . . . P.S. While I can overlook the personal derogations and slurs you cast in ignorance I think you owe it to your readers to clear up the misinformation you dispensed in your columns.

Two days after the marathon, Mayor Lindsay announced that he would request that the Board of Estimate appropriate $5 million to buy the Public Theater and complete its restoration. But his request got postponed, first to September, then to October, then to November. During that time, Papp opened his second 300-seat theater, the New-man, announced the establishment of a 90-seat theater to show the Anthology Film Archives and dealt with the consequences of an off-Broadway strike. That fall of 1970, there were thirty-six staffers at the Public. The Cinque Gallery for young minority artists (directed by Romare Beardon and Ernest Crichlow) dominated the lobby. WBAI's Free Music Store was on the third floor and the Benedict Fernandez Photography Workshop — a tuition-free training program for black and Puerto Rican teenagers — was in the basement. Papp himself was starting work on the next summer's Delacorte season and lobbying hard.

The producer understood the audacity of asking the city to buy a theater in the midst of urban disaster. "This city, like so many cities, has so many problems," Papp wrote in a speech to the Board of Estimate,

that any demand made for funds for anything is resisted. Imagine, then, someone having the temerity to ask for money to put on a play. Ask a garbage collector who has his nose in crap all day and who feels his take home pay is inadequate whether he would support an outlay of several million dollars for a landmark building used for putting on plays. You know his answer — Bull. Ask a city policeman the same question — Bull. Ask the average Black or Puerto Rican in Harlem or the Bronx who has his nose in crap all day and night. . . . We know the answer — Bull. Ask the landlord, the postman, the bus driver, the small property owner — a chorus of Bull! Ask Con Edison, Standard Oil and the big corporations the same question and you'll get a stream of fancy words. But when you remove the decorations, you'll get the same word — Bull!

It is not inconceivable or strange therefore to expect members of the Board of Estimate, representing the attitudes of their constituents, to respond in like manner when confronted with an amendment to the

capital budget for the purpose of the city's acquisition of the former
Astor Library. . . .

In addition to the intrinsic difficulty of getting the city to buy anything, Papp realized that Mayor Lindsay was a weak ally. The second-term
mayor was a Republican in a city dominated by Democrats and a maverick
Republican, who could not even count on the support of members of his
own party. Regarded as a Manhattan "silk stocking" mayor by New
Yorkers who lived in Staten Island and Queens, Lindsay was widely
perceived as a rich liberal, sympathetic to black project dwellers at the
expense of white homeowners, and a politician whose glory days were
behind him. In October, the mayor had stalked out of his first appearance
before the City Council after declining to answer questions about the
fiscal crisis, to cries of "Cop out!" and "Contemptible!" Papp realized
that he had to solidify his base of support. He called, wrote and visited
the city controller, Abe Beame, the City Council president, Sanford
Garelik, the five borough presidents, the thirty-seven city councilmen,
members of the Board of Estimate, the city's legion of publishers, editors,
critics, editorial writers and reporters. His letters were long and highly
personalized, filled with the characteristic Papp mixture of chutzpah,
candor, humor, insult and guile, each one dictated to Gail Merrifield, and
designed to leave its recipient no way out.

It is fashionable in intellectual circles to put down the *Daily News* [he
wrote to its editor]. But to ignore the influence your paper has on
millions of ordinary people is like denying that China exists. No snob-
bery can sniff away the reality of your great circulation.

I was raised in this city and read but one newspaper while growing
up — the *News*. Admittedly, it was the sports section that attracted me
first, followed by movie reviews, The Voice of the People, naturally, the
comics, Bright Sayings and Advice to the Lovelorn. I rarely bothered
with the hard news or the editorials, though I did read the headline
stories.

Many in my family, all living in Brooklyn, continue to read the *News*
as their daily paper. Frankly, I personally read the paper only when I
find it next to me on a seat on the subway or when there is a review
of our play. My interest in detailed news reportage takes me to the
Times and for depth stories to the *Wall Street Journal*.

The *News*, over the past few years, has been not only fair to the work
of the New York Shakespeare Festival, but extremely supportive. . . .
Now you wouldn't be giving us all that space if you had any doubt

that your readership was interested in what we are doing. I find that
to be beautiful because it ties in fully with my reason for being in the
theater. I am basically interested in reaching ordinary people with the
work we do. I come out of ordinary stock and I know and believe in
the potential of the people in the lower economic classes, as well as
those who have just come up the ladder a bit. . . . I try to do "popular"
plays . . . understandable to all without requiring a special cultivation. . . .

My goal, if I can state it without sounding foolish, is to bring the
Times and *News* readers together through a popular theater. It happened before at the Globe Theater. It happens for us during the
summer in Central Park and on the Mobile Unit. I want it to happen
all year round at our Public Theater on Lafayette Street.

But we stand to lose this theater. . . . We need all the help we can
get and I am therefore asking you to consider an editorial supporting
the amendment. [It] will benefit all groups in the city — not just a few.
There is no reason, therefore, that the *New York Times* and the *Daily
News* could not take a similar editorial position on this issue. I thank
you.

Sincerely,
Joseph Papp

The City Planning Commission approved a $5.1 million budget amend-
ment to purchase the Public: $2.6 million for the building as it stood;
another $2.5 million to complete work. But on December 3, the Board
of Estimate rejected the plan 12–6.

The producer's response, of course, was to fight. The acquisition issue,
Papp noted, "played second fiddle to the revanchist and opportunistic
politicking. It is a disgrace that crucial decisions affecting the lives of New
Yorkers remain in the hands of an antiquated political mechanism which
has little reality in contemporary city operations. . . ." Papp immediately
announced that he would resubmit a purchase amendment for $2.6
million — half of what he had originally asked. He stepped up his lobbying of the press, barraging them — especially the metropolitan editor,
chief theater critic and assigned cultural reporter of the *Times* — with
hand-delivered background material.

"A lot of figures have been bandied about," Papp wrote in his notes
to reporter Lou Calta, who had been covering the Festival since the
1950s.

The first $2.6 million represented the actual outlay of privately raised funds for the Shakespeare Festival's acquisition and restoration of the Landmark building . . . the original purchase price plus money spent on creating the Anspacher Theater, the Newman Theater, the Invisible Cinema, and the renovation of other space in the building . . . and this figure was arrived at by a distinguished independent architect, John McNamara, who was engaged by the Bureau of Real Estate at a fee of $25,000 to make a thorough investigation of the building and its actual worth. . . .

The figure of $2.6 million, Papp emphasized, was not a negotiating ploy but the aggregate of actual expenditures and financial obligations he had incurred. The Festival had paid out $1.6 million but owed $360,000 on its mortgage; approximately $475,000 to its contractor; several thousand dollars to its architect; and more to vendors of theater equipment. Its immediate debt, he noted, was just under one million dollars.

The second part — $2.5 million — is the figure estimated by Mr. McNamara as the amount of money necessary to fully complete the restoration of the building. This figure covers such items as total air conditioning, elevator installations, the restoration and creation of a music hall, the creation of an art gallery, the restoration of the main lobby, the creation of new administrative space plus work to be done on the exterior of the Landmark building, particularly the installation of new window frames which are rotted. . . . Despite my feelings that it would be advantageous to the City to do the entire job all at once, the objections raised by the Board of Estimate as to the cost prompted me to request the administration's putting forth a new amendment of $2.6 million which represents the actual worth of the building as it now stands.

As though compelled to explain that he would not personally benefit from the deal, Papp noted that his gross salary was $494.61 per week, or about $31,000 per year.

My salary is determined by the Board of Trustees. I have no authority to raise my own salary and over the years I have resisted proposed increases for two reasons: I cannot tolerate a gap between my income and that of the rest of the staff, actors' salaries are so low it would be immoral from my viewpoint and I would have to raise most of the money anyway.

From 1954 to 1960 I was not on salary at all. In the past 11 years,

I've raised 11 million dollars for the Festival. At this time I have no savings whatsoever and no investments. In comparison with heads of cultural institutions with a $1.6 mill annual budget my salary is at the bottom of the list. In the past ten years I have been offered positions up to $50,000 a year, including stock, plus living quarters — which I have turned down. The Festival and the Public Theater is my life — not a job. I have been subjected to the vulgarity of political hacks year after year — begging for support — hat in hand — in total disregard of any accomplishment — and always starting from scratch. But I have swallowed the indignities and will continue to do so in order to keep the work alive and to serve the city in which I was born and raised.

On a rare self-pitying note, Papp concluded, "It's not easy."

On December 16, he typed out a message to Arthur Gelb, who had reviewed half of *The Taming of the Shrew* at the East River Amphitheater in 1956 and was now metropolitan editor of the *Times*.

DEAR ARTHUR: THIS IS THE LAST TIME I'LL BUG YOU IN 1970. BUT YOU MUST DO THIS ONE THING TO SAVE ME — LET CLIVE DO A SOUL PIECE ON THE IMMINENT LOSS OF THE FESTIVAL FOR THIS FRIDAY. WE TALKED FOR TWO HOURS WITHOUT PAUSE AND HE'S READY TO WRITE A SWINGING PIECE. WE CAN TIE IT IN WITH THE EMERGENCY COMMITTEE TO SAVE FESTIVAL FORMING UNDER ROGER STEVENS. WIRES ARE BEING SENT OUT TO THE MOST IMPOR-TANT PEOPLE IN THE THEATER AND PUBLIC LIFE TO GET TO-GETHER. ALL THIS CAN BE PEGGED TO THE CRISIS IN THE ARTS — THE BATTLEGROUND NOW IS THE FESTIVAL. WHAT'S NEXT? CLIVE'S PIECE CAN SOUND THE CALL. A PROPHECY — THE CASSANDRA. CLIVE HAS THE SPACE. HE NEEDS YOUR BLESSING. I NEED YOUR BLESSING. IN THE NAME OF ATKINSON, O'NEILL AND BARBARA GELB — SAY O.K.! I'LL CALL YOU TOMORROW. . . . JOE PAPP.

On December 17, Papp sent by messenger a set of notes to critic Clive Barnes.

What is really the issue: Fight for the preservation of an idea — not a building. There is a loss in the loss of a building. But the greater loss, by far, would be the demise of a concept about the quality of life at a time of upheaval. . . . We would certainly prefer not to sell the build-ing. Our own independence is compromised in the sale — we become subject to bureaucracy — political opportunism — a loss of options and freedom which we treasure. . . . The sale is merely an instrument — a means of converting . . . bricks and mortar to operating money. . . .

On December 18, Barnes reported that a Committee to Save the New York Shakespeare Festival had been formed and included producer Roger Stevens, actors Julie Harris and George C. Scott, playwright Edward Albee, opera singer Marian Anderson, critic Brooks Atkinson, artist Romare Beardon, museum director Tom Hoving, conductor Julius Rudel, choreographer Robert Joffrey and popular singer Barbra Streisand. In January 1971, *Times* architectural critic Ada Louise Huxtable bemoaned the possible loss of the Public. Finally, on March 10, the City Planning Commission — all mayoral appointees — approved the plan in a 5–0 vote and the PRCA-sponsored amendment went on, once again, to the Board of Estimate.

The Board of Estimate had a packed agenda that March day, and was bitterly divided — as was public sentiment in the entire city — by a public housing controversy in Forest Hills, Queens. It was 6:16 P.M. when the acquisition of the Public came up for discussion, and by that time, tempers were frayed. Papp had just begun to speak when Sidney Leviss, the Queens borough president, interrupted him with the question of what "community" the Festival's board of trustees represented.

"The community of the City of New York," Papp answered.

Leviss noted that his borough of one million residents was "culturally starved" and that the New York Shakespeare Festival was Manhattan-oriented. Something in Papp snapped.

"Listen, that's full of shit," he said.

The two men began to shout at one another, and Leviss demanded that Papp apologize.

"I refuse to apologize," Papp shouted, heedless of the consequences. "I don't care who you represent."

"Well I do," shouted Leviss. "What does this do for the people of Queens?"

"I'm sick of that question," Papp shouted back. "I was the first person to go to Queens with a mobile theater unit — I don't give a damn anymore." Then he turned on his heel, and walked out. It was not a calculated ploy. "Not only was I fed up with this niggling kind of questioning," he later said, "I felt an ingratitude. I was providing something for the city that was needed. I was doing my job. And I felt, *Why do I have to meet this kind of resistance?* I wasn't going to listen to that any longer. I'd had it up to here."

Gail Merrifield and Merle Debuskey were astounded to see Papp stalk out of the chamber and thought everything was lost. But the diplomatic Bernard Gersten leaped up to the podium and spoke for about fifteen minutes, responding in a friendly way to questions. When deputy Brooklyn borough president John F. Hayes noted, "I have seen some turkeys produced by some people who have spoken here today, birds that could not even adorn a Thanksgiving table," Gersten conceded, "We produce some plays that are not good. We are like the Board of Estimate in that respect."

The board voted to defer action on the proposed amendment for two weeks. Then, on March 25, it voted unanimously to buy the Public Theater for $2.6 million and lease it back to the Festival for one dollar per year. Leviss and Papp made a great show of shaking hands. Two days later, the City Council approved the measure 27–10.

The city's acquisition of the Public was widely regarded as a coup for Papp, the victory of one tenacious individual over the gargantuan bureaucracy, a milestone in the history of government support of the arts. But, as when the city built him the Delacorte theater, Papp did not exult. The transfer of ownership, he would later joke, took on aspects of the Nazi occupation of France, with vague ghosts of Stalinist censors and depression landlords hovering in the distance. In June, Papp turned fifty and celebrated with a large raucous party at the Public. Over the summer he produced *Timon of Athens, Cymbeline* and a musical version of *Two Gentlemen of Verona* at the Delacorte, but he was still waiting for the money from the city's purchase of the Public. It was November when Papp, Gersten, Debuskey and Black finally took the subway down to the Municipal Building to pick up their check for $2.6 million. For Bernard Gersten, that day marked the beginning of a new phase for the Festival. "We had a moment, a brief moment, when we were debt-free and had a bankroll," Bernard Gersten remembered. "It didn't last long, because we escalated the stakes, but it was wonderful."

At the same time the Festival received $2.6 million from the city, it was enjoying its first success on Broadway. The previous summer, the Festival had turned away thousands of people who had come to see its adaptation of *Two Gentlemen of Verona*. The success of *Two Gents* had come as something of a surprise to Papp. Mired in city politicking, he had not had much to do with it besides introducing director Mel Shapiro and playwright John Guare to *Hair* composer Galt MacDermot and agreeing that the play, since it was going out on the Mobile, could use more than the usual incidental music. Before long, MacDermot had written a dozen songs and the play had been transformed into a musical the way *The Taming of the Shrew* had become *Kiss Me Kate* two decades earlier. This adaptation of Shakespeare, however, was fueled by MacDermot's driving rock music, an exuberant multiracial cast that included Raul Julia, Clifton Davis, Jerry Stiller and Jonelle Allen, and lyrics such as:

> *Life's a prison and love's the pardon*
> *Love's the gardener and I'm the garden*
> *Love's the doctor and I give in*
> *I was sick but love has driven me sane*

"It was accessible Shakespeare, a wonderful show in the spirit of the time," recalled Bernard Gersten. "Never had any Shakespeare we had done engendered such a response. Various Broadway producers came to us. This was a show virtually asking us to take it to Broadway. It said there were nine, ten thousand people a week who wanted to see it."

Gersten urged Papp to seize the opportunity. In 1964, the Festival had licensed a Delacorte production of *Othello* to Theodore Mann and had lost nothing in the venture. But, in 1967, it had licensed *Hair* to Michael Butler. *Hair* had since contributed more than a million dollars in royalties to the Festival. The *weekly* gross of the four *Hair* companies in the spring of 1970, Gersten pointed out, was larger than the Festival's total *annual* box-office income. But Papp hesitated.

"Where do we get the money," he asked, "to move the show?"

Gersten suggested LuEsther Mertz.

LuEsther Mertz had — at the invitation of her daughter — first walked into the Public Theater for its "Saved From the Wrecker's Ball." A midwesterner and a devout Baptist, LuEsther Mertz and her husband had made millions of dollars by starting a magazine-subscription enterprise called Publishers Clearing House in the basement of their home. Mrs. Mertz had sent back a $2,000 check and asked for four tickets. Danis instructed Papp to pay attention to her and, when she invited him to a party at her home, to attend with good grace.

The New York Shakespeare Festival became Mrs. Mertz's family. She became friends with several staff members and, in a short time, replaced Florence Anspacher as the Festival's chief financial contributor.

In mid-August, Papp and Gersten took her to lunch and explained the situation. *Two Gents* had played at the Delacorte for free for three weeks. On Broadway, it might run for months, put the Festival squarely in the mainstream of American theater and generate the kind of income *Hair* had generated. Various commercial producers had offered to move it to

Broadway but if the Festival licensed it to them, it would receive only a small percentage of profits, as had happened with *Hair.* If, however, someone were to give the Festival the money to move the show to Broadway as a tax-deductible contribution, the Festival would own 100 percent of the profits.

A few days later, Mrs. Mertz wrote Gersten:

> I have thought a lot about 2 Gents and what it will mean to the Shakespeare Festival. And I am more sure than ever that we should not give any part of it away to anyone else. Therefore I am prepared to say that I can and will guarantee a contribution up to the 250M we talked about at lunch. . . . We just simply cannot afford to miss this chance to get on easy street.

When *Two Gents* opened its box office at the St. James Theater, ticket sales were abysmal.

The New York Shakespeare Festival was not widely known enough to draw people to the previews. The Public Theater was very well known downtown. The Delacorte was known by the people who came to Central Park. In 1971, however, the Broadway audience still knew nothing of Joseph Papp.

But the reviewers called *Two Gents* a hit and ticket sales soared. The musical ran for eighteen months and the Festival became the first not-for-profit company to move a show to Broadway and retain all its rights. Papp would soon transfer David Rabe's *Sticks and Bones,* Jason Miller's *That Championship Season* and Shakespeare's *Much Ado About Nothing* to Broadway as well. Four shows running on Broadway at the same time, added to the shows at the Public and the Delacorte and the Mobile, made the Festival seem like a giant enterprise. "It was extraordinary," said Gersten. "To go from screwing chairs into the floor of Emmanuel Church in 1954 to playing on Broadway in 1971 was an amazing arc of achievement." In 1972, a *New Yorker* cartoon would portray all of Manhattan as a Joseph Papp production.

But designer Ming Cho Lee, unlike Gersten, would later cite *Two Gents* as a turning point for the worse. "I felt it was not healthy," he said. "It was the first time I designed a production again and again and again: first for the Delacorte, then for the Mobile, then for Broadway, then for the touring companies. It became a way of sustaining the Public Theater and it diluted the mission."

For the first time, too, Papp began to draw fire from the theater establishment. "Broadway people had not been perturbed by what he did in the park or even at the Public," recalled Merle Debuskey. "Now he

was moving into their turf and into four theaters, with the advantage of
subsidized tryouts downtown. He didn't have to risk his own money
when he brought things to Broadway."

Broadway — enormous step that it was — would turn out to be only
a stepping stone. Within a year, Papp would announce moves into the
first nationally known performing arts complex, Lincoln Center, and into
network television. He would take contemporary American playwrights
with him, particularly the work of his favorite, David Rabe.

THIRTEEN

New Arenas

IN NOVEMBER 1971, Papp opened his second David Rabe play, *Sticks and Bones,* at the Public Theater. For most of that fall, American attention had been riveted on the "Pentagon Papers," the 7,000-page collection of documents detailing United States involvement in Southeast Asia that had been leaked to the press by Daniel Ellsberg, and unremitting protests against the continuing American military operation in Vietnam.

Rabe's first play, *The Basic Training of Pavlo Hummel,* had presented audiences with a disturbing portrait of the young American soldier in Vietnam; *Sticks and Bones* examined his return home. Conceived as a twist on *Ozzie and Harriet,* Rabe appropriated the four characters of the long-running American television comedy. In his surreal variation, Ozzie is still watching football, Harriet is still wearing her apron and Ricky is still playing his guitar. But David has returned from a tour of duty in Vietnam blind. He cannot fit back in and is invited by his family to commit suicide.

"I feel that in life, and particularly in drama, language is something people use to create realities and inflict them on other people," Rabe said. "In *Sticks and Bones,* the fundamental conflict is how to talk about experience. The family wants to use clichés. David wants to use poetry. The clichés are reductive and poetry is expansive. So there's an immediate conflict."

By the time he produced Rabe's second play, Papp was sure he had found the Festival's voice. He told people Rabe was the successor to the first great American playwright, Eugene O'Neill, and that if he were to produce *just* Rabe in his theater, he would be accomplishing something. "Frankly, I stand in awe of his extraordinary talent, which by any existing standard is unmatched in the United States today," Papp wrote to Rabe's parents. "I see David as a national playwright. What that means to me is that he has an acute perception of the American consciousness. This perception in the theater makes it possible for ideas to transcend the limitation of class, color and economic lines."

The intense, laconic Rabe did not fit the stereotype of a playwright. He was not eloquent. He wore cheap, unstylish clothes and lived in Philadelphia. Festival staffers described him as a man "forbidding in the manner of a figure from Norse mythology" or a volcano that might suddenly erupt; one interviewer dubbed him "the Neil Simon of desperation and death." Papp sometimes called him David Rage. "If David didn't write," he often said, "he'd murder someone."

Rabe, like so many other playwrights, found in Papp no mere producer but a patron, no simple contractual relationship but a complicated psychological one in which Papp was both generous and what Rabe perceived as "dangerous" in the extreme. Problems began right away on *Sticks and Bones,* because Rabe had sold the rights to it to his former college roommate, an advertising man with no experience in theater. When Papp told Rabe he wanted the play, Rabe had to tell him that Gerald Paonessa held the rights and wished to participate in the production.

Years later, Papp had no memory of any rights problem. "Paonessa was a gnat to be swatted," Bernard Gersten would recall. "So he had a legal right to it, so what? He was David's friend. It was David's problem." Paonessa and Papp signed a legal agreement providing that he could sit in on rehearsals, receive a credit in the program and retain his Broadway rights. In fact, Papp discouraged his attendance, disregarded the agreement and moved the production to Broadway himself. Attorneys advised Paonessa that he could sue Papp for breach of contract and prevent the play from opening. One offered his services free of charge. But Paonessa, dissuaded by his antiwar politics and friendship with Rabe, decided against taking Papp to court.

Papp's handling of Paonessa was the first of several episodes that made the wary playwright still warier of the producer. After *Sticks and Bones* opened to excellent reviews, Papp determined to move it to Broadway. There had never been a Vietnam play on Broadway before, Papp told Rabe. He wanted it to attract the kind of attention it would not get downtown. Reviews had been positive; they would not be opening blind.

Rabe was ambivalent. "It was an aggressive, unconventional, demanding play, *uncomfortable* for the audience, with a hero it could not like," he later said. "*Sticks and Bones* was doing fine in a 300-seat theater at the Public. Was it prudent to move it? A play can run for one year in a 300-seat theater and close in four days on Broadway. And once you open, there's no going back.

"But that same impulse that made me write the play made Joe want to throw it in the face of a Broadway audience. He said it would be good for me and good for the play. I wasn't sure. I thought it would be good for him. He was an expansionist. He wanted to make his frontal attack on Broadway. It was then I was starting to think of him as I had first seen him: storming through the lobby. And I was now one of those three people following."

The two men debated the pros and cons until Rabe called to agree with Papp's plan. "But he was in a mood I could not have anticipated," Rabe later wrote, "'It's off,' he said. 'Until you decide you want it. . . . It's a risk I want to take, but it's your play I'm risking even if I protect it as much as I can. So you've got to decide to go or not to go. If we did it and it didn't go, I don't want you coming up to me yelling "You sonofabitch, you killed my play."'"

Sticks and Bones, directed by Jeff Bleckner, opened in March 1972 at the Golden Theater, one block away from *Two Gents.* Papp would later recall that he never saw the theater more than half filled. Every week, the producer took $10,000 to $15,000 off the top of Festival income from the musical and applied it to the losses of the Vietnam drama. Such subsidy was a practice he had learned at the Actors' Lab and Papp's way of atoning for having produced a commercial success.

The following month, both shows won Broadway's highest honor, the Tony Award. It was the first time ever that an off-Broadway producer had won, and the first time any producer had won both Best Musical and Best Dramatic Play categories in the same year. Papp appeared on national television and was treated as a celebrity by the press. Earlier that season, *New York* magazine had already featured the producer on its glossy cover, backed up by William Shakespeare and a hippie from *Hair.* It included an examination of Papp's personal life.

Joseph Papp had turned fifty the previous June. He was still living with his wife and two youngest children in an eight-room, rent-controlled apartment at Broadway and 98th Street — an unfashionable, high-crime neighborhood. The Papps, *New York* reported chattily,

> recently celebrated their twentieth anniversary. Joe says, "It shows you I can stick with something," and Peggy acknowledges that there have been stormy years: "It wasn't easy . . . I guess all I can think of is a tremendous struggle — pain and struggle."
>
> Peggy and Joe had no children for the first six years of their marriage. The way Joe puts it is, "If I'd had children I couldn't have done what I wanted to do in the theater — it would have been impossible. It's just that I had to be free." It took him years to come to terms with the fact that he did already have two children. . . . For most of Susan and Michael's childhood, Joe just wasn't there. Peggy thinks the reason their two children mean so much to Joe is "because later on in his life he realized what a tremendous loss that was." Joe says, "To know that you've ruined a part of a child's life — you never forgive yourself for that. But I couldn't do anything else. A child can kill you later for that, he can shoot you and feel perfectly justified." . . .
>
> On the other hand, he's the kind of husband who helps with the dishes and vacuuming on the weekends and makes Peggy's breakfast every Sunday. "That's his most endearing quality. His scrambled eggs are fantastic," she says.

At the time the *New York* story appeared, the Papps' twenty-year marriage was all but over. For six years, he had been addressing part of his intensive therapy to the question of when to initiate his third divorce. And by then, he was romantically involved with his assistant Gail Merrifield.

Merrifield was a hazel-eyed, fine-featured woman whose colleagues invariably described her first as extraordinarily thin. "There ain't much meat on 'er," Papp would joke, appropriating Spencer Tracy's line from the film *Pat and Mike*, "but what there is, is cherce." Some people thought she looked like actress Audrey Hepburn, and found her girlish, ethereal, playful and shy. The thirty-seven-year-old Merrifield kept most things about her to herself — starting with the fact that her great-great-grandfather was actor John Wilkes Booth, who assassinated Abraham Lincoln. Her grandmother was child actress and journalist Izola Forrester. Her parents, distant cousins named Merrifield, were writers. She had grown up in Berkeley, California, where, as a child, she had organized her own basement theater, The Gold Shore Theater of the Air, and —

like Papp — published her own newspaper. She went to college on a
music scholarship in New York and, after marrying a fellow student when
she was nineteen, had worked as an editorial trainee at various publishing
houses, accumulating college credits at night. Her husband became a
journalist and was eventually posted to Mexico City. By the time their
marriage broke up, Merrifield had studied at New York University, City
College, Hunter College, Mexico City College and the Universidad
Nacional de Mexico. When she returned to New York alone at age
twenty-eight, she returned to publishing, as well as taking another course
— this time at the New School for Social Research — to complete her
degree. It was in the New School cafeteria that she met a Yale Law School
graduate who was pursuing a literary career and used the cafeteria as a
place to write. Merrifield, who studied there, began to read his work and
he eventually moved in with her.

They had been together for about seven years when, one Sunday
afternoon, he told her he was hearing voices. That first episode was
followed by spells of violence and disorientation. Although Merrifield
succeeded in having him hospitalized for short periods of time, his parents were unable to comprehend that their grown son was mentally ill
and Merrifield took on the care of her lover alone.

In April 1965, after a year of working as a play-reader at Lincoln
Center, Merrifield interviewed at the Great Northern Hotel for a job in
Papp's office. She had been in Mexico when the Delacorte opened and
knew nothing about the New York Shakespeare Festival. When Papp's
assistant left, Merrifield took on her work.

"I knew she had worked for Harold Clurman and it was obvious that
she was more than a competent secretary," recalled Herta Danis, who
had always kept an eye on her boss's romantic involvements. "You had
to be very bright to work with Joe. He trusted and depended on her.
But she was certainly not the kind of girl he had been romantically linked
with before, and she was not the kind of person to whom I'd say: 'Let's
go have lunch.' She always looked sad. She very rarely smiled. She wore
her hair up in a bun, a little prim. She would walk around in the depth
of winter in a sleeveless brown jumper and I would wonder how she
could stand the cold. She was very reserved and didn't encourage closeness. It never occurred to me that the two of them were involved."

Merrifield had been working at the Festival for three years before Papp
began asking her out to lunch.

"I just thought he was being very decent," Merrifield later recalled.
"We seemed to have a lot to talk about and I was relieved that he didn't
ask me anything about my personal life. I think Joe was relieved I didn't

ask about his. We were mature people, and there's a point in everyone's life when you begin to feel the weight of your past. We were interested in the present. At the time, I read all the scripts that came into Joe's office and we talked about them as well as about everything else you can imagine. Our first real date was to see a play. It was a wonderful evening, but I had very complicated feelings.

"I felt Joe was on the rebound — not from his marriage but from the relationship he had been involved in — and that whatever he was feeling toward me would pass. I was not the best candidate for a relationship. For several years I had been *in* one that was very demanding and I realized that Joe didn't know it. But I felt it would be disloyal to talk about the man I was living with because he was very ill. And he was a writer."

Papp first learned about Merrifield's ancestry in 1970 when, for Christmas, she gave him a copy of *The Mad Booths of Maryland*, with a supplement titled "John Wilkes Booth's Common-Law Family." On the accompanying card she had written: "To Joe with love from Gail (the "family skeleton" is aired in Supplement I)." He discovered he was not the only man in Merrifield's life when, after she called in sick one day and he brought flowers to her apartment, he saw another man at home there. "I was shocked," Merrifield recalled. "I introduced them and Joe didn't stay. He never asked who he was." In his willful way of ignoring any obstacles to the goal on which he had set his sights, Papp continued courting his assistant.

People close to Merrifield would later say that it was to the producer's credit that he had discerned her quirky combination of playfulness, intelligence, refinement of manner and fierce loyalty — all hidden by a self-effacing reclusiveness. "She was just the opposite of show business," said one. "There are many people who, when they're close to power, misuse it," said another. "Gail never abused her power and proximity to Joe."

Merrifield and Papp fell in love as if for the first time. "It was a deep and abiding connection of heart and mind but it was complicated," said Merrifield. "We had no place to be together. For me, it was very difficult to think of leaving the man I was with because he was so dependent on me. Joe felt he could not leave his children, Tony and Miranda. I talked to Tony almost every day. He'd be home after school with the housekeeper and he'd call his father. When Joe was busy, we'd have long conversations about his life, his birds and his gerbil."

Merrifield took a sublet and, for a time, paid two rents, augmenting her meager Festival salary with jobs as a proofreader, typist and publicist. Eventually she convinced her lover's parents to assume responsibility for

their son. Long after Papp and Merrifield were married — in January of
1976 — they would quote from *Othello* to describe their connection.
"She loved me for the dangers I had passed and I loved her that she did
pity them," Papp would sometimes say. Or, reversing the Moor's lines,
"He loved her for the dangers she had passed and she loved him that he
did pity them."

At the office, Festival staffers, attuned to the more flamboyant personalities at the Public Theater, never questioned Gail Merrifield's presence
at the producer's side. It seemed unworthy of remark that she was at
every meeting, taking the producer's notes and accompanying him wherever he went. The couple's romance coincided with the transfer of the
first Festival shows to Broadway. In those first years of the 1970s, Papp
also launched two new theater magazines, kept his Delacorte, Mobile and
Public theaters filled with plays — 23 productions — and moved rapidly
from one project to another. "Within a very brief span of time," Bernard
Gersten would recall, "the Shakespeare Festival suddenly became a major
player in New York theater."

The extraordinary level of activity at the Festival had been noted by
representatives of the William Morris Agency, who met with Papp in May
of 1972 to discuss expanding his activities into network television. Television was becoming the largest source of revenue for the talent agency,
the three national networks were looking for high-prestige "specials" to
beef up their offerings and William Morris was trying to develop a
practice in selling them.

Ten years of working at CBS as a stage manager had left Papp with
few illusions about television. "It was at a far remove from the work we
did — and neither one of us sat around watching TV on Sundays," said
Gersten. "But when an opportunity to produce for TV presented itself,
we embraced it. It was money and new audiences. We didn't see television as diminishing our work but enhancing it."

The choice narrowed down to CBS. Its president, Robert Wood,
seemed interested only in Shakespeare and wanted Papp to do *Romeo and
Juliet*. Papp offered *Hamlet*. Wood demurred. Papp offered to do *Romeo
and Juliet* in exchange for the promise of a second production by a new
playwright — either *The Basic Training of Pavlo Hummel* or *That Championship Season*, which had won a Pulitzer Prize. When the language of
both plays proved unacceptable to CBS, Papp suggested *Sticks and Bones*.

By the end of July, Papp had an $8 million contract to produce
thirteen Shakespearean as well as contemporary plays over a four-year
period. They would be broadcast nationwide over two hundred CBS
affiliates, and each would occupy between ninety minutes and three hours

of prime time. It seemed like a windfall for the Festival and was the largest theater/television deal CBS had ever made.

"To be able to introduce a new writer every year on *network* television?" Papp would later exclaim. "And Shakespeare? It was certainly an artsy idea for network television." It was also a victory for American, as opposed to British, Shakespeare. "There was *The Hallmark Hall of Fame*," Papp noted, "and the Richard Chamberlain *Hamlet,* et cetera. But where were they made? Invariably in England. The networks and sponsors never supported the American theater. Very often I've had productions in the park which I knew were better than some being done in England. But do you think I could interest our networks before this in tackling an American production?"

Papp was unusually gracious at the press conference he held jointly with Robert Wood. He made no mention of his legal history with the network. Television, he said, was "the medium of the people," a natural vehicle through which to extend his long-held goal of reaching new, mass audiences free of charge. The local CBS affiliate had already telecast three of his Delacorte productions; now the network would "reflect the spectrum of work performed by the NYSF and the Public Theater — classics and vital contemporary plays. Our aim is to engage the audience, not alienate it. We are interested in family viewing as well as controversial adult material. We will try not to offend gratuitously, but we will risk offending if the theme is meaningful and serious. We will make every effort to press for broadening the censorship limitations when demanded by artistic considerations. We will strive to apply the same standards in TV that we apply to our work in the theater, both in quality and content."

When reporters asked how CBS would respond to Shakespeare's and Rabe's use of sexually explicit language, Wood replied, "Well, I think we would want to make a very careful judgment . . . we have to be mindful of the many audiences we serve." Papp added, "CBS decides what goes on the air. That's as it should be."

Much later, Papp would say, "If you know what a TV corporation is, you're never disappointed in what they do." And, "I had to get used to the way they talked and the way they made decisions. I knew they were a different breed of people. I couldn't understand how they functioned within this huge, monolithic kind of structure. It sounded alien to my ears when they talked about a play because they weren't thinking — really — about the play. They were worried whether this would be salable or whether people would be offended or understand it."

Within a few weeks of the press conference, Papp arranged to meet with the CBS executives for Program Practices and Program Clearance, whom he perceived as his chief potential adversaries at the network. He wished to discuss any problems likely to arise in regard to either Shakespeare or Rabe, whose two plays Papp had submitted to CBS for the second Festival telecast. *Romeo and Juliet* contained what Papp called "devastating" erotic allusions such as Mercutio's "I conjure thee by Rosalyn's bright eyes, straight leg, quivering thigh, and all the domains that there adjacent lie," which he would quote at the drop of a hat. *Sticks and Bones* could also be construed as profane. *Its* chief challenge to Programming Practices was a scene in which the blind veteran, David, using his cane, raises the hem of a priest's cassock. Papp wanted to get to know his potential censors and, dropping the names of several TV critics, let them know of his close relations with the press.

The producer was well aware of the political context in which the telecast of *Sticks and Bones* was being planned. Papp had memories of Richard Nixon as a lawyer on the side of the inquisitors who had destroyed so many of his colleagues in the theater. Now, Papp followed President Nixon's campaign to decentralize and weaken the power of the media. Vice-President Spiro Agnew had begun his attack on network television during Nixon's first year in office, with a speech written by Pat Buchanan. Less than a year later, Nixon had set up an Office of Telecommunications Policy. Agnew lost no opportunity to portray major newspaper editors and network executives as "Eastern seaboard elitists" with little sense of responsibility to their constituents. At the same time, OTP head Clay Whitehead criticized local station managers "who fail to act to correct imbalance or consistent bias from the networks," and promised to bolster the power of those who *did* correct it by campaigning for a new five-year, rather than three-year, broadcast license.

"Years of contact with station operators . . . have taught me that most of the men who control the country's electronic media bend to two things," broadcasting reporter Les Brown wrote. "Money and political power." When CBS had televised a documentary called *The Selling of the Pentagon,* which investigated the public relations of the Department of Defense, Agnew attacked CBS, noting "the widening credibility gap that exists between the national news media and the American public." CBS president Frank Stanton had responded less than forcefully, and Papp had written him:

> I heard some of your remarks over CBS and I am really amazed. When do liberals ever learn that the only way to handle a bully is to give him a dose of his own medicine? He must be hit and hit hard. This man is

a real threat to democracy — the protégé of Joe McCarthy. Why don't you say out loud what he is attempting to do? Everybody knows it but you want to bury your head in the sand. He is trying to censor the news media. He wants to control the press. He wants to be the arbiter of opinion. He is Mr. Thought Control in person. He is a walking violation of the free speech and free press movement. He is using his position to undermine the only independent means this country has to find out what is going on in it. . . . Of course, be reasonable, but God, man, shout a little.

Stanton, Papp noted, was the man who would be held responsible for CBS's acquisition of *Sticks and Bones*. But Papp did not waste time worrying about his potential response to Rabe's play. Nor did Papp heed the warning of Les Brown, who wrote:

Comes a period of prosperity and one or another network brims with beautiful intentions, the result of which invariably is an extravagant plan to bring something culturally important to the medium, not once but frequently — and not immediately, but in the future.

The press responds from coast to coast and fully half the glory that is to be won occurs at that very moment, in the announcement publicity — a case where the message is the medium. Comes later a disappointing reaction to the first fruit of the project, or worse, a downturn in the economy, and the high-minded plan just sort of fades away. . . .

CBS has already derived a measure of prestige from the announcement itself, and if the Papp dramas, when they are finally presented, should fail to bring equal honor the temptation will no doubt be strong within the CBS precincts to quit the operation. . . . If CBS won some glory with the announcement of the Papp deal, it should rightfully stand to lose prestige if it should fail to fulfill all that was promised.

Papp threw himself into his new project and, typically, ignored potential problems. He leased a floor of office space, commissioned Giorgio Cavaglieri to design an office for a Festival television department and rehired his old Yale student Ted Cornell to run it. He hired an executive producer. He bought himself a small TV camera, worked on production budgets with Bernard Gersten, scouted studios and editing facilities in Toronto and Brooklyn and launched a search for a twelve-year-old Juliet and fourteen-year-old Romeo. Within three weeks, the Festival's casting department had auditioned five hundred people.

But *Romeo and Juliet* had bad karma for Papp. At the Actors' Lab, he had run out of the theater after performing Romeo; at Emmanuel Church, he had been unable to cast the leading male role. Now, he could not find either a Romeo or a Juliet; Franco Zeffirelli's film of the play had just been released. Papp was distracted by other projects. In August, he decided to substitute *Much Ado About Nothing* — then playing at the Delacorte — for *Romeo and Juliet*. In high spirits, he called CBS president Robert Wood to tell him of his change in plans and journalist Stuart Little set down their conversation in this way:

"Joe, you don't realize, television isn't like theater," Wood had said, trying to explain to Papp what seemed obvious to him. "Television is like a large battleship. You have to make a slow turn. There are two hundred affiliates we have to watch out for. And we've promised them *Romeo and Juliet*."

"Well you wouldn't want me to come in with a poor show, would you?" Papp replied. "What's so holy about *Romeo*? CBS audiences wouldn't know the difference between *Romeo and Juliet* and *Much Ado About Nothing*."

When Wood insisted that Papp hold off sending out a press release, the producer interpreted it as tacit consent and announced the news to the personnel of *Much Ado*. Director A. J. Antoon was unhappy with the decision. He knew nothing about television and had no interest in learning to direct for it. He had hoped Papp would move their production to Broadway, a move Bernard Gersten also favored. Papp decided to put *Much Ado* on TV *and* move it to Broadway.

In October, *Newsweek* reported that CBS had a censor present at tapings: "He objected that leading lady Kathleen Widdoes doesn't shave under her arms and questioned the size of a 'respectable bulge' for the men in the bathing scene." In November, when *Much Ado* moved to Broadway, almost everything about the production — Antoon's concept, Ming Cho Lee's set, Peter Link's music, the entire cast — drew applause from the critics. It was seen as the first successful Shakespeare without a major star in Broadway history. A few weeks later, IBM announced that it would sponsor the CBS television version for $1 million.

Over Christmas, *Much Ado* was playing to sold-out audiences, the most popular show on Broadway in a weak season. But toward the end of January, as both CBS and IBM began an intensive promotional campaign for the television show, ticket sales began to falter. On February 7, when an estimated two million New Yorkers and about twenty million people nationwide saw at least part of *Much Ado*, the Winter Garden theater was over half full. But the next day, ticket sales plunged — "I've never seen anything fall so rapidly in my life," Papp recalled. "After the television show there was nobody at the box office." Four days later, after 116 performances and at a loss of $165,000, Papp closed the show.

"We didn't understand the principle that if you gave something away for nothing, people would say 'Why pay?'" he later said. But, at least, the Festival's national TV debut had been widely publicized and very well received and Papp was ready to deliver his second show, *Sticks and Bones*, to the network.

Work on Rabe's play had started against the backdrop of the 1972 presidential elections as voters gave a landslide victory to Richard Nixon over George McGovern and continued through December, when Clay T. Whitehead, head of the White House Office of Telecommunications Policy, made a widely publicized speech criticizing "so-called professionals" who used "ideological plugola" and dispensed "elitist gossip in the guise of news analysis." CBS officials refused to comment on the speech, though a spokesman told the *Washington Post*, "It would be a fair assumption that it's getting read around here."

On January 24, the day *Sticks and Bones* was to have its first screening at the offices of CBS, the *New York Times* carried the banner headline "VIETNAM ACCORD IS REACHED; CEASE-FIRE BEGINS SATURDAY; P.O.W.'S TO BE FREE IN 60 DAYS." President Nixon had announced an agreement to "end the war and bring peace with honor in Vietnam and Southeast Asia." Rabe's play was about the return of a damaged Vietnam veteran to his unscathed family. That evening and for most of the next few weeks, television news would feature the real families of real American POWs and their return home.

That day, Joseph Papp and his people filed into a small screening room high up in the CBS building not knowing what to expect. In the room with them, but seated apart, were some of the CBS executives who had worked most closely with Papp. The group watched the show without much reaction. When it was over, the room was silent. Papp was unable to elicit an air date out of them. A few days later, Papp remarked to a reporter that he expected trouble with the Nixon administration as well as television viewers over his second production.

Papp had no time to brood about the White House or public opinion. He was closely involved in four upcoming Public productions, each of which had pressing problems. "The way I operate is like having a ward with numbers of patients of varying degrees of health," he told a reporter at the end of January 1973. "Each of these patients are related to life and must be preserved, sustained . . . and each one is important."

He was also preoccupied by a new project: discussions with the management of the Lincoln Center for the Performing Arts. Five months earlier, the director of its two theaters had resigned. A committee had been formed to look for a successor, and Papp was asked to help its members choose one.

Lincoln Center for the Performing Arts was a creation of the Rockefeller family and had received mixed reviews upon opening. It was considered an unqualified success by New Yorkers interested in urban development for it had not only replaced blocks of tenements and their inhabitants with pristine white marble cultural arenas, but had triggered a wave of gentrification on the Upper West Side that began in the late 1950s and was still going on more than thirty years later. The project was less successful artistically. Opera-lovers were unhappy with the new Metropolitan Opera House; musicians and concertgoers alike loathed the acoustics of Philharmonic Hall. But both these institutions had the history, wealth and subscriber base to overcome their problems. The 1,100-seat Vivian Beaumont Theater did not.

The Beaumont had been built as a repertory theater, with funds contributed by a department store heiress. The problem was that no repertory company yet existed to fill it. "It was like erecting the Great Pyramid and advertising for a dynasty of pharaohs to go inside," wrote one critic. Its first leaders, celebrated producer Robert Whitehead and director Elia Kazan, put together a repertory company drawing on actors from the Actors Studio, invited Arthur Miller to be their resident playwright and launched an ambitious program. But the two men locked horns with their board. "We were not partners but employees in a vulnerable position, without tenure," Kazan later wrote. "Whom did we work for? Not villains, not bad men but men out of another world, who were not capable of handling the responsibilities they were given. . . ."

In 1964, after Whitehead was fired and Kazan resigned, Papp received a call asking whether he would be interested in taking on the Beaumont. The producer had said he would be interested only if the Festival kept its own board; maintained control of its own program, ticket prices and operation; and if Lincoln Center would pay maintenance costs and underwrite the deficit. Lincoln Center had dropped the matter. Instead, Herbert Blau and Jules Irving from San Francisco had been appointed and had encountered difficulty after difficulty. In 1972, Jules Irving resigned — Herbert Blau had left earlier — and Papp was once again consulted.

"Joe gave himself to the consulting role wholeheartedly," said Gail Merrifield, who had herself worked for Whitehead at Lincoln Center. "The feeling then was that the theater had a rocky history and needed some basic rethinking. Initially, Joe didn't have any desire for this job himself. I went with him to two meetings where he talked about what could be done without his thinking that he himself would do it. But he gradually talked himself into being interested by virtue of talking through his ideas. This often happened to Joe: he'd start probing the reasons he didn't want to do something — especially a play — get deeper into it and end up doing it. Running parallel to this was the financial crisis at the Public. There was a deficit of two million dollars — an extraordinary amount even by today's standards — and I remember Joe and Bernie talking about it all the time, not knowing where the money would come from. Then Joe realized he could raise money if he went to Lincoln Center. The foundations wouldn't be able to say no to him — not even the Ford Foundation — because they had a vested interest in making Lincoln Center work."

Less than two years after receiving a $1.6 million check from the City of New York, the producer was again over one million dollars in debt. "We tended to live with the halcyon view that the cash flow from a popular Broadway show like *Much Ado* gave us latitude," recalled Bernard Gersten. "We went over budget [on the CBS version] by a couple of hundred thousand dollars. Shakespeare on network television was subsidized by us to the tune of three or four percent and that seemed appropriate to the needs of the show and our pursuit of a greater audience. Then we had to close *Much Ado* on Broadway. We were in trouble. But Joe's doctrine was: *When you're in trouble, get into deeper trouble.*"

Papp and Gersten both thought that residency at Lincoln Center would help them raise the kind of foundation money that they had been unable to touch downtown. They thought that the 1,100-seat Beaumont Theater could itself generate income. They thought that Festival playwrights and performers would now have the high visibility they deserved, and that new audiences would be attracted to the Festival.

On Valentine's Day of 1973, Papp went uptown to meet with John Mazzola and the Committee for Theater at Lincoln Center; one week later, with chairman of the board of Lincoln Center Amyas Ames. Just as he had had mixed feelings about selling the Public Theater to New York City, he had mixed feelings about moving uptown. Papp was satisfied with his operation. The Festival had grown tremendously in the past three years. It now employed 110 people, excluding actors. It had its beautifully restored theaters, its own carpentry and costume shops, audio department and casting department, in a building far lovelier than the Berliner Ensemble building he had so admired in 1964. Why would he want to give it up?

Papp sat for hours typing out his thoughts on his old Remington

Standard. Finally, he arrived at a solution: The Festival, unlike the Philharmonic, the Metropolitan Opera or the New York City Ballet, was *not*
becoming part of Lincoln Center; rather, Lincoln Center was becoming
an outpost of the Festival. The move would represent, Papp wrote in his
press statement, "a continuation of the task of bringing thoughtful,
searching, alive plays to the people of the city and the country at large at
those places best suited for the purpose." The park was one place; the
five boroughs on the Mobile Stage were another; the Public Theater
another; Broadway, another; CBS Television another; and now, Lincoln
Center.

He claimed he had no choice but to expand his enterprise. As he told
a writer at the time, "I can't continue on here as I've been going. It's
become too expensive."

In his position papers, Papp took pains to emphasize the continuity of
his philosophy. "The problems of democracy at Lincoln Center are much
more complex than they are in the parks and playgrounds," he wrote.
"By its nature, the leadership here is predominantly white, upper-class
and upper middle-class. This fact is historically rooted, beginning with
the aristocratic arts patron in Shakespeare's time, to individual philanthropy of the 19th century, to the foundation and government subsidies
and grants of the 20th century."

"The Festival," he wrote in a second paper, "unlike most of its fellow
constituents at Lincoln Center, has emerged from popular audience support which includes significant numbers of minority people. By bringing
these sectors of our audience to Lincoln Center, we will convey to the
predominantly white middle-class patrons a feeling of togetherness, rather
than separateness and isolation with its accompanying fears. This psychological evaluation must be part of any consideration of long-range artistic
planning."

Both papers document Papp's continuing commitment to what would
later be called multiculturalism.

> Our progress in democracy can only be measured by the extent of
> economic and social freedom afforded the black in the United States.
> It would be ridiculous for a theater to take as its burden the freedom
> of the black when the entire nation and Government seem to be unable
> or unwilling to deal with the injustice . . . [but] the theater is one area
> in society which can address itself to "giving us our humanity" by
> promulgating changes of a social as well as an artistic nature.

He wished to add at least five thousand black subscribers to the
Lincoln Center Theater's list of forty thousand predominantly white ones

and admit the young and elderly as "passholders" at lower charge. His board at Lincoln Center would reflect the composition of its audience and be, he wrote, "unlike any cultural boards of the past. It will reflect the multi-racial, multi-national and to a great degree, the multi-political character of the city and country. It will not function solely as a 'money force' but principally as a social force."

Assuming that he could put together an audience "of the white and black middle-class — professionals, young people and the elderly, with representatives of the evolving Puerto Rican middle class — we have then to produce a certain selection of plays . . . ," Papp continued. For his first season he envisioned one classic, one contemporary Irish play and three new American plays — one by a black playwright. The difference between plays at Lincoln Center and plays at the Public would lie primarily in a "distinguished actor" policy. He planned to bring to Lincoln Center international stars of stage, film and TV, with special attention to successful black screen and TV actors long associated with the Festival.

The 300-seat Forum Theater beneath the Beaumont, Papp thought, would be home for Shakespeare without the trappings of Central Park productions. "The aim will be to achieve a close-up cameo-style, naturalistic handling of the text and emphasis on character rather than pomp and ritual." Papp anticipated plays moving from downtown to uptown within what would now be a seven-theater complex, as well as moves to Broadway, national tours and television and film projects. He took pains to frame this expansion within the philosophy with which he had begun the Festival. "If there is a single driving force which characterizes the New York Shakespeare Festival," he wrote, "it is its continual confrontation with the wall that separates vast numbers of people from the arts. This wall is spawned by poverty, ignorance, historical conditions and as we joust and engage with this enemy we distill and shape the nature and style of our theater."

At eleven o'clock in the morning, March 6, Amyas Ames, a former investment banker, and Papp held a joint press conference in the plush lobby of the Alice Tully Recital Hall. Short and vivid beside the tall, courtly Ames, and dressed in a modish blue velvet suit, Papp reminded one reporter of "Charlie Chaplin's little tramp" in the province of the "oil barons," although he was about to assume a position of power unprecedented in modern theater history.

When reporters asked why he was making the move, Papp said, "Personal aggrandizement — to establish a cultural power base here in New York so as to take over the rest of the repertory theaters in the country and establish liaisons with China and Russia. And another reason: This is closer to where I live — 98th Street and Broadway." Then: "We're not in too good financial shape at the Public Theater. So why incur a greater financial problem? Traditionally, that's the way we work. At each point of our development, we used our resources to the utmost. It's not expansion but focusing inwards, making the greatest use of our particular resources — our playwrights, actors and directors."

The question of fiscal responsibility — which had plagued both former regimes at the Lincoln Center Theater — had not been resolved between Papp and Amyas Ames. "It was as if we two wanted to get married," noted Ames, "but we didn't have the dowry." Papp added that they had reached a "Vietnamese solution," with each party claiming victory, and that "moving into a prestige area makes it possible to raise more money." His move uptown was contingent, Papp said, on raising $5 million in two months.

When the press conference ended, Papp, Merrifield, Gersten and his wife, Cora Cahan, and journalist Stuart Little, then researching his book on Papp, went back downtown for a celebratory lunch. When Papp picked up his $1.6 million from the city, he had taken the subway back to his theater. Now he drove a leased Mercedes, after flirting briefly with and then rejecting the idea of purchasing a Jaguar. Some Festival staffers noted with displeasure Papp's new means of transportation, but Bernard Gersten, if he thought about it at all, was happy that his old friend had "gotten past his self-imposed culture of poverty." The Festival board had just given them both a hefty raise in salaries, as well as their first package of benefits.

On the way to the Steak Casino, a neighborhood restaurant near the Public Theater, Papp stopped the car by a newsstand. *Time* and *Newsweek* were both carrying advance reviews of the televised *Sticks and Bones*. The show "will drive a nail into your forehead and leave your face hanging like a sack from it all weekend long," reported *Newsweek*. "I cannot recall anything on commercial television of an intensity comparable to this production." The *Time* reviewer wrote, "The greatest national trauma since the Civil War, the U.S. involvement in Viet Nam has yet to be exorcised in drama or fiction. *Sticks and Bones* . . . is strong stuff for commercial TV, stronger even than it seemed on the New York stage." The night before, Papp had received telephone calls from two reporters checking out a rumor that CBS had canceled the show, but since then he had not thought about it.

The Papp party trooped into the restaurant and Papp ordered a round of vodka martinis. "Everyone was feeling exuberant," Gersten later recalled. As the group was boisterously reading through the reviews, a waiter told Papp he had a telephone call. The producer took it at the front of the room.

On the line was Robert Wood, president of CBS Television.

"Great reviews, huh?" Papp later remembered greeting him.

"I have bad news," was Wood's reply. "We can't put that show on." He had just sent a telegram to the general managers of all CBS affiliates explaining that *Sticks and Bones* had been previewed twice for the managements of CBS-affiliated stations, with most of them responding favorably to the powerful show. But a cease-fire had since been declared in Vietnam. The telegram made clear his position that presentation at this time might be unnecessarily abrasive to

> the feelings of millions of Americans whose lives or attention are at the moment emotionally dominated by the returning POWs and other veterans who have suffered the ravages of war.
>
> Never has there been a greater or more serious and responsible sense of concern expressed by our affiliates about a projected program and the timing of its broadcast. It is the conclusion of the CBS Television Network, therefore, that the broadcast of *Sticks and Bones* should be postponed and broadcast at a later date, to be announced, when the context of its showing will be less distressing and its possible application to actual events less immediate. . . .

Papp did not let Wood read his telegram. Instead, he began to shout into the telephone receiver about censorship, government pressure, the First Amendment, the obligation of a network to its viewers. Watching him from the table where he was enjoying a celebratory drink, Bernard Gersten was hoping Papp would not blow the entire twelve-show contract. "I wanted to believe that CBS was motivated not by cowardice but by sensitivity to the POWs," he later said. "You wouldn't run a movie sympathetic to John Wilkes Booth during the week Kennedy was shot. I hoped CBS would run the show later — which it did. We were in the middle of raising money for Lincoln Center. We needed the money from the CBS contract. But Joe perceived it as a threat to his mission, and his response was to bring an enormous amount of public pressure to bear."

The producer returned to the table, announced lunch was over and that they were going to war. For the next few days, in a fury that was fed by years of personal and political experience, Papp would concentrate on nothing else. In 1958, CBS had fired him for his politics. This time, Joseph Papp would — over every radio and television station, in every newspaper and magazine that interviewed him — fire CBS for theirs.

FOURTEEN

Papp and the Press

On THE AFTERNOON of March 6, Joseph Papp launched a press campaign against CBS. "I want to let you know how shabbily you CBS people conduct human affairs," he wrote CBS President Wood.

> Having become desensitized to fraudulent behavior, you proceed through life collecting your wages, finding no contradiction in the face which appears before you in the mirror every morning, avoiding your own eyes, which you must if you are not to cut your throat; finding ersatz substitutes for the real thing which has long disappeared with your honor and your vestige of decency which may at one time have been of some concern to you and your colleagues. I bid you all a fond farewell and leave you to your worm-eaten consciences.

Papp took out an ad in the *New York Times* in protest and press agent Merle Debuskey scheduled interview after interview — with the *Washington Post, Chicago Sun-Times, Des Moines Register, Los Angeles Times, Variety, Time, Newsweek*. The CBS decision, he said, was "virtually unprecedented," "presumptuous" and "dangerous." The network had "backed down because of the implied threats of Clay Whitehead" who had "set up 300 little censors." Moreover, David Rabe was no "effete eastern elitist" on the Agnew model but a bona fide midwesterner from *Dubuque!*

Rabe chose to remain out of the spotlight but, for Papp, "it became an international story, far bigger than the Moses affair," Debuskey would later recall. "It was perceived as a First Amendment issue, an issue related to the Vietnam war and a governmental attempt to control the press. And once again, Joe did something no one else would have done. He stood on principle. He canceled his contract and walked out on millions of dollars."

Papp's Lincoln Center appointment and the CBS cancellation marked a new level in media attention to Papp. Long profiles of the producer appeared in major newspapers and magazines. When warned about over-reach, Papp replied, "They once said that to England, didn't they? I'm the kind of person who is more creative when he has more to do. . . . As important as all this is to me, I could live without it. I could walk out of here tomorrow." Such remarks and the offhand manner in which they were delivered continued to charm reporters, many of whom despised the Nixon administration. Papp was becoming one of a very few people who could get media attention whenever he wanted it, an advantage he would exploit to its fullest and that was to last for the rest of his life.

Unlike Spiro Agnew, Joseph Papp had always liked the press. "When we were living on Boerum Street, I'd cut the letters PRESS from the *Daily News,* paste them on some cardboard, stick it in my father's hat, and go around listening to what people said," he would later recall. "Then I borrowed a typewriter, got some carbon paper and handed out copies of the *Boerum Eavesdropper* to people on the street. There'd be items like 'Who is that shy lad and woman-hater now becoming a ladies' man? Not you, A.B.'" As an adult, Joe Papp brought that earnest, urgent, personal style to his every encounter with the press.

The press and the theater had long had a complicated, volatile rela-tionship almost everywhere in the world, but nowhere had the power of one newspaper to affect theater reached that of the *New York Times.* More than half a century earlier, a twenty-seven-year-old *Times* drama critic named Alexander Woolcott judged a play "tedious." The Shuberts, the show's producers, were furious and demanded that the *Times* send an-other reviewer to their next production. When Woolcott paid for his own ticket, the Shuberts refused to let him into the theater.

The *Times* took the Shuberts to court, which ruled in the producers' favor. But although they won the battle, they lost the war. For a full year, the *Times* refused to accept any advertising for the Shubert organization or to publish the name of any business, production or actor associated with it. Moreover, the *Times* featured the story on its front pages, creating a climate of opinion that shamed the Shuberts, lost them business and eventually forced the producers to invite Woolcott back. The Shuberts never challenged the *Times* again.

Joe Papp understood the relationship. When he was starting out, in the early 1950s, theatergoers read the *Herald Tribune,* the *Daily News,* the *Journal-American,* the *Daily Mirror,* the *Telegram and Sun* and the *New York Post* as well as the *Times.* By the late 1960s, there were only three dailies left, and the *Times* was, by far, the most important and inflluential — its stories were syndicated across the country and picked up all over the world.

From the newspaper's point of view, the theater community had always been one of New York's most glamorous "beats." Readership tended to be educated, and ardent. Theater matters were the stuff of dinner party conversation. For the ambitious editor, reporter or critic, writing well about theater was a surefire way to make a mark. It was also an easy entree into show business and a way to imbibe the thrill of the stage without its difficulties. The line between those who made theater and those who wrote about it was often invisible. Many newspaper editors, critics and reporters had started out wishing to become actors, playwrights or directors. Some managed to work simultaneously in journalism and theater like George S. Kaufman, who was a working playwright and *Times* theater critic for thirteen years. Some used journalism as a stepping stone like Herman Mankiewicz, Kaufman's assistant, who became a Hollywood producer and cowrote *Citizen Kane.*

The men and women who wrote about theater knew their power. They enjoyed such perquisites as free theater tickets, and had the ability to give or hold back press coverage with a nonchalance that would have been somewhat less in evidence had they been reporting on, say, the United Nations or Wall Street. One theater critic reviewing Festival productions submitted his own play to Joseph Papp. The wives of two other journalists covering Papp submitted theirs. (He rejected the first and produced the latter two.)

If journalists found in theater people a way of satisfying their ambitions, vanity or nostalgia for a road not taken, theater people found in journalists a means of advancing their careers. The *Times* was *the* consumer guide to theater, the one journal read by the vast majority of theatergoers. A good write-up in the *Times* could sell thousands of tickets, jumpstart a career, bring a playwright or actor an agent a role or a contract.

The challenge was how to break into the *Times* and how to continue receiving attention. There were thousands of agents, actors, directors and producers to compete with. "If you are running the *Times* cultural section," recalled an editor of the Arts and Leisure section, "people use every form of flattery to manipulate you. Press agents call to tell you what a brilliant job you're doing. They invite you to drinks and say, 'Can I tell you what we're doing this season?' Or, 'We haven't had a story in the paper since that awful one X wrote five years ago.' When I edited the Travel section, one day a messenger — dressed in a tuxedo — arrived and presented me with a beautiful leather clipboard embossed with my name — a *wrong* name as it happened. I kept it as a reminder that people don't really care *who* you are, but that you are the *New York Times*."

Later, people would point out that Joseph Papp could not have forged the media links he did in any other city in America. "He was a Brooklyn boy," recalled Robert Brustein. "His story was, if not the story of many of the people working at the *Times*, then the story of their parents. New York was the most progressive liberal city in America then, and there was something highly attractive about a man who was trying to develop a theatergoing public that was not middle class."

The fight over Free Shakespeare in Central Park established Papp as the proponent of a populist cultural ideology that was attractive to many at the *Times* and as the young Turk who had beat Robert Moses. "People didn't take on Moses in 1959 and survive," recalled Richard Shepard, first a reporter then an editor in the Drama Department. "Even *Times* management was respectful of Moses — he had clout with the publisher's family. And here's Joe, this little *yidl* from Brooklyn coming in and taking him on. That was something that made you sit up and take notice."

The fact that he was a "little *yidl*," literally "little little Jew," the son of poor, unassimilated Eastern European Jews, resonated at the *Times* in a way it would not have resonated at the *Boston Globe*, the *Washington Post* or the *Chicago Tribune*. Many of the men in the Drama Department were sons of immigrants and took pride in success achieved without family connections or family money. Most had been educated at public schools and had started at the *Times* as copy boys or clerks. Like Papp, they learned on the job, arriving at Drama from General Assignment, Shipping or Sports. Few had any training in theater. They were promoted because they were smart, accurate, readable.

"Joe didn't so much cultivate the press as the press cultivated *him*," was how Shepard remembered it. "If you look at the theater world of the sixties and seventies, David Merrick was the big producer. He was very clever and overbearing, and he knew how to play people like a violin the way Joe could. But he was not a public figure. He was interested in making money and being David Merrick. Joe was interested in social and political issues. He could expatiate on the spot about issues of concern to everyone in the city."

From his earliest days as a producer, he had held newspapers accountable for their policies, rarely hesitating to bring pressure to bear on editors. When the *Times* refused to cover Mobile Theater performances in the 1960s, Papp mobilized his audience.

"Dear Audience Member," read the hand-out at the Delacorte and Mobile:

> It is automatic that any play opening on Broadway, though it be the worst piece of junk, ineptly produced and cast, having no other purpose but to satisfy the egos of a number of people with money enough to pay for the expensive adventure — this play will be covered without any question . . . we ask you to join with us in expressing your disapproval of this policy to the Editor of the New York Times, 229 West 43rd Street, New York, New York.

By the mid-1960s, Papp's mixture of innovative projects, charm and relentless lobbying netted him annual coverage far disproportionate to the theater's size and importance. "We covered Joe because actors and directors come and go," recalled one editor. "Joe was the perfect local story: he was going to stay here but he kept changing." The *Times,* noted a critic, was "always very appreciative of anyone who brings in trade. What *else* would they write about?" Another reason for the *Times'* focus on Papp was his long relationship with Arthur Gelb.

Arthur Gelb was another son of Eastern European Jewish immigrants. "My family was not as poor as Joe's was," Gelb would later say. "Depending on the year, they were in and out of the lower middle class." By 1924, when he was born, the Gelbs were living in Harlem, then a largely immigrant neighborhood with a sizable Jewish population. "I grew up knowing a lot of kids like Joe — whether they were Jewish, Italian or Irish. We had common roots. We were native New Yorkers, coming up the same ladder. And, later on, we would talk about our background."

That background was strongly Jewish and forged in the racially and socioeconomically integrated New York City public schools. As a teenager, Gelb had attended Clinton High in the Bronx just as Papp had attended Eastern District in Brooklyn. He, too, remembered looking for work and discovering that many jobs were closed to Jews before becoming a copy boy at the *Times.* By then, he had long been a theater buff, taking the subway down to Broadway, buying fifty-cent second balcony seats to shows. His childhood dream had been to become a playwright. Instead, he became a newspaperman working his way up through the various beats — Police, Health and Hospitals, City Hall — writing feature stories about theater personalities in his spare time. In 1954, just as Papp was founding his Shakespeare Workshop, Brooks Atkinson invited Gelb to join the Drama Department and to cover off-Broadway.

Gelb first met Papp in 1956, when he reviewed the first act of *The Taming of the Shrew* at the East River Amphitheater and came away impressed both by the quality of the production and the philosophy behind Free Shakespeare. He later regarded that review as the one that first put the New York Shakespeare Festival on the city's cultural map and he soon had identified Papp as the best hope of a declining cultural form.

When Gelb first joined the Drama Department, it was, as he recalled, "a hub of activity, an exciting place where there was competition among people for stories, where there were Broadway openings every other night." Over the next decade, as much of the excitement flowed out of theater and into film and television, Papp was one of the few figures who continued to exhibit the charisma of theater people when theater was the main event. "We didn't cover Joe because he was a nice guy," Gelb recalled. "He could be a mean, unforgiving man and he had a terrible temper. But you often find that temperament in people who are great achievers. They go in a straight line and God help anyone who gets in the way — they push them aside. He was a genius — one of the most daring, creative, inventive men ever in the theater. He fought Moses and won. He created an enormous enterprise downtown. He was moving the arts forward. He was always talked about and readers wanted to read about him." Gelb and Papp rose in their respective fields at the same rapid pace. By 1967, when Papp opened the Public Theater, Arthur Gelb was Metropolitan Editor of the *Times*. He was regarded by his reporters as an "idea man" and a strong lobbyist for cultural coverage. "He worshipped the arts," recalled one. "He had a thousand ideas a day, some of them great ideas, and he was always responsive to hearing a good one from someone else. He pushed for more space in the *Times* for the arts and for more writers. But he had his own agenda. He liked to 'discover' people. Once he 'discovered' them, he saw them as his creation and he had a vested interest in maintaining their reputation. He was like a Mafia Don: a fiercely loyal person who took care of his family and friends; a man who would ace you if you were not on his side."

According to his reporters, Joseph Papp became a kind of icon to Gelb. "Arthur always fancied meeting people like Joe," recalled Richard Shepard. "And now he was his friend! There's always the vanity factor to consider. Arthur liked making stories that people talked about and people talked about Joe."

Gelb's closest colleague was A. M. "Abe" Rosenthal, the short, often testy *Times* writer and editor who would later run the *Times*. Rosenthal was another son of working-class Eastern European Jewish immigrants, who grew up in the Bronx. He had also risen up through the *Times* ranks from copy boy to foreign correspondent to a succession of editorial positions. Reporters knew that he would one day run the newspaper and that, when he did, Gelb would run it with him.

During the 1970s, Rosenthal, Papp and Gelb were all in the prime of their working lives and shared a set of core values. All three were born in the early 1920s, all had grown up during the depression, all were young Jewish men when the full extent of the Nazi extermination program became known. The shock of that news as well as their personal experience of anti-Semitism had sharpened their sensitivity to all forms of racism. They were passionate advocates of cultural pluralism. They relished life in New York City and its panorama of ethnic diversity. At the *Times*, Rosenthal and Gelb aimed to better cover that panorama; at the Festival, Papp put it onstage.

The producer began to be invited to cultural lunches at the *Times* and formal dinner parties at the Gelbs' and Rosenthals' homes where he chatted with the city's prominent citizens. "Joe was quite different from everyone else I ever dealt with," recalled William Honan, then editor of the Arts and Leisure section. "I had never met him before and began by making a major mistake — asking what he could tell me about the American Shakespeare Festival. Joe erupted and went off like a rocket. 'I run the *New York* Shakespeare Festival,' he said, and went on at some length denouncing me. That characterized our relationship. I apologized and we tried to move the discussion on to other things. But I always had the feeling that what was important to him was expressing himself and that he was completely unaware of or unconcerned with the possible outcome. I was a new person in his life, someone who would be an important, steady factor and it seemed to me that most other people in his situation would try to figure out who I was or at least be nice to me. He didn't.

"He was among the angriest people I knew and the most unpredictable. During one lunch he told me that he had tried to hide his Judaism when he was younger. Now I'm not Jewish and I always wondered why he told me that. A lot of people try to engineer a name change *sotto voce*. Joe did nothing *sotto voce*. He told me he had been a coward for not owning up to his Jewishness. It became a constant reference in our conversations. We'd be having lunch or dinner and he'd come over

to me and say 'I used to be like that' — 'like that' referring to someone
he thought was trying to 'pass.'"

Papp's personal access to the top editors of the *Times* made things easy
for Merle Debuskey and the Festival's press office. "Part of the relationship was standard: if you wanted to get important coverage, you gave the
story to the *Times* exclusively," Debuskey said. "If you were holding a
press conference, you gave them two days lead time so that they could get
the background work done. But if something important came up suddenly, we'd call and there'd be a reporter down at the Public Theater."

Papp shared information with Gelb, and fed him story ideas. He also
sent him a steady stream of items about his theater, along with specific
requests — often involving theater critic Clive Barnes. "Dear Arthur," he
wrote before the opening of Charles Gordone's *No Place to Be Somebody*,
"I spoke to Clive and with your O.K. he can make the Saturday matinee
at 5:00. I know that the review date coincides with the off-Broadway
Tennessee Williams play, but you have been kind before to work that
out. . . ." Barnes reviewed the play.

Papp never underestimated the power of the *Times* and took great care
to keep his relationship with management in working order. Once, after
a rare blow-up with Gelb, the producer telephoned Rosenthal and asked
if he might drop by the office. When the editor wanted to know what it
was about, Papp said he would tell him in person. When Papp walked
into Rosenthal's office, the producer asked him for a favor: Would the
executive editor of the *Times* walk through the newsroom to the elevator
with him, arm around Papp's shoulders? Rosenthal, chuckling, complied.

By the early 1970s, people were grumbling about the producer's
sweetheart status at the *Times*. Cultural news comprised just two or three
daily pages and one Sunday supplement. Just as New York's arts budget
was sought by many highly competitive parties, newspaper coverage was
sought by several powerful arts communities including classical and
popular music, opera and dance companies and the museums and art
galleries, not to speak of Broadway, off-Broadway and off off-Broadway.
Each contained people with strong egos, dramatic temperaments, and
needs for publicity as urgent as Papp's own. Moreover, by the 1970s Papp
had irritated several critics.

Most critics had applauded Papp's Free Shakespeare from its debut at
the East River Amphitheater in 1956 through the opening of the Delacorte in 1962. They compared it favorably to the Old Vic and the
companies at Stratford, Connecticut, and Stratford, Ontario, and, rather
than differentiating between the work of its several directors, spoke of a
single "American" approach to Shakespeare. They described that style as

"vigorous," "muscular" and "masculine" — in contrast with the "effete" and "elegant" British — in much the same way that the Juilliard String Quartet was being compared to the Budapest Quartet or that the Abstract Expressionists were compared to European artists. "Joseph Papp," wrote Robert Brustein in a representative assessment, "has created a new company, a new style, and a new audience and done so without a single artistic compromise." Even the London *Times* reported Papp's work as distinctly and wonderfully American. "The attacks abound in vitality and virility," wrote their critic. "This is not the Shakespeare of the academy but the Shakespeare whose plays had to compete with bearbaiting."

Detractors would later write that the reviews would have been less glowing had Papp been producing indoors. The spectacular Central Park venue, they pointed out, diverted attention from the production. Also, so long as Papp was producing Shakespeare, he was safe. Until well into the 1970s, the canon of Western literature and Shakespeare's preeminent place in it remained unchallenged. Papp might be maligned for casting the Hollywood starlet of the hour in a leading role or a production concept might be singled out as poor. But the producer was never called upon to defend his taste in playwrights.

His earliest and most savage critic was John Simon, who first critiqued the Festival in 1963 for the *Hudson Review*. "At the beginning of summer, the New York drama critic looks forward to the coming of merciless heat and humidity with roughly equal trepidation as to the coming of Shakespeare," he wrote.

> The Central Park production lacks two things no *Antony and Cleopatra* can do without: grandeur and passion. . . . Colleen Dewhurst's Cleopatra is a dish-faced and pear-shaped matron. . . . As for Michael Higgins's commonplace Antony (also vaguely Irish at times), he was as undrawn to this Cleopatra as she was to him — an aloofness for which, under the circumstances, neither can be blamed. . . . The visual aspects of the production are undistinguished, the supporting cast fair to frightful (the proportion being one fair to six frightful) and Joseph Papp's direction obvious, except in the few places where it was preposterous. . . . As for David Amram's music, the whining of a present-day Arab street singer backed up by a Casbah combo, it was ghastly.

Rather than framing Papp's enterprise as an American response to Britain, Simon saw it as a lower-class, parochial offense to a universal standard of art. In a subsequent piece for *Commonweal* Simon ridiculed Papp's direction, casting policy and the response of his fellow critics:

Out of a laudable integrationist zeal, Mr. Papp has seen fit to populate his Shakespeare with a high percentage of Negro performers. But the sad fact is that, through no fault of their own, Negro actors often lack even the rudiments of Standard American speech. . . . It is not only aurally that Negro actors present a problem; they do not look right in parts that historically demand white performers. . . .

The critical evaluations of Papp's enterprise have been consistently and thoroughly misleading, whether because of the assumption that something free of charge and for the people must be evaluated along democratic, not dramatic, lines, or simply because of the reviewers' abysmal lack of discrimination, it would be difficult to say. . . . The New York Shakespeare Festival had best be considered as an act of charity for underprivileged New Yorkers, and should, as such, be reviewed: by those reporters whom the papers regularly send out to cover charity balls and bazaars. Or is that whom they have been sending all along?

At the time, Simon was writing in small-circulation reviews and was Papp's sole detractor. But by 1965, he was joined by two other disparaging critics.

"In the face of what is plainly virtue," wrote the *Herald Tribune*'s Walter Kerr, "one hesitates to ask for absolute sanctity. But the moment is coming when we shall have to ask more of Joseph Papp's free Shakespeare in the Central Park. . . . The plays are made decently clear, the players speak intelligently and sometimes with a fetching directness, the physical mountings are almost always efficient and attractive. . . . When one has said 'good enough,' however, there is a question left over: good enough for what?"

"Papp has so spectacularly made two blades of grass grow where none grew before, that few critics have had the heart to discuss the quality of his crop," wrote Julius Novick, who had worked at the Festival and now wrote for the *Nation*. "Probably every city with any cultural life to speak of possesses its sacred cows; in New York, the Shakespeare Festival is one such. . . ."

The Festival's status as a sacred cow crumbled entirely after Papp began producing at the Public Theater. Reviews of *Hair* were mixed, but those of Papp's stripped-down *Hamlet* were disastrous. "Poor Mr. Papp! He is desperately trying to be daring and, most of all, provocative," wrote Clive Barnes, then the new *Times* drama critic, "yet he is doing things that undergraduates such as Tony Richardson and William Gaskill were doing at Oxford 20 years ago. . . . No, no, no. I think we need a new approach to Shakespeare but this jejeune nonsense is not it."

Other reviews were equally sharp. Papp packed up his family and fled to Puerto Rico. "I was mercilessly attacked," he would say later. "I thought the production was a complete failure." While he was there, a second set of reviews came out. "To read most critics on his latest production, one would think *Hamlet* is proof of Wilde's 'Each Man Kills the Thing He Loves,'" wrote art critic Emily Genauer.

> But Papp hasn't killed *Hamlet* at all. . . . His technical devices have to do with pop art, with bringing on images bigger and more absurd than they are in life itself. They also have to do with cubism, in that he boldly breaks apart characters, speeches, sequences, familiar conceptions, to put them together again in a new and refreshing light — or even to leave them fragmented, which can be most revealing of all. . . . It's shocking. . . . It's hilariously funny. It sends shafts of intense light on over-familiar passages. It's an esthetic experience, not an evening's entertainment.

Robert Brustein, ever Papp's supporter, wrote:

> I found the whole undertaking to be pretty courageous and while it has drawn a predictable response from those who prefer their Kulcher prepackaged, standardized and wholly digestible like a TV dinner . . . Mr. Papp's group remains, to my mind, the most audacious permanent organization in town, and the only one dedicated not simply to re-mounting familiar masterpieces but to trying to discover what theatre can mean to America in the sixties.

The range of critical reaction to his *Hamlet* validated Papp's faith in himself and helped him formulate a new stance regarding critics. As an inexperienced young producer, he had courted them, writing dozens of notes that fed their vanity and enlisted them in his cause. "Tried to reach you the other day but you were buried in the composing room," he wrote *Tribune* critic Judith Crist, for example. "Your critique was a joy and gave me one of those rare moments of having someone discover exactly what I was attempting to do in the play." Or, to *Times* reporter Milton Esterow, "I am not writing this because you praised our production . . . but I must let you know how much I appreciated your perceptive comments. Most important is that you were attuned to the strange harmonies of this fascinating work and stirred by the same currents that prompted us to produce it. . . . We are most grateful."

By the beginning of the 1970s, Papp was no longer writing borderline mash notes. "Listen," he would say, "when I hear criticism of one of my shows, I know more than most critics what's wrong with it. For every criticism they give, I can give two. But I try to judge the entire work and say: Isn't it an interesting evening in the theater? That's the most important thing." And "A public theater has a duty to criticize critics. The commercial theater is afraid of them. We are not. Critics ought to be made to take responsibility for what they say."

He challenged Clive Barnes to a televised debate about *Hamlet*. And he hit back at John Simon and Walter Kerr, wishing to force them into what he viewed as "personal accountability" for their reviews.

"Mr. Simon's recent denunciation of 'ugliness' on the stage, referring primarily to actresses who are a little fat, or over sixteen, or who perhaps betray some sign of human warmth in their faces," Papp wrote to Simon's editor at *New York*, "is part of his crusade for perfection. Somewhere, way back, little John must have been criticized no end. To regain his loss of self-esteem and to combat the hateful world of nagging women, he cultivated sophisticated techniques to lash back. He became a theater critic and discovered his perfect foil — the artist. A feeling person is no match for someone who has been deprived of that wonderful human attribute — imperfection."

If Simon argued for perfection in the human form, Walter Kerr argued repeatedly for the well-made — rather than loosely constructed or unfinished — play. Papp responded with several drafts of "Joe Papp's Complaint." The first began:

> Walter Kerr never liked me. When I began to read his column a few weeks ago and saw the phrase "Mr. Papp's Public Theater which we all wish well" I thought *OI VAY* (oh my), here it comes. As my father used to say. "From such well-wishers *m'ken gebarget veren*" — one could get killed! And Mr. Kerr proceeded to work us over with his journalistic rubber hose — the innuendo, the sluro, the double reverso.

A second version read, "It is difficult for a policeman not to be affected by his job and the environment in which he functions"; a third:

> Mr. Kerr's understanding of the words success and failure [is] obviously not the same as ours. While it is difficult [to] cry success with a half-empty house, it is equally difficult to regard an S.R.O. show as a success just because every seat is filled. . . . Although Adrienne Kennedy's show played to half-houses, we here consider the work as success and a necessary work for our theater's development. We make long-range investments, Mr. Kerr, which means taking chances on promising writers. . . .

Mr. Kerr fancies himself the champion of "form" and the well-made play. . . . He keeps clamoring for "meaning." What meaning is Mr. Kerr looking for? Is he yearning for *Mary, Mary* or some good old-fashioned musical of yesteryear? Change, Mr. Kerr, is never tidy. You have to do a lot of dirty digging. Come on, grab a shovel.

Papp was particularly incensed by the conclusions critics often arrived at that were based on no knowledge of pertinent facts. He pointed out that they had little knowledge of or interest in the creative process which led to a production and responded solely to product. "To indicate to Mr. Kerr how a choice was made in a particular case might prove edifying," he wrote and began to explain why he had decided against producing a particular play.

The first reason, and always the paramount one, was that we felt the script was weak. We may have been wrong in this, but one can only move by personal taste and experience. Just as important to us, in turning down the play was that it was not our production. Now this may sound like a silly reason to an audience. "Who cares if this production was yours or somebody else's?" Well, we care. Our presenting it would not move our theater forward since we would merely be showcasing someone else's work. There is nothing wrong with show-casing. David Merrick does it all the time and nobody complains. . . . But Mr. Merrick does not operate a theater. He is a collector. We are and try to be, creators. Every play we produce is an experience for our artistic forces and an expression of our collective thinking. . . .

After Kerr blasted Dennis Reardon's *The Happiness Cage*, Papp wrote:

What makes Mr. Kerr's opinion of this new play superior to that of a theater producer — me, for example? . . . I am totally aware that new works may be flawed. Any play which breaks new ground is bound to be imperfect. I never select a play on the basis of its perfection. Is the work serious — does it have dramatic integrity — does it communicate in its own unique way?

A new play comes along by a young man, a talented young man — and Mr. Kerr takes it upon himself to instruct this young man in how to write a play. Theater history has demonstrated time and again that nobody can teach the writer the art of playwriting. Mr. Kerr himself, who has made several unsuccessful attempts, must acknowledge this as a fact.

When, in 1971, Kerr ridiculed a rock musical called *Blood,* the producer typed out on his Remington Standard: "The game playing is over. This is to notify you that you are not welcome at the Public Theater for any of our new presentations. My conscience does not permit me to allow you to annihilate young writers who are the mainstay of the theater. . . . So please stay away. Don't come. Keep out. I don't want you here. You are incapable of judging and evaluating new works." To Kerr's editor, Papp wrote, "This has become intolerable. . . . I cannot permit the executioner Kerr to enter our house."

Because of Papp's favored-theater status with Abe Rosenthal and Arthur Gelb, such letters became the stuff of *Times* folklore rather than provoking retribution of the kind the newspaper had exacted from the Shubert Brothers in 1915. Kerr continued to review Festival productions but Papp was consistently given prime Sunday space to respond to them as he was to the reviews of chief drama critic Clive Barnes.

After Papp threw peanut shells at Barnes during their televised debate over *Hamlet,* the two men had settled into a rough intimacy. "Dear Clive," Papp wrote in one of dozens of letters to the critic:

The other day on the telephone you made a remark that demonstrated to me how far away you are from understanding what really happens here. . . . What distinguishes this theater from all other theaters in New York is that we take chances on unknowns and finance those unknowns as though they were knowns. In other words, we provide the young playwright with first-rate artistic surroundings, a decent wage, and a high-class production — plus a run of his play long enough for it to make an impact. All this costs a lot of money that I sweat to raise.

I believe very strongly in the unknown contemporary American writer, with all his faults — in preference to the accomplished English or international writer. . . . And that's why some of the plays I get on the stage might appear somewhat clumsy, unfinished, sprawling. . . . While you may not wish to accept or approve of the idea, you certainly must accept it. Can you?

Or, after Barnes had reviewed Rabe's *Sticks and Bones:*

I wish you would rethink this play as you have done before (and I thank you for that). . . . I am sending you copies of Douglas Watt's review in the *Daily News,* Martin Gottfried's in *Women's Wear Daily,* and Emory Lewis' in the *Bergen Record.* I think Watt's perspective is the greatest of these and I am glad it's in the *Daily News* because eventually

I hope we will reach that audience. . . . If you want to have lunch to discuss this, I would enjoy it. . . .

With Papp's appointment to Lincoln Center in the spring of 1973, Barnes, like Kerr and Simon, argued for the creation of a national theater or at least a repertory company that would revive European classics. Papp — who had once seen a company as integral to his plans — now regarded it as a fiscal impossibility in New York and the classics as "safe" plays in which he was not very interested. He remained intent on introducing his program of new American playwrights at Lincoln Center. "No country on earth can equal the extraordinary theatrical energy pervading the United States today," he wrote. "Young and talented writers are producing works of depth and literary merit. The influx of black playwrights now entering the mainstream of American theatrical life is a new and powerful force that is growing rapidly. Rock music with its contemporary validity is finding its place on the stage. There is enormous promise here."

Nonetheless, in May of 1973, when he revealed his inaugural program for Lincoln Center, he included, alongside a rock musical and a "black" play either by Festival playwright Ed Bullins or Edgar White or a revival by an all-black company, Strindberg's *Dance of Death* with celebrated Swedish actor Max von Sydow. Leading off would be the contemporary American play *Boom Boom Room* by his favorite playwright, David Rabe.

Subscribers echoed the critics in their dismay at what Papp planned to produce at Lincoln Center and many began canceling months before he opened his first play.

"Dear Mr. Papp," wrote one:

> Since I am one of the lily white subscribers who I think you would like to drop anyway, perhaps this letter is not important to you. I'm not interested in a black company. I'm interested in a good company. I'm not interested in a black playwright. I'm interested in a good playwright. I'm not interested in a rock musical. I'm interested in a good musical. The same holds true for Jewish writers/musicals, Puerto Rican writers/musicals, Black writers/musicals. . . .

And,

> Dear Mr. Papp,
>
> The melting pot of our country has taken numerous minorities, brought them in, and taught them the classics. I believe Euripides, Shakespeare and Ibsen can present the problems of any people far better than the *Pig Pen* or *The Chickencoop Chinamen*. . . . I just hope you don't cause the collapse of the entire Beaumont Theater.

Papp remained unmoved even as the number of cancellations swelled from the dozens into the hundreds. His artistic decisions had never been predicated on market research and he hoped to offset his losses by attracting to Lincoln Center numbers of the African-American and Hispanic middle class.

"I wanted to start with my most important writer," Papp said later. "He represented the Festival at that time." David Rabe was, once again, ambivalent. In two years, he had worked on two Public Theater productions, a Broadway show and the ill-fated CBS special, and had won a Tony Award, which transformed him from an obscure university instructor to a playwright with a reputation.

When Papp told Rabe that he wanted to open Lincoln Center with his new play, *Boom Boom Room*, Rabe said yes although — once again — he felt the play was not ready for a full production. "It needed a workshop," Rabe later said, "But you'd have to be an idiot to turn down a chance at Lincoln Center and I was not prepared to deal with Joe's kind of argument and force."

Boom Boom Room was not, Bernard Gersten would later recall, a "safe" play for a cultural complex accustomed to the traditional fare of the Philharmonic, the Metropolitan Opera and the New York City Ballet. It focused on a working-class Philadelphia girl who quits her job as a supermarket clerk to become a go-go dancer. It examined several varieties of sexual, physical and emotional abuse of women. The incidental music was Motown; the dances, the "Monkey" and the "Jerk." Rabe had not softened his language, which had elicited thirty CBS Programming Practices paper clips for *Sticks and Bones*. But quite apart from those considerations, Rabe thought the play was not ready.

Gail Merrifield thought so too. To her mind, Rabe had written one of the most moving women's roles she had ever read. "But it was a play twenty years ahead of its time," she later said. "It raised issues of abuse that were not then being publicly dealt with. Most of the male critics found it unfathomable." In addition, she knew that the dynamics of Papp and Rabe's intense personal relationship and Rabe's intractability about rewriting under pressure did not bode well for the production.

Papp, in his willfully optimistic way, refused to acknowledge the signals that were coming from the playwright and from his closest associates. He went about propagandizing for his inaugural production with his customary vigor, sweeping the doubters along in his enthusiasm and in his belief that, despite the extraordinarily short pre-production time, everything would fall into place. Although Merle Debuskey discouraged it, he arranged for a Sunday *Times* reporter to trail him as he prepared for the opening of the Beaumont and to interview the playwright, cast and director of *Boom Boom Room*.

What reporter Patty Bosworth saw and heard rivaled the *Hair* experience for offstage drama. Papp had fired Rabe's three-time collaborator, Jeff Bleckner, from a Delacorte production that summer and had to find a new director on short notice. Convinced that a woman should direct the play, he chose Julie Bovasso, a veteran of the experimental theater whose work neither he nor Rabe had ever seen. Bovasso asked the playwright to cut; Rabe steadfastly refused. Papp disliked the $60,000 set and the costumes Bovasso had approved and ordered new ones over her objections. When Bovasso wished to fire a principal actress, Papp stood behind her decision. Then, he fired Bovasso.

"It was like the takeover of two jocks," Bovasso told Bosworth, who was documenting it all. "Two pigs, Joe and David, are threatened by any woman who has strength and individuality."

Papp restaged *Boom Boom Room* in one afternoon and the play opened six weeks after it had been slated to begin previews. After the performance, Papp, Merrifield, Gersten, Debuskey, Rabe, his wife, his sister, his agent and Bosworth repaired to the Green Room to hear the early reviews. Everyone cheered when the first television reviews were broadcast over the small monitor. Then, they listened as the *New York Times* review was read to them over a speaker phone from the composing room.

"The play is full of chic filth," they heard.

> Presumably Mr. Rabe is trying to show a simple girl fighting for individuality as a woman in a man's world. It would have been quicker if he had sent a telegram. The curious thing is how a playwright of Mr. Rabe's unquestioned promise should turn out such an empty and poorly crafted play. . . . Let us hope that the Shakespeare Festival will have better luck next time. There is nowhere to go but up.

Papp let out a torrent of four-letter words and demanded that his press agent give him Barnes's telephone number. Although it was nearly midnight, he went to the telephone and began to shout in full hearing of everyone in the Green Room: "Listen, Clive, you're trying to fuck me up the ass and I'm going to fuck you up the ass. You're trying to kill me and I'm gonna kill you. You son of a bitch. You cunt. I'm gonna get you fired."

The Sunday *Times* article — titled *"Joseph Papp at the Zenith — Was It Boom or Bust?"* — was syndicated throughout the country, minus Papp's language. It treated Rabe's play as representative of Papp's new policy at

Lincoln Center, focused attention on Papp's obscene midnight telephone call and Clive Barnes's response and Rabe again found himself in a maelstrom of publicity. *Time* and *Newsweek* gave the play favorable reviews but only one reviewer, Rabe felt, looked solely at his work — not at the aspirations of Papp or his Shakespeare Festival.

Rabe never forgave him. "In the end, we failed each other at the point of our deepest connection — over the plays," he later said. "If we'd done our work right to begin with, calling Clive Barnes in the middle of the night would not have been necessary. The right thing would have been to do the producer work more thoroughly.

"If I'd been as clear about this then as I am now I wouldn't have kept making the same mistake. But I wasn't. Joe plugged into a certain vulnerability in my character. We had interlocking character flaws. I couldn't say no and walk away. You *had* to be willing to walk, to say no, to risk alienating him when necessary and I didn't do it. I bought enough into Joe's view of himself as my protector and protector of my plays to think he was taking good care of me when, in fact, my needs and the needs of my play were at that point not his needs or the needs of his institution. He was always trying to make up with me. But in this profession, if a play doesn't work, you don't ever catch up. They write their reviews and that's it. You don't get a second chance."

Papp's first season at Lincoln Center was notable for the disappointment it evoked among audiences and the press. *Boom Boom Room* ran for just over one month to half-filled houses. Papp's second play, *The Au Pair Man*, was met with indifference. Only the third, a traditionally structured, all-black drama titled *What the Wine-Sellers Buy*, caused a stir by bringing in an audience unusual for Lincoln Center, one that was 40 percent African-American. That figure represented a first for the theater and was a source of great pride to Papp. But he was unable to convert the one-shot audience into subscribers.

For the first time, the stream of adulatory press seemed to backfire on Papp. "Whom the media would destroy they first make famous," Robert Brustein would write, warning that the "conscious pursuit of success does indeed cripple a man spiritually in this country" and that the press was accessory to the crime. He named Papp alongside radical priest Daniel Berrigan, and novelists Alexander Solzhenitsyn and Norman Mailer, who had been discovered and idealized by the media. So far as Papp was concerned, Brustein wrote, "no one in the theater had worked so hard and so thanklessly in such a good cause." Yet, as the producer had moved from playgrounds and parks to the Public Theater and Lincoln Center, the media virtually canonized him as the savior of the New York stage. . . .

In little more than a year, Papp was tintyped, cover-storied, and interviewed in every organ of the news and, because he possessed a forceful, colorful personality, the public remained focused on his burgeoning activities . . . if he seems to be acting somewhat defensive and irascible these days, this may be because he senses he is an animal being prepared for sacrifice. . . .

The producer, always sensitive to criticism, was incensed at being compared to Norman Mailer and by what he viewed as Brustein's allegation of moral corruption. He spent hours at his Remington Standard, typing rebuttals.

It must take some very fancy mind juggling to write a 5500-word essay assaulting a number of "notables" for giving themselves to the news media . . . and then to submit this essay to the *New York Times* Magazine with an estimated readership of some four million people (not to mention getting paid for the job).

Brustein knows as well as anyone in the theater world that publicity (I'll use that crass word) is the way people get to know not only what you're doing, but what you're thinking. . . . Brustein's article implies that being "newsworthy" is automatically being corrupt or corruptible. We all know that ivy-tower life is not ivory-pure. Corruption does not require mighty issues to test a man. It can out over a breakfast table or at lunch at Sardi's as well as at a faculty meeting. It's not where you are that breeds character but who you are. . . .

As for my relationship with the media, despite great shortcomings, they have been one of the single constructive forces in the development of the New York Shakespeare Festival. . . . But the right to recognition in the press and other media had to be won, in the same way the right to demand government funds to support our work had to be won. . . .

I never sought a confrontation with Parks Commissioner Moses. He was intent on running us out of Central Park and I tried to prevent it. . . . My battles with the Board of Estimate had nothing to do with seeking publicity. It was money we were seeking. . . .

The artistic product is my news. The attempt to broaden the audience for new plays is my news. Finding and producing new writers is my news. Introducing and developing new directors, designers and actors is my news. Raising funds for all these efforts is my news.

Answering Dean Brustein's charges is not my news. I know I might have ignored the distortions of an article read by several million people but I could not.

Papp saw little of himself through the media's lens. In his own mind, he was still, despite his forays into television and Lincoln Center, the outsider, a working-class guy in a middle-class world, the beleaguered head of a theater chronically in need of money. It was a self-image the producer would retain for the rest of his life.

FIFTEEN

A Hotbed of Creativity

DURING THE SUMMER of 1973, Papp moved out of his Upper West Side apartment to Greenwich Village, near the Public Theater. There, with Gail Merrifield, he established a routine in which his professional and private lives were seamlessly interwoven. His old home had been a large apartment filled with heavy Victorian furniture, far from the theater and seldom visited by Festival associates. His new place was small, bright and — except for beds, one couch and one chair — completely unfurnished. "We started from scratch," she said. Papp was fifty-two; Merrifield, thirty-nine years old.

Moving with them was twelve-year-old Tony Papp, the producer's second son. The divorcing couple had agreed to let their children choose which parent they wished to live with and although Tony had chosen him, the producer remained anxious. Giving up Michael, his first son, and losing all contact with him after the age of three had been one of the worst experiences of his life. And Tony Papp, people said, was a small version of his father. Dark-haired, dark-eyed, small and seductive, he had the producer wrapped around his little finger. During the work week,

Papp would sometimes drop what he was doing at the office and go off in search of supplies for Tony's fish tank or bird cage. On weekends at the beach house on the Jersey shore, the producer caved in to appeals to go fishing, do pottery, build sandcastles. "Everything Tony wanted was of great urgency, with great pressure brought to bear on Joe," said Merrifield. "Joe was at his mercy because he wanted so much to hold on to Tony. It was always so intense between the two of them. Very physical as well as emotional."

When Tony turned thirteeen, he had no interest in the Jewish coming-of-age ritual, the bar mitzvah. He was a spiritual child who had become fascinated with stained-glass windows and Catholic ritual. A few years earlier, he had constructed an elaborate altar in his room, which dismayed both Joe and Peggy Papp and which the producer had insisted that he dismantle. By the age of thirteen, on one of his solitary expeditions in the neighborhood of the Public Theater, Tony had wandered into St. Anthony's Church in Little Italy and befriended the priest. Later, he announced that he was getting baptized. His mother and the Public Theater's receptionist went to the ceremony. Papp could not bear to attend.

The producer's relationships with his other children were less intense but also painful. All had to cope with a father whose attention seemed fixed on the people in his theater and with a group of strangers who regarded themselves as Papp's family. All (except his extramarital daughter, Barbara, whom he still had not met) had experienced the bitterness of his divorces. Miranda, who as a child had often waited up for her father to come home, now kept her distance. His older children, Susan and Michael, seldom called. When they did, he took them out to lunch or dinner, was generous when they needed financial assistance, and tried to express interest in their activities. When Michael became involved in Transcendental Meditation, Papp tried it out. But his relations with all four children were troubled.

"Joe could not sustain a line of fathering," Bernard Gersten said. "The essence of being a parent is being steady. Joe was not steady as a parent. He'd think: 'I'm not spending enough time with the kids — I should spend more.' But he could not sustain it. Somewhere Joe preferred the children of the theater to his own children. David Rabe was more intellectually engaging than a twelve-year-old."

As the stepmother to this brood, Gail Merrifield tried to be available to the older three while taking responsibility for the youngest. She supervised Tony's schedule and, responding to his dissatisfaction with school, researched and arranged for a series of transfers from Calhoun to City &

Country to the DeSisto School in Stockbridge, Massachusetts. She worried first about his babysitters and his after-school activities, then about the looming dangers of adolescence. She also worked full-time at the Public Theater.

Unlike Peggy Papp, who led a professional life separate from her husband's, Merrifield worked beside him. Her interest in writers and new writing was as avid as Papp's own and Festival staffers would note that the two were rarely apart for more than a few hours. At the Public, they worked in adjoining offices. Their home — stocked with legal pads, telephones and canisters of pencils — doubled as an office. Festival staffers found Papp's home-like office and office-like home so similar that they sometimes lost track of where they were having a meeting.

By 1973, noted a family friend, Papp's seven years in therapy had had a pronounced effect. "Nobody gets reborn in therapy," she said. "He still had occasional panic attacks. But there were two significant changes he was able to sustain. The first was that he reclaimed his background. His father had been a deeply religious Jew and Joe's departure from Judaism had cost him a great deal — in guilt, alienation and a persistent feeling of wrongdoing.

"The second change was his ability to sustain a successful marriage. All the years Joe was womanizing, he hated himself for it. He felt that he didn't know how to love — which was true. He would see elderly couples walking hand-in-hand, imagine that they had been faithful to one another all their lives and wish he could be that kind of person. He became that kind of person. After years of therapy, he had finally allowed himself to trust a woman."

In the professional sphere, however, Papp changed very little. Although the addition of Lincoln Center had made the New York Shakespeare Festival a large institution, he retained his basketball player style, moving fast, reversing himself without warning. Although the Festival board raised his salary to $75,000 — a respectable figure for the head of a not-for-profit institution — Papp's lifestyle remained modest. His major luxury was smoking the Havana cigars he had been smoking for twenty years. For a time, he drove a maroon Festival-leased Mercedes but, ambivalent about its image, turned it in for a Jeep. He wore suits more often now than in the early years and had bought a tuxedo. But he continued to dress and to view himself as an outsider, driven to confront and change the existing order. Despite the Festival's several forays into television, he felt little attraction to other media where — no matter how high in the hierarchy he reached — he would still be an employee and not his own man. "I'm a person of the theater," he told an interviewer.

"I feel that it's a place where things can grow. It has a kind of joy that's missing in other media. . . . With all due respect to the other media, they are not living situations, although they reflect life and aspects of it. The theater survives because it is a living situation otherwise it would die — especially in this age."

Lincoln Center made that "living" situation difficult. The Beaumont theater, Papp argued, was a "disaster," with a "bastardized" stage that was neither proscenium nor thrust and a cavernous backstage designed to house sets for a revolving repertory it had never seen. The box office and small downstairs theater were controlled by the same thermostat so that, during the day, when the staff needed heat or air conditioning, the empty theater got it as well. And, the Festival had to pay a portion of Lincoln Center's common costs, which included upkeep of the central mechanical plant, maintenance of the grounds — including the Plaza's black marble fountain — security and snow removal, a bill that came to $400,000 each year.

But even more chilling to Papp was the aura of Lincoln Center. "Putting on a new play at Lincoln Center is extraordinarily more important and more significant than putting on that same play either off-Broadway, off off-Broadway, on Broadway or in a regional theater. Now why is that?" he wrote in a note to himself. "Because Lincoln Center represents a certain idea of official culture. . . ." To critic Marilyn Stasio, he described himself as the "cultural capo" of "a huge edifice, built by a lot of foundation money and created in a neighborhood where it exists side by side with low-income housing," serving "the class of people who paid the money."

What was he to do with the subscribers he had inherited? He saw them as fundamentally different from himself: middle-class people interested in plays that reinforced their sense of security and provided reassuring evidence that "not everything is unmoored, that we are not flying through space." There was little tolerance for experimentation on the part of such an audience, he thought, and none at all for failure. "We don't want to lose them," he said. "On the other hand we don't want to suck up to them . . . accept the status quo of those walls. They are crushing, those walls. They want to absorb you, to make you like them. Consequently, twice a day, you have to break those walls down."

Papp did all he could to alter the look of the theater he had inherited. He changed the carpeting in the lobby from red to brown, tried to improve the acoustics and constructed a needed lighting bridge over the stage to make the vast space less imposing. He tried to transform the look of the audience as well, reaching out to African-American, Hispanic and more youthful audiences. But whatever he tried, he felt the Beaumont resembled a mausoleum. "Building concentrated arts centers in a single geographical location, we lend aid and comfort to the colonialist enclave theory — defending the last bastion of western civilization against a hostile native population," he wrote and proposed instead that an art center should be "a fusing force and must find its roots in the earth and not look down on the world from Olympian opera glasses."

As Papp fought against the institution he was running, he battled his public image as well. Although the Festival's real expansion had occurred one year earlier when it moved four shows to Broadway, Papp's twenty-five-year lease at Lincoln Center transformed the way people viewed the producer. The press began to describe him as a czar, creating a persona which challenged that of the radical, anti-Establishment crusader that Papp himself held. At Yale, where he served as an adjunct professor, students accused him of selling out his principles and Papp walked out on them. At the Festival, staffers who had once viewed the theater as Papp's "candy store," now saw it more as a medieval court with a complicated set of fiefdoms. The fiefdoms themselves — the Play Department, the Casting Department, the costume shop, the prop shop — each became as large as Papp's original operation had been. Employees new to the Festival called the producer "Mr. Papp" — not "Joe."

Just as when Papp moved from Emmanuel Church to the East River Amphitheater in 1956 or from the Great Northern Hotel to the Public in 1967, there were Festival veterans who did not like the change. General manager David Black, who since 1957 had been accustomed to walking into Papp's office without second thought, found he now needed to make an appointment. Playwright Dennis Reardon recalled, "I began to perceive myself as a tiny cog in the empire and to perceive how many pressures were on the man. I felt that I owed it to him to take up as little of his time as possible."

Director Gerald Freedman, who had continued to have a loose association with the Festival, finally left in 1974. Designer Ming Cho Lee, who had arrived with Freedman, left soon after. "Suddenly it seemed Joe was hiring people who could have been my students and who preferred to work with their own peers," he recalled. "Then Jerry left and because my work had mostly been with him, I became the odd man out. I was, in name, principal designer. But the new playwrights wanted to work with young directors and the directors wanted to work with designers they knew. Joe handled it poorly. He forgot about family. He said: That's what happens. I was pigheaded too. I said: Where did these people come from?"

Lee found that Papp's almost medieval insistence on loyalty was largely a one-way affair. "My work outside the Festival — at Juilliard or City Opera — upset him a great deal," the designer said. "There would be conflicts between rehearsals and he'd call me up at the opera and say, 'I was there. Where were you?' and hang up on me. I'd hang up on him too. 'If you're principal designer,' he said, 'why are you doing this?' and I said, 'If I'm principal designer of the Festival, why am I not designing the principal productions?' We were quarreling all the time and I felt a real change in his behavior. The number of things he had a hand in was growing: he was becoming a city spokesman. Meeting with him in his office ceased to be a human experience. It was like a press conference."

Because of the continual influx of gifted people into the theater, Ming Cho Lee's place was quickly filled by designers Santo Loquasto and David Mitchell. Theater people began to refer to the Festival's "revolving door," by which they meant that an artist would be favored at the Public for three or four or five years and then be replaced. Papp himself believed that was healthy. When he saw the work of La Comédie Française or Habimah or the Moscow Art Theater, he would comment on the calcified nature of organizations that, through their sinecures, allowed aging actors and actresses to play Romeo and Juliet. "Structure sneaks in on you and before you know it, you're in a rut," he said. "I lose control of a situation as soon as it becomes structured. It's just the reverse of what you'd normally think. In a structure, everybody's doing things right but no one's coming to grips with change."

Papp initially had seen Lincoln Center as a vehicle for providing new sources of funding and new opportunities for the thirty-odd playwrights with whom he had formed relationships. "It has become quite apparent that serious and meaningful American playwrights are being produced off-Broadway only — which means that our most important playwrights cannot make a living in the commercial theater," he wrote. "They are forced to write for a limited audience, which not only means limited income, but limited distribution of significant ideas. This latter loss is the most devastating and it is a loss to the nation. . . . Without a significant national platform, the serious writer will turn to other means for his living. . . ."

"You know what they said about Ziegfeld — he glorified the American Girl," he said. "Well I want to glorify the American Playwright . . . and I want to do it at Lincoln Center." The problem was that Papp, unlike Ziegfeld, refused to cater to his audience. Instead, he insisted the audience accept his own vision of theater, which — in contrast to Ziegfeld — made room for performers and playwrights of color and strictly subsumed entertainment to revelation and instruction. Instead of welcoming his new playwrights, much of the Lincoln Center audience viewed their work as an assault. Instead of flocking to it, they left in droves. And instead of accepting that, Papp responded in his characteristic way: by refusing to take no for an answer.

"Rabe's *Boom Boom Room* — I rushed it up too fast," he explained away his opening production. "It wasn't ready. I was fighting against deadlines. These new works, they have to be generated first, developed downtown first, molded in the workshop . . . after a show's been worked on for a year or more, maybe then it can go uptown." He called Ron Milner's *What the Wine-Sellers Buy* a milestone for bringing African-American audiences to the Beaumont. But during his first two years at Lincoln Center, white audiences remained hostile, complaining to the producer in the lobby whenever they spotted him. Critics panned both his new playwrights at the Beaumont and the chamber Shakespeare he was producing downstairs at the smaller theater, and the criticism took its toll on Papp, who thrived on personal contact and found it difficult to be hated. He never even kept a desk uptown at the Beaumont. Even as he went through the motions of programming for the Beaumont, he withdrew emotionally from Lincoln Center, preferring the freewheeling environment of Lafayette Street.

In the first half of the 1970s, the Public Theater resembled a Victorian greenhouse, with an extraordinary range of theatrical projects and personalities under its roof. All kinds of people worked there: actors who had polished their craft through graduate school, street poets with no formal education, aesthetic experimentalists such as Joe Chaikin, Lee Breuer, JoAnne Akalaitis and even Robert Wilson. Some worked alongside the growing technical staff that occupied the costume, properties and audio shops across Lafayette Street in a building called the Annex, where much activity went unrecorded, let alone reviewed. But it gave the people working there a sense of artistic community that existed nowhere else in the country.

"The building itself seemed charged with energy; one had the sense anything was possible," recalled Festival staffer Lynn Holst. "No day resembled the one before. There was an amazing mix of sensibilities at work on every one of those stages at any given time and no one could ever predict what the result might be.

"Joe tended to respond to plays that had at heart a mystery — something the writers themselves were grappling with — a pain and often an anger that was felt rather than understood. He once commented that he was looking for plays that made the familiar unfamiliar and the unfamiliar *more* unfamiliar. This made attending these productions sometimes as much of a risk as presenting them but for a long time our audiences seemed willing to share in the adventure."

So did actors, directors, poets, dancers and musicians — who brought in projects as often as playwrights. Actor James Earl Jones brought to Lafayette Street the idea of an all-star, all-black *Cherry Orchard*. One of the first generation of Festival actors, Jones had performed in several Shakespeare productions as well as a special Delacorte Theater event of 1966 called *An Evening of Negro Poetry and Folk Music*. The program included writing by Richard Wright, Margaret Walker, Calvin Hernton, Gwendolyn Brooks and Arna Bontemps and drew so much attention that it moved to Broadway for a few performances. More important, it had sent a signal to African-American actors that Papp welcomed their presence and ideas.

When James Earl Jones made his Chekhov proposal, Papp suggested that the actor direct it himself. *"Cherry Orchard!"* a cast member exclaimed years later. "The set was evocative, the cast without peer, the costumes, glorious and oh, how we were cared for. Any other producer would have had our boned undergarments — which no one could see — made of polyester. But ours were made of the silk that the characters we were playing would have worn. Eliot Feld of the Feld Ballet was brought in to serve as dancing master. A Russian expert was engaged to furnish us with the historical background and help us with the Russian words and songs. With Joe's remarkable sensitivity to nuance, the expert was black."

Rehearsals were tumultuous. James Earl Jones, then under the influence of Primal Scream Therapy to which he had been introduced by former Festival director Gladys Vaughan, was directing for the first time — an experiment that Papp would frequently try with his favorite actors and playwrights. The cast rebelled. Papp replaced Jones. The show received mixed reviews but Papp saw it as important for featuring gifted African-American actors in classical roles.

There were, in the early 1970s, three theaters devoted to what was then called "black" work: the New Lafayette Theater, the Negro Ensemble Company and the New Federal Theater. But none had the budget, visibility or production capacity of the Public. An *Ebony* magazine article of the time featured photographs of five African-American women who were working at the Festival, including script-reader Helen Marie Jones, playwright Alice Childress, composer/conductor Margaret Harris, who conducted the orchestra for *Hair* as well as *Two Gents,* and Novella Nelson, who for five years served as a conduit to the minority communities.

Novella Nelson, a striking African-American woman then in her early thirties, was an actress, cabaret singer and director. Born in Brooklyn, she had studied with Eulalie Spence twenty years after Joe Papirofsky graduated Eastern District High School. Walter Jones, the actor/playwright who had brought in *No Place to Be Somebody*, had brought Nelson to the Public as a director. She was interested in learning administration and Papp, typically, hired her to learn on the job. "He saw that I had creative energy," Nelson later said. "The nice thing was that neither of us knew exactly what I would do. He gave me great license and freedom to experiment and I took the opportunity to bring actors, playwrights, poets, musicians from different ethnic groups into the theater. Joe not only was an excellent producer but he was very curious about other kinds of people. I had the impression he was always searching, searching for something he could relate to emotionally and understand but that was *not* his."

Nelson was one of many artists Papp hired to maintain a pipeline to communities that were unrepresented in mainstream theater. Argentine director Osvaldo Riofrancos, who toured the boroughs with El Teatro Movil, was another. There was in New York a traditional Spanish-speaking theater — just as there were Czech and French-language theaters — but it was, in Papp's terms, bourgeois theater that ignored the working-class and slum population that interested Riofrancos. He directed five productions for Papp including *Romeo y Julieta* and *Macbeth*, with one of Mexico's leading actors in the title role. Playing McDuff was Raul Julia, newly arrived from Puerto Rico.

The tall, sonorous-voiced Julia was born to middle-class parents who hoped he would become a lawyer. Instead, as a university student in Puerto Rico, Julia had discovered acting. When he came to New York, he was immediately cast in a Spanish-language production and joined the Theater in the Street, a bilingual troupe led by Papp's former mentor, actress Phoebe Brand. Julia considered Riofrancos's production of *Macbeth* his lucky break. He had acted Shakespeare — in English — in Puerto Rico but, like actress Ellen Holly, found working on the Mobile a formative and deeply rewarding experience.

When he took part in a night of Puerto Rican poetry later that summer at Papp's invitation, Julia recited a patriotic Puerto Rican poem. The Delacorte audience gave him a standing ovation, and Raul Julia's bond with the Festival was cemented. Elsewhere, the young actor found opportunities limited by his Latino accent and looks. In 1968, after struggling to get theater work, and fed up with a series of jobs giving Spanish lessons, selling pens, then magazine subscriptions, a desperate Julia — as desperate as George C. Scott had been a decade earlier — picked up the telephone and, without believing he would reach the producer, called Joseph Papp.

Much to his amazement, the producer took his call. "I told him I needed a job, that I'd clean toilets or floors, anything, that I was ready to kill myself if I didn't get a job in the theater," Julia recalled. "A few minutes later he called back to ask whether I'd ever been a house manager. I said no, but that I'd be the best house manager he had ever had."

Papp found in the warm, emotional Julia a kindred spirit. As a teenager, Julia had also memorized speeches from *Julius Caesar*. He was enthusiastic about the Mobile Theater and, unlike many actors who launched their careers at the Festival, remained an enthusiastic participant, playing a variety of roles from walk-ons to Brecht's Mack the Knife as he became a major American stage and screen actor. He — like many of the older generation of Festival actors — always acknowledged a debt of gratitude to Papp.

By the 1970s, a younger, more streetwise generation saw the producer in a different light, calling him "Massah Joe," referring to the Festival as "Papp's Plantation." Accusations of racial or sexual bias at the Festival became routine. Twice, the Puerto Rican Actors Guild formally accused him of discrimination. And, a few times, the producer received death threats. One morning, Papp even came to work to find seven live white roosters with Spanish-language signs around their necks strutting in the Festival's men's room — someone angry at him had turned to voodoo.

"Never expect gratitude," he would say with a grin. He took pains to distance himself from "the knee-jerk, middle-class liberal guilt," which he believed led so many celebrated New Yorkers to patronize minorities. He said he did not want any "tokens" in his theater. Almost everyone who worked there had a personal connection with him that often stretched back years, whether they were white, black or Hispanic.

At Emmanuel Church in the 1950s, Papp had come into his workshop one day to find his props and swords in disarray. "This young, handsome man walked in and saw that I looked at the costumes with great recognition," recalled Miguel Algarín, then a boy. "I belonged to the Centurion Cadets, one of the church youth organizations, and we had made a mess of his things. He asked my mother if he could speak to me alone. Then he asked if I could help him put the stuff back in order."

Algarín, who was born in Puerto Rico in 1941, had come to New York at the age of nine. He and his mother kept in touch with Papp as Algarín finished high school and went to college and graduate school. By 1970, a university professor, Algarín had established a Puerto Rican Playwrights/

Actors Workshop in Papp's Annex across Lafayette Street, teaching —
among other things — Shakespeare.

Algarín and Julia were not the only Puerto Ricans at the Festival. Soon
Papp brought in playwright Miguel Piñero and director Marvin Camillo.
Newark-born Camillo had worked on and off-Broadway as well as in
Puerto Rico before running workshops for men in prisons such as Sing
Sing and the Bedford Hills Correctional Facility for Men.

In 1973, when his first student had completed his sentence, Camillo
met him at the prison gate and took him to a workshop on the Lower
East Side, not far from where Papp had started. He developed a theater
piece, *New York New York,* which played in Westchester prisons, churches
and parking lots. Less than two years earlier, a thousand prisoners had
rioted at the Attica prison in upstate New York. Governor Rockefeller
had ordered police in, twenty-eight prisoners and nine prison guards
were killed and national attention focused on prison reform. That attention netted Camillo funding, a residency at Manhattan's activist Riverside
Church, and actress Colleen Dewhurst as a sponsor. By the fall of 1973,
he was working with his former student, Miguel Piñero.

At Sing Sing, Puerto Rico–born Piñero had sat at the back of Camillo's
workshop, writing poetry. He had arrived on the Lower East Side at age
four, was sent to a youth house for truancy at age ten, began smoking
marijuana when he was eleven and snorting cocaine at fifteen. Hustling
and burglarizing apartments to support himself, he was arrested and
detained at Riker's Island prison, where he first used heroin. When he
was released, Piñero returned to life as a criminal. After an armed robbery
at an apartment house two blocks from the Public Theater, he received
a five-year sentence and was shipped off to Sing Sing. There he met
Camillo. "I really got hooked on theater," he later told the *New York
Times.* "It was like a shot of dope."

In the fall of 1973, Camillo and his company began a long improvisatory process around Piñero's play, *Short Eyes.* Set in the day room of a
house of detention, the play's chain of violent events is set in motion by
the introduction of a young white child molester, a "short eyes," into
their group. Company members talked about their own prison experiences, their family histories and their expectations now that they were
out. Like the dancers' narratives from which Michael Bennett and his
collaborators would later forge *A Chorus Line,* the men's narratives became the stuff of what would be Papp's first prison play.

"You guys gotta give me background . . . Clap your hands and say . . .
Mambo tu le pop," says Cupcakes, a young Puerto Rican inmate who is

the group's entertainer and courtesan in the play. Then, to their accompaniment,

> It was the night before Christmas . . . and all through the pad . . .
> cocaine and heroin was all the cats had. One cat in the corner . . .
> copping a nod. . . . Another scratching thought he was God. . . . I
> jumps on the phone . . . and dial with care . . . hoping my reefer . . .
> would soon be there . . . After a while . . . crowding my style . . . I saw
> five police badges . . . glaring in my eyes . . . broke down the door . . .
> knock me to the floor . . . and took me away, that's the way I spent
> my last Christmas day. . . . But I didn't care 'cause I was high as hell
> . . . I was cool . . . I was cool . . . You people are the fools . . . cream
> of the top . . . 'cause I got you to say something as stupid as Mambo
> tu le pop.

Short Eyes caused a small sensation when it opened at Riverside Church in January 1974, and Festival staffers as well as Colleen Dewhurst urged Papp to see it. Papp had never forgotten the Living Theater's production of *The Brig*. Piñero's play evoked it. "It was so remorseless," Papp later said. "It was so real. Nobody seemed to be acting."

Papp produced *Short Eyes* at the Public but his desire to educate and shock the middle class led him to move it to Lincoln Center. There, it provided the final straw for much of the audience that had stuck it out from *Boom Boom Room* through the first season. Subscribers who spotted Papp in the lobby demanded that he restore the classics. "Even Joe with all his iconoclasm could only take so much abuse," recalled Robert Kamlot, then the Festival staffer responsible for Lincoln Center. "After *Short Eyes*, the subscriber base dropped to about sixteen thousand. It was the first time I saw Joe capitulate."

Short Eyes won a New York Drama Critics Circle Award and was optioned for a movie. But the hostility it had provoked led Papp to plan for a series of classics. He retained his determination to include at least one "black" production each year at Lincoln Center and planned for an all-black *Peer Gynt*. But he also pursued a white star. In May, he flew to Oslo to meet with Norwegian actress Liv Ullmann, who was playing Nora in Ibsen's *A Doll's House* at the Norsk Theater. Papp had admired Ullmann in Ingmar Bergman's films. He wanted Bergman to direct Ullmann in the play at Lincoln Center.

At the time, Liv Ullmann had never acted on the stage in English but, she later recalled, she needed little persuading. By 1974, Papp's reputation had reached Norway. "He was known as an idealist," she said, "who burned for theater rather than box office. He came to see me in his tennis shoes and jeans — no one over the age of twenty in Norway wore that kind of clothing at that time — and I just loved him." Bergman was unavailable; Ullmann under contract to the Norsk Theater. She could perform in New York only if its director, Tormod Skagestad, could direct. Papp accepted those terms — although he was unexcited about Skagestad's traditional production — and came back to New York with an agreement. Later that year, Bergman's *Scenes from a Marriage,* in which the actress had the starring role, became an international sensation. By the time Ullmann opened in *Doll's House* the following March, she made it the first of Papp's Lincoln Center productions to sell out.

Papp would later regard his producing *A Doll's House* as a "sellout." Even as he booked popular actresses Ruth Gordon and Lynn Redgrave to perform in Shaw's *Mrs. Warren's Profession,* planned to have Ingmar Bergman direct Ibsen's *Rosmersholm* and toyed with a new version of Peter Pan — "the kind of show that would have very wide audience appeal and would be just perfect for Lincoln Center" — he disliked himself and this kind of theater activity.

He had become accustomed to being inside the work rather than outside, thrashing out the problems of play development with Miguel Piñero and the burgeoning group of young male playwrights down on Lafayette Street which now included — in addition to David Rabe and Dennis Reardon — Ed Bullins, John Ford Noonan, Michael Weller, John Guare, Wallace Shawn, Robert Montgomery and Thomas Babe.

"There's something profoundly needful in a writer for the theater," associate producer Bernard Gersten, who stayed out of these relationships, would later say. "Shakespeare was his own producer. But in latter days, playwrights need a producer who — parent-like — takes care of everything. The other side of the coin is that a parent also punishes, becomes angry, is disappointed and can turn against the child. So maybe the distortion wasn't Joe's but part of the behavior of artists with genuine needs. David made Joe a father; Joe didn't make him a son. But I wonder whether it wasn't deeply satisfying to Joe having these surrogate children who filled his own needs. And when one playwright disappointed, he could swing to others."

One of the most promising playwrights then at the Public was John Guare. He had been part of the team that made the musical *Two Gents,* and he looked forward to a long residence at the Public Theater. "It's difficult to convey the sheer vitality of the place then," he recalled. "I loved it. It was like a silent movie studio of the twenties where every door was open, every project was exciting, where you could have an idea and Joe would just say, 'Do it!'"

Guare was planning a second project with Mel Shapiro and Galt MacDermot, and Papp had announced it at a press conference, when Guare received a registered letter from the producer. "It read something like: 'Consider yourself fired from whatever project you're working on! Joseph Papp,'" Guare later recalled. "I went over to his office with the letter. He explained, quite casually, that it was to let me know I could be cut off at any time. He didn't like my way of working — that I wrote in my room and brought him the product rather than including him in the process. 'In this theater, I'm the creative impulse,' he said. Now that I understood this, I should get back to work."

Guare told Papp that he would "consider himself fired" and went to Nantucket, where he helped establish a theater. "It was all one's fears coming to the surface," he said years later. "I loved Joe. I wanted to have a home and it was so much fun to be there. But there was also the constant anxiety that you could be dropped at any moment. I was wary of Joe. I didn't need a father or a best friend. It was too precarious for me to put all my eggs in one basket and there was an anxiety that never went away. I worked in Nantucket and then in Chicago. It was only when Bernie came to see one of my plays and said I should be back at the Public that I went back. He made it possible to live with Joe's eruptions.

"On the other hand, when I was writing *Rich and Famous,* I couldn't get the beginning right. Joe said, 'Go out there and tell the audience you don't have the beginning and these are the problems' — and it was hilarious. You felt at home in that theater. You could say: 'I'm not ready yet.' You could let the audience see how a play is written. That's the degree of intimacy and comfort one felt there."

Another playwright who preferred to come in with finished work was Wallace Shawn, whose plays were produced at the Public from 1973 to 1991. "I did not get mixed up in elaborate personal relations with Joe," Shawn, a son of the then editor of the *New Yorker*, recalled, "which, maybe, accounts for the longevity of our relationship. I already had a father. In fact, my own father was himself a father figure to young writers. Besides, because Joe was clearly governed almost entirely by his feelings, which shifted rapidly from moment to moment, I could tell that a personal relationship with him would be awfully tempestuous, which didn't appeal to me, despite the fact that I was very fond of him. Joe was always quivering with vibrations. His dealings were fraught with emotion. You couldn't spend a simple minute with Joe. After fifteen minutes, it was already extremely complex. I just wanted him to produce my plays. I was much too arrogant to want his opinion. I sneered at the idea of workshops or extensive rewrites. I write slowly and carefully and didn't ever feel capable of rewriting something in a few weeks."

Tom Babe, a Yale Law School graduate who had been a speechwriter for Mayor Lindsay, was one of the playwrights who became closely involved with Papp. For ten years, Papp produced almost all of his work. "I thought that we playwrights represented the kind of children Joe would have liked to have had," Babe later said, "gifted, screwed up in some way, and largely dependent — boys who could kick some ass (aesthetically speaking), absorb the blows and remain loyal, whatever happened. He wanted to help us out of jams, hear of failed romances and broken homes, bail some of us out of jail and advance some others a little cash.

"Straight handouts seemed to strike him as wrong but he was always trying to maximize writers' incomes. He had a deep discomfort with his writers heading off into film or television and was frustrated that writers for the theater couldn't be paid well for their work. I myself had begun writing plays with a certain amount of freedom that came from the generosity of my wife, who was independently wealthy. When my marriage dissolved, Joe saw to it that I got a couple of grants, but even before I qualified for them, he put me on salary at the Public Theater. For a whole year, I drew a check every week, the effect of which was to make me work harder than I would have otherwise. It was a desperately lean time for me, but he never asked anything specific in exchange except that I keep at what I was doing and show up from time to time to bullshit our collective way through the dramatic form. He even hated one play I wrote but went on to produce it successfully.

"This was the height of what one actress described to me as Joe's 'Prince Hal' days, although they struck me more as his 'Hamlet' days. *Hamlet* was Joe's favorite play and there was in him always the spirit of the beleaguered young man unfortunately charged with righting a number of complicated wrongs. It filled Joe's sense of himself and the young men he was interested in as writers. His inclination to mistrust authority was very strong. And to maintain that, you need an army of younger men you trust to change the artistic map."

As the number of young men at the Public grew, Dennis Reardon began feeling as though he belonged to "a select fraternity of *ronin*, a kind of samurai allied to do battle with mediocrity and elevate the standards of theater. We shared a literateness, a fascination with language and theatrical effects, an intensity that seemed to stun and sometimes offend people."

"When I lived at the Public Theater I called it the Bad Boy Syndrome," recalled Elizabeth Swados. "There was David Rabe and David Mamet and Tom Babe and they all seemed like Davids to me. They were good-looking, slightly sweaty straight guys — it always seemed like there were at least ten of them, and that they would close doors louder than the women and sit around and talk about war. I think Joe wanted to lose a few years and hang with them. And when it didn't turn out that way, they'd disinherit each other."

The "Davids" cultivated an aggressively heterosexual style, which included tough language, hard drinking in Papp's office and at the nearby Cedar Tavern and a confrontational stance toward society. "That atmosphere was necessary for Joe and perhaps for all of us in order to keep everything on an even keel," recalled Babe, who went from being a married man raising a daughter, to a divorced man raising a daughter to a man living with another man and raising a daughter while at the Festival. "There wasn't a man who worked with Joe who didn't love him. But we all needed to allay the fear of my generation — and certainly Joe's — that men involved in the performing arts must seem to the world less than men. It was good to know that all these robust, energetic, fucked-up and very gifted guys were otherwise statistically normal males who had made an unusual career decision."

Papp continued to insist that those playwrights working at his theater have the freedom to experiment and fail even though his institution was now in the national spotlight and coming under increasing pressure to produce consistently excellent work. His taste still ran to raw rather than finished productions, to unclear, unfamiliar and nebulous forms rather than to traditional, well-made plays. He took pride in the few reviews that supported his position, such as one of a play by Dennis Reardon: "It is especially gratifying to see the Festival produce *Siamese Connections*. The play is an untidy creation and hardly a success. . . . Manifestly no candidate for transfer to the commercial stage. . . . It is precisely the sort of play which the institutional theater should produce, and Reardon is just the sort of writer whose future artistry can benefit from such a production."

Papp wished to extend the workshop idea to his favorite actors as well as his playwrights. In residence along with Babe, Reardon and Pinero was actor Al Pacino, to whom Papp had given unlimited time and space to explore Bertolt Brecht's *Resistible Rise of Arturo Ui*. Papp had first worked with Pacino in 1968 when he fired him from a production he was directing because the actor mumbled. The actor had become a film star with *The Godfather*, but continued to be interested in theater. When

Pacino asked Papp to underwrite the Brecht project with no guarantee of ever seeing a production, Papp, who thought Pacino a genius, paid a company of thirty — including director Ted Cornell — so that the actor could work on his craft.

The group worked in the Annex, alongside the Puerto Rican Playwrights Workshop and André Gregory's experimental Manhattan Project, "seminaring the play," as Cornell put it, in the slow, deliberate manner of the Berliner Ensemble. The cast was huge. Virtually all its members went off to shoot the film *Dog Day Afternoon* after the first six weeks of work, and some Festival staffers regarded the workshop as an outrageous waste of Festival resources. "*Arturo Ui* was not a cutting edge play," recalled one. "It was what radicals in theater departments around the country were then doing. I didn't think it was a hot idea to do *Arturo Ui* at that time. It was an example of what Joe would do for actors whom he admired."

Papp dropped in to watch the proceedings from time to time, seemed to approve of the work and told Cornell that his cast was exactly right for *Hamlet*, with Pacino in the title role. Two weeks after that conversation, Cornell later recalled, Papp saw a run-through, found it "slow and boring" and, in one of his split-second decisions, decided to end the workshop.

That workshop, like many others at the Public in those years, went unreviewed and unrecorded by the press, a matter of knowledge within the theater community but not outside it. But there was another workshop to which Papp had allocated more money than he had ever invested in the development of any one show. One year earlier, he had been thinking about producing a musical about New York City and remembered *Knickerbocker Holiday,* by Kurt Weill and Maxwell Anderson, about New York's first governor, Peter Stuyvesant. Papp had never seen it but loved the score, which contained the haunting "September Song." As always, finding a director was a problem and he thought of Michael Bennett, a choreographer who Bernard Gersten had recently recommended. Bennett was Broadway incarnate, Papp would later say. But he was also, like the producer himself, a man who had learned what he knew in the streets as well as in school, "down to earth, nothing intellectual about him." Papp had not liked *Follies,* the Broadway show that Bennett had codirected, but he had loved the dancing. Although they had never had a conversation before, Papp called him up and, over the telephone, proposed that he direct *Knickerbocker Holiday* at the Public.

Michael Bennett had no interest in Papp's proposal. He was a Broadway person who had never had the faintest desire to work either off-Broadway or in an institutional theater. Moreover, he disliked revivals. But Bennett told Papp that he had something else on his mind that he wanted to discuss and the producer invited him to come down to the Public Theater.

From the very start of their conversations, Papp was intrigued by the thirty-one-year-old dancer/director. Born Michael Bennett Di Figlia in Buffalo, New York, Bennett was the son of a Sicilian father and a Russian-German-Jewish mother. Since childhood, he had wanted to be a dancer and had dropped out of high school first to tour Europe with *West Side Story* and then to join the chorus of a Broadway musical. Bennett worked in and for chorus lines for over a decade. He loved the work but hated the Broadway conventions that labeled dancers as "gypsies," viewed them as too stupid to be given speaking roles and defined their function as enhancing the star on the stage. He had long wished to create his own musical about dancers and, in January of 1974, had taken a first step. He had invited twenty-one dancers to a midnight gathering, after their respective shows were over, to discuss their lives. They sat in a circle and Bennett asked them to give their name, date and place of birth, talk about their childhood and describe how they first became interested in dancing. They talked for five hours, took a break and then talked until noon the next day. Bennett played some of those tapes for Papp.

"The detail of those tapes was absolutely stunning," Papp later said. "It all had to do with parents and children. Fathers and daughters, fathers and sons, mothers and daughters, mothers and sons. That's all you heard. It was one story after another in the most nonsentimental way, no self-pity."

The two men hit it off. Papp forgot about *Knickerbocker Holiday* and Bennett forgot his preconceptions of off-Broadway. The Public Theater, with its multitude of projects all being developed under the same roof, had immense appeal to Bennett, as did the open-ended working conditions that had been such a draw for actors Al Pacino and James Earl Jones. Bennett had done sixteen Broadway shows under the standard Broadway scenario, which began with five weeks of tightly scheduled rehearsal, a few weeks of out-of-town tryouts and then a New York opening. Workshop conditions at the Public, during which he could develop his idea with a cast of dancers, gave him respite from time and money pressures as well as total control over his project.

"Bennett particularly liked the cachet associated with the title New York Shakespeare Festival," according to one of his biographers. "The only Shakespeare he had read was *Hamlet* in high school. [And] Papp's blue-collar approach to theater, his social-minded plans for developing audiences beyond Broadway's bourgeois limitations, his interest in new, politically relevant material appealed to Bennett."

Papp loved the documentary nature of the project and saw his role as that of a watchdog, whose function was to preserve its character. He offered Bennett space in which to develop his idea for as long as he wished and an across-the-board salary of $100 per week per participant in exchange for the right to produce the show. If the production succeeded, Bennett would receive 5 percent of the gross as director and choreographer as well as 15 percent of operating profits. The Festival would retain 85 percent. Bennett, who had never been offered workshop conditions before, accepted.

Throughout the spring of 1974, Bennett continued to meet with Papp while the producer tended his current productions and planned those for the year to come. In May, the producer took Bennett to Lincoln Center and tried to persuade him to stage his musical there. But Bennett said no. He rejected the Beaumont Theater in favor of a proscenium stage — "It's a chorus *line,* not a chorus *curve,*" he told Papp — and thought the 300-seat Newman Theater at the Public ideal.

As Papp geared up for his seventeenth Central Park season, Michael Bennett updated him on the development of *A Chorus Line* and introduced him to the collaborators he had lined up: Nicholas Dante, a dancer who aspired to be a writer; lyricist Ed Kleban, composer Marvin Hamlisch, who had just won three Academy Awards for his film music but had never worked on Broadway, and set designer Robin Wagner. In August, Papp was invited to sit in at final callbacks for dancers, who auditioned for Bennett's project by reading the transcripts of the tapes some of them had made half a year earlier.

Those who were chosen for Bennett's first workshop began the process of creating *A Chorus Line* — five weeks of working fourteen hours per day in the Newman Theater for $100 per week, with no "book" to work from and only a drummer to help Bennett choreograph the dances. Many of the dancers found the open-ended, improvisatory workshop process difficult and unfamiliar. Others found the ongoing interviewing process, by which both the play and songwriting continued, intrusive and left. The producer kept paying for the experiment.

At the end of five weeks, Bennett had two scenes and a few songs to show Papp. The producer, who was by then preoccupied by problems with a Lincoln Center production — told him to keep working. In October, Papp told his board of trustees that one of the workshops for the coming season would be: "A dance musical by choreographer Michael Bennett based on documentary material about the lives of chorus dancers in Broadway musicals." He added that he viewed the development of such workshops in a supportive environment as an essential part of the Festival's activity. "We expect to fail many more times than we succeed by the critics' yardstick," he added, "and, in fact, insist on the right to fail."

In October, Michael Bennett stopped the workshop process to direct a Neil Simon play, which was a critical failure. The Festival was also bashed by the critics. In November, Papp's Lincoln Center play, *Mert & Phil* — which featured a woman having a mastectomy — garnered notices such as "I have rarely disliked a play more or could, in general terms, recommend a play less. . . . I writhed in my seat at both its coarseness and ineptitude . . . and it will send the squeamish running out of the theater in search of air, water or even brandy. . . ." In the smaller Lincoln Center theater, *Richard III* was called, "one of the most wrongheaded, self-indulgent exercises I've ever seen." In addition to the critical onslaught, Papp faced his usual fiscal problems: the producer had a $6.2 million budget and a million-dollar deficit.

In December, with Lincoln Center continuing to drain funds from the Festival and Papp realizing just how bad his financial problems were, Michael Bennett reassembled his dancers and collaborators for their second workshop. With James Kirkwood, a novelist and playwright, the team placed a huge storyboard over two or three rows of seats in the Newman Theater and plunged into another three months of work, bringing Papp's investment and his anxiety about its development to a high. Gersten met with potential investors Jules Fisher and Jack Lenny, who offered to relieve Festival cash flow problems by investing $125,000 into *A Chorus Line* in exchange for 50 percent of profits. But Papp decided against it. He invited Bennett to his home one evening and the two sat for hours discussing not only the workshop, but Bennett's life story. Finally, Papp asked him, "Do you think you can pull this off?" Bennett said he could. Papp asked the Shubert Organization for an emergency grant to see the Festival through. On March 3, the producer saw the first — four-and-a-half-hour — run-through and gave them the go-ahead to begin a six-week rehearsal process.

On May 21, the day of the press opening, Papp sent Bennett his standard letter to playwrights, inviting him to come back and fail at the Public but by then, almost everyone at the Festival knew that they had something extraordinary in the building. Staffers walked through the offices singing:

"I really need this job;
Please God I need this job."

"Anyone who saw the show would just sit there and weep," recalled a staffer. "There were standing ovations from the beginning."

Most though not all of the critics grasped the extraordinary nature of the show. "The conservative words for *A Chorus Line* might be tremendous or perhaps terrific," wrote Clive Barnes. "The reception was so shattering that it is surprising if, by the time you read this, the New York Shakespeare Festival has got a Newman Theater still standing." John Simon called it "the first musical-verité, the attempt to catch unmediated truth. . . ." And Martin Gottfried wrote, "At a time when producers are taking the choruses out of their musicals for the sake of economy, director Michael Bennett has taken everything else out. . . . a dazzling show, driving, compassionate and finally thrilling. It is a major event in the development of the American musical theater."

On June 11, Bennett and Papp went to Orsini's, an elegant restaurant near Bennett's apartment, to celebrate their success. As usual, Papp was sober rather than joyful. Since childhood, he told Bennett, he had been aware of the corrosive effects of money. He further believed — and his experience had borne him out — that financial success strained or broke connections between people. "Joe thought Michael was a genius and Michael respected Joe," Gail Merrifield recalled. "But Joe worried that, with the success of *A Chorus Line,* the pressures on their relationship would be formidable. That evening, he told Michael that although there was no way to guarantee the permanence of their good feelings for one another, he wanted them to have a reminder of their excellent connection. He wrote a mock-legal agreement for them to sign, but it was not meant as a joke. Joe typed it up himself on his Remington Standard. Michael took to the idea and immediately understood the seriousness of it. It reminded me of pacts you make when you're a kid and seal with blood, and I was honored to be named a witness."

Two days later, Papp and Bennett signed the following statement, in which the *Kol Nidrei* prayer for Yom Kippur echoes as strongly as the monologues of Shakespeare:

Being sound in mind and body and pure in heart, we do solemnly vow, promise, swear, pledge and affirm to perform all the duties, obligations, expectations, as they are construed and understood to apply to the term "friendship" such as loyalty, fealty, mutual assistance, honesty, truthfulness and trust in all dealings, arrangements, both verbal and written, both spoken and unspoken, both at home and abroad, in all companies, at all hours, for all times, to set a shining example of integrity in human affairs, in contradistinction and toward the obliteration of backbiting, undermining, innuendo, opportunism, greed, the devil's larder of subtle seductions preying on man's weakness for aggrandizement at the expense and over the corpus of his fellow.

Be it understood and acknowledged that this signature, though set down in ink, shall be as binding as the power in a blood knot, and whosoever shall attempt to sever or untie it shall suffer the penalty of the damned and remain forever in a dark and empty theater.

SWORN UNTO EACH OTHER THIS 13TH DAY OF JUNE, 1975 IN FAITH AND HOPE: *Joseph Papp   Michael Bennett*

By the time the two men signed this vow, celebrities were vying for the 299 nightly tickets to *A Chorus Line*. In July, with another grant from LuEsther Mertz — this one for $250,000 — Papp moved it to Broadway, where it would win the Festival its third Pulitzer Prize and break all records.

A Chorus Line would also, as Papp had foreseen, break many connections as well. Bennett became a millionaire. The show's several collaborators quarreled and several dancers felt cheated. But Bennett and Papp maintained the cordial relation they had pledged to uphold. Their association was one that Papp would later recall as simple, constant and untroubled. It stood him in good stead as, at fifty-four, he plunged into what would be the most glamorous as well as frustrating period of the New York Shakespeare Festival.

SIXTEEN

The Consequences of A Chorus Line

On JULY 25, 1975, *A Chorus Line* began playing to standing room audiences on Broadway. More than six million people would see it at the Shubert Theater, where it became Broadway's longest-running musical. Millions more would see it elsewhere — in cities across the United States and in twenty countries abroad and, eventually, as a movie. A commercial producer would have earned at least 50 percent of the profits of the musical; Papp himself earned nothing. However, *A Chorus Line* would ultimately bring in about $40 million to the New York Shakespeare Festival, making it for a time the most affluent institutional theater in America.

The musical brought Papp the attention that only great financial success receives in the United States. It was twenty-one years since Joe Papirofsky had founded his Shakespeare Workshop, years spent scrambling for money. Now came the "glory years," as staffers later called them, a time in which the Festival was awash in cash, publicity and goodwill.

"It was no longer a hand-to-mouth existence," recalled Stanley Lowell, the Festival's secretary-treasurer. He urged that 10 percent of the musical's profits be invested in a reserve fund that the producer could not touch: "If we had left it to Joe, he would have spent all the money," Lowell, who had been Papp's supporter since 1957, later said. "This way, he could spend the income but not the capital. It was like an endowment."

The reserve fund, which would peak at $24 million in the mid-1980s, yielded income that allowed Papp to acquire luxuries taken for granted in the corporate world but rare in theater. He hired staff to establish an archive. He bought a large photocopier to process Festival scripts. But, most important, he invested in more work. In 1970–71, Papp had presented or produced twenty-one shows including workshops; in 1977–78, the number was thirty-five.

Ever since Papp had bowed to popular demand by instituting a policy of classics at Lincoln Center and began booking stars for the Beaumont, reporters had been calling him an "impresario." In fact, he had been functioning partly as one. But his primary interest was still Shakespeare on the one hand and new playwrights on the other. For the next ten years, the profits from *A Chorus Line* would subsidize both.

Papp observed the Broadway audiences watching *A Chorus Line* and convinced himself that they were, as Gail Merrifield recalled, "more democratic than the culture consumers who went to Lincoln Center." He further persuaded himself that they were ready for the ornery, untraditional writing of his young playwrights, for what he called his "hunchback" plays. He envisaged a five-play series at the 800-seat Booth Theater. Each would run for four weeks, with tickets priced at a low $2.50. Subscribers could buy five shows for $10 — and twenty thousand tickets were sold. Ever optimistic, Papp sought out foundation support and scheduled Dennis Reardon's *Leaf People* to open alongside *A Chorus Line*.

Leaf People was, according to Reardon, "a fantasia on the theme of genocide" triggered by the encounter of an Amazon Indian culture with a white anthropologist. Partially written in a language of Reardon's creation called Leafish, each line was simultaneously translated by one of two interpreters. The script looked like this:

SECOND INTERPRETER:
But we *are* the leaves. We move like sunlight through the trees. We strike as suddenly as the rain, and our arrows are poisoned raindrops.

GITOUCHO:
Mah Toh she hiwah! Toh gahoolee goh deezhoo bahtjee. Toh bumah eeshee goh lahsh jah tohna treek she mool lahsheek.

"I've always been interested in language," Papp said later. "It was interesting to have a writer create an entire language for a play. The whole piece was so alive, so original, so unusual. Visually, it was very interesting. It was a highly theatrical idea. And I felt he was a terrific writer."

It took two weeks of rehearsal just to prepare a reading. Every script contained a glossary of words, and actors were drilled in the syntax of Leafish. They read for an audience of Festival staffers and playwrights and Reardon remembered the occasion as one of his happiest moments in the theater. "I was simply amazed at how well it read given the overwhelming technical problems of translation," he recalled. "The never-effusive David Rabe came up to me afterwards and Michael Weller's reaction was to shake my hand, and say, 'I see I better get to work,' the gist being 'You've broken new ground and gotten ahead of me and I have to go now and catch up.'"

David Rabe would remember *Leaf People* as "one of the most exquisite plays" he had ever heard. "The beauty was linguistic, primitive, spiritual," he said. "I remember it now, almost twenty years later. And because I was not involved, because it was not *my* play, I could observe what happened to it dispassionately. It seemed emblematic of what happened to most of our plays."

Reardon had written the play specifically for the Beaumont's stage. He was in upstate New York, pruning branches in one of his apple trees, when Bernard Gersten called and asked him to come to Shubert Alley the next afternoon. *Leaf People,* he said, would be opening not the Beaumont but the Booth season on Broadway.

Reardon had no desire to see *Leaf People* on Broadway. "I had always abhorred Broadway," he said. "It had always seemed to be the province of Jewish shysters and pretentious Brits. Why did I not make my opposition known? It was sprung on me late in the game as a *fait accompli.* Second, it wasn't just me involved. My personal fate was bound up with the fates of Weller, Piñero, Babe and John Ford Noonan. Would they have a chance to get to Broadway again if I dug in my heels? Third, I didn't want to feel like a spineless coward and have it appear that I was afraid of Broadway exposure. Fourth, the reading had persuaded me that I had a great play that spoke of things that needed to be heard: tribal genocide, destruction of rain forest habitat — ideas basically fifteen years ahead of their theatrical time. Fifth, he offered me $10,000 — more money than I had yet made from all of my previous efforts combined, pitiful as that now seems. Sixth, it was Joe's express will to do this thing and I did not wish to disappoint him, especially since the Thought

Unspoken was 'Look what I'm doing for you.' I *still* wish I had said Beaumont, Beaumont, Beaumont until he caved. But I didn't.

"I went down to Shubert Alley the next day wearing a T-shirt and blue jeans, with my hair halfway down my back, and there was John Ford Noonan wearing a turban and bib overalls and looking like a pirate, and Miguel Piñero wearing a dashiki and a beret, and Michael Weller in his peacoat. We looked like the counterculture. People presumed that we had shown up looking as offensive as we could. But there was no premeditation involved. No one told us we were going to have our picture taken. And then that photograph became the centerpiece of the ad campaign. Nobody who looked like this had ever gone on Broadway before, and suddenly here was not one but five people looking like escapees from a heavy metal band."

The photograph of the five playwrights appeared under the headline "WANTED!" and was widely reproduced in Festival advertising. Papp enlisted Tom O'Horgan, director of the Broadway production of *Hair* and *Jesus Christ Superstar*. "I thought he was a very good, avant-garde director," Papp later said. "A lot of imagination and also used to doing things that were unorthodox. *Leaf People* was not a normal kind of show. It had a very offbeat kind of quality and I thought he would be ideal."

The match between director and play had been a sore point for Reardon since he had arrived at the Public. "For *Happiness Cage*," he recalled, "Joe assigned me a novice who never directed anything else again. *Siamese Connections* had had a good director in Ann Arbor and I wanted him, but Joe wouldn't hear of it. He gave me a young woman who was pleasant enough but so vague about the script's deficiencies, I couldn't work with her. Joe then linked me up with a young Yalie, who might have been from Mars for all the affinities we shared. He had an aggressively gay perspective which led him to cast a male actor as the play's grandmother. He also wrung many dubious rewrites out of me and after a debacle of a Shakespeare production Papp cut him loose.

"Yet another young Yalie expertly put together the reading of *Leaf People* that was so successful. *His* reward was to be passed over for the Broadway production."

Dennis Reardon grew to detest Tom O'Horgan and felt sure he was destroying his work. "You needed someone with great delicacy and you couldn't go more wrong than with O'Horgan," David Rabe recalled. "It became a kind of muscular play about guys running around in jockstraps. Once you have the wrong director, forget it. It confirmed my worst fears. Five new playwrights on Broadway is a great idea. But if the timetable says fall and it's already spring, you are already not picking the right director for the play but the right director to suit your time frame. *Leaf People* became the vanguard of his new policy at the Booth and carried all that pressure rather than just the burden of having to manifest itself."

After the first preview ran three hours, O'Horgan asked Reardon to cut about a third and to rewrite, as the playwright put it, "in full view of the public." Papp tried to protect the work by postponing the opening. "But when you start cutting like that and they've learned another language, actors start to panic," Reardon said. "I was rewriting twenty hours a day and averaging four hours a night sleep. Meanwhile, we were generating poisonous word of mouth."

Coincidentally, the *Times* published a scathing critique of Papp:

> Every great theater in the world, the Comédie Française, the Abbey, the Moscow Art Theater, the Group Theater, the Royal Shakespeare Company — has been fashioned by a director with a verifiable artistic vision. . . . One is forced to ask whether an impresario . . . is the right man to implement a vision which, in the past, only an artist has been able to construct. . . . He has unearthed no major writing talents. . . . He is lamentably lacking in judgment. The citation of his successes, such as *Hair, That Championship Season* and *A Chorus Line,* does not alter this fact. When a producer has as many throws of the dice as Mr. Papp's various outlets provide, his few successful gambles are easily explained by the law of averages.

Leaf People actors, struggling with Leafish and body paint, were not encouraged.

But no one expected that, a few hours before *Leaf People*'s press opening, Papp would cancel the Booth season. The producer cited a projected $1.2 million Festival deficit, the lack of foundation support and a musicians' union strike that had wiped out $200,000 in expected *Chorus Line* revenues as the reasons for his decision. Following *Leaf People,* he said, the Booth plays would move to the Public.

That night, *Leaf People* was savaged by the press. "Dennis J. Reardon's play is a mess and couldn't be expected to draw even flies at the high-rental house," wrote the *News.* The *Post* noted that the play might not have killed the projected series all by itself, but "after all, Japan didn't surrender the Second World War until a few weeks after the atomic bomb was dropped."

"The critics went after me like mad dogs," Reardon recalled. "If you write a book, reviews trickle in slowly. But in the theater, you get it all the same day. You've worked your ass off for two months not to speak of the *years* you spent writing and then they review a show that seems to have nothing to do with the one you wrote. I was completely unprepared for the violence of it, of being made to feel like a serial killer for writing a play."

Late that night, Papp and Gail Merrifield arrived at Reardon's home, unannounced. "Joe went out of his way to say, 'I want to see your next play. You haven't failed me. I'm still your patron. You still have a home at the Public Theater.' He and Gail were very, very kind." The next morning, Papp called all his playwrights to the Public to participate in a variation on *shiva* — the Jewish mourning ritual — for *Leaf People* in solidarity with the playwright. Papp also called everybody involved in the production to emphasize how proud he was of the work, how important it was, and to praise the actors and designers. Privately, he admitted that *Leaf People* was a botched production and took responsibility for it. The play should not have been produced in a theater with a proscenium stage. It had not been ready for any theater. And it had been crazy to think he could do it as a workshop production under Broadway conditions, at Broadway costs. "This kind of play required a wonderful production to make it acceptable," Papp later said. "I didn't feel the play had been successfully produced. . . . It would have worked better at the Beaumont. It needed that kind of space."

Leaf People ran for twenty-four days. Reardon retreated to upstate New York and did not write another play for several years. David Rabe, who had already gone to the West Coast to investigate prospects in screenwriting, viewed the episode as an important lesson for himself. "You don't get a second chance in theater," he said. "*Leaf People* was a great play and it's gone. Part of the problem by that time was that Joe was spreading himself too thin to be an effective producer. Part of the problem was his impulsive way of making decisions. But the major part was the illusion he fostered of family. He set himself up as our protector and then he didn't protect our work. What an idea to begin with! You can't even protect your own children — how could you protect all the people Joe set out to protect? And I came to realize that the most important thing Joe was protecting was *not* his actors, not Shakespeare, *not* his new American playwrights but his institution. The bigger the place got, the more plays he needed."

Although Papp saw the Booth failure as a major blow, he was already on to his next project. "He saw failure as coming with the territory of a life in the theater," said Gail Merrifield, "and felt that, if people chose that life, they had to pick themselves up, brush themselves off and keep going."

The $500,000 failure of *Leaf People* underlined, for Papp, the continuing precariousness of the Festival. Revenues from *A Chorus Line* disguised but did not change the basic economics of running a not-for-profit theater. The Delacorte was rotting after fifteen years of use and needed about half a million dollars' worth of rehabilitation. The New York State Council on the Arts and the National Endowment, noting Papp's Broadway success, had cut back on their funding of the Festival. Major foundations, which had never been a great source of support, were not coming through now. "If it weren't for *A Chorus Line,* our Festival would be in deep financial trouble," he took to saying in the spring of 1976. Nonetheless, he refused to cut back on productions — "How could I ask for money if I had no deficit?" he sometimes said — and established new programs.

The first $135,000 of *A Chorus Line* income, he told reporters, would be used for Playwrights on Payroll, support for twenty-five writers who would be paid weekly wages up to $10,000 per year and receive medical as well as unemployment benefits. He appointed Ed Bullins head of a Playwrights Unit and put Wallace Shawn, then working as a shipping clerk in Manhattan's garment center, on the payroll. But the sniping that began with Papp's move to Lincoln Center continued — even about such programs. "It all sounds marvelous," observed the *Village Voice,* like Robert Moses nearly twenty years earlier, "but the stratagem behind it is classically expansionist: Never get out of debt, always use any new money to grow, always have a reason to ask people for even more. Become indispensable, then force people to keep you going. This sequence is part of the Papp armamentarium." Some foundation officials felt much the same way. "Papp's a prickly guy, so he doesn't warm the cockles of one's heart," said a Ford Foundation staffer, "but more than that, he's the kind of guy who just goes ahead and does things and says the money's got to be found some way or other, and he always has found it, and that isn't quite the kind of planned procedure and meticulous budgeting control that is most enjoyable to the Humanities and Arts Division of the Ford Foundation. It's a little irresponsible, shall we say."

But Papp's bankrolling of new work attracted a second generation of artists and staffers to the New York Shakespeare Festival. For the most part, they were twenty to thirty years younger than the producer, formed by the 1960s, and less attracted to Shakespeare than to contemporary plays. One was Rosemarie Tichler, an intense thirty-two-year-old casting director, who had been working for regional theaters across the United States. "The Public Theater was the only institution whose work I consistently respected," she said. "The plays there dealt with issues I passionately cared about, issues important not only to me but to the city and the country. I wasn't in the theater to be entertained — I was in it to be changed."

Another was Jason Steven Cohen, a footloose twenty-six-year-old stage manager who would later become associate producer. "I came from politics and I liked it when Joe would say, with a snobby accent: 'I'm not just in the *theah*-ter,'" he recalled. "He was on the political edge and strong enough to take the heat for his positions. He was, to me, a tremendously attractive person: an emotional man, who cared very deeply about people, who had strong feelings including anger. I thought his center was truth."

Politics were also important to Lynn Holst, who was hired at twenty-two and became literary manager of the Festival. "The Public represented a center of creativity with politics, and a counterculture stance that permitted me to feel I wasn't betraying my ideals to join. It meant something to work there. It was being part of a vanguard that mattered to me."

Holst and Tichler, like the first generation of Festival women, were delighted to find a boss for whom gender was beside the point, and who neither patronized nor harassed them. "I had heard that Joe was tyrannical, whimsical and dangerous," Tichler recalled, "so when I interviewed, I told him straight out that I was not the kind of person who could be a rubber stamp. He looked at me and said: 'You want to do it? It's yours.' Joe liked intelligent, strong-willed women. He wasn't threatened by them. I had never before felt such freedom in a professional situation."

The second generation found an institution that was still run "like a Mom and Pop" store, with Papp as the busy, often brusque Pop and Bernard Gersten as the more available, nurturing Mom. They loved the organized chaos of the Public, the range of projects incubating at the same time, and an organizational culture that made room for personal idiosyncrasy, where it was not unknown for staffers with a housing problem to occasionally sleep in the office.

Papp still hired on instinct. "His never asking whether I could type or if I had gone to college made a deep impression on me," said Lynn Holst. "I needed to hold on to my identity as an artist of some kind. I did not want to be seen as a mere secretary, and it was a relief not to be simply categorized. I felt seen and approved of. Joe had an uncanny ability to convey that and it was part of his power over people, particularly people who had lacked that in their lives, I would venture the kind of people who are attracted to the theater."

That approval was felt equally by Tommie King, the usher in a cowboy hat who became a fixture in the Public's lobby. "I was a street person with no theater experience before I came here," said King, whom a friend had brought in to see *No Place to Be Somebody.* "I had no experience at all but they hired me as a carpenter and then a prop master and then a truck driver. For *Black Terror,* they thought I'd be a good understudy since I was inclined to that kind of terrorism. So they sent me up to Joe's office to have a conversation.

"He said, 'You the one trying to take over my theater? I've been hearing a lot about you. Stage manager and understudy? Cost you $200 to join the union but we'll give you a raise to take care of it.' He was writing while he talked — in shorthand — and I thought, 'Wow, this guy knows shorthand, he *got* to be heavy!' He always wrote me little thank-you notes and teased me about moving up in the organization. Joe don't want to lose you and that's a great compliment. He made you feel wanted, like you were someone special. His humanity was what was most important for me. I used to hug him and he'd say, 'That's the best hug I've had today.'"

Papp enjoyed the same kind of closeness with Paul Davis, the Festival's graphic designer. Bernard Gersten had long argued that the Festival needed institutional identification above and beyond each of its productions. "It needed a consistent image," he said, "easily recognizable not only by customers but grantmakers, government arts agencies and their bureaucrats, audiences and performers." Through their advertising agency, they met Paul Davis.

Davis, a painter and graphic artist, was the son of a Methodist preacher who had grown up moving through towns in Montana, Kansas, Arkansas and Oklahoma. Although he liked what he heard about Papp, he had low expectations of working for the Festival. "I thought theater people were dumb when it came to graphics," he recalled. "At that time, typography took up almost all of the space on theater posters. My impression was that they were designed by lawyers and agents thinking only about the size of type in which their client's name would be represented. Those considerations might sell tickets but they restricted the designer's freedom and made for not very interesting posters."

Papp, Davis discovered, was like no client he had ever worked for. He saw theater posters not only as advertisements but as art for those audiences who did not get to see a production or for those who wished to remember it long after it was gone. When he was shown Davis's political posters — a strong, vividly colored portrait of Che Guevara for *Evergreen* magazine, another for the California grape workers — Papp asked the artist to do a poster for *Hamlet,* then playing at Lincoln Center.

Davis worked from a photograph of the actor Sam Waterston, painting a portrait in acrylic paint. When he brought it in, Papp said: "This isn't *Hamlet* storming the barricades. I did that production ten years ago." Paul Davis went home and painted another poster. When he returned with it, Papp reversed himself and accepted the first.

"No client I have ever worked with turned around and accepted something he had rejected," Davis later said. "With most clients, I'd feel anxiety or dread when it came time to see them. They *think* they're asking you to do a sketch but they're really trying to get you to do what they want. I always got excited when it came time to show Joe something. It was fun. He behaved like a co-creator: he was always encouraging me to go beyond myself. Whether he liked what I did or didn't like it, he seemed to have a perspective on it. And it amazed me that he'd have the time to discuss my work.

"There was also the good feeling that I was finally dealing with something real. It's odd to think of the theater as dealing with reality, but compared to Madison Avenue, where they are always manufacturing feelings and desires and images, it was. When Joe talked about characters in a play, he talked about them the way he might talk about people standing in the next room. *He's* having problems with her. *Her* feelings are in conflict. My own work had always been about drama, story-telling, morality. My father was a Methodist preacher in Oklahoma and Joe's theater began to remind me of the Methodist church — a place to bring important issues."

Paul Davis's posters for *Hamlet*, David Rabe's *Streamers*, Brecht's *Threepenny Opera*, and Ntozake Shange's *for colored girls* were displayed on large sheets in subway stations and railroad stations along the Northeast Corridor. Smaller boards were produced for poster collectors, and reductions were published in newspaper ads. Davis's posters did what Gersten thought they would: they provided Festival productions with an instantly recognizable visual image. Public response, Davis recalled, was greater than toward any other work he had produced until that time. And Davis's relationship with Papp affected his work. "It was an adventure. One never knew what was going to happen or who one might see emerging from his office. He created an environment in which creative people could express themselves. He was interested in process as much as product. He surprised me by what he noticed. I never felt he was rejecting something I brought in as much as creating another opportunity for me."

The intensely personal connection that Joseph Papp forged with associates extended into a second generation of actors as well. They were still blood-and-guts types, "muscular, intelligent actors, whose minds you could see working on the stage," said Rosemarie Tichler. "He responded to wonderful speech but cared more for someone's physical imagination or life force than technique. Most of all, he wanted to be surprised. He couldn't abide dullness of any kind."

The generation of actors that came to the Public in the 1970s were almost all college educated. Many had been trained at the professional schools of Yale, Juilliard or New York University. And far from regarding the Festival as marginal, they saw it as the epicenter of the theater world.

"The word in California then was that if you wanted to do socially meaningful theater, you went to the Public," recalled Kathryn Grody, then twenty-two and just out of San Francisco State. "I had pictured a tiny, humble theater — like one wooden room." At Yale, Meryl Streep recalled, "the Public was then considered *the* place to work — the mecca for rigorous, serious dramatists." Streep auditioned as Blanche DuBois in *Streetcar Named Desire,* and Papp walked in during her audition. "The afternoon of the first reading is one I vividly remember because when I got home the phone rang," Streep later recalled. "It was Joe saying, 'How would you like to play Isabella in *Measure for Measure* in the park? And maybe Catherine in *Henry V?* I remember thinking maybe he'd lost his critical faculties and wondering if he was like this with all the actors at the Festival. But I knew the same actors worked over and over at the Public much to the consternation of other actors who felt 'outside' the privileged circle. I had never been shut out. It felt a little like working for a Japanese corporation. You had a job for life."

Like Grody, Streep expected Papp to be an activist, a crusader for social justice, a man who had built a theater. "What I thought was great about him was that he treated me as a peer," she recalled. "Right from the beginning, when I was this unknown, completely ignorant drama student, way before I was ready for it, he admitted me to the discussion as an equal. We shared a birthday — June 22 — and we felt we were partners cosmically. His conviction about me was total but somewhere back in the back of my brain I was screaming: 'Wow! Wow! Look at this! Wow!'"

Streep was pleased by Papp's practice of staggering press openings to relieve psychological pressure on the actors and his apparent indifference to reviews. "Joe encouraged people in spite of their reviews and it was sometimes a defiant endorsement. He would keep shows open that had been panned until word of mouth redeemed them." She also found Papp flexible. During the summer of 1978, Streep worked on *Kramer vs.*

Kramer and Woody Allen's *Manhattan* during the day and performed in *Taming of the Shrew* at night. "Joe had no problem with that schedule as long as I showed up for work and chewed up the scenery nightly in the park," she recalled. "The movie producers, on the other hand, were very nervous about whether or not I'd be able to maintain the concentration and physical stamina necessary to the part of Joanna Kramer. Joe looked at actors as dray horses, muscular and fearsome, while the movies were more prone to molly-coddling. Even now when I see Joanna Kramer in television showings of the movie, I think of her red-haired alter ego, Katherine the Shrew, spitting and sweating all over the first four rows of spectators at the Delacorte."

Mandy Patinkin, who had dropped out of the Juilliard School, was one of the many actors who adopted Papp as an artistic father. "No matter how many other people were saying it, I *knew* I was his true son," he later said wryly. "Joe was better than a real father because there was no childhood baggage, a fantasy father in that he was nurturing and generous and giving. He encouraged me to sing as well as act if I wanted to, not to let myself be pigeonholed."

Papp's relation to Patinkin recapitulated the relationship he had had with his own father. The two men liked to sit together and sing everything from show tunes to Jewish liturgical music. Papp kept tabs on Patinkin's romantic involvement with Kathryn Grody as both became Festival regulars, signed the couple's *ketubah*, the Jewish marriage contract, advised them on amniocentesis and, after their children were born, often celebrated Jewish holidays with their family. When Meryl Streep gave birth to her first child, Papp was among the first at the hospital. When actors Kevin Kline and Phoebe Cates had their first child, they gave him the middle name of Joseph.

New directors also continued to join the family but found that directors still took a back seat to playwrights and actors at the Festival. With the growing number of productions after *A Chorus Line*, Festival staffers scouted vigorously for new directors but found very few. "Young directors need experience," Merrifield recalled. "And although Joe was always giving them a chance, he was more critical than he was of actors. And on their side, young directors would often work for one or two productions, get experience and then go off to work in Hollywood or in television where they could make money."

The first generation of Festival people told stories about Papp's relations with Stuart Vaughan; the second told stories of Papp and Jeff Bleckner. Bleckner had been one of Papp's favorite students at Yale. In

1970, he directed David Rabe's *The Basic Training of Pavlo Hummel,* feeling "incredibly lucky" to be paid the off-Broadway fee of $750. He directed *Sticks and Bones* with great success. But Bleckner always saw himself as the "second" son. "Joe regarded David as the star, his great find," Bleckner, who became an acclaimed television director, recalled. "He saw playwrights as creators — mysterious, fascinating people. Actors and directors were interpreters and in another category entirely. Although I felt I had a lot to do with the success of Rabe's plays, nobody ever gave me a nod for it. When you work as a Festival director, you knock your brains out and constantly hear people say: 'You did that? I thought Joe Papp did that.'"

Trouble between Papp and the young director began when the director accepted a Broadway assignment that conflicted with the CBS taping of *Sticks and Bones.* "There was a slight time overlap and he said: 'I can't wait for you.' We were sitting in his office and to punish me — as I understood it — he picked up the telephone receiver and called Mike Nichols to ask him to direct the show. The tactic misfired: Nichols wasn't there. But I was shocked. Why couldn't he wait for me a few days?"

Rabe and Bleckner's third collaboration, *The Orphan,* was a critical failure. "By that time, David had been done a great disservice by the press," Bleckner recalled. "He was very talented and had always been astute, amenable to changes. Then he got these wonderful reviews, people comparing him to Eugene O'Neill, and he became reluctant to rewrite. *The Orphan* was very dense, long and obscure. If a scene didn't work, it was now the actor's problem or our approach. It became harder and harder to get him to change anything, and the production reflected that."

Papp then assigned Bleckner to direct *As You Like It* in the park. Bleckner had been working with his company just six days when Papp demanded to see a run-through. "I hadn't even started to stage it," Bleckner remembered. "Some people were just standing up and saying their lines. Joe said he wanted to come in and show me how to direct it. I asked: 'Are you firing me?' He said yes.

"In his office, I said: 'Why are you doing this? Are you blaming me for *The Orphan?*' He said yes. And that was that. I was gone. I was absolutely devastated. I was banished from the Public Theater — I couldn't even get a free ticket to a performance. I was thirty years old. My life had centered around the Festival. I had believed I had a place there, that I was part of this family. And all of a sudden I was set loose. I had no structure.

"Joe was a patriarchal figure to me. His approval was terribly important. I might not have had a career without him. But I had to grow up. I went to the West Coast and, after a very hard time, began a career as a television director. In the business, I'm a very late starter.

"Much later, when I was on the East Coast and feeling very healthy, I decided to go and see Joe. We sat in his office, which looked like a shrine, the walls covered with all those theater posters, photographs and framed awards he had received. I told him what I had been doing, that I had directed *Hill Street Blues* and a PBS show — and that I had gotten Emmys for both. He listened. Then he listed *his* television credits.

"It made me smile. There was an element of him that was simply jealous. It was a world he had never conquered. And the fact that he needed to tell me *his* credits — well, it was great for me. It allowed me to put him to bed. He hugged me at the door and said to come back and do a play. As I walked out, I thought: I never realized how short he was. So now, I have very fond memories of Joe."

Papp's dismissal of directors was always a public event. His relationships with writers were usually more private and those selected knew they were an elite group. Their dissatisfactions remained more private. By the mid-1970s, fifty unsolicited scripts *per week* were arriving at Lafayette Street, and Gail Merrifield headed a Play Development Department of three full-timers and twenty-two freelance play-readers and scouts. With the growth of the Festival, Papp had created department heads. Although Merrifield's appointment raised issues of nepotism — the couple married in 1976 — she had been reading plays since 1963, even before coming to work at the Festival, and handling a *de facto* script department since Papp founded the Public.

"Any theater's literary department has the problem of access," said Lynn Holst. "The advantage of Gail's running the literary department was that she was so close to Joe. It was through her that new people were brought to Joe's attention. He was very pressed for time but would actually read what she recommended."

The Play Development Department was installed in a tiny former stock room adjacent to Papp's office and became home to a lively group of readers, many of whom — like writer/director Des McAnuff, actress Kathryn Grody and composer Bill Elliott — concurrently worked in the theater. "Rozanne Ritch, founder of the Drama Book Shop and a former actor, was the first of many many readers who wrote so well themselves that I felt guilty about them using their writing talent to write about other people's work," Merrifield later said. "Author Deborah Eisenberg was another case in point. She wrote *brilliant* reports long before she became recognized as a writer."

The readers not only read scripts but actively scouted productions, playwrights, dancers, poets, composers and directors. Neither of the two most interesting new voices they came across in the mid-1970s were playwrights. One was a composer. One was a poet. Both performed their own work. And both Ntozake Shange and Elizabeth Swados were as serious and brilliant as the coterie of young men they joined.

Ntozake Shange, then in her mid-twenties, was a poet well established in the San Francisco Bay area. Her parents had named her Paulette Williams when she was born in Trenton, New Jersey, and hoped she would go to medical school after graduating Barnard College. By the end of the sixties, she had been radicalized and estranged from a background that was, as writer Michelle Wallace put it, "the upper end of the black middle-class. . . . She lived in a big house in an integrated neighborhood, attended all-white schools, and had live-in maids."

Instead of medicine, Shange studied Afro-American literature and history at the University of Southern California, took an African name, worked in a rape crisis center and became a poet and college instructor. At the time *A Chorus Line* was in its second workshop in the Public, Shange was reading her poetry in Bay area women's bars. "People would come see us for $1.50, and they could drink all the wine and beer that they wanted," recalled her coperformer, Paula Moss. "And we would just get drunk and have two- or three-hour shows. Zaki loves that. If it were up to her, it would still be in a bar. But I always wanted it in a theater."

The two women took the poetry to New York, where Shange's younger sister introduced her to Oz Scott, then a Festival stage manager. He brought in three additional performers and began directing the group in performances at East Side bars. "People would come by to see us and then they'd get up and perform themselves, or we might draw them into it," Shange said. "The adventure was not to set it — the adventure was that it kept changing all the time." It was, at first, unnerving to her to hear actresses read her poems, Shange later said. "I had to deal with the implications of working in theater."

In December 1975, Scott — who had been using the Public to rehearse — gave Papp a manuscript titled *& this is for colored girls who have considered suicide when the rainbow is enuf* and asked the producer to come see it at Demonte's, a nearby bar. The manuscript landed on Gail Merrifield's desk, a thin sheaf of twenty poems including one called "Lady in Red."

without any assistance or guidance from you
i have loved you assiduously for 8 months 2 wks & a day
i have been stood up four times
i've left 7 packages on yr doorstep
forty poems 2 plants & 3 handmade notecards i left
town so i cd send to you have been no help to me
on my job
you call at 3:00 in the mornin on weekdays
so I cd drive 27½ miles cross the bay before i go to work
charmin charmin
but you are of no assistance
i want you to know
this waz an experiment
to see how selfish i cd be
if i wd really carry on to snare a possible lover
if i waz capable of debasin my self for the love of another
if i cd stand not being wanted
when i wanted to be wanted
& i cannot
so
with no further assistance & no guidance from you
i am endin this affair.

this note is attached to a plant
i've been waterin since the day i met you
you may water it
yr damn self

Merrifield responded to what she called "Zaki's language, her self-humor, her vulnerability, and her anger toward a certain kind of man. But it was impossible to know from the page what it would be like as theater. It had to be seen. Joe couldn't get to Demonte's so Oz asked him if he could audition it at the Public."

Shange herself thought theater stuffy, boring, middle class, part of the bourgeois package she had repudiated. "Theater is the most conservative art form," she would later say. "I'm continually leaving it because I get fed up."

But in February 1976, Shange auditioned in the Public's Little Theater. Papp later remembered Shange as "this funny little girl — an earring in her nose, a red bandanna on her head, who didn't even look me in the eye." His reaction to the term "choreopoem" was hardly more enthusiastic. In his producer's lexicon, it meant "the thing that closes in Boston." He told Oz Scott that he had twenty minutes. But Papp remained seated, riveted by Shange's language and material, for over an hour.

Listening to the women speak, he remembered *Wedding Band,* a play by Alice Childress, which he had directed a few years earlier. "Alice's language is so authentic and rich, it's like the loam in the earth," he said. "By itself, that is literature to me. In Zaki's writing, I found that homeyness as well as the twist that a university education gave it. It's a unique style with high flights of poetry intermixed with down-to-earth folk, black material. She has an honesty, a power which makes it dramatic. When someone says something out loud and you're moved by it — that's the first law of drama."

Merrifield was, as she later put it, "overwhelmed" by the reading. "It seemed to be a reflection of my innermost being on the stage even though it was about experiences I had never had and cultural identifications that weren't mine," Merrifield later said. "I could hardly speak afterwards because I was so moved."

Papp had no space immediately available at the Public, but Woodie King, Jr., director of the New Federal Theater who had seen the piece at Demonte's, did. The two men agreed to go ahead with a coproduction, beginning with a limited engagement at King's theater, then more rehearsals and a production at the Public, which gave Papp, Oz and Shange time to work on the material. "When it went into rehearsals here, we had several very strong sit-down meetings," Papp later said, "And I went through it, line by line. They were doing a linear story, starting with being a little kid and then growing up." Papp saw structural problems similar to the ones Bennett and his collaborators had struggled with in *A Chorus Line.* He suggested restructuring the piece, juxtaposing poems and dances differently, and recasting some of the actresses.

Shange proved not at all "tough to deal with." Like David Rabe, she had seen *No Place to Be Somebody* at the Public in 1969 and, from that moment on, regarded Papp as a "remarkable, mystical" person, experienced in a field of which she knew almost nothing. "There is an art to designing a reading and I thought I had perfected it," Shange recalled. "It already worked for me and I was intrigued and somewhat frustrated by the passion with which Joe and Oz wanted to move the poems around. I didn't understand why I had to discuss that with anybody.

"But nobody was asking me to change lines or words. He gave us enormous support just by saying 'I want this thing heard. I want to see it.' And he never acted like I was stupid, and he also never tried to undo my politics, as much opposed to some of them as he was. He didn't try to change me." Ultimately, Shange began to refer to Papp as her "art" father, and when she gave birth to a daughter, named him as godfather.

When *for colored girls* opened at the Public in June of 1976, it was so successful that Papp decided to move it to Broadway's Booth Theater, where *Leaf People* had failed the season before. It represented not just the only serious black work and woman's work on Broadway, but the only serious *American* dramatic work. "What makes it so important to me," he said, "is that it upgrades the entire standard of Broadway. It gives Broadway some dignity. We've introduced the first work of a writer, also the first work of a director. And, for some of the women in it, this is the first time they've played roles of this magnitude and received recognition for it."

Shange was no more enthusiastic about Broadway than Rabe or Reardon. "I knew I wasn't going up there," she said. "My political and aesthetic aims in life were contrary to everything Broadway represented. But Joe said this way more people would be able to see it. Did I want to deny the world an opportunity to know what it was I was talking about? So I said okay but who was going to play my part? He said, I would. Me."

For colored girls opened at the Booth in September of 1976 with Shange lasting three weeks as a performer before she fled. The experience, she later said, forced her to see beyond a leftist, radical feminist perspective: "I was just stunned by the press and applause and I just wanted to get away from it. And so I came down with strep throat, got very sick and went to Europe."

Audiences, a mix of blacks and whites, old and young, adored the show and returned to see it again and again. At board meetings, Bernard Gersten began to report that *for colored girls* was returning a small but steady profit to the Festival as well as to its co-producer, the New Federal Theater. "It's not just that he's absolutely fair as money goes — though that's rare enough, right?" its director, Woodie King, Jr., told a reporter. "It's that he had the guts to go with that play from the beginning. He's a leader, not a follower. Even if *colored girls* hadn't been a success, it would always be a benchmark for any play that really was built on poetry. And he was eager to be out there with it."

Within a few weeks of meeting Shange, Papp saw the work of Elizabeth Swados, then a young composer working with director Andrei Serban at Café La Mama. But his interest in her at that moment was subsumed to his interest in her collaboration with Serban. They had created *Fragments of a Trilogy*, a work based on *Medea, Electra,* and the

Trojan Women, for which they had developed not only music but — like Leafish — a new language, a music of words based on Greek, which served as their text.

Swados and Serban became part of Papp's new strategy for Lincoln Center: matching revivals with nontraditional directors. His first project was *Threepenny Opera,* which had run for six years off-Broadway. Papp had seen a performance there starring Lotte Lenya and later described it as "an experience which I still count as one of the most moving of my life. . . . Although World War II was over, the devastation that Hitler had wrought was still with us, and to me *Threepenny* was a horrendous reminder of the days and climate which brought him to power." In the early 1970s, he tried to obtain the rights, held by Brecht's son, Stefan Brecht, and Lenya. "After long negotiations, Stefan exacted a condition which I heartily embrace," Papp wrote. "He insisted that Richard Foreman direct the work."

Papp had known Richard Foreman for many years. He and Merrifield had attended his Ontological Hysteric Theater on their very first date. "His work was visual, absurdist, full of surprises and bizarre humor," according to Merrifield, "like being in a strange dream, no logic but lots of intimations, sensations and portents." Papp also agreed that a new translation was in order. The 1954 Marc Blitzstein adaptation of *Threepenny,* Papp later wrote, had excised or sweetened Brecht's original lyrics.

> The decision . . . may have been made in deference to stage censorship of twenty years ago, but the result was castrating. . . . One has to remember in *Threepenny Opera* that all human urges — sex and hunger — are set up against a backdrop of starvation caused by a decaying social order. Otherwise the material loses its artistic and political nature and becomes a nightclub act. . . .
>
> The danger of the classic, as demonstrated in productions of Shakespeare, is that it sets up standard expectations on the part of the audience. The Berliner Ensemble, Brecht's own company, had made it a policy in presenting *Threepenny* to consciously make the work less singable by working against the rhythms, which will have the effect of making people listen sharply to what is being said, rather than being lulled by the familiarity of Weill's exquisite music. In producing Shakespeare we are always conscious of the obligation to insist that the audience hear "To Be or Not to Be" not as a nostalgic, operatic rendition, but as a meaningful contemporary statement. . . . When these words are spoken by an actor with a Puerto Rican accent, they suddenly leap out of overladen tradition into the merciless world of now.

Just as Martin Sheen had shocked audiences in Papp's 1968 *Hamlet,* Raul Julia shocked them when, in a Hispanic accent, he declaimed: "What's breaking into a bank compared with founding a bank? What's murdering a man compared with hiring a man?"

Threepenny Opera became a huge and controversial success and Papp conceived of Foreman, Serban and avant-garde director Joseph Chaikin as a triumvirate who might solve his problem at Lincoln Center. Audiences wanted the classics. Well, he would give them the classics — but with his own spin. "Times have changed," he would tell a reporter when, a year later, he announced his new policy. "You can't do the classics conventionally anymore. They lay on you like bagels. Doing the classics doesn't interest me, except with directors who bring them to life."

Tall, thin and cool in manner, Romanian Andrei Serban was a product of the rigorous Eastern European theater world, who found the American scene "sloppy" and "amateurish." Like Swados, he had worked with British director Peter Brook and viewed making theater as an aesthetic and ascetic journey. "Coming here in the 60s and seeing the whole looseness of the avant-garde, where the idea was to be free in this very sentimental way, in this loose way, smoke drugs, let the hair grow — it seemed so cheap to me," he later told a reporter. "There's something in me more connected to discipline and intensity than to this freedom and looseness." Papp's theater, he thought, was like a European theater in that it had a point of view and a clear direction. Like the playwrights who came to Lafayette Street, he found the energy and the mix of work exhilarating.

The two men met for a few hours. Although Serban had never before directed a realistic play, let alone Chekhov, Papp suggested he do *The Cherry Orchard.* He offered him the Beaumont Theater and a roster of brilliant actors. At their second meeting, Papp proposed that Serban take over the Beaumont. Bringing Serban to Lincoln Center, Papp said, "dignifies the situation. . . . It's something we rarely have in the theater, which is so full of fakery. And I feel I am dealing with a colleague, not an employee or a young director. I find an astuteness I've found with only one or two others."

That summer, as *Henry V* and *Measure for Measure* were playing at the Delacorte and *Threepenny* kept on drawing crowds, Papp announced that the show would run until February. He asked the sixteen thousand Beaumont subscribers who had paid for a new season of plays in the fall to "extend their trust" by allowing the Festival to credit their subscriptions toward February or else accept a refund. During the grace period he would gain, Papp told the *Times,* he would make plans for the creation of "an American classical theater company" at Lincoln Center.

It did not work out that way. During the fall of 1976, Papp did indeed think about creating a loose repertory company, directed by Serban. But the project would be expensive and he would have to offer flexible terms that left performers "reasonable breaks" to pursue film and television work. In February 1977, just before Serban's *Cherry Orchard* opened, that was still the plan. Then in April, he presented to the Lincoln Center board a $6.5 million renovation plan for the Beaumont drawn up by architect Giorgio Cavaglieri. The board had no objections to it but also had no funds to commit. By May, Papp had decided to leave the complex. Although Serban's *Cherry Orchard* had been nominated for five Tony Awards and the Beaumont was playing almost at capacity, the Festival, he told his trustees, should be supporting new talent — not Lincoln Center. If *Chorus Line* income continued to be used to subsidize the Beaumont, it would be gone in three years.

Associate producer Bernard Gersten disagreed. "Three companies of *A Chorus Line* — Broadway, national and international — were pumping in the money every week," he argued. "We could afford to stay at Lincoln Center. We had done our time with the bugs and the wind and the rain. We had had several years of small theaters in a wonderful restored building. But now we had an enclosed theater where a subway did *not* run right under the stage, where the whole building did *not* vibrate. And we had the platform, the position that Lincoln Center provides, that gives you a tremendous advantage in everything from critical attention to fundraising. To turn your back on that was like leaving the Garden of Eden.

"We had had some significant successes at Lincoln Center. And with a 1,100-seat theater playing at close to capacity, our earned income combined with contributions could keep the Festival afloat — even without the *Chorus Line* income."

But Papp did not listen. In June, he told board members that he had taken on Lincoln Center to save the Public Theater. True, the Ford Foundation, which had not given the Festival any funds for fifteen years, had made a grant of $1.5 million, followed by the Mellon, Rockefeller and Kaplan foundations. But staying there was simply too expensive, he argued. He was feeding $2 million of *Chorus Line* profits into Lincoln Center every year. Even if plays averaged 90 percent capacity audiences, the Festival would still face a shortfall there of about $3.7 million.

After four years of occupancy, Papp still did not have a desk at Lincoln Center. He had never reconciled himself either to the white marble buildings or the predominantly white, middle-aged, middle-class and — as he conceived of them — middle-European audience. "We cannot fulfill our goals at Lincoln Center," he said. "It does not provide an opportunity to break new ground. We consider leaving an affirmative action."

Contractually, Papp noted, the Festival had a twenty-five-year lease. Lincoln Center could force them to pay $175,000 maintenance on the dark premises but could not force him to produce plays there. He said he had already sought legal counsel and notified Amyas Ames and John Mazzola by telephone of his intent to vacate. The board unanimously voted to vacate Lincoln Center.

"One day, without warning, he called and said, 'I'm having a press conference,'" recalled Robert Kamlot, who managed the Festival's Lincoln Center outpost. "He said: 'I hate the place, this is not what I want to do, we're on a high, we're getting out.'"

"PAPP QUITS LINCOLN CENTER, CITING ARTISTIC-FINANCIAL TRAP" read the front-page *Times* headline, announcing the news. The move startled New Yorkers as well as the international theater community and would leave the Beaumont dark for the next four years. It also drew attention to two basic changes in American culture that had gone unnoticed during what Gersten called Papp's "expansionist period." First, the affluent, freewheeling days of the sixties were gone for good. Costs had risen at a time when there was far less arts funding available either from foundations or from the local, state or federal arts agencies. Second, many of the writers and performers were gone as well, withdrawing their talents from the theater community and investing them in television, film or altogether outside the artistic realm. Some of them would later view 1977 as the highwater mark of Papp's theater. It was the first time they had ever seen the producer retreat.

SEVENTEEN

"A Strategic Retreat Forward"

JOSEPH PAPP called his pull-back from Lincoln Center "a strategic retreat forward." "LAFAYETTE STREET, WE ARE HERE!" proclaimed a press release announcing his first season after Lincoln Center. "The concentration of activities at our home base this season has been a force for change, giving us room to release and expand our energies in new directions. All seven theaters, including the new Theater Cabaret, are continuously lit. . . ."

The press bought the story. "There is a theatrical renaissance taking place at the Public," reported the *New Yorker.* "Joseph Papp's energy is now back home, where it belongs." And, wrote *Newsday,* "The Public Theater is jammed to its skylights with shows. Never before has there been so much activity."

Papp was talking with celebrated director Mike Nichols about producing a play by celebrated novelist E. L. Doctorow. Rock singer Linda Ronstadt came to the Public to talk about appearing in a play. There were new dramas by John Guare, Adrienne Kennedy, Wallace Shawn, David Mamet, Ntozake Shange, Jessica Hagedorn, Tom Babe, Tina Howe and

Sam Shepard; classics such as *The Dybbuk*, Bulgakov's *The Master and Margarita* and Machiavelli's *The Mandrake* directed by experimental directors; and several musicals, two written and performed by women.

Since opening the Public Theater, Papp had developed a string of musicals with nontraditional unlikely subjects, including *Hair* and *Stomp*. The musical *Apple Pie* featured a woman sexually assaulted by the Nazis during World War II, who comes to America and is eventually shot. The musical *Sancocho* showed the adjustment of a Puerto Rican family to life in New York, with episodes at the unemployment and welfare offices. Like *A Chorus Line* and *Hair,* these shows were closer to journalism than to the tradition of American musical theater. They were similar to the serious nonfiction that was contesting the preeminence of novels in the bookstores. But while *Hair* and *A Chorus Line* became landmarks of American cultural history, the others never left the Public.

In 1978, the leading exponent of the Festival's special kind of musical was Elizabeth Swados, who captured Papp's attention and producing energy as no one since David Rabe had done. The slight, intense Swados was then, in some ways, a female version of Joe Papirofsky. For her, theater was a way to change the world. Starting as a teenager, Swados had worked in a variety of extra-theatrical settings — performing on folksinger Pete Seeger's sloop, the *Clearwater;* taking her band into illegal anti-Vietnam army coffeehouses; starting an alternative newspaper in Appalachia. Her theater background included undergraduate work at Bennington, training and touring Africa with director Peter Brook, collaborating with Andrei Serban and other directors in Europe and at the Café La Mama. By 1977, she was, as she later put it, "wanting to connect with the American reality." She wrote Papp a letter asking him to see her work. The letter was passed on to Merrifield, who went to a downtown loft to see her perform.

Swados played her guitar and, with a small group of performers, sang a group of songs from her setting of *Alice in Wonderland,* including one called "Never Play Croquet," chanted in Bob Dylan's nonmelodic style, which made Merrifield laugh out loud.

"She was very very thin, with brown hair down almost to her knees," Merrifield later said. "She appeared extremely young but her face was ravaged, with nothing carefree or happy in her expression. There was an elegaic Jewish sadness in some of her music as well as wacky, funny, wild stuff." When Swados invited Merrifield and Papp to see her work with Serban at Café La Mama, they went.

Their production of Brecht's *The Good Woman of Setzuan* was entirely sung and Papp responded both to Serban's direction and Swados's extraordinary mix of sounds, rhythms and melodies. "Joe came up to me after the show and asked what did I want to do?" Swados later recalled. "There was so much I wanted to do that I found myself trying to come up with an answer that would keep him standing there. I didn't want him to walk away. So I said, 'I think maybe *Alice in Wonderland* but I don't know.'

"A script arrived at my apartment and the next morning Joe called very early. I was sound asleep. 'Why aren't you composing, composer?' he asked. I told him the script was too intellectual, dull and dry for music. Joe didn't hide his annoyance — the play was Tina Howe's *Museum* and it went on to do very well and I enjoyed it tremendously — but told me to come in later that week to discuss *my* projects."

Meanwhile, Swados learned that Papp had engaged Serban to direct *The Cherry Orchard* and *Agamemnon* and was expecting her to compose the incidental music. "I had always felt that Andrei got too much of the credit and critical attention for what had been at least half mine," she recalled, "but Andrei and I were a very good team and even I knew it. And Joe was loyal. Afterwards, he asked me again: 'What do you want to do?'"

Swados still wanted to stage her adaptation of Lewis Carroll's *Alice in Wonderland*. But by the summer of 1977, she had become obsessed by the number of runaways she saw in American cities. Like Michael Bennett, she told the producer she had no more than an idea for a show. Papp agreed to give her full support, including a salary for herself and a seventeen-year-old assistant and a place in the Annex across Lafayette Street in which to work.

Elizabeth Swados worked steadily for the Public Theater for the next five years, writing, composing and directing under Papp's guidance. During the long workshop process for what became *Runaways,* Papp often talked to Swados about his own childhood as well as the trouble he was having with his adolescent son. "He loved Tony's sweetness and innocence but was angry at his inability to get involved in school or other activities that showed an interest in life," recalled Swados. "I thought Tony had problems with dope and depression and the fact that Joe was so fitfully involved with him, but the tenderness of Joe's emotions surprised me. He and Gail asked if Tony could work on *Runaways,* and that began years of his being backstage on my shows and an intimacy with the family."

Through the fall of 1977, Swados interviewed and auditioned more than two thousand city kids, at high schools, basketball courts, settlement houses, museums and shelters for runaways, asking them questions —

What did they smoke during lunch hour? Had any of them ever run away? How would they survive if they did? — and giving them exercises she had developed while touring Africa with Peter Brook. By the end of four months, she had selected eighteen actors between the ages of eleven and twenty-five. "The company did multitudes of improvisations," Swados later wrote. "We ran in place for forty-five minutes sometimes, and then I'd stop and ask them questions. . . . It wasn't a therapy session or encounter group. I wasn't interested in psychological problems or family background. I wanted to absorb their feelings, their movements, and their manner of expressing themselves."

The "kids," as Festival staff called the cast of what became the musical *Runaways,* then spent months wandering around the Public Theater, much like the hippies from *Hair* and *Stomp.* On Halloween, they tricked and treated at the Public; on Christmas, they had their own party there. Swados set their improvisations to salsa, rap, reggae, rock-and-roll. She served as mother and drill sergeant, fining them five dollars when they were late to rehearsals. Half maintained full school loads while carrying out Equity contracts. A few helped support families.

"We were about three weeks into rehearsals when I said, 'You're no longer just the composer. You're the writer,'" Papp later wrote. "She was a little shocked but delighted in a way. She told me the reason she never wrote was that her mother was a writer and she felt in some way that until she was at least thirty, she shouldn't compete. I told her, 'No. You're a writer now.'

"I'm often accused of being a parent figure of some sort. It's not a role I set out to play, nor do I think the people who I deal with are children. When we work together, we're colleagues. A lot of them are much younger than me, so that's a fact, and I'm aware of it. And as the producer, I'm in a supportive position, so there's a similar kind of protective desire on my part. . . . In *Runaways,* Liz saw me as the father of the play and she was the mother . . . it was good, because it didn't make her the child."

Swados herself would later remember Papp as very much of a parent. "At twenty-seven, I was embarrassed and confused by my producer's slipping in and out of professionalism into analysis — even if he was right," she said. "On the occasions which required epic work sessions, he and Gail would drive me out to their house in the country. I liked to watch Joe saw and lift logs and Gail dig her hands into the soil. There was a hammock on the outside porch where sometimes Joe insisted I lie down and he'd rock me. But I was so shy, I couldn't really relax and I was most comfortable inside, where the music system blasted out their new discoveries: Vedic singing, Austrian boy choirs, rock groups from Bulgaria, Hasidic celebrations. And Joe would sing along."

Seven months after their first meeting, Swados showed Papp a run-through. Papp responded with pages of notes on yellow legal pads. "I felt there were a lot of problems with the piece that hadn't been dealt with, or had been dealt with improperly," he later wrote. "Liz had originally conceived it as the story of a group of runaways who were building something together, running their own family. But whenever that was attempted, I felt there was a togetherness that was unreal and reduced the tension of the work. I thought it should be harder, less sympathetic."

Both Papp and Merrifield urged Swados to think structurally, to develop her characters, to write a storyline. But, like Ntozake Shange, Swados resisted dramatic structure and thought character development somewhat extraneous to her interests, preferring the "episodic, poetic, ritualistic," and taking her cues not from any stage production but from the rock albums of Marvin Gaye and the Beatles' *Sergeant Pepper*. The piece that resulted was squarely in the tradition of Public Theater productions. It combined the confessional style of *A Chorus Line,* the poetry of *for colored girls* and the tough street tension of *No Place to Be Somebody* and *Short Eyes:*

> *To boys and girls whose mothers' and fathers'*
> *Minds took long walks down late-night halls*
> *To boys and girls who in baby dreams*
> *Saw mothers and fathers scraping the strength off selves*
> *Like bark off trees. . . .*
> *To boys and girls who now weep*
> *Because you wished you'd meet*
> *Your mother's or father's shadow*
> *On a dark tall porch*
> *In dream rockers*
> *I say,*
> *Make laws against regret. . . .*

When *Runaways* opened in the Public's Cabaret in March of 1978, it was well reviewed. "To call it far and away the best musical of the season is to insult it," wrote *Newsweek*'s critic. The *Times* called it "a serious contemplative musical" and even John Simon liked the show. Papp took it to Broadway and kept it running for seven months at a loss, because he felt the play — like *Sticks and Bones* — needed to be seen there.

Just as *Runaways* opened, Papp was meeting about another musical with Gretchen Cryer and Nancy Ford. Titled *I'm Getting My Act Together and Taking It on the Road,* it was a loose autobiography of Gretchen Cryer, an animated woman in her early forties, who could not have been more different from Swados. Born and raised in rural Indiana, Cryer had graduated from DePauw University and married one of her most promising classmates. While he pursued his graduate studies, she worked as a secretary. When they decided to have children, she stayed home to raise them. By the time Papp met Cryer, she was over forty and divorced but still had, as he put it, "a kind of Midwestern cheerleader quality." She and Ford had written eight musicals together since their sophomore year at DePauw. One, *The Last Sweet Days of Isaac,* had been lauded by the New York critics, but the two women had not managed to build on their success.

Now, Nancy Ford played the piano while Gretchen Cryer described the show, acted all the roles, and sang all the songs. One was called "Dear Tom," a letter to her former husband that Papp kept whistling after the two women had gone:

> *All those years you were living with someone*
> *Who was hiding behind a smile*
> *All those years I was someone else*
> *Deception was my style*
> *I closed you out by asking for nothing*
> *'Cause I needed someone to blame*
> *You couldn't give what I didn't ask for*
> *It was a perfect game. . . .*

"I saw a person who was writing a biography right there on the stage," Papp later said. "It was an admission that things had failed along the way, that a lot of ideology by itself hadn't solved anything. There was great craft in the music and the lyrics had heart, humor and sadness. But I think what intrigued me most was Gretchen's compassion and the man and woman's complicity in victimizing themselves by playing out certain kinds of roles. And their collaboration was so unusual. You're used to seeing Rodgers and Hammerstein, Lerner and Loewe — you never see two women writing a musical together. It was unprecedented."

When the two women had finished, Papp told them he would produce the play on one condition: Cryer would have to play the leading role. "I felt it was so personal that I could not see the work without her," he said. Apart from that note, Papp had little to do with the development of what would become a feminist hit. His contribution would be as a canny marketing strategist.

I'm Getting My Act Together and Taking It on the Road evoked the kind of audience reaction characteristic of revival meetings. Couples in the audience broke into arguments. Women jotted down lyrics and sent them to ex-husbands or lovers. Cryer was accosted as she left the theater by women who thanked her for putting their lives onstage and by men who berated her or confessed that they could change, had changed or at least understood what she was driving at. But the musical, which opened in June of 1978, received poor reviews.

"I got very angry at the stupidity of the reviewers," Papp later said. "I kept thinking: how dumb these men are! They had a preconceived idea of the show and were so deeply entrenched that they could not recognize what it was about. I felt it had life. It was dealing with a major social issue — I read that there were fifty thousand women in New York City at the time who were either not married or whose chances of marriage were slight, for a variety of reasons including that they couldn't find a man to connect with or respect. And I thought: there's an *audience* for this play!"

Papp put money into radio advertising, "far more money," he said, than was warranted by the reviews. By August, the audience built to a steady 65 percent capacity. By winter, the show was selling out and in December, Papp rented the 300-seat Circle in the Square Theater on Bleecker Street in Greenwich Village and moved it there. He recouped $60,000 in moving costs within three months. For most of the next two years, *Getting My Act Together* sold out every weekend and averaged over 90 percent capacity, pulling in a Festival profit of about $4,500 per week or $200,000 each year.

In 1978, Papp was also exploring new ways to do Shakespeare. "In a city like New York," he would often say, "a person should always be able to see a performance of Shakespeare any night of the week." He had produced Shakespeare every summer at the Delacorte and, during his time at Lincoln Center, every winter in the small theater downstairs from the Beaumont. But there had been no Shakespeare at the Public since his 1968 *Hamlet*. By the spring of 1978, propelled by three unrelated issues, Papp had decided to create a black Shakespeare company.

For most of the 1970's, Papp had been troubled by the attenuation of the civil rights movement and the virtual disappearance of political activism. The election of Jimmy Carter had ushered in, he felt, a national mood of narcissism, apathy and lack of interest in social issues. The producer, who had all his life been an avid newspaper reader, now followed the course of what, in June 1978, became known as the U.S. Supreme Court's "*Bakke* decision." Allan Bakke, a white applicant to the University of California, had been denied admission to the medical school at Davis, where sixteen of one hundred incoming slots had been set aside for minorities. He argued that his qualifications were better than those of some of the sixteen minority students accepted and that he had been denied equal protection under the Constitution. The Court ordered that he be admitted to the school.

Papp thought about *Bakke* in the light of his own decisions as a producer. At Lincoln Center, he had retreated from a policy of championing black playwrights. "The direction Papp was heading in was perhaps the most important direction anybody had ever taken in the theater," a critic would write in the African-American newspaper *Amsterdam News.* "He quit on the direction because the pressure was, in his estimation, a greater pressure. I think it was a bad choice." That summer, Ntozake Shange would note that neither Delacorte production — *All's Well That Ends Well* and *The Taming of the Shrew* — included a black performer. And the *Black American,* a New York weekly, would write:

> Joseph Papp presents himself as the major White producer, particularly concerned with the theater of racial minorities. . . . [But] with a few exceptions, all the plays reflect Black street life, emphasizing the wounds and cries of Blacks, ignoring the wholeness and joys of the Black experience. The plays reinforce a stereotyped ghetto image . . . in contrast to the variety and experimentation with forms and styles that Papp offers to White playwrights. . . .

He had hoped, Papp subsequently told the *Amsterdam News,* to see the rise of dozens of black theaters in America during the 1970s. Instead, major black acting and directing talents had been wooed away from New York by Hollywood, the recession had hampered the work of the Negro Ensemble Company and closed down the New Federal Theater. His own all-black *Cherry Orchard* may have inspired a Broadway trend of reviving white plays and musicals with all-black casts, but it had not fundamentally changed prospects for black theater people.

At the same time he was answering African-American critics, he was growing irritated with the white critics who, for many years, had been calling on him to establish a repertory company and national theater. Papp had toyed with the idea of a company for twenty-five years. In 1972, he outlined a $10 million plan for an American National Theater Service Agency, supported by government and foundation funds, which would tour serious new plays around the country, and received an $80,000 grant from the Rockefeller Foundation to explore the idea. By declaring his intent to "break into all that barrenness out there and to restore theater to its rightful place as a creative, social force in this country," he not only offended hundreds of regional and university theaters across the United States but contradicted himself. He knew that an American national theater was a fiscal impossibility and even doubted its worth. "Is the old-fashioned, old-world national theater, a highly structured, highly controlled theatrical institution, the proper instrument for a modern democracy?" he asked. "A national theater is a theater monopoly and like all monopolies . . . effectively destroys new movements which flourish best in a wide-ranging competitive milieu. It is more consistent with our way of life to let every flower bloom."

In yet another development in 1978, Papp was once again infuriated by a problem he thought he had licked twenty years earlier. In February, American public television bought the British Broadcasting Company's complete cycle of Shakespeare's plays. They planned to broadcast them over six years with $3.6 million in American corporate support. Initially, the Corporation for Public Broadcasting had planned to contribute $1.2 million of that money but had been forced to withdraw the grant after protests from American unions.

For Papp, it was as though his twenty-five years of producing American Shakespeare had made no difference at all. "Exxon's consistent support of high quality programming on Public Television deserves the gratitude of all Americans," he wrote to the corporation's president.

> It is most unfortunate, therefore, that the present arrangement makes no provision for meaningful participation by the United States in the producing of the Shakespeare canon. More serious than the loss of jobs (the unintentional, yet painful blow to the pride of American performers and technicians) is the damaging notion a six year series of only British Shakespeare on American Public Broadcasting will have on our young people — the notion that Shakespeare speaks only with a British accent.
>
> Americans have a rich tradition in Shakespeare. It was as commonplace in the last century for American actors to appear in Shakespearean roles on the British stage as it was for British actors to tour here. Some of the great Shakespearean actors of the 19th century were Americans. . . .
>
> In a jointly sponsored program with each country providing half of the 36 plays of Shakespeare we would have the extraordinary opportunity for an unprecedented Anglo-American cultural alliance. . . . There is still time for all parties concerned to re-evaluate the unilateral agreement and explore the means to convert it into a formidable cultural

alliance. . . . I would appreciate discussing this matter further with Exxon. . . .

To the head of New York's PBS affiliate, Papp wrote a letter that expressed his feelings in a more characteristic style. WNET had asked Papp to consult on a series of "wrap-around" programs that would use American actors to introduce the thirty-six BBC productions. "I am struck dumb," Papp replied.

I simply cannot believe that you people are serious. . . . How can you in good conscience dare to suggest that outstanding American performers you name, such talents as George C. Scott, Colleen Dewhurst, Julie Harris, Meryl Streep, James Earl Jones, Estelle Parsons, Ruby Dee, Roberta Maxwell, Zoe Caldwell, all of whom have played major Shakespearean roles with our own and other fine companies in the United States, relegate their function to that of "storyteller" of Shakespeare and not performer of Shakespeare? What sort of thinking goes on in your organization! . . .

Having produced and directed some 62 Shakespeare productions (35 in the canon) and presented them on mobile units in the ghettos, in trade schools, in the parks and in prisons, we have a pretty good idea how a well-produced work of Shakespeare makes itself thoroughly understood. . . .

Please inform your Manager for Children's Program Development that there will be no need to telephone me "later in the week" for consultation. I am available, however, to consult with you and others on a reciprocal exchange of Shakespearean TV productions with BBC and offer my services to this end,

Sincerely,
Joseph Papp

As usual, Papp turned to the press for support but this time he did not get it. Both the *New York Times* and the *Post* came out in favor of the BBC and the *Voice* wrote that Papp had a "Garibaldi complex." The corporate sponsors were angry that Papp had gone to the press without notifying them first; PBS, that Papp was intruding on their internal affairs. In the face of no support, Papp began to think about a creative response. What better way to form the repertory company that critics had been calling for than around Shakespeare? And what could be more American than a company comprised of blacks?

Just as Papp was asking those questions, British director Michael

Langham called to inform Papp he was leaving the Guthrie Theater. Papp
had admired Langham since the 1950s, when he traveled to Stratford,
Ontario, to see Shakespeare Festival productions and often had dinner at
the director's home. A slight, self-effacing man with a reputation for wit
and great charm, Langham was a major figure in the theater world. Like
Brooks Atkinson, his extra-theatrical life was as impressive as his work. "I
had," as Langham put it, "the peculiar honor of being the first British
officer captured in the *Blitzkrieg*. Prison camp was my university. I spent
two years trying to escape, digging tunnels, et cetera. Then gave it up as
a useless activity and started putting on plays before a truly captive
audience. The plays we did really affected people. It stopped some from
committing suicide. I knew then that I wanted to do theater. And plays
that made a better world."

When a reporter once asked Papp whom he would choose to portray
him onstage, the producer replied, "Michael Langham. . . . He's very
gentle, almost fragile, very English, with a subtle kind of smile, very
sweet. He's nothing like me at all, just the opposite. But I have another
side." Papp knew that his idea of an all-black company would appeal to
Langham's social conscience and he saw the audacity of pairing the
director's classic British approach with what he had always regarded as
the rawness and energy of American actors. He asked Langham to lead
a three-month-long workshop to train what he hoped would become a
world-class company of color. "I had never lived in New York before,"
said Langham, "and the idea of getting to know it through its minorities
appealed to me. My wife was to do a play in New York, which made it
very convenient domestically. We agreed to go ahead."

Papp proposed the company work on *A Midsummer Night's Dream*
and *The Merchant of Venice*. Langham proposed two plays about the
nature of governing and leadership, *Julius Caesar* and *Coriolanus*. "I was
going to do it for three months," he recalled. "A workshop with text
work, speech and voice work, movement, combat. I thought it would be
a chance to share something I loved with people from a very different
background from my own and for them to make it their own."

Auditions were held in August. The concept was enlarged to include
Hispanic actors and to guarantee six months' employment. The company
would develop its own apprenticeship program for producing, technical
and administrative staff — all drawn from minority groups.

Why now? Papp was asked. Because a national theater cannot be
created in the United States without the minorities, he told his trustees.
Minorities had become, Papp pointed out, politically powerless in New
York. "When I see that situation," he said, "I, as a white person, feel

threatened — because powerlessness leads to frustration. . . . This is not an act of liberalism at all. I hate it. I don't like 'integration' on the stage because what you get is tokenism. Real integration comes from power, when there is equal justice, equal opportunity, not 'token' opportunity. . . . If you form a fine company that has its own excellence . . . that, to me, is integration. I don't expect the theater to solve the problems of society, but if the theater can stand as a symbol, that such a company can exist and even begin to represent this country — that symbol is not an abstraction, it's very real."

From the start, relations between the white English director and the black/Hispanic company were tense. "It was a very druggy period," Langham recalled. "The company as a whole was wonderful but some of the leading actors were highly erratic and utterly unprofessional. The same people were late to every rehearsal and I was very frustrated. I used to dread going to rehearsals where we'd go over and over the same scene and not get any further. Meanwhile, Joe was getting very excited. He had stereotyped ideas about English people and, one day, when he saw me sobbing my eyes out in the tent scene of *Caesar* — he thought Englishmen were cold and never showed their emotions — he decided we were doing great work."

Julius Caesar later opened to mixed reviews. "There are some thrilling moments in the production," noted the *Times,* "but the fundamental handicap that weighs the production down is its speech. . . . It is not a matter of calling for British accents; it is that the performers' diction lacks, in clarity, variety, and force, what is required by Shakespeare's rhetoric." Langham agreed. "I think Joe was a great romantic," he later said. "I felt I was doing a disservice to these actors, shoving them up onstage before they were ready. But Joe said I was too close to it. It was new to me and I thought: 'Maybe he's right.' He had a childlike enthusiasm that was a tremendously infectious gift but it denied him the perception of the reality. The project became high profile and that was not a good thing. It had a tremendous effect on people's nerves. I knew that some actors with large parts were to be thrown to the lions because they were not up to it." When *Coriolanus* opened, John Simon wrote, "To have a group of black and Hispanic actors, almost totally untrained in Shakespearean acting, do *Julius Caesar* was rashness and folly. To have them do *Coriolanus* ranks as advanced dementia."

By the time that review appeared, Papp had announced that not only was he committing $1.2 million to his black/Hispanic Shakespeare company but inviting in Asian-American actors and calling it the Third World Company. "It is radical today to say to the world at large that we are doing Shakespeare," he said. "I was very much worried that I'd be doing a disservice to the people on the stage, but it began to get better. We knew before *Coriolanus* opened that we had a very strong company.

"Next year, the two plays we are proposing [are] *Mother Courage* and *A Midsummer Night's Dream,* which I feel would give a lot of women the chance to act. . . . We are creating a major company in the United States. It would be ironic in this country to have as its first national theater a multi-colored, multi-racial, multi-national acting company of first-rate quality. I'd love to see that irony. There is going to be an extraordinary amount of fund-raising necessary for us to keep the thing alive. But I suspect that we will obtain the support that we need."

Papp was unable to persuade Michael Langham, who had only committed to a three-month workshop, to continue with the Third World Company. Neither the press nor the funding organizations supported the project and the group — which had included actors Morgan Freeman, Denzel Washington, Gloria Foster and Michelle Shay — disbanded. Associate producer Bernard Gersten later said he had no memory of Papp's preoccupation with it at all. That summer, while Papp was conceiving it, Gersten was focused on a very different kind of project: director Michael Bennett's upcoming musical *Ballroom.*

After *A Chorus Line,* Michael Bennett had cast about for a new project, settling on a reworking of *Queen of the Stardust Ballroom,* a television drama about a widow who finds a new life at a local dance hall. It featured veteran dancers who had retired from the stage and was sentimental in a way that grated on Papp. It was also, he said, a "commercial" show designed for Broadway. After hearing excerpts from the musical, Papp told Bennett he was not excited by the project.

Bennett said he understood. *A Chorus Line* had made the choreographer/director a millionaire who could develop any project he wished to develop by himself. He had bought a building a few blocks away from the Public and was constructing a theater modeled after the Newman, in which he had developed *A Chorus Line.* He had no lack of potential investors in another production.

Bernard Gersten, however, felt that the Festival should coproduce *Ballroom* and tried to bring both Bennett and Papp around to his point of view. Gersten had overseen *A Chorus Line*'s three companies and was close to the choreographer. He was also well aware of Papp's practice of sending his playwrights opening-night notes inviting them to come to the Public with their next play and even "fail" there anytime. "I saw us blowing away an artistic resource," Gersten would later say. "Michael was our star director. Michael gave us *A Chorus Line,* the thing that preserved the Festival. For us not to maintain the alliance was crazy. For us to be judgmental or subjective about *Ballroom* was crazy. We blew zillions on *Leaf People,* and for Michael we didn't have room?"

Gersten was sure that Papp was miffed because Bennett had planned *Ballroom* by himself: "Michael didn't come before Joe, pull his forelock and say, 'Please, Father Joe, let me come to the Public and do this.' Instead, it was as though the son was saying to the father: 'Look — whose dick is bigger?' — and Joe didn't love it."

Gersten had, by then, worked eighteen years as Papp's associate producer. It was thirty years since they had first met at the Actors' Lab. Gersten had become Papp's closest colleague and he was devoted to his job. "The reason Joe and I were together as long as we were is that I never wanted to be Joe," Gersten would later say. "I expressed myself through Joe. I tried to sustain him, support him. There are people who need to be CEOs and there are people who need to be sustainers. I got Joe to perform — *that* was my creative activity. I viewed myself as his handler in the boxing sense of that term. The boxer is in the ring and the handler pours water on his head, rubs his stomach, and whispers in his ear between the rounds. Tells him where the openings are. I tried to steer him in the right direction."

The relationship between the two men had been closer in the earlier days of the Festival — before Gersten married and became the father of two children and before Papp became involved romantically with Gail Merrifield. As he grew older, Papp became more and more demanding of his staffers' time. Many of them all but lived at the theater and one of the rare directors who seemed to be able to be on call for Papp at all hours was Wilford Leach. Leach, who was directing both Central Park productions that summer, was a tall, scholarly man, with the southern manners of his native Virginia. He was born into a poor and, his friends suspected, abusive family and chose theater as a career while in college. Since 1958, he had been teaching at Sarah Lawrence, where he became a tenured professor, writing plays and working regularly at Café LaMama. There, Leach later recalled, "directing the play often meant painting the set and building it and begging someone to help you. And for me, it was easier to do it than to beg somebody to do it."

Papp had called Leach in 1975, asking him to direct Shakespeare at the Delacorte, but Leach turned him down: He had heard how difficult it was to work as a director for Papp, he was uninterested in directing Shakespeare and did not know how. Papp replied that he would teach him how and asked Leach to be his summer assistant on *Henry V* at the Delacorte in 1976. Later that year, Papp asked him to direct part of

Wallace Shawn's *A Thought in Three Parts*, then Machiavelli's *The Mandrake*, which enjoyed a critical success and launched Shawn's acting career. Then Leach directed four successive Shakespeares.

Ultimately Wilford Leach left his teaching position of twenty years to become the Festival's principal director. "He gave up everything for Joe," recalled Wally Shawn, who became Leach's close friend. "I thought he was a fantastic writer but instead of working on his plays, he became totally obsessed with creating a hit for Joe to save the Public Theater. He wouldn't hear anything critical of Joe. He loved Joe and Gail. This was his family. He was like a son in a traditional family in India."

Papp saw in Leach, as he had seen in Andrei Serban, a professional equal. He was grateful that Leach worked out problems without his help, that he prepared and cast brilliantly, designed his shows himself and even built his own models. He also valued Leach's quiet, accepting manner. "Wil was so quiet that most people never paid attention to him," said Shawn. "He made no attempt to be noticed. He was a God-like human being whose entire life was based on the affection he had for other people and virtually the only person I've ever met whose conversation was completely unpredictable." Rosemarie Tichler felt, "You could trust him with the deepest part of your soul, be totally exposed and safe in the knowledge that he would never hurt you." Others, like playwright Ntozake Shange, could not understand what Papp saw in the intellectual, often silent Europe-oriented director.

Just as Gersten and Papp's relationship owed a lot to compatibility and a playfulness that grew out of their twenties, the producer's relationship to Leach grew out of the concerns of his later years. "Joe really listened to Wil," recalled Gail Merrifield. "And since Wil had run La Mama, he empathized with Joe and understood better than anyone else what he was up against. He was extremely calm. He liked to listen to Joe's ideas, and he was also very tolerant. He did not try to win arguments but would say he was more interested in getting things done. He worked long hours. He seemed to have no private life. For the first time, Joe felt he could actually leave the theater for a few days or weeks and it would be in good hands."

During the spring of 1978, Papp — for the first time since the founding of the Festival — had decided to involve himself in a project outside the Public Theater. The owner of the SoHo cabaret The Ballroom had heard Papp sing at a benefit and asked him to put together a nightclub act. Papp was at first reluctant to perform but by June was working with composer Stanley Silverman and director Craig Zadan, choosing, learning and rehearsing a full evening of songs.

In the meanwhile, another project was being planned without his knowledge.

After attending memorial services for two Festival actors earlier that year, Bernard Gersten had been pondering the custom of honoring a person's life only after he or she was dead. "If you're going to honor someone," he told actress Irene Worth, "you should do it while they're still alive." Worth and Gersten discussed a loving celebration of Papp, whose fifty-seventh birthday was in June. With members of the Festival board and staff, they began to plan a huge surprise party in Central Park. Gersten asked playwright John Guare to write a short play and the Festival's Casting Department to cast it. (The players included Chris Sarandon, Edward Herrmann, Carol Kane and Meryl Streep.) The Festival sent out one thousand invitations to a surprise party at the Delacorte, including invitations to the city's mayor and three former mayors. An honorary committee of prominent cultural figures, ranging from playwright Lillian Hellman to actor Al Pacino, was named. Gersten arranged for director Mike Nichols to introduce the evening, for performed segments from *Hair, Much Ado, A Chorus Line, Runaways* and others from the Festival's 267 productions, for a telephone hookup with George C. Scott from California, for all his favorite playwrights and performers to be there. He persuaded chairman of the board LuEsther Mertz to serve as a decoy by inviting Papp to a small birthday party that evening at nine. And he assumed it would not be a problem to get Papp, who rarely left the city during the week, to the Delacorte.

The producer, however, had decided to take his birthday week off in the country with his wife. "We were both exhausted and looking forward to a week of rest," Merrifield later recalled. "The next morning, it was a beautiful day and Bernie called. He explained the scope of the event and told me the task I had: to get Joe back into the city. He told me he had already spoken to the children, who had presents ready for Joe and would appear at the apartment dressed for LuEsther's surprise party.

"Joe and I did not lie to each other and now I had to participate in this ruse. It was a *fait accompli*. No one had involved me in the planning and the reason probably was that they knew the whole thing would strike me as improper. I didn't know how to lie to Joe. It was not a pleasant thing to contemplate. I thought it was outrageous to use me in this way. But I felt trapped. Elaborate preparations had been made, involving the mayors and dignitaries of all kinds. It put me in a terrible state."

Merrifield told Papp that he was expected that evening at a surprise party at Le Poulailler, an expensive uptown restaurant, and Papp, who had just begun to unwind, went into a rage. It was *his* birthday. *He* wanted to be in the country, alone. The last thing he wanted was to drive back to the city to eat in a crowded restaurant. Merrifield tried to stay calm. Papp remained furious all day and during the drive back to Manhattan, where he angered his children by refusing to open presents.

As the Papps were dressing for Le Poulailler, two thousand invited guests streamed into the Delacorte Theater, where they were filmed by a documentary film crew that had been recording all the preparations. Each was given a gourmet picnic basket from Zabar's and a bottle of wine. While they were eating, the second part of the ruse was activated. An actress in *All's Well That Ends Well* telephoned Papp and said there was an emergency — actress Pamela Reed had just walked out on the production.

"I don't want to talk to you," Papp replied. "Let me talk to the director. Put Wil Leach on the line. And you tell Pamela I want her to stay there until I get there." Wilford Leach, who was as uneasy as Merrifield about lying to Papp, asked the producer to hurry to the Delacorte. Two thousand people eating their dinner heard him say — over the speakers broadcasting the conversation — that he would be there soon.

Papp hung up the telephone and told his family that before going to La Poulailler, they were going to the Delacorte. "There was a lot of yelling and shouting and bad humor. The kids were feeling hostile because Joe refused to deal with their presents and I was emotionally wrecked," Merrifield said. "That's the mood we were all in when we got into the car and drove up to Central Park."

Gersten had planted scouts with two-way radios to warn them of Papp's arrival. When, at last, the disgruntled producer came onto the darkened stage, the house lights came up, and two thousand people yelled "Happy Birthday!" and "Surprise!" Papp made a few sputtering remarks: "Oh Jesus Christ! . . . Oh my God . . . I hadn't the remotest idea. . . . It's great to have this in your own lifetime — no posthumous recognition." Then he was conducted to his seat and the entertainment — all filmed by a movie crew which was documenting the party — began.

Mike Nichols served as master of ceremonies. He had asked Gersten, "How rough can I get?" Gersten had replied, "You get first cut. Draw first blood." Now, he opened the show by asking, "Were you really surprised? If Gail really kept this from you, I would worry seriously. I've been asked to be brief and to keep this as much as possible from seeming like a bar mitzvah or a memorial service. . . . Joe doesn't do this all for money, he does it for the sheer love of naked power."

Three mayors — John Lindsay, Abraham Beame and Ed Koch — spoke, with Koch saying, "For me, Joe Papp is Mr. New York," and

Papp and Gail Merrifield, October 1976 *(Chester Higgins, Jr.)*

Irene Worth and George Voskovec in Andrei Serban's production of *The Cherry Orchard* at Lincoln Center *(George E. Joseph)*

A Chorus Line (Martha Swope)

Liv Ullmann and Sam Waterston in *A Doll's House* at Lincoln Center *(George E. Joseph)*

Inmates of Miguel Piñero's *Short Eyes* *(Friedman-Abeles)*

Papp with Michael Bennett and dancers at rehearsal *(Martha Swope)*

(*From L to R*) Rex Smith, Linda Ronstadt and Kevin Kline in *The Pirates of Penzance,* 1981 (*Martha Swope*)

Morgan Freeman and Gloria Foster in *Coriolanus,* 1979 (*George E. Joseph*)

(*From L to R*) Kathleen Quinlan, Meryl Streep, Elizabeth Wilson, Colleen Dewhurst and Dixie Carter in Tom Babe's *Taken in Marriage (Martha Swope)*

Elizabeth Swados and the company of *Runaways,* 1978 (*Martha Swope*)

Papp and his son on his twentieth birthday, 1981 *(Papp Estate)*

Papp (with bullhorn) rallying protesters to block Godzilla's destruction of the Morosco Theater, March 1982 *(Martha Swope)*

Papp personal
advertisement for a
Festival show, 1984 *(Paul
Davis)*

Papp visiting Václav Havel while the
playwright was under house arrest in
Czechoslovakia in 1984 *(Papp Estate)*

Danitra Vance and
Vickilyn Reynolds in
George C. Wolfe's *The
Colored Museum*, 1986
(Martha Swope)

Festival Latino poster
(Paul Davis)

(*From L to R*) Larry
Kramer, Joel Grey,
Michael Lindsay-Hogg
and Papp rehearsing *The
Normal Heart*, 1985
(Martha Swope)

Papp on the steps of the Capitol during 1972 antiwar protest *(Sheldon Ramsdell)*

Opposite, above: Papp's Playwrights *(L to R)* Tom Babe, Miguel Piñero, Dennis Reardon, Michael Weller and John Ford Noonan, at the Booth Theater *(Friedman-Abeles)*

Opposite, below: The second Broadway company of Ntozake Shange's *for colored girls (Martha Swope)*

Merle Debuskey and Papp at press conference, 1975 *(Barry Kramer/Abeles Studio)*

Ellen Greene and Raul Julia in *Threepenny Opera (George E. Joseph)*

Papp and his daughter
Barbara Mosser *(Barbara Mosser)*

(From L to R) Joe Papp,
Kevin Kline, Elizabeth
Mastrantonio and director
Wilford Leach, 1984 *(Papp Estate)*

(Clockwise) Al Pacino,
Edward Herrmann,
Martin Sheen and John
McMartin in Shakespeare
Marathon's 1988 *Julius
Caesar (Martha Swope)*

Papp and George C. Wolfe
in Warsaw, May 1989
(George C. Wolfe)

Papp in his office, 1986
(Eric Kroll)

Papp and playwright
David Rabe, 1989 *(Papp
Estate)*

Kathleen Widdoes and
Diane Venora as Gertrude
and Hamlet, 1982
(Martha Swope)

(*From L to R*) Vet Tom Bird, Gary Beikirch and Papp at Vietnamese orphanage outside Saigon, 1982 *(Robert Holcomb)*

Peter Francis James and Kevin Kline in Papp's 1990 production of *Hamlet (Martha Swope)*

Papp and JoAnne
Akalaitis, 1991 (*Martha
Swope*)

Papp and Emmett Foster
protesting NEA obscenity
restrictions (*Joe
Communale*)

Lindsay repeating one of the producer's favorite jokes: "It's very easy to compare New York to Los Angeles. Last July, when it was 104 degrees in New York, it was 82 degrees in Los Angeles. Last January, when it was 4 degrees in New York, it was 82 degrees in Los Angeles. There are 40,000 interesting people in New York and 82 in Los Angeles."

The authors of *Hair* sang "Aquarius." There were numbers from *Two Gents*, *Runaways* and *I'm Getting My Act Together*, as well as a video of James Earl Jones performing *Lear* beamed onstage. A telephone was brought to Papp's seat so that he could take a call from actor George C. Scott in California. "It was sensational," said press agent Merle Debuskey. "We organized a major extravaganza out of Joe's office and managed to conceal it from him. Two thousand people were sitting in the dark with sparklers, quiet, waiting for a signal. When Joe walked into the Delacorte, he didn't realize anyone was there. Everybody was in heaven. Joe seemed to be having a wonderful time."

Then Bernard Gersten took the microphone. Few of the assembled crowd, he said, had ever spent a day in Papp's office. John Guare had written a play showing what it was like. In it, an irate gun-wielding subscriber burst into the office, demanding to see Papp, and the producer summoned Bernard Gersten to die in his place. Gail Merrifield sat in the producer's lap sucking her thumb and, when an Eskimo playwright with a new script appeared, sank to the playwright's feet, exclaiming about the wonders of a new minority to showcase.

The *Times* called it "the best in-house story ever told." Guare later said that everyone at the Festival congratulated him. "'Finally somebody's told it exactly like it is' was what they said. Everybody adored it. It was authentic. I felt the glee of belonging to a family." Many members of the audience found the playlet brilliant and uproarious. Others found it insensitive and in poor taste.

Tony and Miranda Papp were appalled. "Gail, you should *leave*," Tony Papp advised his stepmother, who was in tears. When Gersten asked that they present the birthday cake to their father, they refused. Papp himself was stunned by the party. His face, as caught by the movie cameras, is youthful, handsome, unguarded, vulnerable. "This is the most overwhelming thing I've ever seen," he said, when he finally addressed the audience. "I've done a lot of shows in my life and I'll tell you — I don't know how Bernie did this. I could never do it. I thought I was pretty good but the sheer *accomplishment* of this show just stuns me. I would say: Bernie Gersten, you are really a genius. I've known that man for almost all of my life. And he's a dear friend and a very fine person. I appreciate him tonight very much. . . ."

Casting director Rosemarie Tichler found herself feeling frightened. "He was so on the edge," she recalled. "I was sitting there with my brother who's a psychotherapist and both of us felt that there, in front of two thousand people, you were watching Joe in the process of working through his conflicting emotions."

"The relationships here are very deep and very personal," Papp said. "Do I really know so many people? Yes, I know every one of these people and I have a special feeling for each of them. . . . I'm not just in the *theah*-tah — I'm interested in articulating a feeling or an idea that is provocative, challenging, that makes you feel glad to be alive. . . . I stand by what I do because that's me. . . . I want to give you back what you've given me. You've given me a tremendous feeling tonight and I'm very pleased I was here to be part of this extraordinary gathering."

The evening ended without incident, but after Papp returned to his country house in Katonah, he began to reflect. "I slowly began to realize that the thing had been done under my nose, without me knowing it, and that money had been spent without my approval," he later told an interviewer. "At the center of all this was Bernie Gersten. He had been in a position to 'protect' me from anything that would be annoying or disturbing, things he felt I didn't have to hear about. You know, when you get too protected, suddenly you are protected from things you should know about. And this party became to me an amazing display of that. How could something on this enormous scale have been perpetrated without me knowing? I thought, 'That's the way revolutions are made or governments are overthrown.'"

Bernard Gersten would remember that night as one of his greatest accomplishments. "The party was just glorious," he later said. "I have never been so congratulated. Joe said most people don't have anything like this until they die. It was my purpose to celebrate Joe while he was alive! There were four mayors there — *four mayors!*" The press was there too. They billed the event as "New York's biggest surprise birthday party," with some reporters noting that the extravaganza was "the first New York Shakespeare Festival show not produced by Joseph Papp" and "financed by profits from *A Chorus Line*, no doubt."

People who knew Papp well anticipated that he would not appreciate a birthday extravaganza, particularly when it cost thousands of dollars. General manager Robert Kamlot saw in his employer "this tremendous ambivalence. On the one hand, he was very moved. Here were all these people and all these segments from his shows. On the other, he was made out to be Gail's puppet. And he had to wonder: 'How is it that someone in my employ could have mobilized all my resources without my knowledge? Who approved the outlay of cash?'"

For most of the next month, Gersten kept irritating Papp by urging him to coproduce *Ballroom*. Papp kept vacillating. "It's a humanistic show," he later told an interviewer. "It's being done by a highly skillful artist. We've had a relationship before. If someone said, 'Oh then you're just doing it for the money?' I would reply 'Well, are you giving us money to survive?' I went through all of that and then said, 'I'm doing it for the wrong reasons. I don't care if it would be the biggest hit ever. I don't identify deeply enough with the play even though it's going to be a very marvelous production. I'm doing it for a money reason, a reason other than the reasons I do things for.' . . . I think the greatest integrity people have is when they really want to go the other way for their own selfish reasons . . . and they're able to turn around. That, to me, takes tremendous integrity. . . . You know, you have only one thing and it's yourself." Papp finally told Gersten that coproducing *Ballroom* violated the nature of the Festival and that he would not do it.

Although Gersten's long relationship with Papp had always been characterized by vigorous arguments over theatrical matters, Gersten had always bowed to Papp's final decision. This time, he challenged Papp head-on. He asked Papp to let him work on *Ballroom* for four months while remaining associate producer of the Festival. Papp dug his heels in and refused. When Gersten said he planned to do so regardless, Papp became convinced that Gersten was asking to be fired.

On August 25, the producer met with the board's executive committee to discuss the situation; two days later, with Stanley Lowell, his oldest adviser. On August 28, he fired Gersten.

"Why did Joe fire me? Sixteen years later, I'm not quite certain," Gersten, managing director of Lincoln Center theater later said. "The shock of being fired was and remains the worst trauma of my life. At a stroke, I was cut off from an organization that I had loved and nurtured for eighteen years. I wasn't just an employee of the Festival — I was Joe's best friend, his confidant, his alter ego. I had walked him on the night streets of London when he woke up sweating with his heart pounding, disoriented from being in a foreign hotel. I had held his son Michael in my arms thirty years before and calmed him on my stomach when he was colicky. I had been at Joe's side for eighteen years, at his side but one step behind to make sure he had the spotlight to himself. I counseled him, I comforted him, I laughed at his jokes and played word games with him. I don't think I could have been more devoted to the Festival than I was and I knew that the Festival *was* Joe and Joe was the Festival.

"At first, Joe asked me to stay on for a couple of weeks for an orderly transfer of my work to undesignated others. But when I arrived the day after he fired me, Joe said I should pack my personal stuff and leave immediately. I emptied my desk drawers, took my rolodex and my old typewriter and within half an hour walked out of the Public Theater for the last time as Joe's erstwhile partner, sidekick and the good cop of the outfit.

"I felt like a live-in mate suddenly turned out of house, home and family. Joe retained everything: the Public Theater, the staff, the work, *A Chorus Line*. I was expunged from the Festival past like some road company Trotsky. Joe even removed my name as associate producer of *A Chorus Line* from the program and billboard at the theater and it was only after a protest by me and others that he restored my billing.

"There was also the matter of supporting myself and my family. I had two young kids, eight and nine. The Festival had been my life's work for eighteen years. The prospect of finding a new life's work was daunting. My sense of loss, my sorrow at being separated from the Festival, which I loved beyond reason, was near devastating. Although I had some knowledge of Joe's capability to behave heartlessly, I couldn't believe that he would have turned against me."

General manager Robert Kamlot was on vacation in Ireland. "It was my thirtieth wedding anniversary," he recalled. "I was in a little town of about six people and I don't know how Joe found me. He said, 'Kamlot, this is Joe Papp. I just fired Bernie Gersten and you better come home.'

"I explained I had to return my car in London. He said, 'All right. Take the rest of your vacation.' The rest of my vacation was a disaster. I couldn't stop thinking about what had happened. His best friend. Bernie and Joe were best friends since the forties. How could he fire him? Bernie was a friend of mine. I didn't want to move into his office. I thought Bernie was unreasonable not to ask for a leave of absence. And Joe was unreasonable not to give him one. But Joe could not stand multiple allegiances. He did not want to share Bernie with Michael."

Merle Debuskey tried to persuade Papp to change his mind. So did others. The press was as intrigued by the break as Festival veterans. "Can Papp run the festival alone?" asked the *Washington Post*. "Can the two be reconciled? Will Gersten come back?" The *SoHo Weekly News* quoted an anonymous source who said: "The deep truth is that the working relationship between Bernie and Joe could no longer exist. People change and grow. People move on and at this point Bernie was ready to move on. . . . In effect the Shakespeare Festival would have been the presenter of a big commercial Broadway musical. It's against the grain, intent, purpose and thrust of the Festival to be presenters."

"It was terribly mishandled," Rosemarie Tichler would later recall. "Joe made no statement to us about firing Bernie. Some of the staff found out when they read the papers. But it was not a total surprise. From the moment I got there, I sensed there were two camps: Bernie's camp and Joe's camp. It was benign, under wraps, with no outward hostility, and Joe, of course, assumed everybody was working for *him*. But I felt Bernie treated Joe as a child — a brilliant child with wonderful ideas — but a child. Later, I understood that Bernie's way of dealing with Joe's ego was by 'handling' him."

Reading the story in Florida, former general manager David Black remembered a memo he had once typed while the Festival was still at the Great Northern Hotel. "I had addressed it to Joe, Bernie and Hilmar, from myself," he said. "Joe called me in and made it clear that he did not wish to be included in a memo addressed to all of them equally. He always had a sense of himself as apart. He was the Festival. The rest of us were employees."

In October, Papp told his board that he had had no choice but to fire Gersten. "Bernie said he would not abide by my decision and it was very clear he would have to resign or be fired. He refused to resign. This is not a democratic institution where everybody has an equal vote. I have to run the organization the way I think best."

EIGHTEEN

Out of Sync

As 1980 began, Joseph Papp was holding down the jobs of two people. Where every other large theater in America was headed by an artistic director and a managing director, both appointed by a board of directors, he presided, alone, over what had grown to a multimillion-dollar institution. He was still a man totally identified with his theater, a workaholic who slept barely five hours a night and had not taken a vacation for several years. But people who knew him well noticed that as the New York Shakespeare Festival entered its fourth decade, he was in crisis.

Although on a good day Papp could look twenty years younger than he was, he would soon turn sixty and was troubled by a variety of ailments. His blood pressure had risen so high that his doctor put him on a strict diet. His stomach gave him so much trouble that, in an effort to make light of it, he wrote Gail Merrifield a memo:

> By nature and habit, I am most effective when I am dancing on the edge of a precipice, emotionally that is. I am not a thrill-seeker in a physical sense; I fear heights, though they sometimes exhilarate me. . . .

My greatest terror is obliteration, falling into the dark, bottomless pit; yet I fall into it because I must know, for my life's sake (ache) that there is a bottom. The pendulum swing is wide — from the Apocalypse to the Messiah and the pendulum is made of flesh and bone, my own. . . . To find the external truth of my life, or better, to understand its impact on me, I must, as it were, throw myself into myself, as in a pot of strange shape and qualities, bury it all under hot sand, turning it to bubbling lava, encase it in a glacier, in short, an upset stomach.

In 1980, Papp stepped off a New York City curb and tore a ligament in his calf that took months to heal. He exercised his leg with an iron boot, then acquired a bicycle, a rowing machine and finally a Universal gym, installing them all in his living room and working out with a personal trainer. In January 1981, without warning, the producer's right eyelid began to droop and within a day, the right side of his face was entirely paralyzed. His doctor diagnosed it as Bell's Palsy. Within two weeks, the producer had recovered, but the experience shook him. He reminded Gail Merrifield that his father, Samuel Papirofsky, had died at seventy-two and began to allude to his "genetic inheritance."

The power of biological ties had been on Joseph Papp's mind since the fall of 1979, when the daughter he had never met — a thirty-four-year-old nurse with his own dark eyes, thick hair and slim, erect figure — had appeared in his office. As far back as Barbara Mosser could remember, she had asked about her biological father.

Her mother, the nurse named Irene Ball with whom Joe Papirofsky had had a wartime navy romance, thought it best to keep Barbara ignorant of the details. She had not tried to contact Papp since 1945, when she wrote him a letter informing him of her pregnancy — a letter that never reached him. Over the years, she had collected news clippings about the successful producer, secreting them away in a drawer, keeping her memories of Joe Papirofsky to herself. Only when Barbara was hospitalized at the age of sixteen and doctors needed to know her family medical history had she telephoned Papp to find out his blood type.

"My maternal grandfather once told me that my mother had been very young when she first married and that shortly after, she had gone into the navy where she met a man who was also married at the time and that I was a product of that relationship," Barbara Mosser later recalled. "My grandfather did not know where my father was, but thought he had something to do with producing — possibly out in Hollywood. He did not know his name. So one piece of the puzzle fell into place: I was illegitimate."

Barbara Mosser never told her mother what her grandfather had told her. She grew up with a stepfather with whom she rarely felt safe, married a career army officer who had served in Korea and Vietnam, had children of her own and was posted with her family to a series of military bases. The Mossers were living in Alaska when, in 1979, Irene Ball was diagnosed with cancer. "We flew to Virginia to be with her," Mosser said. "We were up in her bedroom and she asked me to sit down. Then she asked, 'Would you like to know about your real father?' She walked over to her top dresser drawer and pulled out old newspaper clippings and *Playbills*, spread them out on the bed where I was sitting and said: 'This is your father.'

"In all the scenarios I had conjured up in my mind over the years, not one included a man as well known as my father. I had seen *A Chorus Line* in Washington, D.C. I couldn't believe what I was reading and hearing: They had met in the navy. They lived together in an apartment off base. According to my mother, this was a once-in-a-lifetime relationship. She wanted me to understand that they both wanted me. However, through some circumstance still unclear to me, my father was shipped out before my mother had a chance to tell him she was pregnant.

"My first question was: 'Can I see him?' After a little searching, we were able to get the phone number for the Public Theater. I got up from the bed and stood next to her as she dialed. I remember her saying, 'Would you like to see her?' and his answer: 'Of course I want to meet my daughter.' We took the train to New York and a cab from the train station to the Public Theater. I remember watching every face that walked by, wondering if it could be the one I had been looking for for so many years. Then he came in, we hugged and I started crying. My mother was telling me not to cry and my dad was saying, 'Let her.' One of the first things I verified was his blood type. No one else in my family had B positive blood, so I had to have gotten it from him. I remember saying how I wish I had found him sooner and he said something to me that I have never forgotten: He said the timing might not have been right any sooner, but the timing was right now. I loved him immediately."

During that first meeting between Papp and his daughter, the producer picked up the telephone and called her two children. "Hello, Michael, hello, Stephanie, this is your grandfather calling," he said, and invited them to New York for Christmas.

One year after meeting his grandchildren and third daughter, Papp's younger son graduated from boarding school. Tony had decided against going to college and installed himself in the bedroom he had vacated at age sixteen. The Papps, who had sent him away to school with reluctance, were glad to have him back and supportive of his decision not to attend college. "Joe had never gone to college," Gail Merrifield later said. "I had never finished. Neither of us felt college was going to be the ticket to his future. We wanted him to fulfill his artistic talents, find a direction, be happy and earn a living."

For two years, Tony Papp worked as a waiter and dishwasher in various Manhattan restaurants, without a clue as to what he would eventually do. He was clearly artistic, he loved all kinds of music and certain forms of modern art, but his tastes, like his father's, were very broad. The producer had talks with his son, told him he would finance any education he needed, just as he was financing Miranda's college education at Barnard. But, for what seemed a very long time, Tony did not know what he wanted to do. The most important component of his identity at that time was that he was a homosexual.

At fifteen, Tony Papp had raised the subject with his father. "He was terrified that he was gay and I said, 'Oh no, you're not,'" Papp later told an interviewer. "I wanted to deny it. It's easier to accept gay people who are not in your family than your own child."

Joseph Papp had entertained rather conventional hopes of seeing his son married with children of his own. A friend thought the producer's response prototypically Jewish: He realized that the son he adored would not carry on his name. "But Joe loved Tony so much there was nothing that could jeopardize that love," recalled Gail Merrifield. "He was upset. He blamed himself. He believed that cliché about homosexuality being the result of an absent father and a domineering mother. Even *I* sometimes worried whether there was something I had done to cause this or that I could have done something to make Tony happier. But I came to understand that Tony was born this way. The thing that bothered me was that he was cruising. I wouldn't have liked that in a heterosexual son. I don't think Joe approved of that at all. But the fact that Tony was living with us helped. We talked a lot and his relationship with Joe — after the madness that seems to strike American boys during adolescence — started to improve."

Tony Papp finally decided to follow up on his childhood interest in making artistic objects and entered the Parsons School of Design, specializing in jewelry and metallurgy. He moved into his own apartment in downtown Manhattan and fell in love with an older dancer in *A Chorus Line* with whom he remained for the next several years. Papp's daughter Susan gave birth to a son named Jonathan; his youngest daughter, Miranda, graduated from Barnard College. Although Papp would continue to help all his children with expenses — he paid Tony's apartment and studio rent until his death, for example — all five of his children were now grown.

Papp found the changes in his personal life easier to adjust to than the changes in the political and economic climate of the nation in the late 1970s and early 1980s. In New York, Edward Koch was now mayor. Across the United States, voters were about to elect Ronald Reagan, the most conservative American president since Herbert Hoover. One of the first proposals Reagan would make upon taking office was to cut the National Endowment for the Arts budget in half. One year earlier, Mayor Koch announced cuts in local funding for the arts.

New York City had been in severe financial straits since the mid-1970s, when legal measures were taken to ensure that the mayor balanced the municipal budget. The New York Shakespeare Festival, however, had continued to receive a steady subsidy for Free Shakespeare until Mayor Koch slashed $3.5 million from the Department of Cultural Affairs budget. With the mayor's announcement, the Festival's appropriation of $323,000 — which it had been receiving for five consecutive years — was eliminated. For Papp, this was not a matter merely of cash but of basic philosophy, a signal that "the bedrock of civic responsibility" on which he had built his theater was crumbling.

Other New York cultural leaders protested the cuts. Beverly Sills, director of the New York City Opera, joked publicly that she would have to take the mayor to lunch. The director of the Bronx Zoo warned: "You can't put a dust cloth on a giraffe the way you can on a statue. We will not run an animal slum." City cultural affairs commissioner Henry Geldzahler hastened to raise private funds and the New York Community Trust created an emergency Summer Arts Fund comprised of corporations such as Gulf + Western, Con Edison, American Express and Warner Communications. Geldzahler personally telephoned Papp to let him know that the Festival would be receiving its $323,000 from private sources and that the Festival would continue to be the largest recipient of program funds.

But while other cultural leaders made the best of a bad situation, Papp refused the money and took his case to the press. "I appreciate the offer from the Summer Arts Fund," he told reporters. "But if I took that money I would be letting the city off the hook and I have no intention of doing so." He was particularly furious at Ed Koch, the first mayor for whom he had actively campaigned and by whom he felt personally betrayed and abandoned. He sat down at his Remington Standard and typed out successive drafts of a statement he titled "Et Tu Ed?" and "The

Unkindest Cut of All." In it, he noted that by witholding city aid to Free Shakespeare for the first time in twenty years,

THE ADMINISTRATION HAS EMBARKED ON A LONG BACK-
WARD MARCH AND EARNED ITSELF THE DUBIOUS DIS-
TINCTION OF BEING THE FIRST IN THE LAST FOUR AD-
MINISTRATIONS TO UNDERMINE THE EXISTENCE OF THE
WORLD-RENOWNED CITY-BORN-AND-BRED FREE SHAKE-
SPEARE IN CENTRAL PARK. SOMEONE IS DELIVERING A
MESSAGE THAT THE CITY'S RELATIONSHIP TO ITS CUL-
TURAL RESOURCES IS NOT FUNDAMENTAL, NOT PRI-
MARY. . . . THE CONNECTION BETWEEN THE MUNICIPAL-
ITY AND THE ARTS, ITS MOST PRODUCTIVE ASSET, IS
CRUCIAL AND MUST ENDURE, PARTICULARLY IN TIMES
LIKE THESE AND PARTICULARLY IN NEW YORK CITY. . . .

The Summer Arts Fund was, Papp thought, a pool of private, privi-leged money, an elitist nineteenth-century way of funding the arts, in-stead of the twentieth-century — and socialist — way of using govern-ment funds that Papp had espoused since founding the Shakespeare Workshop. He was tired of repeating arguments he had made since the early 1950s. After testifying before the Board of Estimate, Papp com-plained, "It's demeaning. I hate begging for money. It's like going back to where I was many, many years ago when we were always about to go under."

The future of Free Shakespeare remained a matter of press comment for several months, but 1980 was not 1959. Public interest in Free Shakespeare was tepid compared to the furor Papp had generated by defying parks commissioner Robert Moses. One or two articles expressed outrage: "My grandfather got his education from the free public libraries of New York; my father graduated from the free City College of New York; and I became what I am because of free Shakespeare in the Park," wrote playwright Barbara Garson in the *Voice*. "Cutting free Shakespeare is cutting me out. It means my daughter can't enjoy the advantage I grew up with. It's saying that people like us aren't wanted in this city any more." But most New York cultural leaders adjusted to the cuts and expressed their sympathy with the mayor, saying that in a time of police, hospital and sanitation cutbacks, culture could not hope to be spared. There was little sympathy for and even criticism of Papp's strong stance. *New York* magazine noted: "Papp recently intimated that he might leave

New York if the Mayor doesn't restore his funding, but where would he go? Panama has a Shah."

Papp saw his situation as very different from a shah's. He had been obsessed with Festival finances since *A Chorus Line* profits began creating the impression that the Festival no longer had financial problems. Free Shakespeare in the Park — nearly twenty-five years old now — cost Papp $1.2 million every summer and generated no income. Although the Festival's reserve fund now contained $3 million, generating an annual income of about $300,000 per year, that sum was far from enough to secure his organization's financial base. "We're here to do things which cost money and produce very little revenue — that's the nature of the Festival," he told his board. "How many more years is *A Chorus Line* going to run? We're a fundraising organization, always have been, always should be, and there's something about the success of *ACL* that has somewhat depreciated that fact. We're glad successes happen from time to time but we can't live on that."

Once Papp understood that the city would not fund Free Shakespeare in 1980, he told his board that he would now try to obtain for the Festival its own line on the city budget for maintenance of its plant. The Brooklyn Academy of Music, he said, received "some $700,000 a year." In a letter to Commissioner Geldzahler, Papp wrote that he was willing to reverse the position he had held for years.

> Since the City, in its wisdom, has determined more or less that it is anxious to get out of the business of funding programs, we are prepared to accept this proposition and raise all the money required to produce the free performances from sources other than the City.

In exchange, he expected that the Festival be given its own line on the budget.

> We provide toilet paper, cleaning, ushers, light bulbs, soap, etc. We winterize the stage by painting and caulking. We pay for all repairs — we repair seats in the house when they break and we replace rotten flooring. We, in fact, pay for about everything. . . . In our mutual interest, Henry, I would appreciate you taking the necessary procedural steps to have the New York Shakespeare Festival placed on the City budget line.

In addition to adapting to changes in his political environment, Papp was trying to assess how his theater would fit into the changing American cultural scene of the 1980s. During the 1970s, audiences had reportedly grown for all the arts. Broadway attracted record numbers of people, the number of Shakespeare festivals in America had risen and the number of nonprofit theaters grew from 22 in 1960 to 270 in 1980. Where Papp had once been a lone voice calling for government subsidy for the arts, there were now many. In 1979 the National Endowment for the Arts gave out $150 million to artists. Some artists had become shrewd promoters, marketing their wares like businesspeople. Opera singers, musicians, dancers, poets as well as arts administrators now appeared regularly on television talk shows, pushing their products.

The status of contemporary playwrights had changed as well. Beginning in the 1970s, Playwrights Horizons, the Manhattan Theater Club and Circle Rep began producing new work, and many regional theaters also began producing new plays. "The Festival never acknowledged its growing competition," Rosemarie Tichler later said. "So that even as scripts kept pouring into our offices, a new generation of playwrights such as those coming out of Yale — Chris Durang, Wendy Wasserstein, Albert Innaurato — went elsewhere. There was no attempt to attract them to the Public."

Papp was not interested in producing most of the plays he saw coming out of the new generation of playwrights. He regarded them as "Brustein's playwrights," and saw them as minimally interested in the social issues that continued to constitute the core of Papp's theater. The number of African-American playwrights dropped, and there was little Papp could do about it. "There's no way you can command a play to be written," he said repeatedly. "You can finance someone, you can commission work, but that doesn't necessarily produce the play that is the work of our time. And neither can we know what our time really is. A producer depends on writers."

Writers were an extremely unreliable group. Some stopped writing. Others continued but produced work Papp did not wish to do. Some worked so slowly that Papp was lucky if he saw a play every two or three years. David Rabe spent two or three years rewriting. Some got fed up with trying to support their families as playwrights and went into other fields. "I've been feeling that my theater has not been as effective over the past couple of years as it should be," Papp said. "It's lost the energy of the late sixties. And I want to reach out to a bigger audience."

As Bernard Gersten had foreseen, Papp felt the loss of Lincoln Center's 1,100-seat theater. All the small theaters put together at the Public barely added up to 1,100 seats, limiting audience size, limiting ticket revenue, limiting the impact of a work, limiting income for writers, actors and directors. Papp's quest for a larger theater — a quest that had originally led him to purchase the Public in 1966 — continued to preoccupy him. He asked architect Giorgio Cavaglieri to draw up various plans for expanding his space. One scheme was to roof the Delacorte — he could present four Shakespeare plays there in the winter in addition to two in the summer and perform a public service by bringing Central Park to life at night. Another scheme involved building a mezzanine into the Newman Theater, thereby converting it to a 500-seat house. A third involved building a new theater in Washington, D.C., where his plays could open away from the scrutiny of New York critics and where, he imagined, an audience existed for *his* kind of work. All three projects were stymied. He tried to get approval to construct two extra floors onto the Public Theater but was blocked by the Landmarks Commission. Finally, in an effort to gain more space, he leased a floor of the loft building next door to the Public Theater.

In addition to his frustrated plans for expansion, one project after another failed. After director Michael Langham left the Third World Company, director Mike Nichols resigned as director of the Latino musical *Sancocho*. "He just said, 'This is not my kind of material. I don't know enough about the culture,'" Papp told the *Times*. Nichols also did not wish to direct Shakespeare.

Papp tried to form an all-star classical repertory company where actors worked for $225 per week and performed in Washington's Kennedy Center as well as on Broadway. It's "the major thing I'm working on now," he told reporters. "We've talked to Jill Clayburgh, Al Pacino, Bobby De Niro, Dustin Hoffman and Meryl Streep. . . . When Al Pacino plays Richard III, 99 per cent of the audience go to see Al Pacino. They don't care about *Richard III*, but they find themselves watching him and suddenly they're kind of moved. . . . We hope to start rehearsals in July." But Papp announced the venture before he had the money. The project was canceled, along with Papp's American-Soviet theater exchange.

In 1979, he and Merrifield had traveled to the USSR at the invitation of the minister of culture, with a plan to take *A Chorus Line* to the Soviet Union and bring back the Moscow Art Theater. Papp had been fascinated by the MAT since his days at the Actors' Lab and had kept an eye on its activities. In the late 1970s, he met with Oleg Yefremov, MAT's charismatic actor and director, and empathized with his attempt to bring a huge, two-hundred-member, tenured company into the twentieth century.

Papp and Merrifield had spent ten days in the Soviet Union. They saw two or three plays each day and were driven around Moscow and Leningrad accompanied by an official translator. They attended endless official meetings and receptions. They met officials from the Moscow Art Theater, the All-Russia Theatrical Society, the Gorky Institute of World Literature, the Institute on the Theory and History of the Fine Arts and the American embassy. They were lodged at the party's Sovietskaya Hotel, where they communicated in sign language, certain that their room was bugged. The SALT II agreement was about to be signed by Jimmy Carter and Leonid Brezhnev, the 1980 Olympics were being held in Russia and Papp sensed an opening for cultural exchange. But after many vodka toasts, a discussion of whether the homosexual content of *A Chorus Line* was too "eccentric" for Ministry of Culture censors, a second trip to the USSR by Festival staff, much technical planning and much press, the Russian exchange came to naught. Although the Soviet government agreed to underwrite all Russian costs, Papp could not find a single corporation or government body willing to fund the American side of the deal, estimated at $1 to $1.5 million. In January, after Coca-Cola, IBM, Xerox, American Express, the Chase Manhattan Bank, as well as the International Communications Agency, Armand Hammer and Occidental Petroleum, Vice-President Mondale, four U.S. senators and thirty-nine representatives had turned him down, Papp finally gave up. "We have been unable to raise a penny," he told the *Times*. "My primary interest is preserving the New York Shakespeare Festival and I didn't want to impinge on our own fund-raising efforts. . . . Here we are, the richest nation in the world and we have to grub around for money for this exchange. I feel a little embarrassed."

In board minutes and in conversation with Festival staff, Papp began to stress the need to curtail his expenses and reorganize his own sources of revenue. And he was forced to renege on promises he had made on various projects. "Dear Max," he wrote to Maximillian Schell in regard to plans for the actor to perform *Hamlet* at the Public:

What touched me most when we talked over the telephone earlier was your search for meaning in life as an actor. . . . My response to your openness was great because it coincided with a search of my own, finding a reason to continue running an institution which I had created but which is now facing enormous financial difficulties and the possibility of the end within two or three years. I feel that my theater has the right to exist only if it is possessed with a bold, artistic energy capable of burning through the mediocrity that surrounds and suffocates us. For me, the act of putting on plays holds little interest and to engage in a back-breaking struggle to raise the necessary funds to operate without a new and clear-cut path at this stage of my life in the theater I find debilitating. . . .

I have had to free myself at this particular time from the way we have been working over the past years so that I can clear my head and start afresh. It is necessary that I sort out the kind of program I must do because I love it and want it more than anything else from that which merely perpetuates an institution. What that program will be, I don't know now. I have made commitments to eight playwrights, an equal number of directors, a number of actors and others for the coming season. But I will be painfully informing them that I may be unable to keep my word.

Papp reduced the Public's production schedule to fifteen plays in 1980 and twelve in 1981. He tried to generate work in film and television. He sold some specials and almost launched a midnight talk show called *The Lost Art of Conversation,* which he planned to host live from a table at Luchow's, a famous Manhattan restaurant. But the various projects did not culminate in any major activity. Papp's independent, improvisatory style did not mesh with the corporate world of television. Nor was he able to work comfortably in Hollywood. "It's an antiseptic place," he told the London *Times.* "I flew to the coast a few years ago to look at a three-picture deal which had been set up for me. But after a couple of days there, my stomach started heaving and I came straight back to New York. The deal was off."

For the first time since he had hired Herta Danis in 1960, Papp sought out a professional fundraiser. Fundraising had been one of the many areas former associate producer Bernard Gersten had supervised and, since his firing, it had been neglected. Papp interviewed fundraiser Jane Gullong, who had worked seven years for Lincoln Center. Like most of the new generation of Festival staffers as well as artists, Gullong was highly educated and professionally trained. Her first impressions of the Festival, like Herta Danis's twenty years earlier, were of "a candy store" with outdated records and transactions based in the main on personal relationships. And Papp charmed her as completely as he had Danis.

"He didn't even *inquire* what my salary was and actually offered me less than I was making," Gullong recalled. "But he was compelling and I was interested."

Like Danis, Gullong examined the books. After six weeks, she concluded that fundraising in every category was inadequate and told Papp that the department needed an overhaul. That afternoon, he fired the three people in it, leaving just a startled Gullong and her assistant. She soon discovered that Papp was an unpredictable asset to fundraising. Whereas Beverly Sills could be counted on to enter a roomful of thousand-dollar donors and work it to the nines, Papp was more likely to walk in and out or not show up at all. If he hit it off with a donor or corporate executive, all was well. If he did not, or felt he was being patronized or disbelieved, the producer succumbed to what Gullong called "his fund-raising paranoia," the same set of ambivalent reactions Danis had observed twenty years earlier.

Papp found it difficult to mix personal relations with finances. He was loyal to longtime trustees such as George Delacorte, Judy Peabody and LuEsther Mertz. He not only was reluctant to press them for money, he would not ask them to solicit money from others. He became testy when foundation executives questioned his plans or figures. "He reportedly told one man at the Rockefeller Foundation, 'Don't look down your WASP nose at me,'" said Gullong, "and when I went with him to see CBS president Tom Wyman, it was a disaster. Wyman behaved in a corporate, rather fatherly way, asking for documentation of what Joe was telling him. Joe got mad. And instead of asking for $50,000, he asked for $500,000 which was like throwing the whole meeting out the window. We got nothing. Another time, I had worked for months trying to interest Brooke Astor. Brooke Astor was the *grande dame* of New York philanthropists, the head of the Vincent Astor Foundation. I had finally succeeded in getting her to attend a rehearsal in the Public Theater. There she was — already well into her eighties, and with her busy schedule — right there, and when I went to get Joe, he refused to come out of his office and meet her. He *stood up* Brooke Astor in his own theater! Why? I never figured it out."

Gullong found that foundation support — despite Papp's poor reputation with grants officers — was forthcoming. "The kind of work Joe was doing was exactly what foundations admired in the 1980s," she said. "He was on the cutting edge. He had always run the most multicultural institution in the country and the foundations were beginning to value multiculturalism." Even the Ford and Rockefeller foundations were eager to fund the Festival Latino, with which Papp would become increasingly involved in the 1980s. "The foundations had interests in Latin America and the Festival Latino was important to people there. It's the only time there's been the sense that the U.S. was interested in their culture, and the Latino community in New York felt it was the most recognition they had ever received."

But the Festival had few corporate donors and it was there that Gullong began to work. Like Danis, she sat beside Papp as he made telephone calls, this time to corporate executives. "I would set him up with a vice-president or president," she said, "which was not hard because people wanted to say they had talked to him personally. 'This is Joe Papp,' he would say. 'You're already supporting us but I'm calling to ask you for more money.' He was charming and engaging and compelling. And those telephone solicitations were moderately successful."

Soon after arrival, Gullong had suggested a corporate sponsor to underwrite the costs of Shakespeare in the Park, in the way Texaco underwrote the Metropolitan Opera. "But when I first proposed it," she recalled, "Joe was filled with fears and turmoil. He had spent years arguing that the municipality was responsible for the Delacorte. What would it mean to accept corporate money? What credit would they want? What kind of control? Would they try to influence the work? Getting Citibank to spend $250,000 a year for three years sponsoring Free Shakespeare was relatively easy compared to negotiating the problem with Joe."

Papp met several times with Citibank officials and, to Gullong's relief, seemed to enjoy himself. "They were impressed with him; he was impressed with them," she recalled. "But, in private, Joe had to work through all the issues in the relationship between an artistic institution and a corporate sponsor. I found his arguments intellectually interesting. He stuck to his conviction that the Festival should be supported with government money. But he eventually became comfortable with corporate support. Citibank first became a sponsor — without too much noise — in 1979, the summer of *Othello,* and the Third World Company production of *Coriolanus.* And, of course, in the second summer, when *Pirates of Penzance* became such a hit, they were ecstatic."

Papp had come up with the idea of doing *Pirates of Penzance* when he and his wife were driving with director Wilford Leach to the country one weekend. As he drove, Papp sang the lyrics to a song he had performed more than forty years earlier in high school:

> *Three little maids from school are we*
> *Pert as a schoolgirl well can be*
> *Filled to the brim with girlish glee*
> *Three little maids from school*

He told Leach he was thinking about doing the *Mikado* in Central Park.

By 1980, Leach had replaced Bernard Gersten as Papp's closest friend and colleague, and the two had developed a habit of easy, candid repartee. Leach told Papp that he had always disliked Gilbert and Sullivan, that the notion of American actors pretending to be English people pretending to be Japanese seemed idiotic to him. His high school, like so many others, had mounted a G&S production every year until Leach organized an effort to end the tradition. Papp listened to Leach's objections, then asked him just to listen to the music. Leach bought a record of *Pirates of Penzance* and, much to his surprise, liked it.

Gilbert and Sullivan posed the same kind of challenge for Leach that Shakespeare had initially posed for Papp. There was one, nineteenth-century style of presenting the operettas — fey, stilted, British — hallowed by decades of tradition, immortalized by the D'Oyly Carte Opera. In agreeing to direct *Pirates*, Leach made clear that he would ignore that tradition and treat *Pirates* as though it were a new play. In nineteenth-century England, Leach reflected, opera had been a popular form, like rock music in contemporary America. For his leading actors, Leach determined to use rock singers, happened to glimpse rock star Linda Ronstadt on television and mentioned her to Papp.

As it happened, a *New York Times* reporter had brought Ronstadt to meet Papp one year earlier. "I love this city," she later explained to *Parade* how she came to star in a Festival production. "But I knew if I moved here, I wouldn't be able to stay without a job — it's too rough here, you know? You've got to have a focus or you get too scattered. So I asked Joe for a job and two years later, he gave me one." Papp knew that he would be accused of casting Ronstadt — who had never acted in a play before — for her box-office appeal rather than for her talent. But Papp had liked the rock star and responded to her wish to risk doing something new.

"Get me Linda Ronstadt!" he told his assistant, and the next day she was in his office. "She had a small, very pure voice, a bit like Lily Pons," Papp said. "With coaching that grew and grew." Leach then saw teen rock star Rex Smith's photograph on the cover of a supermarket teen magazine. The Festival's Casting Department obtained his services as well, along with those of Kevin Kline, who had first carried a spear during Stuart Vaughan's all-night *Wars of the Roses* marathon in 1970.

Disregarding traditional stage directions and orchestration, Leach asked composer Bill Elliott to rescore the music. Elliott eliminated all but two of the traditional stringed instruments and added xylophones, synthesizer, marimbas and boobams, a kind of drum. He persuaded the Argentine Graciela Daniele, who had never seen a Gilbert and Sullivan production, to choreograph the show.

As he did with most of his directors, Papp plied Leach with his own ideas for the production, suggesting alternative sets and costumes and finally blurting out that he "just did not like pirates." In his quiet way, Leach told Papp that he could not conceive of a way to do *Pirates of Penzance* without pirates.

The production was heralded by extraordinary publicity. The casting of two rock stars had brought with it unusual press coverage, as had Papp's announcement that since the city had withdrawn its support for Free Shakespeare, he had withdrawn Shakespeare from the city. Citibank had "come to the rescue" of the Festival with a $250,000 summer grant, he said. "We solicited it. We do that all the time for one-shot events. But the continuance of Free Shakespeare in the Park is different. To us Free Shakespeare is an ongoing thing and it should be permanently supported by direct funding in the city budget."

Although critics grumbled predictably about "stunt" casting and it was reported that neither rock star had the stamina to perform eight times per week, the production was an unexpected critical success. "The entire improbable cast has been molded into a seamless and utterly beguiling family by director Wilford Leach," wrote *Newsweek*. "It delivers a dizzying amount of pleasure," wrote the *Times*. "The wild casting, it turns out, is generally first-rate and at times, inspired." Thousands of Festival regulars were joined in line for tickets by thousands of teenage fans of Rex Smith and older fans of Linda Ronstadt. Papp worried over risking $1 million of scarce Festival money, but, like *Two Gentlemen of Verona*, *Pirates* virtually sang itself to Broadway. It opened in January 1981 in Broadway's largest theater, where it once again received rave reviews. It would run for over two years, and join *A Chorus Line* in providing a regular weekly income to the Festival.

Pirates was, by far, the happiest and most rewarding of Papp's projects of the period. Many other of his projects and long-term relationships fell apart. His work with Romanian director Andrei Serban, who had done eight productions with him since 1977, collapsed when Serban encountered such difficulty working with Meryl Streep and Liz Swados in the composer's *Alice* that he quit the Festival. Although the actress retained good relations with Papp, it would also be her last Festival production.

One month earlier, in a highly publicized episode, playwright Sam Shepard had, from California, become engaged in a casting dispute with Papp so acrimonious that *he* told the press he would never allow Papp to produce a play of his again. Papp's two star writers, Ntozake Shange and Elizabeth Swados, were both worn out and tired of the theater. Shange, who had followed *for colored girls* with *A Photograph* and *Spell Number 7* and *Mother Courage*, took a teaching job and returned to the poetry circuit. Swados, who had worked without a break on *Runaways*, *Alice*,

Dispatches and the multicultural *Haggadah* was also burned out. "During *Lullabye and Goodnight,* I felt I had to stop, that I was progressing by rote. I knew I had to leave."

The most painful of Papp's breaks was his final one with David Rabe. Their relationship, which had begun a decade earlier, had been winding down since the mid-1970s. Rabe had gone to Hollywood to try to parlay his stage success into a career as a screenwriter. While there, he had met director Mike Nichols, then sated with filmmaking and looking to get back into theater. The two agreed to work together on Rabe's *Streamers.*

Nichols wanted to do the play outside New York, at the Long Wharf, in Connecticut, and Rabe could not have been more relieved. "By that time, I wanted to see if I really existed apart from Joe," he recalled. The play opened in New Haven and no investor could be found to bring it to New York. "They wouldn't touch it with a ten-foot pole," Rabe recalled, "so I finally called Joe. I took *him* to dinner and he said he didn't want a finished show, that he wasn't a booking agent. But then he saw *Streamers.* It was the kind of play he could not walk away from. It shook people up. It provoked them in a way Joe himself liked to provoke people. Also, it was an opportunity to be a hero, to show up the shmucks who were afraid to take it into New York."

The Long Wharf, however, held the theatrical rights. "That did not sit well with Joe, who suddenly had to negotiate for bringing the man he regarded as his own creation back to his theater," recalled Robert Kamlot. "Joe didn't want to present the Long Wharf production of anything. The Long Wharf refused to let us have the set or props until the contract — which had a provision which read *Joseph Papp presents the Long Wharf Theater Production of Streamers* — and Joe wouldn't sign it. Bernie had negotiated a compromise which read *a NYSF/Long Wharf Theater Production,* and said it was taken care of. Joe was in Philadelphia. Nichols would not start rehearsals unless he had the set. So I called the Festival attorney and asked if I could sign the contract myself.

"A couple of days later, Joe sees a program and blows his stack. He said that if I had been in the army, I would have been shot for insubordination. He took the Long Wharf name off the program. Long Wharf took us to court. Joe called their managing director a 'fucking shit' in front of the judge. The judge ruled that Joe had to reinstitute the Long Wharf's credit."

In 1981, Rabe gave Papp a new play, *Goose and Tom Tom,* which would have two productions at the Public Theater. Rabe directed the first himself in workshop and asked that it be closed to critics. It was followed by a second production, with another director. "He was doing me a favor," Rabe later said. "It was about patching up a relationship instead of doing plays." *Goose and Tom Tom* was difficult, with the playwright discovering what it was he had written during the rehearsal process. Rabe was reluctant to face the critics and Papp agreed that he would not open the play unless the author felt comfortable. However, after two months of performance, the actors were distressed at not being reviewed. "Joe called me every day and badgered me until I finally said: 'What's this about? Are you going to continue this until I say yes?' Then one day I pick up the paper and see that the play was opening. I tried to save the play and sent telegrams to the critics disavowing it. And that was the end."

There were many other playwrights eager to take his place. Papp was still producing Tom Babe, Len Jenkins, Des McAnuff, Richard Wesley, Wallace Shawn, James Lapine and David Henry Hwang, a young Asian-American playwright whose *FOB* and *The Dance and the Railroad* had come to the Festival from the New Federal Theater. But there were no more workshops for new plays, and audiences, accustomed to finished shows like *A Chorus Line* or *Pirates*, expected more polished productions than the Public's standard. The work came under increasing scrutiny by critics, and it seemed to Papp that the tone of the criticism had changed with the times, that it was too often mean-spirited and abusive.

Some playwrights, like Wallace Shawn, agreed and responded by arranging for their work to debut out of New York City. Longtime Festival actor Michael Moriarty was so enraged by John Simon's vituperative reviews that he wrote a play about him, which Papp produced in 1981. In a separate but equally problematic development, Actors Equity eliminated the showcase contract governing off off-Broadway production. That contract provided for minimal actors' salaries and had made the Public Theater's long workshop process possible. In part, the change was a response to *A Chorus Line*. Millions of dollars had accrued to the New York Shakespeare Festival, Michael Bennett and his official collaborators. Several of the dancers who had originally contributed autobiographical material had been locked out. The code was reformulated so as not to allow that to happen again and each theater was constrained to negotiate its own agreement with Actors Equity.

Papp campaigned against the reformulation, arguing that it would kill play development, but lost. All the productions in his theater were placed on off-Broadway contracts, substantially raising his costs and curtailing the long workshop process that had nurtured *Runaways, for colored girls* and *A Chorus Line*. "Now readings became the rule," Rosemarie Tichler recalled. "Everything Gail and the play development people worked on went through lots of drafts but usually there was no development process with actors."

Playwright John Guare, who had worked at the Public since 1971, decided to pull out of a scheduled production in 1979. "I saw that it would be a difficult six weeks," he later said. "Plays were not so much nurtured as hyped and flung on. There was no chance to grow there. When I told Joe, he burst into tears. I said I was sorry but that I needed to work on the play more."

Increasingly, playwrights as well as other theater people began to feel that Joe Papp, after years of keeping up an inhuman pace, had grown tired — as well as tired of theater. Papp was, in fact, tired. Tired of raising money, tired of fighting with the city, tired of the hundred and one daily crises of the theater. For the first time, Papp also complained publicly about his role as a nurturer of talent. "Some people don't look at me as a nurturer," he said in 1982. "Wilford Leach doesn't and neither does JoAnne Akalaitis. There are some people who are mature. When artists are very young, they expect to be taken care of. They think I'm like their father. Which means that they want everything from you and they don't want to give anything back."

Festival literary manager Lynn Holst later recalled that, by the early 1980s, Papp was feeling trapped by the institution he had created. Holst herself was feeling frustrated at the Festival. She left to try to resuscitate the Provincetown Playhouse in Greenwich Village. When she told Papp of her intention in her new job to ignore critics deliberately, not to advertise, to see if an audience would discover her theater and support it on their own, Papp responded by saying that he envied that. "Joe told me he sometimes wished he could go back and do that himself," she later recalled. "But, of course, he couldn't go back. He had several hundred people he employed now and felt he had a responsibility to the artists, who needed a written record of their work.

"Working at the Festival for so long I was familiar with his tendency to work in two- or three-year creative spurts, similar to those of an artist, after which he lost direction for a while until he discovered a new one. When he lost his sense of purpose or meaning, he could not proceed until he had gained new direction. Some people faulted him for this but I thought it was a great quality. He was not afraid of change and seemed to be invigorated by it. He was at his best when up against a wall and faced with some impossibility."

Now Papp — for the first time in his life — longed to get away. He had often been offered opportunities to travel, receiving scores of official and unofficial invitations from abroad and turning them down. In the fall of 1981, he accepted an unlikely excuse to leave his theater — an invitation to deliver a keynote address before the International Association of Theater Critics, meeting in Tel Aviv.

Papp had never been to Israel — and certainly not on vacation. He had not grown up with the habit of taking vacations and did not understand what to do with leisure. He did not like to be away from the Public Theater. He spoke no foreign language. He was a homebody, allergic to hotels. "I was always cautious about unpacking our bags," Gail Merrifield said. "If the lobby passed muster, you held your breath that the room would be okay." Papp carried a camera but rarely took pictures. He seldom visited popular tourist attractions.

In the fall of 1981, however, Papp not only flew to Israel, but instead of staying away for a scheduled two weeks, stayed away for five. Like almost every Jew arriving in Tel Aviv for the first time, Papp — for whom Hebrew had been the language of prayer — was thrown into a state of confusion. He was shocked by the first airport sign he saw printed in Hebrew, by Hebrew in the mouths of customs officials and policemen and by the total absence of Yiddish which — for him — was the everyday language of Jewish people. Merrifield later remembered that during his stay, "he never got over an emotional feeling that Hebrew was the sacred language he knew from his childhood and not for this other use."

Like most visitors to Israel, he was overwhelmed by the intensity of the country, the control exerted by the ultra-Orthodox Jews, the hourly news broadcasts reporting military incidents, the constant presence of uniformed soldiers — men and women — carrying guns, the heated argument that constituted Israeli conversation. But, as in the Soviet Union, he saw the country through the prism of its theater. Every day, he saw plays, met with Palestinian and Israeli theater people, gave interviews about theater, attended official receptions. In some Israeli plays, he told reporters, he was struck by a loathing of Yiddish and European-Jewish culture, but also by the higher societal value placed on Jews of European origin than on those of North African descent. In the split, Papp came down on the side of the North Africans. In Jerusalem, he attended a concert of classical music and was surprised to see that the program was all-German. At the Wailing Wall, Papp did not walk up to the ancient stones because men and women were separated by a fence and he could not pray with his wife beside him. "This is the most complicated country I've ever seen in my life," he told the *Jerusalem Post*. In conversations with dignitaries like Jerusalem mayor Teddy Kollek, or with his Israeli driver, Papp focused on the issue of Jewish survival: what did it mean?

what would it cost? How many people would have to die each year to keep the state alive?

He spent one afternoon with his father's younger brother, Sol Pepper, an Auschwitz survivor, and his wife. The couple, then in their seventies, had an Israeli-style afternoon spread — herring, tomatoes, gefilte fish, pickles, rye bread, chopped liver, pound cake — ready and waiting when the Papps arrived in their small, bare Tel Aviv flat. Sol Pepper had the straight, compact posture that ran in the Papirofsky family and was visibly pleased to see his nephew. But after a warm embrace and greeting, the two ran out of conversation. Ruth Pepper, trying to find common ground, asked: Did Joe know it was her mother who brought his father to the States? And introduced his parents to each other? Papp behaved, as Merrifield later put it, "like a restless son" — the only time she had ever seen him behave that way — but she expressed interest and Sol went into the bedroom, returning with several albums of Papirofsky photographs. Moshe Papirofsky and his wife Bayla had eight children born in Kielce, Ruth Pepper explained. There were four girls and four boys: Simon, Rose, Chaya, Shmuel, Eydele, Isaac — Look! There was a studio portrait of a handsome young man in a jaunty fedora, the photographer in Kraków! The Papirofskys were listed at Yad Vashem, the Israeli Holocaust memorial. Five of Papp's aunts and uncles had died in the Holocaust, as had Sol's first wife and two children. Only three survived.

Papp finished his sandwich and said they had to leave. He had an appointment arranged by the American ambassador, to discuss cultural exchange. Ruth Pepper was dismayed but agreed that one shouldn't be late to such an appointment. She insisted he take some pound cake, and the Papps arrived at their meeting with time to spare. "Joe was relieved to be out of there but he didn't talk about it," Merrifield said later. "My feeling was that Joe did not want to deal with the fact that his family had been destroyed. He didn't want to hear it. It was too painful. He never mentioned it."

Papp's visit to Israel also had moments that were entirely carefree, and Merrifield would later say that it was in Israel that she first saw Papp truly enjoy himself while traveling. One of their guides insisted the couple see the Sinai desert before it was returned to Egypt, and the two signed up for a "Sinai Safari" — a three-day camping trip with four other couples and two guides: one a burly Israeli just out of the army, the second a slender Bedouin named Ahmed Abou Ayesh. No one in the group had ever heard of Joseph Papp or the New York Shakespeare Festival, and the producer slept in a sleeping bag, sang camp fire songs and climbed to the summit of Mount Sinai without complaint. He befriended his Bedouin guide, compared the Bedouins' relation to women with that of Petruchio in *The Taming of the Shrew* and wound up promising to find him a job if he came to America.

While they were in Israel, news of Papp's presence in the Middle East had reached theater people in Egypt and, instead of flying back home, the producer accepted an invitation to speak to students at the American University in Cairo and the University of Alexandria. Anwar Sadat had been assassinated a few weeks earlier and many of the people he met with were still shaken by the event. The only worthwhile Egyptian theater, they were told, was the academic theater. But Papp found the Egyptian versions of *Othello* and *The Merry Wives of Windsor* he was taken to see so boring that he determined to seek out the commercial theater that had been described as cheap and common.

"We went to a show called *Welcome Doctors,* a comedy about two country boys who become doctors, in which a famous Egyptian comic actor was appearing," Merrifield recalled. "It lasted five hours but people wandered in and out at will. No one cared if babies cried or adults chatted. Vendors with trays of food circulated constantly. Part of the virtuosity of the actors was that they improvised brilliantly so that it was never the same show twice. We loved it."

When they left Egypt for what was to be a short stopover in London, where *Pirates* was being filmed, Papp found a message from Polish director Andrzej Wajda, asking him to see his production of *Hamlet* in Kraków. Wajda was a director Papp admired as well as a prominent member of the Solidarity movement; his film portrait of political leader Lech Walesa had won top prize at the Cannes Film Festival the previous spring. Papp decided to obtain a visa. "We went several times to the Polish visa office in London," recalled Merrifield. "Mostly, we found it closed. Poland was in turmoil. There were no visa-seekers except us and a sportsman going to Poland to shoot game. When someone finally opened the door, we were told it was not possible to visit Poland.

"Joe demanded to see the director. No, this was impossible. The director wasn't there. Joe was very scornful of this and said he'd met with the minister of culture in the Soviet Union — why shouldn't he see the head of the Polish visa office? We should come back the following day at ten. Of course, the next day at ten the office was closed. When we finally got to see the director, Joe delivered a passionate tirade on behalf of theater and world culture, civilization and the artist and the reasons why he and I should be granted visas to visit Poland. The director listened attentively. When Joe was finished, he said, 'Mr. Papp, do you ski? There is very good skiing in Poland. Why don't you go there and ski?' There was a pause. Then Joe said, 'Yes, we'd like to do that.' As we left, Joe thanked him, to my amazement, in Polish that he suddenly remembered from his childhood."

Papp was disappointed in Andrzej Wajda's *Hamlet*. The actor playing Hamlet was short, pudgy and continually downcast; the play seemed very long and the theater, very hot. The audience, however, seemed electrified. Papp kept his reservations about the production to himself and met with Wajda, aware that his attention to the director might prove helpful to him in a worsening political situation. In Warsaw, he met with the director of the Jewish State Theater, where actors learned their Yiddish lines by rote since none spoke the language.

Papp's journey to the country his father had left seventy years earlier depressed him. As in the Soviet Union, he ate in local restaurants, which offered next to nothing to eat as well as in official party restaurants which overflowed with imported specialties. He saw untended Jewish cemeteries desecrated by vandals. He remarked on the absence of Jews in Krakow and Warsaw but on the persistence of anti-Semitism.

On December 13, after five weeks abroad, the Papps returned to New York. That same evening, they attended the Broadway opening of Michael Bennett's new musical, *Dream Girls*. Just before they left for the theater, they learned martial law had been declared in Poland. It was evident that supporters of Solidarity would be at risk and that leaders like Andrzej Wajda would be arrested.

"Joe sat through *Dream Girls* gritting his teeth," Merrifield recalled. "Such a depressing frame of reference — so narcissistic and banal after the people and situations we had seen abroad." Broadway had never been Joseph Papp's theater of choice, but, with both hit musicals *A Chorus Line* and *Pirates of Penzance* running strong, he was one of its leading producers. Dressed in his tuxedo, standing among his colleagues on a Broadway opening night, Papp was disoriented. The theater, which had once appeared to be such a large, challenging world to conquer, now seemed to him very small.

NINETEEN

Beyond Theater

IN THE SPRING of 1982, Joseph Papp made a significant move that he did not announce to the press. He rented the fifth floor of the loft building next door to the Public Theater and moved his office into it. The directory at 419 Lafayette Street listed the New York Shakespeare Festival, but not the producer's name. With him, Papp took Gail Merrifield, artistic director Wilford Leach and only a handful of staff.

For twenty-five years, since moving into the Heckscher Theater, Papp had kept the door to his office open and thrived on an idiosyncratic management style. "He used to meet me in the john and we'd make a decision standing at the urinals," recalled Robert Kamlot, who had taken over many of Bernard Gersten's administrative duties. The Festival's evolution from a shoestring to a multimillion-dollar operation had not significantly changed Papp's operational style. The Festival's management structure while Bernard Gersten was associate producer had resembled a bicycle, with the spokes of the two wheels converging at their hubs. Since Gersten's departure, there was only one hub and one wheel, whose spokes converged at Papp's office.

By 1982, Papp had grown tired of the endless demands on his time and attention. His daily calendar was so jammed with appointments that there was hardly any white space. The traffic in and out of his doorway seemed constant. His telephone rarely stopped ringing. He wanted a conventional office with a conventional secretary who screened people and problems out rather than letting them flood in. In an uncharacteristic move, he fired his longtime assistant and moved out.

Gail Merrifield was unhappy with the move. "I was very attached to the Public and I worried about his absence from the building," she said. "People at 425 now had to phone over to see if Joe was free instead of just poking a head in the door. It was like the captain of a ship moving out, but I understood that somehow he had used up the office in the Public Theater, emotionally and psychologically. It was like a house in which a love affair had been conducted or where a family had been raised and which was filled with memories of something that was over. He wanted to be in a different relationship to everything around him. He didn't live there anymore."

Writers and directors who worked closely with Papp had always noted that the producer preferred the world to the world of the theater. Director Richard Foreman would later remember the producer urging him to maintain a sense of perspective in the face of problems with a production. "You know, we think we're in a life-and-death situation, Richard, but out in the big world very few people will give more than a passing thought to what we do. It's just a play after all."

By the 1980s, Wallace Shawn, like many other Festival playwrights, had become dismayed. "You were living out a very pleasing fantasy to have your work produced at the Public Theater," Shawn said. "The words spoken in that building continued to have a weight in the world. And it continued to be important to me that Joe was intelligent, handsome and charming, as well as encouraging of my work. But I noticed he became less and less interested in theater. In some ways, I admired that. I *loved* the fact that he was interested in the real world. I think anyone who is only obsessed with theater is pitiful. But I regretted that the man running the Public Theater had lost interest in the theater."

As the 1980s evolved into a decade pervaded by symbols of self-aggrandizement — Reaganomics, yuppies, the various scandals of Wall Street — Papp hoped American playwrights would respond. Instead, he saw them eschewing social issues and writing "story" plays about personal relationships. "The theater is supposed to be a living force which absorbs in some way what is happening in the world," he said. "I'm not interested in plays that have to do with relationships. It's not that those relationships are unimportant, but what is happening in the world now is so extraordinary that you need something more cosmic. . . . I don't want to see another coffee cup on the stage or a refrigerator. Or someone eating an apple." Or, to a student at Brown University: "It's your generation we're having trouble with. Why aren't they saying something?"

In addition to being disappointed in his playwrights, Papp was unhappy with the theater world itself. Living in the New York theater had always been like living in a small town. But Papp's rise to prominence had coincided with the shrinking of that world as theater — beset by rising costs and the flight of middle-class audiences to the suburbs — took an ever more distant third place to movies and television. Only half of New York City's forty-four Broadway theaters were actually lit during the first half of the 1980s, and most were showing revivals, British imports and/or traditional musicals that Papp continued to regard as "fluff." The cost of mounting a Broadway show had reached $5 million, and top seat prices were now $45. Off-Broadway and off off-Broadway theater seemed to have run out of steam. When asked by the *Wall Street Journal* how he envisaged leisure activities in the year 2011, Papp said with bravado that people would still wish to see live actors performing onstage and that there'd be a production of *Hamlet* playing somewhere. To the *Daily News,* he was less sanguine. "People keep saying 'Don't worry about the theater; it's a fabulous invalid. It'll go on forever and ever.' I don't want to be the one to say theater is dead but it's certainly sick. And it's not fabulous at all."

As the major employer in an ailing industry, Papp had become the obvious target for criticism of all kinds. For many years he had enjoyed a kind of immunity from the malice of the theater community. In the 1980s, while he continued to be lionized by many artists and New Yorkers as a risk-taker, friend and advocate, *New York* magazine noted that it had become "very hip to knock Joe Papp." New writers were disgruntled that after years of accepting unsolicited scripts, Papp had announced that his Play Development Department would now read only those sent by agents. All were disgruntled by a subsidiary-rights policy that gave the Public Theater 40 percent of their royalties for a period of twenty years. The policy was modeled on the standard Broadway playwright's contract and had been instituted in 1966, but by the 1980s, off-Broadway, regional and English theaters were offering a far better deal. "The 40 percent was a kind of enforced gratitude," said Wallace Shawn. "Just in case you didn't happen to feel like giving 40 percent of your income to the Public Theater, it was compelled. I resented it so much I would have almost given up writing plays than sign a contract like that again. I fought to have it changed with *Aunt Dan and Lemon*. It was nonnegotiable. It was only out of personal loyalty to Joe that I didn't take the play elsewhere."

Hundreds of young actors who had never known an earlier, less powerful Papp vied for jobs at the Festival and, when they failed to obtain them, called it exclusionary. New directors and designers complained about their pay, which was low compared to that at the regional theaters. Longtime NYSF actors, directors and designers felt neglected, hurt and abandoned. The road to Papp's success, some said, was "strewn with corpses." He "carried no baggage," had a "revolving door" that used people up and then spit them out when they were no longer needed. Papp, aware of these sentiments, would say defensively, "You cannot build a theater and have strong relationships at the same time, except with those people who are working with you. Everyone expects you to be there all the time and it's just not possible for me to be there for one person all the time."

Most critical were the people who had helped create the New York Shakespeare Festival — Bernard Gersten, Stuart Vaughan and Merle Debuskey. Gersten thought Papp had become the powerful Establishment figure captured in a Paul Davis poster for the producer's cabaret performance at The Ballroom. While some saw a handsome, irreverent, patently successful man enjoying himself, for Gersten the image "could have been a balloon in Macy's Thanksgiving Day parade. So blown up, so full of himself. For Joe to have pushed himself forward as a performer represented the culmination of that inflated ego, encouraged by sycophants, egged on by sycophants." Debuskey came to believe that part of the job description for staffers at the Festival was "an unqualified adoration of the producer."

Since his adolescence at Eastern District High School, Joe Papirofsky had demanded attention. As a young man challenging Robert Moses, he had been cocky, imperious, insistent. Those qualities had been seen as assets. Now, as head of the nation's most important theater, those same qualities had become liabilities. People who had once viewed his imperiousness as a startling but necessary, even engaging, feature of a young idealist were in the 1980s offended by it. They remembered a rough but accessible Papp in dirty boots and shirtsleeves. Now they saw a glib, expensively dressed Papp posing for American Express Card advertisements (his fees went to the Festival) and heard him singing radio commercials for his shows: "*The bells are ringing, for me and* Top Girls; *That's*

why I'm singing, 'cause we've the top girls. . . . Hi, Joe Papp here at the
Public in case you couldn't guess . . ." For a time, he even agreed to the
use of his name as the Festival's information line: 861-PAPP.

Merle Debuskey, who, in the late 1950s, had persuaded the young
producer to become the "voice" of the Festival, began to feel that Papp
had succumbed to the classic corruptions of fame and power. "He began
pruning away all those people who shared the credit for building the
Festival," Debuskey said, "so that even I was part of something he no
longer wished to acknowledge. He became susceptible to the most outrageous forms of flattery. And he stopped talking like a normal person.
He used to be such a pleasure to have a conversation with. He *listened*.
Now, if you didn't accept what he said, he'd abuse you. You had to be a
devotee, a Vestal Virgin. He would not go anywhere without a retinue,
a trail of people attending him."

Debuskey had been one of the people who had tried to reconcile Papp
and Gersten. In November 1985, after more than thirty years of close
collaboration, Papp would fire the press agent, on the grounds that his
$18,000 annual consulting fee was a luxury the Festival could no longer
afford. Debuskey, who had worked for Papp *pro bono* during the Festival's
first decade, was outraged. Like Gersten, he now viewed the producer
less as Hamlet or Prince Hal than as Lear demanding unreasonable proofs
of love.

In the 1950s, staffers had compared the Festival to a corner candy store.
In the 1980s, they compared it to a dysfunctional American family or a
troubled Shakespearean kingdom. Papp was the still powerful but aging
King attended by his retinue; Memfield, the self-effacing Queen, attended
by hers. Then there were the Princes: the mysterious artistic director,
Wilford Leach; the earthy casting director, Rosemarie Tichler; the less
visible and virtually autonomous Andrew Mihok and Milo Morrow, who
presided over the technical and costume departments; the chatty Richard
Kornberg, who ran the press department; and Jason Steven Cohen, who
had come to be known as Papp's constant shadow and chief henchman.

Cohen, who had served briefly as assistant to Long Island politician
Allard Loewenstein, had been twenty-six when he began working for the
Festival in 1971 and in his early thirties when he began assuming some
of Bernard Gersten's former duties. Cohen shared with Papp an avid
interest in social and political issues. He understood the code of loyalty
that Papp expected from his employees and was prepared to live by it. "I
spent the last twenty-one years *not* talking about Joe," he said in an
interview after the producer's death. "Anyone who knew Joe knew the
importance he placed on loyalty, honor, obligation. The thing that would

drive him crazy was anyone being disrespectful of him in his house —
which was the theater." Cohen's description of his relationship with Papp
echoed Gersten's. "You could never *tell* Joe anything," he said. "You had
to suggest it. He'd say it was impossible. He'd tear into you. And then
he'd come up with the idea as if it had been his own all the time. How
did I cope? There were only two ways of coping: First, you never lost
your sense of humor. Second, I left my ego in the medicine cabinet every
morning when I shaved. It was part of the deal. We had extraordinary
arguments in private, but in public — nothing."

Many staffers believed that Papp had finally found in Cohen the "good
son" he wanted. "Steve became his shadow, available seven days per week,
twenty-four hours per day," said one. "Joe would push a button and
Steve was there. Service to Joe was what gave his life meaning." Some
staffers saw that in Cohen, Papp had found a male he could banter with.
"They talked about women and had these back-room boy-jokes that I
found offensive," said Jane Gullong. Many people found Cohen rude as
well as mean-spirited and could not understand why Papp gave Cohen
everything he asked for, including Bernard Gersten's former title — a
promotion that provoked general manager Robert Kamlot, one of the
Festival's most respected staffers, to quit. Papp interpreted Kamlot's
decision to leave as a defection; Kamlot felt that the producer should have
understood that he himself had made remaining impossible. "But instead,
Joe was furious at me," Kamlot later said. "He wouldn't speak to me. He
accused me of deserting culture for commerce."

In his relationship with the press, Papp became more like other celebrities or CEOs of large organizations: one could gain access to him
exclusively through his organization's Press Department. But by the
1980s, the press had also undergone a generational change. Young critics
and reporters had no experience of Papp as a scrappy, idealistic local hero.
They saw an established showman who straddled the commercial and
not-for-profit sector, enjoyed the use of a city-owned theater and a
city-owned Central Park amphitheater, and seemed accountable to no
one. "To me," recalled Frank Rich, the new chief drama critic for the
Times, "he came out of another era: an old-time show-biz background
with the kind of impresario's skills more reminiscent of great Broadway
producers than of the kind of artistic types who had come out of drama
school or off off-Broadway. He was like Kermit Bloomgarten and David
Merrick in that he knew that a big part of a producer's job was to beat
the drums and promote his wares. Part of the motive was the same —
ego. But what made Joe different was that he was driven not to make
money but to make a place for the plays he believed in."

Papp did not lunch or correspond with Frank Rich as he had with Brooks Atkinson or Clive Barnes. He maintained his relationships with *Times* editors Arthur Gelb and Abe Rosenthal, and enjoyed the company of some reporters, but, increasingly, when Papp gave interviews, they tended to be on his own terms. "Reporters would ask him a question and instead of answering it, he would go off into a discursive lecture on anything that crossed his mind," said Merle Debuskey. "He spoke authoritatively on any subject. People became disenchanted. They stopped wanting the assignment of covering him. They'd call me up and ask: 'What's wrong with him?' I said Joe had become like an imperial palm, those trees you see in Florida. Almost all the fronds are gone. The only ones left are those which are currently growing. It stands tall, majestic and lonely."

A decade earlier, critic Stanley Kauffman had been a lone voice when he characterized Papp as an opportunist who had used Shakespeare and the not-for-profit theater for personal gain. "The fact . . . that he had no sheerly creative gifts, no artistic talent, could be submerged in matchmaking between Shakespeare and the several ghettos, by making the theater accessible and enjoyable to all previously excluded and/or ignored groups," Kauffman wrote in the *American Scholar.* By the time the producer had acquired the Public Theater:

> Papp seemed to succumb to the age-old and most dangerous seduction of success, the belief that it couldn't have happened to him if he hadn't deserved it. . . . If we disregard the big commercial managements as irrelevant to our discussion, then Papp is the only person who has made a considerable mark in the theater . . . without extraordinary talent, without exemplary taste, without an aesthetic imperative, without intellectual distinction. If I run through all the names that come to mind . . . I can find no one who has had so great an effect on the theater of his time as Papp, for whose talent and taste I have so little respect.

By the 1980s — encouraged by the aggressive nastiness that informed the decade — many critics took up where Kauffman left off. Papp's years as an object of criticism had not made him any less sensitive to its sting, but his response remained to persist in doing what he had always done. "When you get shot down by a critic, even people who have a lot of confidence and a solid track record begin to lose that confidence," he said. "Actors may be most immediately crippled by a bad review — they have to go on and perform on the very day the audience is reading about how terrible they are. But playwrights are more permanently affected. I have seen writers stop writing because of critics, or give up the theater. You hear stories of actors killing critics. That's not so far-fetched. There are times you feel you could actually commit an atrocity because your feelings are so intense.

"Over the years, I've repeated the same thing over and over again to the artists I work with: 'Try to find your satisfaction in the work itself. Theater is a collective effort. You have to have faith in yourself and the people with whom you are working. The work you do may not please everyone but you created something that did not exist before. The critic has created nothing. He or she would have no job without you. That basic fact can give you the stamina to withstand any criticism you receive.'"

Throughout the 1980s, Papp held firm to the eclectic mix of plays that was his trademark and produced an extraordinary amount of work. Artists and staffers new to the Public were as excited as their counterparts had been a decade earlier to be working in what seemed to them a paradise, a hothouse of creativity. "The theater was always run according to his taste and his faith in talent," Robert Brustein, who had watched Papp since the 1950s later wrote, "so the offerings varied wildly, from the most commercial to the most arcane. . . . Papp was able to operate at the same time as the most successful producer on Broadway and as a primary New York facilitator for the avant-garde."

Papp also remained committed to nontraditional audiences, paying close attention to the changes in the city's population. Not only was New York rapidly losing its white middle class, but the composition of its minority segments was changing. Where once the Latino presence had been marginal and predominantly Puerto Rican, it now numbered close to two million people from Cuba, El Salvador, Ecuador, Peru, Colombia, the Dominican Republic, Chile, and Argentina as well as Puerto Rico. In 1976, when Argentinian director Oscar Ciccione and his Salvadoran wife, Cecilia Vega, asked to use the Public for a Latino festival that August, Papp agreed. Ciccione and Vega were founders of Teatro Quatro, and, like Papp, interested in drama that addressed contemporary political and social issues. New York's Latino theater, they said, had traditionally reflected "the empty bourgeois" theater tradition of Latin America and Spain. "With time, the needs of the Latin American immigrant in New York went beyond cultural nostalgia," they wrote in the first program of the Festival Latino. "The political turbulence in the United States during the 1960s served as a catalyst. . . . Toward the end of the last decade, popular Latin American theater in this city took its first tentative steps. Using theater, young people from various Latino communities attempted to present their problems, the crises and tensions that plagued the daily life of the immigrant. The theater left its halls and went to the streets and parks. . . ." The Festival Latino would become part of the Festival in 1984, an annual, one-of-a-kind event that attracted international attention and occupied more and more of Papp's time.

Papp also stepped up another longtime interest: his quest for a non-traditional musical. His artistic interest in the form was reinforced by a financial one. Profits from *A Chorus Line* had dropped steadily from an annual high of seven million dollars to under one million. Although he did not like to admit it, he knew that the only way for the Festival to survive financially was by finding another musical hit like *A Chorus Line* and successfully transferring it to Broadway. The problem was not only that this way of thinking was against Papp's nature and philosophy but that no one could predict with certainty what would become a hit.

Gail Merrifield and Wilford Leach devised a long-range project to solicit ten-minute musicals, to attract composers, singers and other people who had never before worked in the theater and who might become interested in developing full-scale works. Leach developed musical projects of his own such as an English translation of Puccini's *La Bohème* and William Finn's *Romance in Hard Times*. Other projects such as Ntozake Shange's and jazz musician Baikida Carroll's collaboration on *Betsey Brown* underwent development financed by the Festival, as did Des McAnuff's *The Death of Von Richthofen as Witnessed from the Earth*. Mounting a musical at the Public was very costly, but despite the failure of *Von Richthofen* and Papp's unsuccessful transfer of Galt MacDermot's through-composed adaptation of William Saroyan's *The Human Comedy* — which Papp loved — to Broadway, the producer kept trying.

He also found ever different ways of producing Shakespeare. With a few exceptions, Papp had been producing at least two Shakespeare plays every year since 1956, sometimes as many as five. He had often declared that in a city the size of New York, a theatergoer should have the opportunity to see a Shakespeare play any night of the year and in 1982, declared that he would begin a new, year-round schedule with *Hamlet*, featuring a relatively unknown actress named Diane Venora in the title role. Although she was not the first woman to ever play Hamlet, Papp's choice of a female startled the theater community. So did the passion with which he threw himself into directing the play and his conviction that the space in the Anspacher Theater was inadequate. He had all the seats in the center section removed and the concrete block beneath them jack-hammered out. After wrecking the section, Papp said he had been wrong and had the center seating rebuilt.

Another manifestation of Papp's frustration with routine was his reversal of a twenty-five-year-old policy of ignoring contemporary British playwrights. In Britain, playwrights were responding to Margaret Thatcher's government with a rash of plays that addressed the social and economic costs of conservative policies. One of them was *Plenty*, a play by David Hare, whose work Papp had first produced in 1971. *Plenty* centered around a contemporary Englishwoman obsessed by memories of her days as a courier for the French underground, when she had lived the finest, most thrilling moments of her life.

Like *The Human Comedy*, the play addressed the time of World War II, a phase of Papp's own life that was becoming ever more meaningful to him as he grew older. "There was a time in the thirties and during the war when everything you did had an importance," he said later. "It wasn't that there weren't boring things and a lot of waiting and hanging around, but I felt I was alive, and there was something vital. . . ." Increasingly, Papp felt the legacy of his years as the child of an Orthodox Jewish father, as his own idiosyncratic kind of Communist, as a sailor in the service of his country. He had retained the spirit in which he had embraced communism but found himself becoming more and more patriotic. "It's vulgarized here by flag-wavers and super-patriots who talk about freedom," he said. "But if you take away that vulgarization, you find there is a meaning to that word and you become very aware of it when you travel to other countries. You find yourself supporting this government to the hilt — not this particular administration — but what we stand for."

David Hare, the first of several British playwrights Papp would produce during the 1980s, was preoccupied with such questions. During the late 1970s, Papp had developed a relationship with one of Hare's close associates, Max Stafford-Clark, the director who had brought Wallace Shawn's *A Thought in Three Parts* to London. Papp had subsequently engaged Stafford-Clark to direct at the Public and discovered that his taste in plays was similar to his own. Stafford-Clark became head of the Royal Court Theater, a small, financially beleaguered theater independent of both the West End and the establishment loop of the National Theatre and Royal Shakespeare Company. Located in Sloane Square, it had introduced playwrights Papp admired, such as John Arden and Arnold Wesker. Papp saw plays there whenever he was in London and, in 1982, proposed an exchange of work. He liked Stafford-Clark, he liked the Royal Court and he liked its hit play, *Top Girls*, by Caryl Churchill. *Top Girls* was a portrait of a successful Thatcherite businesswoman against the two backdrops of contemporary Britain and feminist history; it opened the Royal Court Exchange in the fall of 1982.

Papp drew criticism for abandoning American in favor of British play-

wrights, but he persevered through hard negotiations and problems with
both British and American unions. Although the principle of exchange
was based on the notion of equality — one American play would be
produced at the Royal Court in exchange for one British play at the
Public; both would run for an equal number of weeks — neither Stafford-Clark nor Papp could control the number of characters for which
the playwrights would write, so a scheme was devised whereby an imported production would run first, to be followed by a second production with a local cast. Within the next five years, nine more plays would
be exchanged, including Churchill's *Serious Money,* Wallace Shawn's *Aunt
Dan and Lemon,* Tom Babe's *Buried Inside Extra,* the Vietnam Veterans
Ensemble Company's *Tracers,* Larry Kramer's *The Normal Heart* and
George C. Wolfe's *The Colored Museum.* When Stafford-Clark later faced
a loss of subsidy from the British Arts Council, Papp responded with a
dollar-for-pound challenge grant and by assuming the greater proportion
of the costs of the exchange.

The plays were almost all well received, but Papp was accused of an
inconsistent artistic policy and of abandoning American writers. "American writers in the past few years have been writing in their own heads
and bellies. That tires me out," he replied. "Hare's play certainly deals
with a woman's personal life, very deeply psychologically true, but it's
about the world. . . . Caryl Churchill writes extraordinarily compassionate things but she's in the world. There's a social viewpoint." Papp
argued that American drama had grown "too domestic" and that he had
been forced to turn to England and Europe for relief.

By 1983, Papp and Stafford-Clark were talking seriously about ex-
changing jobs for one year. That Joe Papp would even contemplate
leaving his theater in someone else's hands was startling. But increasingly,
Papp mentioned Wilford Leach as his successor at the Public, of wishing
to travel more and function in a wider arena.

In March 1982, Papp did. For a month, he led an attempt to block
the demolition of two irreplaceable Broadway theaters to make way for
a Marriott Marquis hotel complex in Times Square.

The hotel project had first been proposed ten years earlier, under the
Lindsay administration. Atlanta-based architect and developer John Portman, designer of Detroit's fortress-like Renaissance Center and San Francisco's Embarcadero, had designed a similar $150 million, 2,000-room,
fifty-story luxury hotel complex to run between 45th and 46th streets
west of Broadway, just down Shubert Alley from where *A Chorus Line*
was playing at the Shubert and where *for colored girls* and *Leaf People* had
played at the Booth. The new hotel would require the demolition of

three legitimate theaters — the Morosco, the Helen Hayes and the Bijou — two movie houses and the 550-room Piccadilly Hotel. In their place, across the street from Shubert Alley would be the sheer dark windowless wall of a multi-story garage. A rooftop revolving restaurant, dozens of shops, and — Portman's signature feature — a huge atrium with trees, fountains, escalators and bubble-lit glass elevators would all be hidden inside. Portman planned to replace the "eliminated" theaters with a new 1,500-seat theater.

New York City's mid-decade fiscal difficulties had killed the project, but by 1978 Mayor Koch had resuscitated it. Portman asked the National Advisory Council on Historic Preservation for permission to raze the Helen Hayes Theater, although it was on the National Register of Historic Places. The owners of the Piccadilly Hotel refused to sell and, when the city condemned the property, went to court. Meanwhile, the City Planning Department estimated that New York would collect $12 million in annual taxes from the hotel once it opened. New York's two U.S. senators, most of its business community, the *New York Times* and the Shubert Theater organization — Papp's sometime supporters, and landlords for *A Chorus Line* — all viewed the project as the salvation of Times Square. The theater district had become a disaster, they argued. Pornography shops and movie houses, massage parlors and three-card monte dealers all did lively business. Prostitutes, pimps, panhandlers, drug dealers and runaway teenagers dominated the streets and made the area unsavory as well as dangerous — not unlike the Upper West Side before Lincoln Center. The Morosco and Helen Hayes needed millions of dollars' worth of repairs. The Marriott Marquis would transform the neighborhood, provide more than nineteen hundred construction and two thousand permanent jobs, and attract tourist and convention business to the theater district. And it would bring the city federal funds — $21.5 million in an Urban Development Action Grant from the U.S. Department of Housing and Urban Development. In 1980, the city's Environmental Impact Study determined that the hotel project would have no adverse impact on the neighborhood, and the Board of Estimate approved the project.

Ostensibly a fight about local real estate development, it became for Papp, as well as many others in the theater community, a fight for the future of American theater. Papp met with the several groups — arts activist Joan Davidson's Save Our Broadway Committee, the Natural Resource Defence Council and Actors Equity's Committee to Save the Theaters — opposed to it. For them, the construction of the Marriott Marquis symbolized the triumph of the city's real estate interests over ordinary citizens as well as over the theatrical community. In 1981, lawyers for the Natural Resource Defense Council, Actors Equity and six other unions brought legal action to delay the demolitions. They had commissioned an architect to evaluate a plan to build the hotel *over* the Morosco Theater and emphasized that they were opposed not to the construction of a hotel but to the destruction of historic (and functioning) theaters. They argued that pornography, prostitution and panhandling were *not* problems on 45th Street as they were in Times Square and that the Morosco and Helen Hayes theaters were irreplaceable dramatic houses — as irreplaceable as Carnegie Hall was to musicians — whose acoustics were so sound that they carried an actor's whisper. Moreover, each contained a minihistory of the American drama. When it was announced that New York State and New York City planned to augment the $21.5 million federal grant with local subsidies and tax abatements worth another $33 million in public funds, actors protested that no part of the $55.5 million had been used to explore alternatives to destroying the theaters.

In retrospect, it seems odd that Papp dropped all business at the Public to try to rescue the Broadway theaters. Opinion among Broadway theater producers was divided about the proposed demolitions. Members of the Shubert Organization and others thought the old theaters obsolete and fully supported the hotel project. But Papp, schooled in the philosophy of adaptive reuse by his architect Giorgio Cavaglieri, and always susceptible to appeals for rescue, disagreed. It was also one of the many paradoxes of his life that while he hated and denigrated Broadway, he also honored it. Since the early 1970s, when he had brought Charles Gordone's *No Place to Be Somebody,* Jason Miller's *That Championship Season* and David Rabe's *Sticks and Bones* to Broadway, Papp was determined to put his playwrights at center stage, in the mainstream of American theater tradition, and center stage had always been Broadway. For him, tearing down the Morosco and Helen Hayes, smaller dramatic houses, rather than the larger theaters in which musicals pulled in profits, presaged the end of an art form. "A large hunk of Broadway theater, the dramatic play hunk, was in danger of disappearing," he later wrote. "To state the case as simply as possible: a serious play, a drama, cannot possibly survive on Broadway."

By November 1981, the opposition succeeded in having the Morosco placed in the National Registry of Historic Places. It was then that U.S. secretary of the interior, James Watt, and President Ronald Reagan's chief aide Lyn Nofziger both telephoned the Advisory Council on Historic Preservation to "expedite" discussion on the Morosco. Their intervention was reported by the *Washington Post* and *New York Times*, with the note that the Marriott Corporation was a longtime contributor to the Republican party. Despite this revelation, the director of the Advisory Council signed an agreement permitting demolition.

The first theater, the Bijou, was demolished in January amid a flurry of legal activity. Appeals were brought before state and federal courts to delay the demolitions, and last-minute opposition to the hotel project broadened. Portman's projects, wrote one architect in the *Wall Street Journal*, "have an almost medical antipathy to the street . . . are like giant spaceships . . . always adamant about their alien status. . . . In its outward scale, massing and texture, the Portman Hotel is an affront to the cityscape, unresponsive to the particulars of its immediate context or to the special building traditions of the city. From almost every angle it will look like an enormous box, a 5-story wall blocking views and helping obliterate the rhythm and liveliness of this part of town." One of the features would be a "sidewalk" café located on the hotel's seventh floor. The new theater would be located on the second floor. Political cartoonist/playwright Jules Feiffer drew a cartoon about the "Vietnamization of Broadway" in the *Village Voice* and, in the *Times*, said, "Of course it would help clean things up — we'd get rid of a lower class of thieves and import a higher class of thieves; it's just changing the color of the people who are doing the robbery."

Before 1982, Papp had made only a few public statements on the Marriott Marquis controversy, emphasizing the value of the Morosco and Helen Hayes theaters and opposing the use of public funds as subsidy for a business enterprise. But in the spring of 1982, Papp all but dropped Festival business to lead the Save the Theaters campaign. It was a lackluster season at the Public, with two musicals by an exhausted Liz Swados, the last of David Rabe's plays, *Goose and Tom Tom*, and JoAnne Akalaitis's experimental *Red and Blue*, which one staffer would later call one of the all-time "out there" Festival plays, about a pair of light bulbs, whose lines were recited by actors speaking offstage.

The Save the Theaters campaign was a crisis unfolding within a block from where *A Chorus Line* was becoming the longest-running musical on Broadway, and a battle tailor-made for Joseph Papp. Broadway producer Alexander Cohen might lend his name to the cause, but it was Papp who provided the resources. He recruited Merle Debuskey, who had organized publicity during the fight against Robert Moses in 1959 and CBS in 1973. He telephoned dozens of celebrated actors: "I need you on 45th Street tomorrow at noon." He provided audio, lighting and technical crews, rented a suite in the Piccadilly Hotel, transforming it into twenty-four-hour headquarters, and — for two weeks — lived there. "The point is if you fight this in offices and over the telephones it's deadsville," he told a reporter from the *Washington Post*. "I say keep the street scene alive. Keep the drum beat going. Let people know you're alive."

On March 1, a U.S. appellate court upheld the demolition plans, and Papp led a protest rally of five hundred actors in front of the Morosco. On March 4, Justice Thurgood Marshall of the U.S. Supreme Court issued an injunction preventing demolition through the weekend, and a nineteen-day "Save the Morosco and Helen Hayes Theater Vigil" began. Police had roped off a block of 45th Street, and Festival staffers constructed a stage mounted on a truck — much like the early Mobile Theater — in front of the Morosco, where excerpts from seven Pulitzer Prize–winning plays that had originated there were read by leading actors.

During the vigil, Papp met with lawyers, met with the architect who had written the build-over proposal, met and sought meetings with representatives of Manufacturers Hanover Trust and Equitable Life Insurance — two of the hotel's backers. When he flew to Los Angeles to discuss the film of David Hare's *Plenty*, he kept in touch by phone, managing his Festival staff, which was leading the protest on 45th Street. Some staffers felt the producer was misusing Festival resources. Papp himself conceded that the extent of his involvement was only partly triggered by the issues. "What this whole Portman thing is fucking up is my work on plays at the Public," Papp told the *Washington Post* with the frankness that captivated a second generation of reporters. "I've taken away a lot of people from their jobs here to help with the demonstrations. . . . All the energy I'm putting into the fight I should be putting into the theater itself. Back in the 60s and 70s . . . there was a tremendous amount of ferment. The biggest ferment we've had recently is this Portman battle. . . . If the times were ripe, I'd be producing fantastic plays dealing with the nuclear problem, with war and survival . . . but you can't generate that stuff by yourself. . . . The reason I'm so goddamned caught up in this Portman campaign is because the theater today is not satisfying me in terms of what it's doing. And when the theater gets less of life than what is on the outside, I've got to be out there doing something."

On March 19, the state Supreme Court rejected a new petition to halt demolition and Papp threatened to lie down in front of the bulldozers to stop the demolition of the Morosco. "There was an element of testing his own value and existence in the world," Lynn Holst would later recall. "Joe was brought to life by a fight. There was something in him that needed to struggle and to rescue, that thrived on a cause. He had been traveling and had seemed bored with producing, but now he was available again, energetic and happy."

On Monday, March 22, a forty-ton Caterpillar Traxcavator nicknamed Godzilla was scheduled to wreck the Morosco. "Joe had the empty lot where Godzilla was parked occupied by two hundred people who refused to move," recalled Gail Merrifield. "The demolition could not proceed with people standing in the lot, and Joe orchestrated the timing so that they would be covered on the evening news." Television shows, newspapers and magazines ran shots of Papp and celebrated actors being led off by policemen, some of them in tears. The "Morosco 200" were arrested on 45th Street and taken to the local precinct on 54th Street. Papp himself was arrested, put in a paddy wagon and taken to the precinct. Then — resuming the Festival obligations which had piled up while he was politically engaged — he flew to Washington, D.C., for the opening of *Pirates of Penzance*.

His intervention came two years too late to do any good, wrote *New York* magazine, and Papp himself admitted that he had entered the fight too late to win. But, although the Morosco and Helen Hayes were torn down, public attention turned to the theater district. The Morosco was demolished on the same day that the New York City Planning Commission issued its new West Side Zoning Plan, which encouraged moving new development from the east to west side of Manhattan. Alarmed Landmarks officials began surveying the theater district to determine what should be preserved. Mayor Koch appointed a Theater Advisory Council, which included Joe Papp.

The producer spoke with federal legislators about the feasibility of having the theater zone declared an historic district, met with city planners and, for the next three years — though frustrated by city bureacracy and the polarization of the council into factions — dutifully wrote papers and attended council and subcommittee meetings. "Joe was never a cynical person," said Gail Merrifield. "He also had this extraordinary quality of going into a situation that other people regarded as hopeless and — despite all evidence — believing that there was a possibility to change things. He did it out of a sense of civic responsibility."

It was that sense of civic responsibility, his frustration with the limits of American theater — and, critics said, his inability to refuse any opportunity to feed his ego — that led Papp to accept more and more invitations to lead rallies and lend his name to various causes. By the 1980s, he had loaned it to such groups as Relief to Cambodian Refugees, the Vietnam Veterans Ensemble Theater Company, Amnesty International, the various groups formed to protest the imprisonment of dissidents in Poland and Czechoslovakia, the YIVO Institute for Jewish Research, and AIDS research activists.

He also began to accept invitations to travel abroad. Two months after the Morosco protest, he took off to Southeast Asia as part of a nine-member delegation of the group Vietnam Veterans of America meeting with officials in Hanoi. The United States had no diplomatic relations with Vietnam, and the delegation was briefed by the State Department as to American policy toward the Hanoi government. The Vietnam Veterans Memorial in Washington had not yet been completed; few welcome-home parades for Vietnam war veterans had taken place. But Papp viewed the interests of Vietnam veterans as akin to his own.

His involvement, typically, grew out of a personal encounter. From 1978, Papp had been helping fledgling producer and veteran Tom Bird develop VETCO, a Vietnam veterans' theater company. In December 1981, Bird was one of the first four veterans to go back to Vietnam to discuss with Hanoi officials the twenty-five hundred American soldiers still missing in action, the estimated fifty thousand Amerasian children and the aftereffects of the chemical defoliant Agent Orange used by the American military. Papp was one of the few prominent people who encouraged him.

"It was 1981, and we were embarrassing the Reagan administration by going to Hanoi forcing these issues. When we got tremendous international press coverage, the right-wing hit squads went in action," Bird recalled. "We were called traitors and 'Commie sympathizers' in part because we had visited the tomb of Ho Chi Minh. Joe was the first person of any stature who embraced us. I'd often heard Joe talk about cultural exchange as a way of warming up relations between countries. We had discussed cultural exchange with the Vietnamese, and I suggested Joe come back with us as cultural affairs adviser on our second trip."

Papp threw himself into preparing for the Vietnam mission, flying down to Washington, D.C., for a briefing at the State Department, boning up on American policy. He liked the tall, courteous, open-faced Tom Bird. "My father and Joe were both in the Aleutians in World War II and that confluence bonded me to him in a strong way," Bird later said. "Being a war veteran is a brotherhood, and Joe was very proud of belonging. [In the 1980s] there weren't too many veterans around the New York Shakespeare Festival and it always shocked people when I introduced him as such. It was a side he rarely showed in public — he was identified with the antiwar movement."

Papp looked forward to the respite from Festival business and, to assure the mission publicity, contacted the CBS show *60 Minutes.* "We were sitting in his office," Bird recalled, "and suddenly he said, 'I have an idea — get me Don Hewitt.' Joe explained what we were doing and they offered to send Harry Reasoner with us. He put his hand over the receiver and asked: 'How's Harry Reasoner?' We said Mike Wallace would be better, so he said into the phone, 'We think this would be a good assignment for Mike Wallace.'"

The delegation, accompanied by Wallace and his crew from *60 Minutes,* flew to Bangkok. There, the producer discovered that though he was well supplied with French brandy, American cigarettes, a personal medical kit and several rolls of toilet paper, he lacked an airplane ticket to continue on to Hanoi. He bought one for $150 in American cash, but it was only one-way, and as he flew above the rice paddies in what he later called "the nearest thing to a flying sauna," Papp was glad Mike Wallace was there.

Papp had first met Wallace in the late 1950s, as a CBS stage manager. "Mike Wallace is one of the great provocateur television journalists," he later wrote. "His interviews are masterly demonstrations of entrapment through a mixture of guile and true blue curiosity. With all my knowledge of Mike and his methods, I must confess that under his interrogation, to me very warm and supportive, I felt totally assured that it was free from any conniving or intent to do me injury. My life experience informed me this notion is naiveté of the first order. But I cannot help being fond of this twentieth century muckraker and to trust him where I am concerned."

The plane landed in Hanoi, with *Times* correspondent Colin Campbell and AP correspondent Dennis Gray along to report on proceedings. The delegation set to work filling out customs forms and Papp again felt — as he had during the Morosco campaign — that sense of being in the world. "Turning to the window at the extraordinary sound of a passing MIG 21 which disappeared as soon as it appeared, the memory of the war and all of the heartache it produced swept over me," he wrote. "Just a few hours ago, I had left a luxurious suite in an internationally acclaimed hotel in Bangkok and a few days before that I had been in London looking at the edited film of the *Pirates of Penzance* and a new production of it on the West End. Back in the States I had left behind me three new productions about to go into rehearsal and a nervous staff of people wondering what the effects of my absence would have on the progress of this work. In my new surroundings, all of these so recent experiences seemed remote and frankly, of no great importance. Another MIG whooshed and screamed by. . . ."

He recalled his associations with the name "Hanoi": the newspaper headlines, the description of the "tricky and unyielding" troops that had defeated the French at Dien Bien Phu, who kept rebuilding the Ho Chi Minh trail after bombings. "Hanoi had always sounded to me like a hard name, the foe, an enemy name," he wrote. "The war was over and except for the MiGs, the airfield appeared to me as menacing as the back-lot of a gas station in some small Southern town. . . ."

Papp found himself slowing down in Vietnam as he never had in New York. As the eldest of the delegates and unencumbered by a personal history in the country, he was often able to defuse tensions between the veterans and officials with the charm so striking in his early career. "He was wonderful with John Holdridge, the assistant secretary of state for Southeast Asia, who was a true hard-line cold warrior," said Tom Bird. "And he charmed Madame How, a former guerrilla fighter who had lived in tunnels with the Vietcong for ten years and hated us. Joe spoke to her in French. He sang for her and turned this woman around."

An approximation of French was only one of the unexpected things that issued forth from Papp. In Saigon, the delegation was driven past a guardhouse and through two sets of black steel gates to an old French villa, whose beautiful lawns and trees and gardens were confined by eight-foot walls topped with crushed glass. "We all thought it was a wonderful place," Bird recalled, "but Joe got paranoid and said he couldn't stay there, that this had happened to his people once before and he wouldn't allow it to happen to him. Mike Wallace was staying in a hotel downtown and he wanted to be housed there, where he could feel less confined. I had to negotiate with the Vietnamese and threaten to report them to the foreign minister before they finally gave him a suite in the hotel."

Papp was grateful to Bird for his intervention and even more impressed when, after several delegation members said they wished to remain in Saigon and spend a day shopping, Bird insisted that they drive toward the Cambodian border to see the effects of Agent Orange. On a long ride to Vung Tau, gazing out through the lace curtains of an air-conditioned limousine at the rice paddies and water buffaloes, the producer fell into the confessional mood that often strikes travelers far from home, a mood that startled Tom Bird. "Out of nowhere he started telling me his life story, talking about his family, how he'd been so driven by his work and building his organization that he'd been remiss as a father and how proud he was of his children nonetheless," recalled Bird. "He felt that his relationship with his daughter Barbara was on solid footing even though she had been born out of wedlock and hadn't known about him for much of her life. He was concerned about his youngest son, Tony, and the choices he needed to make about what he was going to do with his life. Tony was drifting and had been angry at him. Joe hoped he could work things out. He talked about his marriages — and how at one point he had decided to never marry again but changed his mind when he met Gail because finally he had found someone who was always there for him, someone he could trust. He seemed to make trust and loyalty paramount to what he was looking for in a woman.

"I was pretty blown away, but I didn't know what to do but listen. Then, after telling me his whole story, he asked, 'How can I help you?' I said VETCO needed some space to do workshops. He said, 'Workshops? You don't need workshops. I'll tell you what you need. You need a hit. Here's what I'll do. We'll do a two-play deal and I'll challenge you 3–1.' I'm the most stunned person on the planet at that point. Not only have I heard his life story but by the time we got to Vung Tau, he offered me a deal."

When Papp returned from Vietnam, he spent a few weeks trying to arrange for a young Vietnamese pianist to play in the United States as the opening wedge of a cultural exchange between the two countries. But his efforts produced no results. The State Department was opposed to the initiation of any cultural exchange. However, international cultural exchange — in which he had first become interested during his trip to the Soviet Union three years earlier — was again drawing his interest. "I wouldn't mind being called upon by the government to do something of a cultural nature," he told *New York* magazine. "For example, if the United States government appointed me to be cultural ambassador-at-large, I would be interested."

The Reagan administration had no such plans, and Papp proceeded to engineer his international cultural exchanges alone. In 1984, he traveled to Cuba, England, Sweden, the USSR, Czechoslovakia and Brazil; in 1985, back to London and Sweden, to Spain, Venezuela and Puerto Rico. His travel to Spanish-speaking countries was in the service of the Festival Latino, which was beginning to attract the interest of several governments. In Brazil, Papp shopped for plays and playwrights. In Cuba, he accepted cigars, met with the minister of culture, spent a day touring a showcase collective farm with Fidel Castro's older brother, Mungo, and performed a scene from *Twelfth Night* — in which he spoke English, and Bibi Andersson spoke Swedish — before a Cuban audience. "There are no tractors or photographs of Castro in the streets," Papp told *Variety* when he got back. "They are so far removed from the

Soviets, they make it seem as if socialism can be fun. . . . We went to nightclubs like the Copacabana and the Tropicana. They reminded me of the Folies Bergère and the Cotton Club in Harlem. The music is excellent, very much alive. . . . The Cubans know Americans. They take our television off satellites. They are anxious to have relations with the U.S. . . . Cuba is the natural ally of the U.S. Not only because it is only 90 miles from us, but also because the culture, the music, the art is all very much interlocked with ours. Culturally, I hope we get past all this confrontation business." Of all he saw in Cuba, it was the show at the Tropicana that he wished to bring to New York.

In Sweden, Papp was invited to the premiere of Ingmar Bergman's *King Lear,* which marked the director's return to the stage. Papp also flew to Prague and made a trip out into the Czechoslovak countryside where dissident playwright Václav Havel was living under house arrest, bringing Havel his Obie Award from 1968 for *The Memorandum.* Since his 1979 trip to the USSR, despite the Reagan administration's foreign policy, the Russian invasion of Afghanistan and other cold war battles, Papp had been pursuing his idea of theater exchange. For five years he kept open negotiations for rights to Victor Rozov's *The Nest of the Wood Grouse,* a play about the family of an obtuse Soviet foreign ministry official, with an interesting set of characters and candid arguments about abortion and religion. Finally, in 1983, he had acquired the rights. After directing the production at the Public, Papp proposed a joint Soviet-American TV production and flew to Moscow for meetings. NBC's *Today* show interviewed Papp on the roof of the Rasia Hotel overlooking the Kremlin, talking about the benefits of cultural exchange.

His travels abroad, particularly to Latin America, influenced his work in New York, where he became ever more interested in the Spanish-speaking population. That interest soon meshed in his mind with his thoughts about Koch's Theater Advisory Council, which produced a report for which Papp was largely responsible and which was ignored by the mayor. Papp had concluded, in opposition to the strict preservation-ists, that it made no sense to save theaters if they were to remain empty. "If you don't have an audience for serious plays, you may as well not save those dramatic houses," he said. "What's the good? You're just saving buildings. You save them because you want them to operate, not because you want to preserve the buildings. . . ." He saw the theater crisis as akin to the crisis of the American automobile industry and insisted that the theater, like the Chrysler Corporation, needed government bailout. He drew up a plan for what he called "a National Theater." In it, five unused theaters would be leased and operated by a consortium of New York and regional nonprofit theaters such as Des McAnuff's La Jolla Playhouse and Gordon Davidson's Mark Taper Forum. The consortium would be financed by a combination of subscriptions and government and foundation grants as well as the sale of development rights belonging to the theaters. He planned such economies as paying star actors minimal wages, negotiating lower rents from theater owners and concessions from the various theater unions, holding costs down to under $500,000 per show.

But the theater world had never been known for cohesion or cooperation among its producers or landlords. Moreover, Papp had not cultivated relationships with other theater heads. He was a loner rather than a coalition builder and was unsuccessful in persuading other theaters, regional or in New York City, to adopt his idea. Here, too, he forged ahead by himself, coming up with the outlines of what would, a few years later, become the Belasco Project.

The Belasco Project coupled the Save the Theaters campaign with Papp's interest in what was now being called "multiculturalism." Braiding together the issues of unused Broadway theaters, the absence of black or Hispanic playwrights from the Public, the changes in New York City demographics and the declining theater audience, Papp returned to Shakespeare and the schools population. In the first decade of the Festival, he had worked closely with New York City's Board of Education bringing Shakespeare to high school students. But that arrangement had fallen apart in 1970 when New York City schools were decentralized and it became too difficult to put together a touring schedule. If he wanted to develop new urban audiences as an alternative to the suburban or business-account audience of Broadway, he had to begin with kids. "What you are trying to do is restock a lake where all the fish are dead," he told the *Daily News*. "You have to get the dead fish out and put some live ones in and spawn them. It's the most important part of this job. Writers will begin to write if they know they have a theater and an audience to write for." High school students would be bussed to Broadway with their teachers and their families who, reflecting the change in New York's demographics, were now African-Americans, Latino and Asian immigrants, many of whom had never been inside a theater or seen a Shakespearean play.

The Belasco — like the Delacorte and the Mobile Theater — would function outside the money economy. He negotiated with the Shubert Organization, which gave him the 1,000-seat Belasco Theater rent-free. He negotiated with school chancellor Nathan Quinones for $1 million — he would eventually receive half that amount — in underwriting from New York City. He negotiated for wage concessions with the eleven

Broadway unions. In addition to the financial support he intended to get
from the city, Papp planned to attract corporate sponsors. His experience
with the Third World Company had taught him that such a project
needed a suitable director and he began to look for one.

While Papp devoted time and energy to cultural exchange and the
Belasco, the growing number of film, television and cable deals, and the
running of an organization that now employed nearly 150 people, he
increasingly left the development of new work at the Public Theater to
his wife. It was Gail Merrifield and her staff who were charged with
finding the socially relevant, poetic and provocative plays that had engaged Papp since 1966. And it was during this time that, finally, a political
play with the explosive anger and urgency of David Rabe's work on
Vietnam arrived in her department. The playwright was Larry Kramer.
Papp had never heard of him.

Gray-haired and professorial in appearance, Larry Kramer was, in
1984, a controversial figure in the gay community, a man who equaled
Papp in candor, confrontational style and explosive anger. A Yale graduate, he had had a career in film production, most of it in London. In
1970, he had received an Academy Award nomination for his screenplay
adaptation of D. H. Lawrence's *Women in Love,* directed by Ken Russell.
In 1978, he wrote the novel *Faggots,* which he described as "an exploration of what it was like to be gay in the 1970s." *Faggots* took the reader
into the discos, bars, city neighborhoods and beaches of the fast-lane gay
community, critiquing the hedonistic lifestyle it documented. It received
a mixed reception from critics. Kramer later said he received thousands
of letters from readers "who liked that I said it like it was: that people
were so desperate for love that in their desperation they overdosed on it,
that people had been locked in closets for so long that this was their only
outlet." The *Gay Community News* called *Faggots* "appalling" and "offensive." Manhattan's one gay bookstore did not carry the novel. Critics
called him a self-hating homophobe, whose Jewish upbringing had fused
with Puritanism into anti-eroticism. The party set viewed him as a neurotic, hellbent on spoiling their party.

By 1981, Kramer had noticed that several of his friends were getting
sick. When he read a *Times* article that summer titled "Rare Cancer
Found in 41 Homosexuals," he was moved to action. After physicians
Linda Laubenstein and Alvin Freidman-Kien urged him to raise money
for research on the disease, Kramer hosted a fundraiser in his apartment,
and by January 1982 had pushed the group into establishing the Gay
Men's Health Crisis. In March 1983, he published a cover story in New
York's gay publication, the *New York Native,* titled "1,112 and Count-

ing." It was an investigative reporting piece on the disease and what journalist Randy Shilts would later call "one of the most influential works of advocacy journalism of the decade." Kramer began his piece by writing, "If this article doesn't scare the shit out of you we're in real trouble. If this article doesn't rouse you to anger, fury, rage and action, gay men may have no future on this earth." He then attacked the medical establishment, the *New York Times,* the gay community and Mayor Edward Koch — "With his silence on AIDS, the mayor of New York is helping to kill us" — for ignoring the problem.

After watching several friends die, Kramer became obsessed with AIDS. That obsession and his personal abrasiveness made him a pariah in some circles. During the summer of 1983, he had been booted out of GMHC, the organization he had helped establish. "The organization was founded to spread information and fight," he said, "and it turned into a bunch of candy-stripers." Some people found such a remark offensive; Kramer found it true.

Hurt and at loose ends, Kramer flew to Europe. In London, he saw *A Map of the World,* a play by David Hare soon to be produced by Papp, that reminded him of the impact Hare's *Plenty* and Caryl Churchill's *Top Girls* had had on him in New York. In Munich, he took a side trip to the concentration camp at Dachau. When he read that the camp had begun operating in 1933 — eight years before America entered the Second World War — he identified the indifference of the world toward the annihilation of the Jews, homosexuals and others that the Nazis termed undesirable with the indifference of the world to the annihilation caused by AIDS.

He returned to the U.S. with a sense of personal mission and began writing a play that he viewed as a call to arms. "I wanted Ed Koch and Ronald Reagan and the *New York Times* to change and I was naive enough to believe that a play would help do that. To my mind, everything in the play was the truth." Taking his title from a line of a poem by W. H. Auden, he named it *The Normal Heart.*

The Normal Heart was turned down by every major agent in New York, Kramer later said, and by many directors including Tommy Tune, Arthur Penn and Mike Nichols. Like so many other playwrights, Kramer thought the best place for the play was the Public Theater, and he gave it to Emmett Foster, Papp's personal assistant and a volunteer at GMHC, who passed it on to the Play Department. Kramer, who had been encouraged by the quick and sympathetic readings of the three directors, was irritated by continuing silence from the Public. "I used to send periodic letters to Joe Papp, whom I had never met," he later said. "'Mike Nichols said that this play should be done at the Public. Tommy Tune said it moved him so much he was afraid to direct it. So why am I not hearing from you?'" At the same time, Kramer was fearful of what might happen when he met the producer, given both their tempers. He also suspected that, like many 1930s radicals, Papp was radical about everything but homosexuality.

It was true that Papp occasionally made a thoughtless remark regarding homosexuals. "Now I hope I won't be attacked by the Gay Liberation group," he told the *Intellectual Digest* in 1973, "because I don't discriminate against anyone for sex, race or color, but the fact is my theater is a strongly heterosexual theater, both in its playwrights and the kind of plays we put on." But that remark was mild compared to his pronouncements on other matters, and the fact was he had employed both closeted and uncloseted homosexuals since the late 1950s as his closest associates. "I was not ever uncomfortable as a gay man around Joe," said David Black, who had started working in the office under the stairs at the Heckscher and remained with Papp for eighteen years. "I think now in retrospect that Joe was uncomfortable with the fact that he was *not* uncomfortable with gay men. He never, ever, made any derogatory remarks about gay men in my presence nor did he ever slight me because I was gay."

Playwright Tom Babe noted that Papp "didn't seem to know who was gay and who wasn't, or didn't seem to want to know. He never expressed any thoughts to me about the people we worked with one way or the other, nor did he make any easy jokes. Rather, what I saw was a wall of silence, the casual inadvertence, the hesitancy to ask pointed questions. Only once did he say to me of a director we both knew to be gay, 'A different sort of director, you see, would have gotten it.' I felt sad about Joe's inability to separate an artistic failure from what he perceived as a kind of psychological crippling."

The reason Kramer did not hear from Papp was that his letters — one of which berated Papp for ignoring a play about AIDS although he had a homosexual son — were intercepted long before they reached Papp's office and because the Festival employed many gay staffers who thought Kramer an impossible man. The Public's Play Department had received several plays about AIDS that had been returned to their senders because staffers knew Papp recoiled from plays about illness. Several play-readers thought Kramer's script poor. Moreover, they dreaded his telephone calls and tried to protect both Papp and Merrifield from him.

"It was a mess, two plays in one," Merrifield recalled thinking, when she finally saw the play. "Way too long and overwritten but after I finished it, I cried. It must have been in February [of 1984] that I called Larry and told him I liked his play very much. We met and I liked him. He had a grizzled gray beard, in his mid-forties, stocky, a very warm, very bright man who always brought his dog, Molly, with him. He had written one play before, called *Sissies' Scrapbook*."

For the next eight months, Kramer and Merrifield met regularly to work on the script. She asked him question after question and, in response, Kramer began rethinking and rewriting his script. There was no contract between them and no promise of pay — only the hope that Papp would like the result. For months, the two honed the primary characters: writer Ned Weeks, based on Kramer himself; his heterosexual brother, Ben; his lover, a *Times* fashion reporter; and Dr. Emma Brookner, a wheelchair-bound physician crusading for AIDS research. "Gail started asking me all these questions and she noticed that I answered with great passion," Kramer later said. "She would say: 'Can't you see how excited this makes you? Why didn't you put that into the play?' And I would say: 'I didn't know that stuff like that could go into the play.' She'd say: 'Put everything in!' The main reason the family stuff went out is the political stuff came in. I was extraordinarily fortunate. A great editor does not tell you what to do. A great editor makes you sense what you want to do and facilitates *your* doing it. Going home to write after our sessions was like taking the lid off the volcano. The whole process was electric. It was like firecrackers going off for me all the time. I had never had such energy. This play was going to change the world."

As he rewrote, Kramer continued sending out his script to various theaters: Playwrights Horizons, the Manhattan Theater Club, Yale, the Circle Rep. "I'm very pragmatic," he said. "I was angry I had no commitment from the Public but I also knew that because of Gail my play was getting better. And I was hoping that if someone else made me an offer I'd be able to say to Joe: 'Put up or shut up.'"

The next step was to have Papp read it. Over the years, some staffers had left Play Development in frustration because they had failed to draw the producer's attention to pet projects. The playwright's best hope was Gail Merrifield, but even she often failed. "Gail would say: 'I met a very interesting writer today' and Joe would say, very quietly: 'Why was he so interesting?' and Gail would have to defend her choice," a Festival staffer recalled. "It was difficult for anyone to stand up to Joe and, for Gail, being his wife, there was so much at stake when she liked a writer or a play." In championing *The Normal Heart*, Merrifield knew she was up against her husband's strongest antipathies: "Gail, I don't want to read a play about AIDS," he said when she introduced it. "I don't want to *do* a play about AIDS. I hate to do plays about cancer. I hate to do plays about illness. It'll only depress me. It's too long. I have no time to read it."

Merrifield went out on a limb as she had done for rock composer Rupert Holmes and *The Mystery of Edwin Drood*. When finally Papp read it, he had objections. "There's so much junk in this thing, I can't get through it," Papp complained. "It's overwritten. It's overblown. . . . Some of the stuff is so poor and so outrageous and there's a moment here and there. . . . This is one of the worst things I've ever read." But by the time he had finished, as Papp later put it, "plowing his way through it," he was crying. "Here was a play," he later said, "that I felt was putting us in touch with the world again."

Despite their common objectives in seeing *The Normal Heart* to success, neither Kramer nor Papp looked forward to a meeting. Each had been amply warned about the other. Their similarities were obvious: Both were smart, blunt, impatient New York Jews. Both were social activists, imbued since childhood by a strong moralistic sense and a passion for social justice. Papp wanted to schedule a reading followed by a workshop. Kramer implored him to go straight to a production. Papp agreed.

"It was a wonderful relationship and both of us were moved and enriched by it," Kramer would later recall. "He didn't really become involved until we started the previews. He came to auditions, was concerned with casting it properly, didn't get on very well with director or set designer but didn't interfere. Bill Hart was pretty much the man on the scene. Joe insisted on shifting two scenes in the second act. The thing about Joe was that some ideas he had were great and others were terrible but everything was delivered as an ultimatum so you had to learn how to walk through the minefield carefully. I shifted the scenes. The only fight we had was about a line he wanted taken out that Ed Koch was gay. I said I wouldn't. He said, 'Then I'm not going to do the play' and hung up. I went back to rehearsal, told everybody Joe said he wasn't going to do the play and that was the last that was ever said about that." In *The Normal Heart*, the protagonist says:

> Time is not on our side. If you won't take word to the Mayor, what do we do? How do we get it to him? Hire a hunky hustler and send him up to Gracie Mansion with our plea tattooed on his cock?

The playwright would later describe the care with which the production proceeded in the same glowing terms as had the playwrights who had preceded him since 1967. Although agreeing on a director had at first been a problem between Kramer and Papp, the playwright marveled at the expertise of the Casting Department, the designers and technicians and at the producer's unwavering personal support.

The Normal Heart opened April 21, 1985, to mixed reviews. "Although Mr. Kramer's theatrical talents are not always as highly developed as his conscience, there can be no doubt that *The Normal Heart* is the most outspoken play around," wrote Frank Rich in the *Times*. "The aesthetic failings of Larry Kramer's *The Normal Heart* — as plentiful as bacteria in a human mouth," wrote Michael Feingold in the *Village Voice,* "are balanced by the truth of what Kramer has to say: historically, politically, epidemiologically." Some critics called it a masterpiece of political theater, comparing the play to Ibsen's *An Enemy of the People*. Others found fault with it and noted other AIDS plays, including William A. Hoffman's *As Is,* which had opened earlier. "Kramer's play — probably more autobiographical, informed, and data-filled, but also more intemperate and biased — is less literate and poetic than *As Is,*" wrote John Simon, "but more rousingly polemical, more politically and morally challenging."

For Papp, no other AIDS play existed. On opening night, he sent Kramer a card. "Dear Larry," he wrote. "Once every ten years or so a play comes along that fulfills my original idea of what role my theater must play in society. *The Normal Heart* is that play — and it fills me with pride (and tears) in being the producer of this play — Thank you, dear friend, for your noble fire. Love, Joe."

Audiences who came to see *The Normal Heart* responded to the play in the tradition of audiences for *Sticks and Bones, for colored girls* and *A Chorus Line*. They laughed and wept in recognition and, when the play ended, many did not move from their seats. Audience size fluctuated, but Papp could not bring himself to close *The Normal Heart*. Although it lost money there, it became the longest-running show ever at the Public Theater. In less than a decade, it would be given more than six hundred productions throughout the world.

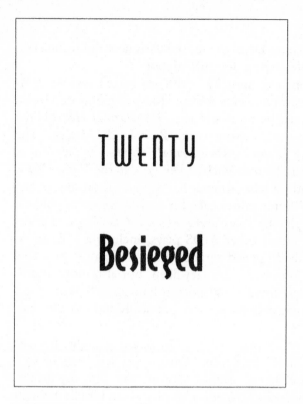

TWENTY

Besieged

O<small>N</small> APRIL 1, 1987, Joseph Papp had his annual physical. For months, he had been complaining of aches in his ribs and back but his heavy schedule had kept him from seeing a doctor. He had begun interviews for the New York Shakespeare Festival's Oral History Project; he was supervising several shows, including *The Knife,* another wildly nontraditional musical about a married man with three children who decides to have a sex-change operation. The playwright David Hare and leading man Mandy Patinkin were very nervous, as was Papp, who had invested more than half a million dollars into the show.

In February, just before *The Knife* was to open, Papp flew to the Soviet Union, where he had been invited to a conference on nuclear disarmament and where he continued negotiating a Soviet-American coproduction of a television series. On his return, he performed in a benefit for the YIVO Institute for Jewish Research, testified on the arts in Albany, New York, and was planning the summer season in Central Park.

Artistic director Wilford Leach was to have directed the first of the

Delacorte plays. But he had telephoned from London, where he was directing *Drood,* and said he was ill with a bronchial infection. When Papp asked questions, Leach talked about the damp London weather, then began to sob. He said he felt terrible about letting Papp down but he would be unable to direct *Two Gentlemen of Verona* in the park that summer. When Papp offered to fly to London, Leach asked him to remain in New York. Papp told him to take whatever time he needed to get well and pushed the conversation to the back of his mind.

By 1987, the producer had received many odd calls concerning illness. The first had been about Robert Yodice, the set designer for twelve Festival shows. Yodice suddenly began disposing of his paintings, giving the Papps a hermaphrodite nude. Later, they learned he had been diagnosed with AIDS and had committed suicide. Then *Pirates of Penzance* orchestrator Bill Elliott had left for the West Coast in pursuit of film work. A few months later, he had died of AIDS. Actor/director Charles Ludlam of the Ridiculous Theater, whom Papp had asked to direct the Central Park production following *Two Gentlemen of Verona,* canceled his engagement. He was hospitalized with AIDS.

"At least 20 people who worked here have died," Papp had told a reporter in 1985. "The first time we were surprised that a person so young — he was 23 — was stricken. We had a memorial for him, and then another and another for other victims. At one point we had a memorial every few months. It's horrible to see."

Papp was involved with AIDS activists: playwright Larry Kramer had cofounded the Gay Men's Health Crisis; Papp's son Tony, his personal assistant Emmett Foster and his longtime board member Judy Peabody all worked as volunteers there. But the producer had never before connected AIDS with Wilford Leach. Leach had never brought a lover to the Papps' home. Neither he nor Merrifield had ever had a conversation with Leach about his private life. They assumed he was celibate or gay and respected his reticence on the subject.

When Papp finally went to his annual physical, he was worried more about Leach than about himself. He was prepared to hear the conventional wisdom, that as a sixty-six-year-old man he could expect some aches and pains and should think about slowing down. Instead, the doctor found a lump in his prostate gland. He ordered tests. And a few days later, he telephoned to report that they indicated cancer.

"I've never seen Joe so stunned and immobilized," Merrifield later recalled. Her response was to find everything ever written about the disease. Papp, faced with four days of waiting for final test confirmations, flew to Mexico City. He had been scheduled to fly by helicopter into the jungle of the Yucatán Peninsula to see the work of El Laboratorio Teatro y Indigena and he proceeded with his plans.

When he returned to New York, his test results were confirmed. He and Merrifield spent hours in tears, holding one another and consulting with New York medical personnel who, as Merrifield said, "had only frightening and contradictory advice to offer." Ultimately, they called the prostate cancer specialist at Boston's Dana-Farber Cancer Institute, Dr. Marc Garnick. Garnick's assistant had seen Papp on television and in *People* magazine. His research nurse had grown up hearing about Joseph Papp, seen *A Chorus Line* ten times and felt as though she owed him something. He was booked for an appointment the following day.

When the Papps arrived in Boston's Logan Airport, they looked like smaller, grayer versions of themselves. But when he spoke, Papp was unchanged. He talked in his usual rapid-fire, stream-of-consciousness way, in control, as though fighting cancer would be like fighting Moses or CBS or City Hall. "Gail has done a tremendous amount of research," he said. "There's no cure for prostate cancer — just a treatment to slow the progression of the disease. It involves chemical or actual castration. I'm not prepared to do that at this time. It's unacceptable to me. Maybe if I were in great pain. Maybe if I believed I were dying. . . ."

At Dana-Farber, the Papps were ushered into the office of Dr. Garnick, a forty-year-old physician who for fifteen years had been researching prostate cancer. Garnick looked at Papp's stack of medical records and took a history. His examinations and lab tests indicated prostate cancer. His bone scan showed multiple "hot spots" in the ribs, spine, joints, hip and pelvis. Papp had, Garnick thought, one of the most advanced states of prostate cancer he had ever seen at a first consult. With his degree of disease, Papp could be dead within six months.

But Garnick was, by nature, an optimist and the kind of doctor who listened closely to his patients. The Papps did not ask how long the producer had to live and Garnick himself had never seen the point in setting a time limit on any patient's life. Also, although he himself had never heard of the producer, he had noticed the effect Papp's name had on his wife, his nurse and his assistant — all of whom had impressed upon him what an unusual man he was. His own clinical observations included the note that Papp looked and acted far younger than his stated age of sixty-six and that his relationship with his wife seemed unusually close. Often the married couples he saw were "in very different places psychologically with the disease creating a gulf between them." The Papps behaved like one unit.

Garnick addressed them as such. The disease had metastasized far into the bone, he told them. There were only three modalities of treatment: surgical castration, chemical castration using DES and a third, hormonal, experimental option — a course of dual-hormone therapy that blocked the pituitary gland's release of hormones that induced the production of testosterone. The problem with this third option was that *before* it blocked the release of hormones, it stimulated them. If Papp's tumor had grown close to his spinal cord, the treatment was high risk.

Garnick asked the Papps if they had any questions. He was never sure how much people actually took in. They needed time to process the data. Often, he had to go over the same facts again and again for months. But the Papps were already familiar with all three options. Merrifield handed the startled specialist a 400-page computer printout from the National Library of Medicine that she had compiled.

"Everything about them was unique," Garnick later recalled. "Usually I spend an hour with patients the first time. But we spent three or four." Papp seemed to view his illness as a major but workable problem demanding a solution. He would be an exacting patient, Garnick thought, like some of the CEOs he treated. But the chemistry between them was good. The Papps would not play one doctor against another. But Garnick wondered why they were seeking treatment in Boston, two hundred miles away from their home.

Papp explained that he did not relate to the doctors he had seen in New York and that he was concerned about word getting out that he was sick. It would curtail his ability to attract talent and funding to the Festival. And no matter how sympathetic people might be, he said, they would write him off.

Did he wish to take the weekend to mull over the options?

No, said Papp. He was ready to begin treatment that afternoon. Garnick said that was impossible. Papp had to have more tests and he himself had to obtain one of the two drugs, which was "investigational" and not yet approved by the FDA. (It would be two and a half years before the treatment was legal.) He promised that if he could legally obtain an FDA waiver and supplies of the drug, Papp could begin treatment by the following weekend.

It was only after the Papps had left that Garnick realized neither of them had asked for a prognosis. Over the next four and a half years they never did.

"I felt really proud that he chose me to be his doctor," Garnick later said. "Joe didn't only want a doctor — he wanted a friend. I knew he chose special people in his life and I felt as though I couldn't let him down. With Joe, nothing was routine. It was like playing basketball with Larry Bird or Magic Johnson — it raised the level of the game. It raised my physician's skills to a higher level. I always had to be thinking five steps ahead."

After the Papps returned to New York City that April weekend in 1987, the producer told only a few people of his condition. He called his children, his former therapist, his assistant Barbara Carroll, his casting director Rosemarie Tichler, his associate producer Steve Cohen, and actors Meryl Streep, Mandy Patinkin and Kathryn Grody, Kevin Kline and Phoebe Cates. And he asked Kline and Cates, who had met and married while at the Festival, to get into a cab and come over.

"Joe told us he was very sick," Kline later recalled. "We were both taken aback. It was the first time I had seen Joe not in total control, as though the rug had been pulled out from under him. I asked questions and said corny things like 'You'll beat it. You're a fighter, Joe. With your spirit, you'll live to be a hundred.' And then he went right into his plans for a Shakespeare marathon. He wanted to do the whole canon and said that I had to play Hamlet again, even though I had just played it the year before. It became a strangely professional conversation under the circumstances. But the connection between his illness and the Marathon was clear to me. He wanted a commitment from me right then and there.

"He had said he was returning to Boston for tests. When Phoebe and I got home, we called back and offered to go to Boston with him and keep him and Gail company. He said, 'Let me think about it.' Then he called back and asked us to come with him. We were surprised. He was always the person other people came to with their needs. It was the first time I had ever seen him acknowledge any kind of personal need at all."

By 1987, the thirty-nine-year-old Kevin Kline had emerged as Papp's featured actor much as George C. Scott had emerged thirty years before. He had come to the Festival as a spear-carrier in 1970 but it was not until ten years later, when he played the Pirate King in *Pirates of Penzance*, that he got to know Papp.

"I had loved being the Pirate King and working with Wil Leach for five weeks in Central Park," he recalled, "but doing it eight times a week for a year on Broadway nearly killed me. There was a free-for-all atmosphere at the core of the production that occasionally took its toll. I'd signed on for this long run and one day I was so frustrated, I kicked the door of my dressing room off its hinges. Joe came to talk to me. He said: 'You know we're *renting* this theater. I think expressions of temperament can be a good thing, but we're going to have to fix that door.' I was touched by his way of indulging me and at the same time cautioning me not to make it a regular event. I said: 'Are you telling me I have to pay for it?' He said: 'Oh no, no, no — we'll take care of it.' It was a side of Joe I'd never seen before."

It was during that year, Kline recalled, that their friendship began. The Acting Company, of which Kline was a founding member, was honoring the producer with the John Houseman Award. Papp indicated that in place of an acceptance speech, he would sing a duet with Kline. "He chose the song 'Stouthearted Men' — with the idea of our accompanying ourselves on kazoos," Kline recalled. "Well, during a rehearsal in his apartment when we started doing these elaborate kazoo riffs, we lapsed into a childlike lunacy and wound up literally on the floor, laughing until we cried. He had this wonderful silly streak which jibed with my own. I started to see that this guy — this producer who could instill fear — was also an inveterate punster who could not — even on the most serious occasions — pass up an opportunity to make a joke. Also, he was not the disciplinarian I expected him to be. He was more like a nagging conscience or a kind of forceful paternal figure I did not have in my life: a *demanding* father."

Kline, Cates, Papp and Merrifield all checked into Boston's Ritz-Carlton Hotel and Papp began a week of extensive tests. "We walked around Boston and we stayed up all night talking," Kline later recalled. "At times, he was in very good spirits — as if there was nothing wrong. He believed in the treatment. He learned to give himself injections. And man-to-man, he confessed to feeling uneasy about tampering with his hormones. He said things like 'I start wondering whether I'll lose what makes me a man' or 'I don't know the extent to which I'm going to lose something of myself.' He was very vulnerable."

The Garnicks, the Klines and the Papps dined together and, on April 26, Papp began the dual-hormone treatment. "Everything about the process was extraordinary," said Garnick. "My relationship to both Joe and Gail; our decision-making process; the way Joe was able to articulate what was happening to him. He was the only man I've ever treated who was able to verbalize how his physical, emotional and sexual being was being modulated by the therapy. He was not only *able* to talk about the effects of the lowered testosterone but to talk about it with lucidity. He was thoroughly in touch with his feelings in all their aspects. And the length of time he remained in good health was extraordinary. Instead of six months, he had four good years."

On May 4, Dr. Garnick wrote in his assessment that Papp was doing exceptionally well and, two days later, Papp and Merrifield flew to London to attend the press opening of *Drood*. When he arrived, Papp learned that Wilford Leach had turned the show over to choreographer Graciela Daniele and disappeared. For two weeks, no one was able to find him. Then he surfaced in a Manhattan hotel where he had checked in under another name. Leach had AIDS. He was no longer able to direct a show. He could no longer function as the Festival's artistic director.

The producer decided to direct *Richard II* that summer and asked Stuart Vaughan to direct *Two Gentleman of Verona* in place of Leach. To sweeten the offer, he told Vaughan — with whom he had not spoken in over a decade — that he planned to establish a resident classical company that the director would head. "Well, hell, that's what he should have been doing all along," Vaughan later said. "He knew I was the guy who saved the bacon and also — because he thought he was dying — he was making peace with everyone in sight."

That May, although two theaters were closed for renovation, the Public was busy. George C. Wolfe's *The Colored Museum,* a satire of African-American theater history and stereotypes, had been playing for several months. Performance artist Eric Bogosian was rehearsing *Talk Radio,* his first full play. Papp himself worked on directing *Richard II,* studying the play, reading books on the historical background, meeting with set, lighting and costume designers, and, at the end of the month, began a ten-to-seven rehearsal schedule from Tuesday to Sunday. He had decided to produce three plays that summer, following *Richard II* with its sequel, *Henry IV, Part I,* and immersed himself in the story.

"Richard isn't necessarily a martyr," he told an interviewer, "for in Shakespeare, the character who controls language is the character who controls the play. On any stage, and particularly on the Shakespearean stage, language is power and language is life."

As he prepared *Richard II,* he sat for two Festival Oral History interviews as well as others with National Public Radio and *Gentlemen's Quarterly* magazine, sang at a benefit for Marvin Camillo's theater group, traveled to Philadelphia to accept an honorary doctorate from the Philadelphia College of Arts and visited Wilford Leach at New York Hospital.

He also fought — as he had for thirty years — with the city. He wrote to Mayor Koch's chief of staff, Diane Coffey:

> I am sorry to learn that the Executive Budget for fiscal year 1988 shows a decrease in support for the New York Shakespeare Festival. . . . I am in rehearsal, directing *Richard II* for the Delacorte Theater. My day off is Monday and I would be happy to get together at a mutually agreeable time within the next few weeks. . . .

To city controller Harrison J. Goldin, in an attempt to persuade the city to double its subsidy of the Belasco Shakespeare project on Broadway:

This is a unique program of Shakespeare for students and teachers performed by a multi-racial cast, in strong collaboration with the Board of Education and its leadership. . . . Over 100,000 New York City junior and senior high school students, hundreds of teachers and hundreds of parents as well as entire families attended performances (in repertory) of *Macbeth*, *As You Like It*, and *Romeo and Juliet*. All you need to do is ask the Chancellor, Nathan Quinones, Robert Wagner Jr., any teacher that brought a class to the Belasco, and their students themselves, what these performances meant to them. You will get unanimous raves. . . . I hope you and your colleagues on the Board of Estimate will seriously consider the importance and impact of the Belasco project on this city and will be moved to keep it alive with a one million dollar appropriation.

To the mayor himself:

We have been negotiating a 99-year lease for the Public Theater for almost three years. . . . All of our fundraising is predicated on the durability of the Public Theater building and now as we celebrate . . . 33 years as an institution, born out of the very streets of New York in partnership with the City of New York, being denied a long-term lease would indeed be a disservice to all of us. . . .

Who could write these letters after he was gone? Papp wondered. He was unwilling to step down immediately. But, with Wilford Leach no longer on the scene, he needed to groom someone who could step into his role, someone, he later said, with "knowledge of good theater, with an orientation toward theater with meaning. But executive ability too, the ability to handle a lot of money, because artistic decisions are ultimately business decisions. A good sense of music — that's very important. Plus a capacity to raise funds. . . . Maturity too — preferably in his or her early forties or late thirties. Once people get past a certain age, a kind of cynicism sets in, a kind of worldliness. That's okay, as long as they're still idealistic too. . . . It's like trying to find someone for the Supreme Court."

His first candidate was Meryl Streep. The film star, then in her late thirties, had first worked at the Public more than a decade earlier in a succession of plays including Elizabeth Swados's *Alice, The Cherry Orchard, Measure for Measure* and *The Taming of the Shrew*. She enjoyed a reputation for impeccable work, a quick intelligence and good sense. In the late 1970s, Papp had shepherded Streep and her boyfriend John Cazale through the medical labyrinth when Cazale was diagnosed with cancer. When Papp called, she responded with alacrity.

"I came in from Connecticut to see him and thought it was about doing something in the park with Kevin Kline," Streep later recalled. "I had wanted to do something for a while but I was usually pregnant or in a movie — postpartum or preproduction — and it was difficult for me to schedule things as far in advance as Joe needed. I sat opposite him in his office, surrounded by the pictures and memorabilia of my favorite times in the theater, all ready with my reasons for why, yet again, I couldn't do it.

"He was abrupt and to the point. He said he realized that he wasn't going to be able to head up the Public full-time because of his health and he wanted to bring someone in part-time at first to be able to take over the helm when he finally couldn't continue. He said he wanted that someone to be an artist — not an administrator, someone who was dedicated to what the Public stood for, someone who had a history with the Festival and loved it as much as he did. He said, 'I want you to do it.'

"I remember thinking how asking me to run it was a way of keeping it in the family. It was also a demonstration of how Joe, for all his shrewd street-bred tough business exterior, was led in decisions by his heart and his hopes. *If I wish it, I can make it so* was his modus operandi. He *wanted* me to be the right person for this task — as if the strength of his wishing could make it so. I couldn't have been a more impractical choice and, much as I loved him and understood why he wanted me to fit into this role, I knew I couldn't have been more unsuited to it.

"I hadn't been in a play for ten years. I had abandoned the theater for films in part because the shooting schedules allowed me more time for my three little children. He knew I'd moved out of New York City because I hated the danger of raising kids there — all the cultural advantages notwithstanding. I lived more than a two-hour drive from the city and I had told Joe more than once that I'd never felt anything but relief at having left.

"Finally, a big part of Joe's job was fundraising, *shmoozing* at Washington and Manhattan dinner parties and important events, constantly keeping the Festival and its head in the news, courting publicity, making news, pushing the face and fact of the theater into the spotlight. This was something Joe was great at and something that gives me hives just to contemplate. Joe *had* to know this about me; he just didn't want it to interfere.

"I said no right away. He said, 'You have to think about it longer than that.' We kissed and parted. I went back to Connecticut stupefied and touched and sad. I was unspeakably touched that he would choose me to be his successor, stupefied that he could misconceive me so thoroughly, and sad to realize that there was no one, *no one*, who could fill his shoes."

In July, director Michael Bennett, who had developed *A Chorus Line* at the Festival, died of AIDS. He had telephoned Papp a few weeks earlier and told him that he planned to "tap-dance his way to heaven." Although Papp had not worked with Bennett since *A Chorus Line*, he was fond of the director and felt his loss as a blow. And each time he visited Leach, he saw his friend and closest colleague growing progressively weaker.

Shortly after Bennett's death, Papp met with Mike Nichols, whom he saw as a master stage director with a social conscience. He asked Nichols to take over the Festival, suggesting that he could hire people to handle the administrative end of the job. But Nichols also turned him down.

That summer of 1987, Papp produced *Richard II, Two Gentlemen of Verona* and *Henry IV, Part I,* recalling the halcyon 1960s in Central Park when three productions were the rule and Festival members worked day and night. In the face of so much illness and his own uncertain prognosis, he reveled in an abundance of Shakespeare.

After *Henry IV* opened, Papp spent two weeks at his country home in Katonah, where he sat for another Oral History interview and worked with Betsy Kirkland, a young Shakespeare scholar, on thirty-six introductions to the thirty-six plays in Bantam Books' complete set of Shakespeare. His direction of two plays that summer, combined with discussions of the entire Shakespearean canon, had reminded him of his plan to produce all Shakespeare's plays in succession. At first, he thought of producing it at the Belasco. Mike Nichols would direct Kevin Kline and Meryl Streep in *Much Ado About Nothing;* Stuart Vaughan would direct Sam Waterston and Martin Sheen in *Julius Caesar;* he himself would direct Marlon Brando and Jack Nicholson in *King Lear* and Mandy Patinkin in *The Merchant of Venice*. It would be a marathon.

Although he never asked for a prognosis, Papp repeatedly asked his doctor what results he could expect from the treatment. Garnick had answered that, although his libido would disappear, his bone scan would revert to normal, his biochemical markers would revert to normal, his prostate gland would shrink and he would feel good. From a medical standpoint, the treatment continued to be an extraordinary success. "It was unbelievable," Garnick recalled. "You can take some of Joe's scans when he was in remission and they look almost normal. I had thought his chance of going into a complete remission was under 5 percent.

Instead, for four years, it was 100 percent. I don't think the Papps ever realized how unusual and lucky they were. For four years, they lived a totally normal life, running all over the place. They thought it was going to go on forever and so did I — although, deep down, I knew it could not."

Deep down, Joe Papp also knew it could not. By autumn of 1987, he had made a will and had met with his new accountant, Aaron Shapiro, to go over his personal finances. Shapiro discovered that, in 1986, Papp had earned $182,000. He had almost no savings or investments — only the tax-deferred annuities that the Festival had set up, which would come due upon retirement or death. Moreover, he had many expenses. He had been paying his third wife alimony for more than a decade. He had been underwriting professional expenses for his son Tony, who had completed his education at Parsons and had launched an artistic but unprofitable career as a jewelry designer. (The producer paid Tony's apartment and studio rent and had guaranteed a ten-year lease for a small store in Trump Tower.) He also knew that he would be facing huge medical expenses. Shapiro advised him of his budgetary needs, suggested a study of his retirement benefits and a raise in his compensation. The producer, who had in the past refused salary raises when they were offered and had all his life turned over whatever teaching or advertising fees he received to the Festival, now asked his board to approve a hefty raise for himself.

Papp was in rehearsal with *Henry IV* when Tony asked him and Gail Merrifield to accompany him to a doctor's appointment. Both Papps were exhausted. They had been visiting Wilford Leach in the hospital as well as Merrifield's mother, who had suffered lung failure. Merrifield herself was on crutches because she had broken her leg in a bicycle accident. The doctor told them that Tony, then twenty-six, was HIV positive.

"We had feared all along that Tony would get AIDS," Merrifield later said. "He had already had two years of symptoms that were precursors. Nevertheless, when you hear it said to you, it comes as a blow. We went home and couldn't sleep. We spent many nights, both of us, just crying. There's no remedy for that kind of despair. But we felt we had to be strong for Tony."

People close to the producer thought that Tony's illness was more painful to Papp than his own. He was helpless in the face of AIDS, unable to protect his son. "We had known Tony and Miranda since they were children," said Judy Peabody, the longtime Festival board member who had become an AIDS activist. "When he was diagnosed, Joe said: 'Tony likes you. He trusts you. Maybe you could talk to him.' The sicker Tony got, the harder it was for Joe to see his young, adored son dying. I thought it was the cruelest torture imaginable. It became very hard for him to keep going. He retreated into himself. I don't think a lot of people knew how hard it was for him or how he remained a fantastic, loyal friend who always had time for other people in trouble."

He had less and less time for discussions that led nowhere. In October, Papp resigned from the Mayor's Theater Advisory Council on which he had served for five years, when Koch ignored its recommendation that a tax on real estate interests finance new Broadway projects and proposed instead that theatergoers pay for them with a $1 surcharge on tickets. He denied rumors of his illness. When writer Ross Wetzsteon, who had followed Papp's career since East 6th Street, interviewed him for the *Village Voice,* Papp did not confide in his old acquaintance. "'Ill?' he says, amused at the preposterous notion. 'I'd be the first to know, wouldn't I? I was operating at full capacity all year.'" When Wetzsteon pressed him for a successor, Papp replied, "You have any good ideas? . . . Hardly a day goes by that I don't consciously consider this question. I keep looking — just like I keep looking for the perfect Juliet."

By November, the producer was ready to announce what he was now calling the "Shakespeare Marathon." He had lined up celebrated directors and stage and screen actors, many of whom had established their careers at the Festival. Six plays would be presented each year for six years at an estimated total cost of $33 million. The first, *A Midsummer Night's Dream,* had just begun rehearsals. And, he reminded reporters, he was still doing twelve new plays. "You keep Shakespeare alive by having a contemporary theater side by side," he said. "This can be a shot in the arm for the theater. Certainly, it's a shot in the arm for me."

Although some critics deplored "the selling of the Bard," the Shakespeare Marathon or Shakespeare-with-Stars, as some called it, was regarded as a shot in the arm for New York, where just a few weeks earlier, the stock market had crashed. The Festival lost $3 million of its endowment and, in December, Papp realized he faced the largest cash shortfall in his organization's history — a projected $4.8 million deficit. He canceled three of his upcoming productions and decided to seek independent funding for *Betsey Brown,* Ntozake Shange's musical that he had been developing for seven years. But he refused to fire any of the 130 people working at the Festival and its various shops. "Even to drop fifteen people," he said, "you begin to destroy the organization."

Instead, Papp took out a jaunty full-page advertisement in the Sunday *New York Times* headed "FOR THE FIRST TIME IN AMERICA, SEE *ALL* OF SHAKESPEARE," soliciting charter members who would receive an *I've Seen It All* T-shirt, a $50 discount on the price of tickets, preferential treatment at performances in Central Park, and, on September 15, 1993, at 8:15 P.M., the opportunity to drink a glass of champagne with Papp at the Public Theater.

Over the next four months, thirteen hundred people purchased subscriptions for the six-year series at prices ranging from $400 to $2,500, and Papp talked up his new venture to the press. "I can't compete with the movie industry financially, but I can certainly negotiate," he told an interviewer, casting himself as David faced with yet another version of Goliath. "I can get the people [to whom] they pay $3 million for $400 because I offer them something very important to their artistic lives. . . . You can't be an outstanding actor unless you have played outstanding roles. You can't be an outstanding actor if you are only doing films."

That Christmas, the Papps took what was only their second vacation in over a decade. They flew to Captiva Island off the coast of Florida for two weeks. Papp rested and read *Cymbeline* aloud to his wife, thinking it might be a good play for JoAnne Akalaitis to direct. The progress of his disease seemed to have been arrested. "Mr. Papp continues to do exceptionally well some nine months into therapy," Dr. Garnick noted in January 1988. "He has really no difficulties whatsoever." By that time, Garnick understood his role not only as Papp's physician but as one of his chief sources of hope and support.

The year at the Public began with an exuberant first Shakespeare Marathon production, *A Midsummer Night's Dream*, directed by A. J. Antoon, followed by an all-star *Julius Caesar*, directed by Stuart Vaughan. They were followed by two contemporary plays: *American Notes*, directed by JoAnne Akalaitis, and *Wenceslas Square*, a serious comedy about an American professor's experiences in Prague before and after the Russian invasion of 1968, directed by Jerry Zaks.

Papp paid closer attention than usual to the work of these directors, observing not only their artistic choices but their interactions with other people. He did not consider Vaughan or Antoon as candidates for his job, because he felt they were temperamentally unsuited for it. But when Jerry Zaks's production of *Wenceslas Square* opened at Washington's Kennedy Center, he approached the director as he had Meryl Streep and Mike Nichols.

Zaks was forty-two years old. He had first worked at the Festival over a decade earlier as an actor. In 1985, he had directed a production of a new play at the Public, and Papp admired his work on *Wenceslas Square*. Zaks had also directed John Guare's *The House of Blue Leaves* and the hit musical revival *Anything Goes* at Lincoln Center, and Papp was impressed by his versatility.

"He asked if I'd be interested in taking over the Public Theater and I was totally taken aback," Zaks would later recall. "You'd have to know me and my particular variety of neuroses to understand how shocking it was, in part because of who he was and in part because of my own self-image which I've been working on for the past three thousand years. I needed to walk around with it for a little bit — to savor the fact that he had been willing to entrust me with his theater. But once I got over being shocked and flattered, I realized it was not what I wanted.

"I like to direct plays. My love affair with theater does not include running one. I don't have that kind of vision. Also, I have two young daughters and I knew that if I accepted that job and did it the way it should be done, I would have had to sacrifice my family. I couldn't do that. I must have apologized twenty or thirty times when I told Joe. It meant a great deal to me, and still does, that he asked."

At the time, during the spring of 1988, Zaks was well aware of the burdens of running the Public Theater. A few months earlier, Papp had opened *Serious Money,* by Caryl Churchill, to excellent reviews at the Public. Because of those reviews and because Churchill had never had a play on Broadway, Papp had decided to transfer it to Broadway. "*Serious Money* was a tour de force both as writing and performance," Gail Merrifield recalled. "It was also relevant to our own inside trading scandals on Wall Street, which no American had written about." But *Serious Money* closed after only twelve days and, when *Times* critic Frank Rich wrote an essay examining the reasons why, Papp held *him* responsible.

"One would imagine that the most influential newspaper critic in America would have bent all of his efforts to advocate a show he had recently extolled Off-Broadway," Papp wrote in one of his passionate letters to the *Times.*

> But instead he chose incredibly to leave the country a few days prior to the long-announced opening for a jaunt to London, not on assignment, but as a voluntary choice trip, leaving the one serious play he called one of the year's ten best subject to the vagaries of Broadway.
>
> He was aware . . . that the play was controversial and not to everyone's taste . . . he must also have been aware that without the strength of the *Times'* critic's heavy endorsement, this play would go down. And yet, he left . . . he chose to leave his post at a most critical time and must share in the blame for the closing of *Serious Money.* It was a time when his voice needed to be heard and he was elsewhere.

Papp's fury at Rich was matched by his fury at still having to worry endlessly about money. The Festival's financial difficulties were now being reported in such magazines as *Forbes*. In April, that journal noted that *A Chorus Line,* then in its fourteenth year on Broadway, would barely break even and that New York's Chemical Bank had just extended to the Festival a $1 million line of credit. Even though he had been with his back to the wall many times before, Papp felt the stakes had reached a new high. "It's the greatest pendulum you can imagine," he had told an interviewer a few months earlier. "You can go from the most ecstatic heights to the depths of despair. Last night, I was watching the Baltimore Orioles' manager Earl Weaver. They were way behind the Red Sox. . . . I was watching his face. . . . they couldn't win the game. He was grim, grim, grim. I thought baseball is somewhat similar to trying to make it in our field. How many times has this man gone through it? He's in his sixties, maybe seventies. I thought, my God, you know, he has to win this game. It's like putting on a play. You've got to win it, and then a whole season, and then another season. . . ."

AIDS continued to take its toll at the Festival. In June 1988, one day after playwright Miguel Piñero died, Papp was told of the death of his friend and closest colleague Wilford Leach. He never talked much about it but mourned his loss in a preface to the book *Poets for Life: Seventy-Six Poets Respond to AIDS,* which he began by recalling the 1930s.

> . . . bleak times, the worst of times. I am working in a laundry after school on 15th Street in Manhattan. I pass a newsstand and my heart stops; the headline: MADRID FALLS. Not wanting to spend the money, I sneak a glance at the front page. Half the story is concealed by an iron weight, carefully placed by the vendor to encourage customer curiosity and a sale. I make out a few of the lines: "Generalissimo Francisco Franco enters . . . Hitler jubilant as he . . . Democracies silent." I head home for Brooklyn. This is without a doubt, I think, the worst time in my life. At least I thought it was — at 17. . . .
>
> In the spirit of 1939, I find myself writing "Like enemy propaganda in war, words play a vital role in winning that war." I continue with grim determination: "All of us, people with AIDS and people without, are in this together." I feel an ache around my heart. My fingers are growing numb. The ache is overwhelming and my throat is terribly tight. I look at the half-written page and I am surprised to find it smudged. It is wet. I am crying. My God! I am writing a poem!

> *MY THOUGHTS ARE OF SCHOOL DAYS*
> *OF BROTHERS AND SISTERS,*
> *PARENTS AND TEACHERS,*

FRIENDS . . .
AT THE WORD
MY EYES BEGIN TO DIM
MY HEART ACHES OF AN ABSENCE
AND A GREAT LONGING SWELLS UP WITHIN ME
LIKE THE CRY OF A WILD BIRD
I HEAR THE NAME . . . WILFORD, WILFORD . . .

Ah, dear friend whose radiant humanity touched all who had the good fortune of knowing you, how I miss the wonder of you. My fallen comrade. Dear, dear friend.

That year, Papp flew to London twice, and to Venezuela, where the minister of culture presented him with the Order of Andres Bello in recognition of his efforts on behalf of Latin American theater. He flew to Greece as a delegate to the United Nations Symposium on Culture Against Apartheid, organized by the Greek minister of culture, actress Melina Mercouri, whose husband, Jules Dassin, Papp had known at the Actors' Lab. He flew to Madrid to discuss with cultural officials and investors a possible film of *Don Quixote* with actor Kevin Kline playing both Cervantes and Quixote. And he grew more and more involved with Jewish causes, organizing famous actors to celebrate the Jewish holidays and lending his name to the Joseph Papp Yiddish Theater, which would produce the Yiddish musical revue *Songs of Paradise.*

Meanwhile the Festival produced *Romeo and Juliet* followed by *Much Ado About Nothing, King John, Coriolanus, Love's Labor's Lost* and *The Winter's Tale* — all featuring movie stars and directed by a variety of men including Festival veterans Stuart Vaughan and Gerald Freedman and relative newcomers such as Steven Berkoff and James Lapine.

James Lapine was thirty-nine years old. He had first come to the Festival in 1981, as the playwright/director of *Twelve Dreams,* based on a Jungian case history, and had built his directorial reputation with the Stephen Sondheim musicals *Sunday in the Park with George* and *Into the Woods.* Papp found Lapine both entrepreneurial and artistic, sensible and imaginative, as well as "graceful under pressure," Merrifield recalled. At one of their early meetings about *The Winter's Tale* Papp asked Lapine point-blank if he would be interested in running the Public Theater.

"I remember saying, 'Well, where are *you* going?'" Lapine later said. "He didn't talk about his illness and he didn't put a timetable on it. He said it could be a couple of years off. But I just didn't think I could do it. You can't spend time with your family and direct and run a theater properly. I told him right away that I wasn't a social person. I hate parties and meeting new people and fundraising. I remembered Joe greeting critics on opening nights and donors at benefits, being very comfortable holding court. That's something I'm not.

"Joe suggested we put together a consortium. I met with Steve Cohen to talk about it but Joe sensed my ambivalence — which is, of course, my hallmark. I felt that by not accepting, I was being not as generous as he had always been, that in our generation there was no altruism left in the theater, that no one was doing things anymore for the city or for the culture. He always made me feel that if you have something to give, you give it. He created a place that created an incredible amount of work and a place for people to come together. But, I couldn't do it. I wanted to write. I wanted to work in film. He said: 'Think about it; you don't need to decide now.' He didn't want me to close the door on it and he would raise the issue with me again."

The issue of succession was facing other, less public heads of New York institutions at the time. At the *New Yorker,* editor William Shawn had reigned for decades. At the *New York Times,* A. M. Rosenthal was slated to retire. Many candidates coveted those two jobs, which offered their holder power but protection from regular public review. Few candidates appeared to covet the leadership of the New York Shakespeare Festival as a new generation of theater critics, faced with a shrinking purview and the Shakespeare Marathon — the largest ongoing project in the industry — focused their attention on its producer and wrote ever more savage reviews.

In February 1989, the *Times* ran a long Sunday piece titled "Peaks and Valleys in Papp's Marathon" by Frank Rich.

When it comes to amassing culture, Americans like to collect the complete set. . . . So it was no surprise that the public rushed to enlist in Joseph Papp's Shakespeare Marathon. . . . Always a shrewd impresario, Mr. Papp had once again succeeded at a task few of his peers in the theater would even attempt: selling Shakespeare to a broad public. Why does he bother? The reasons, by now well enshrined in New York City folklore, are not venal. An impoverished child of immigrant Brooklyn, Joseph Papirofsky discovered Shakespeare, and a liberating view of life and culture, in a Williamsburg public library. Out of that childhood came the mission that has propelled the New York Shakespeare Festival for over 30 years: Joseph Papp believes in Shakespeare, especially free Shakespeare, for a mass urban audience, particularly a student audience that might be spiritually transported from the same grinding poverty he experienced in his youth. . . .

Still, legitimate criticism of Mr. Papp persists. One can admire the producer's motives and calling without necessarily endorsing the results — which have been erratic. . . . Might the worst Papp stagings be more counterproductive than no Shakespeare at all? . . . Why, promotional expediency aside, is there a need for a marathon? Would it be more worthwhile to do some of Shakespeare's plays with deliberate care rather than to mount three dozen at a sprint simply so the culturally acquisitive can say "I've seen it all"?

Rich argued that the Marathon had so far included "good productions, in-between productions and barely nominal productions" with "no unifying principle other than the rubric 'Joseph Papp presents.'" He faulted Papp for his haste in assembling the project, particularly for his inability to line up more effective directors, and proceeded to a play-by-play critique.

The Marathon's "most embarrassing failure," he wrote, had been a *Julius Caesar* "turned over to three heroic American actors of the kind Mr. Papp admires: Al Pacino, Martin Sheen, Edward Herrmann. The production was straightforward, the stars in theory well cast, but the slovenliness of the acting . . . assassinated the play well before its hero reached the Ides of March. . . ."

Papp's two marathon successes, in Rich's view, were the work of two highly talented directors, particularly the *Coriolanus* of English actor/playwright/director Steven Berkoff. *Coriolanus*, Rich wrote:

demonstrated the importance of mating a play with a director who has a real passion for it, rather than merely doling out the marathon assignments haphazardly, as seems to happen half the time, to whichever Shakespeare Festival regular might be available. That Mr. Berkoff would have such a passion for *Coriolanus* was no surprise to anyone (including, one assumes, Mr. Papp) who had seen the director's own plays in England. . . .

The director . . . must have some compelling reason for doing a given work, and be capable of firing up a cast with that compulsion. The failed marathon productions have been those without an animating impulse, an inner drive — those that seem to have been put on for no other reason than to fill the marathon's relentless march of scheduling shots or to capitalize on this or that name actor. These second-tier productions announce themselves to audiences immediately . . . the consistency of the mediocrity is inevitable: a director who is merely putting the play up because it is there communicates his dispassion to the entire production team, from the lightman to the lowliest bit player.

Were Mr. Papp never to produce another Shakespeare play, his legacy to Shakespeare production in the United States would still be incalculable. He has long since fought and won the war to prove that American actors of all types need not be second to the English in performing the canon; he has kept Shakespeare a constant in a New York theater that has changed radically in every other way during the three decades since free Shakespeare began. But the marathon, which so far has too frequently seemed like a mechanical winding down to the finish line of the Festival's mission, offers Mr. Papp the opportunity for a new beginning. It's his chance to build an audience for the next generation, to cap his career with a magical flourish worthy of Prospero. He will have succeeded if the "I've Seen It All" crowd that gathers at the Public Theater on September 15, 1993 has not relegated Shakespeare's complete plays to the dusty shelf of dutiful cultural collectibles but is instead as eager as Mr. Papp has always been to return to them again and again.

Rich's piece angered Papp more than any single piece of writing had for years. He found it snide, condescending, self-important and — his major complaint about theater critics for the previous thirty years — wilfully ignorant of the facts behind the production process, which, he thought, could be easily ascertained. He shot off a letter to Arthur Gelb, asking for a face-to-face confrontation with Rich, then sat down at his Remington to refute him point by point. Papp wrote best when he was furious, and the *Times* reprinted his letter in its entirety:

The Shakespeare Marathon has been characterized in this newspaper as an enterprise lacking a unifying vision and having no unifying principle other than "Joseph Papp presents." Needless to say, I consider such charges baseless and I resent them.

To build his case the critic begins by trotting out a heart-rending tale of my early years . . . "Grinding poverty," he suggests, is what did it. The facts, however, are much different. Poor, yes; impoverished, hardly. "Life and culture" was not discovered in a library but at home, in the streets, at school and shul (synagogue), all places rich in culture. There was music, both classical and jazz. I sang boy soprano in a Jewish choir, danced the Lindy Hop, read tales of adventure as well as poetry; played marbles after shul and won enough to pay for a five-cent Charlie Chaplin movie, harmonized at home with my father and brother and two sisters. And taste — the ability to distinguish a good ballplayer, dancer, actor, song writer, marble player, hot dog or knish from a mediocre one — was ever present. Anything and everything was always being judged, compared, and commented on, and there was no need for sophisticated jargon. We all knew that Frank Sinatra was a better singer than Bing Crosby. . . .

With the poverty-to-Shakespeare theory out of the way, we can move to our critic's fundamental objections to the Marathon. He begins with the all-encompassing query known in my circles as the "Why don't you drop dead?" question: "Might the worst Papp stagings be more counterproductive than no Shakespeare at all?" Well, I find that question difficult to answer. How is anyone to foretell what will end up as "the worst stagings"? Our critic admits that the Marathon has produced, at the least, two unreservedly fine stagings. Yet the beginnings of one of them, *Coriolanus,* did not augur well at all. . . .

In fact, Steven Berkoff had absolutely no outward passion for the play. It was I . . . who felt that Steven Berkoff was the man for the job. But he remained uncertain and later revealed to me that he had made numerous inquiries among his friends as to his being the proper director. . . . Complicating the passion theory even more is the fact that Mr. Berkoff was performing in London and unable to come to the United States to cast the play. At which point, with the assistance of Rosemarie Tichler, our casting director, I passionately set out to second-guess Maestro Berkoff by casting the show. . . .

Even the first week of rehearsals was so lacking in anything resembling passion that the concept of a set had yet to be found. There were, I admit, some passionate disagreements along the way, which caused the temporary departure of one of the leading actors, the costume and the lighting designer. To an outsider, it would have appeared that *Coriolanus* was heading for a fiasco of unprecedented dimensions. And one must assume that our critic, had he the authority, would have called it quits at this juncture. But the producer, trained through years of experience to discern any signs of life in what appears to be an irreversible catastrophe, was able both to detect and to keep faith with the spark of Berkoff's genius that finally caught fire in a production of unusual style and interest.

With poverty and passion out of the way. . . . Lest anyone be tempted to accept one man's definition of failure, I must remind the reader that *Julius Caesar* received some of the best reviews of the Marathon. . . . In one review, Al Pacino's Marc Antony was called superior to Brando's. And the most important test of success or failure, as we in the theater understand the term, is attendance. *Julius Caesar* sold out every performance of its run.

The weight of our critic's displeasure with this production fell on the backs of some of the leading actors, "the kind Mr. Papp admires." I certainly do admire Al Pacino, Martin Sheen and Ed Herrmann. Who doesn't? . . . These actors, eager to grow in their work, put their reputations on the line and took a sizable risk in appearing in a New York production, knowing what perfect targets they make for any journalistic marksman ready to shoot them down. If our critic was sincere, he would appreciate the courage these men showed and not vent his displeasure in a manner that can't help but discourage not only these actors but the many others who aspire to similar risks. . . .

Perhaps our critic's most insidious complaint comes when he asks, "Would it be more worthwhile to do some of Shakespeare's plays with deliberate care rather than mount three dozen at a sprint . . ." Deliberate care is a constant process at the New York Shakespeare Festival. The notion that by engaging in the Marathon we are so harried and *fartootzt* we are unable to pay proper attention to the oncoming or ongoing production is untrue. We have had many instances (over a 35-year period) of plays approached with the greatest and most deliberate care which failed to receive unanimous approval. On the other hand, we have literally thrown shows together which happen to have the right writer, director and actors, all of whom combine to create a harmony and a chemistry that all the preparation in the world could not achieve. I'm not in favor of these situations, but the truth is, you cannot plan or predict them. Nobody knows what will make a show work until it does. . . .

"Why," our critic asks, "promotional expendiency aside, is there a need for a Marathon?" Here, once more, is the Why Don't You Drop Dead question. After having thrown accolades at me for my deep and abiding interest in Shakespeare . . . how could our critic then accuse me of embarking on such a momumental theatrical journey, spending inordinate sums of hard-to-raise money to produce six works of Shakespeare each year, staking my professional reputation on the results of such an effort, all for the sake of "promotional expediency"? . . .

I can come up with only one word to describe his thinking: cynicism. What is being promoted? And for what purpose? Is the Marathon proving to be helpful in raising money? It is not. Does the Marathon have even the remotest possibility of paying for itself? Because of our small theaters at the Public, it does not. Even if part of the reason for launching the Marathon was to bring stronger attention to an institution that, lacking the basic underwriting of such companies as the Royal Shakespeare, struggles day in and day out to stay alive, how could such a huge effort by so many people over the course of six years be fundamentally inspired by "promotional expediency"?

Is there a "need" for a Marathon? Come on. We are living in a country where philistinism and violence ride high, where education, in the best sense of that word, is at a new low. Our critic speaks of my "mission," calls me a believer in "Shakespeare for a mass urban audience, particularly a student audience that might be spiritually transported from the same grinding poverty he experienced in his youth." But even the middle class needs a lift these days.

The Marathon is an act of cultural affirmation. It proclaims Shakespeare alive. It opens up all kinds of possibilities for programs to reach our young people as well as the loyal elderly. It is doing that now. It is causing lots of people to read and reread the plays of Shakespeare. There is a destination, a road to follow, and thousands of people are on it. Is there a need for a Marathon? What a question!

Papp did not write that the Marathon was his way of bargaining with God, that he was hoping to be drinking champagne with his subscribers on September 15, 1993. That same mind-set framed his response when Papp was presented with the first draft of the *Oral History of the New York Shakespeare Festival*. "Is this the oral history of the NYSF?" he wrote in the notes he made while reading it.

It is an assemblage of angry, frustrated, revengeful theater people, who get off on taking me on — and me without armor. . . . When my voice is heard, I come off benign, even-tempered, almost a kind of jerk with his head in the clouds — and here are all these others, yapping away, quoting me as the too-tough guy, the frustrated director (I directed 25-30 plays), the publicity hound, the maker of bum decisions — I take the rap for every failure and am denied any credit for the successes! What kind of fool must I be to be party to the publication which can only misrepresent and muddle the fundamental achievement of the Festival in a mud bath of invective and neurotic reflexes to authority, power, or whatever you want to call being a leader or a boss. The fundamental achievement, if you will, cannot be articulated in the success or failure of this play or that — certainly not by blaming me for every show that failed. . . . This litany of theater stories about neurotic theater people pays no service to the meaning of the long life of the Festival. It certainly does not justify a book — one that I had hoped to be a serious appraisal of the history of my organization.

Papp returned his advance to Bantam Books and advised the journalist who had spent two years on the work that he was withdrawing the project.

The next three productions of the Marathon — James Lapine's *Winter's Tale,* JoAnne Akalaitis's *Cymbeline* and Harold Guskin's *Twelfth Night* — were all trashed by the major critics. *Twelfth Night,* with movie stars Michelle Pfeiffer, Gregory Hines and Jeff Goldblum, was the greatest popular success in the Festival's history, drawing a very young crowd of which thousands had to be turned away but the worst reviews. "It's a terrible delusion that you get free Shakespeare in Central Park," wrote John Simon of *Twelfth Night.* "You leave in darkest ignorance or unutterable disgust. Either of those is too high a price to pay for Shakespeare." The *New Yorker,* which had replaced Papp fan Edith Oliver with Mimi Kramer, noted, "The most depressing thing yet in Joe Papp's ongoing marathon is . . . turning the Delacorte stage into a symbol of commercial theater at its cheapest and most sterile. . . . With Papp behind you, you can strip Shakespeare of all poetry, feeling and meaning and still call what you have a hit." And the *Daily News* wrote, "The Marathon, instead of being the culmination of 30-odd years of serious endeavor, only shows how much lower our standards are now than they were before Shakespeare became the domain of Papp."

Papp himself felt that *Twelfth Night* was a poor production but would not publicly criticize the director. To critics who attacked what they dubbed his "Shakespeare-with-Stars policy," Papp replied that he had conceived it for the benefit of actors and audiences.

There are actors who work in Hollywood for magnificent salaries who feel the need to work onstage as part of their craft. Our movie actors have very little opportunity to play classics. We must give them a chance because, from an actor's viewpoint, there's no real growth in making movies. Everything is shot in fragments. The actors are not required to give a sustained performance. And what other stars than movie stars are there? There *used* to be Broadway stars. Now, you name one! All the good actors are working in film.

The second reason to use stars is to develop audiences. When you go to a conventional theater with few exceptions the members of the audience are white, affluent and 50 to 70 years old. At the Delacorte we did a survey. The average age of people waiting on line to get a ticket is 28. They are black, Hispanic, Asian as well as white. Many of them have never been to the theater before even though they live in what is regarded as the cultural capital of the United States. This is no different from the situation when I first started the Festival. Many of these people come *because* we have star actors. If you want to get a new audience, you must get actors with big reputations.

In addition to attacking individual productions, some critics once again called into question Papp's casting policy. *New York* magazine's John Simon, reviewing *The Winter's Tale*, described actors Mandy Patinkin and Alfre Woodard in terms that far outdid his attack on Colleen Dewhurst decades earlier. As King of Sicilia, Patinkin "doesn't know what to do with his hands," Simon wrote, "he tends to keep them behind his back, as if he were handcuffed or an international financier. This, combining with his bulky, hulking head further swelled by a mass of raven hair, makes him look rather like a caricature in the notorious Nazi publication *Der Sturmer*." As Paulina, Woodard was "visually a cross between Topsy and Medusa" and "aurally . . . a pretty fair impersonation of Butterfly McQueen. If Miss Woodard weren't black, one might suspect her of racism; as it is one suspects her merely of not having the foggiest notion about how to play a classical role."

Although protests were immediately lodged by the NAACP, the Anti-Defamation League and Actors Equity — Colleen Dewhurst, now president of the union, called for Simon's removal — it was Papp who led the public rebuttal of the critic. "What Simon says is an insult to blacks and Jews and all fair-minded people," Papp told the press. "It goes beyond cruelty, Simon's favorite weapon, into bigotry."

That spring of 1989, Joseph Papp still had the energy to mount spirited defenses of his policies, his actors and his theater. Both he and his son Tony were, despite their diagnoses, in good heath. The twenty-eight-year-old jewelry designer was working hard in his studio. The sixty-seven-year-old producer had merely added a few minutes of attending to his daily injections and pills to a frenetic schedule. In addition to warring with the critics, negotiating with the city for the new ninety-nine-year lease he wanted on the Public and fundraising, Papp was once again directing a contemporary play. He chose *The Forbidden City* by Bill Gunn, an African-American poet, playwright and director whose *Black Picture Show* Papp had directed at Lincoln Center more than a decade earlier and with whom he had a long, complicated personal relationship similar to the one he had with David Rabe. Gunn, who was returning to stage writing after years in film, insisted that Papp direct his new play. Then he did not appear for rehearsals. *The Forbidden City* opened April 6, the night the playwright died of AIDS.

In July, another kind of criticism came down on Papp after he reversed a decision to produce the Palestinian theater group El-Hakawati, at the Public. Its play, *The Story of Kufur Shamma,* had been performed in Israel and was the story of a Palestinian who returns to his family's village looking for survivors of the 1948 Arab-Israeli war. Papp had never seen the group's work. He had agreed to present *Kufur Shamma* at the Public that summer at the suggestion of the Play Development Department, which had been corresponding with the group for years and had found them a theatrical touring agent in the United States. In May, he went to Baltimore to accept an honorary doctorate from Baltimore Hebrew University. In his acceptance speech, he said there was a great need for Arabs and Jews to get together and that he was planning to bring El-Hakawati to his theater. "Two days later," he said at the time, "I get a letter from Baltimore: 'From one Jew to another, Mr. Papp, I think you're a wonderful person but how can you possibly put this show on in your theater? My son was shot and killed in the war.' It's amazing what a single letter can do. I came to the idea that maybe I would not do it. I'd never before canceled a show. I had no plays running at the Public at the time. It would have been the only play. The bus [terrorist] incident had just happened in Israel. I thought it would look like an arrogant statement on my part. Like a damn fool, I told the truth. That I didn't want to make this statement now. I offered to help him find another theater. I felt bad reneging on my commitment to them but I did not want to do it. It felt inappropriate to me."

The theater company was quick to use Papp's action as a news peg for their own publicity. "While the Israeli public remains sharply divided on whether representatives of the Palestine Liberation Organization should speak with its Government," wrote theater critic Alisa Solomon on the *Times* Op-Ed Page, "producer Joseph Papp has decided that Palestinian actors should not speak to New York audiences. . . . Mr. Papp has demonstrated an understanding of theater's unique ability to put a human face on political issues, to bring them to the earthly visceral level of personal experience. So when he excuses his cancellation of El Hakawati by saying, 'I've never produced an Israeli play,' you have to wonder what makes this maverick suddenly so concerned about balance — as if presenting an Israeli play would even provide it." A *Daily News* columnist wrote a column titled "All world's a stage — except to Papp." The *New Yorker* ran a feature on the company as the lead item in its "Talk of the Town."

"You are a hero to so many of us," wrote one of Papp's many dismayed admirers. "You are one of those who perennially make us proud of being New Yorkers. How can you shame us and yourself by canceling the appearance of the El-Hakawati troupe? And to give comfort to our enemies by seeming to confirm that indeed there is a Jewish Mafia that has veto power over New York's cultural life. Fie! Give us back the fighting Joe Papp we've been proud of!"

Papp subsequently met with the American-Arab Relations Committee of the National Council on Islamic Affairs and at the joint press conference that followed was photographed embracing its president, Dr. Mohammed Mehdi. He later joked he had given El-Hakawati more publicity by canceling their show than if he had presented it. But he was bitter about the alacrity and vehemence with which he had been criticized. "It's very painful," he said. "They're so fast to throw you off the horse. They want you to be a hero as long as you say what they believe in. But as soon as you say something they don't believe in, you're no longer a hero. No one stopped and asked: *why* did Joe Papp do this?"

The controversy over El-Hakawati would soon die down. A far bigger one was shaping up. The fight over the National Endowment for the Arts would be played out on a grand scale, in New York, Washington and venues across the nation. It was the last political battle that Papp would wage.

TWENTY-ONE

The
Last Battles

IN JANUARY 1989, *Piss Christ* — a photograph of a plastic crucifix floating in a container of the artist's urine — had been among the works in an exhibit shown by the Virginia Museum of Fine Arts. The photographer was Andres Serrano. The show had originated in North Carolina with support from the National Endowment for the Arts. Outraged museumgoers had written letters of complaint to the American Family Association — a direct-mail Christian fundamentalist group in Mississippi — and its director had by April organized a massive response.

The following month, thirty-seven senators, led by Jesse Helms of North Carolina and Alfonse D'Amato of New York, expressed their indignation in the Senate and to the NEA. A few weeks later, they were reinforced by television evangelist Pat Robertson and 107 congressmen protesting another show on its way to Washington's Corcoran Gallery, where photographs by the late Robert Mapplethorpe included portraits of sadomasochistic homosexual acts.

On June 12, bowing to congressional pressure, the Corcoran's director canceled the Mapplethorpe show, triggering nationwide protest and focusing national attention on the NEA. In the House of Representatives, one congressman moved to abolish the $171 million endowment and two others offered amendments to reduce it. In an attempt at compromise, the amendment that punished the NEA by reducing funding by $45,000 — the amount of its funding of the Serrano and Mapplethorpe exhibits — passed 361–65. But, two weeks later, Senator Helms offered yet another bill, proposing that no NEA funds be used for "(1) obscene and indecent material, including but not limited to depictions of sado-masochism, homoeroticism, the exploitation of children, or individuals engaged in sex acts; or (2) material which denigrates the objects or beliefs of the adherents of a particular religion or nonreligion; or (3) material which denigrates, debases or reviles a person, group, or class of citizens on the basis of race, creed, sex, handicap, age or national origin."

On July 26, the Senate approved the amendment and Papp was among the first to respond. "We could offend everybody with what we've done," he told *Newsday* the next day. He noted that Shakespeare's *Merchant of Venice* would probably have had trouble obtaining NEA funding "because there are aspects of the play that reflect the anti-Semitism of Shakespeare's time. But I would produce it. In fact, when the Jewish Board of Rabbis protested the play, I refused to go along with that even though I'm a religious Jew."

At first, reaction to the Helms amendment was confined largely to the museum and gallery communities; in August, Papp was among the few theater people to join a protest demonstration. In September, he spoke on a panel organized by Volunteer Lawyers for the Arts and hosted, at the Public, a discussion on censorship. In October, a Senate-House compromise bill cleared Congress, prohibiting the funding of "obscene art." It used an obscenity standard determined by a 1973 Supreme Court decision and it was the first time that content had been restricted in the award of federal arts grants.

A few weeks later, the NEA chairman, John Frohnmayer, canceled a $10,000 NEA grant to a New York City gallery because the catalogue of its AIDS exhibit *Witnesses: Against Our Vanishing* attacked Senator Helms, Cardinal John O'Connor, and Congressman William Dannemayer for their opposition to homosexuality. The next day, Papp told an interviewer, "The ramifications go far beyond art gallery exhibitions. It certainly will affect the theater. . . . Any interesting play that deals with the contemporary scene has political aspects to it . . . all through Shakespeare, he mixes politics and sex. . . . Sexuality is very much a part of art. Nobody, even artists themselves, can separate politics or sexuality from art. . . .

"The attitude of a democratic society toward the spiritual nature of art and the cultural life should be a reflection of the life of the country. The money should reflect the basic tenets of a democratic society. It should embody the principles of freedom of expression. . . . The money is granted as a cultural symbol — a manifestation of democracy at work. To say that because the government gives money, it therefore has something to say about the content — that's not appropriate."

This time, the NEA decision triggered much more widespread reaction. Conductor Leonard Bernstein refused the National Medal of Arts in protest. *Witnesses* opened to large crowds. Chairman Frohnmayer reinstated the NEA grant with stipulations that funds could not be used toward the catalogue and Papp refocused his attention on his theater.

He was busy piecing together a new organizational structure that would allow him to groom a successor. Once again, he conferred with directors Jerry Zaks and James Lapine about running the Public Theater. The two men turned him down. Then he turned to JoAnne Akalaitis.

JoAnne Akalaitis seemed, at first, as unlikely a choice as Meryl Streep. While Streep was a mainstream American movie star, Akalaitis was a member of the international avant-garde. An outspoken feminist and cofounder of the experimental Mabou Mines theater company, she was admired for the integrity and aesthetic rigor of her work.

Akalaitis had worked at the Public Theater even longer than Meryl Streep and, in some ways, she was closer in profile to the producer. Like Papp, she came from a working-class background — in her case, a Lithuanian Catholic family in Cicero, Illinois, which expected that as the first in her family to attend college, she would become a physician. Akalaitis had, in fact, been a pre-med student at the University of Chicago and then pursued doctoral studies in philosophy at Stanford. But, thanks to an intensely Catholic girlhood and a drama teacher much like Papp's Eulalie Spence, she had always loved theater. By the early 1960s, Akalaitis was hanging out at San Francisco's Actors' Workshop, where she sold orange juice and worked with actors Lee Breuer and Ruth Maleczech. Then she became part of the English-language theater scene in Paris, where she met composer Phillip Glass. When the couple returned to New York in 1970, they formed Mabou Mines. Café La Mama's Ellen Stewart sponsored the group, which lived communally in Manhattan. First, they paid the bills from Glass's earnings as a plumber. Later, she worked as chef at FOOD, a SoHo restaurant with the rest of Mabou Mines members serving as waiters and dishwashers. During that time Akalaitis moved from performing to directing. "At Mabou Mines, you had artistic license to be all things," she said. "The work was so intelligently collaborative it

empowered all theater artists to understand all the aspects of theater."
When Papp invited the group to perform at the Public, "the Public
seemed like a very straight scene, the Establishment," Akalaitis recalled.
"I remember Richard Schechner telling us that if we accepted we were
going to lose our souls.

"It was a wonderful beginning of a long relationship which took lots
of forms. Joe subsidized us in various ways. Sometimes he took on the
entire budget for a show, sometimes part of it. Sometimes he would lend
us money with interest, sometimes without. I was grateful for that but it
was so subjective and patriarchal that it made me crazy. When one was
the object of his largesse it put you in a debt that was neither professional
or fair. I thought there should be a policy instead of a benign dictator
dipping into his pot. But Joe thought of Festival money as his money.
And in some ways, it was. No other theater in America was indentified
with one man the way the Public was identified with Joe."

At first, as Akalaitis remembered it, Papp assumed that her cofounder
Lee Breuer spoke for Mabou Mines. "He had no idea who I was or that
I directed. But after he saw *Dressed Like an Egg*, he told me, 'You're an
artist.' Then, in 1980, he saw a work-in-progress of *Dead End Kids* at
P.S. 122. With both, he saw a little piece of it, he invited the show to the
theater and then we would work out our financial relationship. *Dead End
Kids* ran at the Public for a long time. We had discussions on Friday
nights and Joe would come — he loved the idea of his theater being used
as a political forum. He asked me to direct for him. Often I was busy
with Mabou Mines, but there was always the prospect of work for me
there."

Akalaitis worked at the Public for more than fifteen years but chose to
eschew a close personal relationship with Papp. "Like everybody else I
was enchanted by Joe and drawn to his charisma," she said, "but I saw
right away that he was a man ruled by his emotions and that it wreaked
havoc. I was also very wary of the other side of him that was dark and
sometimes quite cruel. He could say terrible things to people about their
work or their ideas and I was often angry about his cracks at women —
'Oh, pretty good for a woman' or 'Haven't you put on a little weight
around your hips?' — the kinds of things he would never say to a black
person. Sometimes I walked out; sometimes I stood up to him. But I
found it very hard to stand up to Joe."

When Papp first broached the issue of her taking over the Public
Theater, Akalaitis was ambivalent. "I didn't understand why *anyone* would
want to run an institution," she said. "I had resigned from Mabou Mines
and I was happy to go from job to job as a freelance director. I *like*

directing." In 1989, she was preoccupied with two big productions: Genet's *The Screens* at the Guthrie Theater in Minneapolis and *'Tis Pity She's a Whore* at the Goodman in Chicago. But during the winter, after thinking more about Papp's offer, Akalaitis decided to accept it. "The question became not *why* do it but why *not*? It was a chance, in the most idealistic sense, to do some good. I felt I shared part of Joe's aesthetic agenda and political ideas. So I told Joe I was interested."

Akalaitis was concerned about how the succession would work but reticent about raising the subject with Papp. Although she had long heard rumors to the effect that he had cancer, Festival staffers denied that Papp was seriously ill. And, like everyone at the Festival, she found it difficult to fight what had become Papp's habit of controlling the agenda of meetings and conversations. The terms of her employment as well as who, exactly, she would be working with seemed fluid to Akalaitis that winter. Papp viewed them as fluid, too. Without informing Akalaitis, he told actor Kevin Kline that he wanted him to assume greater responsibility at the Festival. And he also talked with George C. Wolfe, the writer/director of *The Colored Museum*, about launching an autonomous African-American theater within the Public, with Wolfe as its artistic director. He also moved to cultivate a second tier of younger directors, including Michael Greif, David Greenspan and Melia Bensussen.

As 1990 began, Papp was again worried about the Festival's finances. After fifteen years, *A Chorus Line* was about to close and he sorely needed another hit musical. But instead, the two musicals that the Festival had been developing opened to poor reviews. Papp did not argue with the critics. He was particularly disappointed in *Romance in Hard Times*, with book and music by William Finn. Finn had collaborated with James Lapine on the successful musicals *March of the Falsettos* and *Falsettoland*, and Papp considered him a genius. He felt the show, set in a New York City soup kitchen during the depression, was misconceived by its director and blamed himself.

Times critic Frank Rich would later remember wondering what was going on at the Festival. "*Romance in Hard Times* was clearly not well produced," he later recalled. "There was a collapse in quality control — it was misdesigned, misdirected and not ready to open. It said to you: No one's minding the store. It was also set in the depression and I began to think about the fact that a whole series of productions — *The Human Comedy, Songs of Paradise, Café Crown* — had been sentimental choices. *Café Crown* didn't draw an audience in 1942 — why would Papp think it would in 1988? It was an incredibly sentimental choice — an old commercial piece, beautifully produced and nicely acted but revived for reasons that had nothing to do with artistic merit, and I thought: 'He must be dying' — it was like someone taking stock and going back to his roots."

In fact, that winter many artists with whom Papp had deeply rooted relationships were working at the Public for the first time in several years. Raul Julia played the title role in *Macbeth;* Elizabeth Swados staged her Old Testament cantata *Jonah;* Kathryn Grody appeared in her own one-woman show, *A Mom's Life.* But Papp was also casting his Shakespeare Marathon with movie stars who had never worked at the Festival, such as Denzel Washington, whom he asked to play Richard III.

It was February 1990 when Papp was hit with his first medical setback. His PSA level, a marker for prostate cancer, rose slightly, indicating a resurgence of cancer activity, and the interpretation of his bone scans became ambiguous. But he did not feel ill. He was busy and when, on March 16, the Festival received formal notification of its $50,000 NEA grant for the Festival Latino, he was focused on Washington politics.

On March 3, Congressman Dana Rohrabacher announced that he would submit a bill ending all government funding for the arts. Four days later, Citizens for Community Values in Ohio announced their intention to halt the exhibit of Robert Mapplethorpe photographs, now due to open in Cincinnati. On March 9, the *Washington Post* reported that an anti-obscenity clause had been added to the NEA contract, which all recipients of grants were obliged to sign.

On March 15, Papp discussed at a board meeting the Festival's shrinking endowment — down to $17.5 million — the chronic $2 million annual deficit and a recent cut in city funding. *A Chorus Line,* which had earned $38.8 million for the Festival, was scheduled to close on April 28. Yet he felt sure that he could not sign what, to him, evoked the loyalty oaths of the McCarthy era. "Dear Mr. Frohnmayer," Papp wrote the NEA chairman:

> Your letter pressed me to note that acceptance of this grant was predicated on my observance of the restrictions contained in a recently passed piece of legislation affecting obscenity and N.E.A. grant giving. . . .
>
> As head of a major theatrical institution, I have always cherished my freedom, defending it whenever it was challenged. My privileged right to make my own judgment in choosing this over that and that over this regardless of great varieties of societal pressure have been matters of principle, taste and artistic standards. To be asked, after meeting the tests of 35 years, to yield to circumscription and legislative prohibitions

in the most vulnerable and inexplicable area of the arts, its content, is unthinkable, if not downright subversive.

Even if I did submit to the signing of what amounts to a loyalty oath, how am I to decide what others consider obscene? My personal views of what constitutes art and morality may, and probably do, widely differ from those legislators who conceived the obscenity measure.

And must I play the censor too, subject all plays and films from Latin America to microscopic scrutiny for some clue to sexual "aberration"? Who knows where sex may be lurking and in what disguise? I have no way of invoking community standards as some would have it. With what yardstick am I to measure the community standards of Rio de Janeiro?

With some dismay I have learned that a number of my colleagues will accept N.E.A. grants despite the restrictive clause in their agreements. The rationale is completely understandable: it is difficult to stand on principle when the need is so great. Further, it seems they are confident that reauthorization of N.E.A. funding will pass, and, in all likelihood, minus the restrictions.

I wish I could share this optimism. Perhaps time will prove this assessment to be correct. At the moment, I have serious doubts that reauthorization can make it through without some accommodation to the foes of the N.E.A. I hope I'm wrong.

Right now, we need the $50,000 for the Latin Festival. To obtain this money, I am being asked to be a party to a design which, in my opinion, is an abuse of the fundamental ethic in artistic endeavor. I have no desire to grandstand on this delicate issue. I certainly have not the slightest desire to push you into a corner. I do not want to break the law. I do not wish to relinquish the $50,000 grant. I do not wish to go through the motions of "signing" our agreement with the knowledge that I am bound, at one point or other, to violate, unwittingly, the prohibition I promise to observe. Is this a dilemma, or isn't it?

Frohnmayer replied that the federal obscenity law was not of the NEA's asking and regretted it caused such concern. "I hope you will be able to accept the grant," he wrote. "It is richly deserved."

Both letters appeared on the *Times* Op-Ed page of April 24. On April 26, Papp wrote another letter to Frohnmayer, turning the grant down:

I cannot in all good conscience accept any money from the National Endowment for the Arts as long as the Helms inspired amendment on obscenity is part of our agreement. I am therefore turning down the recently awarded $50,000 grant for the Latino Festival. Further, while we will be applying for 1990 grants in the amount of $550,000 (last year we received $350,000), we are prepared not to accept this money should it be awarded while the Helms restriction remains in force. . . .

Letters of support, telephone calls and checks poured in to Papp as they had done after his HUAC testimony in 1958. Television producer Mark Goodson sent Papp a check to replace the $50,000 he refused from the NEA and others sent smaller contributions, which totaled about $10,000. He even received a note from Senator Alfonse D'Amato which read "Congratulations on your principled stand in support of artistic freedom. As you know, I opposed the Helms amendment and continue to believe that limiting language is wrong. Be assured, I will closely follow the reauthorization of the N.E.A."

A few weeks later, on letterhead that listed Meryl Streep, Raul Julia and Mike Nichols as members of his board alongside such old-timers as George Delacorte, Judith Peabody and Stanley Lowell, Papp wrote a letter addressed to "Friends and Colleagues of the New York Shakespeare Festival" in which he urged them to oppose the restrictions on the NEA. He appeared on the cover of *Theater Week* with the headline: "Just Say No." He made pages of notes on the NEA controversy, designing his own "guidelines" for the religious right, which read:

In light of recent revelations of obscene and criminal behavior by two major TV evangelist preachers — Jimmy Swaggart and Jimmy Bakker — would it not be appropriate for the U.S. government to require Pat Robertson, president of the tax-exempt, not for profit, Christian Coalition (and the rest of television's religious leaders) to take the following pledge:

1. I will not commit adultery
2. I will not steal
3. I will not engage in deception
4. I will not undermine the morals of any in my congregation
5. I will not use my tax-exempt status to promote hate and dissension in all my preachings and practices. I will carefully observe America's fundamental constitutional separation of church and state.

At the Public Theater, members of the audience were given fliers and forms with which to protest. At every performance there, and later in the park, one of the leading actors would speak to the audience about the issue. Papp sent a top hat worn by one of the dancers in *A Chorus Line* to President George Bush with a letter: "Dear Mr. President: My hat's off to you. Your recent remarks on freedom of the arts . . . were the most crucial in this ongoing congressional debate in which the fate of the NEA hangs in the balance. . . . Enclosed are some 130 letters which I received in the past week (many of which had checks attached to them) reflecting that there are many, many thoughtful Americans out there who care deeply about the freedom of the arts and the survival of the NEA." He sent other versions of the letter to members of Congress, made himself available to any news organization and arts group that asked and helped mobilize a network of artists, lawyers, theater people and legislators to fight against the obscenity clause.

At the same time, he struggled with the fear that his three-year remission from cancer was over.

"In late May, Joe began experiencing the first symptoms of intense pain," Gail Merrifield recalled. "It came and went. It corresponded to the rise in his PSA and we were very scared. Joe had not been given any drugs for pain. We hadn't been *told* anything about pain. We thought this might be the beginning of the end."

On May 29, the *New York Times* reported that Papp had reorganized the Festival, naming JoAnne Akalaitis as his "artistic associate" and George C. Wolfe, Michael Greif and David Greenspan as resident directors. Akalaitis, Papp said, would be "the key artistic force of this institution." *Variety* reported that Papp had "handed over the reins" to Akalaitis but not yet "left his post" as "helmer" of the $14 million organization. It also related his choice of Akalaitis to "his political activism and concern over NEA-bashers like Senator Jesse Helms."

Akalaitis later recalled that, even then, she did not know what she was getting into. Neither her exact role nor her salary had been determined. Papp had not explained how he envisaged their relationship, did not invite her to staff meetings and made no other effort to introduce her to the workings of the Festival. Akalaitis, who later described herself as a person "more interested in black holes than in filling in the blanks" did not press Papp to do so. He still had not told her that he was ill, and Akalaitis felt no sense of urgency about getting oriented to the Festival. She understood how difficult it was for him to appoint a successor and did not obsess about the fact that, as she later said, "Joe's hand seemed to be pulling back as soon as he offered me the job."

Press coverage of Akalaitis's appointment broke at the same time as news from Papp's doctor. "I was waiting for the relapse," recalled Marc Garnick. "This was three-plus years after diagnosis. I knew that the PSA was slowly creeping up but I realized that I had to put things in the most optimistic light possible in order not to have the disease consume their lives. They were able to deal with it as long as I put it in terms of 'brush fires.' Nothing calamitous: a series of 'brush fires' that needed to be put out. I raised the idea of a course of radiation to address the hip pain."

The Papps adopted Garnick's terminology and radiation as the solution to his hip pain. Meanwhile, armed with Tylenol and Percodan, Papp focused on the NEA fight. A reauthorization bill backed by President Bush had been sent to Congress and Papp flew to Washington twice to testify on its behalf.

On June 28, Papp met with his board. He screened a segment of the television news show *Face the Nation* in which he had debated Congressman Dana Rohrabacher. The board approved a resolution "to affirm the action of its President and Artistic Director" in refusing the NEA grant and his view that "as long as this restriction applies, the NYSF cannot accept grants from the N.E.A." Papp told board members he was deferring a decision on applying for grants totaling $323,000 until the reauthorization bill was passed. The following day, NEA chairman John Frohnmayer vetoed four Theater Program grants to individual artists approved by peer review — on the basis of the new obscenity guidelines.

"You cannot legislate art or put controls on it any more than you can legislate the human spirit," Papp wrote in the *Los Angeles Times*.

Art takes the raw material that is life and interprets it, giving us new ways to see and hear and perceive. No artist knows for sure what the outcome will be when he or she begins to work. One of the very wonders of art is its unpredictability, its power to surprise, to make an original and startling statement. . . .

Democracy is true to itself when it protects the arts, not when it curbs them. Stop the invasion of the artistic process and the scapegoating of American artists by opportunistic legislators seeking reelection. . . . Get on with the original democratic mandate of the National Endowment for the Arts by encouraging the uncensored creation of art and its dissemination throughout the land.

On July 12, taking his cue from Capitol insiders who reported that congressmen "loved meeting movie stars," Papp returned to Washington with actors Kevin Kline, Kathleen Turner, then appearing in *Cat on a Hot Tin Roof* on Broadway, and Morgan Freeman, about to open in *The Taming of the Shrew* at the Delacorte. They met with members of the Congressional Arts Caucus, House Speaker Tom Foley and Republican Senate Minority Whip Alan Simpson. Papp was heartened by the news that choreographer Bella Lewitzky had turned down an NEA grant of $72,000.

Two days later, he arrived at a Cambridge condominium he had sublet, for nearly a month of radiation therapy. In addition to clothing, Merrifield had packed a fax machine and Papp's bulging rolodex. From nine in the morning until late at night, the producer — dressed in a gray sweatsuit, swallowing his hormones and painkillers on a rigid schedule, was on the phone — coordinating congressmen, lawyers, law professors and arts administrators.

Three times each week, he drove to the Dana-Farber Cancer Institute for radiation therapy and, when necessary, back to New York City. Many people were unaware that Papp was away. It was summer. In Central Park, *The Taming of the Shrew* — the fourteenth Shakespeare Marathon production — was well received. At the Public Theater, George C. Wolfe's *Spunk*, three one-acts based on Zora Neale Hurston's work, continued to bring in audiences. At both theaters, audiences were urged to lobby their representatives to reauthorize the NEA. Voting on the bill had been postponed until October, and theatergoers were invited to fill out forms that were then sent by Festival staffers to senators and congressmen.

In mid-August, his radiation therapy complete and apparently successful, Papp met with his new artistic associate, JoAnne Akalaitis. "What can I do for the Public this coming fall and winter?" she had written in response to a telephone conversation.

I envision a getting acquainted with the structure of the theater and some kind of more in depth understanding of the various departments. I already see the potentially problematic position I am in as someone who has always been on the outside (as directors and designers traditionally are) becoming an insider in an organization where everyone works for one person. I think the Public is the most dramatic example of an institution being identified with a sole vision and personality. My awareness of this does not intimidate me. My philosophy about running a theater is akin to the way I direct. I come at it sincerely in openness, some kind of innocence, naivety, terror and dread. I always allow the work to lead me. It tells me what to do. My vision comes in the midst of work. It is constantly changing in the works, renewed, redefined. . . . Which is not to say that there is not enormous preparation and planning. . . .

As for the three directors: They are already on their respective tracks. I don't see myself "supervising" anyone — rather, and sincerely helping if they need/want it. It should be director to director. Can we talk more about this? Here are some philosophical/practical questions: What do you expect from me? How do you see a one person operation becoming a two person operation? How do we negotiate and reconcile differences (if they exist) in matters of taste, management, budget? What is my relationship to the Board? What about potential Broadway projects for which I have little interest and instinct?

There are several very important issues I want to address at the Public. I want to lobby for artists' fees being more equitable with the demands of a normal standard of living. I want to urge the various departments to work for the artists in the production, not the needs of the department, the producer or the image of the organization. Artists must have a voice. I do hear stories of designers feeling slighted and playwrights betrayed by broken promises. . . . As for the Shakespeare Marathon . . . [it] is so far along and it has a very specific investment and imprint from you. How do you see me relating to it? That's all for now, except to say that I am wildly enthusiastic about my association with this rich place.

Love
JoAnne

On August 20, 1990, Papp and JoAnne Akalaitis had their second meeting since her appointment. He praised her letter and indicated that they would discuss it sometime later. "As often happened with Joe, we discussed what was on his mind at the moment," Akalaitis — who had no idea the producer had just received massive radiation — later recalled. "Falstaff was often on his mind. He liked to talk about Falstaff's wisdom and Falstaff's humor. And, when I think about it in retrospect, *Henry IV* is in some ways Shakespeare's most eloquent meditation on death. Our discussions were very moving to me although — because we talked over the telephone rather than in person — I did not understand how close he was to death himself."

That August, Akalaitis did not insist on addressing the troubling issues in her letter. By then, Papp had told her that she would be working in a managerial triumvirate with Jason Steven Cohen as managing director and Rosemarie Tichler, but when she moved into the Public Theater, in September, she was assigned one of several desks set up in Wilford Leach's old office. George C. Wolfe, Michael Greif and David Greenspan were working at the other desks and when, one day, Melia Bensussen appeared, saying that Papp had told her to work there, Akalaitis moved her assistant to give Bensussen space to work.

The month Akalaitis moved in, Papp had proposed a salary of $30,000. The director, though accepting her temporary office arrangements, was taken aback. "I told him: this is too tacky for me to argue. Then I asked for $50,000. I had *no idea* that Steve was getting a six-figure salary and that most other senior department heads were making more than the future artistic director." She also began, as tactfully as she knew how, to inform Papp of her dismay at the state of the Public Theater. "Production had atrophied," she later said. "The infrastructure was rotting. The place closed down on weekends. No one answered the phone. In Minneapolis, people knocked themselves out to do things for me. At the Public, a director was the enemy. My designers never wanted to work there again after *Cymbeline*. The lines of communication were not functioning. Everybody was answering to Steve Cohen and Steve was not in touch with the real world of theater. He did not serve Joe in the way Bernard Gersten had. Gersten was a grown-up, an intelligent manager who loved the theater, who had links with the foundation community, the unions — who knew how to look at a season. But it was very hard for me to say to Joe: 'Listen, you gotta fix this place up because it's falling apart and everybody in the theater world knows it.' He seemed to listen and said to go around to the departments and see what I could do."

Akalaitis was well aware of Papp's defensiveness and his reluctance to give up running his theater. The press also emphasized Papp's unreadiness to turn over the Public to a successor. In a *Village Voice* cover story that September, Don Shewey noted the difficulties for the head of any organization to groom a successor and noted that Papp had been seriously ill. Papp replied, "No, I've never been ill. I've never been ill at all. I've had certain things I've had to attend to, but I'm not very ill and my life is not at stake. . . . I'm 69 years of age. You can't run a theater forever. I began to think seriously about this when I turned 50. How does this continue? Or does it continue?"

In November, the *Daily News* ran a full-page article showing Papp, Akalaitis, Greif, Greenspan and Wolfe at a restaurant table, but Papp told the reporter, "No one's sitting at my desk. I'm exercising more authority than I ever did before. I'm taking this step of maintaining this theater for the next 100 years by creating the conditions under which it can exist both financially and artistically. I'm trying to find a way to make an institution work past the time when I or the next person is here. . . . These four people may not be here next year."

At the time Papp gave that interview, Akalaitis was totally concentrated on her production of the Marathon's *Henry IV, Parts 1 and 2*. Instead of attending development or marketing meetings, she was rehearsing. And although Papp's illness was common knowledge in the theater community, both she and Festival staffers continued to be unaware of just how sick Papp really was.

That winter, it was Papp's institution that seemed in the most danger. The value of its endowment had fallen precipitously as had production. In November of 1990, Papp notified thirty of his employees that he would be closing the electric, scenery, sound and prop shops to save the Festival $750,000. He was also considering closing the costume shop for an additional annual saving of $522,000. For years, Papp had resisted cutting back. Now he felt he had no choice.

At home, Papp faced another devastating situation. His son had developed symptoms of cytomegalovirus, an opportunistic AIDS-related disease that affects the eyes. Tony Papp was hospitalized, underwent surgery, lost vision in one eye and decided he was no longer able to live by himself. With his friend Rosemary Jordan, he moved back into the room of the Papps' apartment that he had lived in as a child.

"I didn't know what his parents would think," recalled Jordan, who had met Tony at his health club, where she was a fitness manager. "When I first met him, I was involved in a relationship with a woman. We knew each other for about a year before I found out he had AIDS. Then I found myself falling in love with him and it was a little weird. Neither of us were used to being with members of the opposite sex. Both of us felt like we were coming out of the closet the other way around. After his operation, I wanted to be with him but it was a little strange, at first, moving into his parents' house."

Papp and Merrifield welcomed them with their usual hospitality. Peggy Papp, too, was grateful that Tony had fallen in love at a time when he desperately needed a companion. She and Rosemary Jordan would become his primary caretakers in his last months of life.

The producer's own disease seemed to be in remission. He worked out at home and took long walks in Katonah, race-walking uphill. Over Christmas, the Papps spent time there with Tony and Rosemary, and with Papp's brother, Phillip Martel, whose wife had recently died. LuEsther Mertz, for years the Festival's chief benefactor, also died that month. "There was snow on the ground and we took pictures of the deer," Merrifield recalled. "Joe had also become very interested in birds and birdlife as a sign of environmental health. He ordered many birdhouses and had twenty of them situated around the property so that in the spring, certain species would be attracted back to the land. He had worked out the most remarkable design with designer Robin Wagner for a birdhouse that was a replica of the Globe Theater and could function as a nesting place, refuge and feeder."

In January, JoAnne Akalaitis's *Henry IV, Parts 1 and 2* opened at the Public with Papp absent on opening night. She had spoken to him over the telephone during previews and thought he sounded "spirited but weak" and unresponsive to her questions of what, exactly, she was expected to do or how, exactly, she would share decisions with associate producer Steve Cohen. Understanding that Papp was not going to orient her as artistic director, she began interviewing department heads herself. Meanwhile, in an interview with the *New York Observer* that month, Papp said that the Festival endowment, once $24 million, was now $13 million, in part because it had been used to make up deficits of $2.5 million a year. He hoped to build a $35 million fund, he said, which would produce enough income to restore the Festival to fiscal health. When asked where he hoped to find that money, Papp replied, "I don't know." When asked if it were possible, "I have to think so. Yes."

He worked in his office part-time but complained of a stiff neck, shoulder and back pain. Tony had begun radiation therapy for Kaposi's sarcoma. "Tony and Joe would get home from work and each would collapse on a living room couch," recalled Rosemary Jordan. "Joe would be exhausted and in pain. Tony would be nauseous. Gail and I would stand there between the couches and look at each other. It was pretty intense."

From Boston, Dr. Garnick recommended a second course of radiation therapy for the producer and, this time, suggested Manhattan's Sloan-Kettering Hospital as a more convenient site. Papp began therapy there on February 1, every day, before and after work. But his bone pain did not disappear as it had in August. He began taking Percoset around the clock and stopped going out in the evening. On February 14, he appeared in his tuxedo for the last time at an Asian-American benefit in Chinatown where he presented actor B. D. Wong with a "Justice in Action" award. That month, the London *Times* ran an old photograph of a smiling, exuberant Papp with a caption that read "If my theater isn't being criticized for being extreme, there's something wrong."

A few days later, he stopped going to the office.

By March, Tony Papp was hospitalized for the third time and the producer was doing business strictly over the telephone. He was in continual touch with his pain specialist at Sloan-Kettering, who had prescribed Dilaudid, and asked first for a cane, then for a wheelchair for use in his apartment. "Nobody knew how sick he really was because he saw few people in person and had reversed his initial impulse to tell people about his illness," said Merrifield. "He realized he was going to be written off before he finished what he wanted to do. Also, it was a dispiriting and defeating prospect that people were going to relate to him purely on the basis of his being mortally ill. So we started covering our tracks."

Papp stopped taking calls from many people, including his own children. Apart from the people he lived with, he wanted to see only his brother, Phillip, set designer Robin Wagner — who had designed *A Chorus Line* and later became Papp's close friend — a few actors, *Times* editor Arthur Gelb and his former therapist. He ate little, slept a great deal and rarely left the apartment. Sometimes he talked as energetically and volubly as ever; sometimes he remained silent for hours at a time.

On March 18, *Theater Week* ran a cover story on Papp and Akalaitis. It reported that Akalaitis was reluctant to discuss her role as artistic associate at the Public. "It's in the process of being defined although I can say I would like to have a voice in the future of this organization," she told the writer in what she later termed as "a cover for the lack of planning or structure." "Papp echoes the sentiment, refusing to go into detail either. 'We're negotiating a three-year contract right now,' Papp says. 'I won't retire. I'll have to be killed off.'"

That day, unable to negotiate a trip by air, Papp, Merrifield and Papp's personal assistant, Emmett Foster, were setting out by car for Boston with a stopover in Katonah. Papp had decided to have a consultation with Dr. Garnick in Boston.

Emmett Foster had come to New York from Santa Monica, California, at age twenty-five to become an actor. Instead, for eighteen years he had served as Papp's chauffeur and gofer, occasionally performing on the side. "In the beginning, I only planned to stay a year or two — then I'd be a star," Foster later said wryly. "That's how many people got to the Festival. But because I was alone with him a lot, we developed a close personal relationship. I told him about my childhood, being raised Mormon in California, and discovering I was gay and leaving the church. He told me about when he was a poor Jewish boy in Brooklyn and I began to understand him better. He was a typical American man — he wanted to be seen as this tough guy. But I learned how very dependent he was on other people to make him feel supported and secure. It actually hurt his feelings if I said I didn't want to have dinner with him, that I had something else to do.

"It's only in retrospect that I realize how much it was a codependent relationship, that Joe relied on me and other people in the office as much as I relied on him. My mother had been married nine times and I had seen a lot of stepfathers come and go. My relationship with him was the longest relationship I had ever had with any man. I had no boundaries with him. I could not leave him even if it meant not pursuing my own life." Papp dubbed him "Emmett the Good."

By the time Papp, Merrifield and Foster arrived in Boston, the producer could no longer stand unassisted. Dr. Garnick prescribed three weeks of lumbar radiation starting immediately and changed his pain medication from Dilaudid to MS Contin, or oral morphine. The Papps and Foster had not planned for a long stay. But they settled into their accommodations at the Charles Hotel and Foster and Merrifield scoured the Boston area for medical accessories and hospital supplies that would make Papp feel more comfortable. Foster even persuaded a store manager to deliver a hospital bed on Easter Sunday. Papp could no longer walk, dress, bathe or get in or out of bed unassisted and was in unremitting pain. The pain required more morphine and the morphine brought on terror, nausea, hallucinations and paranoia.

Gail Merrifield drove with him back and forth from the hospital and tried to keep up with events at their Greenwich Village apartment, where Tony Papp had begun to have seizures. By phone, she tried to orchestrate family members, friends and Festival staff into a rotating schedule that would provide Tony with a companion at all times. Meanwhile, the pain-wracked producer had become so demanding that even the devoted Foster began to crack.

"I had not had a vacation in two and a half years," he later said. "Whenever I said, 'This seems like a good time for me to take a few days off,' Joe would say, '*I'll* tell you when it's a good time. Just because I'm a little bit better doesn't mean you can go away.' In March, when I had to take a break, he started yelling, 'You people don't know what I'm going through!' For the first time in eighteen years, I was determined to stand up to him. I said: 'You don't know what *we're* going through.' He yelled, 'Nobody understands me,' and started crying. That was excruciating for me but thank God Gail was there supporting me. Later on, he apologized and said: 'Take the days.'"

On March 28, the *Daily News* noted that Papp had missed the Passover *seder* for the stars that he had planned in New York because "a major flare-up of an old back problem forced him out of town for treatment." On March 29, *USA Today* ran a feature titled "Joseph Papp Enters A New Stage." It read, "Preserving what he has built over the last thirty-five years, a non-profit theater that gives approximately 15 productions per season of classics and experimental theater, is utmost in Papp's mind. Prior to this season, he admits he had become bored with his own theater and found it much more interesting to oppose National Endowment for the Arts grant restrictions." "I've been a political figure all my life," Papp is quoted as saying. "I was arrested during the Vietnam situation and if I had more energy I would be arrested more recently." The story was accompanied by an excellent photo of Papp taken the previous year.

That week, Papp's contact with the Festival was close to nil. When his assistant Barbara Carroll called daily from New York, Foster or Merrifield would take the telephone and say, "He's a little better today" or "He's a little worse." Neither one of them could bear to report Papp's actual condition. At the Festival, "it felt like the last days of Stalin or Mao," Akalaitis would later recall. Staffers speculated on how sick or drugged he seemed when he spoke over the telephone and they worried about their futures. There was no mechanism in place for anyone but Papp to approve projects and Festival staffers treaded water. "Nobody there had the nerve to ask Joe whether he was dying," Foster recalled. "It was horrible for them not to know what was going on but they, too, went into a kind of denial."

On April 12, deeply disappointed that the producer was still unable to walk, the Papps drove from Boston back to Katonah, where they planned to stay the night before returning to Manhattan. There Papp was hit with hip pain so intense that Dr. Garnick recommended even more radiation at a Westchester Hospital. The couple, accompanied by Foster, decided to stay in Katonah.

"Joe still could not walk, but gradually, with some physical therapy, he began to take a few steps holding on to the edge of the kitchen counter," Gail Merrifield recalled. "This was a tremendous difference and I was so moved by his struggle.

"He had lost an appalling amount of weight since the beginning of the year. His body was as emaciated as anyone in a concentration camp. Joe was unwilling to wear walking shorts or short-sleeved shirts as it got warmer because they would show the true condition of his arms and legs. So the illusion set in that Joe's physical deterioration wasn't as severe as in fact it really was. He sat on the deck in the sun. His face was tanned and seemed to get younger with the loss of weight."

When he felt up to it, Papp telephoned his office and his son Tony, who was becoming delusional for long periods at a time. Although it was spring, he believed Christmas was coming. Papp sang him carols over the telephone, then hung up exhausted. He sat dozing for hours on the deck, looking out into the woods, not speaking for days at a time. He had become so depressed and anxious that Merrifield consulted a local doctor, who prescribed psychotropic medication to supplement the morphine. "He slept most of the time, both day and night," she said. "He regarded sleep as a delicious blessing, a boon, something he devoutly desired and regretted waking up from. He slept for days and weeks."

From Boston, Marc Garnick wrote:

> Joe, The last four months have been the most difficult four months of your life. You have had to endure things that most people have never had to think about. . . . The situation with Tony has been equally traumatic and painful to even the most casual, detached observer. To experience both these major traumas simultaneously and emerge in any recognizable form is itself testimony to your extraordinary strength and constitution. The fact that you have not crashed is unbelievable. . . .
>
> You're turning the corner, Joe. The worst is behind you. . . . You must get back to familiar surroundings. You must get back to the Shakespeare Festival. . . . Joe, you will recover, but it's not going to be an easy task. . . . You have got to get back in control of the things which form your essence. You have got to get back to your creative environs. This is the "medicine" which is now prescribed.

Later, Garnick would defend his prescription. "You don't tell people they're going to die unless they're ready to hear it," he said. "Joe had been through the wars by then. He needed to hear how well he had done. If you took away the positive in the medical reports, it was like shooting both of them. The only way to get through the illness was to put a positive spin on things. If a bone scan showed cancer activity, I would say: 'Look at all the places that are disease-free.' If one of them had asked me: 'Am I going to die this year?' I would have tried to answer them. But I would never initiate that conversation myself. Of what value would it be? I tried to maintain his productivity."

In mid-May, after Rosemary Jordan warned them that Tony, who moved in and out of coma, was declining rapidly, Papp and Merrifield drove into the city. Papp was wheeled into his own apartment for the first time in two months. His bedroom was now a storage area for medical equipment; the living room, a waiting area for doctors, nurses and visitors. Tony lay in a hospital bed in his old room, hooked up to an IV. He could no longer speak but squeezed his father's hand. Papp played his son a recording of their favorite piece of music, Mendelssohn's violin concerto. "Tony was crying," remembered Rosemary Jordan. "All Joe could say was 'I'm here' and 'I love you, son,' and he just couldn't deal with it. Both of them were dying. One was a mirror for the other but Tony was embracing death more easily than Joe. He had reached another level of being. He wasn't scared. Joe was in terror of dying." They drove back to Katonah.

On May 29, Papp and Merrifield moved back into Manhattan. Bernard Gersten, now executive director of Lincoln Center Theater who had been following with alarm the recurrence of his friend's illness, loaned Papp his apartment. Gersten and his wife, Cora Cahan, commuted to work in the city every day from their country house in Katonah, where he and Papp had once talked about living out their old age together. In the theater world, Gersten's generosity and their reunion were considered remarkable signs of healing. Papp spent three weeks, mostly asleep, in Gersten's apartment. Merrifield, Foster, Robin Wagner, Papp's brother, Phillip, and his former therapist alternated sitting by his bedside. The therapist was there holding his hand when the telephone rang on the evening of June 1, and Merrifield told Papp that Tony had died.

"Oh my son!" Papp cried out. He was unable to attend the funeral, which was held at a nearby church, unable to emerge from the bedroom of Gersten's apartment to greet guests at the reception afterward and unable to perform *shiva,* the seven-day Jewish mourning ritual. Actor Mandy Patinkin appeared one evening and managed to say prayers with Papp. But, most of the time, the producer stayed in bed and slept. During the brief intervals when he was awake, he took telephone calls. He spoke to *Times* managing editor Arthur Gelb, to Gersten and to Kevin Kline. "When he told me about Tony's death," said Kevin Kline, "he let out a high-pitched, anguished cry. I had never heard that sound come out of anyone's mouth before."

Shortly after Tony's death, the Papps moved back into their own apartment and the producer suddenly came alive again. He spoke to staffers at the Festival and talked with friends over the telephone. After dismissing a series of New York physicians who, he felt, treated him like a dying man, Papp found what he called "an optimistic oncologist," in the person of Dr. Larry Norton. On June 21, he felt well enough to call a staff meeting at his apartment to discuss the upcoming 1991–92 season.

Most of his visitors had not seen him since February but many had talked to him over the telephone. "There was no sense of being called to his deathbed," Rosemarie Tichler later recalled. "He had a gaunt look but I did not think that he was dying." Before they arrived, Papp dressed in loose clothing that would disguise his thinness and positioned himself carefully on the couch. After JoAnne Akalaitis, Steve Cohen, Rosemarie Tichler, Melia Bensussen, David Greenspan and his assistant Barbara Carroll had all sat down, Papp began the meeting. "Once everybody was in the room, Joe was reminded of the serious problems he'd left behind

him a few months earlier," Merrifield recalled. "He was concerned that
JoAnne did not yet have a signed contract. He conducted the meeting
with all his old aplomb, fielding ideas, reinforcing good ones, skillfully
orchestrating people. It was an amazing performance." Several staffers
left Papp's apartment certain that he would soon return to the office.
"He looked frail but he was still able to yell at people," Melia Bensussen
would later recall. "We were trying to program the season and at one
point Steve Cohen said 'What about the Shakespeare Marathon?' and Joe
said, 'Forget the Shakespeare Marathon!' and I remember thinking that
there was no one else who could say something like that, ignore the
subscribers and the board and totally reverse himself and come up with
a new plan. I didn't think he was dying. I thought he could beat the
cancer if only he could get over Tony's death."

The Shakespeare Marathon was not the producer's only surprising
reversal. For days, Papp had been telling Merrifield that the management
structure he had pieced together was incomplete and that there was a
"hole" in the producing area. The day before he met with his staff, Papp
had called the executive director of the New York Public Library for the
Performing Arts, Robert Marx. "I want you to come see me," said Joseph
Papp. "It's about the future of the New York Shakespeare Festival."

Robert Marx was forty-one years old and a product of both New York
City public schools and the Yale School of Drama. He had met Papp in
1968, interviewing the producer for his student newspaper. In 1976, he
began discussions with him again, this time as head of the theater division
at the New York State Council on the Arts. For several years Marx was
the Festival's grants officer at NYSCA. Later, he became artistic associate
of the Mark Taper Forum, worked at international theater festivals and
served as director of the NEA Theater Program before taking his current
job. Papp's most recent glimpse of Marx had been as a speaker at a
colloquium arguing against censorship of the arts. He was an arts advocate, but not himself an artist. Marx agreed to come to Papp's apartment
the following day.

Emmett Foster seated Marx in the living room where he waited for
about ten minutes. Marx had heard rumors that Papp was in a wheelchair
and was surprised to see the producer walk into the room, looking frail
but behaving in his usual take-charge manner. "He did not waste a
minute," Marx recalled. "He said he had decided to pass on control of
the Festival, that he had a list of names and kept coming back to mine.
He wanted me to be producer of the Festival.

"I was surprised and overwhelmed. But I also felt that everything in
my professional life had led me to that point. It became a one-and-a-half-

hour job interview: questions like 'What do you bring to this job?' I asked about JoAnne, whom I regarded as a friend, and Joe said that she was an artist — not a producer. It did not occur to me to ask whether she or Steve Cohen had been informed. I brought up the fact that I had a contract with the New York Public Library. Joe said I should talk immediately to the library's president about a release, and deliver an artistic and institutional proposal by Monday. I brought up my lack of producing experience — I had produced only one off-Broadway play — and he said: 'Don't worry — I'll be there for you.'"

That weekend, Marx wrote Papp a detailed proposal of how he would run the Festival. Early on June 25, he talked with the library's leadership about Papp's offer and obtained their support. That same day, Papp called members of the executive committee of his board to his apartment. In the morning, he told them he had made an offer to Marx, and took the extraordinary measure of tape recording their meeting. In the afternoon, he informed artistic associate JoAnne Akalaitis, casting director Rosemarie Tichler and associate producer Steve Cohen.

All three were stunned that Papp had made an offer to Marx without consulting them. After leaving his apartment, they went to a nearby café to discuss what Marx's appointment would mean. Akalaitis telephoned Papp and said she would not work for Marx or anyone else and would resign immediately if the plan was implemented. Cohen said he would remain so long as Papp was alive but then resign. "Joe was so alarmed when Steve said this," Merrifield recalled, "that he started to hyperventilate and it took me quite a while to calm him down."

On June 27, Papp called Marx, told him he had to deal with threats of resignations, that he would work things out and get back to him. That afternoon, he roused himself sufficiently to drive to Central Park and greet the company of *Othello,* which was opening at the Delacorte. He sat for a while with director Joe Dowling and Raul Julia by Belvedere Lake and returned in the evening to see part of the show. Then, for most of July, he sank back into sleep. On July 26, the Festival board met, formally appointed JoAnne Akalaitis artistic director and notified Marx that he would not be hired.

In August, Papp seemed to rally. Dr. Norton had asked him to keep a journal and, that month, he began to fill it with observations about his illness, poetry and Festival business. "Call Kevin Kline," he wrote August 6. "Board of Advisors in the future. Meryl Streep wants to accept Cochairmanship. Kevin is Chairman. Bernie Gersten temporary coordinator as discussed."

On August 11, he mustered his energy to drive into Central Park and greet Caca Rosset's São Paulo theater company, Teatro Ornitorrinco, which was opening *A Midsummer Night's Dream* at the Delacorte. The Brazilians made a "magic circle" around the producer chanting in Portuguese for his well-being. Too weak to speak in the open air, Papp thanked them by blowing kisses.

That same day, he called *Times* critic Frank Rich, who, Papp learned, had just lost his mother. The producer had, in the past, attacked Rich as angrily as he had attacked Clive Barnes, John Simon or Walter Kerr. "His voice sounded normal, articulate and forceful," Rich later recalled. "We had this emotional conversation that went on for about half an hour, which was fascinating since we had never had a close relationship. He was incredibly compassionate, not perfunctory. Sweet and warm. I told him I had heard about his son and couldn't imagine what that was like. I didn't know what to say about his illness. Arthur Gelb gave conflicting reports from week to week and for the longest time did not believe that Joe was seriously ill. Joe said that he had always thought I loved the theater and whatever squabbles we'd had, we were on the same side. And I told him how I felt about him and that I had always felt that bond even though we didn't know each other. We told each other that we loved each other. I had just gotten married and that he wished me happiness with Alex, my wife, who had worked at the Public. I said we'd love to have him over sometime when he felt like it. Both of us were crying. It was an unstated good-bye. I remember getting off the phone and saying, 'He's never going to come to dinner.'"

On August 13, he met with JoAnne Akalaitis, finally began to discuss with her the future of the Festival, and wrote in his diary: "Good meeting with JoAnne regarding goals, ideas, objectives, finances, small groups, short and long views, strategy, and leadership development. Putting the Festival into orbit with colleagues and audience. . . . Gail and I talked about my nervousness. She suggests I opened up the Festival's future plans which I had buried away and the thoughts of it are scary because they were brought forth from their hiding places."

On August 16, Papp prepared himself for what he knew would be an exacting interview with *Times* reporter Alex Witchel. "Gail let me sleep through 4 AM pills almost four hours plus, perhaps to imbue me with stamina," he wrote in his diary. "Gait slightly better. If walking and ribs improve, I will become much more of a participant in day's events, planning and decision-making power — all of which are absolutely necessary for the progress and development of the institution." With a burst of energy that astonished Merrifield, Papp roused himself for what would be the last and most difficult interview of his life.

Witchel had an insider's view of the producer. She had worked at the Festival as a college intern, had recently married drama critic Frank Rich and was herself a tough reporter and caustic writer. Papp — who had not given an in-person interview in several months — was nervous. He was about to confirm the rumors of his illness and announce his stepping down as artistic director of the New York Shakespeare Festival. He wanted to make his announcement with grace and dignity.

"I knew he had been sick for a very long time," Witchel recalled. "But whenever I had spoken to him over the phone he was focused and in charge. He always made me feel that his theater was a place where something was happening and that theater was not a moribund art form.

"He was such a hero of mine, I never believed he was going to die and I did not believe it during that interview. He answered the door wearing slippers and socks and sweatpants. He looked bad. But the way he spoke was at total odds with the way he looked. He had such conviction and strength in the way he spoke. He was not saying that he was going to die, he was saying 'I'm going to do less now than before,' and I sort of believed that the structure he was setting up would actually work for a season with him in charge. He had always done what he said he would do. I believed that he could have gotten up the next morning, gotten dressed and gone to his office. I think what motivated him to give the interview the way he did could only have been his rage at dying and losing his theater."

The head of the Festival's Press Department, Richard Kornberg, had told Witchel that Papp was not up to being photographed. Like everyone else at the Public Theater, Kornberg spent much of his time denying rumors about Papp's failing health. Witchel, for her part, did not think it unreasonable that Papp did not wish to be photographed while he was not feeling well. The piece might well run on the front page of the newspaper, she thought. There was no paucity of good photographs of Papp in the *Times* archive. The one chosen was taken six years earlier.

In her piece, Witchel reported that Papp had appointed JoAnne Akalaitis to succeed him "effective immediately," that Jason Steven Cohen would be promoted from associate producer to managing director, and Rosemarie Tichler from casting director to artistic associate. "Mr. Papp has been absent from the theater since last spring," she wrote. "He has lost a great deal of weight and, when he crossed the room of his Greenwich Village apartment, his walk was slow and uncertain. But when he sat down to talk, his manner was as vigorous as ever. His determination to fight for the survival of his own theater, and of the theater in general, has not abated. . . ."

Witchel described the cutbacks in staff — which now totaled forty-three because the costume shop had finally been closed. She noted the 50 percent cutback in new productions; the shrinking of the Festival's operating budget from $13.5 million to $10.5 million; the drop in government funding — a 33 percent cut in municipal funds, a 60 percent cut in state funds, and a total cut in federal funding since Papp would not accept money from the NEA.

> But the tough economic times, Mr. Papp said, are an opportunity for the Festival's rejuvenation, and he calls JoAnne Akalaitis . . . the perfect person to guide it. . . . "I will not censor JoAnne in any way," he said. "She is the artistic director now. I'm the producer and can provide the overall view. It remains to be seen what will happen, but isn't that exciting?" . . .
>
> His health, however, must remain a priority. "I've been going through treatment at Sloan-Kettering," he said, "as part of some kind of experiment that has to do with a new drug." And he added firmly, "It looks like I'm improving."

Witchel concluded on an upbeat note. "He mentioned that he had been reading a new translation of the French classic novel *Les Liaisons Dangereuses* and he talked about the complexity of the language and how the adaptor had mastered it. 'You know,' he said with admiration in his voice, 'there are still so many ways to say something new.'"

Gail Merrifield called the week in which he gave his last interview "the week of one thousand firsts." He welcomed a visit from one of his favorite actors, Al Pacino, and wrote many poems, including one he dedicated to Merrifield "and close friends and to children everywhere":

> *Life is everywhere*
> *there is no end*
> *What we have sown, we reap*
> *Nothing disappears but is retained*
> *in the crucible of memory . .*
> *Never say never — dear ones,*
> *the key word*
> *is always, always will be —*
> *ever.*

The day after his *Times* interview, Papp went into his office and, for two hours, sat at his desk reading his mail, making calls and greeting staffers who happily welcomed him back to work. From the Public, Papp and Merrifield drove to Katonah. "Walked around grounds — uphill, saw the coming of fall on the trees, the vines, the stillness of the place," he wrote in his diary. "Stand on the highest roof of the land and shout Hooray! No matter how overwhelming is the force which dampens human COURAGE, youth will have its day, its own generation's SHOW, a real EXTRAVAGANZA — LESSONS LEARNED AND MINDS ATTUNED TO WHAT THE WORLD MUST UNDERTAKE AS IT MOVES THROUGH THE 90s."

For the next few days, Papp walked, talked and dined with friends, including Bernard Gersten. The two men had set aside the painful episodes in their history and been able to reconnect to the warmth and simple camaraderie that was the best part of their long relationship. At Gersten's urging, Papp and Merle Debuskey had a long telephone conversation as well. The producer urged the press agent to put aside their differences and invited Debuskey to visit. The press agent demurred. He never forgave Papp for firing Gersten or himself.

The people who saw him every day — Gail Merrifield, Emmett Foster, Phillip Martel, Robin Wagner and Papp's therapist — rarely felt that Papp behaved like a dying man. "The boundaries of his life got smaller and smaller," said his brother. "But he was still sarcastic, opinionated, always volatile." Robin Wagner would later say that he did not remember a sad or maudlin moment with the producer, even in the hospital when he was coming in and out of delusions. "He never lost his sense of humor," said Wagner. "And we never talked about death. I had no idea how close he was." When numerous and effusive press tributes followed Alex Witchel's story, the producer joked that he was the only person in history granted the privilege of reading his own obituaries. He also never lost the rage that had fueled him in so many previous crises. *"An urgent letter to a dear Friend,"* he wrote in his diary, after being shown the new Festival brochure with JoAnne Akalaitis's name beside his own, disliking it, and — for the first time since he had founded the theater — feeling unable to change what he disliked. "OR KING LEAR ON A RAMPAGE. I'M FURIOUS AT HAVING TO BEG FOR SOMETHING THAT HAS BEEN MINE OVER MANY YEARS — MY FLESH AND BLOOD — MY MIND. . . ."

That August, *glasnost* and *perestroika* had culminated in a neo-Communist coup attempt in the Soviet Union. "I can't even begin to think about Russia and the international crisis," Papp wrote in his diary on August 20, as Mikhail Gorbachev was being held prisoner in his vacation home in the Crimea, "and this is a first in my active politically conscious life — a real first — so the impact of what my body is going through must be devastating."

The producer would go in and out of denial of his impending death. One day Papp helped chop onions for a stew that his wife was learning to prepare. Afterward he dozed and when he awoke, said abruptly, "I don't know how to do this — I don't know how to die." When a friend asked him what he viewed as his most important accomplishment in life, he snapped back:

"Why you asking?" he demanded.

"I'm just curious," was the reply.

"Yes, you probably are." And then he said, "Producing David Rabe's plays. And my marriage to Gail."

On August 27, depression once again set in. "Is one great chance all?" he wrote in his diary a few days later. "Is there any space left for an old-comer, a man who has known the fruits of children, the consuming passions of love and still has been permitted to love & be loved on. Isn't that more than anyone can ask for? I don't want to think so. . . . My resistance to this concept is powerful and exceedingly painful. . . ."

On August 30, he wrote a poem to his brother, Phillip, as he had written one to his therapist and several to his wife.

During the next two months, Papp was hospitalized twice. For days at a time, Gail Merrifield did not leave the darkened room to which he would admit virtually no one but his brother, his therapist and Robin Wagner. Once, when Mandy Patinkin tried to visit, Papp screamed, "Why do you let people I love in here?" and refused to see him. When Merrifield had to get some sleep, Emmett Foster would sit by Papp's bed.

"Gail?" Foster would later recall him whispering. "'No, it's Emmett,' I would say. 'My trusted Emmett. What would I do without you?' He would have never said that before he got sick. Sometimes he'd start singing in a thin, weak tenor and I was amazed. He sang on tune, he knew the words and he had just enough strength to hold the notes. He told me a story of his life, a version that began with his creating the Festival. He had a son and his son got AIDS and then he got cancer and then he died. I'd say, 'You didn't *die,* Joe — you're still *alive,*' and he'd say, 'Well what the hell are you guys doing — I'm trying to die, can't you see?' And I couldn't tell whether he was making a joke or hallucinating.

"He had talked to me years earlier about dying — maybe because of all the people he knew who were dying of AIDS. He said, 'I would help you die if that's what you wanted; would you help me?' I said yes. In September of 1991, he had had it one day. Gail went out of the room and he said to me 'Do you remember the pact we made? Now's the time. I've nothing to live for. I'm only going to get worse. Gail's a young woman. Do whatever you have to do. Get whatever you have to get. Go to Robin Wagner or whoever you need to and get me something.'

"I'd been trained for eighteen years that when Joseph Papp said to do something, I did it. Usually, I could even anticipate his needs, and my immediate reaction was to go ahead and do it. I was just vibrating with it. But I couldn't go over Gail's head and help him kill himself. It was too much for me. Instead I went to the hospital psychiatrist, trusting his confidentiality. The psychiatrist told his doctor who went into Joe the next morning and told him it was inappropriate for him to be talking to Emmett and Gail about suicide."

Papp astounded his hospital nurses and physicians by punning — in and out of delirium. He insisted on going back home as soon as possible. In his Greenwich Village apartment, he drifted in and out of sleep. Heavy medication had slurred his speech, but he would periodically muster his energy for an incisive chat over the telephone. On September 20, the *Washington Post* reported that the Senate had adopted another Helms amendment on NEA guidelines for another year but that Helms and other critics "complained that the endowment continues to award grants to dubious endeavors including $323,000 to the New York Shakespeare Festival which presented a version of *Midsummer Night's Dream* performed by a Portuguese-speaking cast clad nude, topless and in G-strings."

On October 27, Papp spoke over the telephone with his former playwright Václav Havel, now president of Czechoslovakia and in the United States on government business. On October 29, he saw actors Kevin Kline and Phoebe Cates with their newborn son, to whom they had given the middle name Joseph. For days he lay on the open living room couch surrounded by his books, an oxygen machine and an IV unit. An exhausted Merrifield and equally exhausted Foster sat in the soft lamplight. A home aide was on call in one of the bedrooms.

The Papps had consistently refused to have professional nurses come to the apartment. They had also refused to contact hospice workers, for that contact would be an admission that Papp's illness was terminal. For much of the summer and the fall, Merrifield had been telling callers, members of Papp's biological and theater families alike, that it would be better to talk with him when he was feeling better, that now was not a good time.

Foster would later recall that in the very early morning of October 31, Papp had a sudden burst of energy. He sat straight up and tried to stand, saying he wanted to go to his own room. The producer had not left the

couch in several days, Foster was terrified that he would fall, and he
wrestled him down while Merrifield brought over his wheelchair. By the
time they had settled Papp in his own bed he was breathing in a way that
Foster understood was a prelude to death.

"My mind is teeming with ideas," he had told Merrifield a few hours
earlier. And, "Do you love me?" And some time after that, "Am I going
to die?"

PAPP died shortly after 2:00 A.M., October 31. A few days earlier, Congress had reauthorized the NEA for three years, eliminating explicit restrictions on the type of art that might be funded but requiring that grantees take into account a "general standard of decency and respect for the diverse beliefs and values of the American public." The NEA announced it was eliminating its obscenity pledge.

JoAnne Akalaitis served as artistic director from the day of Papp's death, until March 1993. On March 15, 1993, the New York Shakespeare Festival board of trustees fired JoAnne Akalaitis and named George C. Wolfe producer. Jason Steven Cohen became managing director. Rosemarie Tichler and Kevin Kline became associate producers. Gail Merrifield Papp became a member of the board of trustees.

The experimental therapy Papp received for his illness has become a standard treatment for prostate cancer.

Acknowledgments

FOR MY RESEARCH I enjoyed unrestricted access to the New York Shakespeare Festival Archive and the personal papers of Joseph Papp. The New York Shakespeare Festival Archive, now part of the Billy Rose Theater Collection of the New York Public Library for the Performing Arts, contains more than one thousand cartons of documents, video and audiocassettes pertaining to Joseph Papp and his theater from 1954 to 1991. Former Festival archivist Serge Mogilat served as my guide to this material. Joseph Papp's personal papers are also part of the Billy Rose Collection. They include thirty-five years' worth of letters, position papers, notes, poems and diary entries, and his oral history interviews. Of vital importance was Papp's daily appointment calendar, which elucidates the chronological evolution of some of his projects.

The original Shakespeare Workshop scrapbooks — which contain clippings, photographs and programs from the earliest years of Papp's venture — were the starting point of my research in 1976 as well as in 1991 and are now on microfilm. Equal in importance are reel-to-reel taped radio interviews and television footage from the 1950s now transposed to cassettes. Early Festival history is further documented in two unpublished manuscripts commissioned by Papp: David Black's *History of the New York Shakespeare Festival 1952–1961* and Sean Cronin's *History of the New York Shakespeare Festival*. Another view of the Festival and aspects of Papp's life is provided by the collection of tapes and transcripts of the *New York Shakespeare Festival Oral History* compiled by Kenneth Turan and owned by the Papp Estate. There are also two excellent master's dissertations — Robert Michael Newman's *S.R.O. Culture: The Development of the New York Shakespeare Festival* (Cornell University, 1967) and David Harry Watrous Smith's *The Roots of the New York Shakespeare Festival* (Hunter College, 1967) — and Yoko Hashimoto's comprehensive *Joseph Papp and the New York Shakespeare Festival,* an unpublished doctoral dissertation written at the University of Michigan in 1972.

The Archive maintained files on every Festival production. For some, there is one file folder. For others (for example, *A Chorus Line*) there are dozens. These files contain production budgets, programs, reviews, feature articles on the production, its cast members, playwright, director and designers, and related issues (for example, files on *The Normal Heart* include news reports and analyses of AIDS research and casualties). Files of the board of trustees' minutes were a rich source of data, as were the Festival's annual reports, files of Papp's correspondence with critics, with politicians and with subscribers, and Papp's many position papers on such subjects as Shakespeare in the schools, the role of critics, the state of large arts complexes, government funding for the arts and the future of Broadway theaters.

In addition to the Archive, I enjoyed access to and a most unusual collaboration with Gail Merrifield Papp, former director of play development at the New York Shakespeare Festival and wife of Joe Papp. Gail has been a friend since 1977 and it was she who suggested that I write Papp's biography. At the time of the producer's death, I was at work on another book and did not wish to interrupt it. But there were compelling reasons to do so. First, I admired Papp and his work, and had observed him closely for fifteen years. Second, I had twice started to write a book with him and had already amassed boxes full of research material. Third, I could draw on Gail's knowledge and resources. Papp had often referred to their marriage as one "of heart and mind." As the producer's wife and closest colleague, Gail's insight into Papp and the Festival is unique. I agreed to write this biography only on the condition that she work with me as consultant and researcher.

This idea struck almost everyone we knew (including Gail herself) as misguided. However, I, knowing how multifaceted Papp's life was and how difficult it would be to negotiate the massive Festival Archive, refused to do the book without her. I felt that the value she brought to the project had to be addressed in monetary terms and we drew up a contract of collaboration. When Papp and I planned to write his "as-told-to" autobiography, he planned to give his portion to the New York Shakespeare Festival (as he did all fees he received for teaching, speaking and doing advertisements). In a similiar decision, Gail decided that *her* royalties would go to a nonprofit foundation.

Another issue that we addressed in our contract was editorial control. Many authorized biographers trade access to their subject's personal papers for final approval of their work by the estate. Gail agreed that I would retain editorial control. I knew that she respected the integrity of the writing process and that she would not attempt to subvert it. Some skeptics assumed that as the producer's widow, she would try to "whitewash" Joe Papp. Certainly Gail acted as Papp's advocate on many controversial issues. But she never imposed her convictions on me. Some friends viewed our enterprise as a feminist experiment. Others observed that it would destroy either our project or our friendship. At times, we thought both. We discovered new — sometimes unattractive — aspects of one another. And I found that portraying the producer the way I saw him turned out *not* to be the problem. The difficulty for me — bound by the constraints of friendship — turned out to be portraying Gail who, perhaps, appears in the narrative as less complete a personality than she is in life.

Working together in the way we did was unorthodox journalism. But I feel that that unorthodoxy paralleled Papp's approach to theater and encouraged me to go beyond conventional interviewing. I knew many Festival staffers and artists personally before I began my research and had the advantage of being able to use what I already knew about their relations with Papp. I also conducted new, formal interviews. Over a period of two years, I was able to consult as needed with Papp's therapist (who wishes to remain anonymous), with his personal assistant of eighteen years, Emmett Foster, and with his physician Marc Garnick, who were all generous with their time. I gave my principal interviewees "quote approval" and returned transcripts of our conversations to them, asking for corrections, clarifications and amplification. In previous work, I had never given interviewees this option. Journalistic convention assumes that the interviewee will self-censor and that the journalist will lose valuable material thereby. I am happy to report satisfaction with this highly collaborative process and gratitude toward my interviewees for letting painful or very personal material stand.

In addition to mining the Festival Archive and the resources of Gail Papp, I am the grateful beneficiary of help from the eight excellent librarians of the General Reference Services of the Research Library division of the Boston Public Library, who answered dozens of my queries, and from Harvard University's Barbara Burg. My West Coast research was aided by librarian Janet Lundblad at the *Los Angeles Times* library. My research on the Robert Moses controversy, well documented by Robert Caro in *The Powerbroker*, was augmented by material from the City of New York Parks Department Archives. Correspondence between Moses, his staff and Papp was identified and assembled by the intrepid Elaine Shapiro, ex-librarian and master sleuth.

I began my research on the 1970s with the work of two journalists: former *Herald Tribune* columnist Stuart W. Little and *New Yorker* writer Philip Hamburger. Little's book, *Enter Joseph Papp*, tracks the producer closely during the year 1973. Philip Hamburger's five boxes of notes and materials covering the years 1971–1980 are in the Rare Books and Manuscripts Collection of the New York Public Library.

My paper research was supplemented by formal interviews and informal chats with hundreds of people to whom Papp was important, ranging from his closest associates, his siblings and children to strangers on whom he had left an enormous impression by speaking at their school or engaging in one significant conversation. Quotations from interviews other than my own appear by permission of the interviewees and copyright owners.

Members of Joseph Papp's family who gave of their time to this project were Papp's elder sister, Rhoda Lifschutz, and his younger brother, Phillip Martel. I would also like to thank Peggy Papp, Sylvia Faulkner, Irene Neth, and Barbara Mosser for their generosity of spirit and time. Equal in that generosity were Joseph Papp's two long-time colleagues — press agent Merle Debuskey and executive director of Lincoln Center Theater Bernard Gersten — who not only put up with my many telephone calls and interviews but read my final manuscript for factual errors. Former Festival members David Black, Barbara Carroll, Serge Mogilat, Lynn Holst and current associate producer Rosemarie Tichler also provided invaluable help. Former New York City budget director David Grossman was kind enough to read a chapter concerning Papp's financial negotiations with the City of New York. Papp's financial adviser, Aaron Shapiro, was helpful in providing details of Papp's personal finances.

All journalists rely on the groundwork laid by their colleagues. I am the beneficiary of the writing or personal recollections of Philip Hamburger, Arthur Gelb, William Honan, Richard Shepard, Milton Esterow, Grace Glueck, Mel Gussow, Judith Crist, Lou Calta, Meyer Berger, Michiko Kakutani, Patricia Bosworth, Leo Lerman, Frank Rich, John O'Connor, Michael Feingold, Richard Goldstein, Ross Wetzsteon, Stuart W. Little, John Simon, Catherine Breslin, Les Brown, Alex Witchel and many other cultural reporters of the *New York Times, Newsday,* the *New York Post,* the *Daily News,* the *Los Angeles Times,* the *Washington Post,* the *Philadephia Inquirer, Variety* and the *Wall Street Journal.*

Last, I would like to thank friends who read the manuscript: Margo Jefferson, Gina Mallet, Sandra Fairbank, Susan Sachs, Jill Harkaway. I would also like to thank my husband, who not only read the manuscript but labored over the page proofs, washed the dishes, took the children out of the house, and continues to brave the indignities of being a writer's spouse. I thank Susan Erony — who reproduced some of the photographs — and writer Kathryn Grody, consultant without bounds. And my editor Jennifer Josephy — mistress of grace under pressure — my copyeditor, Mike Mattil, and my agent, Peter Ginsberg.

Notes

THIS IS A WORK of journalism and these notes are intended to give the reader insight into how I went about my reporting as well as provide more detail than there was room for in the narrative. For a guide to the journalistic literature on Papp, I refer the reader to two excellent — though far from complete — annotated bibliographies: Brenda Coven and Christine E. King's *Joseph Papp and the New York Shakespeare Festival: An Annotated Bibliography* (New York, 1988) and Barbara Lee Horn's *Joseph Papp: A Bio-Bibliography* (New York, 1992). In general, reviews of Festival productions appear in newspapers the day after opening night and, in magazines, within the following two weeks. Articles of unusual depth or interest are cited in my chapter notes.

INTRODUCTION

My account of Joseph Papp's funeral is based on personal observation and interviews with participants. Bernard Gersten offered me the use of his personal record of the event. I also read the broadcast logs of WOR and WCBS/AM radio stations and the AP wire service story. The quotations come from interviews I conducted later that year. The seven pallbearers were actors Kevin Kline, Mandy Patinkin and Martin Sheen; director James Lapine and designer Robin Wagner; NYSF associate producer Steve Cohen and executive director of Lincoln Center Theater Bernard Gersten. The five mayors with whom Papp had worked during his lifetime were Robert Wagner, John Lindsay, Abraham Beame, Edward Koch and David Dinkins. The parks com-

missioners were Robert Moses, Newbold Morris, August Heckscher, Henry Geldzahler, Bess Myerson and Mary Schmidt Campbell. The *Times* critics were Brooks
Atkinson working 1926–1971; Howard Taubman, 1960–1965; Stanley Kauffman,
1966; Walter Kerr, 1966–1983; Clive Barnes, 1967–1978; Richard Eder, 1979;
Frank Rich, 1980–1993.

My own involvement with Joseph Papp began in November of 1976, when
William Honan, then editor of the *New York Times* Arts and Leisure section, assigned
me to write a profile of the New York Shakespeare Festival. I was then twenty-nine,
an untenured journalism professor at New York University and a freelancer who often
wrote profiles of classical musicians for the *Times*. The piece was published February
27, 1977, and I began to see the Papps frequently that spring in New York and at
their country place in Katonah. It was during those weekends that Papp and I
discussed my idea for his biography. The editor he called was Robert Gottlieb, then
editor-in-chief at Knopf. When Gottlieb asked for a written statement from Papp
pledging his full cooperation, Papp backed out of the project.

The next I heard about a book was in the spring of 1985. Papp had met with
editor Nessa Rapoport at Bantam Books to discuss a possible project about the
Festival. Rapoport had edited Lee Iacocca's bestselling autobiography and asked
Papp if he would be interested in writing one. Papp said no and countered by
suggesting an oral history. Merrifield and Rapoport asked me if I would undertake
the interviews but I was pregnant and unavailable to travel. The search for an
appropriate interviewer continued well over one year until Papp and Rapoport agreed
on Kenneth Turan, then a freelance writer. Papp contracted with Turan as a writer-
for-hire, signed the contract with Bantam Books for an oral history on January 19,
1987, and sat for his first interview that month. Turan gave Papp the first draft of
his book in June 1989. Papp canceled the project in a perfunctory letter to Turan
and a colorful one to Bantam executive Linda Grey (both in the Billy Rose Theater
Collection). He then asked me to revive my 1977 book proposal. By 1989, I was
forty-one, married, and living in Massachusetts with two toddlers. I told Papp that
I would be willing to work on the book from home, interview him by telephone,
order his memories, do additional research and have my credit read "as told to Helen
Epstein." He would retain complete editorial control of the content. I wrote an
extensive proposal. We worked on two sample chapters — one on his childhood, one
on his communism. We taped several interviews but he became more and more
ambivalent about the project. The first time this had happened, I had written *Children of the Holocaust*. This time, I applied for an appointment at Harvard's Center
for European Studies and began research on a memoir of the women in my family
of Czech Jews. In November 1991, a few weeks after the producer's death, Gail
Merrifield asked me to write Papp's biography.

CHAPTER ONE
For this chapter I relied on interviews with Joe Papp, Peggy Papp, Gail Merrifield,
Papp's therapist, Aaron Shapiro and his siblings Rhoda Lifschutz and Phillip Martel.
There are also dozens of published remarks by Papp about his childhood — an
affecting one appears in a *Times* magazine profile by Michiko Kakutani of June 23,
1985. Memories of one's parents are, of course, highly subjective and Papp's older
sister and younger brother have memories of Shmuel and Yetta Papirofsky that are
different from Papp's own. Rhoda Lifschutz recalls that although the Papirofsky
parents spoke Yiddish to one another, Yetta Papirofsky spoke an unaccented English
to her children. Both she and Phillip Martel remember her as warm, sensitive and
even-handed with her four children — even though she was often ill. They also
disagree with the view that she was depressed. "Momma did more than just clean
the house and feed the family," says Phillip Martel. "Both she and Poppa instilled in

all of us a sense of dignity (poverty notwithstanding), compassion and sensitivity to others. I am sure she felt she had accomplished quite something in keeping a husband and four children together during this country's worst depression." Both Lifschutz and Martel concur with Papp that, from the time he was a child, he spent more time in the streets than at home.

Background material on Williamsburg and Brownsville comes from two wonderful books: David W. McCullough's *Brooklyn and How It Got That Way* (New York, 1983) and Eliot Willensky's *When Brooklyn Was the World* (New York, 1986). My interviews with Joseph Papp, Aaron Shapiro, Rhoda Lipschutz and Phillip Martel provided the details specific to the Papirofskys' life at this time.

For an overview of the world of the Jewish immigrants from Eastern Europe, there is no better source than Irving Howe's *World of Our Fathers* and Irving Howe and Kenneth Libo's *How We Lived*. Michael Gold's *Jews Without Money* — one of Papp's favorite books as a teenager — and the work of Jewish working-class writer Anzia Yezierska were also important to my understanding of that world, as were my conversations with art historian Meyer Shapiro, who grew up in Brownsville, Brooklyn. For background on all Jewish matters, I used the *Encyclopedia Judaica*. For a sharply contrasting view of the 1920s in New York, written by another Jew from an immigrant family who became a major figure in the theater, see Harold Clurman's *The Fervent Years* (New York, 1975). Clurman was one of the founders of the Group Theater, some of whose members founded the Actors' Laboratory, which was the major influence on Papp's own theater.

Joseph Papp's family documents and history were assembled and ordered by Gail Merrifield Papp for her husband after their first trip to Israel in 1981 and are in the Billy Rose Theater Collection. They include marriage and divorce documents, birth certificates and naturalization papers. Papp's paternal grandparents were Moshe Papirovski and Baila Paiserkoski of Kielce, Poland. His maternal grandparents were Josef Miritch and Rose Sefts of Kovno, Lithuania. His mother, Yetta Miritch, was born March 18, 1893, in Kovno and his father, Samuel Papirovski, was born in Kielce January 20, 1892. Yetta arrived in New York in February of 1909 on the SS *Korea* and immediately began to do factory work. Samuel Papirovski arrived in New York on the SS *Bremen* in 1913, and in 1917 was drafted into the American Expeditionary Forces. When they were married on September 11, 1917, the marriage certificate notes her employment as "shop girl" and his as "trunkmaker." Their first child, Rhoda, was born August 9, 1918; Joseph was born June 22, 1921; Murray, who later changed his name to Phillip Martel, was born October 1, 1924; and Anna, July 16, 1930. Joseph Papirofsky finally became Joseph Papp in the eyes of the law on October 13, 1959, by an Order to Change Name issued by the Supreme Court of New York County. His brother, Murray Papirofsky, had his name changed to Phillip Martel in 1952. Some of the Papp family history has been published by the *Jewish Daily Forward*.

Between 1918 and 1923, the Papirofskys lived on Siegel Street; from 1923 to 1926 on Maujer Street; from 1926 to 1928 on Boerum Street; from 1928 to 1932 on Manhattan Avenue; from 1932 to 1936 at two locations on Boerum and from 1936 to 1938 on Prospect Place.

For background on Papp's learning environment and educational policy of the time, I interviewed people who had been pupils in the New York City public school system of the time. I also found useful the works of educational reformer Thomas Dewey and social reformer Jane Addams, whose influence on the teaching profession at the time was significant, and recommend Addams's *Spirit of Youth* (New York, 1917).

For my discussion of *The Jazz Singer* — originally a short story by Samson Raphaelson — and its importance for the Jewish community, I drew on Neal Gabler's excellent *An Empire of Their Own: How the Jews Invented Hollywood* (New York, 1988). For a sense of how it affected young Jews who saw it in the late 1920s and early 1930s, I interviewed Papp's contemporaries Arthur Gelb, Merle Debuskey and Stanley Lowell. Papp and I first wrote this chapter together.

CHAPTER TWO
For this chapter I have drawn on the diaries of Phillip Martel, the letters of Bina Rothfeld Mozell, Papp's annotated high school yearbook and junior high school autograph book, as well as interviews with Papp, Lee Cahn, Bina Rothfeld Mozell, Mary Geller Lichtman and Phillip Martel. I also drew on previous research of my own into the Brownsville childhood of Meyer Shapiro (*ARTnews*, May and June 1981).

Papp's discussion of his attraction to communism as a teenager derives from a chapter that Papp and I originally prepared together.

A sense of how Joe Papirofsky was regarded by his teachers in high school is conveyed in the letter written by Esther Hersh to Joe Papp on February 8, 1972, now in the Billy Rose Theater Collection: "Dear Joe: Some day the definitive biography of Joseph Papp will be written — large and bold — and how could I withhold from it this bit of memorabilia. We've followed your doings only during the last ten years or so. Before that we were sort of looking for news of Joel Parker, Superstar. Remember him? I could go on with all sorts of recollections but I remember that even at 17, you were impatient with the trite and the obvious, and your tastes ran way above those of the ordinary ghetto kid. There's a nice quote for your biographer! . . . Fondly, Esther C. Hersh."

The first time Joe Papirofsky was exposed to professional dramatic theater was when he saw two productions of *Hamlet* in 1936. He later told Gail Merrifield that the two excursions into Manhattan were underwritten by the philanthropist Mrs. August Belmont. The John Gielgud *Hamlet* opened at the Empire Theater on October 8 and its cast included Judith Anderson as Gertrude and Lillian Gish as Ophelia. It was directed by Guthrie McClintic, was judged a huge success and played 132 performances, becoming the longest-running *Hamlet* in Broadway history. The Leslie Howard *Hamlet* opened at the Imperial Theater on November 10. He and John Houseman directed with choreography by Agnes DeMille and music by Virgil Thomson. It did not get good notices and closed within a month.

A note on Michael Gold and *Jews Without Money:* Gold was for a time Joe Papirofsky's favorite writer, and he identified closely with the world of the novel. Born a generation earlier than Papp, Gold was the son of Romanian immigrants who had left school and started working at age thirteen to help support his family. He had joined the Communist party soon after its formation in the United States and became the editor of one of its chief publications, *New Masses*. Throughout the 1930s, he wrote a column for the *Daily Worker*, as well as plays and stories. Gold's work offended many observant Jews because it drew a portrait of a rigid, moribund Judaism. It also offended the growing number of Jewish intellectuals — Communists and anti-Communists — who found Gold crude, uneducated and an embarrassment. For writer Irving Howe, "Gold was an inveterate low-brow who, if he had not turned radical, would have made a superb police reporter; he was a hater of refinements of thought, partly because he could not distinguish them from refinements of manners. . . . The writing that Gold accepted and encouraged was notable for a naive arrogance, a sweaty earnestness, an utter lack of literary awareness or modulation." For Joe Papirofsky, Gold was a writer who articulated his experience of the world. Some of the same words and phrases Howe used to describe Gold would be used by theater critics to describe the productions of Papp.

A note on name changes and anti-Semitism of the 1920s and 1930s: Many Jewish men — although few women — changed their names in order to have or to advance their careers. Papp's brother, Phillip Martel, changed his name in 1952. "It was extremely common for people in our age bracket — first-generation children with names of all nationalities — to change names," he explained. "For me, the issue was raised initially in the army, where the illiterate Southern cadre ridiculed anyone with a 'furrin' name, calling me PapiLOUSky, PapRIOWsky and similar wince-inducing appellations at each roll call. The situation was aggravated after discharge in 1946 when I worked for a pan-American export and import agency and I ran into 'How do you spell that?' when I gave my name." *New York Times* editor Arthur Gelb, who did not change his name, recalled many instances of job discrimination based on anti-Semitism in the 1930s and later, with A. M. Rosenthal, wrote a book about the pressures on many Jews which led to self-hatred, titled *One More Victim*. He empha- sized to me how as a young man he had been aware of the prevalence of Nazi sympathizers in New York City as well as across the country, the legacy of Father Coughlin's anti-Semitic radio broadcasts of the 1930s, and widespread discrimination against Jews in the universities, in corporate America and in housing. Papp's close colleague, longtime NYSF trustee Stanley Lowell, echoed Gelb's observations to me. Lowell changed his name from Loewenbraun for the reasons Gelb articulated. Al- though a graduate of Harvard Law School, Lowell thought his real name would stand in the way of his professional advancement.

CHAPTER THREE

My understanding of Joe Papirofsky during the 1940s has come from interviews with Irene Ball, Sylvia Faulkner, Phillip Martel, Phoebe Brand, the late Ruth Nelson and Bernard Gersten, as well as transcripts of the NYSF oral history.

In the navy, Joe Papirofsky received the American Theater Medal, the Victory Medal, the Asiatic Pacific Theater Medal, the European Theater Medal and the Japanese Occupation Medal. His navy papers, which I requested for this book, are part of the Billy Rose Theater Collection.

For background on the Actors' Laboratory Theater and how it grew out of the Group Theater, I relied heavily on Nora Delia Salvi's UCLA doctoral dissertation, *The Actors' Laboratory Theater* (1969), Harold Clurman's *The Fervent Years*, Wendy Smith's *Real Life Drama: The Group Theater and America* (New York, 1990) and Lee Strasberg's *A Dream of Passion* (Boston, 1987). Speech teacher Margaret Pren- dergast McLean's two books were *Good American Speech* and *Oral Interpretations of Forms of Literature*. Lab founders included Jules Dassin of the Jewish Art Theater and J. Edward Bromberg, Roman Bohnen and Mary Virginia Farmer of the Group Theater. The Lab's executive board during the latter part of the 1940s included Roman Bohnen, Phoebe Brand, Lloyd Bridges, Morris Carnovsky, Hume Cronyn, Jules Dassin, Ruth Nelson, Rose Hobart, Will Lee, Larry Parks, Ed Dymytryk, George Tyne, Hy Kraft, John Wexley and Abraham Lincoln Polonsky. Among the Lab's Audience Sponsors were Alvah Bessie, Mrs. Ira Gershwin, Jay Gorney, Gene Kelly, Ring Lardner Jr., Mrs. Peter Lorre, Albert Maltz, Clifford Odets, Gregory Peck, Earl Robinson, Gale Sondergaard, Donald Ogden Stewart and Dalton Trumbo.

For background on the Tenney Committee, I read the excellent book by Edward L. Barrett, Jr., *The Tenney Committee* (Ithaca, 1951), as well as its proceedings.

The Hollywood Ten were writer Alvah Bessie, director Herbert Biberman, writer Lester Cole, director Edward Dymytryk, writer Ring Lardner Jr., writer John Howard Lawson, writer Albert Maltz, writer Sam Ornitz, writer-producer Robert Adrian Scott and writer Dalton Trumbo. The Tenney Report of 1948 cites the letterhead that the Lab was using in February of 1948. Joe Papirofsky is listed as a member of its executive board. Papp made his journalistic debut in the *Los Angeles Daily News* of September 16, 1948, and the *Los Angeles Daily People's World*. The *World* quotes

"Joe Papirofsky, Public Relations Director for the Actors Laboratory" as stating "We come under the Veterans' Administration and have many Negro ex-GIs acting and studying under the best traditions of the theater in non-segregated workshops." I found the clipping in Papp's FBI file, which I obtained under the Freedom of Information Act.

For background on the Lab's growing political problems, the clippings from the *Los Angeles Times,* which included some quotations from other newspapers, were of great help. Important background on the period and its consequences for American actors, writers, directors and other theater and movie people can be found in Alvah Bessie's *Inquisition in Eden* (New York, 1965); Cedric Belfrage's *The American Inquisition* (New York, 1973); Eric Bentley's *Thirty Years of Treason: Excerpts from Hearings Before the House Un-American Activities Committee 1938–1968;* Harold Clurman's *The Fervent Years;* John Cogley's *Report on Blacklisting* (New York, 1956); Hallie Flanagan's *Arena* (New York, 1940); Walter Goodman's *The Committee* (New York, 1968), quoted on p. 65; Gordon Kahn's *Hollywood on Trial* (New York, 1948); Stefan Kanfer's *A Journal of the Plague Years* (New York, 1973); Hy Kraft's *On My Way to the Theater* (New York, 1971).

CHAPTER FOUR

My interviewees for this chapter include Sylvia Faulkner, Peggy Papp, Phillip Martel, Bina Rothfeld Mozell, David Black, Merle Debuskey and Bernard Gersten. Much of the data was drawn directly from the NYSF scrapbooks. I also made use of the FBI's dossier on Joseph Papp — despite the fact that many sections are entirely deleted and therefore useless to the researcher.

I found the two unpublished manuscripts — Sean Cronin's *History of the New York Shakespeare Festival* and David Black's *History of the New York Shakespeare Festival 1952–1961* — invaluable. Also helpful are the master's theses — Robert Michael Newman's *S.R.O. Culture: The Development of the New York Shakespeare Festival* (Cornell University, 1967) and David Harry Watrous Smith's *The Roots of the New York Shakespeare Festival* (Hunter College, 1967). Other useful sources included the *Cambridge Guide to World Theatre* (Cambridge, 1988); David Amram's *Vibrations* (New York, 1968); Beryl and Samuel Epstein's *Who Says You Can't?* (New York, 1969) and Stuart W. Little's *Off Broadway* (New York, 1972).

Joseph Papp had at least five Irish friends at the time: Joseph Carroll, Liam Lenihan, Sean Cronin, Paul Lambert and Lloyd Gough. Papp loved the way the Irish used language and he loved the way his Irish friends sang. His childhood best friend, Jerry Winthrop, was Irish, and Papp later remembered that Jerry's parents spoke with an Irish brogue that intrigued and enchanted him. He became acquainted with the Irish theatrical tradition at the Actors' Laboratory, where Sara Allgood came from Dublin's Abbey Theater to star in *Juno and the Paycock* and where Dion Boucicault's *The Streets of New York* opened the Lab's New Globe Theater. His friend Joe Carroll had written a one-act play called *The Unbreakables,* based on the book *The Gates Flew Open* by Peadar O'Donnell, which Joe Papirofsky directed in 1951. In a 1990 interview with a Latin American reporter, he would recall the year in which he was working with Irish and Hispanic actors at the same time. "These two seemingly opposite groups had one thing in common," he said. "Their great spontaneity and enthusiasm. It was not a matter of actors but simply of people who loved to sing and recite." The FBI's dossier on Joseph Papirofsky contains additional evidence of his interest in Sean O'Casey. On July 14, 1952, it shows that an issue of *Show Business* carried the following ad: "Joe Papirofsky, Director and Co-Producer of the recently presented plays by Sean O'Casey, is looking for an actor interested in devoting the summer to a thorough analysis of his work. The project will emphasize an organized

approach to a part through detailed step-by-step exploration from script to performance and will include one other actor. Anyone interested should be prepared for
intense work. . . ." Interviews could be arranged by phoning his home number
before noon or his extension at CBS.

Papp's first production to be reviewed, *The Curious Savage,* played December
6–8, 1951, and was reviewed in an unidentified community newspaper serving
Stuyvesant Town. The review, by Michael M. Kaufman, dated December 13, 1951, was
titled "Oval Players Called Tops in their latest offering" and was accompanied by a
photograph. I found references to Papp's direction of Federico García Lorca's *The House
of Bernarda Alba* during the same period — he used as actors Puerto Rican women
from the neighborhood — but no materials such as photographs, programs or reviews.

For reference material on the golden age of television, I used Les Brown's
Encyclopedia of Television (New York, 1982) and *Television Drama Series Programming: A Comprehensive Chronicle 1947–1959* (Metuchen, NJ, 1980). The oral history
transcripts of Joe Papirofsky's colleagues at CBS made for very interesting background reading. Of particular interest is a videocassette of a special edition of Garry
Moore's *I've Got a Secret* from 1957 in which behind-the-scenes CBS technicians
perform. Papp is shown delivering Marc Antony's speech that he had memorized in
junior high school.

The Shakespeare Workshop received provisional tax-exempt charter #6699 from
the New York State Board of Regents on behalf of the New York State Education
Department on November 19, 1954. The charter was made absolute in January of
1960 and the Workshop's name changed to the New York Shakespeare Festival.

CHAPTER FIVE
For this chapter I interviewed Sylvia Gassell, Elsa Raven, Stuart Vaughan, Merle
Debuskey, Bernard Gersten, Peggy Papp, Roscoe Lee Browne, Richard Shepard,
Stuart Little and Arthur Gelb and drew once again on the Festival's scrapbooks and
historical outlines supplied by Merle Debuskey and David Black's *History of the New
York Shakespeare Festival 1952–1961.* David Harry Watrous Smith's *The Roots of the
New York Shakespeare Festival* contains a detailed discussion of the technical aspects
of productions, reviews and cast lists. Robert Michael Newman's *S.R.O. Culture: The
Development of the New York Shakespeare Festival* was also useful here, as were the
NYSF oral history transcripts that pertain to this period. Stuart Vaughan's *A Possible
Theatre* (New York, 1969) is an invaluable window onto this period in Festival
history. There are several position papers, letters and a prospectus for Wooden-O
productions in the NYSF folders marked "1953–54 Joseph Papp." The most inter-
esting magazine articles are J. M. Flagler's "Onward and Upward with the Arts
Gentles All" in the *New Yorker,* August 31, 1957, and Jerry Tallmer's "Three
Shakespeares by Two Rivers" in the *Village Voice,* July 4, 1956. Arthur Gelb's seminal
review of *The Taming of the Shrew* ran August 11, 1956, in the *New York Times* and
Brooks Atkinson's follow-up on August 26.

CHAPTER SIX
My interviews included: Papp, Merle Debuskey, Bernard Gersten, Peggy Papp, Stuart
Vaughan and David Black. I prepared the first draft of this chapter with Joseph Papp
in 1989 and later expanded it. The 1957 summer season was financed by grants and
donations. The foundations were the Doris Duke Foundation, which gave the NYSF
$10,000; the New York Foundation, which gave it $10,000; the Rodgers and Hammerstein Foundation, $1,000; ANTA, $1,000; producer Herman Levin and friends,
$2,000; the John Golden Fund, $1,000; the Old Dominion Fund, $5,000.

Joseph Papp's testimony is taken from the transcript of "Communism in the New

York Area (Entertainment)": Hearings before the Committee on Un-American Activities, House of Representatives, Eighty-fifth Congress, Second Session (US Government Printing Office, Washington, 1958). For press coverage of Papp's testimony before HUAC and its consequences, I have used all the city dailies of the time as sources.

An interesting note to Papp's successful fight for reinstatement at CBS was that the American Newspaper Guild had unsuccessfully challenged the *New York Times* over the dismissal of an employee with an alleged Communist background in 1956 and challenged the *San Francisco Examiner* in 1958. As far as I could ascertain, Papp was extremely rare, if not unique, in regaining his job after being fired for his politics.

CHAPTER SEVEN

For this chapter I am indebted to Elaine Shapiro, who was my representative at the City of New York Parks Department Archives at Department of Records, 31 Chambers Street, New York City. I also used legal files prepared by the firm of Paul, Weiss, Rifkind & Garrison and gratefully acknowledge the help of Judge Samuel Silverman. Press materials prepared at the time were supplied to me by Merle Debuskey. I interviewed Joseph Papp, David Black, Edward Bernays, Peggy Papp, Merle Debuskey, Robert Montgomery, Samuel Silverman and Stuart Vaughan.

Understanding Robert Moses and the extent of his power was facilitated by Robert Caro, whose *The Powerbroker: Robert Moses and the Fall of New York* (New York, 1974) is a journalistic classic. Although I differ with him in his assessment of Moses's opinion of Papp, his work was crucial to my own. My other sources include David Black's *History of the New York Shakespeare Festival 1952–1961;* Jules Cohn's "The Fight for Free Shakespeare in the Park" in *Man, Culture and Society* (Brooklyn College, 1959); and Stuart Vaughan's *A Possible Theatre.* Once again, I relied for news clippings on the NYSF scrapbooks, which contain clips from the *New York Times,* the *Daily News,* the *New York Post,* the *Herald Tribune,* the *Daily Mirror,* the *World Telegram and Sun,* the *Journal-American.* There are also several pertinent NYSF oral history tapes.

CHAPTER EIGHT

Major sources for this chapter were Peggy Papp, Eldon Elder, David Black, Herta Danis, Vera Gold, Ellen Holly, Gerald Freedman, Stanley Lowell, Merle Debuskey and Dorothy Senerchia. As a guide to Central Park, I used Victor Laredo's *Central Park: A Photographic Guide* (New York, 1979). Some of Eldon Elder's work of the time is collected in *Eldon Elder: Designs for the Theatre* (Catalogue of Amsterdam Gallery, New York Public Library at Lincoln Center, December–March 1978–1979).

Papp's history with the Ford Foundation is worthy of special mention. All his development directors would note his hatred of the Ford Foundation and its directors. Foundation officials reciprocated his dislike. Three years into his fruitless correspondence with the Ford Foundation, Papp applied for a director's fellowship. "Were I selected for a grant," he wrote, "I would wish to spend a ten-month season with the Berliner Ensemble Repertory Company in East Berlin. This extraordinary company, formed by Bertolt Brecht, is producing some of the most exciting theater in Europe and maintains a company of some 300 people. I am particularly interested in their techniques of production, which is a blend of the modern and the classical approach. . . . Experience gained in this area would be of tremendous value to myself, as well as to institutions I am and will be connected with." He did not receive the grant or any other grant from the foundation until he took up residence at Lincoln Center in 1973. Ford Foundation theater division head W. McNeil Lowry had fixed ideas about how theater should be run and "Free Shakespeare" did not fit his paradigm. By contrast, he became a great supporter of Tina Packer, the British founder of Shakespeare & Company in Lenox, Massachusetts, who received her first Ford Foundation grant in 1974. Lowry's comments on Papp are available in Ford Foundation oral history transcript in the Ford Foundation Archives.

The Yale Club luncheon was hosted by R. Peter Straus, president of New York radio station WMCA and, in the producer's mind, the epitome of the "uptown" assimilated Jew that Joe Papirofsky had labeled the enemy as a boy soprano whose father did not have the $35 required to attend High Holiday services at synagogue. Straus also chaired that year's Mayor's Committee, whose 150 members had pledged to raise $285,000 for the coming season.

CHAPTER NINE

This chapter draws on interviews with David Amram, Giorgio Cavaglieri, Anne Resch, David Black, Bernard Gersten, Merle Debuskey, Peggy Papp, Robert Brustein and Harry Friedman, materials from the New York Shakespeare Festival Archive as well as David Amram's *Vibrations* (New York, 1968); Robert Brustein's *The Third Theatre* (New York, 1969); Samuel and Beryl Epstein's *Who Says You Can't?*; Elia Kazan's *A Life* (New York, 1988); Ming Cho Lee's "Rebuilding a Landmark" in *Theatre Crafts*, July/August 1967; Mark Wischnitzer's *Visas to Freedom: The History of HIAS* (New York, 1956) and Harmon H. Goldstone and Martha Darymple's *History Preserved: A Guide to New York City Landmarks and Historic Districts* (New York, 1974).

On Hispanic theater: Osvaldo Riofrancos had founded El Primer Teatro Español several years before and, using local teenagers, had been presenting street productions since 1962. In a 1990 interview, Papp dated his interest in Hispanic culture to a fondness for his high school Spanish teacher and to his emotional involvement in the Spanish Civil War. In a transcript of an interview he gave in the fall of 1990, Papp said, "I think the greatest connection comes from the time of the Spanish Civil War. . . . I met a lot of people who went to fight in that war and did not return. . . . When I was 15 years old, I tried to enlist, but I was not allowed to do so, being considered too young. I learned all the revolutionary songs and I shall never forget the voice and words of that extraordinary woman whom they called La Pasionara. . . . I wept when I saw the announcement in the newspapers of the fall of the Spanish Republic. I found fault with the position taken by President Roosevelt for in some way we knew perfectly well that the war was a test run of the Second World War. The years passed and my love for English continued being the most important thing for me but people from Puerto Rico were beginning to move into the neighborhood. The community passed from being predominately Jewish to being Latin. Among the Puerto Rican youngsters there were some poets. . . . Will you believe me if I tell you that the first play I directed was *La Casa de Bernarda Alba* by García Lorca? It allowed me to use the women of the neighborhood as actors."

A note on the Mobile: It consistently drew large numbers of children and teen-agers and the following year Papp presented actor Robert Hooks's teenage theater workshop production of *We Real Cool*, with skits about the Little Rock school integration and other racial issues. "Most children's theater is now geared to middle class children who are accompanied by their parents and it tends to be dance, mime, puppetry or romanticized drama," Papp told his trustees. "Our material must be different, vivid and direct. The Company itself should be composed of Negro and Puerto Rican actors and dancers with whom the audience can identify."

Papp and Amram's opera of *Twelfth Night* was produced by the Lake George Opera Company in 1968. The opera was subsequently produced in its entirety seven times, most recently in March of 1992 at the LaMont School of Music at the University of Denver. However, Amram says that arias from the opera are frequently performed in concerts throughout the U.S.

Papp's suit against a New Jersey motel was written up by the *New York Post* of January 2, 1964: "Joseph Papp Wins Jersey Bias Fight: A New Jersey State Division of Civil Rights announced a settlement of a complaint brought by Papp against a motel for refusing to provide accommodations for his black housekeeper last summer. The motel has agreed to cease discrimination and has invited the Papps and their housekeeper to return at any time."

Some financial notes: As per board minutes of January 19, 1965, total receipts for 1964 had been $797,321 and the Festival had a savings bank balance of $176,173. Running expenses for permanent staff were $10,000 per month. In 1962, Papp earned $17,372 gross; in 1963, $18,939; in 1964, $19,830; in 1965, $24,176.

Additional notes about the acquisition and reconstruction of the Public Theater: In fact, according to Giorgio Cavaglieri, construction would take until 1980 to complete and cost close to $3 million. Papp was originally interested in building a large 800- to 1000-seat house so that he could expect some kind of return on ticket sales. Instead, he was forced by fire regulations and the economics of reconstruction to build a theater with less than half that number of seats. The small size of his theaters would become a problem that later plagued Papp. But, in the 1960s, he was not yet aware just how much of a factor size would become. He was more preoccupied with financing his new theater and relied heavily on advice from August Heckscher, former Kennedy administration adviser and then president of the Twentieth Century Fund, and producer Roger Stevens, chairman of the new National Endowment for the Arts, to guide him through the government funding maze.

Papp's therapist makes her first appearance in this chapter and remains unnamed at her request. After Papp completed his work with her, she became a close family friend, a regular member of the Festival audience and a frequent guest in the Papp home. She was also one of the handful of people who attended Papp in the last months of his life.

The people who moved into the Public Theater office suite were Joseph Papp, artistic director Gerald Freedman, associate producer Bernard Gersten, general manager David Black, production coordinator Andrew Mihok, fundraiser Herta Danis, casting director Dolores Pigott and assistants Wendy Shepard and Gail Merrifield.

CHAPTER TEN
My interviewees for this chapter included Robert Brustein, Alonso Alegria, Jeff Bleckner, Ted Cornell, Tom Aldredge, Gerald Freedman, Bernard Gersten, Adrienne Kennedy, Gail Merrifield, Galt MacDermot, and Ming Cho Lee. My bibliography for this chapter includes Eileen Blumenthal's *Joseph Chaikin: Exploring the Boundaries of Theater* (Cambridge, 1984); Robert Brustein's *Making Scenes* (New York, 1981), Cheryl Crawford's *One Naked Individual* (New York, 1977); Martin Gottfried's *A Theater Divided: The Postwar American Stage* (Boston, 1967), Howard Greenberger's *The Off-Broadway Experience* (New York, 1971), Kenneth Tynan's *Show People* (New York, 1979), Yoko Hashimoto's *Joseph Papp and the New York Shakespeare Festival* (unpublished doctoral dissertation, University of Michigan, 1972); Adrienne Kennedy's *In One Act* (Minneapolis, 1988), *Deadly Triplets: A Theatre Mystery and Journal* (Minneapolis, 1990) and *The Alexander Plays* (Introduction by Alisa Solomon) (Minneapolis, 1992), Mindy N. Levin's *New York's Other Theatre* (New York, 1981), Yakov Lind's *Ergo* (New York, 1967) and *Counting My Steps* (1969) and Stuart W. Little's *Off-Broadway: The Prophetic Theater* (New York, 1972).

John Gruen reviewed Frank Zajac's play for the *World Journal Tribune* February 7, 1967: "There is a certain irony in opening an Off-Off Broadway program sheet and reading a list of Who's Who in which actors have appeared on Broadway and are, with this production, making their Off-Off Broadway debut," he wrote. "What's disheartening is the particular play upon which this kind of professional interest is being lavished. . . . Zajac's play is an exercise in unrelieved grimness, well coated with deeply juvenile allusions to life, love, disillusionment and self-deception. . . . But [Papp] obviously believed in Frank Zajac's talents. The playwright is hard at work on a new, full-length work commissioned by the Shakespeare Festival."

Joseph Papp's teaching career began at Long Island University, October 1965–February 1966, where he was a "Distinguished Seminar Professor." He later taught at Columbia, Yale and Florida State.

CHAPTER ELEVEN

Material in this chapter was gathered from the New York Shakespeare Festival Archives and my interviews with David Black, Ted Cornell, Merle Debuskey, Gerald Freedman, Bernard Gersten, Ellen Holly, Gail Merrifield, Peggy Papp, David Rabe, Dennis Reardon and Ming Cho Lee.

Although he produced only one more of her plays, *A Movie Star Has to Star in Black and White,* Papp maintained his personal relationship with Adrienne Kennedy until the time of his death. "In the mid-1970s," Kennedy recalled, "I was trying to get my sons through high school and I would run out of money. One night I called Joe Chaikin and told him I was two months behind in the rent. Two hours later, Joe Papp called and said I'd have the money in the morning. At 8:30 that morning the phone rang and somebody from the Festival asked whether I could come down to get it myself or whether I was too upset. So it's not only that he paid my rent. In 1991, when he was very sick, just a few months before he died, the phone rang and he said, 'I gave your play to George Wolfe to read and he doesn't much like it but I wanted you to know that I'm not neglecting you.' It's not only that he came through, but that he thought about my feelings. I never understood: how did he find the time for that?"

It was not until 1983 that Papp produced another play by Václav Havel. Then he produced three one-acts, *Interview, Private View* and *Protest.* He visited Havel in 1984, when the playwright was under house arrest in Czechoslovakia. Papp produced Havel's *Largo Desolato* in 1986, and *Temptation* in 1989. As president of Czechoslovakia, Havel made several attempts to visit Papp during the last months of his life. They had their last telephone conversation two days before the producer's death.

NYSF files on *No Place to Be Somebody* contain several profiles of Gordone as well as a collection of the reviews his play garnered. For example: "Charles Gordone is the most astonishing new American playwright to come along since Edward Albee" (Walter Kerr, *New York Times*). "Mr. Gordone is struggling, practically alone, beyond the clichés of racial relations" *(Wall Street Journal).* The play "stalks the Off-Broadway stage as if it were an urban jungle, snarling and clawing with uninhibited fury at the contemporary fabric of black-white and black-black relationships. Gordone is too honest to lie about a bright tomorrow, but in thunder and in laughter he tells the racial truth about today" *(Time).*

Sambo also stirred controversy: a Harlem minister protested the title to Mayor Lindsay and parks commissioner Heckscher. In response to criticism in the *Amsterdam News,* Papp wrote: "I sincerely regret that you find the title *Sambo* objectionable. . . . I had raised the question with the author on numerous occasions which led to hours of discussion. At the conclusion, Mr. Steward held to his viewpoint that the title was indigenous to his concept of the work. . . . If there was the slightest suggestion in his material of demeaning or derogating the dignity of the great rights struggle now being waged with such anguish, please know I would not be a party to it."

CHAPTER TWELVE

For this chapter I relied on the NYSF Archive, my interviews with David Black, Merle Debuskey, Bernard Gersten, Lindsay administration budget director Frederick O'Reilly Hayes, deputy budget director David Grossman and Gail Merrifield. Two helpful books pertinent to Papp's activities during this period are August Heckscher's *Alive in the City: Memoir of an Ex-Commissioner* (New York, 1974) and John Lindsay's *The City* (New York, 1969).

By the time Papp acquired the Public Theater, his costs had grown enormously. Producing Free Shakespeare at the Delacorte now cost about $395,000 as compared to $160,000 seven years earlier. The Mobile productions cost $337,500. The schools tour cost $101,500. In the *Herald Tribune* of March 15, 1966, Papp had spelled out to Stuart Little the annual amount of yearly contributions to the Festival: $60,000 in 1961; $100,000 in 1962; $100,000 in 1963; $313,000 in 1964; $402,000 in 1965.

Long before the musical *A Chorus Line* would become the Festival's cash cow, royalties from the musical *Hair* had helped keep the Festival afloat. By 1970, Gersten told *Mademoiselle* magazine (June 1971), it had contributed $1 million in income to the Festival. In just one week, four concurrent companies of *Hair* grossed $330,000. Total Festival box office income for the 1970–71 season was $305,000.

CHAPTER THIRTEEN

I am indebted in this chapter to the reporting of Stuart W. Little in his book *Enter Joseph Papp* (New York, 1974). Little discussed this period of Papp's life with me. I also found useful Les Brown's *Television: The Business Behind the Box* (New York, 1971); Fred Friendly's *The Good Guys, the Bad Guys, and the First Amendment* (New York, 1977); Jeremy Turnstall's *Communications Deregulation: The Unleashing of America's Communications Industry* (New York, 1986); Stanley Kimmel's *The Mad Booths of Maryland* (New York, 1969) and David Savran's *In Their Own Words* (New York, 1988). In addition to consulting the usual newspapers, I found the *Philadelphia Sunday Bulletin*, *Broadcasting* magazine and *Variety* useful. My main interviewees were David Rabe, Bernard Gersten, Stuart Little, Merle Debuskey and Gail Merrifield.

News coverage of Joseph Papp began to snowball in the early 1970s. *New York* magazine ran its cover story on Papp November 29, 1971. This was followed by Papp's first mention in the *New Yorker*'s annual "Greetings Friends!" and by a *New Yorker* cartoon by William Hamilton in October of 1972, naming Papp as a desirable celebrity party guest along with Tom Hoving, Susan Sontag and Philip Roth. *Newsweek* ran a cover story on Papp on July 3, 1972; *Time*, its own non-cover story the same week; the *Economist*, a profile on September 2, 1972; *Show*, November 1972. In addition, Papp received much local broadcast and newspaper coverage. He received his first *New York Times Magazine* cover story on November 9, 1975.

During the time of the Papps' courtship, the Festival moved *Two Gents, Sticks and Bones, That Championship Season* and *Much Ado* to Broadway, and launched the quarterly *Performance* and the monthly *Scripts*. In 1971 there were eighteen productions at the Public Theater (Anspacher, Newman, Other Stage and Annex); four at the Delacorte and Mobile and one on Broadway. In 1972, there were fifteen productions at the Public, four at the Delacorte and Mobile, and four on Broadway. Papp's first meeting with the William Morris Agency was on May 12, 1972, as per Papp's appointment calendar. The CBS contract called for *Romeo and Juliet* and *Sticks and Bones* to be broadcast in 1973, three more "specials" in 1974 and four each in 1975 and 1976.

The first CBS/Festival special, *Much Ado About Nothing*, received Nielsen ratings 25 percent lower than usual Friday night prime-time CBS shows. Its audience share was 17 percent — or upwards of 2 million people in the NYC metropolitan area — with an 11 percent share of audience in Los Angeles. After postponing *Sticks and Bones* for several months, CBS broadcast the play on August 17 with this introductory announcement: "This special broadcast is intended for mature audiences. It is a powerful tragedy of man's inhumanity to man as revealed by the callous rejection by his own family of a veteran returning blinded from war. If you believe the subject matter of this strong drama or its compelling manner may distress you or others in your family, you may want to refrain from watching it."

CHAPTER FOURTEEN

I have relied in this chapter on interviews with Merle Debuskey, Bernard Gersten, Bill Honan, Robert Brustein, Milton Esterow, Richard Shepard, Grace Glueck, John Simon, Arthur Gelb, Gina Mallet and Stuart Little and on the following books for background: Brooks Atkinson's *Broadway* (New York, 1970); John E. Booth's *The Critic, Power, and the Performing Arts* (New York, 1991); Robert Brustein's *The Third Theatre* (New York, 1969); Robert Metz's *CBS: Reflections in a Bloodshot Eye* (New York, 1975); Julius Novick's *Beyond Broadway* (New York, 1969); Joseph Papp's *William Shakespeare's "Naked" Hamlet* (New York, 1969); John Simon's *Uneasy Stages* (New York, 1975). For background on the *New York Times,* there is still no better book than Gay Talese's *The Kingdom and the Power* (New York, 1969).

Papp's Lincoln Center appointment and his feud with CBS resulted in another burst of press coverage. Long articles about him appeared in the *Christian Science Monitor, Sunday News, Newsweek, Time,* the *New York Times Magazine, World, Intellectual Digest, Vogue, Show,* and the *Economist.*

The influence of the *New York Times* on the cultural life of the United States would make a fascinating book of its own. The only newspaper that was its equal in influence that I know of was Vienna's *Neue Freie Presse* in *fin-de-siècle* Austria-Hungary. For a close examination of the Shubert-*Times* affair, see Lee Israel's "The Shuberts vs. The *Times*" in *TheaterWeek,* November 30, 1992. It is also discussed in Gay Talese's *The Kingdom and the Power.*

The critic who submitted his own play to the Festival was Martin Gottfried, then reviewing for *Women's Wear Daily.* Papp wrote him the following letter on March 18, 1969: "Dear Mr. Gottfried, If the play your agent sent us is the kind of junk you would expect us to put on our stage, forget it. . . . I suggest you examine your whole approach to criticism and discover the source of your hostility. Only a frustrated playwright can adopt the stance that you have consistently taken in regard to our plays at the Public Theater, in contrast to the majority of other critics who have no axes to grind. Since you find your experiences here so unbearable, may I suggest that you spare us your erudition in the future. We can certainly use the seat." In later years, Papp would consider work by Anastazia Little, wife of theater columnist Stuart Little, and produce *My Gene,* a one-woman play by Barbara Gelb, co-author with her husband Arthur Gelb of a biography of Eugene O'Neill. Arthur Gelb first met Papp as an off-Broadway theater critic in 1956. He became metropolitan editor in 1967, assistant managing editor in 1976, and managing editor in 1986.

John Simon first reviewed the New York Shakespeare Festival for the *Hudson Review* in its Autumn 1963 issue. In view of the opinions he expresses in this book, it is interesting to note that John Ivan Simon was born just four years later than Papp, but that belonging to the same generation was one of their few points in common. Raised in the multicultural Subotica, Yugoslavia by parents from the Hungarian minority, John Simon's first language was German, but like much of the local upper middle class in what was formerly the Habsburg Empire, he learned several languages as a child. Although his surname was an indication that his father's family included some Jews, Simon, when asked, identified his immediate family as Christian. He arrived in the United States in 1940 due to a business trip undertaken by his father. On the eve of Yugoslavia's occupation by German forces, Simon left his country of origin. After completing one year of public school in Cambridge, England, the future drama critic arrived in Cambridge, Massachusetts, where he spent the next decade taking three successive degrees. While working on his doctorate in comparative literature, he began to teach and propound the cultural views he would hold to as a drama critic. Like so many other Harvard men, Simon saw himself as first a student, then a teacher, then a critic of Culture rather than "a culture," and its defender from the vulgar, crass and unschooled. Joseph Papp, he decided early on, belonged among them.

Some quotes from reviews of Papp's *Hamlet* of 1968: In addition to Clive Barnes's devastating *Times* review, the *News* called it "Not so much a happening as a mishap"; the *Post*, "a lunatic burlesque, at times satirically amusing, at others seemingly pointless." Walter Kerr called it "an enterprise exactly like the shows idiot children used to put on in their basements (admission 2 cents if you had 2 cents)." By that time, Kerr had a decade-long history of argument with Papp. When Papp was first starting out in Central Park, Kerr had joined Robert Moses in advising Papp to charge admission to Shakespeare — and Papp had never forgotten. Papp's defenders were Emily Genauer, writing in *Newsday,* and Robert Brustein, writing in the *New Republic.*

CHAPTERS FIFTEEN AND SIXTEEN

Useful background reading for these chapters includes Kevin Kelly's *One Singular Sensation: The Michael Bennett Story* (New York, 1990); Ken Mandelbaum's *A Chorus Line and the Musicals of Michael Bennett* (New York, 1989); Robert Viagas et al., *On the Line: The Creation of A Chorus Line* (New York, 1990); and materials in the New York Shakespeare Festival Archive. My interviews include Bernard Gersten, Merle Debuskey, Ted Cornell, Gail Merrifield, John Guare, Wallace Shawn, Tom Babe, Elizabeth Swados, Lynn Holst, Rosemarie Tichler, Ming Cho Lee, Miguel Algarín, Roscoe Lee Browne, Ellen Holly, Paul Davis, Novella Nelson, Liv Ullmann, Kathryn Grody and Dennis Reardon.

Papp's Booth season of hunchback plays by outlaw playwrights included *Leaf People* by Dennis Reardon; *Fathers and Sons* by Thomas Babe; *Listen to the Lions* by John Ford Noonan; *The Sun Always Shines for the Cool,* by Miguel Piñero; and *Lucky Joe and the Powers That Be* by Michael Weller.

The roster of young actors at the Public in the mid-1970s included Christopher Walken, Marybeth Hurt, William Hurt, Mandy Patinkin, John Lithgow, Meryl Streep, Chris Sarandon, Trazana Beverley, Ron Silver, Kathryn Grody, Michelle Shay, Dianne Wiest and Kevin Kline. Readers in the Play Department included Alfred Levinson, an older playwright Merrifield had met at Lincoln Center, Rozanne Ritch, an actress who went on to open New York's Drama Bookshop; writer Deborah Eisenberg; actress Kathryn Grody; directors Des McAnuff, Meir Ribalow and Robert Ackerman; and composer Bill Elliott. All were paid $5 per play report. Lynn Holst, now vice-president of creative affairs at American Playhouse, worked in the Play Department from 1972 to 1981, eventually becoming literary manager. Kathryn Grody, then twenty-two and just out of San Francisco State, described what auditioning at the Public was like then: "The word in California then was that if you wanted to do socially meaningful theater, you went to the Public," she recalled. "I had pictured a tiny, humble theater — like one wooden room — and figured I'd spend three years waitressing in New York before maybe I got a chance to audition for Joseph Papp. Instead, on the second day, Martin Sheen — for whose family I had been a nanny — took me to two places: Horn & Hardart's Automat and to meet him. I planned to tell Joe Papp I came from Berkeley and we'd discuss socially relevant theater. Instead, Martin disappeared, a lady came out and said, 'Kathryn, would you look at page twelve, please?' and I was ushered into this room full of people.

"I read a scene and Joe Papp said, 'Great, great.' And then he said: 'Kathryn, do you sing?'

"I looked around the room. There was no piano and I thought: 'He's not going to ask me to sing *now*.' And I said, 'Yeah. Yeah, I sing,' even though I never sing, not even in the shower. And he said, 'Could you sing something for me?'

"All the people in the room got dim and hazy. I rose very slowly and there I was on my second day in New York City singing for Joe Papp the only song that I knew:

> *I wear my pink pajamas in the summer when it's hot*
> *I wear my flannel nightie in the winter when it's not*
> *And sometimes in the springtime and sometimes in the fall*
> *I jump between the sheets with nothing on at all.*

"There was this silence. This huge silence. Then Joe looked at me, with absolutely no expression on his face, and said, 'Do you know anything else?'

"That response always struck me as an example of his bottom-line optimism. The only other song that came to mind was a Leonard Cohen song, 'That's No Way to Say Goodbye.' I held on to the back of a chair and did an imitation of Judy Collins singing it.

"'That's great,' Joe said. 'That's just the quality I'm looking for,' and I backed out of the room saying, 'Sorry. Thank-you. Thank-you. Sorry. Please don't blame Martin.' And the next day, after exposing everyone in that room, I came down with chicken pox. I stayed away for four years."

CHAPTER SEVENTEEN

For this chapter I interviewed Bernard Gersten, Stanley Lowell, Elizabeth Swados, Gretchen Cryer, Wallace Shawn, Ntozake Shange, Adrienne Kennedy, Bernard Gersten, Merle Debuskey, Gail Merrifield, Michael Langham, Paul Davis, Lynn Holst and Rosemarie Tichler.

I viewed and reviewed the highlights of Papp's fifty-seventh-year surprise birthday party many times on a short videocassette made of the evening, but find it difficult to account for the wide discrepancies of opinion about it. Many differing ones can be read in the transcripts of the NYSF oral history. Lynn Holst later called the whole evening "a passive-aggressive roast." Artist Paul Davis said he had begun to feel uneasy at the very beginning of the evening when Mike Nichols began speaking. Actress Kathryn Grody was outraged at the way Merrifield had been caricatured in that night's performance. "Gail was portrayed as a bimbo," she later said. "I know it was supposed to be a farce, but the character had nothing to do with who she is. Gail's such a private person and here was this horrendous thing taking place in front of everyone she knew."

Within a week of being fired, Bernard Gersten went to work for Michael Bennett as co-producer of *Ballroom*. It opened in December of 1978, was not well received and closed in February 1979. Gersten then worked for two years as executive vice-president of creative affairs at Francis Ford Coppola's Zoetrope Studios in California, for two years as executive producer of Radio City Music Hall and for one and a half years as partner to producer Alexander H. Cohen. Seven years after being fired by Papp, he became executive producer of Lincoln Center Theater first in partnership with Gregory Mosher and then André Bishop. "This previously beleaguered theater has become one of the country's most thriving theaters," Gersten said in 1994, "with an enviable body of work and an organizational structure and stability without precedent at Lincoln Center. Amazingly, getting fired by Joe Papp proved to be the best thing that ever happened to me."

CHAPTER EIGHTEEN

My interviews for this chapter included Barbara Mosser, Irene Neth, Gail Merrifield, Peggy Papp, Jane Gullong, Robert Kamlot and Rosemarie Tichler.

A note on Papp's television projects: Since Papp's cancellation of his $8 million CBS contract in 1973, the Festival had worked with ABC, NBC, PBS and the new cable networks. Papp had tried to develop one television series with Jakov Lind and another with Israel Horovitz. The second was a television pilot for a series that came out of *The Cherry Orchard*, dramatizing the incursion of real estate developers into country forests. By 1981, NBC had bought Elizabeth Swados's *Alice* with Meryl Streep, ABC Cable had bought David Hwang's *The Dance and the Railroad*, and PBS, Andrei Serban's production of Beckett's *Happy Days*.

When Gullong analyzed Festival fundraising efforts during the summer of 1979, she found that during the previous fiscal year, only $1.7 million had been raised from all sources. The largest source of funding came from the city, state and federal governments: $823,250. The second largest source was small individual gifts, the majority of which, just as two decades earlier, came in dribs and drabs of under $50: $317,261. The third source was the board. Though large and wealthy, it had raised only $311,340. In fourth place were the foundations: $205,608. She made it her priority to ensure funding for Free Shakespeare in the Park and, for the next three years, Citibank Corporation would provide it. On May 8, 1980, Citibank senior vice-president Richard M. Kovacevich was quoted in *Show Business* as saying, "Joseph Papp's New York Shakespeare Festival has presented us with an unparalleled gift of artistic excellence in theater for more than a quarter of a century. The tradition of free theater in Central Park and in our city's neighborhoods must be continued. Citibank is proud to support this tradition and we urge other New Yorkers to join us by helping to ensure its future."

Meryl Streep later recalled *Alice at the Palace* in its concert version as one of her best experiences at the Public: "We put the show together quickly, wildly, energeti-cally and it was a huge success. Huge means maybe a thousand people saw it over three nights but it was definitely a hot ticket in town. I then came back to do a fully staged production of *Alice* — which was my worst experience at the Public. I remem-ber a day when Joe came to the rehearsal hall and took each cast member at five-minute intervals and told them whether they were fired or that they could continue with the production and why. As each person got up from their audience with him at the other end of the great hall you immediately knew who had been beheaded and who had not. It was a truly horrible thing to do and a gruesome way to do it. The surviving cast members gathered our dispirited selves together and went through with the production and there were nights when it seemed like a good show but the massacre had taken the joy from the piece and that had been its distinguishing feature. Joe contracted with PBS to tape the show for television and I was desperate to do anything else but I was unable to say no to him. We taped something that was a stilted, uninspired rendering of the material that had lived so exuberantly in its first incarnation."

CHAPTER NINETEEN

My interviewees for this chapter included Robert Kamlot, Rosemarie Tichler, Lynn Holst, Steven Jason Cohen, Gail Merrifield, Wallace Shawn, Emmett Foster, Merle Debuskey, Jane Gullong, Frank Rich, Tom Bird, Larry Kramer and Kevin Kline. For background on AIDS and Larry Kramer, I relied on Randy Shilts's *And the Band Played On* (New York, 1987) and the abundant material in the NYSF files.

I am indebted to archivist Serge Mogilat for putting together research material for the Save the Theaters Campaign from NYSF press kits and reporting by the *New York Times*, the *New York Post*, the *News*, the *Washington Post*, the *Wall Street Journal* and video material from WCBS, WABC and WNBC November 1981–April 1982.

CHAPTER TWENTY

My interviewees were Papp and Merrifield, Kevin Kline, Meryl Streep, James Lapine, Jerry Zaks, JoAnne Akalaitis, Marc Garnick, Kathryn Grody, Steve Cohen, Rosemarie Tichler, Aaron Shapiro and Nessa Rapoport.

My sources for this chapter are my own notes made at the time, the medical reports of Dr. Marc Garnick and a retrospective chronology written by Gail Merrifield in early 1992. The dual-hormone therapy that was being tested at the LaBrie Clinic in Quebec City comprised the drugs Flutomide and Leuprolide. Flutamide had not yet been approved by the FDA and Garnick obtained it through the generosity of Dr. George Prout at the Massachusetts General Hospital with approval from the Sherring Plow Corporation.

Kevin Kline attended graduate school at Juilliard and became a founding member of John Houseman's Acting Company. It was not until 1977, when he understudied Raul Julia in *Threepenny Opera*, that he worked for the Festival again. After his starring role on Broadway in *Pirates of Penzance*, Kline played the title roles in *Richard III* in 1983, *Henry V* in 1984 and *Hamlet* in 1986. During July 1988 he opened as Benedick in *Much Ado About Nothing* and in the film *A Fish Called Wanda*, for which he won an Academy Award. In 1990 he both directed and played the title role in *Hamlet* at the Public Theater.

A note on Papp's salary: It rose from no compensation in the first few years of the Shakespearean Theater Workshop to $31,714 in 1970; $60,000 in 1973; $85,000 in 1975; $105,000 in 1979; $155,000 in 1984. For some of that time, Papp refused salary raises initiated by his board members. He also turned over all his teaching and advertising fees to the Festival. In 1987, when he met with accountant Aaron Shapiro, he was still earning under $200,000 and his attitude toward money was, as Shapiro put it, "unfocused." He had well under $50,000 in savings. He had large mortgages on both his Katonah country home and his Manhattan apartment, which contributed to expenditures of about $200,000 per year. Shapiro suggested that he augment his salary considerably and the Festival board approved the raises Papp proposed. In 1990, his last full year, his salary was $291,760. This was an extremely high salary for the director of a not-for-profit theater but commensurate with arts managers in the music world. As leader of the Shakespeare Festival, Papp served the dual roles of artistic and managing director. Compared to the salaries of many charitable foundation heads (as per a 1992 study by the *Chronicle of Philanthropy*), his salary was in the upper third. Compared to commercial producers, his earnings were low. Had Papp taken a producer's share of *A Chorus Line*, he would have pocketed at least $15 million.

Following Black Monday of 1987, the value of the Festival's Reserve Fund plummeted as well, with investment income dropping from $4.7 million in 1987 to $1.3 million in 1988. An analysis of the Festival's financial standing of the last years can be found in the unpublished case study, "New York Shakespeare Festival" (UCLA, Program in Arts Management, 1992).

CHAPTER TWENTY-ONE

My interviewees were: Papp and Merrifield, Bernard Gersten, Merle Debuskey, Robert Marx, Frank Rich, Alex Witchel, Arthur Gelb, JoAnne Akalaitis, Rosemarie Tichler, Steve Cohen, Stanley Lowell, Marc Garnick, Kathryn Grody, Mandy Patinkin, Kevin

Kline, Melia Bensussen, Rosemary Jordan, Emmett Foster, Robin Wagner and Phillip Martel.

The definitive source for the NEA controversy is the excellent and comprehensive *Culture Wars: Documents from the Recent Controversies in the Arts,* edited by Richard Bolton (New York, 1992). Interesting for its very different point of view is John Frohnmayer's *Leaving Town Alive: Confessions of an Arts Warrior* (Boston, 1993). My special thanks to Barbara Carroll for assembling research materials on Papp and the NEA campaign. Although hostility to the arts has a very long history in American political discourse, the NEA controversy can fairly be said to have started in 1989 with the Andres Serrano photograph of a crucifix submerged in the artist's urine, which was part of a show juried by the Southeastern Center for Contemporary Art in Winston-Salem. The man who organized a direct-mail campaign against NEA funding for such work was Donald E. Wildmon, a former minister and anti-obscenity-in-the-media crusader in Tupelo, Mississippi, who is also director of Christian Leaders for Responsible Television. The Robert Mapplethorpe photographs included one of a man urinating into the mouth of his partner; one man's arm disappearing into his partner's rectum; and a self-portrait of the artist with a bullwhip implanted into his rectum. The director of the Corcoran Gallery was Dr. Christina Orr-Cahall. The congressmen most prominent in the debate were freshman member Dana Rohrabacher, who moved to abolish the NEA, and Congressman Sidney Yates, who offered the compromise amendment in hopes of minimizing damage to the NEA. The obscenity clause approved in October of 1989 read: "None of the funds authorized to be appropriated . . . may be used to promote, disseminate, or produce materials which in the judgment of the National Endowment for the Arts . . . may be considered obscene, including but not limited to depictions of sadomasochism, homoeroticism, the sexual exploitation of children, or individuals engaged in sex acts and which, when taken as a whole, do not have serious literary, artistic, political, or scientific value." The $10,000 grant Chairman Frohnmayer canceled was to the Artists Space in Manhattan. The show was *Witnesses: Against Our Vanishing.* The catalogue included an essay by artist David Wojnarowicz that criticized Jesse Helms and John Cardinal O'Connor among other prominent figures who had spoken against homosexuality. In his letter to "Friends and Colleagues of the New York Shakespeare Festival," Papp wrote, "I am hopeful that as many of you as possible will join us in an effort to rid future grants of any restrictions. I am happy to provide you with information on a 1-900 phone number the American Arts Alliance has set up which makes it very easy to register your feelings on this issue with your elected representatives at minimal cost. You simply call this number, provide your name, address, zip code and telephone number and telegrams are automatically sent to your Congress members and two senators. In addition to making these calls yourselves, I would ask that you contact family and friends from across the country and ask them to do the same. . . . This battle will be waged over the next two months and it is important that pressure be maintained throughout that time. If you have questions or would like additional information, please call the Shakespeare Festival's Development Office. . . . Thank you, Joseph Papp" (May 22, 1990).

Secret Rapture ran at the Public September 8–27, 1989, with no press opening, since Papp planned to move it to Broadway. Recent *Times* policy was to review the original production of a play only one time in New York. It had its first preview at the Barrymore Theater on October 10 and closed after twelve regular performances, on November 4, following mixed reviews from Rich and other critics. Both David Hare and Joseph Papp held Frank Rich responsible for the failure of the production. Hare vowed never to allow his work to be performed in New York City again.

On July 11, Robert Marx wrote Papp confirming that he had spoken with

Timothy Healy, president of the New York Public Library, and that the library had agreed to release him from his contract. On July 26, he once again wrote Papp to confirm that he had spoken with board member Larry Condon, who had told him that the board had decided against bringing him to the Festival and that, although it did not work out, his proposal had meant a great deal to him. "In the meantime, all the best. I do hope that things go well for you and Gail and that your wonderful drive and determination remain as strong as ever."

New York Shakespeare Festival Production List, 1954–1991

1954

Emmanuel Church

AN EVENING WITH SHAKESPEARE AND MARLOWE, directed by Joseph Papp.

1955

Emmanuel Church

SHAKESPEARE'S WOMEN CHARACTERS, by William Shakespeare, directed by Joel Friedman, James Lipton, Terence Killburn and Joseph Papp.

MUCH ADO ABOUT NOTHING, by William Shakespeare, directed by Joel Friedman.

CYMBELINE, by William Shakespeare, directed by Joseph Papp.

AS YOU LIKE IT, by William Shakespeare, directed by Joel Friedman.

TWO GENTLEMEN OF VERONA, by William Shakespeare, directed by John Heldabrand.

ROMEO AND JULIET, by William Shakespeare, directed by Joel Friedman.

1956

Emmanuel Church

MUCH ADO ABOUT NOTHING, by William Shakespeare, directed by Joel Friedman.

THE CHANGELING, by Thomas Middleton and William Rowley, directed by Joseph Papp.

TITUS ANDRONICUS, by William Shakespeare, directed by Frederick Rolf.

East River Park Amphitheater

JULIUS CAESAR, by William Shakespeare, directed by Stuart Vaughan.

THE TAMING OF THE SHREW, by William Shakespeare, directed by Stuart Vaughan.

1957

Mobile Theater

ROMEO AND JULIET, by William Shakespeare, directed by Stuart Vaughan.

Central Park, Belvedere Tower Area

TWO GENTLEMEN OF VERONA, by William Shakespeare, directed by Stuart Vaughan.

MACBETH, by William Shakespeare, directed by Stuart Vaughan.

Heckscher Theater

RICHARD III, by William Shakespeare, directed by Stuart Vaughan.

1958

Heckscher Theater

AS YOU LIKE IT, by William Shakespeare, directed by Stuart Vaughan.

Central Park, Belvedere Lake Theater

OTHELLO, by William Shakespeare, directed by Stuart Vaughan.

TWELFTH NIGHT, by William Shakespeare, directed by Joseph Papp.

1959

Heckscher Theater

ANTONY AND CLEOPATRA, by William Shakespeare, directed by Joseph Papp.

Central Park, Belvedere Lake Theater

JULIUS CAESAR, by William Shakespeare, directed by Stuart Vaughan.

1960

Central Park, Belvedere Lake Theater

HENRY V, by William Shakespeare, directed by Joseph Papp.

MEASURE FOR MEASURE, by William Shakespeare, directed by Alan Schneider.

THE TAMING OF THE SHREW, by William Shakespeare, directed by Gerald Freedman.

1961

Heckscher Theater

ROMEO AND JULIET, by William Shakespeare, directed by Joseph Papp.

Central Park, Wollman Memorial Skating Rink

MUCH ADO ABOUT NOTHING, by William Shakespeare, directed by Joseph Papp.

A MIDSUMMER NIGHT'S DREAM, by William Shakespeare, directed by Joel Friedman.

RICHARD II, by William Shakespeare, directed by Gladys Vaughan.

1962

Heckscher Theater

JULIUS CAESAR, by William Shakespeare, directed by Joseph Papp.

Delacorte Theater

THE MERCHANT OF VENICE, by William Shakespeare, directed by Joseph Papp and Gladys Vaughan.

THE TEMPEST, by William Shakespeare, directed by Gerald Freedman.

KING LEAR, by William Shakespeare, directed by Joseph Papp and Gladys Vaughan.

HARKNESS DANCE FESTIVAL

·Heckscher Theater

MACBETH, by William Shakespeare, directed by Gladys Vaughan.

CBS-TV

THE MERCHANT OF VENICE, by William Shakespeare, produced and directed by Joseph Papp, co-director Gladys Vaughan.

1963

Delacorte Theater

ANTONY AND CLEOPATRA, by William Shakespeare, directed by Joseph Papp.

AS YOU LIKE IT, by William Shakespeare, directed by Gerald Freedman.

THE WINTER'S TALE, by William Shakespeare, directed by Gladys Vaughan.

HARKNESS DANCE FESTIVAL

Heckscher Theater

TWELFTH NIGHT, by William Shakespeare, directed by Joseph Papp.

CBS-TV

ANTONY AND CLEOPATRA, by William Shakespeare, produced and directed by Joseph Papp.

1964

Delacorte Theater

HAMLET, by William Shakespeare, directed by Joseph Papp.

OTHELLO, by William Shakespeare, directed by Gladys Vaughan.

ELECTRA, by Sophocles, translated by H. D. F. Kitto, music by John Morris, directed by Gerald Freedman.

HARKNESS DANCE FESTIVAL

Mobile Theater

A MIDSUMMER NIGHT'S DREAM, by William Shakespeare, directed by Jack Sydow.

Spanish Mobile Theater

THE SHOEMAKER'S PRODIGIOUS WIFE, by Federico García Lorca, directed by Osvaldo Riofrancos.

THE PUPPET THEATRE OF DON CRISTOBAL, by Federico García Lorca, directed by Osvaldo Riofrancos.

Heckscher Theater

A MIDSUMMER NIGHT'S DREAM, by William Shakespeare, directed by Cyril Simon.

Playhouse in the Park, Philadelphia, PA

HAMLET, by William Shakespeare, directed by Joseph Papp.

OTHELLO, by William Shakespeare, directed by Gladys Vaughan.

Martinique Theater

OTHELLO, by William Shakespeare, directed by Gladys Vaughan.

Imperial Theater

HURRAHS! AND FARE THEE WELLS, Memorial to Sean O'Casey, based on Sean O'Casey's autobiographies, adapted by Paul Shyre, directed by Joseph Papp and Paul Shyre.

CBS-TV

HAMLET, by William Shakespeare, music by David Amram, directed by Joseph Papp.

1965

Delacorte Theater

LOVE'S LABOR'S LOST, by William Shakespeare, directed by Gerald Freedman.

CORIOLANUS, by William Shakespeare, directed by Gladys Vaughan.

TROILUS AND CRESSIDA, by William Shakespeare, directed by Joseph Papp.

HARKNESS DANCE FESTIVAL

AN EVENING OF POETRY IN THE PARK/LOVE POETRY OLD AND NEW

NEWPORT FOLK FESTIVAL 1965: PREVIEW

THE GEORGIA SEA ISLAND SINGERS

AN EVENING OF PUERTO RICAN POETRY AND FOLK MUSIC

Delacorte Mobile Theater

HENRY V, by William Shakespeare, directed by Joseph Papp.

THE TAMING OF THE SHREW, by William Shakespeare, directed by Joseph Papp.

Mobile Theater

WE REAL COOL (A LIVE TEENAGE SHOW), directed by Ron Mack and Robert Hooks.

Spanish Delacorte Mobile Theater

ROMEO AND JULIET, by William Shakespeare, translated by Pablo Neruda, directed by Osvaldo Riofrancos.

School Tour

HENRY V, by William Shakespeare, directed by Joseph Papp.

1966

Delacorte Theater

ALL'S WELL THAT ENDS WELL, by William Shakespeare, directed by Joseph Papp.

MEASURE FOR MEASURE, by William Shakespeare, directed by Michael Kahn.

RICHARD III, by William Shakespeare, directed by Gerald Freedman.

HARKNESS DANCE FESTIVAL

NEWPORT FOLK FESTIVAL 1966: PREVIEW

AN EVENING OF PUERTO RICAN POETRY AND FOLK MUSIC

AN EVENING OF NEGRO POETRY AND FOLK MUSIC

Mobile Theater

MACBETH, by William Shakespeare, directed by Gladys Vaughan.

POTLUCK! — A DANCE AND SONG SHOW FOR KIDS, conceived and directed by Bernard Gersten and Lotte Goslar.

Spanish Mobile Theater

MACBETH, by William Shakespeare, translated by Leon Filipe, directed by Osvaldo Riofrancos.

School Tour

MACBETH, by William Shakespeare, directed by Gladys Vaughan.

1967

Delacorte Theater

THE COMEDY OF ERRORS, by William Shakespeare, directed by Gerald Freedman.

KING JOHN, by William Shakespeare, directed by Joseph Papp.

TITUS ANDRONICUS, by William Shakespeare, directed by Gerald Freedman.

HARKNESS DANCE FESTIVAL

AN EVENING OF YIDDISH POETRY AND FOLK MUSIC, directed by Bernard Gersten.

NEWPORT FOLK FESTIVAL 1967: PREVIEW

POETRY AND FOLK MUSIC OF AMERICAN NEGROES, directed by Roscoe Lee Browne.

MUSIC AND POETRY OF PUERTO RICO, directed by Pedro Santaliz.

Mobile Theater

VOLPONE, by Ben Jonson, directed by George Sherman.

LALLAPALOOZA — A SHOW FOR KIDS, devised and directed by Lotte Goslar and Bernard Gersten.

VOLPONE, by Ben Jonson, a Spanish translation.

1967–68

Anspacher Theater

HAIR, book and lyrics by Gerome Ragni and James Rado, music by Galt MacDermot, directed by Gerald Freedman.

HAMLET (modern version), by William Shakespeare, directed by Joseph Papp.

ERGO, by Jakov Lind, directed by Gerald Freedman.

THE MEMORANDUM, by Václav Havel, translated by Vera Blackwell, directed by Joseph Papp.

THE SERPENT, presented by the Open Theater.

Public Theater School Production

HAMLET, by William Shakespeare, directed by Ted Cornell from the original production by Joseph Papp.

Delacorte Theater

HENRY IV, Part I, by William Shakespeare, directed by Gerald Freedman.

HENRY IV, Part II, by William Shakespeare, directed by Gerald Freedman.

ROMEO AND JULIET, by William Shakespeare, directed by Joseph Papp.

Mobile Theater

HAMLET, by William Shakespeare, directed by Joseph Papp.

TAKE ONE STEP, book and lyrics by Gerald Freedman and John Morris, music by John Morris, directed by Gerald Freedman.

Anspacher Theater

HUUI, HUUI, by Anne Burr, directed by Joseph Papp.

CITIES IN BEZIQUE ("The Owl Answers" and "A Beast's Story"), by Adrienne Kennedy, directed by Gerald Freedman.

INVITATION TO A BEHEADING, adapted by Russell McGrath from the novel by Vladimir Nabokov, directed by Gerald Freedman.

NO PLACE TO BE SOMEBODY, by Charles Gordone, directed by Ted Cornell.

The Other Stage

THE EXPRESSWAY, by Robert Nichols, directed by Crystal Field.

UNTITLED, by Michael Graham, directed by Ted Cornell.

ROMANIA, THAT'S THE OLD COUNTRY, by Allen Joseph, directed by Amy Saltz.

THE FIGURES AT CHARTRES (two one-acts), by Edgar White: "The Cathedral of Chartres," directed by Ted Cornell; "The Mummer's Play," directed by Lisle Wilson.

DOWN THE MORNING LINE, by Ramon G. Estevez, directed by Michael Lessac.

NO PLACE TO BE SOMEBODY, by Charles Gordone, directed by Ted Cornell.

Martinson Hall

THE FREE MUSIC STORE, in association with WBAI (series of informal concerts).

Delacorte Theater

PEER GYNT, by Henrik Ibsen, translated by Michael Meyer, songs and music by John Morris, lyrics by Gerald Freedman and John Morris, directed and adapted by Gerald Freedman.

TWELFTH NIGHT, by William Shakespeare, directed by Joseph Papp.

HARKNESS DANCE FESTIVAL

REPERTORY DANCE THEATRE

Mobile Theater

BLACK ELECTRA, by Sophocles, directed by Gerald Freedman.

TAKE ONE STEP, book and lyrics by Gerald Freedman and John Morris, music by John Morris, directed and choreographed by George and Ethel Martin.

ANTA Theatre

NO PLACE TO BE SOMEBODY, by Charles Gordone, directed by Ted Cornell.

1969-70

Anspacher Theater

SAMBO, book and lyrics by Ron Steward, music by Ron Steward and Neal Tate, directed by Gerald Freedman.

MOD DONNA, book and lyrics by Myrna Lamb, music by Susan Bingham, directed by Joseph Papp.

Martinson Hall

STOMP, with The Combine, written and directed by Doug Dyer.

THE MAGIC WOOFER-TWEETER, by Tom Johnson, directed by Michael Lessac (children's show).

The Other Stage (Workshop Series)

THE WONDERFULL YEARE, by Edgar White, directed by Ted Cornell.

KUMALIZA, by C. L. Burton, directed by David Patterson.

PLAY ON THE "TIMES," written and directed by Amy Saltz.

TRELAWNY OF THE "WELLS," by Sir Arthur Wing Pinero, directed by Robert Ronan.

THE HAPPINESS CAGE, by Dennis Reardon, music by Ronny Cox, directed by Tom Aldredge.

X HAS NO VALUE, by Cherrilyn Miles, directed by Walter Jones.

Delacorte Theater

THE WARS OF THE ROSES: THE CHRONICLES OF KING HENRY VI, First Part, by William Shakespeare, directed by Stuart Vaughan.

THE WARS OF THE ROSES: THE CHRONICLES OF KING HENRY VI, Second Part, by William Shakespeare, directed by Stuart Vaughan.

THE WARS OF THE ROSES: RICHARD III, by William Shakespeare, directed by Stuart Vaughan.

DANCE FESTIVAL

Mobile Theater

SAMBO, book and lyrics by Ron Steward, music by Ron Steward and Neal Tate, directed by Michael Schultz.

1970-71

Anspacher Theater

TRELAWNY OF THE "WELLS," by Sir Arthur Wing Pinero, directed by Robert Ronan.

SLAG, by David Hare, directed by Roger Hendricks Simon.

SUBJECT TO FITS, by Robert Montgomery, directed by A. J. Antoon.

MONADNOCK MUSIC CONCERTS

Newman Theater

THE HAPPINESS CAGE, by Dennis Reardon, music by Ronny Cox, directed by Tom Aldredge.

JACK MACGOWRAN IN THE WORKS OF SAMUEL BECKETT, adapted by Jack MacGowran.

SIOBHAN MCKENNA IN HERE ARE LADIES, written, directed and designed by Sean Kenny.

THE BASIC TRAINING OF PAVLO HUMMEL, by David Rabe, directed by Jeff Bleckner.

LAR LUBOVITCH DANCE COMPANY

Martinson Hall

BLOOD, written and directed by Doug Dyer.

FREE MUSIC STORE (series of informal concerts).

SUNDAY AFTERNOON SERIES

South Hall

THE GREY LADY CANTATA, NO. 2, EMILIA

THE QUEST, presented by the Bread and Puppet Theater (limited engagement).

CANDIDE, presented by The Organic Theater Company of Chicago.

The Other Stage

UNDERGROUND: "Jazznight" by Walter Jones, and "The Life and Times of J. Walter Smintheus" by Edgar White, directed by Walter Jones.

DANCE WI' ME (or THE FATAL TWITCH), by Greg Antonacci, directed by Joel Zwick.

The Other Stage (Workshop Series)

WILLIE, by Joe Ponzi, directed by Robert Jordan.

FUGA, by José Varona, music by Keith Gates, directed by Osvaldo Riofrancos.

COOCOOSHAY, by Robert Auletta, directed by Jeff Bleckner.

SUBJECT TO FITS, by Robert Montgomery, directed by A. J. Antoon.

SLAG, by David Hare, directed by Roger Simon.

OUT OF THE DEATHCART, written and directed by Charles Mingus.

THE AMBASSADORS, by Mba Acaz, music by David Patterson, directed by Damon Kenyata.

Delacorte Theater

TIMON OF ATHENS, by William Shakespeare, directed by Gerald Freedman.

TWO GENTLEMEN OF VERONA, musical version of William Shakespeare's play adapted by John Guare and Mel Shapiro, lyrics by John Guare, music by Galt MacDermot, directed by Mel Shapiro.

THE TALE OF CYMBELINE, by William Shakespeare, directed by A. J. Antoon.

NEW YORK DANCE FESTIVAL

Mobile Theater

TWO GENTLEMEN OF VERONA, musical version of William Shakespeare's play adapted by John Guare and Mel Shapiro, lyrics by John Guare, music by Galt MacDermot, directed by Mel Shapiro.

1971–72

John Golden Theater

STICKS AND BONES, by David Rabe, directed by Jeff Bleckner.

St. James Theater

TWO GENTLEMEN OF VERONA, musical version of William Shakespeare's play adapted by John Guare and Mel Shapiro, lyrics by John Guare, music by Galt MacDermot, directed by Mel Shapiro.

The Young Vic (London)

IPHIGENIA, from Euripides' IPHIGENIA IN AULIS, adapted and directed by Doug Dyer, music by Peter Link.

Anspacher Theater

STICKS AND BONES, by David Rabe, directed by Jeff Bleckner.

OLDER PEOPLE, by John Ford Noonan, directed by Mel Shapiro.

DON'T FAIL YOUR LOVIN' DADDY, LILY PLUM, by Anastazia Little, music by Peter Schlosser, directed by Ron Van Lieu (part of the Admission Free Series, the workshop series formerly presented at the Other Stage).

Newman Theater

THE BASIC TRAINING OF PAVLO HUMMEL, by David Rabe, directed by Jeff Bleckner.

THAT CHAMPIONSHIP SEASON, by Jason Miller, directed by A. J. Antoon.

Martinson Hall

IPHIGENIA, from Euripides' IPHIGENIA IN AULIS, adapted by Doug Dyer, Peter Link and Gretchen Cryer, music by Peter Link, directed by Gerald Freedman.

PROSPECTIVE ENCOUNTERS (evenings with the New York Philharmonic).

The Other Stage

THE BLACK TERROR, by Richard Wesley, directed by Nathan George.

THE CORNER: "Andrew," by Clay Goss, directed by Carl "Rafic" Taylor; "His First Step," by Oyamo, directed by Kris Keiser; "The Corner," by Ed Bullins, directed by Sonny Jim Gaines.

FOUR FOR ONE: "You Gonna Let Me Take You Out Tonight, Baby?" by Ed Bullins, directed by Carl "Rafic" Taylor; "One: The 2 of Us," by Ilunga Adell (aka William Adell Stevenson III), directed by Ilunga Adell; "His First Step" (Part I), by Oyamo, directed by Kris Keiser; "The Corner," by Ed Bullins, directed by Sonny Jim Gaines.

Annex

BLACK VISIONS: "Cop and Blow," by Neil Harris, directed by Kris Keiser; "Players Inn," by Neil Harris, directed by Kris Keiser; "Gettin' It Together," by Richard Wesley, directed by Kris Keiser; "Sister Son/JI," by Sonia Sanchez, directed by Novella Nelson; "One: The 2 of Us," by William Adell Stevenson III, directed by Novella Nelson.

THE HUNTER, by Murray Mednick, music by Peter Link, directed by Kent Paul.

DIONYSIUS WANTS YOU, presented by Folger Library Group, music by Bill Danoff and Taffy Nivert, directed by Richmond Crinkley (part of the Free Admission Series).

SLAUGHTERHOUSE PLAY, by Susan Yankowitz, music by Robert Dennis, directed by Richard Vos (part of the Free Admission Series).

JUNGLE OF CITIES, by Bertolt Brecht, adapted and translated by Anselm Hollo, music by Ken Guilmartin, directed by Paul Schneider (part of the Free Admission Series).

Delacorte Theater

HAMLET, by William Shakespeare, directed by Gerald Freedman.

TI-JEAN AND HIS BROTHERS, written and directed by Derek Walcott.

MUCH ADO ABOUT NOTHING, by William Shakespeare, directed by A. J. Antoon.

NEW YORK DANCE FESTIVAL

Mobile Theater

TI-JEAN AND HIS BROTHERS, written and directed by Derek Walcott.

1972–73

Wintergarden Theater

MUCH ADO ABOUT NOTHING, by William Shakespeare, directed by A. J. Antoon.

Booth Theater

THAT CHAMPIONSHIP SEASON, by Jason Miller, directed by A. J. Antoon.

O'Keefe Center (Toronto)

TWO GENTLEMEN OF VERONA, musical version of William Shakespeare's play adapted by John Guare and Mel Shapiro, lyrics by John Guare, music by Galt MacDermot, directed by Mel Shapiro.

Phoenix Theatre (London)

TWO GENTLEMEN OF VERONA, musical version of William Shakespeare's play adapted by John Guare and Mel Shapiro, lyrics by John Guare, music by Galt MacDermot, directed by Mel Shapiro.

Anspacher Theater

WINNING HEARTS AND MINDS, adaptation of "Winning Hearts and Minds: War Poems by Vietnam Veterans," adapted and directed by Paula Kay Pierce.

THE CHERRY ORCHARD, by Anton Chekhov, production conceived by James Earl Jones, directed by Michael Schultz.

THE ORPHAN, by David Rabe, music by Peter Link, directed by Jeff Bleckner.

Newman Theater

WEDDING BAND, by Alice Childress, directed by Alice Childress and Joseph Papp.

Martinson Hall

CONEY ISLAND CYCLE, presented by the Bread and Puppet Theater.

The Other Stage

THE CHILDREN, by Michael McGuire, directed by Paul Schneider.

MORE THAN YOU DESERVE, book by Michael Weller, lyrics by Michael Weller and Jim Steinman, music by Jim Steinman, directed by Kim Friedman.

Annex

SIAMESE CONNECTIONS, by Dennis Reardon, directed by David Schweizer.

Workshop

THE CHERRY ORCHARD, by Anton Chekhov, directed by James Earl Jones.

CONCERNING THE EFFECTS OF TRIMETHYLCHLORIDE and RAINBOWS FOR SALE, by John Ford Noonan, directed by Ed Rombola.

Delacorte Theater

AS YOU LIKE IT, by William Shakespeare, directed by Joseph Papp.

KING LEAR, by William Shakespeare, directed by Edwin Sherin.

NEW YORK DANCE FESTIVAL

OLU CLEMENTE: THE PHILOSOPHER OF BASEBALL, by Miguel Algarin and Jesus Abraham Laviera, directed by Miguel Algarin.

PLEASE DON'T LET IT RAIN!: A Midnight Concert in Central Park, music by Peter Link, lyrics by A. J. Antoon, Michael Cacoyannis, C. C. Courtney, Ragan Courtney, Euripides, Peter Link, Susan McGonagle, and William Shakespeare.

A TRIBUTE TO JACK MACGOWRAN

Mobile Theater

TWO GENTLEMEN OF VERONA, by William Shakespeare, directed by Kim Friedman.

CBS-TV

MUCH ADO ABOUT NOTHING, by William Shakespeare, directed by A. J. Antoon with Nick Havinga.

1973-74

Royal Alexandra Theatre (Toronto)

THAT CHAMPIONSHIP SEASON, by Jason Miller, directed by A. J. Antoon.

Anspacher Theater

LOTTA, by Robert Montgomery, directed by David Chambers.

BARBARY SHORE, adapted from the novel by Norman Mailer and directed by Jack Gelber.

SHORT EYES, by Miguel Piñero, directed by Marvin Felix Camillo.

Newman Theater

MORE THAN YOU DESERVE, book by Michael Weller, lyrics by Michael Weller and Jim Steinman, music by Jim Steinman, directed by Kim Friedman.

THE KILLDEER, by Jay Broad, directed by Melvin Bernhardt.

THE ELIOT FELD BALLET

Martinson Hall

THE EMPEROR OF LATE NIGHT RADIO, by Terry Miller, directed by Meir Zvi Ribalow.

BURNING, by David Rabe, directed by Robert Hedley.

WHERE DO WE GO FROM HERE?, by John Ford Noonan, music by Kirk Nurock, directed by David Margulies.

The Other Stage

LES FEMMES NOIRES, by Edgar White, directed by Novella Nelson.

THE RESISTIBLE RISE OF ARTURO UI, by Bertolt Brecht, directed by Ted Cornell.

LA GENTE, by Edgar White, directed by Dennis Tate.

Vivian Beaumont Theater (Lincoln Center)

BOOM BOOM ROOM, by David Rabe, directed by Joseph Papp.

AU PAIR MAN, by Hugh Leonard, directed by Gerald Freedman.

WHAT THE WINE-SELLERS BUY, by Ron Milner, directed by Michael Schultz.

THE DANCE OF DEATH, by August Strindberg, directed by A. J. Antoon.

SHORT EYES, by Miguel Piñero, directed by Marvin Felix Camillo.

Mitzi E. Newhouse (Lincoln Center)

TROILUS AND CRESSIDA, by William Shakespeare, directed by David Schweizer.

THE TEMPEST, by William Shakespeare, directed by Edward Berkeley.

MACBETH, by William Shakespeare, directed by Edward Berkeley.

Delacorte Theater

PERICLES, by William Shakespeare, directed by Edward Berkeley.

THE MERRY WIVES OF WINDSOR, by William Shakespeare, directed by David Margulies.

THE NEW YORK DANCE FESTIVAL

Mobile Theater

WHAT THE WINE-SELLERS BUY, by Ron Milner, directed by Woodie King Jr.

CBS-TV

STICKS AND BONES, by David Rabe, directed by Robert Downey.

PBS-TV

KING LEAR, by William Shakespeare, produced by Joseph Papp, directed by Edwin Sherin.

ABC-TV

WEDDING BAND, by Alice Childress, directed by Joseph Papp and Jack Sameth.

1974-75

Anspacher Theater

IN THE BOOM BOOM ROOM, by David Rabe, directed by Robert Hedley.

KID CHAMPION, by Thomas Babe, music by Jim Steinman, lyrics by Jim Steinman and Thomas Babe, directed by John Pasquin.

Newman Theater

WHERE DO WE GO FROM HERE?, by John Ford Noonan, music by Kirk Nurock, directed by David Margulies.

FISHING, by Michael Weller, directed by Peter Gill.

A CHORUS LINE, book by James Kirkwood and Nicholas Dante, lyrics by Edward Kleban, music by Marvin Hamlisch, conceived, directed and choreographed by Michael Bennett.

THE ELIOT FELD BALLET

Martinson Hall

SEA GULL, by Anton Chekhov, performed by The Manhattan Project, directed by André Gregory.

OUR LATE NIGHT, by Wallace Shawn, performed by The Manhattan Project, directed by André Gregory.

Anspacher Theater

SWEET TALK, by Michael Abbensetts, music by Leopoldo F. Fleming and Leroy Henley, directed by Novella Nelson.

The Other Stage

THE LAST DAYS OF THE BRITISH HONDURAS, by Ron Tavel, directed by David Schweizer.

THE CONJURER, words and music by Michael Sahl and Eric Salzman, directed by Tom O'Horgan.

HEAT, by William Hauptman, directed by Barnet Kellman.

APPLE PIE, by Myrna Lamb and Nicholas Meyers, directed by Rae Allen.

THE TIME TRIAL, by Jack Gilhooley, music by David Maloney, lyrics by Jack Gilhooley, directed by Peter Maloney.

NYSF Public Theater

NAKED LUNCH, based on the novel by William Burroughs, directed by Don Sanders (Chicago Project/New York).

Vivian Beaumont (Lincoln Center)

MERT AND PHIL, by Anne Burr, directed by Joseph Papp.

BLACK PICTURE SHOW, written and directed by Bill Gunn.

A DOLL'S HOUSE, by Henrik Ibsen, a new version by Christopher Hampton, directed by Tormod Skagestad.

LITTLE BLACK SHEEP, by Anthony Scully, directed by Edward Payson Call.

Mitzi E. Newhouse (Lincoln Center)

RICHARD III, by William Shakespeare, directed by Mel Shapiro.

A MIDSUMMER NIGHT'S DREAM, by William Shakespeare, directed by Edward Berkeley.

THE TAKING OF MISS JANIE, by Ed Bullins, directed by Gilbert Moses.

Delacorte Theater

HAMLET, by William Shakespeare, directed by Michael Rudman.

THE COMEDY OF ERRORS, by William Shakespeare, directed by John Pasquin.

THE NEW YORK DANCE FESTIVAL

Mobile Theater

SHOE SHINE PARLOR, by James Lee, music by Tito Goya, directed by Marvin Felix Camillo.

1975–76

Shubert Theater

A CHORUS LINE, book by James Kirkwood and Nicholas Dante, lyrics by Edward Kleban, music by Marvin Hamlisch, conceived, directed and choreographed by Michael Bennett (later with national and international companies).

Booth Theater

THE LEAF PEOPLE, by Dennis Reardon, music by Xantheus Ruh Leempoor, directed by Tom O'Horgan.

Anspacher Theater

THE SUN ALWAYS SHINES FOR THE COOL, by Miguel Piñero, directed by Marvin Felix Camillo.

APPLE PIE, by Myrna Lamb, music by Nicholas Meyers, directed by Joseph Papp.

FOR COLORED GIRLS WHO HAVE CONSIDERED SUICIDE/WHEN THE RAINBOW IS ENUF, by Ntozake Shange, directed by Oz Scott.

Newman Theater

LATIN AMERICAN POPULAR THEATER FESTIVAL

THE ELIOT FELD BALLET

RICH AND FAMOUS, by John Guare, music and lyrics by John Guare, directed by Mel Shapiro.

REBEL WOMEN, by Thomas Babe, music by Catherine MacDonald, lyrics by Barbara Bonfigli, directed by Jack Hofsiss.

The Other Stage

JESSE AND THE BANDIT QUEEN, by David Freeman, directed by Gordon Stewart.

THE LOCAL STIGMATIC, by Heathcote Williams, directed by David Wheeler.

SO NICE THEY NAMED IT TWICE, by Neil Harris, directed by Bill Lathan.

Martinson Hall

JINXS BRIDGE, by Michael Moran, production conceived, directed and designed by members of the Manhattan Project.

WOYZECK, by Georg Buchner, directed by Leonardo Shapiro.

REHEARSAL and PRIVATE HICKS, by Albert Maltz, directed by Jon Fraser.

LuEsther Hall

SO NICE THEY NAMED IT TWICE, by Neil Harris, directed by Bill Lathan.

The Little Theater

THE LOST ONES, by Samuel
Beckett, music by Philip Glass,
adapted and directed by Lee Breuer.

GOGOL: A Mystery Play, written and
directed by Len Jenkin.

Vivian Beaumont (Lincoln Center)

TRELAWNY OF THE "WELLS," by
Sir Arthur Wing Pinero, directed by
A. J. Antoon.

HAMLET, by William Shakespeare,
directed by Michael Rudman.

MRS. WARREN'S PROFESSION, by
George Bernard Shaw, directed by
Gerald Freedman.

THREEPENNY OPERA, by Bertolt
Brecht and Kurt Weill, translated by
Ralph Manheim and John Willett,
directed by Richard Foreman.

Mitzi E. Newhouse (Lincoln Center)

THE SHORTCHANGED REVIEW,
by Michael Dorn Moody, directed
by Richard Southern.

STREAMERS, by David Rabe,
directed by Mike Nichols.

Delacorte Theater

HENRY V, by William Shakespeare,
directed by Joseph Papp.

MEASURE FOR MEASURE, by
William Shakespeare, directed by
John Pasquin.

Mobile Theater

MONDONGO, book by Ramiro
(Ray) Ramirez, music by Willie
Colon and David Barron, lyrics by
Lon Ivey, directed by Dean Irby.

Manhattan Theatre Club

IN THE WINE TIME, by Ed Bullins,
directed by Robert Macbeth.

1976–77

Booth Theater

FOR COLORED GIRLS WHO
HAVE CONSIDERED
SUICIDE/WHEN THE
RAINBOW IS ENUF, by Ntozake
Shange, directed by Oz Scott.

Anspacher Theater

FOR COLORED GIRLS WHO
HAVE CONSIDERED
SUICIDE/WHEN THE
RAINBOW IS ENUF, by Ntozake
Shange, directed by Oz Scott.

GOGOL: A Mystery Play, written and
directed by Len Jenkin.

ASHES, by David Rudkin, directed by
Lynne Meadow.

Newman Theater

THE ELIOT FELD BALLET

MARCO POLO SINGS A SOLO, by
John Guare, directed by Mel Shapiro.

CREDITORS/THE STRONGER, by
August Strindberg, directed by Rip
Torn.

MISS MARGARIDA'S WAY, written
and directed by Roberto Athayde.

The Other Stage

THREE SHORT PLAYS, by Wallace
Shawn: "Summer Evening," directed
by Wilford Leach; "Youth Hostel,"
directed by Leonardo Shapiro; "Mr.
Frivolous," directed by Lee Breuer.

ON THE LOCK-IN, by David
Langston Smyrl, directed by Robert
Macbeth.

UNFINISHED WOMEN CRY IN
NO MAN'S LAND WHILE A
BIRD DIES IN A GILDED CAGE,
by Aishah Rahman, directed by Bill
Duke.

CRACK, by Crispin Larangeira, music
by Tom Mandell, directed by John
Braswell.

1976–77 (*continued*)

The Old Prop Shop Theater

A PHOTOGRAPH: STILL-LIFE WITH SHADOWS/A PHOTOGRAPH: A STUDY OF CRUELTY, by Ntozake Shange, directed by Oz Scott.

DRESSED LIKE AN EGG, from the writings of Colette, directed by JoAnne Akalaitis.

Martinson Hall

A MOVIE STAR HAS TO STAR IN BLACK AND WHITE, by Adrienne Kennedy, music by Peter Golub, directed by Joseph Chaikin.

HAGAR'S CHILDREN, by Ernest Joselovitz, music by Randy Lee Ross, directed by Robert Small.

DOOR, by the Pittsburgh Factory Theatre, directed by Zbigniew Cynkutis (benefit).

LuEsther Hall

MUSEUM, by Tina Howe, directed by Richard Jordan.

QUEENS SYMPHONY CHAMBER ORCHESTRA (Sunday concerts).

ON THE LOCK-IN, by David Langston Smyrl, directed by Robert Macbeth.

The Little Theater

GUNTOWER, by Miguel Piñero, directed by Reinaldo Araña.

CASCANDO, by Samuel Beckett, directed by JoAnne Akalaitis.

B. BEAVER ANIMATION, written and directed by Lee Breuer.

Vivian Beaumont (Lincoln Center)

THREEPENNY OPERA, by Bertolt Brecht and Kurt Weill, translated by Ralph Manheim and John Willett, directed by Richard Foreman.

THE CHERRY ORCHARD, by Anton Chekhov, translated by Jean-Claude van Itallie, directed by Andrei Serban.

AGAMEMNON, by Aeschylus, translated by Edith Hamilton, conceived by Andrei Serban and Elizabeth Swados, music by Elizabeth Swados, directed by Andrei Serban.

Mitzi E. Newhouse (Lincoln Center)

STREAMERS, by David Rabe, directed by Mike Nichols.

Delacorte Theater

THREEPENNY OPERA, by Bertolt Brecht and Kurt Weill, translated by Ralph Manheim and John Willett, directed by Richard Foreman.

AGAMEMNON, by Aeschylus, translated by Edith Hamilton, conceived by Andrei Serban and Elizabeth Swados, music by Elizabeth Swados, directed by Andrei Serban.

NEW YORK DANCE FESTIVAL

Mobile Theater

UNFINISHED WOMEN CRY IN NO MAN'S LAND WHILE A BIRD DIES IN A GILDED CAGE, by Aishah Rahman, directed by Bill Duke.

Manhattan Theatre Club

ASHES, by David Rudkin, directed by Lynne Meadow.

BILLY IRISH, by Thomas Babe, directed by Barry Marshall.

Henry Street Settlement, New Federal Theater

DADDY, by Ed Bullins, directed by Woodie King, Jr.

Los Angeles Actors' Theater

A MIDNIGHT MOON AT THE GREASY SPOON, by Miguel Piñero, directed by William H. Bushnell Jr.

Academy Festival Theater (Chicago)

LANDSCAPE OF THE BODY, by John Guare, directed by John Pasquin.

Royal Court Theatre (London)

CURSE OF THE STARVING CLASS, by Sam Shepard, directed by Nancy Meckler.

1977–78

Booth Theater

PAUL ROBESON, by Phillip Hayes Dean, directed by Lloyd Richards.

Ambassador Theater

MISS MARGARIDA'S WAY, written and directed by Roberto Althayde.

Plymouth Theater

THE WATER ENGINE and MR. HAPPINESS, by David Mamet, directed by Steven Schachter.

RUNAWAYS, written, composed and directed by Elizabeth Swados.

Anspacher Theater

THE MISANTHROPE, by Molière, translated by Richard Wilbur, music by Jobriath Boone, Margaret Pine, and Arthur Bienstock, directed by Leonardo Shapiro, then by Bill Gile.

A PRAYER FOR MY DAUGHTER, by Thomas Babe, directed by Robert Allan Ackerman.

I'M GETTING MY ACT TOGETHER AND TAKING IT ON THE ROAD, book and lyrics by Gretchen Cryer, music by Nancy Ford, directed by Word Baker.

Newman Theater

MISS MARGARIDA'S WAY, written and directed by Roberto Althayde.

LANDSCAPE OF THE BODY, by John Guare, directed by John Pasquin.

THE DYBBUK, by S. Ansky, new version by Mira Rafalowicz and Joseph Chaikin, directed by Joseph Chaikin.

CURSE OF THE STARVING CLASS, by Sam Shepard, music by Bob Feldman, directed by Robert Woodruff.

WINGS, by Arthur Kopit, directed by John Madden.

SGANARELLE (An Evening of Molière Farces), by Molière, translated by Albert Bermel, directed by Andrei Serban.

The Other Stage

IN THE WELL OF THE HOUSE, by Charles C. Mark, directed by Davey Marlin-Jones.

FLUX, by Susan Miller, directed by Annabel Leventon.

A PRAYER FOR MY DAUGHTER, by Thomas Babe, directed by Robert Allan Ackerman.

THE MANDRAKE, by Niccolò Machiavelli, translated by Wallace Shawn, music by Richard Weinstock, directed by Wilford Leach.

THE QUANNAPOWITT QUARTET, PART ONE: HOPSCOTCH, by Israel Horovitz, directed by Jack Hofsiss.

THE QUANNAPOWITT QUARTET, PART TWO: THE 75TH, by Israel Horovitz, directed by Jack Hofsiss.

MANGO TANGO, by Jessica Hagedorn, directed by Regge Life.

MAN-WO-MAN (two one-act plays): "Michael," written and directed by Ed Bullins; "Passion Without Reason," by Neil Harris, directed by Ernestine Johnston.

The Old Prop Shop Theater

SHAGGY DOG ANIMATION, written and directed by Lee Breuer.

TAUD SHOW (from the life and work of Antonin Artaud), by Jerry Mayer, directed by John Pynchon Holms.

Martinson Hall (Theater/Cabaret)

TALES OF THE HASIDIM, by Martin Buber, music by Fred Kaz, adapted and directed by Paul Sills.

WHERE THE MISSISSIPPI MEETS THE AMAZON, written and performed by Jessica Hagedorn, Thulani Nkabinde and Ntozake Shange, directed by Oz Scott.

THE WATER ENGINE, by David Mamet, directed by Steven Schachter.

RUNAWAYS, written, composed and directed by Elizabeth Swados.

VISUAL ALCHEMY, by Jeff Sheridan.

LuEsther Hall

DRESSED LIKE AN EGG, from the writings of Colette, directed by JoAnne Akalaitis.

THE LOST ONES, by Samuel Beckett, adapted and directed by Lee Breuer.

A PHOTOGRAPH: A STUDY OF CRUELTY, by Ntozake Shange, directed by Oz Scott.

MUSEUM, by Tina Howe, directed by Max Stafford-Clark.

THE APPLEGATES, by C. K. Alexander, directed by Robert Livingston.

The Little Theater

INTIMATIONS, written and directed by Crispin Larangeira.

THE LOST ONES, by Samuel Beckett, adapted and directed by Lee Breuer.

TAUD SHOW (from the life and work of Antonin Artaud), by Jerry Mayer, directed by John Pynchon Holms.

Lunch Time Theater

GUM, by Walter Corwin, directed by Susan Gregg.

Delacorte Theater

ALL'S WELL THAT ENDS WELL, by William Shakespeare, directed by Wilford Leach.

THE TAMING OF THE SHREW, by William Shakespeare, directed by Wilford Leach.

NEW YORK DANCE FESTIVAL

Mobile Theater

EVENING AT NEW RICAN VILLAGE, poetry by Pedro Pietri and Sandra Esteves, directed by Eduardo Figueroa.

Manhattan Theatre Club

CATSPLAY, by Istvan Orkeny, directed by Lynne Meadow.

1978-79

Plymouth Theater

RUNAWAYS, written, composed and directed by Elizabeth Swados.

National Tour

FOR COLORED GIRLS WHO HAVE CONSIDERED SUICIDE/WHEN THE RAINBOW IS ENUF, by Ntozake Shange, directed by Oz Scott.

Circle in the Square (Downtown)

I'M GETTING MY ACT
TOGETHER AND TAKING IT
ON THE ROAD, book and lyrics
by Gretchen Cryer, music by Nancy
Ford, directed by Word Baker.

Anspacher Theater

I'M GETTING MY ACT
TOGETHER AND TAKING IT
ON THE ROAD, book and lyrics
by Gretchen Cryer, music by Nancy
Ford, directed by Word Baker.

JULIUS CAESAR, by William
Shakespeare, directed by Michael
Langham.

CORIOLANUS, by William
Shakespeare, directed by Michael
Langham.

SPELL #7, by Ntozake Shange, music
by Butch Morris and David Murray,
directed by Oz Scott.

Newman Theater

DRINKS BEFORE DINNER, by
E. L. Doctorow, directed by
Mike Nichols.

WONDERLAND IN CONCERT
(Concert), based on *Alice in
Wonderland* and *Through the Looking
Glass* by Lewis Carroll, music,
additional lyrics and direction by
Elizabeth Swados.

TAKEN IN MARRIAGE, by Thomas
Babe, directed by Robert Allan
Ackerman.

THE WOODS, by David Mamet,
directed by Ulu Grosbard.

HAPPY DAYS, by Samuel Beckett,
directed by Andrei Serban.

SPRING AWAKENING, by Frank
Wedekind, adapted by Edward
Bond, directed by Liviu Ciulei.

The Other Stage

UNFINISHED WOMEN CRY IN
NO MAN'S LAND WHILE A
BIRD DIES IN A GILDED CAGE,
by Aishah Rahman, directed by
Thomas Bullard.

FATHERS AND SONS, by Thomas
Babe, music by Brad Burg, directed
by Robert Allan Ackerman.

NEW JERUSALEM, by Len Jenkin,
directed by Garland Wright.

LEAVE IT TO BEAVER IS DEAD,
written and directed by Des
McAnuff.

REMEMBRANCE, by Derek Walcott,
directed by Charles Turner.

SPELL #7 (workshop), by Ntozake
Shange, directed by Oz Scott.

POETS FROM THE INSIDE
(compilation of poems by prisoners,
mental patients, children, the deaf
and the aged), directed by Jeremy
Blahnik.

The Old Prop Shop Theater

WHITE SIRENS, by Lois Elaine
Griffith, music by Claude Cave II,
directed by Eleo Pomare.

NASTY RUMORS AND FINAL
REMARKS, by Susan Miller, music
by Ken Guilmartin, directed by A. J.
Antoon.

A PRELUDE TO DEATH IN
VENICE, written and directed by
Lee Breuer.

Martinson Hall (Theater/Cabaret)

THE UMBRELLAS OF
CHERBOURG, book by Jacques
Demy, music by Michel Legrand,
English translation by Sheldon
Harnick, in association with Charles
Burr, directed by Andrei Serban.

DISPATCHES, a rock-war musical, based on the book by Michael Herr, adapted, composed and directed by Elizabeth Swados.

JAZZ AT THE PUBLIC

LuEsther Hall

THE MASTER AND MARGARITA, by Mikhail Bulgakov, a project by Andrei Serban.

QUANNAPOWITT QUARTET, PART THREE: STAGE DIRECTIONS, by Israel Horovitz, directed by Jack Hofsiss.

SANCOCHO, book by Ramiro (Ray) Ramirez, music and lyrics by Jimmy Justice and Ramiro (Ray) Ramirez, directed and choreographed by Miguel Godreau.

WAKE UP, IT'S TIME TO GO TO BED! A Concert of Contemporary Music, conceived, written and directed by Carson Kievman.

The Little Theater

FILM AT THE PUBLIC

Delacorte Theater

CORIOLANUS, by William Shakespeare, directed by Wilford Leach.

OTHELLO, by William Shakespeare, directed by Wilford Leach.

NEW YORK DANCE FESTIVAL

Mobile Theater

THE MIGHTY GENTS, by Richard Wesley, music by Baikida Carroll, directed by Ntozake Shange.

Performance Garage

SOUTHERN EXPOSURE, written and directed by JoAnne Akalaitis.

BBC-TV

KISS ME PETRUCHIO (film documentary of the New York Shakespeare Festival 1978 Delacorte production of *The Taming of the Shrew* by William Shakespeare, music by Richard Weinstock, directed by Wilford Leach).

1979–80

Anspacher Theater

SPELL #7, by Ntozake Shange, music by Butch Morris and David Murray, directed by Oz Scott.

SALT LAKE CITY SKYLINE, by Thomas Babe, directed by Robert Allan Ackerman.

SUNDAY RUNNERS IN THE RAIN, by Israel Horovitz, directed by Sheldon Larry.

Newman Theater

HAPPY DAYS, by Samuel Beckett, directed by Andrei Serban.

THE ART OF DINING, by Tina Howe, directed by A. J. Antoon.

MARIE AND BRUCE, by Wallace Shawn, directed by Wilford Leach.

MOTHER COURAGE AND HER CHILDREN, by Bertolt Brecht, adaptation by Ntozake Shange, lyrics adapted by Louisa Rose, music by William Elliott, directed by Wilford Leach.

PEARL LANG DANCE COMPANY

The Other Stage

SORROWS OF STEPHEN, by Peter Parnell, directed by Sheldon Larry.

TONGUES, a collaboration by Sam Shepard and Joseph Chaikin, music by Skip Laplante, Harry Mann and Sam Shepard, directed by Robert Woodruff.

HARD SELL, conceived and directed by Murray Horwitz.

SCENES FROM THE EVERYDAY LIFE, by Ned Jackson, directed by Elinor Renfield.

The Old Prop Shop Theater

A PRELUDE TO DEATH IN VENICE, written and directed by Lee Breuer.

SISTER SUZIE CINEMA, written and directed by Lee Breuer.

Martinson Hall

O'NEILL AND CARLOTTA, by Barbara Gelb, directed by Robert Allan Ackerman.

SORROWS OF STEPHEN, by Peter Parnell, directed by Sheldon Larry.

THE MUSIC LESSONS, by Wakako Yamauchi, directed by Mako.

FOB, by David Henry Hwang, directed by Mako.

LuEsther Hall

MERCIER AND CAMIER, by Samuel Beckett, adapted and directed by Frederick Neumann.

THE HAGGADAH, A Passover Cantata, adapted, composed and directed by Elizabeth Swados.

The Little Theater

FILM AT THE PUBLIC

Delacorte Theater

THE PIRATES OF PENZANCE, book by W. S. Gilbert, music by Arthur Sullivan, directed by Wilford Leach.

Mobile Theater

UNDER FIRE, composed and directed by Elizabeth Swados.

Eisenhower Theater (John F. Kennedy Center for the Performing Arts, Washington, D.C.)

THE ART OF DINING, by Tina Howe, directed by A. J. Antoon.

PBS-TV

HAPPY DAYS, by Samuel Beckett, produced by Joseph Papp, directed by Andrei Serban.

1980–81

Uris Theater (then Minskoff Theater as of 8/12/81)

THE PIRATES OF PENZANCE, book by W. S. Gilbert, music by Arthur Sullivan, directed by Wilford Leach.

Ahmanson Theater (West Coast Company)

THE PIRATES OF PENZANCE

Anspacher Theater

AN EVENING OF SHOLOM ALEICHEM, new translations by Joseph Singer, directed by Richard Maltby, Jr.

ALICE IN CONCERT (A musical adaptation based on Lewis Carroll's *Alice in Wonderland* and *Through the Looking Glass*), by Elizabeth Swados, directed by Joseph Papp.

LONG DAY'S JOURNEY INTO NIGHT, by Eugene O'Neill, directed by Geraldine Fitzgerald.

Newman Theater

2ND LATIN AMERICAN POPULAR THEATER FESTIVAL (UTEPO)

THE SEA GULL, by Anton Chekhov, adaptation by Jean-Claude van Itallie, music by Elizabeth Swados, directed by Andrei Serban.

1980–81 (*continued*)

PENGUIN TOUQUET, written, directed and musically scored by Richard Foreman.

TEXTS, by Samuel Beckett, adapted by Joseph Chaikin and Steven Kent, directed by Steven Kent.

IL CAMPIELLO, A VENETIAN COMEDY, by Carlo Goldoni, adapted by Richard Nelson, directed by Liviu Ciulei.

WAITING FOR GODOT, by Samuel Beckett, directed by Alan Schneider.

A MIDSUMMER NIGHT'S DREAM, by William Shakespeare, directed by David Chambers.

CROWSNEST — MARTHA CLARKE (dance)

MAY O'DONNELL CONCERT DANCE COMPANY

THE PEARL LANG DANCE COMPANY

The Other Stage

GIRLS, GIRLS, GIRLS, by Marilyn Suzanne Miller, music by Cheryl Hardwick, lyrics by Marilyn Suzanne Miller, directed by Bob Balaban.

DEAD END KIDS, conceived and directed by JoAnne Akalaitis.

WRONG GUYS, from *Wrong Guys* by Jim Strahs, created by Ruth Maleczech.

WIE ALLES ANFING/HOW IT ALL BEGAN, An adaptation of the autobiography of former West German terrorist Michael "Bommi" Baumann, written and compiled by the members of Group X of the Stage Division of the Juilliard School, edited by John Palmer, directed by Des McAnuff.

The Old Prop Shop

YOU KNOW AL HE'S A FUNNY GUY, written and performed by Jerry Mayer, directed by John Pynchon Holms.

Martinson Hall

TRUE WEST, by Sam Shepard, directed by Robert Woodruff.

THE HUNCHBACK OF NOTRE DAME, adaptation of Victor Hugo's novel *Notre Dame De Paris: 1482,* by Ron Whyte, music by Louise Tiranoff, directed by Ted Cornell.

LuEsther Hall

PRESENTING ALL OF DAVID LANGSTON SMYRL (OR IS IT?), written and composed by David Langston Smyrl, arranged and directed by James Milton.

MARY STUART, by Wolfgang Hildesheimer, English version by Christopher Holmes, directed by Des McAnuff.

THE HAGGADAH, A Passover Cantata, adapted, composed and directed by Elizabeth Swados.

Delacorte Theater

THE TEMPEST, by William Shakespeare, directed by Lee Breuer with Ruth Maleczech.

HENRY IV, Part 1, by William Shakespeare, directed by Des McAnuff.

The Little Theater

FILM AT THE PUBLIC

PBS-TV

THE HAGGADAH (live television broadcast from the Public Theater), adapted, composed and directed by Elizabeth Swados.

1981–82

Anspacher Theater

THE DANCE AND THE RAILROAD, by David Henry Hwang, directed and choreographed by John Lone.

THREE ACTS OF RECOGNITION, by Botho Strauss, translated by Sophie Wilkins, directed by Richard Foreman.

DEAD END KIDS, conceived and directed by JoAnne Akalaitis.

Newman Theater

FRESH FRUIT IN FOREIGN PLACES (a rap musical), story, music and lyrics by August Darnell.

FAMILY DEVOTIONS, by David Henry Hwang, directed by Robert Allan Ackerman.

LULLABYE AND GOODNIGHT, written, composed and directed by Elizabeth Swados.

CHARLOTTE, by Peter Hacks, directed by Herbert Berghof.

GOOSE AND TOM-TOM, by David Rabe, directed by John Pynchon Holms.

THE KLEZMORIM (one evening).

The Other Stage

THE LAUNDRY HOUR, by Mark Linn-Baker, Lewis Black, William Peters and Paul Schierhorn, music by Paul Schierhorn, directed by William Peters.

WRONG GUYS, from *Wrong Guys* by Jim Strahs, created by Ruth Maleczech.

ZASTROZZI, by George F. Walker, directed by Andrei Serban.

RED AND BLUE, by Michael Hurson, directed by JoAnne Akalaitis.

Martinson Hall

TWELVE DREAMS, written and directed by James Lapine.

THE KATHRYN POSIN DANCE COMPANY

ANTIGONE, by Sophocles, new translation by John Chioles, music by Richard Peaslee, directed by Joseph Chaikin.

RUMBA, A Voyage through Cuban Folklore, by Leopoldo Fleming, directed and choreographed by Poli Rogers.

LuEsther Hall

DEXTER CREED, A Satirical Fable, by Michael Moriarty, directed by James Milton.

SPECIMEN DAYS, conceived, composed and directed by Meredith Monk.

THE HAGGADAH, A Passover Cantata, adapted, composed and directed by Elizabeth Swados.

The Little Theater

FILM AT THE PUBLIC

The Public Theater

POETS AT THE PUBLIC

JAZZ AT THE PUBLIC

Delacorte Theater

DON JUAN, by Molière, translated by Donald M. Frame, directed by Richard Foreman.

A MIDSUMMER NIGHT'S DREAM, by William Shakespeare, directed by James Lapine.

Shakespeare and Company (Celebrate Brooklyn 1982 — Prospect Park Music Pagoda)

TWELFTH NIGHT, by William Shakespeare, directed by Tina Packer.

Riverside Shakespeare Company (New York City Parks Tour)

THE COMEDIE OF ERRORS, by William Shakespeare, directed by Gloria Skurski.

American Theatre of Actors

A FEW GOOD MEN, by John Sedlak, directed by Robert Graham Small.

NBC-TV Project Peacock

ALICE AT THE PALACE — A Music Hall based on Lewis Carroll's *Alice in Wonderland* and *Through the Looking Glass,* by Elizabeth Swados, directed by Joseph Papp.

ABC-Cable

THE DANCE AND THE RAILROAD, by David Henry Hwang, music by John Lone, directed by Emile Ardolino.

1982–83

Plymouth Theater

PLENTY, written and directed by David Hare.

Anspacher Theater

THIRD LATIN AMERICAN THEATER FESTIVAL

HAMLET, by William Shakespeare, directed by Joseph Papp.

Newman Theater

THE DEATH OF VON RICHTHOFEN AS WITNESSED FROM EARTH, written, composed and directed by Des McAnuff.

PLENTY, written and directed by David Hare.

TOP GIRLS, by Caryl Churchill, directed by Max Stafford-Clark.

PEARL LANG DANCE COMPANY

The Other Stage

UNCLE VANYA, by Anton Chekov, translated by Ann Dunnigan, directed by Peter Von Berg.

WHAT EVERYWOMAN KNOWS, by Tulis McCall, in collaboration with Nancy-Elizabeth Krammer.

COMPANY, by Samuel Beckett, directed by Honora Fergusson and Frederick Neumann.

EGYPTOLOGY (My Head Was a Sledgehammer), text, staging and musical scoring by Richard Foreman.

Martinson Hall

MEN INSIDE and VOICES OF AMERICA, two solos by Eric Bogosian; with Eric Bogosian.

BURIED INSIDE EXTRA, by Thomas Babe, directed by Joseph Papp.

GOODNIGHT LADIES!, devised by the company Hesitate and Demonstrate.

FUNHOUSE, written, designed and performed by Eric Bogosian, co-directed by Jo Bonney.

EMMETT, A ONE MORMON SHOW, written and performed by Emmett Foster.

LuEsther Hall

NECESSARY ENDS, by Marvin Cohen, music by Robert Dennis, directed by James Milton.

COLD HARBOR, conceived and directed by Bill Raymond and Dale Worsley.

HAJJ, a performance poem conceived in collaboration by Ruth Malezcech (performer), Craig Jones (video), Lee Breuer (poem and direction).

FEN, by Caryl Churchill, directed by Les Waters.

The Little Theater

FILM AT THE PUBLIC

The Public Theater

POETS AT THE PUBLIC

JAZZ AT THE PUBLIC

Delacorte Theater

RICHARD III, by William Shakespeare, directed by Jane Howell.

NON PASQUALE, a pop opera based on *Don Pasquale* by Gaetano Donizetti and Giovanni Ruffini, directed by Wilford Leach.

Shakespeare & Company (Celebrate Brooklyn 1983 — Prospect Park Theater)

COMEDY OF ERRORS, by William Shakespeare, directed by Tina Packer.

Riverside Shakespeare Company (New York City Parks Tour)

MERRY WIVES OF WINDSOR, by William Shakespeare, directed by Timothy Oman.

Royal Court Theatre (London)

BURIED INSIDE EXTRA, by Thomas Babe, directed by Joseph Papp.

Universal Pictures

THE PIRATES OF PENZANCE (The Film), produced by Joseph Papp, directed by Wilford Leach.

ABC-Cable

SWAN LAKE, MINNESOTA, conceived and directed by Kenneth Robins.

A MIDSUMMER NIGHT'S DREAM, by William Shakespeare, directed by Emile Ardolino.

REHEARSING HAMLET, the work process of the Public Theater stage production directed by Joseph Papp.

1983–84

Royale Theater

THE HUMAN COMEDY, based on the novel by William Saroyan, music by Galt MacDermot, libretto by William Dumaresq, directed by Wilford Leach.

Anspacher Theater

THE HUMAN COMEDY, novel by William Saroyan, music by Galt MacDermot, libretto by William Dumaresq, directed by Wilford Leach.

A MIDSUMMER NIGHT'S DREAM, by William Shakespeare, adapted and directed by Amy Saltz.

FOUND A PEANUT, by Donald Margulies, directed by Claudia Weill.

Newman Theater

ORGASMO ADULTO ESCAPES FROM THE ZOO, by Franca Rame and Dario Fo.

NO MORE BINGO AT THE WAKE, by Pedro Pietri, directed by Eduardo Figueroa.

LENNY AND THE HEARTBREAKERS, by Kenneth Robins, music by Scott Killian and Kim D. Sherman, lyrics by Kenneth Robins, Scott Killian and Kim D. Sherman, staged and choreographed by Murray Louis and Alwin Nikolais.

FEN, by Caryl Churchill, directed by Les Waters.

THE NEST OF THE WOODGROUSE, by Victor Rozov, translated by Susan Layton, directed by Joseph Papp.

The Other Stage

MY UNCLE SAM, written and directed by Len Jenkin.

1983–84 (*continued*)

EMMETT, A ONE MORMON SHOW, written and performed by Emmett Foster.

COMPANY, by Samuel Beckett, directed by Honora Fergusson and Frederick Neumann.

SERENADING LOUIE, by Lanford Wilson, directed by John Tillinger.

ICE BRIDGE, by John F. Forster, directed by Ted Cornell.

Martinson Hall

A PRIVATE VIEW, by Václav Havel, translated by Vera Blackwell, directed by Lee Grant.

PIECES OF 8 (eight one-acts), conceived and directed by Alan Schneider: "The Unexpurgated Memoirs of Bernard Mergendeiler," by Jules Feiffer; "The Black and White," by Harold Pinter; "The Tridget of Greva," by Ring Lardner; "The Sandbox," by Edward Albee; "The (15 Minute) Dogg's Troupe Hamlet," by Tom Stoppard; "Come and Go," by Samuel Beckett; "Foursome," by Eugene Ionesco; "I'm Herbert," by Robert Anderson.

THE THIRD ANNUAL YOUNG PLAYWRIGHTS FESTIVAL, Peggy C. Hansen, producing director, Gerald Chapman, artistic director. *Full Productions:* "Romance," by Catherine Castellani, directed by Elinor Renfield; "Fixed Up," by Patricia Durkin, directed by Shelly Raffle; "Meeting The Winter Bike Rider," by Juan Nunez, directed by Elinor Renfield; "In The Garden," by Anne Harris, directed by James Milton; "Tender Places," by Jason Brown, directed by Shelly Raffle. *Staged Readings* (Admission Free Series): "Liars," by Joseph Yesutis, directed by Jerry Zaks; "Buddies," by Kevin Hammond, directed by Billie Allen; "Always Open," by Rebecca Gilman, directed by Billie

Allen; "Tender Places," by Jason Brown, directed by Kay Matschullat; "We Three Kings," by Alexander Frere-Jones, directed by Billie Allen; "Living in the USA," by Julie Tayco, directed by Kay Matschullat.

LuEsther Hall

SOUND AND BEAUTY, by David Henry Hwang, directed by John Lone.

CRIME AND PUNISHMENT BENEFIT

CINDERS, by Janusz Glowacki, translated by Christina Paul, directed by John Madden.

The Little Theater

FILM AT THE PUBLIC

The Public Theater

JAZZ AT THE PUBLIC

FOURTH LATIN AMERICAN FESTIVAL

Delacorte Theater

HENRY V, by William Shakespeare, directed by Wilford Leach.

THE GOLEM, by H. Leivick, translated from the Yiddish by J. C. Augenlicht, directed by Richard Foreman.

FOURTH LATIN AMERICAN FESTIVAL

Riverside Shakespeare Company (New York City Parks Tour)

ROMEO AND JULIET, by William Shakespeare, directed by John Clingerman, associate director Mary Lowry.

Shakespeare & Company (Celebrate Brooklyn 1984 — Prospect Park)

A MIDSUMMER NIGHT'S DREAM, by William Shakespeare, directed by Tina Packer and Kevin Coleman.

ROMEO AND JULIET, by William Shakespeare, directed by Tina Packer and Dennis Krausnick.

1984–85

Anspacher Theater

LA BOHEME, music by Giacomo Puccini, original libretto by Giuseppe Giacosa and Luigi Illica, adaptation and new lyrics by David Spencer, directed by Wilford Leach.

SALONIKA, by Louise Page, directed by John Madden.

THE NORMAL HEART, by Larry Kramer, directed by Michael Lindsay-Hogg.

Newman Theater

THE BALLAD OF SOAPY SMITH, by Michael Weller, directed by Robert Egan.

VIRGINIA, by Edna O'Brien, directed by David Leveaux.

THE MARRIAGE OF BETTE AND BOO, by Christopher Durang, directed by Jerry Zaks.

The Other Stage (name of theater changed to Susan Stein Shiva Theater on 10/29/84)

THROUGH THE LEAVES, by Franz Xavier Kroetz, translated by Roger Downey, directed by JoAnne Akalaitis.

Susan Stein Shiva Theater

TRACERS, conceived and directed by John DiFusco.

PUBLIC SCHOOL PROGRAM IN PLAYWRITING

Martinson Hall

HANDY DANDY: A COMEDY BUT, by William Gibson, directed by Kay Matschullat.

COMING OF AGE IN SOHO, written and directed by Albert Innaurato.

RAT IN THE SKULL, by Ron Hutchinson, directed by Max Stafford-Clark.

LuEsther Hall

TOM AND VIV, by Michael Hastings, directed by Max Stafford-Clark.

THE NORMAL HEART, by Larry Kramer, directed by Michael Lindsay-Hogg.

The Little Theater

FILM AT THE PUBLIC

GLOBAL VILLAGE 11TH ANNUAL DOCUMENTARY FESTIVAL

Public Theater

JAZZ AT THE PUBLIC

P.O.W. THEATRE FESTIVAL (1st Annual Professional Older Women's Theater Festival — Elsa Rael, founder/producer).

FIFTH LATIN AMERICAN FESTIVAL

Delacorte Theater

MEASURE FOR MEASURE, by William Shakespeare, directed by Joseph Papp.

THE MYSTERY OF EDWIN DROOD, by Rupert Holmes, suggested by the unfinished novel by Charles Dickens, directed by Wilford Leach.

FIFTH LATIN AMERICAN FESTIVAL

John F. Kennedy Center for the Performing Arts (Washington, D.C.)

THE NEST OF THE WOODGROUSE, by Victor Rozov, translated by Susan Layton, directed by Joseph Papp.

St. Clement's Church

THE GARDEN OF EARTHLY
DELIGHTS (based on Hieronymus
Bosch's painting), conceived and
directed by Martha Clarke.

*Riverside Shakespeare Company (New
York City Parks Tour)*

THE TAMING OF THE SHREW, by
William Shakespeare, directed by
Maureen Clarke.

*Shakespeare & Company (Celebrate
Brooklyn 1985 — Prospect Park)*

MUCH ADO ABOUT NOTHING,
by William Shakespeare, directed by
Derek Goldby.

Public School #29 (Brooklyn)

THE SHOOTING OF DAN
McGREW, written and directed by
Jacques d'Amboise.

1985–86

Imperial Theater

THE MYSTERY OF EDWIN
DROOD, by Rupert Holmes,
suggested by the unfinished novel by
Charles Dickens, directed by Wilford
Leach. (Title later shortened to
Drood.)

Longacre Theater

CUBA AND HIS TEDDY BEAR, by
Reinaldo Povod, directed by Bill
Hart.

Anspacher Theater

THE NORMAL HEART, by Larry
Kramer, directed by Michael
Lindsay-Hogg.

AS YOU LIKE IT, by William
Shakespeare, directed by Estelle
Parsons.

ROMEO AND JULIET, by William
Shakespeare, directed by Estelle
Parsons.

FESTIVAL LATINO: *Sobre el Amor y
Otros Cuentos Sobre el Amor* (About
Love and Other Stories About
Love), created and directed by
Norma Aleandro; *La Zapatera
Prodigiosa* (The Shoemaker's
Prodigious Wife), by Frederico
García Lorca, directed by Margarita
Galban; *Fight,* book and lyrics by
Manuel Martin, Jr., music by Felix
Mendez, directed by Manuel
Martin, Jr.; *Quintuples* (Quintuplets),
written and directed by Luis Rafael
Sanchez; *Tiempo Muerto,* adapted by
Rosalba Colon, directed by Ramon
Albino; *Los Tiempos del Ruido,*
collective creation by Grupo La
Mama, translated by Rodney Reding
and Martha Avellaneda, directed by
Eddy Armando.

Newman Theater

A MAP OF THE WORLD, written
and directed by David Hare.

HAMLET, by William Shakespeare,
directed by Liviu Ciulei.

VIENNA: LUSTHAUS, conceived
and directed by Martha Clarke.

FESTIVAL LATINO: *La Tras-escena*
(Behind the Scenes), written and
directed by Fernando Penuela;
Guadalupe Años Sin Cuenta
(Guadalupe Countless Years),
collective creation by cast, translated
by Fernando Torres, directed by
Santiago Garcia; *Toda Nudez Sera
Castigada,* written by Nelson
Rodriguez, adapted and directed by
Jose Antonio Teodoro; *Lo Que Esta
en el Aire* (Something in the Air),
written by ICTUS and Carlos
Cerda, directed by Nissim Sharim
and Delfina Guzman; *Temporada de
Danza Contemporanea* (Ballet
Moderno y Folklorico),
choreography direction by Julia Vela;
Bolivar, by Jose Antonio Ral,

directed by Carlos Gimenez;
Memory, written and directed by
Carlos Gimenez.

Susan Stein Shiva Theater

TRACERS, conceived and directed by
John DiFusco.

RUM AND COKE, by Keith Reddin,
directed by Les Waters.

CUBA AND HIS TEDDY BEAR, by
Reinaldo Povod, directed by Bill
Hart.

FESTIVAL LATINO: *Introduction to
Chicano History 101,* written and
directed by Anthony J. Garcia; *The
Place Where the Mammals Die,* by
Jorge Diaz, translated by Naomi
Nelson, music by Felix Mendez,
directed by Carlos Carrasco; *Box
Plays* (INTAR's Playwrights-In-
Residence Laboratory); *Culture
Clash,* written and directed
collectively by cast; *Retrato de Mujer
Sola con Espejo* (Portrait of Woman
alone with Mirror), written by Pedro
Corradi, directed by Duman Lerena;
The Many Deaths of Danny Rosales,
written by Carlos Morton, directed
by Marvin Camillo.

Martinson Hall

THOMAS COLE, A WAKING
DREAM, written and directed by
Donald Sanders.

AUNT DAN AND LEMON, by
Wallace Shawn, directed by Max
Stafford-Clark.

FESTIVAL LATINO: *Pranzo di
Famiglia* (Family Dinner), written
by Roberto Lerici, translated by
Nina Miller, directed by Tinto Brass;
Los Musicos Ambulantes (The
Strolling Musicians), collective
creation based on texts of Luis
Henriquez and Sergio Baraotti,
adapted and directed by Miguel
Rubio Zapata; *Sombras de Agua*
(Shadows of Water) and other
works, choreography by Eva

Gasteazoro, directed by Tony
Gillotte; *Chupate Esta en lo Que Te
Mondo la Otra,* conceived by Merian
Soto and Pepon Osorio; *The Birds
Fly out with Death* (Los Pajaros Se
Van con la Muerte), by Edilio Pena,
directed by Vicente Castro; *Alguna
Cosita Que Alivie el Sufrir* (A Little
Something to Ease the Pain),
written by Rene R. Aloma,
translated by Alberto Sarrain,
directed by Mario Ernesto Sanchez.

LuEsther Hall

JONIN', by Gerard Brown, directed
by Andre Robinson, Jr.

LARGO DESOLATO, by Václav
Havel, translated by Marie Winn,
directed by Richard Foreman.

CUBA AND HIS TEDDY BEAR, by
Reinaldo Povod, directed by Bill
Hart.

The Little Theater

FILMS AT THE PUBLIC

FIFTH NATIONAL LATINO FILM
AND VIDEO FESTIVAL 1985
(October 18–20, 1985)

FESTIVAL LATINO FILMS 1986
(August 15–31, 1986)

The Public Theater

JAZZ AT THE PUBLIC

Delacorte Theater

TWELFTH NIGHT or WHAT YOU
WILL, by William Shakespeare,
directed by Wilford Leach.

FESTIVAL LATINO: *La Verdadera
Historia de Pedro Navaja* (The True
Story of Pedro Navaja), written and
directed by Pablo Cabrera;
Jazmines-Tango (an original
tango-ballet), based on the idea of
Ana Maria Stekelman with Jorge
Romano, script by Ana Maria
Stekelman and Niko Vasiliadis,
directed by Ana Maria Stekelman;

Cumbre Flamenca (gypsy dance of southern Spain), directed by Francisco Sanchez.

MEDEA, by Euripides, directed by Yukio Ninagawa.

Mobile Theater

AS YOU LIKE IT, by William Shakespeare, directed by Estelle Parsons.

ROMEO AND JULIET, by William Shakespeare, directed by Estelle Parsons.

New Heritage Repertory Theatre, Inc.

JONIN', by Gerard Brown, directed by André Robinson, Jr.

Town of Thompson Park in Monticello

FESTIVAL LATINO: *Bodas de Sangre* (Blood Wedding), by Federico García Lorca, directed by Maria Alicia Martinez Medrano.

The Royal Court Theatre (London)

TRACERS, conceived and directed by John DiFusco.

AUNT DAN AND LEMON, by Wallace Shawn, directed by Max Stafford-Clark.

Cable Channel L-TV on Group W and Manhattan Cable

FESTIVAL LATINO IN VIDEO (August 18–28, 1986)

1986–87

Belasco Theatre

AS YOU LIKE IT, by William Shakespeare, directed by Estelle Parsons.

ROMEO AND JULIET, by William Shakespeare, directed by Estelle Parsons.

MACBETH, by William Shakespeare, directed by Estelle Parsons.

Newman Theater

THE KNIFE, music by Nick Bicat, book by David Hare, lyrics by Tim Rose Price.

THE COLORED MUSEUM, by George C. Wolfe, directed by L. Kenneth Richardson.

FESTIVAL LATINO: *Las Bacantes* (The Bacchae), written and directed by Salvador Tavora; *La Señorita de Tacna* (The Lady from Tacna), written by Mario Vargas Llosa, directed by Emilio Alfaro.

Susan Stein Shiva Theater

THE COLORED MUSEUM, by George C. Wolfe, directed by L. Kenneth Richardson.

FESTIVAL LATINO: *Pancho Diablo* (Pancho Devil), written by Carlos Morton, directed by Vicente Castro; *Las Bohemias, Concierto in Hi-Fi* (The Bohemias, Concerto in Hi-Fi), by Mirelsa Modestti, musical direction by Giselle Solis, theatrical direction by Valli Marie Rivera.

Martinson Hall

MY GENE, by Barbara Gelb, directed by André Ernotte.

TALK RADIO, by Eric Bogosian based on an original idea by Tad Savinar, directed by Frederick Zollo.

LuEsther Hall

FESTIVAL LATINO: *El Renidero* (The Cockpit), written by Sergio DeCecco, directed by Carlos Gimenez; *La Tragicomedia de Calisto y Melibea* (The Tragicomedy of Calisto and Melibea), written by Miguel Sabido and Margarita Villasenor, directed by Carlos Gimenez; *Los Payasos de la Esperanza* (The Clowns of Hope), written by Raul Osorio and

Mauricio Pesutic, directed by Claudio DiGirolamo.

Little Theater
FILM AT THE PUBLIC

The Public Theater
JAZZ AT THE PUBLIC

Delacorte Theater
RICHARD II, by William Shakespeare, directed by Joseph Papp.

TWO GENTLEMEN OF VERONA, by William Shakespeare, directed by Stuart Vaughan.

HENRY IV, Part 1, by William Shakespeare, directed by Joseph Papp.

Kings County Shakespeare Company, Inc. (Celebrate Brooklyn 1987 — Prospect Park)
ALL'S WELL THAT ENDS WELL, by William Shakespeare, directed by Steve Zimmer.

Eisenhower Theater (John F. Kennedy Center for the Performing Arts)
VIENNA: LUSTHAUS, conceived and directed by Martha Clarke.

Terrace Theater (John F. Kennedy Center for the Performing Arts)
MY GENE, written by Barbara Gelb, directed by Andre Ernotte.

East Coast Arts at Wildcliff
OLD BUSINESS, written and directed by Joe Cacaci.

INTAR Hispanic American Center
ROOSTERS, by Milcha Sanchez-Scott, directed by Jackson Phippin.

Opera at the Academy
THE MAGIC FLUTE, by Wolfgang Amadeus Mozart, directed by Eric Fraad.

The Royal Court Theatre (London)
THE COLORED MUSEUM, by George C. Wolfe, directed by L. Kenneth Richardson.

1987–88

Royale Theatre
SERIOUS MONEY, by Caryl Churchill, directed by Max Stafford-Clark.

Anspacher Theater
A MIDSUMMER NIGHT'S DREAM, by William Shakespeare, directed by A. J. Antoon.

ROMEO AND JULIET, by William Shakespeare, directed by Les Waters.

THE DEATH OF GARCIA LORCA, by Jose Antonio Rial, translated by Julio Marzán, directed by Carlos Gimenez.

FESTIVAL LATINO: *Made in Lanus,* by Nelly Fernandez Tiscornia, directed by Luis Brandoni.

Newman Theater
SERIOUS MONEY, by Caryl Churchill, directed by Max Stafford-Clark.

JULIUS CAESAR, by William Shakespeare, directed by Stuart Vaughan.

MIRACOLO D'AMORE, conceived and directed by Martha Clarke.

Susan Stein Shiva Theater
OLD BUSINESS, written and directed by Joe Cacaci.

AMERICAN NOTES, by Len Jenkin, directed by JoAnne Akalaitis.

1987–88 (*continued*)

OLD NEW YORK: NEW YEAR'S DAY, from the Edith Wharton novel, adapted and directed by Donald T. Sanders.

THE IMPERIALISTS AT THE CLUB CAVE CANEM, by Charles L. Mee Jr., directed by Erin B. Mee.

STRANGER HERE MYSELF: Songs of Kurt Weill, performed by Angelina Réaux, directed by Christopher Alden.

Martinson Hall

TALK RADIO, by Eric Bogosian, based on an original idea by Tad Savinar, directed by Frederick Zollo.

WENCESLAS SQUARE, by Larry Shue, directed by Jerry Zaks.

FESTIVAL LATINO: *The Island* (Mosquito), by Athol Fugard, John Kani and Winston Ntshona, music by Juan Marcos Blanco, translated into Spanish and directed by Filander Funes; *Mariameneo, Mariameneo,* written and directed by Juan Sanchez; *Bang Bang Blues,* by Charles Gomez, directed by Jules Aaron.

LuEsther Hall

LA PUTA VIDA TRILOGY (This Bitch of a Life), by Reinaldo Povod, directed by Bill Hart.

ZERO POSITIVE, by Harry Kondoleon, directed by Kenneth Elliott.

FESTIVAL LATINO: *De la Calle* (From the Street), by Jesús Gonzáles Dávila, music by Salvador Matías Fabián, Arturo Cornejo Vargas, Rafael Matías Fabián, directed by Julio Castillo; *El Martirio del Pastor* (The Pastor's Martyrdom), by Samuel Rovinski, music by Adrián Goizueta, directed by Alfredo Catania.

Little Theater

FILM AT THE PUBLIC

Delacorte Theater

MUCH ADO ABOUT NOTHING, by William Shakespeare, music by John Morris, directed by Gerald Freedman.

KING JOHN, by William Shakespeare, music by Peter Golub, directed by Stuart Vaughan.

FESTIVAL LATINO: *Concerts for Peace and Friendship,* Tania Libertad (Peru) and Inti-Illimani (Chile).

Terrace Theater (John F. Kennedy Center for the Performing Arts)

WENCESLAS SQUARE, by Larry Shue, directed by Jerry Zaks.

Annenberg Center (University of Pennsylvania)

MY GENE, written by Barbara Gelb, directed by André Ernotte.

The Plaza Theatre (Dallas, Texas)

MY GENE, written by Barbara Gelb, directed by André Ernotte.

Dock Street Theatre (Spoleto Festival U.S.A.)

MIRACOLO D'AMORE, conceived and directed by Martha Clarke.

Opera at the Academy

LA CALISTO, written by Francesco Cavalli, musical direction by Paul C. Echols, stage direction by David Alden.

Liberty State Park (Jersey City, New Jersey)

FESTIVAL LATINO: *In Concert,* Tania Libertad (Peru) and Willie Colon (U.S.A.); *El Martirio del Pastor* (The Pastor's Martyrdom), by Samuel Rovinski, music by Adrián Goizueta, directed by Alfredo Catania.

1988-89

Anspacher Theater

CORIOLANUS, by William Shakespeare, directed by Steven Berkoff.

THE WINTER'S TALE, by William Shakespeare, directed by James Lapine.

MANDY PATINKIN: DRESS CASUAL, Songs performed by Mandy Patinkin.

ROMANCE IN HARD TIMES, written and composed by William Finn, directed by David Warren.

FESTIVAL LATINO: *El Gran Circo EU Craniano* (The Great U.S. Kranial Circus), written, directed and translated by Myrna Casas; *El Paso o Parabola del Camino* (El Paso or Parable of the Path), a collective creation of the La Candelaria company, translated by Nina Miller, directed by Santiago Garcia; *The Miracle,* written and directed by Felipe Santander.

Newman Theater

CAFÉ CROWN, by Hy Kraft, directed by Martin Charnin.

LOVE'S LABOR'S LOST, by William Shakespeare, directed by Gerald Freedman.

CYMBELINE, by William Shakespeare, directed by JoAnne Akalaitis.

FESTIVAL LATINO: *El Coronel No Tiene Quien le Escriba* (No One Writes to the Colonel), from the story by Gabriel García Márquez, adapted and directed by Carlos Gimenez; *Sueno de una Noche de Verano* (A Midsummer Night's Dream), by William Shakespeare, adapted by Manuel Rueda, translated by Melia Bensussen, directed by Ramon Pareja.

Susan Stein Shiva Theater

WHAT DID HE SEE?, written and directed by Richard Foreman.

SONGS OF PARADISE, based on the biblical poetry of Itsik Manger, book by Miriam Hoffman and Rena Berkowicz Borow, music by Rosalie Gerut, directed by Avi Hoffman.

JACKIE MASON AT THE PUBLIC, by Jackie Mason.

MY BIG LAND (Sailors' Silence), by Alexander Galich, directed by Oleg P. Tabakov.

Martinson Hall

FOR DEAR LIFE, by Susan Miller, directed by Norman Rene.

JACKIE MASON: LONDON-BOUND, by Jackie Mason.

TEMPTATION, by Václav Havel, translated by Marie Winn, directed by Jiri Zizka.

FESTIVAL LATINO: *Peggy and Jackson,* libretto by Michael Alasa, music by David Welch, directed by Michael Alasa, co-directed by Mary Lisa Kinney; *Adios Tropicana,* book and lyrics by Chuck Gomez, music by Mark Pennington, directed and choreographed by Mark Pennington; *Amazonia,* by Larry Herrera, translation by Jack Agueros, directed by Oscar Ciccone.

LuEsther Hall

GENESIS: MUSIC AND MIRACLES, From the Medieval Mystery Plays, book and lyrics by A. J. Antoon and Robert Montgomery, music by Michael Ward, directed by A. J. Antoon.

THE FORBIDDEN CITY, by Bill Gunn, directed by Joseph Papp.

FESTIVAL LATINO: *No+* (No More), written and directed by Raul Osorio; *Fantasma,* libretto by Edward Gallardo, music by Marc Allen Trujillo, directed by Bill Castellino.

Little Theater

FILM AT THE PUBLIC

Delacorte Theater

TWELFTH NIGHT, by William Shakespeare, directed by Harold Guskin.

TITUS ANDRONICUS, by William Shakespeare, directed by Michael Maggio.

FESTIVAL LATINO: *Concert for Peace and Friendship,* Roy Brown (Puerto Rico) and Dizzy Gillespie (U.S.A.), August 21, 1989.

Brooks Atkinson Theatre

CAFÉ CROWN, by Hy Kraft, directed by Martin Charnin.

Annenberg Center (University of Pennsylvania)

TEMPTATION, by Václav Havel, translated by Marie Winn, directed by Jiri Zizka.

Opera at the Academy

DIDO AND AENEAS, music by Henry Purcell, libretto by Nahum Tate, epilogue by Thomas D'Urfey, directed by Christopher Alden.

1989–90

Ethel Barrymore Theater

THE SECRET RAPTURE, written and directed by David Hare.

Anspacher Theater

MACBETH, by William Shakespeare, directed by Richard Jordan.

HAMLET, by William Shakespeare, directed by Kevin Kline.

FESTIVAL LATINO: *Los Rayos Gamma in New York* (The Gamma Rays in New York), book and lyrics by Silverio Perez, directed by the company; *Andar por la Gente* (Walking among the People), directed, designed and performed by Inda Ledesma; *Mondo Mambo, a mambo rap sodi,* written by Pedro Pietri, conceived and directed by Adal Alberto Maldonado.

Newman Theater

THE SECRET RAPTURE, written and directed by David Hare.

ROMANCE IN HARD TIMES, written and composed by William Finn, directed by David Warren.

ONE OF THE GUYS, by Marilyn Suzanne Miller, directed by Arthur Penn.

ICE CREAM with HOT FUDGE, by Caryl Churchill, directed by Les Waters.

FESTIVAL LATINO: *Cronica de una Muerte Anunciada* (Chronicle of a Death Foretold), a spectacle by Salvador Tavora, based on a text by Gabriel García Márquez, translated by Melia Bensussen, directed by Salvador Tavorachis; *Sin Testigos* (Without Witnesses), adapted from a play by Sofia Prokofieva, directed by Inda Ledesma; *O Doente Imaginario* (The Imaginary Invalid), by Molière, translated by Marcia Abujamra, directed by Caca Rosset.

Susan Stein Shiva Theater

CARNAGE, A COMEDY, by Adam Simon and Tim Robbins, directed by Tim Robbins.

KATE'S DIARY, by Kathleen Tolan, directed by David Greenspan.

A MOM'S LIFE, by Kathryn Grody, directed by Timothy Near.

B. BEAVER ANIMATION, written and directed by Lee Breuer.

FESTIVAL LATINO: *De Donde?*, by Mary Gallagher, translated into Spanish by Rosario Santos, directed by Sam Blackwell; *Voces de Acero* (Voices of Steel), a collective creation by Pregones Theater Group, directed by Alvan Colon Lespier.

Martinson Hall

KINGFISH, by Marlane Meyer, directed by David Schweizer.

JONAH, adapted, composed and directed by Elizabeth Swados.

SPUNK, Three Tales by Zora Neale Hurston, adapted and directed by George C. Wolfe.

LuEsther Hall

UP AGAINST IT, based on the screenplay by Joe Orton, adapted by Tom Ross, music and lyrics by Todd Rundgren, directed by Kenneth Elliott.

JACKIE MASON . . . BRAND NEW #1, by Jackie Mason.

JACKIE MASON . . . BRAND NEW #2, by Jackie Mason.

FESTIVAL LATINO: *La Misma Sangre* (The Same Blood), by Carlos Velis, with two texts by Jose Roberto Cea from *Memoria en Carne Propria* (Memory of My Own Flesh) and *Poema de Amor* (Love Poem) by Roque Dalton, translated by Melia Bensussen, directed by Emilio Carballido; *El Palomar* (The Pigeon House), by Carlos Catania, translated by Melia Bensussen, directed by Alfredo Catania; *Matatangos*, by Marco Antonio de la Parra, directed by Abel Lopez and Hugo Medrano; *La Secreta Obscenidad de Cada Dia* (Secret Obscenities), by Marco Antonio de la Parra, directed by Hugo Medrano and Sonia Castel.

The Little Theater

FILM AT THE PUBLIC

Delacorte Theater

THE TAMING OF THE SHREW, by William Shakespeare, directed by A. J. Antoon.

RICHARD III, by William Shakespeare, directed by Robin Phillips.

FESTIVAL LATINO: *Concert for Peace and Friendship; Romeo and Juliet*, by William Shakespeare, directed by Maria Alicia Martinez Medrano.

Alice Tully Hall

REVELATION IN COURTHOUSE PARK, written and composed by Harry Partch, directed by Jiri Zizka.

The World Financial Center

FESTIVAL LATINO PREVIEW

1990-91

Anspacher Theater

THE BIG FUNK, by John Patrick Shanley, directed by John Patrick Shanley.

Newman Theater

THROUGH THE LEAVES, by Franz Xavier Kroetz, directed by JoAnne Akalaitis.

HENRY IV, Parts 1 and 2, by William Shakespeare, directed by JoAnne Akalaitis.

Susan Stein Shiva Theater

INDECENT MATERIALS (Two one-act plays): "Indecent Materials," text by Senator Jesse Helms, R-NC, adapted by Edward Hunt and Jeff Storer, directed by Jeff Storer; "Report from the Holocaust," from the book *Reports from the Holocaust:*

The Making of an AIDS Activist by Larry Kramer, adapted by Edward Hunt and Jeff Storer, directed by Jeff Storer.

GONZA THE LANCER, by Chikamatsu Monzaemon, translated by Donald Keene, directed by David Greenspan.

THE FEVER, by Wallace Shawn.

DEAD MOTHER, written and directed by David Greenspan.

THE WAY OF THE WORLD, by William Congreve, directed by David Greenspan.

Martinson Hall

CAUCASIAN CHALK CIRCLE, by Bertolt Brecht, adapted by Thulani Davis, directed by George C. Wolfe.

LuEsther Hall

MACHINAL, by Sophie Treadwell, directed by Michael Greif.

A BRIGHT ROOM CALLED DAY, by Tony Kushner, directed by Michael Greif.

CASANOVA, by Constance Congdon, directed by Michael Greif.

The Little Theater

FILM AT THE PUBLIC

Delacorte Theater

OTHELLO, by William Shakespeare, directed by Joe Dowling.

FESTIVAL LATINO: *Sonho De Uma Noite De Verao* (A Midsummer Night's Dream), by William Shakespeare, translated, adapted and directed by Caca Rosset; *La Tempestad* (The Tempest), by William Shakespeare, directed by Carlos Gimenez.

The author gratefully acknowledges the following for permission to reprint material:

Hirschfeld drawing. Copyright © by Al Hirschfeld. Drawing reproduced by special arrangement with Hirschfeld's exclusive representative, the Margo Feiden Gallery, Ltd., New York.

Excerpt from *A Chorus Line*. Words by Edward Kleban and music by Marvin Hamlisch. Copyright © 1975 by Edward Kleban and Marvin Hamlisch. By permission of Wren Music Co. and American Compass Music Corp.

Exerpt from Foreword by Joseph Papp in *Poets for Life: Seventy-six Poets Respond to AIDS*, edited by Michael Klein. Copyright © 1989 by Joseph Papp. By permission of Persea Books.

Exerpt from "Air" from *Hair*. Words by James Rado and Gerome Ragni and music by Galt MacDermot. Copyright © 1966, 1967, 1968, 1979 by James Rado, Gerome Ragni, Galt MacDermot, Nat Shapiro and EMI U Catalog Inc. By permission of CPP/Belwin, Inc.

Photographs from the Billy Rose Theater Collection are used with the permission of The New York Public Library for the Performing Arts and the Astor, Lenox and Tilden Foundations.

Exerpt from "Lady in Red" by Ntozake Shange. By permission of Ntozake Shange.

Exerpts from McNeil Lowery's oral history transcript are used with the permission of the Ford Foundation.

All exerpts from letters and plays are used with the individual author's and copyright holder's permission.

Index

Papp (Papirofsky) (*continued*)
New York's financial crisis, 372–374;
planned American-Soviet theater
exchange, 376, 377, 410, 418; trips to
Soviet Union, 376–377, 418; and Festival
Latino, 379, 397–398, 409; and
corporate sponsorship, 380, 382; break in
relations with Rabe, 383–384; wearies of
work and theater, 385–386, 391; trip to
Israel and Egypt, 386–388; trip to
Poland, 388–389; moves office out of
Public Theater, 390–391; criticisms of
imperiousness of, 392–394, 395–396;
singing radio commercials, 393–394;
firing of Debuskey, 394, 469; on theater
critics, 396–397, 436; interest in Latino
theater, 397, 410, 487; and British
playwrights, 398–400; exchange program
with Royal Court Theater, 399–400; in
resistance to demolition of Broadway
theaters, 400, 401, 402, 403–405; on
Koch's Theater Advisory Council, 405,
410, 429; Belasco Project for Shakespeare
in schools, 411–412, 425; and oral
history of Shakespeare Festival, 418, 424,
427, 439–440, 480; and Shakespeare
Marathon, 422, 429–430, 434–439,
440–441, 449, 464; awarded honorary
doctorates, 424, 442; search for successor,
425–427, 429, 431, 433–434, 446,
464–465; writes introductions for Bantam
edition of Shakespeare, 427; Palestinian
theater group controversy, 441–443;
involvement in NEA controversy, 443,
445–446, 453, 454, 496; and Akalaitis as
successor, 447–448, 452, 454–456,
457–458, 459, 464, 465, 466, 467, 468;
refusal of NEA grant, 449–452, 453, 468;
USA Today feature on, 460–461;
interview with Alex Witchel, 466–468,
469; teaches at Long Island University, 489
Papp, Miranda (daughter; later Miranda
Papp Adani), 8, 363; birth of, 117, 197;
childhood of, 221, 303; Papp's
relationship with, 303, 371
Papp, Peggy Bennion (third wife), 8; acting
career, 72, 87, 95, 96, 105, 106, 110,
131, 167; friendship with Papp, 72–73;
marriage to Papp, 73, 74, 75; on Papp's
personality, 73, 79–80, 106, 197, 221;
and Papp's communism, 74–75, 120; on
Papp's work, 84, 170, 205; children born
to, 117, 119; career as psychotherapist,
174, 196, 304; trip to Europe with Papp,
182, 183; marital counseling with Papp,
196, 197, 221; divorce from Papp, 267;
and son Tony, 303, 457
Papp, Susan (daughter; later Susan Papp
Lippman), 8, 197, 267, 303, 371

Parks, Larry, 67, 122, 126, 128
Patinkin, Mandy, 335, 418, 422, 441, 463, 470
Paton, Alan, 168
Patrick, John, 74
Peabody, Judith, 184, 379, 419, 428, 451
Peer Gynt (Ibsen), 313
Penn, Arthur, 413
Pennsylvania Station, 187
Pentagon Papers, 264
People's World, 64, 66, 67
Pepper, Ruth (aunt), 387
Pepper, Sol (uncle), 387
Pfeiffer, Michelle, 440
Philadelphia, Pa., 117, 130, 141
Philadelphia College of Arts, 424
Philharmonic Hall, 276
Phoenix Theater, 120
Photograph, A (Shange), 382
Piccadilly Hotel, 401
Pietà di Novembre, La (Brusati), 210
Piñero, Miguel, 312, 313, 314, 326, 327, 432
Pinter, Harold, 203
Pirates of Penzance (Gilbert and Sullivan),
380–382
Piss Christ (Serrano), 444
Place, Dick, 199
playwrights: Papp on, 203, 375, 391–392;
Papp's relations with, 205, 219, 222,
223–224, 228, 230, 314–316, 317;
salaries, 219, 330; blacks, 226, 296, 353,
375; at Public Theater, 233, 239, 314,
317; contemporary, 375, 391–392; critics'
influence and, 396
Playwrights Horizons, 375
Plenty (Hare), 399, 404
*Poets for Life: Seventy-Six Poets Respond to
AIDS*, 432
Pogany, Willy, 116
Poland, 388–389
Polansky, Abe, 67, 122
Polish Theater Laboratory, 182
Popkin, Henry, 207
Portman, John, 400, 401, 403, 404
Premice, Josephine, 101
Price, Leontyne, 101
Primer Teatro Español, 487
Prospect Park (Brooklyn), 136
Prout, George, 495
Public Broadcasting Service (PBS), 354,
355, 494
Public Theater: development of new plays
at, 5, 239, 308, 319, 330–331, 334,
346–347, 391, 412; Shakespeare Festival
moves into, 26, 197, 223; construction of
theaters in, 194–195, 204–205, 210, 234,
249, 254, 257, 488; opening of, 213,
214, 291; Astor Library renamed as, 221;
mortgage and renovation costs, 240, 241,
257; ticket prices, 241; sale to city by